Introduction to Clinical Mental Health Counseling

To all those individuals who have dedicated their lives to a profession that benefits their communities in countless ways. May you enjoy your careers as professional counselors as much as I have and count yourself blessed.

JCW

To the loves of my life, Erika and Koralie, who continuously believe in me. I am truly blessed.

MKS

Introduction to Clinical Mental Health Counseling

Contemporary Issues

Joshua C. Watson

Texas A&M University–Corpus Christi

Michael K. Schmit

Texas A&M University–Commerce

Los Angeles | London | New Delhi
Singapore | Washington DC | Melbourne

FOR INFORMATION:

SAGE Publications, Inc.
2455 Teller Road
Thousand Oaks, California 91320
E-mail: order@sagepub.com

SAGE Publications Ltd.
1 Oliver's Yard
55 City Road
London EC1Y 1SP
United Kingdom

SAGE Publications India Pvt. Ltd.
B 1/I 1 Mohan Cooperative Industrial Area
Mathura Road, New Delhi 110 044
India

SAGE Publications Asia-Pacific Pte. Ltd.
18 Cross Street #10-10/11/12
China Square Central
Singapore 048423

Acquisitions Editor: Abbie Rickard
Editorial Assistant: Elizabeth Cruz
Production Editor: Astha Jaiswal
Copy Editor: Mark Bast
Typesetter: C&M Digitals (P) Ltd.
Proofreader: Sally Jaskold
Indexer: Robie Grant
Cover Designer: Candice Harman
Marketing Manager: Zina Craft

Printed in the United States of America

Library of Congress Cataloging-in-Publication Data

Names: Watson, Joshua C., author. | Schmit, Michael K., author.

Title: Introduction to clinical mental health counseling / Joshua C. Watson, Texas A&M University-Corpus Christi, Mississippi State University, Michael K. Schmit, University of North Texas, Denton.

Description: Los Angeles : SAGE Publications, Inc., [2020] | Includes bibliographical references and index.

Identifiers: LCCN 2018045029 | ISBN 9781506323756 (pbk. : acid-free paper)

Subjects: LCSH: Mental health counseling.

Classification: LCC RC466 .W38 2020 | DDC 362.2/04256—dc23
LC record available at https://lccn.loc.gov/2018045029

This book is printed on acid-free paper.

19 20 21 22 23 10 9 8 7 6 5 4 3 2 1

BRIEF CONTENTS

DETAILED CONTENTS

Chapter 6 • Documentation and Record Keeping in Clinical Settings   135

Chapter 7 • Working With Managed Care and Third-Party Reimbursement Agencies   171

SECTION II • CURRENT AND EMERGING TRENDS IN CLINICAL MENTAL HEALTH COUNSELING 215

PREFACE

MOTIVATION FOR THIS PROJECT

The motivation to write this book stems from our personal experiences as mental health counselors. In our professional careers, as both clinicians and academicians, we have witnessed a great many changes in the practice of counseling. Some changes have presented new challenges, but most have positively impacted the profession. The experiences Michael and I have had training future counselors and working with clients firsthand has allowed us to see the unlimited potential clinical mental health counselors have to make a positive impact in their local communities. As a result, our goal in writing this book is to help spark your passion for mental health counseling so you too can be a part of this change we know to be possible. As you are the next generation of clinical mental health counselors, your willingness to work with clients in the community who are experiencing a wide range of issues and actively use contemporary, evidence-based practices will be of vital importance as the counseling profession continues to evolve its identity and more effectively serve those in our society most in need.

OVERVIEW AND ORGANIZATION

From the beginning, our overarching goal for this project has been to create a resource for beginning counselors introducing them to contemporary issues and trends in clinical mental health and provide them with the knowledge and aptitude needed to successfully put theory into practice in real-world settings. As we were formulating our vision for this book, we decided early on that we wanted it to be a resource that would really speak to our readers and touch on the issues and trends we see driving the counseling profession today. Specifically, we wanted to create a book that helped counselors familiarize themselves with a variety of topics they likely will encounter as they begin working across clinical settings. As such, we have adopted a more conversational tone throughout the book that speaks to the ways you can use the material we present in any number of clinical mental health settings. Additionally, case illustrations and guided practice exercises are included in every chapter to help you begin to see the application and utility of the content with all types of clients.

The first section of the book provides a global overview of clinical mental health counseling, touching on the more foundational components of modern-day clinical practice. In Chapter 1, we talk about professional identity and help you see what it is clinical mental health counselors do and how this differs from counselors in other settings as well as individuals in the other helping professions. We also provide an overview of how clinical mental health counseling as a specialty area of practice originated and grew into the profession we see today. In Chapter 2, we address the evolution of clinical mental health counseling. The figures, organizations, legislation, and landmark events that helped found and grow the counseling profession are presented to help you the reader appreciate your chosen profession's origins. Our goal in Chapter 3 is to present you with an overview of the counseling theories and models germane to working in clinical mental health counseling settings. This chapter is intended to supplement the richer orientation to counseling theories in general you likely receive in other courses throughout your counselor training program. In Chapter 4, we highlight the policies, laws, and regulatory issues impacting the work of clinical mental health counselors and how counselors can become more active in professional advocacy issues at the local and national level.

The remaining four chapters in Section I focus more on practice-related issues. Here we try to cover some of the day-to-day activities clinical mental health counselors likely will need to perform in their careers. In Chapter 5, we discuss legal and ethical issues. The counseling profession is guided by a set of ethical principles. Along with state and federal legislation, the practice of counseling is regulated and governed in a way that ensures the clients we serve receive the highest possible quality of care. The content in this chapter addresses these legal and ethical guidelines as they relate to both historical and emerging areas of practice. Aware of the ever present need to document services provided, we structure Chapter 6 to include a variety of tips and strategies for effectively documenting clinical work provided. This chapter contains a host of examples related to all types of documentation appearing in a client's case file. In Chapter 7, we address the process through which mental health counselors communicate with managed care and third-party reimbursement agencies. Knowing how to communicate with these groups facilitates the process of gaining approval of services provided and ultimately receiving reimbursement for the work you do. In the final chapter of this first section, Chapter 8, we include a discussion of clinical supervision. Throughout your career you likely will be required to either seek supervision or supervise others. Familiarity with the various models of supervision and how they can be applied will be useful in this process.

The second section of the book, Chapters 9 through 15, incudes the content we are most excited to share with you. In these chapters we address what we see as the issues and trends becoming more prevalent in the practice of clinical mental health counseling. These topics often are addressed briefly in other classes, so we take a more in-depth look at these issues in our book. In Chapter 9, we talk about the incorporation of evidence-based practices into your counseling work. As you may be aware, the current emphasis in mental health service provision is on using evidence-based practices. In this chapter you will learn what it means for a practice or technique to be termed *evidence-based*, how to locate evidence of a treatment, and how to evaluate the quality or merit of that evidence. In Chapter 10, we look at behavioral medicine and the current push toward interdisciplinary care. Here you will learn more about the ways counselors can participate on multidisciplinary treatment teams and effectively communicate with a variety of mental and behavioral health service providers to provide clients with the holistic services they need. Similarly, in Chapter 11 we provide you with an overview of basic principles of psychopharmacology. As the number of clients receiving medications to address their mental health concerns increases, it will be important for you as a counselor to have a basic understanding of what medications do, how they might affect client presentation, and what some of the current medications being prescribed are.

In Chapter 12, we provide a basic understanding of how neuroscience is being integrated into counseling practice. After reading this chapter you should have a greater appreciation for how the mind works and how we as counselors can help clients reshape their brains and evoke a change in thinking, feeling, and behaving. A growing number of clients seek counseling services to cope with challenging events in their lives. In Chapter 13, we talk about how counselors can address issues of bereavement, trauma, loss, and crisis in their work with clients. A variety of strategies, techniques, and interventions are included to help you expand your skill set when working with clients who have suffered. In Chapter 14 we discuss issues surrounding assessment, diagnosis, and treatment planning. In addition to teaching students how to use a six-step differential diagnosis process, this chapter walks students through a five-step process of developing treatment plans using illustrative examples. Finally, we conclude this book with Chapter 15. In this chapter, we address strategies for working with specific client populations. Especially in clinical mental health settings, some of the clients you will encounter may have complexities and additional issues to work through based on who they are and where they come from. We tried to identify a wide variety of client populations you may encounter and offer some insight and targeted suggestions when working with these individuals in the future.

ACKNOWLEDGMENTS

Completing a project of this scope could not have been accomplished without the support and assistance of many individuals. Michael and I would like to extend our sincere appreciation to each of you for helping us create a product we believe will become a true asset to the counselor-training profession. To our families, we thank you for your love and support as the many long hours spent invested in this project were certainly made easier by your positivity and well-timed words of encouragement. To our friends and colleagues, thank you for stimulating our creative process, sharing your expertise, and supporting our writing efforts. Because of you, new generations of counselors continually are being trained to provide much-needed mental health services in communities across the country. We hope you know the lives of many are positively impacted by the work you do. To Rick Parsons and Naijian Zhang, thank you for allowing us to be a part of this project and contributing to this timely series. Thank you to our contributing authors: Rochelle Cade, Karisse Callender, Ted Chapin, Samantha Klassen-Bolding, Caroline Norris, Lori-Russell-Chapin, Erika Schmit, Justin Tauscher, Michelle Wade, and Julia Whisenhunt. Finally, we would like to thank those at SAGE who helped shepherd our vision into reality, especially acquisitions editor Abbie Rickard, whose constant enthusiasm, patience, and unwavering commitment to the project did not go unnoticed.

Finally, we would be remiss if we did not mention the many individuals who reviewed our manuscript throughout the process: Dr. Kathryn Dziekan, New Mexico Highlands University; Arie T. Greenleaf, Seattle University; Susan V. Lester, University of Saint Joseph; Melissa A. Odegard-Koester, Southeast Missouri State University; Kristina A. Peterson, Roosevelt University; Dr. Betsy St. Pierre, Nicholls State University; Jenny Wagstaff, Campbell University; Ben T. Willis, University of Scranton; Dr. Carlos Del Rio, Bellevue University; and Abby E. Dougherty, Drexel University College of Nursing and Health Professionals. We strongly believe the feedback we received from these talented counselor educators helped us produce a more polished product in the end.

ABOUT THE AUTHORS

Joshua C. Watson, PhD, LPC, NCC, ACS, is a professor and chair in the department of counseling and educational psychology at Texas A&M University–Corpus Christi. Dr. Watson has more than 18 years of clinical experience working in a variety of community mental health and private-practice settings and has been active in various professional organizations. In addition to being a past president of the Association for Assessment and Research in Counseling (AARC) and former member of the American Counseling Association (ACA) Governing Council, he currently serves as editor for the *Journal of College Counseling* and is an elected member of the Texas Counseling Association Board of Directors. A renowned scholar, Dr. Watson has authored more than 90 publications and presented at state, national, and international professional counseling conferences. In recognition of his contributions to the profession, Dr. Watson has received numerous awards, including the David K. Brooks Jr. Distinguished Mentor Award, Arthur A. Hitchcock Distinguished Professional Service Award, American College Counseling Association (ACCA) Outstanding Contribution to Professional Knowledge Award, and the Ralph F. Berdie Memorial Research Award. In 2018 he was named an ACA fellow, an honor bestowed on less than 1% of the ACA membership. Dr. Watson resides in Corpus Christi, Texas.

Michael K. Schmit, PhD, LPC, is an assistant professor in the department of counseling at Texas A&M University–Commerce. Dr. Schmit has more than 6 years of clinical experience working with persons across the life span in a variety of clinical mental health settings. Prior to his current role as a counselor-educator, Dr. Schmit was a program administrator at an integrated community mental health center. As an active member of numerous national, state, and local professional counseling organizations, Dr. Schmit is most proud of his service to the *Journal of College Counseling* as an associate editor and the *Journal of Counseling & Development*, the flagship journal of the counseling profession, as a reviewer. In recognition of his contributions to the profession, Dr. Schmit was recently identified as an emerging leader in the field by the Association for Assessment and Research in Counseling (AARC) and the recipient of two national awards, the Glen E. Hubele National Graduate Student Award, in 2016, and the Best Practices Research Award, in 2018, provided by the American Counseling Association for his research on integrated care treatment.

FOUNDATIONS OF CLINICAL MENTAL HEALTH COUNSELING

SECTION I

BECOMING A
CLINICAL MENTAL
HEALTH COUNSELOR

Professional Identity Issues

When you began your training to become a counselor, you might have had an image in your head of what the job entailed. This image likely was formed based on personal experience or seeing a counselor portrayed in a book, movie, or television series. Although there is some validity to what you thought previously, the truth is the roles counselors fill are much more varied. By this point in your counselor training you should be developing an appreciation for the diversity that lies within the counseling profession. Every day, professional counselors make significant differences in the lives of the clients they serve across multiple settings and career fields. Although all professional counselors should be aspiring to empower their clients to accomplish mental health, wellness, education, and career goals (American Counseling Association [ACA], 2016), the manner in which they do so varies depending on their area of specialization. Unlike the general practice of professional counseling, counseling specializations are narrowly focused and require advanced training and knowledge in the field (Myers & Sweeney, 2001). Examples of counseling specializations include school counseling, addictions counseling, rehabilitation counseling, and clinical mental health counseling. In this chapter, we begin examining in depth the distinct field of clinical mental health counseling.

Our goal in writing this chapter is to introduce readers to the field of clinical mental health counseling. Whereas other chapters delve deeper into the specifics of various elements of clinical mental health counseling, this chapter provides a general overview of this unique specialty area. By the end of this chapter, readers should have a greater understanding of the characteristics differentiating clinical mental health counseling from all other counseling specialty areas, minimum educational requirements necessary for practice as a clinical mental health counselor, contemporary issues related to the credentialing and licensing of clinical mental health counselors, current and future employment outlook for individuals with a clinical mental health counseling degree, and the ongoing professional advocacy efforts designed to improve clinical mental health counselors' abilities to best meet the needs of their communities and the clients they serve.

LEARNING OBJECTIVES

After reading this chapter, you will be able to do the following:

- Articulate the scope and mission of clinical mental health counselors

- Describe the origins and history of the clinical mental health counseling specialty area (CACREP 5C-1-a)

- List the educational requirements for practice as a clinical mental health counselor (CACREP 5C-2-k)

- Identify the importance of credentialing for professional counselors (CACREP 5C-2-k)

- Differentiate between clinical mental health counselors and other mental health providers

- Describe various workplace settings employing clinical mental health counselors (CACREP 5C-2-a)

- Summarize current professional advocacy efforts clinical mental health counselors are engaged in at the local, state, and federal level (CACREP 5C-3-e)

CLINICAL MENTAL HEALTH COUNSELING DEFINED

Counseling is far from a homogenous profession. Depending on where a counselor works, the client populations served, and presenting issues addressed, the practice of counseling can look substantively different from setting to setting. For example, the skills and techniques used when working with an adolescent experiencing test anxiety in a primary school setting may be inappropriate for use with an adult client experiencing symptoms of post-traumatic stress disorder (PTSD) following return from a recent overseas military deployment. Clearly, a one-size-fits-all approach would not work for both clients. Because of the diversity in need among clients presenting for help, counselors often find they need localized knowledge of counseling approaches and interventions specific to the setting in which they plan to work to be effective. To meet the unique demands of counselors in all these settings, training needs to be specialized. Recognizing the diversity of experiences in the work counselors do, and the value of promoting specialization, the American Counseling Association (ACA) Governing Council adopted a formal definition of specialty areas within the profession of counseling in 1997. In this definition, counseling specialty areas were conceptualized as narrowly focused areas of practice requiring members to have advanced knowledge and expertise in that area beyond the basic standards and requirements established for the general practice of professional counseling (ACA, 2004; Myers & Sweeney, 2001). Clinical mental health counseling is an example of a specialty area of practice, complete with its own established national standards for education, training, and clinical practice.

So, what is clinical mental health counseling? Although clinical mental health counseling is recognized as a distinct counseling specialty area, defining the practice is challenging. To do so, we first need to understand what counseling is. According to the ACA, **counseling** is defined as "a professional relationship that empowers diverse individuals, families, and groups to accomplish mental health, wellness, education, and career goals" (Kaplan, Tarvydas, & Gladding, 2014; p. 368). By extension, **clinical mental health counseling** can then be defined as the provision of counseling services in institutions of higher education and community-based human service agencies. If you think this definition seems ambiguous, you should know that you are not alone, and others share your confusion. Because the practice of clinical mental health counseling is typically regulated at the state level, the actual definition of what clinical mental health counseling practice looks like varies from state to state. In other words, what a mental health counselor's role would be in, say, New York would be different from what a mental health counselor's role would look like in Minnesota. Because of this lack of uniformity, a better way to understand the practice of clinical mental health counseling is to examine what clinical mental health counselors do in their day-to-day activities. Clinical mental health counselors are highly skilled professionals whose primary goal is to promote optimal states of mental and emotional health for their clients. To accomplish this altruistic goal, clinical mental health counselors benefit from conceptualizing clients from both a developmental and holistic lens (Hershenson & Power, 1987), and artfully combine elements of traditional psychotherapy with a practical problem-solving approach to create a dynamic and efficient path for change and problem resolution (American Mental Health Counseling Association [AMHCA], 2015). As noted on the AMHCA website, practicing clinical mental health counselors offer a full range of services, including these:

- Assessment and diagnosis

- Psychotherapy

- Treatment planning and utilization review

- Brief and solution-focused therapy

- Alcoholism and substance abuse treatment

- Psychoeducational and prevention programs

- Crisis management

Clearly, the role of the clinical mental health counselor has become increasingly more expansive and the practice of clinical mental health counseling more scientific over the years (Calley, 2009). To illustrate this point, O*Net OnLine (www.onetonline.org), the U.S. Department of Labor–sponsored website used for career exploration and job analyses, lists 26 distinct job tasks and professional activities performed by clinical mental health counselors (see Table 1.1). Although several of these duties are performed by counselors in all settings, most are specific to the practice of counseling in a clinical mental health setting and are addressed throughout this textbook.

TABLE 1.1 ■ Job Tasks Listed in the O*Net Summary Report for Clinical Mental Health Counselors
Maintain confidentiality of records relating to clients' treatment.
Encourage clients to express their feelings and discuss what is happening in their lives, helping them to develop insight into themselves or their relationships.
Collect information about clients through interviews, observation, or tests.
Assess patients for risk of suicide attempts.
Fill out and maintain client-related paperwork, including federal- and state-mandated forms, client diagnostic records, and progress notes.
Prepare and maintain all required treatment records and reports.
Counsel clients or patients, individually or in group sessions, to assist in overcoming dependencies, adjusting to life, or making changes.
Guide clients in the development of skills or strategies for dealing with their problems.
Perform crisis interventions with clients.
Develop and implement treatment plans based on clinical experience and knowledge.
Evaluate clients' physical or mental condition, based on review of client information.
Act as client advocates to coordinate required services or to resolve emergency problems in crisis situations.
Modify treatment activities or approaches as needed to comply with changes in clients' status.
Evaluate the effectiveness of counseling programs on clients' progress in resolving identified problems and moving toward defined objectives.
Meet with families, probation officers, police, or other interested parties to exchange necessary information during the treatment process.
Discuss with individual patients their plans for life after leaving therapy.
Collaborate with other staff members to perform clinical assessments or develop treatment plans.
Counsel family members to assist them in understanding, dealing with, or supporting clients or patients.

(Continued)

TABLE 1.1 ■ (Continued)
Monitor clients' use of medications.
Plan, organize, or lead structured programs of counseling, work, study, recreation, or social activities for clients.
Learn about new developments in counseling by reading professional literature, attending courses and seminars, or establishing and maintaining contact with other social service agencies.
Refer patients, clients, or family members to community resources or to specialists as necessary.
Gather information about community mental health needs or resources that could be used in conjunction with therapy.
Supervise other counselors, social service staff, assistants, or graduate students.
Plan or conduct programs to prevent substance abuse or improve community health or counseling services.
Coordinate or direct employee workshops, courses, or training about mental health issues.

Source: This page includes information from O*NET OnLine by the U.S. Department of Labor, Employment and Training Administration (USDOL/ETA). Used under the CC BY 4.0 license. O*NET® is a trademark of USDOL/ETA.

Despite being a new specialty area, clinical mental health counselors find themselves uniquely qualified to meet the challenges of providing high-quality care cost-effectively. In the following section we examine how clinical mental health counseling came into existence. Through understanding the origins of the profession, clinical mental health counselors will have a better understanding of current practices and outlined goals for the future.

ORIGINS OF CLINICAL MENTAL HEALTH COUNSELING

Counseling, as a profession, has been around for well over 120 years. However, prior to the 1960s, counseling services were most often delivered by professionals working in schools and universities rather than in local communities as you will read more about in Chapter 2. Community-based services were still far and few between (Smith, 2012). However, this all changed with the passage of the Community Mental Health Act (also known as the Mental Retardation and Community Mental Health Centers Construction Act). Signed into law by President John F. Kennedy in 1963, the CMHA transformed the way counseling services were delivered by creating a network of community-based comprehensive mental health centers easily accessible to all Americans. Each center was required, at a minimum, to provide five essential services: consultation and education on mental health, inpatient services, outpatient services, emergency response services, and partial hospitalization services. To make this a reality, federal funding was allocated to establish and support over 1,500 mental health centers nationwide.

Passage of the CMHA was both fiscally and socially motivated. Prior to the law, most federal and state resources for mental health treatment were directed toward institutional-based systems of care. Individuals experiencing severe mental illness were hospitalized, often for months or years at a time, in facilities with deplorable conditions. Between

1900 and 1950, the number of people institutionalized for mental illness grew exponentially. By the late 1950s, over 500,000 adults and children were institutionalized across the United States. Treating such a large population taxed available resources. With the CMHA, rather than having to be institutionalized for an indefinite period, individuals could instead receive treatment in their local communities, maintain employment, and attend to family responsibilities. As these community-based treatment facilities were created, so too were opportunities for counselors to work in the community. By the 1970s, a large number of counseling graduates were finding employment in various community and nonschool settings (Weikel, 1985). According to Seiler and Messina (1979), these individuals defined their work as "an interdisciplinary multifaceted, holistic process of (1) the promotion of healthy life-styles, (2) identification of individual stressors and personal levels of functioning, and (3) preservation or restoration of mental health" (p. 6).

The 1970s also saw the emergence of the American Mental Health Counseling Association (AMHCA). The growing number of community-based counselors lacked a true professional home. At the time, the American Personnel and Guidance Association (APGA, now known as the ACA) had a reputation for serving those counselors working in school settings. No organization specifically focused on the professional needs of masters-level counselors working in community-based mental health settings. In 1976, Jim Messina and Nancy Spisso, codirectors of the Escambia County (Florida) Mental Health Center, founded the AMHCA as the professional home for clinical mental health counselors. By 1977, the AMHCA held its first professional conference. Since its inception, the AMHCA has enjoyed strong and steady growth. Today, thousands of clinical mental health professionals are members. As an organization, the AMHCA has played, and continues to play, an important role in the history and development of the clinical mental health counseling profession.

In addition to the development of a professional home for clinical mental health counselors, another important stage in the history of the profession was the establishment of standardized training guidelines. The clinical mental health counseling specialization is a relatively new addition to the counseling profession. First recognized as a distinct specialty area in 2009 by the Council for the Accreditation of Counseling and Related Educational Programs (CACREP), clinical mental health counseling represents a merger of the former community counseling and mental health counseling specializations. The combination of these specialty areas resulted in a new training model that prepared counselors to address the needs of the whole person in their clinical work. According to Gerig (2011), applying wellness and remedial approaches to the assessment, diagnosis, and treatment of individuals and their related systems within relevant ecological contexts are hallmarks of the clinical mental health counseling specialization, and position clinical mental health counselors in an ideal spot to lead the effort in integrating health care. In the following section, you will learn about the specific educational requirements in place to become a clinical mental health counselor.

EDUCATIONAL REQUIREMENTS FOR CLINICAL MENTAL HEALTH COUNSELORS

Clinical mental health counselors have a foundational skill set distinct from those of other behavioral health disciplines. According to the American Mental Health Counseling Association, prior to calling yourself a clinical mental health counselor you will need to satisfy a number of educational requirements and training standards. Specifically, you will need to earn a master's degree in clinical mental health counseling. In the past, clinical mental health degree programs varied in length across institutions. However, recent efforts by the AMHCA have sought to unify the training process. Beginning January 1, 2016, all clinical mental health counseling degree programs were required to be 60 semester hours in length. In addition to specifying program length, the AMHCA also delineated specific curricular experiences to be included in a clinical mental health training program.

Core Curriculum

Although counseling practice is specialized, there are common competencies all counselors, regardless of work setting, should be able to demonstrate. As a result, the common core areas identified by the Council for the Accreditation of Counseling and Related Educational Programs (CACREP) as being representative of the foundational knowledge required of all entry-level counselor education graduates are included in clinical mental health counseling training programs. Based on the 2016 CACREP standards, the common core areas included in graduate clinical mental health counseling training programs are the following:

- Professional counseling orientation and ethical practice

- Social and cultural diversity

- Human growth and development

- Career development

- Counseling and helping relationships

- Group counseling and group work

- Assessment and testing

- Research and program evaluation

Within these eight common core areas, 88 separate standards must be addressed throughout the counseling curriculum for accredited programs.

Supporting classroom instruction across these eight core areas is the requirement for clinical practice. Students in masters-level clinical mental health counseling programs are required to complete practicum and internship experiences as part of their degree plans. The scope and intensity of these experiences vary by institution, with some programs having their own counseling clinics and facilities on campus and others partnering with local community mental health providers for student intern placement. CACREP regulations are specific in terms of the types of counseling and counseling-related activities a practicum or internship experience should include. A required number of hours of individual counseling, group counseling, and supervision are required. The goal of these experiences is to help orient the counselors in training to the professional world of counseling and build their skill sets. In addition to practicing the core skills you learn in the course areas just identified, you also will have the opportunity to demonstrate the skills and knowledge gained that are specific to your specialized area of training.

Specialized Clinical Mental Health Counseling Training

In addition to the common core areas, CACREP standards also delineate certain competencies specific to the specialization area in which students are earning their counseling degree. Standards associated with the foundations, contextual dimensions, and practice of clinical mental health counseling help ensure students intending to specialize as clinical mental health counselors are equipped with the knowledge and skills needed to address a wide variety of circumstances within the context of clinical mental health counseling (CACREP, 2016). Table 1.2 includes the CACREP clinical mental health counseling specialty standards. As you proceed through this text, you will see that the learning objectives identified at the beginning of each chapter are aligned to these specialty area standards.

TABLE 1.2 ■ 2016 CACREP Clinical Mental Health Counseling Specialty Area Standards

1. FOUNDATIONS

   A. History and development of clinical mental health counseling

   B. Theories and models related to clinical mental health counseling

   C. Principles, models, and documentation formats of biopsychosocial case conceptualization and treatment planning

   D. Neurobiological and medical foundation and etiology of addiction and co-occurring disorders

   E. Psychological tests and assessments specific to clinical mental health counseling

2. CONTEXTUAL DIMENSIONS

   A. Roles and settings of clinical mental health counselors

   B. Etiology, nomenclature, treatment, referral, and prevention of mental and emotional disorders

   C. Mental health service delivery modalities within the continuum of care, such as inpatient, outpatient, partial treatment and aftercare, and the mental health counseling services networks

   D. Diagnostic process, including differential diagnosis and the use of current diagnostic classification systems, including the *Diagnostic and Statistical Manual of Mental Disorders* (DSM) and the *International Classification of Diseases* (ICD)

   E. Potential for substance use disorders to mimic and/or co-occur with a variety of neurological, medical, and psychological disorders

   F. Impact of crisis and trauma on individuals with mental health diagnoses

   G. Impact of biological and neurological mechanisms on mental health

   H. Classifications, indications, and contraindications of commonly prescribed psychopharmacological medications for appropriate medical referral and consultation

   I. Legislation and government policy relevant to clinical mental health counseling

   J. Cultural factors relevant to clinical mental health counseling

   K. Professional organizations, preparation standards, and credentials relevant to the practice of clinical mental health counseling

   L. Legal and ethical considerations specific to clinical mental health counseling

(Continued)

TABLE 1.2 ■ (Continued)

3. PRACTICE

A. Intake interview, mental status evaluation, biopsychosocial history, mental health history, and psychological assessment for treatment planning and caseload management

B. Techniques and interventions for prevention and treatment of a broad range of mental health issues

C. Strategies for interfacing with the legal system regarding court-referred clients

D. Strategies for interfacing with integrated behavioral health care professionals

E. Strategies to advocate for persons with mental health issues

Source: CACREP®

MENTAL HEALTH COUNSELOR CREDENTIALING

Throughout your career as a mental health counselor, credentialing will be an important part of your continued growth and development as a professional. **Credentialing** refers to a formalized process of obtaining, verifying, and assessing the qualifications and competence of an individual by a third party with the relevant authority to issue such credentials. During the credentialing process, mental health professionals must provide documentation evidencing their educational background, training, clinical experience, licensure status, and successful satisfaction of other relevant qualifications. Whereas some credentials are mandatory to practice as a mental health counselor, others are voluntarily pursued. Counselors choosing to pursue various credentials often do so to increase their sense of professionalism and demonstrate their expertise in the field (Neukrug, 2017). Additionally, credentialing serves to protect the public by helping individuals identify counselors whose training, clinical experiences, and skill proficiency meet established standards of practice (Foster, 2012). In this section we examine three forms of credentialing most relevant to the practice of mental health counseling: registration, certification, and licensure.

Registration

The least restrictive form of credentialing is registration. In the **registration** process, individuals are recognized for successfully completing requirements mandated for the practice of mental health counseling. Typically, a registry listing the individuals who have satisfied these mandated requirements is made available to the public and acts as a form of advertising for the counselor. To qualify for a registry, the state legislature where a counselor resides and intends to practice must have passed a law allowing professional associations to document or list the individuals within the profession who have met specific standards (Watson, Erford, & Eliason, 2017).

Many state branches of the American Counseling Association provide a list of counselors in their jurisdiction to benefit individuals seeking counseling services. For example, the Texas Counseling Association provides a referral bank of counselors on its website (www.txca.org). Individuals seeking help can customize their search by narrowing the pool of potential counselors by gender, language spoken, specialty areas practiced, and even geographic location. In addition to state counseling associations, national associations also are an option for counselors seeking to promote their services. The American Association of Christian Counselors (www.aacc.net) is one example of a national association providing a registry of its members to the public. For each of these registries, information on local counselors is provided as a public service only. No endorsement is made regarding the skills or qualifications of the counselors listed. Everyone accessing these registries is responsible for researching potential counselors and selecting the individual whom they believe they can work most effectively with in addressing their needs.

Other registries not connected to professional associations also exist. In these cases, counselors can gain listing by signing up and creating an online profile. These services typically come at a cost, with counselors either needing to pay an initial cost to join or monthly payments to keep their profile active and viewable. Given the number of individuals who use the Internet to search for counselors, including one's services in these registries often makes the cost associated with these services a worthy investment for practicing mental health counselors. There are several sites available, but counselors should do their homework and choose those most likely to be accessed by potential clients.

Certification

Certification is the process by which counselors are identified as meeting national standards set by the counseling profession. Certification credentials are typically offered through an accredited professional group. The process of seeking certification is voluntary at the national level and is not required to practice as a mental health counselor. However, seeking certification is one way counselors enhance their expertise, assert their professional identity, and bolster their resume (Paterson, 2006; Sweeney, 1995). For clinical mental health counselors, the National Board for Certified Counselors (NBCC) is the primary credentialing body with which you should be familiar. Established in 1982, the NBCC was developed by the American Counseling Association to be an independently run credentialing body for counselors. By design, the NBCC recognizes counselors voluntarily seeking to meet standards set by counseling professionals rather than state legislators. According to the NBCC (2016), the benefits of obtaining national certification are numerous and include the following:

- To show the public and employers that you have met national standards for education, training, and experience based on research completed by professional counselors working in the counseling profession

- To enhance your professional reputation and credibility and provide a sense of personal accomplishment

- To offer both you and your clients the protection of an enforceable code of ethics

- To demonstrate your commitment to continued professional development and skills expansion

- To increase your opportunities for career advancement and earnings

- To provide you opportunities to advocate on behalf of the counseling profession

The most established, and perhaps most widely recognized, national counseling certification offered through the NBCC is the **national certified counselor** (NCC) credential. As of 2016, more than 60,000 professional counselors worldwide held the NCC credential. According to Paylo, Protivnak, and Kress (2015), the primary benefit of becoming an NCC is to confirm a minimal knowledge, skill, and ability to practice. To become an NCC, an individual needs to (a) hold a degree from either a CACREP-accredited counseling program or from a master's-level program in counseling with a minimum of 48 graduate-level semester hours or 72 quarter hours, (b) document a minimum of 100 hours of counseling supervision, (c) complete a minimum of 3,000 clock hours of postmaster's counseling experience within a 24-month period, (d) demonstrate satisfactory performance on the national counselor examination (NCE), and (e) ensure that his or her behavior adheres to the standards identified in the NBCC's Code of Ethics. Graduate coursework must cover the following nine content areas: human growth and development theories in counseling, social and cultural foundations in counseling, helping relationships in counseling, group counseling theories and processes, career counseling and lifestyle development, assessment in counseling, research and program evaluation, professional orientation to counseling, and counseling field experience. In response to a changing professional landscape, the NBCC has announced it will be changing its requirements for the NCC certification. Beginning January 1, 2022, individuals applying for the NCC credential will need to hold a graduate degree from a CACREP-accredited counselor education program. For current NCCs who did not graduate from CACREP-accredited programs, the NBCC has announced that it will enact a grandfathering clause and continue recognizing these individuals as certified counselors so long as they keep their certification current and remain in good standing.

Another credential with which you likely will want to become familiar is the **certified clinical mental health counselor** (CCMHC) specialty credential. Established in 1993 jointly by the National Academy of Clinical Mental Health Counselors (NACMH) and the NBCC, the CCMHC credential was designed to establish a set of uniform competency standards for professional clinical mental health counselors. Like the NCC, the CCMHC is a voluntary credential. However, several insurance carriers require their providers to hold the CCMHC credential to be included as mental health providers in their network (Litchfield & Watson, 2009). Currently, there are over 1,500 credentialed CCMHCs. To become a CCMHC, an individual needs to (a) hold a degree from either a CACREP-accredited counseling program or from a master's-level program in counseling with a minimum of 60 graduate-level semester hours or 90 quarter hours, (b) document a minimum of 100 hours of counseling supervision, (c) complete a minimum of 3,000 clock hours of postmaster's clinical client contact within a 24-month period, (d) demonstrate satisfactory performance on the National Clinical Mental Health Counseling Examination (NCMHCE), (e) provide a video or audio recording of a clinical session, and (f) ensure that his or her behavior adheres to the standards identified in the NBCC's Code of Ethics. Graduate coursework must address the following 10 content areas: theories of counseling psychotherapy and personality, counseling and psychotherapy skills, abnormal psychotherapy and psychopathology, human growth and development, group counseling and psychotherapy, career development, professional orientation to counseling, research, testing and appraisal, and social and cultural foundations.

As a clinical mental health counselor, there may be other certifications important for you to pursue depending on your area of practice and the work you plan to do. For example, should you see yourself working in addictions, it might be a good idea for you to consider certification as a master addiction counselor (MAC). Or perhaps you plan to practice in a virtual environment. Counselors who work online often investigate becoming certified as distance credentialed counselors (DCC). Both credentials are offered through the Center for Credentialing and Education (www.cce-global.org) and might be added ways to establish credibility with potential clients. Although it may be tempting to add as many certifications as possible, my advice to you is to research the different certifications you are interested in and choose those that best relate to your ability to work with your clients. Your goal should be positioning yourself to be more effective as a counselor rather than amassing an impressive array of "alphabet soup" after your name.

CASE ILLUSTRATION 1.1

I have been a national certified counselor (NCC) since 2000. For me, the NCC is an important part of my professional identity as a mental health counselor. Not only does it establish my credibility among potential clients, it also serves as a testament to my dedication to provide my clients with the best possible services I can. As an NCC, I am required to keep my clinical skills sharp and accrue continuous professional development. Through attending conferences and participating in local and online workshops, I can learn new and innovative ways counselors are working with their clients and adapt them to my own practice. Participating in these professional development opportunities keeps me energized about the work I do and excited for the future of our profession. Although maintaining this credential is not *required* to do my job, I cannot envision a scenario in which I would not renew my certification. As a counselor educator, national certification is something I strongly advise all my students to pursue as they begin their professional careers.

—*JCW (coauthor)*

State Licensure

Another form of counselor credentialing is state licensure. **Licensure** refers to the process by which individual state legislatures regulate the use of title and practice of a profession in their jurisdiction to individuals with specific training and certification. Essentially, licensure laws spell out who can legally use the term *licensed counselor* and

GUIDED PRACTICE EXERCISE 1.1

Think about your upcoming career as a professional counselor. Have you thought of the type of work you would like to do? Perhaps you are interested in working with a certain client population (e.g., children, adolescents, elderly, military veterans, indigent, incarcerated) or certain presenting issues (e.g., addictions, family issues, career/vocational). Based on your responses, search online to determine whether specialty credentials you might be able to pursue to establish your credibility in these areas exist. What would you need to do to earn these credentials, and how can you begin planning to meet those requirements?

who can provide counseling services in a state. Within the counseling profession, state licensure stands as the most inclusive and prestigious credential to obtain. Unlike certification, which is trade-sanctioned and granted by individual professional guilds (e.g., NBCC), licensure is a government-sanctioned credential issued by state licensing boards. According to the American Counseling Association (2016), individual states have the right and obligation to pass laws and take other such actions as they may deem necessary to protect the health, safety, and welfare of their citizens. The licensing process provides states one way to assure that only individuals with the appropriate academic preparation and experience are working with the public. Although licensure laws vary by state, most modern licensure laws include information related to the eligibility criteria, description of a scope of practice, education and certification requirements, penalties for licensure violators, licensing fees, and establishment of a licensure board (Mester et al., 2009).

Motivated by passage of the Community Mental Health Act of 1963, and the psychology profession's subsequent efforts to block counselors from continuing to seek psychology licensure (Goodyear, 2000; Lawson, 2016), the counseling profession, led by the American Personnel and Guidance Association (APGA; now the American Counseling Association [ACA]), began a focused campaign to pursue licensure for counselors in the early 1970s. These efforts proved successful, and Virginia became the first state to enact a counseling licensure law in 1976. Since then, the counseling profession has worked diligently to overcome many obstacles and at times opposition from other professions to achieve the goal of having counseling licensure laws enacted in all 50 states. In 2009, that goal finally became reality when the California legislature supported a counseling licensure law. Today, all 50 states as well as Puerto Rico and the District of Columbia license mental health counselors.

One of the benefits afforded individuals granted licensure by their appropriate state credentialing agencies is the ability to use the approved professional title in their state. Across the country, several titles are used to refer to licensed counselors, for each state is free to choose how they refer to their license credential. In some states, a single license to practice is issued. This license is commonly referred to as a **licensed professional counselor** (LPC). In other states, specialty licenses are awarded to LPCs who have completed advanced clinical requirements. Examples of these advanced specialty license titles include the licensed clinical professional counselor (LCPC), licensed professional clinical counselor (LPCC), licensed mental health counselor (LMHC), licensed professional counselor of mental health (LPCMH), and licensed clinical mental health counselor (LCMHC). Although each state has its own requirements for obtaining licensure, there are some basic licensing requirements related to education, supervised counseling experience, satisfactory performance on state licensing examinations such as the National Counselor Examination (NCE) or National Clinical Mental Health Counselor Examination (NCMHCE), and adherence to established ethical codes and standards of practice. The website of each state licensing board is included in a tremendous resource provided by the NBCC (www.nbcc.org/directory). By clicking on the state in which you are interested in working, you can find the contact information for the licensing board and additional information helpful in beginning the licensing process. By beginning to plan now, you will be able to take courses or select practicum and/or internship sites that will facilitate you meeting the educational and practice requirements outlines in the licensure regulations for your state. Because all states have their own set of requirements, it may be helpful to consider states in which you may have interest working and research their specific requirements for licensure.

GUIDED PRACTICE EXERCISE 1.2

Research the state licensure requirements for your current home state and two additional states where you might aspire to practice. This may require you to use multiple sources (e.g., Internet, telephone, personal visit) to gather the information you need. Once you have reviewed the licensure requirements in the states you chose, answer the following questions for each state:

1. What is the name of the license in this state?

2. What types of degrees qualify one for licensing in this state?

3. How many semester hours of graduate coursework are required to become license-eligible?

4. How many total clock hours are required for licensure? How many of these hours can come from predegree supervised practicum and internship experiences?

5. How many hours of postdegree supervision are required? Are there specific requirements for these supervision services and the professionals who provide them?

6. Are candidates required to pass any examinations to be licensed? If so, what examinations?

7. How often must counselors renew their license? What must counselors do to maintain the status of their license yearly?

8. Does this state practice reciprocity? If so, with which states?

With licensure in hand, clinical mental health counselors have a wide variety of options available to them regarding workplace setting. In the following sections, we look at how clinical mental health counselors differ from other mental health professionals working with clients in community and agency facilities and examine some of the many workplace settings clinical mental health counselors find employment and what it is like to function in each of these types of settings.

CLINICAL MENTAL HEALTH COUNSELORS AND OTHER MENTAL HEALTH PROVIDERS

In addition to clinical mental health counselors, several other mental health professionals are trained to help individuals address behavioral or psychological problems. Psychologists, social workers, and psychiatrists are but a few of the treatment providers with whom clients may interact throughout their care. In this section we briefly examine the differences between these similar professions in terms of the treatment models they follow and the training required to join these professions.

Psychologists

Probably most similar to clinical mental health counselors are psychologists. Psychologists mainly study the human mind and human behavior. Trained in the scientist-practitioner model, psychologists look to determine the root causes of client distress and mental illness by gaining empirical evidence. Guided by their clinical experience, psychologists posit hypotheses regarding their clients' conditions and look to collect data in the form of signs and symptoms to either prove or disprove their hypotheses. As a result, assessment and diagnosis are major components of the clinical process when psychologists work with clients.

Psychologists are trained in American Psychological Association (APA)–accredited graduate training programs. To practice as a licensed psychologist, an individual must complete a doctoral degree program as well as a clinical residency. Doctoral-level psychologists can earn either a doctor of philosophy (PhD) or doctor of psychology (PsyD) degree. The difference between the degrees deals with whether the training emphasis was more on research (PhD) or clinical practice (PsyD).

Social Workers

Social workers are masters-level clinicians who help individuals, groups, and communities improve social functioning. They advocate for their clients and arrange for the provision of needed social services. As a profession, social work is based on the social-ecological model of treatment. In this model, the complex interplay among individual, relationship, community, and societal factors is considered when developing treatment plans and working with clients. The overlap between these factors (see Figure 1.1) illustrates the influence each factor has on the others.

To practice as a social worker, one needs to complete at minimum a 4-year college degree. However, to be considered for licensure as a licensed clinical social worker (LCSW), a graduate degree in social work as well as 2 years of postgraduate supervised clinical experience are required. The LCSW credential is available in all 50 states and allows individuals to move from state to state to practice.

FIGURE 1.1 ■ Social-Ecological Treatment Model

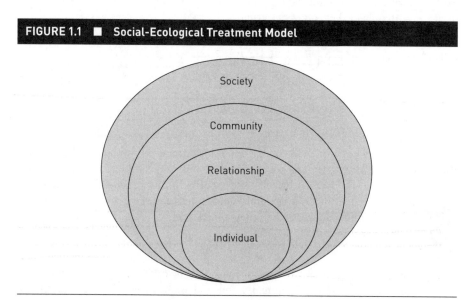

Society

Community

Relationship

Individual

Psychiatrists

Psychiatrists are medical doctors (i.e., physicians) certified to treat and diagnose mental disorders. Traditionally, psychiatrists have adhered to a biomedical model as the primary approach toward client care. In the biomedical model, all mental illness is thought to be the product of a biological defect, with any symptoms that cannot be explained in biological terms being excluded from consideration when making a diagnosis. However, a more modern approach espoused by many psychiatrists addresses the reductionist nature of the biomedical model by also examining psychological and social roots to clients' problems. In terms of interventions, pharmacotherapy remains the primary treatment provided by psychiatrists.

To become a psychiatrist, an individual must complete medical school and earn either a doctor of medicine (MD) or doctor of osteopathic medicine (DO) degree. Following degree completion, a 4-year residency with a specialization in psychiatry is required. Written and oral examinations allow one to become licensed and certified. Licensure occurs at the state level, and certification is available through the American Board of Psychiatry and Neurology. Table 1.3 compares these mental health professions.

TABLE 1.3 ■ Comparison of Mental Health Professions				
	Counselors	**Psychologists**	**Social Workers**	**Psychiatrists**
Orientation	Wellness, developmental model	Scientist-practitioner model	Social-ecological model	Biomedical model
Training	Graduate (MS) or advanced graduate (PhD) degree	Graduate (MS) or advanced graduate (PhD or PsyD) degree	4-year college degree or graduate (MSW) degree	4-year college degree; medical school with special training in psychiatry
Credentialing	State licensure with MS degree and supervised work experience	State licensure with PhD or PsyD degree and clinical residency	State licensure with MSW degree and supervised work experience	State licensure with MD or DO degree and clinical residency
Main Professional Organization	American Counseling Association	American Psychological Association	National Association of Social Workers	American Psychiatric Association

GUIDED PRACTICE EXERCISE 1.3

As we read in this chapter, there are several different mental health professions. What was it about counseling, specifically clinical mental health counseling, that drew you to this profession? In small groups of three to four students, share your responses and see if any common themes emerge. What was it about counseling that drew members of your group in, and how do they see their careers developing?

WORKPLACE SETTINGS FOR CLINICAL MENTAL HEALTH COUNSELORS

Clinical mental health counselors find employment in a variety of settings and can work with many different client populations addressing a variety of presenting issues. No matter what your professional interests, you likely will be able to find a setting where you can do the kind of work you enjoy and find rewarding. This is often mentioned as one of the best parts of being a counselor. There are multiple ways an individual can help others, and all serve a valued purpose in improving our neighborhoods and communities. As a bit of an introduction, the following are examples of some of the many sites and settings you might find employment as a clinical mental health counselor. A more comprehensive list of workplace settings for clinical mental health counselors is included in Table 1.4.

Outpatient Community Mental Health Centers

Outpatient community mental health centers are perhaps the most common setting in which clinical mental health counselors work. At this level of care, a wide variety of services are offered to clients including outpatient therapy, 24-hour emergency services, day treatment and partial hospitalization programs, and psychosocial rehabilitation services. Counselors working in community mental health centers often serve as the first contact many clients have with a help provider, so another part of the work clinical mental health counselors do is screening and triage of client presenting issues. Because most community mental health centers operate on state or federal funding, there is an increased need to focus on counselor productivity. In this sense, **productivity** refers to the number of billable hours a counselor generates (Newsome & Gladding, 2014). Additionally, mandates from managed care organizations require the use of evidence-based treatments when working with clients. As a clinical mental health counselor, it will be important for you to have a strong working knowledge of evidence-based therapies and how they can be integrated into established treatment plans for the clients you serve. In Chapter 9 we focus more on evidence-based treatment and how you as an emerging clinical mental health counselor can find and implement these treatments.

Residential Care Facilities

Mental health counselors also find employment in residential care facilities. A residential care facility is a place where individuals in need of continuous monitoring

GUIDED PRACTICE EXERCISE 1.4

Depending on the setting in which you work, the clients with whom you interact are likely to also have contact with several other mental health care professionals. How would you describe to a client what it is that you do as a clinical mental health counselor? What would you say are the key differences between you and these other mental health care professionals?

TABLE 1.4 ■ Workplace Settings for Clinical Mental Health Counselors
Cancer care facilities
Career development centers
Colleges and universities
Community mental health centers
Corrections facilities (jails and prisons)
Domestic violence shelters
Employee assistance programs (EAPs)
Health maintenance organizations (HMOs)
Hospice units
Hospitals
K–12 school settings
Outpatient medical clinics
Private practice
Psychiatric facilities
Substance abuse treatment centers

and supervision are housed temporarily. Residential care facilities exist for all types of populations, including children, adults, and the elderly. According to the American Residential Treatment Association (ARTA, 2018), residential care facilities offer mental health treatment for a variety of diagnoses including but not limited to the following:

- Bipolar disorder
- Schizophrenia
- Depression
- Personality disorders
- Mood disorders
- Anxiety disorders
- Post-traumatic stress disorders
- Substance abuse disorders
- Autism spectrum–related disorders

Residents in these facilities are often voluntarily placed, meaning they are free to discontinue treatment when they like. Counselors in these facilities often facilitate group counseling sessions, conduct individual counseling sessions, coordinate care with families, and provide psychoeducational content to assist clients with their eventual discharge from the facility and return to home. Individuals typically receive treatment at a residential care facility when they are leaving a hospital or acute psychiatric care facility as a way of transitioning to full independent living.

Psychiatric Hospitals

Psychiatric hospitals, or behavioral health centers, employ clinical mental health counselors to provide individual and group counseling services to children, adolescents, young adults, adults, and families. Clients hospitalized in these facilities are either seen as an imminent threat to themselves or others or need to have their current medication regimen regulated. Issues typically treated at this level of care include the serious conditions of clinical depression, schizophrenia, and bipolar disorder. Counselors working in these settings often assist in the admission of clients and work with them throughout their hospitalization until discharge. Whereas in the past most individuals hospitalized for mental illness could expect lengthy stays, the current treatment emphasis is on helping individuals gain control of their own lives and transition to a lesser (e.g., outpatient) level of care as soon as possible. Within the inpatient setting, clinical mental health counselors participate as members of an interdisciplinary treatment team that includes both mental health and medical personnel working to address the client's needs through a combination of pharmacotherapy and psychotherapy.

Substance Abuse Treatment Centers

Clinical mental health counselors also may find gainful employment working in substance abuse treatment centers. In this setting, the clinical mental health counselor works with individuals whose relationship with alcohol and/or illicit drugs is currently causing problems in one or more aspects of their lives. A range of services are offered in these settings. Clinical mental health counselors may work with clients individually or in groups. Typical services offered in these settings include detoxification, inpatient treatment, outpatient treatment, partial hospitalization, and psychoeducation. In addition to working with the individual user, there is a strong possibility that clinical mental health counselors also will work with the family and friends of the user. Additional training and/or certification may be needed to work in some substance abuse treatment facilities, but in general, a masters-level counseling license is a sufficient practice credential.

Hospitals

Hospitals or other medical settings provide opportunities for clinical mental health counselors to ply their trade. Many hospitals have counselors on staff to work in emergency departments for cases involving mental health or substance use–related presenting concerns. Clinical mental health counselors working in this setting may be asked to triage clients who present for emergency services, arrange for inpatient hospitalization if needed, or participate in the involuntary commitment process for those clients deemed to be a current danger to self or others. Working in an emergency department is often fast-paced and challenging. Counselors often have no idea what a workday will look like when they arrive. In addition, the ability to quickly assess and preliminarily diagnose clients are essential skills. If working in an emergent care setting does not seem to be a fit for you, other opportunities to work in hospital settings are a little less fast-paced. Clinical mental health counselors also may find employment working with hospitalized patients who indicate either a current need for counseling or an ongoing counseling treatment. Here, you would be able to help these individuals by establishing referrals for them upon their discharge or communicating with their current mental health providers if needed.

CASE ILLUSTRATION 1.2

I have worked at the local community mental health center for the past 11 years. In that time, I have filled many roles. Initially, I was hired as a case manager. While working on my licensure hours I managed the counselors' caseloads and made sure records and files were always updated. Although I did not get to participate in actual therapeutic counseling with the clients we served, I did feel I was playing a role in their treatment. After becoming licensed I transitioned into a therapist position. This is the role I still hold today. Although the work is demanding, I love being a counselor.

Each day I get a chance to make a positive impact in people's lives. What I most like about the setting in which I work is the fact that I never know what my day will hold in advance. Sure, I have an established caseload, but new issues emerge all the time in my clients' lives, and this requires me to always be sharp clinically. I have colleagues who also have worked in community mental health settings and they also describe similar experiences. Although this may not be the ideal work setting for all counselors, for me I know it is where I am meant to be, and it is where I can help the most.

K–12 School Settings

In some districts, clinical mental health counselors find employment in school settings. Often, these school administrators contract with local mental health agencies to provide clinical services to students on campus and support the efforts of professional school counselors. School-based mental health services include a broad spectrum of assessment, prevention, intervention, postvention, counseling, consultation, and referral activities and services. As funding issues have reduced the number of school counselor positions, the number of available mental health professionals who can work with the growing number of students presenting with diagnosable disorders becomes problematic. As a result, many public school systems have turned to community mental health agencies for assistance. These services, often referred to as *school-based mental health services*, provide outpatient services to children and their families within the school environment through individual and family counseling, case management, and referral and access to psychiatric services if needed (Baker, 2013). Recent legislation regarding the implementation of school-based mental health services (i.e., the Mental Health in Schools Act of 2013) further supports the identified need for additional services for our youth (Corthell, 2014).

Colleges and Universities

Clinical mental health counselors also work on college and university campuses. In this setting, mental health counselors interact with students presenting with a host of issues and concerns. Some of the issues college counselors deal with include academic challenges, relational problems, stress management, homesickness, and difficulties adjusting to the college environment. Adding to these issues, college students are increasingly coming to school with a wide range of existing mental health concerns. According to recent studies, an estimated 11% of college students are dealing with symptoms of mental health warranting a clinical diagnosis (Gallagher, 2011), and as many as 25% of students are being prescribed psychotropic medications as part of their current treatment protocol (Guthman, Iocin, & Konstas, 2010). Working in this type of setting, clinical mental health counselors can expect to work as part of an interdisciplinary treatment team. Along with psychiatrists and psychologists, you may find yourself interacting with medical personnel, for many college counseling centers operate closely with campus student health services. Currently, a push is being made for more licensed professional counselors to be on the clinical staff of college counseling centers. In my home state of Texas, this is one of the advocacy efforts the state counseling organization is working on as a way of promoting the profession and ensuring clients are receiving the services most likely to be of benefit to them.

Employee Assistance Programs

An employee assistance program (EAP) is a work-based intervention program designed to identify and assist employees in resolving personal problems (e.g., martial, financial, or emotional problems; family issues; or substance abuse or usage-related problems) that may be having an adverse effect on an employee's job performance, health, and well-being (Society for Human Resource Management [SHRM], 2014). Established in the 1940s to address the negative impact of alcoholism on productivity and organizational performance, EAPs have expanded their services throughout the years. Today, most EAPs are full-service treatment providers operating as a member benefit and providing services to employees and their immediate families at little or no out-of-pocket cost. Clinical mental health counselors working in corporate EAP programs provide employees with individual, group, and family counseling services; psychoeducational training; testing and assessment; consultation; and treatment referrals. In addition to working with employees, EAP counselors also might be asked to work with management by providing advanced planning for unique situations such as organizational change or restructuring, legal considerations, emergency planning and preparedness, and help in response to unanticipated traumatic events (United States Office of Personnel Management [OPM], 2016). EAP counselors often have master's degrees in either clinical mental health counseling or addictions counseling.

Private Practice

Many clinical mental health counselors ultimately decide to work for themselves and go into private practice. Depending on the counselor, these practices can serve several different issues and client populations. There are many advantages to working in a private practice setting. For one, you get to be your own boss. This means you set your own hours, determine the structure and policies of your practice, and decide on the types of services that will be provided. However, before starting a private practice, counselors should look to gain clinical experience first working in one of these other settings. Working in an agency setting allows you to develop your skill set, build established referral networks with colleagues, and earn a guaranteed income. In time, you can begin transitioning into a private practice as an established mental health provider in the community. When you do, it is important to make sure you have a strong business plan and have consulted with other private practice clinicians to ensure you are taking the appropriate steps to be successful. Organizations such as the ACA and AMHCA offer a variety of resources to their members interested in going into private practice, including online tools, podcasts and webinars, books, and professional development courses. If you are willing to work hard, landing a lucrative private practice is well within reach for the masters-level clinical mental health counselor.

Correctional Facilities

Some mental health counselors may find themselves working in correctional facilities. Working with individuals in the prison system, clinical mental health counselors provide counseling services to inmates throughout the duration of their incarceration. In addition to evaluating all new inmates, counselors in these settings also provide mental health and educational services to individuals in need. For inmates being discharged, counselors aid in preparing the individual for the transition to life outside prison and what that will look like. A primary focus of the work a counselor does in the criminal justice system is relapse prevention. Counselors work to build skills clients will need to prevent recidivism and refrain from a life of crime and illegal activity.

PROFESSIONAL IDENTITY

Hopefully you now see that the counseling profession provides you unique opportunities to help others. There are many possibilities available to you in terms of the training you receive, credentials you seek, clients you serve, and settings in which you may find yourself working. No matter where you find yourself in the future, it is important that you continually seek to strengthen and crystallize your professional identity. Knowing who you are professionally, what you stand for, and what is important to you and your clients improves the quality of care you provide and strengthens the profession. As your professional identity develops you also may find it important to begin advocating for professional counselors in other settings. Although we all may work in different areas, counselors are bound by a shared passion and vision for helping. Despite the good we as counselors do, the profession itself still faces many challenges that hinder efforts to provide quality mental health care. As a result, professional advocacy becomes an important component of your role as a mental health counselor. We touch on the issue of professional advocacy at several points throughout this book to highlight its importance.

PROFESSIONAL ADVOCACY

The term **advocacy** refers to those actions taken by counselors to remove the environmental barriers hampering client well-being. In this sense, advocacy is an important part of the work clinical mental health counselors do. However, this is not the only type of advocacy they engage in. Clinical mental health counselors also engage in professional advocacy and support the continued growth of the profession. As noted by Myers and Sweeney (2004), "Advocacy of the profession has the potential to place counselors in positions where they can advocate effectively for the causes of their clients" (p. 466). However, many clinical mental health counselors do not engage in professional advocacy efforts. Or, when they do, their efforts are often ineffective (Reiner, Dobmeier, & Hernandez, 2013). Fortunately, this does not have to be the case. In terms of professional advocacy efforts, there are several ways clinical mental health counselors can support their profession and ultimately benefit the clients served by clinical mental health counselors in communities nationwide. As you will see in the suggestions that follow, professional advocacy does not have to be complex.

One easy way clinical mental health counselors can advocate for their profession is by contributing to the establishment of a singular professional identity. One of the biggest issues that has plagued the counseling profession in general is the lack of a single voice articulating who counselors are and what they do. With so much variance, it is easy to see how the public can get confused about how counselors might be able to help them. As we collectively work to promote professional identity this confusion will subside. So how can you contribute to professional identity? The answer is simple—become involved. Join professional organizations. As clinical mental health counselors, organizations such as the ACA and AMHCA should be your professional homes. Stand with your colleagues and help shape the way clinical mental health counseling services are viewed and delivered. In addition to joining these organizations, become involved. Whether at the local or national level, look to contribute to the organization's mission by becoming an active advocate.

A second way in which you can advocate for the profession is by participating in lobbying efforts. At the national level, several counseling organizations are engaged in efforts to increase recognition of the profession. You too can play a valuable role in this process. Contact your local elected officials and share with them the valuable work counselors do and how clients and the community benefit from having these services available. Many state counseling associations sponsor advocacy days in which counselors gather in the capitol and lobby their representatives to endorse initiatives that promote counseling and increase access to services for a greater number of individuals. The AMHCA website has a link for individuals to see the current advocacy efforts the profession is taking and how one can get involved (www.amhca.org/?page=advocacy). Every voice counts and supports the profession and the clients it serves.

A third way counselors can advocate for the profession is by demonstrating professional pride and accountability. For some of your clients, their interaction with you is their only exposure to counseling. How you act has an important influence on how that individual ends up viewing the counseling process and what they share with others about you and counseling in general. As a result, you should strive to maintain high standards

GUIDED PRACTICE EXERCISE 1.5

Identify a current mental health issue in your home state (can be local to your community or statewide) and develop an advocacy initiative around that issue. In your description of the advocacy project, include your rationale for this initiative; the type(s) of advocacy it involves; and all community, state, national, and international resources to which you may refer a client in need of these resources. Additionally, address your plans for marketing and promoting your work so that it is seen, heard, and experienced by the appropriate audience(s) and stakeholders in the community.

of practice and professionalism. Treat clients and their families with respect and always practice in an ethical manner. Finally, be proud of the work you do. Demonstrate pride in being a counselor and others will take notice, seeing your passion as a sign that the work being done is valued.

CASE ILLUSTRATION 1.3

Throughout my career I have been fortunate to have had several positive experiences in my role as a counselor. One that truly stands out to me is participating in one of the American Counseling Association's *Day at the Capitol* events. During these events, the ACA organizes a group of counseling professionals to visit with their elected officials in Washington, DC, to advocate for the profession. Meeting with these legislators helped me realize how important it is that we as counseling professionals advocate for the work we do. Many people simply do not know what counselors do or how they benefit local communities. I can remember my congressman being shocked by some of the statistics I shared regarding the number of persons who go without adequate mental health care for financial reasons. He seemed receptive to my message and promised to educate himself more on the issue. I realize legislators hear pitches like this every day from various groups and constituencies, but knowing that I at least kept counseling and mental health care on his mind was satisfying. As professional counselors, more of us should look to take part in similar activities. If not at the national level, then certainly at the state and local level, advocating for the care our clients need and deserve.

Keystones

- Clinical mental health counseling is a profession that meets the needs of community members using various counseling interventions and treatment models.

- The practice of clinical mental health counseling differs from other helping professions in terms of treatment paradigms followed, training received, and professional activities engaged in as part of client care.

- Certain educational requirements are in place to become a clinical mental health counselor. In addition, practicing counselors should seek to obtain appropriate credentials (licensure or certification) to practice in their communities.

- Clinical mental health counselors find employment in many different venues and work with varied client populations.

- Clinical mental health counselors should engage in professional advocacy efforts as

a way of supporting their profession and promoting the visibility of counseling in the communities in which they work and live.

Key Terms

Advocacy 24

Certification 11

Certified clinical mental health counselor 12

Clinical mental health counseling 4

Counseling 4

Credentialing 10

Licensed professional counselor 14

Licensure 13

National certified counselor 12

Productivity 18

Registration 10

Web Resources

American Association of State Counseling Boards (www.aascb.org)

American Counseling Association (www.counseling .org)

American Mental Health Counselors Association (www.amhca.org)

Council for the Accreditation of Counseling & Related Educational Programs (www.cacrep.org)

National Board for Certified Counselors (www.nbcc .org)

onetonline.org
aacc.net
cce-global.org

References

American Counseling Association. (2004). Definition of professional counseling specialty. Retrieved from http://www.counseling.org/news/updates/2004/07/26/definition-of-professional-counseling

American Counseling Association. (2016). What is counseling? Retrieved from https://www.counseling .org/about-us/about-aca

American Mental Health Counseling Association. (2015). Facts about mental health counselors: What is a clinical mental health counselor? Retrieved from http://www.amhca.org/?page=facts

American Residential Treatment Association. (2018). Treatment for a variety of mental health conditions. Retrieved from https://artausa.org/

Baker, C. (2013). School-based mental health services: What can the partnership look like? Retrieved from http://ct.counseling.org/2013/01/school-based-mental-health-services-what-can-the-partnership-look-like/

Calley, N. (2009). Comprehensive program development in mental health counseling: Design, implementation, and evaluation. *Journal of Mental*

Health Counseling, 31(1), 9–21. doi:10.17744/mehc
.31.1.u018125603371233

Corthell, K. (2014). The role of mental health counselors in public schools. Retrieved from http://scholarworks.gsu.edu/cgi/viewcontent.cgi?article=1117&context=cps_diss

Council for the Accreditation of Counseling and Related Educational Programs. (2016). 2016 CACREP standards. Retrieved from http://www.cacrep.org/for-programs/2016-cacrep-standards/

Foster, L. H. (2012). Professional counselor credentialing and program accreditation in the United States: A historical review. *Journal for International Counselor Education, 4*, 42–56. Retrieved from http://digitalcommons.library.unlv.edu/jice

Gallagher, R. P. (2011). National survey of counseling center directors. Retrieved from http://collegecounseling.org/wp-content/uploads/2011-NSCCD.pdf

Gerig, M. S. (2011). *Foundations for clinical mental health counseling: An introduction to the profession* (2nd ed.). Upper Saddle River, NJ: Pearson.

Goodyear, R. K. (2000). An unwarranted escalation of counselor-counseling psychologist professional conflict: Comments on Weinrach, Lustig, Chan, & Thomas (1998). *Journal of Counseling & Development, 78*(1), 103–106. doi:10.1002/j.1556-6672.2000.tb02566.x

Guthman, J. C., Iocin, L., & Konstas, D. D. (2010, August). *Increase in severity of mental illness among clinical college students: A 12-year comparison.* Paper presented at the Annual Meeting of the American Psychological Association, San Diego, CA. Retrieved from www.apa.org/news/press/releases/2010/08/students-mental-illness.aspx

Hershenson, D. B., & Power, P. W. (1987). *Mental health counseling: Theory and practice.* New York, NY: Pergamon Press.

Kaplan, D. M., Tarvydas, V. M., & Gladding, S. T. (2014). 20/20: A vision for the future of counseling: The new consensus definition of counseling. *Journal of Counseling and Development, 92*, 366–372. doi:10.1002/j.1556-6676.2014.00164.x

Lawson, G. (2016). On being a profession: A historical perspective on counselor licensure and accreditation. *Journal of Counselor Leadership and Advocacy, 3*(2), 71–84. doi:10.1080/23276716X.2016.1169955

Litchfield, M., & Watson, J. C. (2009). Mental health counseling. In American Counseling Association (Ed.), *The ACA encyclopedia of counseling* (pp. 101–103). Alexandria, VA: ACA.

Mester, J. L., Trepanier, A. M., Harper, C. E., Rozek, L. S., Yashar, B. M., & Uhlmann, W. R. (2009). Perceptions of licensure: A survey of Michigan genetic counselors. *Journal of Genetic Counseling, 18*(4), 357–365. doi:10.1007/s10897-009-9225-0

Myers, J. E., & Sweeney, T. J. (2001). Specialties in counseling. In D. C. Locke, J. E. Myers, & E. L. Herr (Eds.), *The handbook of counseling* (pp. 43–54). Thousand Oaks, CA: Sage.

Myers, J. E., & Sweeney, T. J. (2004). Advocacy for the counseling profession: A national survey. *Journal of Counseling and Development, 82*(4), 466–471. doi:10.1002/j.1556-6678.2004.tb00335.x

National Board for Certified Counselors. (2016). Benefits of certification. Retrieved from http://www.nbcc.org/Certification/BenefitsOfCertification

Neukrug, E. S. (2017). *A brief orientation to counseling: Professional identity, history, and standards* (2nd ed.). Boston, MA: Cengage Learning.

Newsome, D. W., & Gladding, S. T. (2014). *Clinical mental health counseling in community and agency settings.* Upper Saddle River, NJ: Pearson.

Paterson, J. (2006). Sorting out certification. Retrieved from http://ct.counseling.org/2006/10/sorting-out-certification/

Paylo, M. J., Protivnak, J. J., & Kress, V. E. (2015). Professional credentialing. In V. F. Sangganjanavanich & C. Reynolds (Eds.), *Introduction to professional counseling* (pp. 267–292). Thousand Oaks, CA: Sage.

Reiner, S. M., Dobmeier, R. A., & Hernandez, T. J. (2013). Perceived impact of professional counselor identity: An exploratory study. *Journal of Counseling and Development, 91*(2), 174–183. doi:10.1002/j.1556-6676.2013.tb00084.x

Seiler, G., & Messina, J. J. (1979). Toward professional identity: The dimension of mental health counseling in perspective. *American Mental Health Counselors Journal, 1,* 3–8.

Smith, H. L. (2012). The historical development of community and clinical mental health counseling in the United States. *Turkish Psychological Counseling and Guidance Journal, 4,* 1–10.

Society for Human Resource Management. (2014). Employee assistance program (EAP): General: What is an employee assistance program? Retrieved from https://www.shrm.org/resourcesandtools/tools-and-samples/hr-qa/pages/whatisaneap.aspx

Sweeney, T. J. (1995). Accreditation, credentialing, professionalization: The role of specialties.

Journal of Counseling & Development, 74(2), 117–125. doi:10.1002/j.1556-6676.1995.tb01834.x

United States Office of Personnel Management. (2016). Work-life: Employee assistance programs. Retrieved from https://www.opm.gov/policy-data-oversight/worklife/employee-assistance-programs/

Watson, J. C., Erford, B. T., & Eliason, G. T. (2017). Professional counseling organizations, licensure, certification, and accreditation. In B. T. Erford (Ed.), *Orientation to the counseling profession: Advocacy, ethics, and essential professional foundations* (3rd ed., pp. 35–68) Columbus, OH: Pearson.

Weikel, W. J. (1985). The American Mental Health Counselors Association. *Journal of Counseling & Development, 63,* 457–460. doi:10.1002/j.1556-6676.1985.tb02833.x

EVOLUTION OF CLINICAL MENTAL HEALTH COUNSELING

Imagine the latter years of your professional career as you begin contemplating retirement. For some of you that could be a few years away. For others, retirement could be a distant goal 20, 30, or even 40-plus years in the future. Regardless of how far off this point in your career might be, envision what you think the profession will look like. What types of issues are you likely to be addressing with clients? What kind of services will you be offering, and how will they be offered? Will there even be professional counselors in the future? Only time will tell what the profession looks like in the future. What is for sure is the fact that counseling as a profession will look markedly different than it does today. This has always been the case for our profession and will continue to be so into the future.

Your ability to practice today and look toward the future was made possible by several pioneering individuals whose vision for a better society helped form the foundation of the mental health counseling profession. Through an exploration of the historical roots of the profession, today's practicing counselors are more knowledgeable and better equipped to face the evolving challenges facing the counseling profession as it continues to grow and mature.

LEARNING OBJECTIVES

After reading this chapter, you will be able to do the following:

- Articulate the history and development of clinical mental health counseling (CACREP 5C-1-a)
- Describe the origins of current theories and models related to clinical mental health counseling (CACREP 5C-1-b)

- Name the important contributors, organizations, and legislation that have shaped the field through the years
- Understand the current state of the profession and the scope of mental health counseling practice across various settings
- Identify trends shaping the future of clinical mental health counseling practice

MENTAL HEALTH COUNSELING: PAST, PRESENT, AND FUTURE

In Chapter 1 we introduced you to the specialized practice of clinical mental health counseling. Although community-based mental health services are relatively new, the practice of counseling extends well over 120 years. In those early times, several individuals, decisions, and events helped pave the way for the profession of today to emerge. Awareness of our past helps us understand where our profession is at and where it can go from here. In this chapter, we delve a bit deeper into the clinical mental health counseling profession by reviewing the past, examining the present, and looking toward the future.

In the 19th century, counseling was practiced very differently than it is today. Early counselors were seen more as teachers or social advocates who gave advice and educated their clients on the resources available to them for help. As such, in the first half of the 1900s the focus for and growth of the emerging counseling profession were educational institutions (Sangganjanavanich & Reynolds, 2015). However, evolving societal demands brought about the need for more structured services. At the turn of the century, a period commonly referred to as the Progressive Era, changes across three professional movements—guidance counseling and educational reform, mental health reform, and the emergence of psychometrics as a scientific discipline—helped form the foundation of counseling practice as we know it today. Without the vision of early pioneers dedicated to improving the lives of others and helping create a better society, these social reform movements likely would not have occurred.

PIONEERS IN THE PROFESSION

During the Progressive Era (1900–1920), the United States experienced a tremendous amount of growing pains associated with the rise of industrialization and immigration. Local governments struggled to keep pace with the large numbers of people moving to America's cities in search of better lives for themselves and their families. Lacking the proper infrastructure to support their growth, many cities became rife with political corruption, disease, and debilitating social inequities. Social reformers sought to combat the negative consequences of urbanization and create a better environment in which people could prosper and thrive. These community activists focused on humanitarian concerns, child and adult welfare, public education and guidance, legal reform, and immigration management (Smith, 2012). It is within this social reform movement that the counseling profession was born. In this section, we introduce you to a sample of progressive reformers whose efforts in the first half of the 20th century were instrumental in establishing the foundation from which the counseling profession would emerge. Collectively, they made it possible for individuals like you to train for a career as a mental health counselor.

Frank Parsons

Frank Parsons (1854–1908) was a bit of a renaissance man whose work made an indelible mark on the counseling profession. Born in Mount Holly, New Jersey, on November 14, 1854, Parsons was an inquisitive child whose quest for knowledge allowed him to excel academically. At the age of 15 he was admitted to Cornell University where he earned a degree in civil engineering in only 3 years. Upon graduating, Parsons became a railroad engineer in western Massachusetts. This position would prove to be short-lived, for the depression of 1873 bankrupted the railroad company and sent Parsons into unemployment. After initially finding work as a day laborer, he eventually accepted a position with the Southbridge public school system teaching courses in history, mathematics, and French. While teaching, he was encouraged by his friends and colleagues to pursue a career in law. Studying independently, Parsons passed the Massachusetts bar examination in 1881 and opened a small private practice in Boston. However, practicing law did not appeal to Parsons so he began writing legal textbooks for a local publishing house. Ultimately, he became a lecturer at the Boston University school of law, a position he held from 1892 to 1905 at which time his varied research and civic interests forced him to resign.

While in Boston, Parsons experienced firsthand the exponential population growth caused by the continued industrialization of America. An avid social reformer who was active in populist and progressive causes, Parsons noted the struggles newcomers experienced and tirelessly advocated for the improved living conditions of those adversely affected by the Industrial Revolution (Aubrey, 1983). In addition, he spoke out on the need for more systematic vocational guidance programs designed to help Boston's new citizens identify careers for which they were best suited. Consequently, with an initial staff of three and an advisory board comprised of local civic leaders, Parsons opened the Vocation Bureau in Boston in 1908. There Parsons and associates provided vocational assessment interviews, counseling, and information to aspiring young workers (Protivnak, 2009). Specifically, they worked with individuals to find careers in which they would excel using the following three principles of career choice that would become the basic tenets of the trait and factor approach to vocational counseling:

1) Developing a clear understanding of the individual including that person's aptitudes, interests, values, ambitions, resources, strengths, and weaknesses

2) Developing a knowledge of the world of work including an understanding of the requirements and conditions of success, advantages and disadvantages of various jobs, training needs, compensation, current opportunities, and prospects in that specific field of work

3) Successfully merging the two previous characteristics, matching talent to job requirements, to facilitate satisfaction and success

Using these principles, the Vocation Bureau staff served 80 men and women in its first 4 months of existence. And, as Parsons (1909) noted, "according to their own spontaneous statements, all but two . . . received much light and help. Some even declaring that the interview with the Counsellor was the most important hour of their lives" (p. 30).

Though Parsons would pass away before the end of the bureau's first year, his work provided the foundation on which modern career counseling practices are based (Savickas, 2011), securing his legacy as father of the vocational guidance movement. As Brewer (1942) noted, in a brief period of approximately 2 years, Frank Parsons had accomplished the following:

1) Furnished the idea for the Vocation Bureau and began its execution

2) Paved the way for vocational guidance in schools and colleges by advocating their role in it and offering methods they could use (35 cities had adopted the Boston vocational guidance model by 1910)

3) Began the training of counselors

4) Used all the scientific tools available to him at the time

5) Developed "steps" to be followed in the vocational progress of the individual

6) Organized the work of the Vocation Bureau in a way that laid the groundwork for groups to model in schools, colleges, and other agencies

7) Recognized the importance of his work and secured for it the appropriate publicity, financial support, and endorsements from influential educators, employers, and other public figures

8) Laid the groundwork leading to the continuance and expansion of the vocational guidance movement by involving friends and associates and preparing the manuscript for *Choosing a Vocation*.

GUIDED PRACTICE EXERCISE 2.1

To gain a better understanding of Parsons's trait and factor approach, explore your own career choice and how it relates to you as an individual. Using the RIASEC Markers Scales (https://open psychometrics.org/tests/RIASEC/) you can see how your individual constellation of personality traits match up with your chosen profession. What do your results suggest? Are you in the right field? Does your personality lend itself to the types of skills needed to be an effective mental health counselor? Should the results of this screening be taken as a valid and reliable indicator of whether counseling is a suitable profession for you? Share your results with a peer in class.

Clifford W. Beers

Clifford W. Beers (1876–1943) was another influential early-20th-century social reformer whose work proved pivotal to the development of modern-day clinical mental health counseling practice. Recognized as the founder of the mental hygiene movement, Beers's personal experiences with mental illness led to him becoming a staunch advocate for the improved treatment of the mentally ill. Born in New Haven, Connecticut, Beers was the second youngest of five children. As a child, he experienced significant familial losses, including an older sibling who died during infancy and an older brother who was diagnosed with epilepsy as a teenager and ultimately died at a young age as well. These losses had a profound effect on Beers, who himself would go on to suffer from multiple bouts of depression as both a child and young adult. Despite his struggles with mental illness, he excelled academically. After graduating from Yale University in 1897, Beers began working as a financier in New York City. During this time, he became increasingly more anxious and depressed and feared he too would one day suffer the same fate as his brother. In 1900, during a bout of depression, Beers attempted suicide. At his family's Connecticut home, he let himself fall from a top-floor window to the ground below. Amazingly, he survived by narrowly missing the concrete alley and fencing behind the home and landing on a small patch of grass, shattering every bone in both legs. He subsequently would spend the next 3 years in various mental health institutions.

Although some staff members treated Beers well, the majority physically abused and subjected him to various forms of degrading treatment while institutionalized. This mistreatment troubled Beers and spurred his interest in championing reform. Following his release from treatment in 1903, Beers began writing about his experiences. His writings would ultimately be published in 1908 as book titled *A Mind That Found Itself*. The book brought newfound attention to the way patients were treated in mental health institutions, leading to public outcry for change. Though he voluntarily would be institutionalized again in 1904, Beers continued leading efforts to improve the quality of institutional care, challenge the stigma of mental illness, and promote mental health (Parry, 2010). In 1909, he founded the National Committee for Mental Hygiene (renamed the National Mental Health Association [NMHA] in 1950 and Mental Health America [MHA] in 2006). According to MHA's (n.d.) website, the organization "is the nation's leading community non-profit dedicated to addressing the needs of those living with mental illness and promoting the overall mental health of all Americans." Today, MHA staff and volunteers from over 200 affiliates across 41 states are leading grassroots advocacy efforts to help Americans live mentally healthier lives by educating the public on mental illness and reducing barriers to treatment and services. Mental Health America would not be possible were it not for Beers sharing his personal struggles and promoting improved treatment conditions for others with similar afflictions.

Jesse B. Davis

Jesse B. Davis (1871–1955) is another early counseling pioneer whose efforts helped shape modern-day clinical mental health practice. Davis was working as a high school counselor in Detroit, Michigan, when he was appointed principal of Central High School on the west side of the state in Grand Rapids. Influenced by such progressive American educators as Horace Mann and John Dewey, Davis was a huge proponent of vocational guidance being an integral part of a child's education. As principal, he sought to increase the amount of didactic guidance students received and implemented what would become the first school-based systematic guidance program. In his program, all English teachers in Grades 7 through 12 required students to write weekly essays on topics related to vocational choice, career plans, and the type of person they hoped to become. Davis believed prompting students to think about their future and vocational choices would help address current challenges in American society, build moral character, and prevent problems. His pioneering work in establishing school-based vocational guidance programs in Michigan provided the foundation for the modern-day career counseling specialization (Pope, 2009).

In addition to his local work, Davis made an impact nationally. In 1912, at the second National Guidance Conference held in New York, Davis was appointed to an organizing committee tasked with exploring the possibility of establishing a national association that would advance the vocational guidance movement in response to growing economic, educational, and social demands (U.S. Bureau of Education, 1914). Following a year of meetings, the committee presented their findings in October 1913 at the third National Guidance Conference held in Grand Rapids, primarily because of Davis's presence and work in that community. Their report was well-received, leading to the creation of the National Vocational Guidance Association (now known as the National Career Development Association [NCDA]). According to its founding constitution, the purpose of NVGA was to "promote intercourse between those who are interested in vocational guidance; to give stronger and more general impulse and more systematic direction to the study and practice of vocational guidance; to establish a center or centers for the distribution of information concerning the study and practice of vocational guidance; and to cooperate with the public school and other agencies in the furtherance of these objects" (Feller, 2014). Inaugural officers also were voted on at the conference, with Davis being selected to serve as the NVGA's first secretary.

Abraham and Hannah Stone

The efforts of Abraham and Hannah Stone helped expand the scope of counseling services outside of school-based and institutional facilities. Abraham Stone (1890–1959) was a urologist whose research interests included reproductive health issues including family planning, birth control, sterility, fertility, sexual relations, and global overpopulation. Together with his wife Hannah (1894–1941), also a physician whose pioneering work as an advocate for the birth control movement led to her being named the founding director of the Margaret Sanger Research Bureau, they established the first family and marriage counseling center in New York City. There they counseled thousands of couples with relationship and sexual problems. The approach they used deviated from any used previously to address issues such as these. They would go on to publish their counseling techniques in a book titled *A Marriage Manual: A Practical Guide-book to Sex and Marriage* (1931). This was one of the first books of its kind exploring marital relations and communication skills among couples. The work of Abraham and Hannah Stone was significant in that it marked a shift in counseling practice where career and vocational issues were the only focus of discussion.

Edmund Griffith ("E. G.") Williamson

Edmund Griffith ("E. G.") Williamson (1900–1979) was a lifelong academic. After completing his doctorate in psychology, he joined the faculty at the University of Minnesota at the age of 31. Between 1931 and his retirement in 1969, Williamson remained affiliated with the university in various capacities including professor, director of testing and counseling, coordinator of student services, and dean of students. It was here that Williamson made his mark on the counseling profession.

During the 1930s, the Minnesota Employment Stabilization Research Institute was established at the University of Minnesota to assist those whose careers had been lost due to the Great Depression (Chartrand, 1991). Working at the institute, Williamson began applying many of the same principles Parsons was using in Boston at the Vocation Bureau. His approach, trait and factor theory, or the Minnesota point of view as it was called, is widely regarded as the first true comprehensive counseling model. Trait and factor theory expands on the concept of vocational matching by integrating psychometric data gathered in addition to client interviews to match dimensions. In fact, one of the career assessment instruments that emerged out of this work was the *Strong Interest Inventory*. After collecting data, the counselor would then analyze it using statistical techniques to quantitatively evaluate individuals and their potential career fits. The entire counseling process consisted of six steps designed to systematically assist college students with their career development concerns. The six steps in this process were (1) analysis, (2) synthesis, (3) diagnosis, (4) prognosis, (5) counseling, and (6) follow-up (see Table 2.1).

Carl Rogers

Carl Rogers (1902–1987) was one of the most influential psychologists of the 20th century. However, psychology was not always his career goal. He initially attended the University of Wisconsin with the intention of majoring in agriculture. While enrolled, his interests changed and he switched majors often, first to history and then to religious

TABLE 2.1 ■ Six-Step Sequence of the Trait and Factor Theory	
Step	**Tasks Performed**
Analysis	Examination of the presenting problem; gathering of existing records, available test scores/results, and additional background on the client
Synthesis	Collating available information to identify patterns and develop a working hypothesis of the client's presenting problem
Diagnosis	Interpretation of the problem based on all available information
Prognosis	Estimating the likelihood that the client would be better adjusted under different conditions or career options
Counseling	Working collaboratively with the client to establish potential solutions to the presenting problem
Follow-up	Ensuring the client is satisfied with the resolution obtained and establishing safeguards and support systems for the future should the presenting problem reemerge or new problems arise

studies with an eye toward a career in ministry. While at the University of Wisconsin he participated in a study-abroad program and spent 6 months in Beijing, China, attending a World Student Christian Federation Conference along with nine other students. While in China, seeds of doubt were spread as Rogers began questioning his religious beliefs as he was exposed to new cultures and religious dogma. Upon his return to the United States, and subsequent graduation in 1924, Rogers moved to New York City and enrolled in Union Theological Seminary. In seminary he attended a student-led seminar titled "Why Am I Entering Ministry?" that led to his turning away from religion personally (he became an atheist) and professionally (he left the ministry). After 2 years in seminary he transferred to Columbia University Teachers College where he worked with John Dewey and earned his doctorate in clinical psychology in 1931.

After an initial clinical appointment, Rogers transitioned to a life in academe. He held faculty positions at the University of Rochester, Ohio State University, University of Chicago, and the University of Wisconsin. While at Ohio State University, Rogers began developing his theory of client-centered change. There he wrote *Counseling and Psychotherapy* (1942) in which he posited that clients who can build a strong working relationship with an accepting and empathic counselor would be able to resolve any problems they faced and gain the insight needed to live happier and healthier lives. His ideas represented a radical deviation from current therapeutic approaches that relied heavily on behavioral principles. For Rogers, behaviorism was too simplistic. He believed the approach had low ecological validity and completely neglected the fact that individuals could make their own decisions (free will). Initially, these ideas were not widely supported.

Undeterred, Rogers moved to Chicago in 1945 and continued refining his ideas regarding clinical work. There he founded a counseling center and wrote two of his more influential works, *Client-Centered Therapy* (1951) and *Psychotherapy and Personality Change* (1954). At his last academic appointment at the University of Wisconsin, Rogers wrote perhaps his most famous book, *On Becoming a Person: A Therapist's View of Psychotherapy* (1961). In it, he suggested that individuals have the innate ability to resolve their own conflicts and facilitate personal growth. Further, he outlined a process through which counselors could help their clients achieve self-actualization. According to Rogers (1959), we all have an actualizing tendency that is deeply rooted in our genetic makeup. This **actualizing tendency** is what guides us to grow and reach our full potential. True self-actualization occurs when a person's ideal self, who one would *like* to be, is congruent with one's real self, who one *actually* is (see Figure 2.1). In other words, we all can achieve our hopes, dreams, and aspirations in life. Our ability to do so depends on whether we are fully functioning persons (see Table 2.2).

FIGURE 2.1 ■ Carl Rogers's Conceptualization of Self-Actualization

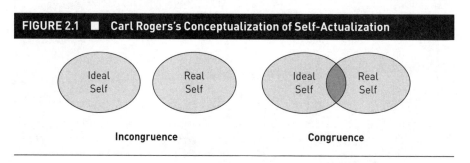

GUIDED PRACTICE EXERCISE 2.2

Consider your own ideal and real selves. Are you living in congruence? If not, what changes might you need to make to better align your ideal and real self? Additionally, consider what currently prevents you from doing so. How might these obstacles or barriers to self-actualization be like those experienced by your clients? Knowing yourself and your own challenges, how would you go about helping your clients overcome their barriers to self-actualization?

TABLE 2.2 ■ Characteristics of a Fully Functioning Person	
Open to new experiences	Acceptance of both positive and negative emotions. The individual realizes that life has its ups and downs, and low points represent opportunities to be resilient and work through these negative issues.
Existential living	Being able to live in the here-and-now and appreciate the moment. The individual can experience life as it is without the filter of any preconceptions or prejudices.
Trust in feelings	Individuals should trust their basic instincts. Gut reactions should be acknowledged and trusted. Everyone is in the best position to make the right decision for himself or herself.
Creativity	A fully functioning individual is willing to take risks in life. Rather than playing it safe, these individuals seek adventure and positively adjust to changes in their world.
Fulfilled life	Individuals who are happy and satisfied with life. Individuals who are open to new challenges and experiencing all life has to offer.

Rogers's work was influential in that it ushered in a new school of thought known as humanism. Deviating from the dominant treatment approaches of the time, behaviorism and psychoanalysis, counselors began focusing less on symptom reduction and more on client empowerment. Clients became active participants in the counseling process and were viewed as experts in their own lives. Rather than providing solutions for client problems, Rogers believed counselors should instead work to create an environment conducive to growth for their clients. This environment included the need for what Rogers would call the core conditions of counseling: genuineness, acceptance, and empathy. Because of Rogers's efforts the humanistic approach flourished, with counselors referring to it as the "third force" in psychology (Maslow, 1968). This new perspective redefined the therapeutic relationship and how counselors interacted with their clients.

C. Gilbert Wrenn

Gilbert Wrenn (1902–2001) had a long and distinguished career that impacted the counseling profession in a profound way. A counseling psychologist by trade, Wrenn was one of the first presidents of the American Psychological Association's Division of Counseling and Guidance (now the Division of Counseling Psychology) and the founding editor of the *Journal of Counseling Psychology*. In 1962, his seminal work

The Counselor in a Changing World introduced a shift in thinking for counselors in placing greater emphasis on developmental needs than career and vocational issues. Wrenn (1962) noted that individuals should not be viewed in isolation; rather, they needed to be seen as part of a larger system in which environmental and societal influences are considered. This perspective provided a foundation for which school counseling programs should be constructed in a society with changing views on human behavior and the role of school personnel (Gibson & Mitchell, 2011). Specifically, Wrenn (1962) thought school counselors should fill four primary functions: (a) counseling students; (b) consulting with parents, teachers, and administrators; (c) studying changing student demographics and interpreting this information for school administrators; and (d) coordinating school-based counseling services as well as school-community partnerships.

Wrenn's approach changed community-based mental health counseling services as well, for throughout the 1960s and beyond counselors began focusing more on the influence of cultural diversity and client background in the counseling process (Gladding & Newsome, 2018).

INFLUENTIAL PROFESSIONAL ORGANIZATIONS AND ASSOCIATIONS

As the mental health counseling profession began to grow and expand its scope, counselors nationwide began moving to establish professional organizations that would help promote the profession, provide networking opportunities for practitioners, and champion a new unified voice for the profession. Several organizations and associations emerged throughout the 20th century, but the following groups merit mentioning for the lasting impact they have had on the profession.

American Personnel and Guidance Association

The American Personnel and Guidance Association (APGA) was founded in 1952 to formally organize groups interested in guidance, counseling, and personnel matters (Gladding & Newsome, 2018). At a joint convention in Los Angeles, members of four professional organizations, the National Vocational Guidance Association (NVGA), the National Association of Guidance and Counselor Trainers (NAGCT), the Student Personnel Association for Teacher Education (SPATE), and the American College Personnel Association (ACPA), convened to find a way to collaborate on their shared interests and vision. These groups would become the first four divisions of the APGA. According to the new association's ethical standards, the APGA was established as an educational, scientific, and professional organization dedicated to service to society (APGA, 1961).

In 1983, the organization rebranded itself as the American Association of Counseling and Development (AACD). This name change was made to reflect changes and commitment to the counseling field and more accurately represent the evolving professional orientation of the organization's membership (Vacc & Loesch, 2000). Finally, in 1992 the organization adopted its current name, the American Counseling Association (ACA), to reflect the common bond among association members and to reinforce their unity of purpose (ACA, 2018). Today, the ACA functions as a not-for-profit organization comprised of 19 chartered divisions, four regions, and 56 branches across the United States, Europe, and Latin America that works to grow and enhance the counseling profession. Table 2.3 describes the ACA's core values.

American Mental Health Counseling Association

The American Mental Health Counseling Association (AMHCA), established in 1976, is the leading national organization for licensed clinical mental health counselors. In the 1970s, many counselors began to secure employment in nonschool settings. Community agencies, counseling centers, and private practice settings became popular sources of employment for mental health counselors. Despite this vocational shift, the primary professional organization at the time, the APGA, still focused primarily on counseling in school settings and had no distinct division for those counselors working out in the community. Seeking to rectify this situation and give a professional home to community and agency counselors, counselors in Florida and Wisconsin began lobbying efforts aimed at establishing a new APGA division that represented mental health counselors. At its July 1976 meeting, APGA leaders met to consider the proposal from AMHCA leadership to become a new divisional partner. Optimism was high, however, the APGA board instead passed a resolution placing a moratorium on any new divisions until further research could be conducted to gauge whether expansion would be beneficial. Undaunted, the leaders of the AMHCA incorporated the organization in Florida and began operating independent of the APGA. It would not be until the summer of 1978 that the AMHCA would officially become a division of the APGA.

Capitalizing on the uniqueness of mental health counseling and the counseling skills, developmental approach, and preventative strategies employed by its members, the AMHCA continues to use its influence to generate legislation more favorable to mental health counselors and to propose programs aimed at better health care (Weikel, 1985). Today, AMHCA leaders work to address such current professional issues as the role of mental health counselors

TABLE 2.3 ■ Core Values of the American Counseling Association	
Diversity, equity, and inclusion	Values individuals for the diversity of identity, ideas, and interests they bring to the group and actively works to engage them in the association and profession
Integrity	Leadership and staff commit to being honest, transparent, and values-based in their communication, action, and advocacy efforts.
Proactive leadership	Serves as a leader in the counseling field, both creating a vision and taking action to advance the profession
Professional community and relationships	Creates opportunities for counselors to network, collaborate, and enhance their skills through lifelong learning
Scientific practice and knowledge	Espouses evidence-based methodologies and practices and supports their use in counseling research, practice, supervision, and teaching
Social justice and empowerment	Commits to being a champion for the provision of high-quality mental health care to all individuals

in business and industry through employee assistance programs (EAPs), health maintenance organizations (HMOs), hospital privileges for counselors, counselors' roles and rights related to diagnosis, interprofessional liaisons, and full parity for mental health counselors in state and federal legislation as well as health care insurance plan coverage.

National Board for Certified Counselors

The National Board for Certified Counselors (NBCC) was established as a not-for-profit, independent certification organization in 1982 (NBCC, 2018). Today, the NBCC serves as the premier certification body of the profession and advances the counseling profession representing over 64,000 national certified counselors in 40 countries. In addition to offering the national certified counselor (NCE) credential, the NBCC also administers several specialty certifications including the certified clinical mental health counselor (CCMHC), master addictions counselor (MAC), and national certified school counselor (NCSC) credentials. The leadership at the NBCC is dedicated to advancing the counseling position. This dedication is evident in the role it plays in state and national advocacy and lobbying efforts.

CASE ILLUSTRATION 2.1

I have called the American Counseling Association my professional home since I began my career as a mental health counselor in 1998. Looking back at my time as a member, I would say it has been beneficial to my professional development and would encourage others to strongly consider joining. The association provides so much to its members, with many services available free of charge. In addition, participation in the ACA and attendance at conferences each year has helped me build a strong and supportive network of colleagues nationwide. These individuals are those I turn to for advice, counsel, and support. I also appreciate that the ACA advocates for me professionally. Their lobbying efforts on behalf of counselors and commitment to promoting counseling and counselor identity are important to me and represent a value for the membership dues I pay.

I also would recommend beginning counselors actively involve themselves in the ACA. Your membership is enhanced when you take an active role in helping the association grow and meet its goals and objectives. Throughout my career, I have had the opportunity to participate locally and nationally in a variety of roles and functions. I have served as a program proposal reviewer, committee member, state branch representative, division president, and member of the ACA's Governing Council and Executive Committee. Active participation lets me take ownership in helping build the profession. When students ask me whether they should get involved or what they should look to be doing I often respond that every little bit helps. Everyone can play a part in helping the organization be successful, and volunteers are always welcome.

—JCW

Chi Sigma Iota

Chi Sigma Iota (CSI) is the international honor society of professional counseling and for professional counselors. Established by Dr. Tom Sweeney in 1985 at Ohio University, CSI serves to provide recognition for outstanding achievement as well as outstanding service within the profession. CSI currently has over 120,000 initiated members, making it one of the largest single member organizations of professional counselors in the world (CSI, 2018). Members, who must meet stringent academic standards, have access to the CSI newsletter, *Journal of Counselor Leadership and Advocacy*, and are eligible for a series of awards, grants, scholarships, and fellowships. Many counselor training programs house local CSI chapters. Mental health counseling students often find CSI membership beneficial because it helps establish a professional identity and affords members opportunities to network with professionals nationwide through virtual and live meetings.

CASE ILLUSTRATION 2.2

Being a member of Chi Sigma Iota (CSI) is much more than a line on your curriculum vita. Rather, it means being a part of a counseling community whose focus is on excellence in counseling through leadership, service, advocacy, and scholarship. As counselors, service and advocacy do not stop when the last client leaves for the day. It is part of our professional identity and responsibility to be agents of change outside our offices. As a student, CSI provided me with opportunities to positively impact others within my own community and within the counseling field. With programs like the Leadership and Fellow Intern Program, it created an avenue for me to foster innate leadership qualities but also develop those I did not possess. Through opportunities like CSI Days at the American Counseling Association conferences, writing for publication in the Counselor's Bookshelf, participating in the free online webinars, and offering chapter and research grants,

CSI was instrumental in establishing my burgeoning scholar identity. These programs and initiatives also gave me the chance to collaborate with colleagues and professors, to teach and be taught.

This guidance and encouragement has continued as I transitioned to a counselor educator and chapter faculty advisor. I can share that I have undeniably found a supportive home in Chi Sigma Iota. It is an affordable counseling organization that strives for excellence and caters to the needs of students, practitioners, and counselor educators. I encourage students, faculty, and alumni to stay active members of their local chapter. Being a member of CSI has most certainly been a worthwhile endeavor that has aided in my own personal and professional development as a counselor and counselor educator.

—J. Gerlach
Assistant Professor of Counselor Education

American Association of State Counseling Boards

The American Association of State Counseling Boards represents state boards regulating the practice of counseling. Created in 1986 by an AACD (now ACA) steering committee, the AASCB was established to encourage communication among individual state licensing boards. Specifically, the AASCB collects, interprets, and disseminates information on legal and regulatory matters directly and indirectly impacting the ability of licensed professional counselors to engage in independent practice. Today, the AASCB seeks to promote regulatory excellence and serve as the premier resource for information related to counselor licensing and regulation, test development, and standards for licensing. According to the AASCB (2018) website, the overarching goal of the group is to accept "competent counselors into the arena of professional practice rather than excluding individuals based on arbitrary or unreasonable criteria."

Fair Access Coalition on Testing

Fair Access Coalition on Testing (FACT) is an independent group of professionals formed in 1996 dedicated to protecting and supporting public access to professionals and organizations demonstrating competence in the administration and interpretation of assessment instruments including psychological tests (FACT, 2018). Representatives from the following professional organizations, in addition to public members, sit on the FACT board of directors:

- American Association for Marriage and Family Therapy
- American Counseling Association
- American Mental Health Counselors Association
- American Speech-Language-Hearing Association
- Association for Assessment and Research in Counseling
- Association of Test Publishers
- National Association of School Psychologists
- National Board for Certified Counselors

The FACT coalition was established to protect the rights of counselors who use assessments and tests to develop treatment plans, provide appropriate referrals, and assess treatment progress of their clients. They also monitor state and national legislation and regulatory actions to assure that all qualified professionals are permitted to administer test instruments (FACT, 2018). Unfortunately, many counselors have been adversely affected by policies or legislation that includes unfair requirements or restrictive clauses that impede counselors' ability to provide quality care to their clients (Watson & Sheperis, 2010). In recent years, FACT has assisted counselors in defeating proposed legislation in Indiana, Kentucky, and Wisconsin that would have significantly limited, and in some cases prohibited, counselors' use of various tests and diagnostic assessments.

COUNSELING PROFESSION TODAY

The preceding sections were intended to provide you with foundational knowledge related to your profession's origins and development. The individuals and organizations included have made, and in some cases continue to make, invaluable contributions to the continued growth and maturation of mental health counseling. According to U.S. Bureau of Labor Statistics, mental health counseling is one of the few professions expected to grow at a rate almost 3 times the national average for all other forms of employment. In recent reports, the number of available mental health counseling positions was expected to grow 29% between 2012 and 2022. This growth represents the increasing demand for mental health services as well as the effect advocacy efforts of professional organizations like those previously mentioned have had to increase public recognition of professional counseling and the quality care its members provide. Subsequent chapters in this book address contemporary practice issues in mental health counseling we hope will allow you to become a more well-informed and competent practitioner.

EMERGING PROFESSIONAL TRENDS

Where the clinical mental health counseling profession goes in the future is anyone's guess. Although the destination may be unknown, we do know the profession will continue to evolve to meet the changing needs of persons across the globe as it has since the early parts of the 20th century. In addition to a growing need for mental health counselors, a changing professional landscape awaits those about to enter the profession. Shifting paradigms, evolving standards of care, and technological advances all are having a direct impact on the way mental health counselors practice, the services they deliver, and the clients with whom they will work. As a result, it is imperative for counselors to remain abreast of changes that may affect the work they do. In the remainder of this chapter, we attempt to forecast the future and identify some of the issues and potential challenges mental health counselors will face. We realize our list is by no means exhaustive and is likely to exclude issues and challenges that have not yet emerged.

Telehealth

The emergence of telehealth technologies is transforming the delivery of health care services for millions of persons (Dorsey & Topol, 2016) as providers, patients, and treatment funders all seek more effective and cost-efficient ways to deliver care. Although imperfect, telehealth services represent a promising treatment alternative for clients living in rural, remote, and underserved areas where sufficient health care options are lacking (Valentino, 2016). Several definitions of telehealth exist, with many states opting to create their own operating descriptions. At the federal level, the Health Resources and Services Administration (HRSA, 2018) defines **telehealth** as the use of electronic information and telecommunication technologies to support and promote long-distance clinical health care, patient and professional health-related education, public health, and health administration. These technologies include several different service delivery strategies and employ multiple mediums such as terrestrial and wireless communications, the Internet, streaming media, and videoconferencing.

Although still in its infancy, telehealth has been shown to have a positive impact on individual health care. In a recent Altru Health System survey, an anticipated 7 million patients were expected to use telehealth services in 2018, up nearly 2000% from 2013. Further, an estimated 70% of employers had plans to begin offering telemedicine services as an employee benefit. These increases show individuals being receptive to this type of delivery method and providers adapting their practice to meet the needs of their patients. Among the benefits provided by telehealth services are these:

- Increased access to care

- Reduced travel time and costs

- Improved satisfaction with the health care system

- Reduced delays in care

- Ability to ensure continuity of care

- Ability to consult with specialists in the field

- Reduced stigma associated with seeking mental health services

Mobile Health Apps

Smartphones have become ubiquitous fixtures in the lives of billions of users since their creation in the mid-2000s. In 2017, roughly three quarters of Americans (77%) owned a smartphone, a statistic more than double (35%) the amount reported in 2011 (Statista, 2018). Among millennials, smartphone ownership is even more pronounced; over 90% of Americans ages 18 to 29 reported owning a smartphone. As the number of smartphone users continues to grow, so too does the number of multimedia applications (apps) being developed. In 2016, there were over 6 million apps available for download with total time spent engaged in app usage topping 1.6 trillion hours globally (Hollander, 2017).

As app usage becomes a more ubiquitous part of everyday life, it only makes sense that mental health care providers explore ways to use this technology. Based on recent statistics, it appears this is the case. From 2009 to 2015, the National Institute of Mental Health awarded 404 grants totaling $445 million for technology-enhanced mental health intervention (NIMH, n.d.). Apps for self-management, mood tracking, passive symptom tracking, skills training, improved thinking skills, illness management and supported care, screening and assessment services, and mindfulness are all readily available. With the proliferation of apps being added to the marketplace daily, it can be difficult to distinguish quality tools from those that are not. To assist counselors in knowing which apps to use and recommend to their clients, the American Psychiatric Association has developed an online evaluation model to rate mental health apps (see Web Resources). The model includes five steps: (1) gather background information, (2) risk/privacy and security, (3) evidence, (4) ease of use, and (5) interoperability. Steps 2 through 5 are presented in sequence so that apps rating unsatisfactory at a lower level need not be evaluated at a higher level. In this model, it is important to note that there are no specified guidelines for how many criteria need to have been met for an app to be considered good or useful. Like all interventions and techniques, you the counselor must ultimately decide its utility for the clients you counsel. Table 2.4 highlights some of the advantages and disadvantages of mental health apps that counselors should consider.

CASE ILLUSTRATION 2.3

As part of their dissertation research, two former students in the doctoral program at the university I am affiliated with created a mobile mental health app to serve as a free psychoeducational tool to support pregnant women and new mothers who may be experiencing perinatal and/or postpartum depression. Their app, VeedaMom, is one of the first to use technology to detect depression during pregnancy. It is a multifunctional app a woman can use and share with her physician. The app allows women to complete self-screening assessments, manage symptoms of perinatal depression, and

address personal wellness. As their two dissertations show, the initial research on the app and
its efficacy looks promising. Qualitative data show
that when women use the educational material in
the app, they face their feelings and thoughts in
positive ways, and our quantitative results have
shown that using the app reduces depression by
15% in postpartum mothers compared with just
information provided on paper. The students note
that women who used the app have taken time for
self-care, and this focused attention is reflected
in their results. VeedaMom is a great resource for
women who may be hesitant to seek counseling
due to stigma, lack of resources, or accessibility
issues. Like other mobile mental health apps,
this technology helps to make mental health services more readily available and broadens our
reach in local communities. Working with these
two amazing students and seeing the impact their
work is having has helped me gain a stronger
appreciation for mobile app use in mental health
counseling.

—JCW

TABLE 2.4 ■ Advantages and Disadvantages of Mental Health Apps	
Advantages	**Disadvantages**
Convenience	Scant research evidencing their effectiveness
Anonymity	Challenging to address client individuality
Low-risk introduction to mental health care	No guidance for clients seeking services
Reduced cost	Privacy concerns
Access for those in remote areas	Limited regulation and practice guidelines
24-hour, around-the-clock service availability	Product overselling by developers
Consistent treatment experiences	
Added support for traditional counseling	

Neurocounseling

In recent years, mental health counselors have become increasingly interested in learning more about and applying principles of neuroscience in their counseling work with
clients (Bray, 2018). The term **neurocounseling** has emerged to refer to the "integration of neuroscience into the practice of counseling, by teaching and illustrating the

GUIDED PRACTICE EXERCISE 2.3

Locate three to five mental health apps. There are
several available for free download in both the App
Store and Google Play. You also can search the
Internet and find several websites with lists of current and popular mental health apps. After you have
identified some apps you think might be helpful to
you in your work as a mental health counselor, use
the APA App Evaluation Model to rate each of them.
Upon closer inspection, are these apps you still
would feel comfortable using with clients? What
would you need to see for you to introduce an app
into the counseling relationship with your clients?

GUIDED PRACTICE EXERCISE 2.4

In small groups, discuss the advantages and disadvantages of integrating neuroscience into counseling practice. Is this something you would use with all clients, or are there certain client groups for whom you believe this approach would not be appropriate? After discussing with your group, share with the rest of class. Did you notice differences among groups in terms of how and when neuroscience would be integrated?

physiological underpinnings of many of our mental health concerns" (Russell-Chapin, 2016, p. 93). Attesting to the increased popularity of neurocounseling and its utility in counseling practice, the *Journal of Mental Health Counseling* introduced a new section titled "Neurocounseling" in its January 2017 issue with plans for it to be a regularly featured section. In addition to helping counselors teach their clients how their physiology and brain work to influence their behaviors and emotions (Russell-Chapin, 2016), principles of neurocounseling can help counselors better understand their clients' concerns, conceptualize cases, and plan treatment by using a brain-based perspective (Field, Jones, & Russell-Chapin, 2017). Further, researchers are now demonstrating that neurocounseling can be effectively used to establish more objective, measurable, and physiologically based therapeutic outcomes (Russell-Chapin, 2016). A more detailed introduction to and description of neurocounseling appears in Chapter 12.

Positive Psychology

One of the fastest growing areas of mental health, **positive psychology** refers to the scientific study of what makes life worth living (Peterson, Park, & Sweeney, 2008). What started as inquiry into happiness has evolved into an analysis of human flourishing (Seligman, 2012). Today, positive psychology has become an increasingly popular, evidence-based theory grounded in the foundational belief that personal happiness is derived from both emotional and mental factors. Its popularity among mental health counselors could be related to its close alignment with many of the fundamental principles of counseling that differentiate it from other helping professions. As Duckworth, Steen, and Seligman (2005) noted, positive psychology is a field concerned with well-being and optimal functioning that aims to broaden the focus of clinical psychology beyond suffering and its direct alleviation.

Positive psychology as a therapeutic approach is applicable to the counseling field in many ways. As Kress and Paylo (2014) have noted, counselors are more frequently employing a strengths-based approach with their clients, and the core focus on positive events and influences in life including positive experiences, states and traits, and institutions found in positive psychology make for a natural fit. Within the positive psychology paradigm, positive psychology interventions readily can be applied. **Positive psychology interventions** (PPIs) are interventions within the positive psychology framework that aim to create positive outcomes for clients (Gander, Proyer, & Ruch, 2016). Seligman and Csikszentmihalyi (2000) identify the following as examples of positive outcomes clients may be able to realize:

GUIDED PRACTICE EXERCISE 2.5

Identify two positive psychology–based interventions you could use with the client population(s) you intend to work with when you graduate. Practice implementing these interventions with your peers or in simulated counseling experiences you may have in your counseling training program. Become familiar with these interventions and how you will implement them now, so you can be more confident in your abilities when you are counseling in the future.

- Well-being, contentment, and satisfaction with the past

- Flow and happiness in the present

- Hope and optimism for the future

Since *positive psychology* was introduced into the professional lexicon by Martin Seligman in the 1990s, multiple theorists have posited various conceptualizations and actively are trying to shape the field. As these new conceptualizations emerge, mental health counselors should explore how this perspective might be useful in their work with clients presenting with a variety of concerns.

Holistic Wellness Counseling

According to researchers, concepts related to holistic wellness continue to inform best practices for counselors and other mental health professionals (Moe, Perera-Diltz, & Rodriguez, 2012). **Holistic wellness counseling** is a therapeutic approach in which counselors take the entire human experience into account when assessing and treatment planning. Various wellness models exist for counselors to follow. A thorough review of each is not possible here. However, we do want to introduce you to one model widely used and researched, the indivisible self model of wellness (IS-Wel; Hattie, Myers, & Sweeney, 2004).

Since its creation over 10 years ago, support for the IS-Wel model has grown exponentially. Developed through structural equation modeling of a large database, the IS-Wel model (see Figure 2.2) reflects a strength-based, choice-oriented, multidimensional approach emphasizing the interconnectedness of various dimensions of an individual's life. Conceptually, the factor structure of IS-Wel incorporates three levels of dimensions. At the center of the model is the higher-order factor labeled total wellness. According to Myers (1992), total wellness is best conceptualized as everyone's drive and ambition to achieve maximum functioning that encompasses the mind, body, and spirit. Comprising this higher-order total wellness factor are five second-order factors: creative self, coping self, essential self, social self, and physical self. Each of these second-order factors was conceptualized and labeled through a series or confirmatory and factor analyses performed on the 17 discrete wellness dimensions identified in previous wellness research (Hattie et al., 2004; Sweeney & Witmer, 1991). In addition to these dimensions, various local (basic safety), institutional (laws, policies, cultural views), global (current world events), and chronometrical (developmental lifespan) contextual variables also play an important role in the model.

FIGURE 2.2 ■ **Higher order total wellness factor labeled 'The Indivisible Self'.**

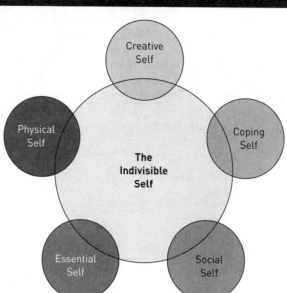

Spirituality

Spirituality is a diverse concept that carries a unique meaning for everyone. Broadly speaking though, **spirituality** refers to an individualized practice extending beyond religious dogma and practice that serves to connect people to a power greater than themselves and bring them peace. Scholars have long advocated for the importance of discussing issues surrounding spirituality as a valuable part of the work we do with clients. As Corey (2006) noted over a decade ago, counseling is most effective when it addresses the body, mind, *and* spirit. Further, the counseling literature indicates that the recognition and validation of a client's spirituality in the counseling process has become increasingly important for mental health counselors (Matise, Ratcliff, & Mosci, 2018). As such, beginning mental health counselors should be cognizant of the role spirituality plays for their clients and how it influences psychosocial functioning.

When discussing spirituality, it is important to remember that it can either help or hinder the healing process (Plumb, 2011). Whereas spirituality can be a critical source of strength for some clients (Corey, 2006), others may view it as a salient part of their presenting problem. Resources are available to help counselors incorporate spiritual issues in counseling. The Association for Spiritual, Ethical, and Religious Values in Counseling (ASERVIC) has developed a set of competencies for addressing spiritual and religious issues in counseling. The competencies address acknowledgement of both client and counselor worldview as well as application to various parts of the counseling process (e.g., assessment, diagnosis, treatment planning). A copy of the ASERVIC competencies can be found on the association's website (www.aservic.org). Adhering to these competencies will help counselors serve clients who espouse diverse religious and spiritual beliefs and contribute to the formulation of their culturally competent professional identity (Cashwell & Watts, 2010).

Social Justice

Social justice is a growing force within the counseling profession (Chang, Crethar, & Ratts, 2010). Like spirituality discussed earlier, the concept of social justice can be broadly interpreted. In general, the concept of **social justice** is often used to describe the promotion of equity and fairness in terms of the distribution of opportunities, resources, and privileges among all members of a society. Advocates for social justice seek to address examples of institutional oppression present in society and adversely affecting people's lives (Shin, 2008). They both acknowledge and understand how issues of unearned power, privilege, and oppression link with psychological stress and the potential manifestation of mental health disorders (Ratts, D'Andrea, & Arredondo, 2004).

In the counseling profession, social justice refers to a multifaceted approach in which counselors strive to simultaneously promote human development and the common good through addressing challenges related to both individual and distributive justice (Crethar & Ratts, 2008). More than an ethical or moral issue, social justice is a foundational belief for counselors and serves as one of the core values of the ACA. Because of the work you will do as a professional counselor, you will be uniquely positioned to be a strong social justice advocate. Through various outlets, you will have opportunities to advocate for social justice at the individual (micro), community (meso), and public policy (macro) levels (Decker, Manis, & Paylo, 2016). Resources such as the Multicultural and Social Justice Counseling Competencies (Ratts, Singh, Nassar-McMillan, Butler, & McCullough, 2015) assist counselors by providing a framework from which they can implement multicultural and social justice competencies in theory, practice, research, and supervision. Further, organizations such as the ACA division Counselors for Social Justice (CSJ) provide a way for social justice advocates to collaborate and connect.

CASE ILLUSTRATION 2.4

Historically marginalized populations face adversity at alarming rates throughout their life span. Adversities, to name a few, include experiencing childhood abuse and neglect, being low-income or economically disadvantaged, having a racial and ethnic minority status, facing oppression and discrimination, or being exposed to violence. Individuals who face these types of adversities are more at risk for suboptimal physical and emotional health outcomes and poor relationship quality. Considering these dire outcomes, social justice and advocacy are integral to my role as a counselor and counselor educator. I also firmly believe acting is critical to achieving the goal of equity for historically marginalized populations.

I promoted healthy relationships and family stability in my clinical work with low-income individuals and couples living 200% below the federal poverty threshold. I provided case management and brief counseling services and facilitated evidence-based relationship education interventions. These efforts provided access to community resources, improved relationship outcomes, and reduced the risk of family fragmentation.

(Continued)

(Continued)

Next, in my role as an educator, I encourage counseling students to develop awareness of their sociocultural identities. I then prompt them to think about contextual and socioeconomic barriers, as well as adversities prevalent among historically marginalized populations. Finally, I challenge counseling trainees to consider these obstacles and disadvantageous experiences as they conceptualize their clients and create socioeconomically responsive treatment plans that support positive client outcomes.

—*S. Griffith*
Assistant Professor of Counselor Education

Mindfulness

According to Brown, Marquis, and Guiffrida (2013), mindfulness is a relatively new construct in counseling that is rapidly gaining interest as it is applied to people struggling with a myriad of problems. In general, **mindfulness** refers to a way of being in which individuals focus their attention on what is happening in the present and how they are experiencing the moment. It includes awareness of personal thoughts, feelings, and sensory experiences (Mayorga, De Vries, & Wardle, 2016). The origins of mindfulness practices can be traced to Eastern meditation practices and Buddhist teaching (Baer, 2003), but their integration into Western healing practices dates to the work of Jon Kabat-Zinn in the 1990s. These practices have been shown to yield positive client outcomes (Brown et al., 2013).

Counselors integrating mindfulness strategies into their work look to bring about cognitive and behavioral changes in their clients. Specifically, counselors work to help their clients (a) observe their thoughts, feelings, and sensations; (b) act with greater awareness; (c) describe their inner experiences; (d) remain nonjudgmental toward their inner experiences; and (e) maintain nonreactivity to their inner experiences (Baer, Smith, Hopkins, Krietemeyer, & Toney, 2006). Several mindfulness-based strategies are available for counselors to use. We recommend those of you interested in incorporating mindfulness in your counseling work explore the current literature because new approaches are consistently being developed and researched. Further, new approaches such as mindfulness-based cognitive therapy (MBCT), which combines traditional theoretical paradigms with elements of mindfulness, are emerging as compelling ways to approach counseling (Schwarze & Gerler, 2015).

Keystones

- The counseling profession was born out of the Progressive Era and is a by-product of the influential work of several social reformers invested in helping individuals displaced by the Industrial Revolution or unemployed due to the Great Depression.

- Early forms of counseling were vocational in nature and naturally fell under the purview of educators and college personnel.

- In response to growing demands for mental health services, federal legislation paved the way for increased access to mental health services. The Community Mental Health Act of 1963 authorized federal funding for the establishment of a nationwide network of public, nonprofit community mental health centers.

- The establishment of the American Mental Health Counselors Association along with other counseling organizations in the 1970s and 1980s provided a professional home for mental health counselors and a voice for a profession seeking recognition and parity with established health care specialties.

- Technology has helped counselors extend services to clients who previously were unable or unwilling to access treatment through traditional methods. When using

technology as a counseling medium, it is important for counselors to be aware of the limitations and ethical ramifications of this approach.

- The counseling profession continues to redefine itself. The integration of neuroscience, positive psychology, and holistic wellness into service delivery models will continue to alter the way counseling services are provided.

- The continued expansion of integrated health care models is closing the loop on treatment services provided to clients. Being able to competently and effectively work as part of a multidisciplinary treatment team is becoming required knowledge for counselors working in clinical mental health settings.

Key Terms

Actualizing tendency 36
Holistic wellness
    counseling 47
Mindfulness 50

Neurocounseling 45
Positive psychology 46
Positive psychology
    interventions 46

Social justice 49
Spirituality 48
Telehealth 43

Web Resources

American Association of State Counseling Boards (www.aascb.org)

American Counseling Association (www.counseling.org)

American Mental Health Counselors Association (www.amhca.org)

American Psychiatric Association (APA) Mental Health APP Evaluation Model (www.psychiatry

.org/psychiatrists/practice/mental-health-apps/app-evaluation-model)

Association for Spiritual, Ethical, and Religious Values in Counseling (www.aservic.org)

Chi Sigma Iota International (http://csi-net.org)

Fair Access Coalition on Testing (www.fairaccess.org)

National Board for Certified Counselors (www.nbcc.org)

References

American Association of State Counseling Boards. (2018). About AASCB. Retrieved from http://www.aascb.org/aws/AASCB/pt/sp/about

American Counseling Association. (2018). Our history. Retrieved from https://www.counseling.org/about-us/about-aca/our-history

American Personnel and Guidance Association. (1961). Ethical standards. *Journal of Counseling and Development, 40*(2), 206–209. doi:10.1002/j.2164-4918.1961.tb02428.x

Aubrey, R. F. (1983). The odyssey of counseling and images of the future. *Personnel and Guidance Journal, 62*(2), 78–82. doi:10.1111/j.2164-4918.1983.tb00151.x

Baer, R. A. (2003). Mindfulness training as a clinical intervention: A conceptual and empirical review. *Clinical Psychology: Science and Practice, 10*, 125–143. doi:10.1093/clipsy.bpg015

Baer, R. A., Smith, G. T., Hopkins, J., Krietemeyer, J., & Toney, L. (2006). Using self-report assessment methods to explore facets of mindfulness. *Assessment, 13*, 27–45. doi:10.1177/1031911105283504

Bray, B. (2018, March). Why neurocounseling? *Counseling Today.* Retrieved from https://ct.counseling.org/2018/03/why-neurocounseling/

Brewer, J. M. (1942). *History of vocational guidance.* New York, NY: Harper & Brothers.

Brown, A. P., Marquis, A., & Guiffrida, D. (2013). Mindfulness-based interventions in counseling. *Journal of Counseling and Development, 91*(1), 96–104. doi:10.1002/j.1556-6676.2013.00077.x

Cashwell, C. S., & Watts, R. E. (2010). The new ASERVIC competencies for addressing spiritual and religious issues in counseling. *Counseling and Values, 55*, 2–5. doi:10.1002/j.2161-007X.2010.tb00018.x

Chang, C. Y., Crethar, H. C., & Ratts, M. J. (2010). Social justice: A national imperative for counselor education and supervision. *Counselor Education and Supervision, 50*(2), 82–87. doi:10.1002/j.1556-6978.2010.tb00110.x

Chartrand, J. M. (1991). The evolution of trait-and-factor career counseling: A person x environment fit approach. *Journal of Counseling and Development, 69*(6), 518–524. doi:10.1002/j.1556-6676.1991.tb02635.x

Chi Sigma Iota. (2018). About CSI. Retrieved from https://www.csi-net.org/page/About_CSI

Corey, G. (2006). Integrating spirituality in counseling practice. *Vistas Online, 25*, 117–119. Retrieved from https://www.counseling.org/resources/library/vistas/vistas06/vistas06.25.pdf

Crethar, H. C., & Ratts, M. J. (2008). Why social justice is a counseling concern. *Counseling Today,* 24–25.

Decker, K. M., Manis, A. A., & Paylo, M. J. (2016). Infusing social justice advocacy into counselor education: Strategies and recommendations. *Journal of Counselor Preparation and Supervision, 8*(3). http://dx.doi.org/10.7729/83.1092

Dorsey, E. R., & Topol, E. J. (2016). State of telehealth. *New England Journal of Medicine, 375*, 154–161. doi:10.1056/NEJMra1601705

Duckworth, A. L., Steen, T. A., & Seligman, M. E. P. (2005). Positive psychology in clinical practice. *Annual Review of Clinical Psychology, 1*, 629–651. doi:10.1146/annnurev.clinpsy.1.102803.144154

Fair Access Coalition on Testing. (2018). What FACT does. Retrieved from http://www.fairaccess.org/aboutfact/whatfactdoes.html

Feller, R. (2014). *The first conference of the National Vocational Guidance Association: Roots of the National Career Development Association #2.* Retrieved from https://www.ncda.org/aws/NCDA/pt/sd/news_article/70380/_PARENT/CC_layout_details/false

Field, T. A., Jones, L. K., & Russell-Chapin, L. A. (2017). *Neurocounseling: Brain-based clinical approaches.* Alexandria, VA: American Counseling Association.

Gander, F., Proyer, R. T., & Ruch, W. (2016). Positive psychology interventions addressing pleasure, engagement, meaning, positive relationships, and accomplishment increase well-being and ameliorate depressive symptoms: A randomized, placebo-controlled online study. *Frontiers in Psychology, 7,* article 686. doi:10.3389/fpsyg.2016.00686

Gibson, R. L., & Mitchell, M. H. (2011). *Counseling: Yesterday and today.* Retrieved from https://www.counseling.org/resources/library/VISTAS/2011-V-Online/Article_01.pdf

Gladding, S. T., & Newsome, D. W. (2018). *Clinical mental health counseling in community and agency settings* (5th ed.). Columbus, OH: Pearson.

Hattie, J. A., Myers, J. E., & Sweeney, T. J. (2004). A factor structure of wellness: Theory, assessment, analysis, and practice. *Journal of Counseling and Development, 82*(3), 354–364. doi:10.1002/j.1556-6678.2004.tb00321.x

Health Resources and Services Administration. (2018). Telehealth programs. Retrieved from https://www.hrsa.gov/rural-health/telehealth/index.html

Hollander, R. (2017). App usage is growing, but only a few apps are reaping the benefits. Retrieved from http://www.businessinsider.com/app-usage-growing-benefits-2017-10

Kress, V. E., & Paylo, M. J. (2014). *Treating those with mental disorders: A comprehensive approach to case conceptualization and treatment.* Columbus, OH: Pearson.

Maslow, A. H. (1968). *Toward a psychology of being* (2nd ed.). New York, NY: D. Van Nostrand.

Matise, M., Ratcliff, J., & Mosci, F. (2018). A working model for the integration of spirituality in counseling. *Journal of Spirituality in Mental Health, 20,* 27–50. doi:10.1080/19349637.2017.1326091

Mayorga, M. G., De Vries, S., & Wardle, E. A. (2016). Mindfulness behavior and its effects on anxiety. *Journal of Educational Psychology, 9*(4), 1–7.

Mental Health America. (n.d.). About Mental Health America. Retrieved from http://www.mentalhealthamerica.net/our-history

Moe, J. L., Perera-Diltz, D. M., & Rodriguez, T. (2012). *Counseling for wholeness: Integrating holistic wellness into case conceptualization and treatment planning.* Retrieved from https://www.counseling.org/docs/default-source/vistas/vistas_2012_article_31.pdf?sfvrsn=49a00ded_13

Myers, J. E. (1992). Wellness, prevention, development: The cornerstone of the profession. *Journal of Counseling and Development, 71,* 136–139. doi:10.1002/j.1556-6676.1992.tb02188.x

National Board for Certified Counselors. (2018). About us. Retrieved from http://www.nbcc.org/About

National Institute of Mental Health (n.d.). Technology and the future of mental health treatment. Retrieved from https://www.nimh.nih.gov/health/topics/technology-and-the-future-of-mental-health-treatment/index.shtml

Parry, M. (2010). From a patient's perspective: Clifford Whittingham Beers' work to reform mental health services. *American Journal of Public Health, 100*(12), 2356–2357. doi:10.2015/AJPH.2010.191411

Parsons, F. (1909). *Choosing a vocation.* Boston, MA: Houghton Mifflin.

Peterson, C., Park, N., & Sweeney, P. J. (2008). Group well-being: Morale from a positive psychology perspective. *Applied Psychology: An International review, 57,* 19–36. doi:10.1111/j.1464-0597.2008.00352.x

Plumb, A. M. (2011). Spirituality and counselling: Are counselors prepared to integrate religion and spirituality into therapeutic work with clients? *Canadian Journal of Counseling and Psychotherapy, 45,* 1–16. Retrieved from https://files.eric.ed.gov/fulltext/EJ930782.pdf

Pope, M. (2009). Jesse Buttrick Davis (1871–1955): Pioneer of vocational guidance in the schools. *Career Development Quarterly, 57*(3), 248–258. doi:10.1002/j.2161-0045.2009.tb00110.x

Protivnak, J. J. (2009). Career development, key people in. In American Counseling Association

(Ed.), *The ACA encyclopedia of counseling* (pp. 80–82). Alexandria, VA: American Counseling Association.

Ratts, M. J., D'Andrea, M., & Arredondo, P. (2004). Social justice counseling: A "fifth force" in the field. *Counseling Today, 47*, 28–30.

Ratts, M. J., Singh, A. A., Nassar-McMillan, S., Butler, S. K., & McCullough, J. R. (2015). *Multicultural and social justice counseling competencies*. Retrieved from https://www.counseling.org/docs/default-source/competencies/multicultural-and-social-justice-counseling-competencies.pdf?sfvrsn=20

Rogers, C. (1959). A theory of therapy, personality, and interpersonal relationships as developed in the client-centered framework. In S. Koch (Ed.), *Psychology: A study of a science. Volume 3: Formulations of the person and the social context* (pp. 184–256). New York, NY: McGraw Hill.

Russell-Chapin, L. A. (2016). Integrating neurocounseling into the counseling profession: An introduction. *Journal of Mental Health Counseling, 38*(2), 93–102. doi:10.17744/mehc.38.2.01

Sangganjanavanich, V. F., & Reynolds, C. A. (2015). *Introduction to professional counseling*. Thousand Oaks, CA: Sage.

Savickas, M. L. (2011). Special section: The 100th anniversary of vocational guidance—introduction to the special section. *Career Development Quarterly, 57*(3), 194–288. doi:10.1002/j.2161-0045.2009.tb00104.x

Schwarze, M. J., & Gerler, E. R. Jr. (2015). Using mindfulness-based cognitive therapy in individual counseling to reduce stress and increase mindfulness: An exploratory study with nursing students. *The Professional Counselor, 5*(1), 39–52. doi:10.15241/mjs.5.1.39

Seligman, M. E. P. (2012). *Flourish: A visionary new understanding of happiness and well-being*. New York, NY: Free Press.

Seligman, M. E. P., & Csikszentmihalyi, M. (2000). Positive psychology. *American Psychologist, 55*(1), 5–14. doi:10.1037//0003-066X.55.1.5

Shin, R. Q. (2008). Advocating for social justice in academia through recruitment, retention, admissions, and professional survival. *Journal of Multicultural Counseling and Development, 36*(3), 180–191. doi:10.1002/j.2161-1912.2008.tb00081.x

Smith, H. L. (2012). The historical development of community and clinical mental health counseling in the United States. *Turkish Psychological Counseling and Guidance Journal, 4*(37), 1–10.

Statista. (2018). Number of smartphone users worldwide from 2014 to 2020 (in billions). Retrieved from https://www.statista.com/statistics/330695/number-of-smartphone-users-worldwide/

Sweeney, T. J., & Witmer, J. M. (1991). Beyond social interest. Striving toward optimum health and wellness. *Individual Psychology, 47*, 527–540.

U.S. Bureau of Education. (1914). *Vocational guidance* (Bulletin 1914, no. 4). Retrieved from https://www.ncda.org/aws/NCDA/asset_manager/get_file/59456?ver=10671

Vacc, N. A., & Loesch, L. C. (2000). *Professional orientation to counseling* (3rd ed.). Philadelphia, PA: Taylor & Francis.

Valentino, T. (2016). Five factors influencing telemental health. *Behavioral Healthcare, 36*(3), 58–60.

Watson, J. C., & Sheperis, C. J. (2010). *Counselors and the right to test: Working toward professional parity* (ACAPCS-31). Alexandria, VA: American Counseling Association.

Weikel, W. J. (1985). A brief history of the American Mental Health Counselors Association. Retrieved from http://www.amhca.org/Go.aspx?MicrositeGroupTypeRouteDesignKey=430fca37-b93a-492b-8d69-277eef72bd9b&NavigationKey=a159b7c4-8cca-42da-8016-291ce825bc87

Wrenn, C. G. (1962). *The counselor in a changing world*. Washington, DC: American Personnel and Guidance Association.

CONTEMPORARY THEORIES AND MODELS OF CLINICAL MENTAL HEALTH COUNSELING

Imagine it is your first day of clinical practice after graduating with your master's degree in counseling. You've landed a counselor position at a regional community mental health agency. Your first client, a 34-year-old Asian American transgender woman, enters your office. She appears anxious but is reserved. She graciously completes the intake paperwork, and you both review the informed consent and professional disclosure statement forms. You further clarify for her the limits to confidentiality and then you both sign. You ask her what brings her into the clinic today. She cautiously discloses that she has felt anxious for the past 6 months. She goes on to say that at first the anxiety was situational, mostly occurring at work. However, now she feels anxious all the time: at work, at home, when walking to her car, at the grocery store, and especially when alone. Suddenly, her voice lowers and she quietly adds that her partner seems ambivalent about their relationship, and to cope with the relational strain she has begun using marijuana.

Although not an uncommon scenario in clinical mental health counseling, the question begs to be asked: How would you proceed? Would you focus on one presenting issue at a time? How will you determine which issue to focus on first? Or should you focus on them all at once? If you happen to be entertaining these or similar questions, you are in the right frame of mind. The answer is simple and yet not so simple: It depends. It depends on personal factors, such as your values, beliefs, and biases; professional factors, such as education and training; and a combination of both—your counseling theoretical orientation (e.g., person-centered theory, cognitive theory, cognitive behavioral theory).

Counselors working in clinical mental health settings may experience another challenge, one not openly discussed, of having to work within a theoretical framework or model adopted by the clinical setting that clashes with their own. Although this may sound anxiety provoking, at least initially, counselors can certainly honor their personal counseling theory while adhering to agency-adopted models or theories of practice. This may require counselors in training to expand on how they conceptualize both theory and model as it relates to clinical mental health counseling.

We begin by identifying the similarities and differences between a model and a theory of practice. The remainder of this chapter focuses on introducing five applied models found in clinical mental health counseling. When applicable, the underlying theory is presented alongside each applied model. Although numerous other counseling theories and models (e.g., psychodynamic, humanistic, constructivist) can be found in clinical mental health counseling, the intent of this chapter is not to duplicate what a counseling theories course would cover in most counselor training and preparation programs. Rather, we highlight theories and models most commonly used by counselors in a variety of clinical mental health settings that are practical and lend themselves to managed care and third-party insurance payments.

LEARNING OBJECTIVES

After reading this chapter, you will be able to do the following:

- Identify the similarities and differences between a model and a theory of practice

- Describe five applied models (and underlying theory when applicable) used in clinical mental health counseling (CACREP 5C-1-b)

- Differentiate between the various principles, techniques, and interventions found in each applied model of clinical mental health counseling (CACREP 5C-3-b)

Before we dive into each model and underlying theory, it is important to understand the similarities and differences between a model of practice and a theory of practice. It is not uncommon for counselors and other helping professionals to use these terms synonymously. In fact, the two are closely related and each can be thought of as a constituent of the other. However, without a doubt, clear differences exist. A **theory of practice** is a set of principles or guidelines that describes and explains a particular phenomenon (Nilsen, 2015). Theories are often broader than models and tend to describe the "what," "how," and "why" aspects of a particular phenomenon. Hence, a theory can predict. For example, in person-centered therapy, Rogers (1951, 1959) described how personality develops from an early age and how the environment plays a significant role in its construction. He also shed light on the personality change process, which occurs by experiencing what Rogers identified as the core conditions necessary for change (i.e., unconditional positive regard, genuineness, empathy). Finally, Rogers identified the *why* aspect characteristic of a theory. He proposed that human beings are motivated to do and be good, although they have the capacity to do and be the opposite. However, Rogers conceptualized human motivation as something positive and forward moving, into one's full potential, a process known as the actualization tendency. Based on his theory, Rogers was able to explain personality development and the change process necessary for self-actualization.

GUIDED PRACTICE EXERCISE 3.1

In groups of three to four students, differentiate between a theory of practice and model of practice. Here are a few questions to help develop and organize your discussion:

1. What are the characteristics of a theory of practice?

2. What are the characteristics of a model of practice?

3. What are the similarities and differences between a theory and a model of practice?

4. What challenges do you foresee, if any, in implementing a model of practice that is incongruent or dissimilar with your own personal theory of counseling?

Once complete, come together as a class to explore your group's answers to the questions.

Unlike theory, a **model of practice** describes a phenomenon or an aspect of a phenomenon in simplistic terms (Nilsen, 2015). Thus, models of practice are snippets of theory extracted and expanded to describe the *what* aspects helpful in facilitating the practical side of counseling. As you will learn in your counselor preparation and training program, models (e.g., ethical decision-making models; see Forester-Miller & Davis, 2016; Schmit, Schmit, Henesy, Klassen, & Oliver, 2015) can be atheoretical, that is, absent of the *hows* and *whys* provided by theory. However, this does not mean that models are less useful in counseling. In fact, the opposite is true. Counselors use models to simplify decision-making processes or to ensure that clients receive a consistent level of care. For instance, a licensed professional counselor-supervisor who supervises using the discrimination model (Bernard & Goodyear, 1992) is practicing from an atheoretical perspective. The supervisor attends to the supervisee by focusing on three specific areas related to the supervisee (i.e., process, conceptualization, personalization) while engaging in three different roles (i.e., teacher, consultant, counselor). As you can see, the *what* aspects of the discrimination model are easily understood: roles and areas of focus. However, where the model falls short is specific to answering the *hows* and *whys*. Why should supervisors adopt these specific roles and address these specific areas of focus? How should a supervisor engage in each role and area of focus? Although the how and why aspects of the discrimination model go unaddressed, it offers supervisors a practical framework from which to operate.

We explore five applied models (and underlying theory when applicable) of practice found in clinical mental health counseling: cognitive-behavioral-based approaches, the biopsychosocial model, the collaborative (integrated) care model, the population-based prevention model, and the recovery model. Keep in mind our previous discussion on theories and models of practice as you are introduced to each applied model found in clinical mental health counseling.

COGNITIVE-BEHAVIORAL-BASED MODELS

All cognitive-behavioral-based models emerged from the theoretical framework of cognitive theory, in response to behaviorism, and are most recognizable in counselor practice as cognitive-behavioral therapy (CBT). *Cognitive-behavioral therapy* is now recognized as an umbrella term used to classify similar therapeutic approaches such as acceptance and commitment therapy (ACT), rational emotive behavior therapy (REBT), cognitive therapy (CT), dialectical behavior therapy (DBT), trauma-focused cognitive-behavioral therapy (TF-CBT), and mindfulness-based cognitive therapy (MBCT), just to name a few. To truly appreciate the cognitive-behavioral-based models discussed, you must first understand the cognitive theory framework from which they were built. **Cognitive theory** asserts that a person's perceptions (thoughts) of an event are the primary determinant of one's behaviors, emotions, and physiology (Beck, 2011). To better understand this premise, let's examine Figure 3.1, adapted from Judith Beck (2011).

As you can see, the cognitive model is composed of three separate but related parts: situation/event (S/E), automatic thoughts (AT), and reaction (R). From a cognitive theory perspective, it is a person's automatic thoughts (AT) about an event or situation (S/E) that results in behavioral, emotional, or physiological reactions (R). Therefore, it is not the situation or event itself that results in a reaction but rather the cognitive process (e.g., automatic thought, memory, attention) related to said event that best accounts for a reaction (Beck, 2011). For instance, Steven, a 47-year-old combat veteran diagnosed with post-traumatic stress disorder, suddenly heard gunfire (S/E) in his residential neighborhood. Due to the sound of gunfire (S/E), Steven experienced an automatic thought of *I'm going to die* (AT) while at home. As a result of Steven's automatic thought that originated from the gunfire (S/E) he heard, both his heart rate and level of anxiety increased significantly, and he quickly dove for cover behind his sofa (R). Steven's cognitive process (*I am going to die* [AT]) is the product of an event (gunfire [S/E]) he experienced, which resulted in both emotional and behavioral consequences (anxiety and diving for cover [R]). This same framework holds true for cognitive-behavioral-based models.

Most, if not all, clinical mental health setting and third-party payers favor cognitive-behavioral-based models. Treatment tends to be structured or manualized, empirically

---

FIGURE 3.1   ■   Cognitive Model Diagram

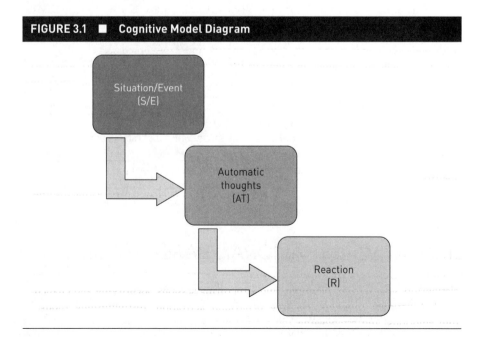

GUIDED PRACTICE EXERCISE 3.2

Given the expansiveness and popularity of cognitive-behavioral-based models, it is important to understand the theoretical framework from which they were built. With an in-class partner, using Figure 3.1 as a guide, take turns explaining the cognitive model, in your own words, to your partner. Next, develop an example that is representative of the cognitive model and share it with your in-class partner. Take turns in trying to identify the situation/event (S/E), automatic thoughts (AT), and reaction (R) in the other's example.

supported, goal-oriented, brief, cost-effective, and adaptable to a wide variety of mental health issues. Perhaps what makes this approach most appealing is that clients learn an array of cognitive and behavioral skills that can be implemented outside of treatment, creating self-sufficiency in addressing their own problems over time. To further your understanding of cognitive-behavioral-based models, let's dive into five practice models commonly found in clinical mental health counseling: cognitive behavioral therapy, trauma-focused cognitive-behavioral therapy, cognitive processing therapy, dialectical behavior therapy, and eye movement desensitization and reprocessing.

Cognitive-Behavioral Therapy

Cognitive-behavioral therapy (CBT) refers to a classification of cognitive and behavioral interventions and techniques that draw on the ideology of unwellness maintained by maladaptive cognitions (Hofmann, Asnaani, Vonk, Sawyer, & Fang, 2012). According to Beck (1970) and Ellis (1957), these maladaptive thought processes contribute to and perpetuate behavioral problems and emotional distress. To meet the complex health issues of clients in treatment, it is not uncommon for counselors who practice from a CBT framework to do so atheoretically, that is, without theoretical concern, unless the chosen behavioral and cognitive techniques are grounded in cognitive theory (Beck & Weishaar, 2014). Regardless of whether counselors approach CBT from a theoretical or an atheoretical perspective, one thing is clear: CBT has been shown to be an effective model of treatment.

CBT has demonstrated varying degrees of effectiveness with children (Silk et al., 2016), teens (Sprich, Safren, Finkelstein, Remmert, & Hammerness, 2016), and adults (Hans & Hiller, 2013; Stewart & Chambless, 2009). It has been used to treat a wide range of mental health disorders, such as depression (Lepping et al., 2017), anxiety (Stewart & Chambless, 2009), alcoholism (Olthuis, Watt, Mackinnon, & Stewart, 2015) and substance use (Acosta et al., 2017), bipolar disorder (Ye et al., 2016), eating disorders (de Jong et al., 2016), and aggression (Chen et al., 2014). It is applicable in a variety of treatment settings, such as school (Drmic, Aljunied, & Reaven, 2017), outpatient (Taylor, Rybarczyk, Nay, & Leszczyszyn, 2015), inpatient (Owen, Sellwood, Kan, Murray, & Sarsam, 2015), and web-based (Acosta et al., 2017). Although CBT varies from counselor to counselor, treatment components generally consist of establishing the counselor-client relationship; goal setting, planning, and structuring sessions; identifying and challenging dysfunctional thoughts; eliciting behavioral activation; distinguishing thoughts from emotions; and establishing and maintaining cognitive and behavioral change in and out of the treatment setting. However, the interventions and techniques counselors use to elicit cognitive and behavior change vary. Common interventions and techniques found in CBT include Socratic questioning, cognitive restructuring, functional analysis, thought record, journaling, decision-making, exposure and imaginary exposure, role-playing, progressive muscle relaxation, controlled breathing, mindfulness, and so forth. It is beyond the scope of this chapter to review each treatment component and technique or intervention in detail, but we recommend reading Beck's (2011) *Cognitive Behavioral Therapy: Basic and Beyond* and Parsons and Zhang's (2014) *Counseling Theory: Guiding Reflective Practice*. For both sources, see chapter references.

Trauma-Focused Cognitive-Behavioral Therapy

Trauma-focused cognitive-behavioral therapy (TF-CBT) is a leading evidence-based approach developed to treat children and adolescents with exposure to trauma (Cohen, Mannarino, Kliethermes, & Murray, 2012). A trauma event can be a single or reoccurring experience of mental, physical, emotional, or sexual abuse or the result of grief or violence that results in symptoms associated with post-traumatic stress or mood dysregulation (Psychology Today, 1991–2018). Similar to CBT, TF-CBT addresses mental and emotional needs by modifying distorted thoughts and unhealthy behavioral and emotional reactions. As a trauma-sensitive approach, TF-CBT has demonstrated varying degrees of effectiveness in reducing trauma symptoms associated with post-traumatic stress in youth (Cary & McMillen, 2012; Cohen, Berliner, & Mannarino, 2010; de Arellano et al., 2014; Dorsey et al., 2017; Lenz & Hollenbaugh, 2015). What differentiates TF-CBT from CBT is the incorporation of trauma-sensitive interventions and family therapy. As a short-term approach (approximately 12–16 sessions), TF-CBT includes elements easily identifiable by the acronym PRACTICE: psychoeducation and parent training, relaxation guidance, affect expression and coping, cognitive processing and coping, trauma narrative construction, in vivo exposure, conjoint sessions, and enhancing safety and the future (Cohen, Mannarino, & Deblinger, 2006).

Psychoeducation is used to describe the various treatment components of TF-CBT and explain how treatment works. Both children and caregivers learn of natural childhood responses to trauma and how trauma impacts the child. Psychoeducation methods can include open discussions, handouts and worksheets, books and other resources, and games. Parent training serves to enhance the caregiver-child relationship and the child's ability to adjust emotionally and behaviorally. Parents learn an array of strategies such as praise, selective attention, instruction, rewards and consequences, setting limits, establishing play and one-on-one times, and behavior management. Relaxation guidance skills are learned to reduce distress. Skills learned include progressive muscle relaxation, mindfulness, yoga, and controlled breathing. Affect expression coping are skills taught to both parents and children to manage and cope with an array of emotions. The goals are to identify one's feelings, expand one's current feeling repertoire, and link appropriate expression to a situation. Cognitive processing and coping skills help both child and parent learn how to identify automatics thoughts about the trauma that lead to unhealthy behaviors and emotions. A common technique used to identify thinking mistakes is the cognitive triangle. A triangle shape is used to represent the interconnectedness among one's automatic thoughts related to an event and one's corresponding feelings and behaviors related to the automatic thoughts. Once unhealthy negative thoughts have been detected, they can be modified to healthier cognitions. Trauma narrative construction provides the child an opportunity to tell the story of the trauma using analogies, poems, audio recordings, drawings, and other nonthreatening means. Once the trauma narrative has been constructed, the counselor and youth collaboratively identify and reorient inaccurate or unhelpful thoughts into healthier ones. Techniques used can include Socratic questioning, classifying thoughts, role-playing, showing the evidence, and so forth. The next module is in vivo exposure, where the child learns to master the fear response directly related to the trauma event and then focuses on innocuous triggers associated with the trauma event. The goal is to reduce emotional and behavioral patterns that interfere with normal daily functioning. Conjoint sessions provide the child the opportunity to share the trauma to a trusted parent or adult, enhancing both communication and family connectedness. The last phase of treatment is enhancing safety and the future. In this phase, counselors may develop situation-specific safety plans, provide additional psychoeducation, and facilitate role-plays between child and caregiver. Given the structure and evidence of TF-CBT, it seems clear why this approach is adopted by many clinical mental counselors.

Cognitive Processing Therapy

Similar to TF-CBT, cognitive processing therapy (CPT) is an evidence-based treatment approach designed to help people recover from post-traumatic stress disorder (PTSD). Across 12 sessions, CPT systematically addresses vital post-traumatic themes—safety, trust, power and control, self-esteem, and intimacy—through modifying unhelpful beliefs and reprocessing trauma memories (Forbes et al., 2012). According to pioneers Resick and Schnicke (1993), trauma memories need to be activated in the present, in a therapeutically safe environment, to correct erroneous thoughts that inhibit healthy functioning. Resick and Schnicke (1992) first applied CPT to the treatment of post-traumatic stress symptomology present in rape victims in group format. Since then, CPT has been administered individually (Chard, 2005; Resick, Nishith, Weaver, Astin, & Feuer, 2002) and continues to occur in group format (Resick et al., 2015; Resick et al., 2017) with a variety of populations. CPT has demonstrated effectiveness with active-duty military (Resick et al., 2017), veterans with and without military sexual trauma (Voelkel, Pukay-Martin, Walter, & Chard, 2015), refugees (Schulz, Resick, Huber, & Griffin, 2006), and motor vehicle accident survivors (Galovski & Resick, 2008).

CPT integrates aspects of CBT and information processing to help survivors of trauma reconceptualize their trauma and associated negative symptomology in order to live healthy and functional lives. It is not uncommon for persons who experience trauma to engage in avoidance; however, CPT treatment hinges on the fact that avoidance negatively impacts the healing process and inhibits the client from evaluating emotions and cognitions surrounding the trauma event. Therefore, treatment begins with psychoeducation regarding the symptoms associated with PTSD and how thoughts, feelings, and behaviors are not mutually exclusive of one another. During this phase of treatment, it is paramount the counselor establishes a strong therapeutic alliance for what lies ahead. Within the education phase, often the first session, the counselor and client work in collaboration to define the traumatic event. This is usually a written account of the event from the client's perspective. The written trauma account is important in CPT because it establishes a baseline and provides the counselor a snapshot of the client's maladaptive thoughts and stuck-points (Resick, Monson, & Chard, 2006). Emphasis is placed on teaching the client to identify maladaptive thoughts related to the trauma.

Once the trauma narrative is developed and stuck-points and automatic thoughts have been identified, the emotional reprocessing of the trauma can take place through repeated exposure. Repeated exposure occurs though further development of the trauma narrative, perhaps asking the client to detail the narrative by including sensory information or by focusing only on a specific part of the narrative. Throughout this process the counselor and client are attempting to disrupt the client's pattern of avoidance, thereby allowing the emotions to surface and an opportunity to modify stuck-points into more accurate cognitions. Counselors may find themselves using Socratic questions to guide clients to their discovery of new cognitions surround the trauma. Throughout the course of treatment, clients are given homework to continue the work that occurred in session. Homework can include constructing a trauma narrative, identifying stuck-points and maladaptive thoughts, identifying emotions, ABC worksheets, and so forth. In the final phase of CPT, the counselor helps the client reinforce the coping skills learned in earlier sessions. It is likely that not all trauma events or aspects of the trauma explored in treatment are completely resolved; rather, clients leave treatment feeling confident in their ability to identify, appraise, and modify deleterious thoughts concerning a trauma where necessary (Resick et al., 2006). To learn more about CPT, we recommend Resick, Monson, and Chard's (2016) book, *Cognitive Processing Therapy for PTSD: A Comprehensive Manuel* (see References at end of chapter).

Dialectical Behavior Therapy

A modified form of CBT, dialectical behavior therapy (DBT) was designed to help persons with borderline personality disorder (Linehan, Armstrong, Suarez, Allmon, & Heard, 1991), but applications of DBT can be found in the treatment of substance use and eating disorders, self-harming behaviors and suicidality, and other forms of mental illness. Developed by psychologist Marsha M. Linehan, DBT assumes that problem behaviors result from skill deficits when attempting to cope with an emotionally charged situation. For instance, after 20 years of marriage, a husband was just informed by his wife that she wanted a divorce. Rather than take a "time-out" to process his emotions, he becomes enraged and threatens to end his own life. Although this behavior may provide some temporary relief, it certainly does not solve the marital discord in the long term. An important aspect of DBT is acknowledging the dialectical in a given situation. In simplistic form, **dialectic** describes two opposing sides that can be true at the same time. Using our previous example of the couple whose marriage is in dismay, the husband could be enraged and yet not want to take his own life. Another example: A client could be unhappy with his or her counselor and counseling can still continue. It doesn't have to result in the termination of the counseling session. Acknowledging the dialectical in any situation is important in DBT because it creates an opportunity to accept where we are and acknowledges the need for change.

Although the list of effectiveness studies is exhaustive, here is a brief presentation of more recent outcome studies. DBT has been shown to be effective for adults with borderline personality disorder (Linehan et al., 1991; Linehan et al., 2015), eating disorders (Safer, Robinson, & Jo, 2011), and mood disorders (Van Dijk, Jeffrey, & Katz, 2013) and for adolescents with repeated suicidal ideations and self-injury (Mehlum et al., 2016) and bipolar disorder (Goldstein et al., 2015). A key difference of DBT from CBT is the emphasis on accepting one's uncomfortable thoughts, feelings, and behaviors, that is, coming to realize they exist so that change is possible. The DBT counselor helps clients find a balance between acceptance and change though talk therapy. Individual talk therapy provides opportunities for clients to challenge maladaptive thoughts and engage in newly learned coping skills in a supportive and encouraging environment. DBT skills training groups help clients develop the skills necessary to enhance their capacity to cope and change unhealthy behaviors. DBT skills training groups consist of four modules: mindfulness, distress tolerance, interpersonal effectiveness, and emotion regulation (Behavioral Tech, 2017).

Clients in DBT commit to a full year of treatment at the onset of therapy. During the 1-year treatment period, clients meet in a skills group for 2.5 hours weekly to learn the four modules. It takes approximately 24 weeks to complete the curriculum, which is then repeated (Behavioral Tech, 2017). Individual therapy takes place concurrently with the skills group, once a week, for the treatment's duration. Features unique to DBT include phone coaching by the counselor for real-time support when clients are faced with difficult situations, teaching clients how to be their own case manager to create self-sufficiency, and supporting counselors with DBT consultation teams (Behavioral Tech, 2017). As you can see, DBT is an exciting and multifaceted approach to working with adults and adolescents with a range of mental illness; the topic could be a chapter on its own. Therefore, for those of you interested in learning more about DBT, we recommend Linehan's (2014, 2015) *DBT Skills Training Manual* and *DBT Skills Training Handouts and Worksheets* (see References).

Eye Movement Desensitization and Reprocessing

Based on the theory of information processing and similar to CBT in its desensitization and reprocessing (Salkovskis, 2002), eye movement desensitization and reprocessing (EMDR), an eclectic approach developed by Fiona Shapiro, attempts to reduce the distress associated with PTSD that results from traumas such as military combat, physical assault, motor vehicle accidents, natural disasters, and rape. However, what differentiates EMDR from other CBT approaches is that maladaptive thoughts are not directly challenged, nor is extended exposure required. Rather, the client recalls a distressing trigger, memory, or belief while receiving bilateral stimulation in the form of audio, visual, or tactical stimuli. Using their eyes, clients follow the bilateral stimulation for a short period. This may occur multiple times within a single session. According to Shapiro (1995), bilateral stimulation reduces disturbances that result from negative thoughts and emotions. Although a theory is still in development, exploration into areas of working memory and the orienting response have garnered the attention of EMDR researchers (Lee & Cuijpers, 2013). Some researchers question the need for bilateral stimuli used in EMDR (Davidson & Parker, 2001) and its effectiveness compared to other trauma-specific therapies (e.g., TF-CBT; Bisson, Roberts, Andrew, Cooper, & Lewis, 2013).

GUIDED PRACTICE EXERCISE 3.3

First, on your own, describe the similarities and differences between the five cognitive-behavioral-based models. Focus on the most salient characteristics, such as the focus of treatment, target population, interventions and techniques (when appropriate), and so forth. Use the Web Resources section at the end of this chapter to further your comparisons. What aspect(s) of each model resonated with you as a counselor in training? Next, share your discoveries with an in-class partner, noting areas of agreement and disagreement for further discussion.

EMDR is praised as a relatively brief treatment that follows specific protocols and procedures across eight treatment phases: Phase 1: history and treatment planning; Phase 2: preparing the client for EMDR; Phase 3: assessment of trauma memory; Phase 4: desensitization to negative thoughts, beliefs, emotions and bodily sensations; Phase 5: installation of positive beliefs; Phase 6: body scan of physical sensations; Phase 7: closure back to a state of equilibrium; and Phase 8: reevaluation of EMDR effects (Shapiro, 1995). For more details on each phase of EMDR, we recommend Shapiro's (2018) *Eye Movement Desensitization and Reprocessing (EMDR) Therapy: Basic Principles, Protocols, and Procedures* (see References). As a final note, certification in EMDR is available to only master's level or higher mental health professionals who are licensed or certified to independently practice and able to complete the basic training through a certified EMDR training provider.

BIOPSYCHOSOCIAL MODEL

The biopsychosocial model of care is a philosophical approach to understanding health and illness across the life span. Throughout life, biological (genetic and physiological factors), psychological (e.g., personality, stress, behavior), and social (e.g., culture, socioeconomic status, technology, religion) systems continuously interact and contribute to one's health. When it was developed, the biomedical model dominated the field of medicine, focusing on disease in a cause-and-effect way. Engel's (1977, 1980) biopsychosocial model revolutionized the way practitioners conceptualized health and illness, although not without criticism and disdain from supporters of the biomedical model. For more in-depth information on the biopsychosocial model and how systems interact, fast-forward to Chapter 10: Behavioral Medicine: A Holistic Look at Health and Illness. The remainder of this section briefly explores the underlying theory of the biopsychosocial model proposed by Engel (1977, 1980). But before heading in that direction, it is important to realize that the philosophy of the biopsychosocial model is enacted by health practitioners' manner of practice, regardless of whether they are working in a hospital, agency, or private practice setting. When you are empathetic to your clients, treat them with respect and dignity, and honor their right to autonomy, you are practicing from the biopsychosocial approach as Engel intended: to treat the person as a person and not as an ailment, disorder, or disease. The repercussive effect of being treated as a person may influence clients' positive behavior, dismantle the stigma associated with mental health treatment, or motivate a person toward optimum health and wellness.

Even though the biopsychosocial model is considered a philosophy of care, Engel (1977, 1980) posited that it closely aligns with general systems theory (GST; von Bertalanffy, 1968). GST attempts to explain how complex systems (e.g., human beings) are composed of separate but interrelated parts, influenced by the environment, sharing organization principles of governance (von Bertalanffy, 1968). A system can be classified by its structure and function (e.g., biological, psychological, social). Given the dynamic principle of GST, it is believed that a change in one part of the system will result in change in another. For instance, when parents argue, the dynamic of the household may shift to establish some semblance of equilibrium. This may take the form of children walking on eggshells so as to not further aggravate the parents. If the argument goes unresolved, there may be a carryover effect that results in one parent seemingly checking out while the other overcompensates to maintain the household and thereby reestablish equilibrium. Note that any two systems with similar biological, psychological, and social characteristics could follow a differential process (method of establishing equilibrium) that results in a similar outcome. In other words, no two processes of achieving health and wellness are ever the same. From a practice standpoint, how does one translate the ideology of the biopsychosocial model into client care? Perhaps the answer lies within the practice of collaborative or integrated care.

CASE ILLUSTRATION 3.1

Coralie, a 37-year-old Caucasian female who identifies as being middle-class, recently completed a biopsychosocial assessment. The assessment was used to identify her needs to treat and personal strengths. She identified bouts of depression that lasted for more than 2 weeks, which have occurred for longer than 7 months. She noted a higher intensity of depression symptoms over the past month. She also reported that she recently found out she has high cholesterol and an elevated blood sugar level, both of which are common in her family. She currently lives at home with her parents, but she described the environment as hostile and aggressive, desiring to seek a place of her own one day soon. A strength identified by Coralie is working part-time at a day care center for the past 10 months. From the biopsychosocial model, Coralie's health status is considered within the context of her biological, psychological, and social systems and their interactions. Her unwellness is not simply the result of her current living situation or genetics; rather, it is understood within the context of her psychological factors such as stress, personality, and coping skills; her social factors such as family circumstances, socioeconomic status, culture, and education; and her biological factors such as gender, genetics, medication effects, and physical health—and the interaction among the systems. Using GST and the biopsychosocial model, Coralie's treatment would emphasize holistically addressing her overall health through interventions of individual and family counseling, meditation, physical activity, nutrition and diet, self-help group, and community involvement. This would take advantage of the synergistic effects that result when addressing the entire person.

COLLABORATIVE (INTEGRATED) CARE MODELS

Collaborative care is an umbrella term used to describe a health care philosophy that systematically combines treatment of mental illness, substance use, and disease in primary or behavioral health care settings. This could include partnerships among health care providers, health care providers sharing the same physical space, or health care providers working together as teams that operate in the same physical space. Other terms commonly referring to this systematic approach include *integrated care, primary care in behavioral health, integrated primary care*, and *integrated behavioral and primary health care treatment*. As you can tell, the lack of consistency in terminology can certainly create confusion among both health care professionals and consumers of health care services. Rather than getting stuck on terminology, it is important to understand that collaborative or integrated care exists on a continuum of service integration: collaborative, co-located, and integrated. The continuum of service integration and description of integrated care treatment are provided in Chapter 10. The remainder of this section focuses on an example of integrated care treatment commonly found in clinical mental health settings.

Primary Care in Behavioral Health

The goal of integrating primary care into behavioral health settings is to reduce a health disparity observed in the mental health population: A diagnosis of comorbid mental illness and/or substance abuse and a primary health care disease (e.g., diabetes, hypertension) results in persons dying sooner than those in the general population with only primary health care concerns. By offering primary health care services within behavioral health settings, those with comorbid primary and mental health illnesses have greater access to primary care services, the possibility of early detection and prevention of primary health care illnesses, and the opportunity to receive a more holistic approach to treatment (Substance Abuse and Mental Health Services Administration [SAMHSA], n.d.).

From this approach, experts in primary health care (i.e., primary care physician, nurse practitioner, nutritionist) are integrated within the mental health setting and work collaboratively (depending on the level of service integration) with mental health experts such as psychiatrists, counselors, and case managers to provide health screenings, diagnose and treat both mental health and primary care illnesses, and partake in preventative education and promotion of health initiatives. It is common for health care professionals, especially in a fully integrated model, to follow a team-based approach. A team-based approach includes experts in both primary health care and mental health collaborating and communicating in a way that shifts the perspective from specialty care to holistic care in understanding and treating illness. Thus, each member of the team is important, and each contribution to understanding and treating illness is equally valued regardless of role and expertise.

Schmit, Watson, and Fernandez (2018) found that persons receiving integrated behavioral and primary health care treatment experienced a 24 times greater improvement in overall functioning, across a 12-month period, when compared to persons with similar mental and primary health care illnesses who received only behavioral health services. Essentially, those who participated in behavioral health–only services were responsible for seeking out and coordinating their own primary health care treatment. This study, although not without its shortcomings, provides evidence of how impactful collaborative care models are in outpatient clinical mental health settings.

CASE ILLUSTRATION 3.2

Derivatives of population-based prevention strategies can be found in clinical mental health settings such as agencies or hospitals. Persons with severe and persistent forms of mental illness such as major depression, bipolar disorder, and schizophrenia have shown a higher prevalence of primary health care diseases such as types 1 and 2 diabetes, cardiovascular disease, and hypertension. This phenomenon can be attributed to behavioral choices—for example, poor diet and exercise habits, excessive alcohol consumption and substance use, and smoking—made by persons in this population. A significant consequence among the comorbid mental illness and primary medical disease population is persons dying 25 years sooner than those in the general population with only primary care disease. In response to this loss of life, community mental health agencies have begun implementing population-based prevention strategies that impact the entire population receiving service at the particular setting. Most, if not all, community mental health agency settings have banned smoking within

so many feet of the facility. To support this initiative, agencies are offering smoking cessation programs, free of charge, to those interested. Furthermore, clients are provided free nicotine replacement therapy options for a certain period. Agencies are also placing posters throughout the treatment setting to educate their clientele on the dangers of smoking and health benefits of quitting. For clients unwilling to quit, agencies will offer nicotine replacement options such as nicotine gum to clients waiting to see their counselor. To further support this initiative, most settings have also banned smoking for employees and in return offer them free nicotine replacement therapy. As you can see, the population-based prevention strategy of the smoking cessation program impacts every person within the agency setting, with the intent of preventing persons with severe and persistent mental illness only from also developing primary health care diseases. Likewise, persons with comorbid mental illness and primary health care diseases also benefit from the smoking cessation program.

POPULATION-BASED PREVENTION APPROACH

Population-based prevention approaches focus on improving the health status of a population or subset of the population. Geoffrey Rose (1985, 1992), an epidemiologist, developed and demonstrated the principle of prevention by targeting the general population rather than the high-risk population to observe the population's average decrease in a particular disease or illness. If disease rates continue to rise, this increase would be more readily apparent in the general population than the population considered high-risk (Mackenbach, Lingsma, van Ravesteyn, & Kamphuis, 2012). Some population-based prevention programs or movements you may be familiar with include D.A.R.E. America, school-based immunization programs, youth antismoking campaigns, and Drug Free America, all of which target the general population.

It is important to recognize that a prevention approach may not address the health disparities experienced within a subset of the general population (i.e., a high-risk population). For instance, persons with chronic mental illness are more likely to experience primary health care diseases due to personal factors (e.g., diet, alcohol and substance use, symptoms associated with mental illness), perceived or actual barriers that limit access to mental health and primary care services, and the stigma associated with mental illness (Clement et al., 2015). In this case, the high-risk population, persons with comorbid mental illness and primary health care diseases, is not necessarily the target of a population prevention approach. Rather, prevention strategies such as education, early detection, and ease of access to health care services are implemented to capture the general population, which, in theory, may prevent persons in the general population from becoming considered at-risk. Fortunately, high-risk prevention strategies exist in many clinical mental health settings to capture individuals or groups within the general population that are at higher risk for a specific disease or illness.

RECOVERY MODEL

The ideology of recovery has increasingly become more evident in mental health treatment across the United States. In 2003, the New Freedom Commission on Mental Health provided general policy recommendations to transform mental health treatment based on the principles and guidelines of recovery. Despite the garnered support for recovery, policymakers, legislators, and practitioners are unclear as to how recovery should be defined. Additionally, empirical evidence in support of recovery is scarce, which can be attributed to the absence of an overarching theoretical framework adopted by legislators, policymakers, and practitioners explaining how the principles and guidelines of recovery translate into mental health programs and practices.

Although the terms *treatment* and *recovery* are used interchangeably in clinical mental health counseling, each represents two distinct philosophical views to understanding health and illness. The term *treatment* suggests that a problem can be resolved by applying an intervention. For instance, a person with type 1 diabetes can receive the intervention of insulin medication. Approximately 2 to 3 months after the initial diagnosis, the physician can run a glycated hemoglobin (AC1) test to determine blood sugar level and compare this finding to a previous one. Hence, treatment suggests a tangible outcome that can be measured across time. However, unlike treatment, recovery takes on a whole different meaning. This is not to say that treatment is not part of recovery; rather, recovery extends beyond an intervention or treatment and is considered both an intra- and interpersonal process of health and wellness. According to the Substance Abuse and Mental Health Services Administration (SAMHSA; 2010), **recovery** is "a process of change through which individuals improve their health and wellness, live a self-directed life, and strive to reach their full potential" (p. 3). From this perspective, health, illness, disease, and everything else in between are considered a normal part of development across the life span (Clossey, Mehnert, & Silva, 2011).

The recovery model is a treatment ideology loosely affiliated with the consumer/survivor social movement, placing a person with mental illness in control of making decisions about his or her own life (Mancini, 2008). Thus, persons with bipolar disorder, for instance, could choose not to take medication so long as they are not a danger to themselves or others. This concept sharply contrasts the previously held ideas of both the biomedical model and mental illness; that is, from a biomedical model perspective, mental illness when left untreated results in a prognosis of functional decline and diminished quality of life (Clossey et al., 2011). Although health care professionals differ regarding which model seems more appropriate to health and illness, the recovery model seems to better align with the counseling profession's values of "autonomy, nonmaleficence, beneficence, justice, fidelity, and veracity" (American Counseling Association, 2014, p. 3).

According to SAMHSA (2010), recovery has four important dimensions to support health and wellness: health, home, purpose, and community. The dimension of *health* is related to the act of taking control of one's illness or symptoms to support well-being. Rather than acting as passive participants, persons with mental illness in recovery make informed decisions about their care that lead to optimal health and well-being. The dimension of *home* is grounded in the fact that every person needs a safe and stable environment in order to engage in the recovery process. Without a foundation of safety and support, recovery becomes almost impossible. The next dimension, *purpose*, reflects that people gravitate toward wanting to finding purpose and feel accomplished and useful to self and society. Activities such as working, volunteering, and obtaining an education give people in recovery a sense of both purpose and independence. The last dimension, *community*, emphasizes the importance of interpersonal relationships and social connectedness. Initially, this may be facilitated by the clinical mental health counselor working with the person in recovery. However, the goal of recovery is self-sufficiency. Therefore, mutually satisfying relationships with family, friends, and community can serve as a long-term support system to the person in recovery. In addition to the four dimensions, SAMSHA (2010) identified 10 guiding principles of recovery: hope, self-determination, multiple pathways, holistic, peer support, relational, addressing trauma, culturally informed, involving others' strengths and responsibilities, and respect. Based on these four dimensions and 10 guiding principles recovery is possible.

The process of recovery for persons with mental illness is highly personal and can occur through different mechanisms based on goals, strengths, coping skills, resources, and limitations. Goals developed at the onset of treatment are meaningful to the person in recovery and not specific to a set of outcomes. It is common to find persons in recovery attending counseling and 12-step recovery programs (e.g., Alcoholics Anonymous, Narcotics Anonymous), receiving peer support, engaging in community activities, meeting with their primary care physician and/or psychiatrist regularly, practicing self-care, and exploring their religion and/or spirituality. Continual growth toward optimal health and wellness is defined by the person in recovery. As such, recovery is not a linear process. Rather, it ebbs and flows with the blessings and tragedies of life. Therefore, hope, resiliency, and optimism play a significant part in the recovery process for persons with mental illness.

GUIDED PRACTICE EXERCISE 3.4

It can be difficult to organize one's thoughts surrounding the various theories and models discussed in counseling. Therefore, to help facilitate the understanding of theories and models discussed in this chapter, on your own, develop a short paragraph, three to four sentences, that summarizes each model discussed: cognitive behavioral based, biopsychosocial, collaborative (integrated) care, population-based prevention, and recovery. Upon completion of this independent exercise, feel free to share with classmates outside of class time.

Keystones

- Differentiating between a model of practice and theory of practice is important in clinical mental health counseling. A theory of practice is a set of principles or guidelines that explains a particular phenomenon. It often answers the what, how, and why aspects and is predictive in nature. Unlike theory, a model of practice attempts to simplify aspects of a theory, focusing more on the practice side of counseling. In other words, models provide counselors a framework (answering the *what*) from which to practice that allows for flexibility.

- Cognitive-behavioral-based approaches such as CBT, TF-CBT, CPT, DBT, and EMDR are grounded in cognitive theory. Cognitive theory asserts that a person's perceptions, thoughts, and beliefs determine one's behaviors, emotions, and physiology. Cognitive-behavioral-based approaches attempt to restructure unhealthy thoughts into healthier ones and are favored by third-party payers and most clinical mental health settings due to the structure, empirical support, cost-effectiveness, and brief nature of treatment they provide.

- The biopsychosocial model is best understood as a philosophy to understanding health and illness across the life span. According to Engel, the biopsychosocial model closely aligns with general systems theory, that is, biological, psychological, and social systems interact and contribute to one's health or illness. A major criticism of the biopsychosocial model is how to translate this philosophy into clinical practice. Evidence of the biopsychosocial model can be found in the fields of psychiatry, medicine, counseling, social work, and nursing.

- Collaborative or integrated care describes a health care practice that systematically combines the treatment of mental illness and/or substance use and primary health care disease in either primary care or behavioral health settings. Differing degrees of collaboration exist, depending on the level of service integration, within the treatment setting. Service integration exists on a continuum and can range from collaborative to co-located to fully integrated. Integrating primary care in behavioral health is one example of an integrated/collaborative approach that relies on a team-based approach, particularly if a fully integrated model is being used.

- A population-based prevention approach focuses on improving the health status of the entire population by using prevention strategies such as education, early detection, and easing access to health care services. Prevention strategies target the general population rather than the high-risk population to observe a population's average decrease in a particular disease or illness. Although unintentional, population prevention strategies may create health disparities among members of the population considered high-risk.

• The recovery model is based on the ideology that disease and illness are a normal development across the life span, which

is in sharp contrast to the biomedical model and mental illness. Recovery can be defined as a process of change through which individuals improve their health and wellness, live a self-directed life, and strive to reach their full potential. Salient concepts found in the recovery model include hope, self-determination, multiple pathways, holistic, peer support, relational, addressing trauma, culturally informed, involving others' strengths and responsibilities, and respect.

Key Terms

Cognitive theory 58
Collaborative care 66

Dialectic 62
Model of practice 57

Recovery 68
Theory of practice 56

Web Resources

Beck Institute for the Cognitive Behavior Therapy (https://beckinstitute.org/cognitive-model)

Behavioral Tech: A Linehan Institute Training Company (https://behavioraltech.org)

Cognitive Processing Therapy (www.apa.org/ptsd-guideline/treatments/cognitive-processing-therapy.aspx)

Cognitive Processing Therapy: For Post-traumatic Stress Disorder (https://cptforptsd.com)

EMDR Institute (www.emdr.com)

National Child Traumatic Stress Network (www.NCTSN.org)

Overview of Dialectical Behavior Therapy (https://psychcentral.com/lib/an-overview-of-dialectical-behavior-therapy)

Recovery and Recovery Support (www.samhsa.gov/recovery)

SAMHSA-HRSA Center for Integrated Health Solutions (www.integration.samhsa.gov/integrated-care-models)

TF-CBT Therapist Certification Program (https://tfcbt.org)

Trauma-Focused Cognitive Behavior Therapy (www.psychologytoday.com/therapy-types/trauma-focused-cognitive-behavior-therapy)

World Health Organization: Population-Based Prevention (www.who.int/whr/2002/chapter6/en)

References

Acosta, M., Possemato, K., Maisto, S., Marsch, L., Barrie, K., Lantinga, L., . . . Rosenblum, A. (2017). Web-delivered CBT reduces heavy drinking in OEF-OIF veterans in primary care with symptomatic substance use and PTSD. *Behavior Therapy, 48*(2), 262–276. doi:10.1016/j.beth.2016.09.001

American Counseling Association. (2014). *ACA code of ethics*. Alexandria, VA: Author.

Beck, A. T. (1970). Cognitive therapy: Nature and relation to behavior therapy. *Behavior Therapy, 1*(2), 184–200. doi:10.1016/S0005-7894(70)80030-2

Beck, A. T., & Weishaar, M. E. (2014). Cognitive therapy. In D. Wedding & R. J. Corsini (Eds.), *Current psychotherapies* (10th ed., pp. 231–264). Belmont, CA: Brooks/Cole.

Beck, J. S. (2011). *Cognitive behavioral therapy: Basic and beyond* (2nd ed.). New York, NY: Guilford Press.

Behavioral Tech. (2017). What is dialectical behavior therapy (DBT)? Retrieved from https://behavioraltech.org

Bernard, J. M., & Goodyear, R. K. (1992). *Fundamentals of clinical supervision*. Boston, MA: Allyn & Bacon.

Bisson, J., Roberts, N. P., Andrew, M., Cooper, R., & Lewis, C. (2013). Psychological therapies for chronic post-traumatic stress disorder (PTSD) in adults. *Cochrane Database of Systematic Reviews, 12*(12), CD003388. doi:10.1002/14651858.CD003388.pub4

Cary, C. E., & McMillen, J. (2012). The data behind the dissemination: A systematic review of trauma-focused cognitive behavioral therapy for use with children and youth. *Children and Youth Services Review, 34*, 748–757. doi:10.1016/j.childyouth.2012.01.003

Chard, K. M. (2005). An evaluation of cognitive processing therapy for the treatment of posttraumatic stress disorder related to childhood sexual abuse. *Journal of Consulting and Clinical Psychology, 73*, 965–971.

Chen, C., Li, C., Wang, H., Ou, J., Zhou, J., & Wang, X. (2014). Cognitive behavioral therapy to reduce overt aggression behavior in Chinese young male violent offenders: CBT to reduce aggression behavior. *Aggressive Behavior, 40*(4), 329–336. doi:10.1002/ab.21521

Clement, S., Schauman, O., Graham, T., Maggioni, F., Evans-Lacko, S., Bezborodovs, N. . . . Thornicroft, G. (2015). What is the impact of mental health-related stigma on help-seeking? A systematic review of quantitative and qualitative studies. *Psychological Medicine, 45*, 11–27. doi:10.1017/S0033291714000129

Clossey, L., Mehnert, K., & Silva, S. (2011). Using appreciative inquiry to facilitate implementation of the recovery model in mental health agencies. *Health & Social Work, 36*(4), 259–266. doi:10.1093/hsw/36.4.259

Cohen, J. A., Berliner, L., & Mannarino, A. (2010). Trauma focused CBT for children with co-occurring trauma and behavior problems. *Child Abuse & Neglect, 34*(4), 215–224. doi:10.1016/j.chiabu.2009.12.003

Cohen, J. A., Mannarino, A. P., & Deblinger, E. (2006). *Treating trauma and traumatic grief in children and adolescents*. New York, NY: Guilford Press.

Cohen, J. A., Mannarino, A. P., Kliethermes, M., & Murray, L. (2012). Trauma-focused CBT for youth with complex trauma. *Child Abuse and Neglect, 36*, 528–541. doi:10.1016/j.chiabu.2012.03.007

Davidson, P. R., & Parker, K. C. H. (2001). Eye movement desensitization and reprocessing (EMDR): A meta-analysis. *Journal of Consulting and Clinical Psychology, 69*, 305–316.

de Jong, M., Korrelboom, K., van der Meer, I., Deen, M., Hoek, H. W., & Spinhoven, P. (2016).

Effectiveness of enhanced cognitive behavioral therapy (CBT-E) for eating disorders: Study protocol for a randomized controlled trial. *Trials, 17*(1). doi:10.1186/s13063-016-1716-3

Dorsey, S., McLaughlin, K. A., Kerns, S. E. U., Harrison, J. P., Lambert, H. K., Briggs, E. C., . . . Amaya-Jackson, L. (2017). Evidence base update for psychosocial treatments for children and adolescents exposed to traumatic events. *Journal of Clinical Child & Adolescent Psychology, 46*(3), 303–328. doi:10.1080/15374416.2016.1220309

Drmic, I. E., Aljunied, M., & Reaven, J. (2017). Feasibility, acceptability and preliminary treatment outcomes in a school-based CBT intervention program for adolescents with ASD and anxiety in Singapore. *Journal of Autism and Developmental Disorders, 47*(12), 3909–3929. doi:10.1007/s10803-016-3007-y

Ellis, A. (1957). Rational psychotherapy and individual psychology. *Journal of Individual Psychology, 13*, 38–44.

Engel, G. (1977). The need for a new medical model: A challenge for biomedicine. *Science, 196*(4286), 129–136.

Engel, G. (1980). The clinical application of the biopsychosocial model. *American Journal of Psychiatry, 137*(5), 535–544.

Forbes, D., Lloyd, D., Nixon, R. D. V., Elliott, P., Varker, T., Perry, D., . . . Creamer, M. (2012). A multisite randomized controlled effectiveness trial of cognitive processing therapy for military-related posttraumatic stress disorder. *Journal of Anxiety Disorders, 26*(3), 442–452. doi:10.1016/j.janxdis.2012.01.006

Forester-Miller, H., & Davis, T. E. (2016). *A practitioner's guide to ethical decision making.* Alexandria, VA: American Counseling Association.

Galovski, T. E., & Resick, P. A. (2008). Cognitive processing therapy for posttraumatic stress disorder secondary to a motor vehicle accident: A single-subject report. *Cognitive and Behavioral Practice, 15*(3), 287–295.

Goldstein, T. R., Fersch-Podrat, R. K., Rivera, M., Axelson, D. A., Merranko, J., Yu, H., . . . Birmaher, B. (2015). Dialectical behavior therapy for adolescents with bipolar disorder: Results from a pilot randomized trial. *Journal of Child and Adolescent Psychopharmacology, 25*, 140–149. doi:10.1089/cap.2013.0145

Hans, E., & Hiller, W. (2013). A meta-analysis of nonrandomized effectiveness studies on outpatient cognitive behavioral therapy for adult anxiety disorders. *Clinical Psychology Review, 33*(8), 954–964. doi:10.1016/j.cpr.2013.07.003

Hofmann, S. G., Asnaani, A., Vonk, I. J., Sawyer, A. T., & Fang, A. (2012). The efficacy of cognitive behavioral therapy: A review of meta-analyses. *Cognitive Therapy and Research, 36*(5), 427–440. doi:10.1007/s10608-012-9476-1

Lee, C. W., & Cuijpers, P. (2013). A meta-analysis of the contribution of eye movements in processing emotional memories. *Journal of Behavior Therapy and Experimental Psychiatry, 44*(2), 231–239. doi:10.1016/j.jbtep.2012.11.001

Lenz, A. S., & Hollenbaugh, K. M. (2015). Meta-analysis of trauma-focused cognitive behavioral therapy for treating PTSD and co-occurring depression among children and adolescents. *Counseling Outcome Research and Evaluation, 6*, 18–32. doi:10.1177/2150137815573790

Lepping, P., Whittington, R., Sambhi, R., Lane, S., Poole, R., Leucht, S., . . . Waheed, W. (2017). Clinical relevance of findings in trials of CBT for depression. *European Psychiatry, 45*, 207–211. doi:10.1016/j.eurpsy.2017.07.003

Linehan, M. M. (2014). *DBT skills training manual* (2nd ed.). New York, NY: Guilford Press.

Linehan, M. M. (2015). *DBT skills training handouts and worksheets* (2nd ed.). New York, NY: Guilford Press.

Linehan, M. M., Armstrong, H. E., Suarez, A., Allmon, D., & Heard, H. L. (1991). Cognitive-behavioral treatment of chronically parasuicidal borderline patients. *Archives of General Psychiatry, 48*(12), 1060–1064. doi:10.1001/archpsyc.1991.01810360024003

Linehan, M. M., Korslund, K. E., Harned, M. S., Gallop, R. J., Lungu, A., Neacsiu, A. D., . . . Murray-Gregory, A. M. (2015). Dialectical behavior therapy for high suicide risk in individuals with borderline personality disorder: A randomized clinical trial and component analysis. *JAMA Psychiatry, 72*(5), 475–482. doi:10.1001/jamapsychiatry.2014.3039

Mackenbach, J. P., Lingsma, H. F., van Ravesteyn, N. T., & Kamphuis, C. B. M. (2012). The population and high-risk approaches to prevention: Quantitative estimates of their contribution to population health in the Netherlands, 1970–2010. *European Journal of Public Health, 23,* 909–915. doi:10.1093/eurpub/cks106

Mancini, A. D. (2008). Self-determination theory: A framework for the recovery paradigm. *Advances in Psychiatric Treatment, 14,* 358–365. doi:10.1192/apt.bp.107.004036

Mehlum, L., Ramberg, M., Tørmoen, A. J., Haga, E., Diep, L. M., Stanley, B. H., . . . Grøholt, B. (2016). Dialectical behavior therapy compared with enhanced usual care for adolescents with repeated suicidal and self-harming behavior: Outcomes over a one-year follow-up. *Journal of the American Academy of Child & Adolescent Psychiatry, 55*(4), 295–300. doi:10.1016/j.jaac.2016.01.005

Nilsen, P. (2015). Making sense of implementation theories, models and frameworks. *Implementation Science, 10,* 53. doi:10.1186/s13012-015-0242-0

Olthuis, J., Watt, M., Mackinnon, S., & Stewart, S. (2015). CBT for high anxiety sensitivity: Alcohol outcomes. *Addictive Behaviors, 46,* 19–24. doi:10.1016/j.addbeh.2015.02.018

Owen, M., Sellwood, W., Kan, S., Murray, J., & Sarsam, M. (2015). Group CBT for psychosis: A longitudinal, controlled trial with inpatients. *Behaviour Research and Therapy, 65,* 76–85. doi:10.1016/j.brat.2014.12.008

Parsons, R. D., & Zhang, N. (2014). *Counseling theory: Guiding reflective practice.* Thousand Oaks, CA: Sage.

Psychology Today. (1991–2018). Trauma-focused cognitive behavior therapy. Retrieved from https://www.psychologytoday.com/therapy-types/trauma-focused-cognitive-behavior-therapy

Resick, P. A., Monson, C. A., & Chard, K. M. (2006). *Cognitive processing therapy: Veteran/military version.* Retrieved from http://alrest.org/pdf/CPT_Manual_-_Modified_for_PRRP%282%29.pdf

Resick, P. A., Monson, C. A., & Chard, K. M. (2016). *Cognitive processing therapy for PTSD: A comprehensive manual.* New York, NY: Guilford Press.

Resick, P. A., Nishith, P., Weaver, T. L., Astin, M. C., & Feuer, C. A. (2002). A comparison of cognitive-processing therapy with prolonged exposure and a waiting condition for the treatment of chronic post-traumatic stress disorder in female rape victims. *Journal of Consulting and Clinical Psychology, 70*(4), 867–879.

Resick, P. A., & Schnicke, M. K. (1992). Cognitive processing therapy for sexual assault victims. *Journal of Consulting and Clinical Psychology, 60,* 748–756.

Resick, P. A., & Schnicke, M. K. (1993). *Cognitive processing therapy for rape victims: A treatment manual.* London, England: Sage.

Resick, P. A., Wachen, J. S., Dondanville, K. A., Pruiksma, K. E., Yarvis, J. S., Peterson, A. L., . . . and the STRONG STAR Consortium. (2017). Effect of group vs individual cognitive processing therapy in active-duty military seeking treatment for posttraumatic stress disorder: A randomized clinical trial. *JAMA Psychiatry, 74,* 28–36. doi:10.1001/jamapsychiatry.2016.2729

Resick, P. A., Wachen, J. S., Mintz, J., Young-McCaughan, S., Roache, J. D., Borah, A. M., . . . Peterson, A. L. (2015). A randomized clinical trial of group cognitive processing therapy compared with group present-centered therapy for PTSD among active duty military personnel. *Journal of Consulting and Clinical Psychology, 83*(6), 1058–1068. doi:10.1037/ccp0000016

Rogers, C. (1951). *Client-centered therapy: Its current practice, implications and theory.* London, England: Constable.

Rogers, C. (1959). A theory of therapy, personality and interpersonal relationships as developed in the client-centered framework. In S. Koch (Ed.), *Psychology: A study of a science* (Vol. *3*, pp. 184–256). New York, NY: McGraw Hill.

Rose, G. (1985). Sick individuals and sick population. *International Journal of Epidemiology, 14,* 32–38.

Rose, G. (1992). *The strategy of preventive medicine.* Oxford, England: Oxford University Press.

Safer, D. L., Robinson, A. H., & Jo, B. (2011). Outcome from a randomized controlled trial of group therapy for binge eating disorder: Comparing dialectical behavior therapy adapted for binge eating to an active comparison group therapy. *Behavior Therapy, 41,* 106–120.

Salkovskis, P. (2002). Review: Eye movement desensitization and reprocessing is not better than exposure therapies for anxiety or trauma. *Evidence-Based Mental Health, 5*(1). doi:10.1136/ebmh.5.1.13

Schmit, M. K., Schmit, E. L., Henesy, R., Klassen, S., & Oliver, M. (2015). Constructing an integrated model of ethical decision making in counselor education and supervision: A case conceptualization. *VISTAS Online.* Retrieved from http://www.counseling.org/knowledge-center/vistas

Schmit, M. K., Watson, J. C., & Fernandez, M. A. (2018). Examining the effectiveness of integrated behavioral and primary healthcare treatment. *Journal of Counseling & Development, 96,* 3–14. doi:10.1002/jcad.12173

Schulz, P. M., Resick, P. A., Huber, L. C., & Griffin, M. G. (2006). The effectiveness of cognitive processing therapy for PTSD with refugees in a community setting. *Cognitive and Behavioral Practice, 13*(4), 322–331. doi:10.1016/j.cbpra.2006.04.011

Shapiro, F. (1995). *Eye movement desensitization and reprocessing: Basic principles, protocols and procedures.* New York, NY: Guilford Press.

Shapiro, F. (2018). *Eye movement desensitization and reprocessing (EMDR) therapy: Basic principles, protocols, and procedures* (3rd ed.). New York, NY: Guilford Press.

Silk, J. S., Tan, P. Z., Ladouceur, C. D., Meller, S., Siegle, G. J., McMakin, D. L., . . . Ryan, N. D. (2016). A randomized clinical trial comparing individual cognitive behavioral therapy and child-centered therapy for child anxiety disorders. *Journal of Clinical Child & Adolescent Psychology,* 1–13. doi:10.1080/15374416.2016.1138408

Sprich, S. E., Safren, S. A., Finkelstein, D., Remmert, J. E., & Hammerness, P. (2016). A randomized controlled trial of cognitive behavioral therapy for ADHD in medication-treated adolescents. *Journal of Child Psychology and Psychiatry, 57*(11), 1218–1226. doi:10.1111/jcpp.12549

Stewart, R. E., & Chambless, D. L. (2009). Cognitive-behavioral therapy for adult anxiety disorders in clinical practice: A meta-analysis of effectiveness studies. *Journal of Consulting and Clinical Psychology, 77*(4), 595–606. doi:10.1037/a0016032

Substance Abuse and Mental Health Services Administration. (n.d.). SAMHSA's primary and behavioral health care integration program. Retrieved from https://www.integration.samhsa.gov/about-us/pbhci

Substance Abuse and Mental Health Services Administration. (2010). SAMHSA's working definition of recovery. Retrieved from https://store.samhsa.gov/shin/content/PEP12-RECDEF/PEP12-RECDEF.pdf

Taylor, H. L., Rybarczyk, B. D., Nay, W., & Leszczyszyn, D. (2015). Effectiveness of a CBT intervention for persistent insomnia and hypnotic dependency in an outpatient psychiatry clinic: CBT for insomnia in an outpatient psychiatry clinic. *Journal of Clinical Psychology, 71*(7), 666–683. doi:10.1002/jclp.22186

Van Dijk, S., Jeffrey, J., & Katz, M. R. (2013). A randomized, controlled, pilot study of dialectical behavior therapy skills in a psychoeducational group for individuals with bipolar disorder. *Journal of Affective Disorders, 145,* 386–393.

Voelkel, E., Pukay-Martin, N. D., Walter, K. H., & Chard, K. M. (2015). Effectiveness of cognitive processing therapy for male and female U.S. veterans with and without military sexual trauma: CPT for veterans with and without MST. *Journal of Traumatic Stress, 28*(3), 174–182. doi:10.1002/jts.22006

Von Bertalanffy, L. (1968). *General systems theory: Foundations, development, application* (Rev. ed.). New York, NY: George Braziller.

Ye, B., Jiang, Z., Li, X., Cao, B., Cao, L., Lin, Y., . . . Miao, G. (2016). Effectiveness of cognitive behavioral therapy in treating bipolar disorder: An updated meta-analysis with randomized controlled trials: CBT for bipolar disorder. *Psychiatry and Clinical Neurosciences, 70*(8), 351–361. doi:10.1111/pcn.12399

4

POLICIES, LAWS, AND REGULATORY ISSUES RELEVANT TO THE PRACTICE OF CLINICAL MENTAL HEALTH COUNSELING

Since passage of the Community Mental Health Act in 1963, the practice of clinical mental health counseling has been shaped by an everchanging sociopolitical landscape. The profession you currently are learning about in your respective training programs looks markedly different than it did 50, 25, or even 10 years ago. Further, it is likely the profession of tomorrow will bear little resemblance to contemporary practice. For example, when I began practicing as a counselor nearly 20 years ago, the idea of telehealth or distance counseling was barely on the radar. In addition to technology not being where it needed to be, acceptance of this form of practice was uncommon. Many counselors viewed computer-based or online counseling to be poor alternatives to traditional service delivery methods because immediacy and human connection, hallmarks of the counseling profession, largely were absent. However, advances in technology have helped change perceptions of these practices. Today, telehealth is becoming a widely accepted form of practice and is being used to help meet the needs of clients in geographically remote areas who otherwise would not have access to the help and services they need.

To function in this shifting professional climate, it is imperative that all clinical mental health counselors recognize and be informed of the current trends and professional issues impacting their ability to practice. As a beginning clinical mental health counselor, this awareness is especially important for it will allow you to start developing the skills and expertise needed to work in a variety of roles and settings today and into the future.

To assist you in preparing for a career in this shifting professional marketplace, this chapter introduces you to a few of the current sociopolitical issues shaping the future of counseling and how services will be delivered. Many of the issues discussed have been the focus of professional advocacy efforts at both the national and grassroots levels for several years and only recently have begun affecting clinical practice. Others remain works in progress that hopefully will soon lead to increased access to quality mental health care for scores of underserved populations. In addition to describing these emerging trends, we also provide guidance for how you, the emerging counselor, can actively advocate for your profession. Working together, counselors can help realize the changes they seek.

LEARNING OBJECTIVES

After reading this chapter, you will be able to do the following:

- Differentiate between laws, policies, and regulations governing the delivery of clinical services and defining the scope of practice for clinical mental health counselors

- Articulate the history and development of clinical mental health counseling service delivery in response to changing client demographics and community needs (CACREP 5C-1-b)

- Describe current legislation and government policy relevant to clinical mental health counseling (CACREP 5C-2-i)

- Identify contemporary legal and ethical considerations specific to the practice of clinical mental health counseling (CACREP 5C-2-l)

- Employ the skills necessary to collaborate with integrated behavioral health care professionals (CACREP 5C-3-d)

- Develop strategies for advocating for persons with mental health issues (CACREP 5C-3-e)

POLICIES, LAWS, AND REGULATIONS

The practice of counseling is highly regulated and influenced by several external forces. Professional counselors learn their craft in accredited training programs, gain their ability to practice through meeting strict licensing requirements, and are bound to practice by a series of professional ethics and standards of care. Further, the venues in which counselors can practice, the clients they can serve, techniques and interventions they can use, and even their ability to bill for services delivered are influenced by a variety of agencies. As you begin your career as a professional mental health counselor, it would be helpful for you to be aware of the policies, laws, and regulations impacting counselors today and how they may continue to guide practice when you begin working with clients. With that in mind, let's start by reviewing the differences among policies, laws, and regulations.

A **policy** is a document that outlines what a governing body hopes to achieve for its constituents and the methods and principles it will use to achieve its goals. Several bodies make policies impacting the practice of clinical mental health counselors including federal and state governments, professional trade associations, state licensing boards, and any third-party agencies who might fund counseling services. Examples of policies relevant to clinical mental health counseling include the profession's view on access to treatment, improved quality of treatment, reduced recidivism, and increased focus on early intervention and prevention services (Mental Health America [MHA], 2018). It is important to note here that policies are merely stated objectives. Neither do they mandate action nor are they enforceable. Additional work is needed to establish the framework for how the ideas expressed in policies are put into practice.

Laws help create the framework transforming idea to practice. **Laws** are sets of rules decided on by legislative bodies for the purpose of governing a particular activity within society (Wheeler & Bertram, 2015). They can originate at the federal, state, or local level. Unlike policies, laws are compulsory and must be followed. Specific provisions regarding punishment for individuals who break or do not follow laws are included in these statutes. An example of a federal law impacting the practice of clinical mental health counseling is the Privacy Rule included in the Health Insurance Portability and Accountability Act (HIPAA) of 1996. The HIPAA Privacy Rule provides individuals certain privacy rights and protections related to their personal health information, including how health care providers (including counselors) and health plans can use this information and to whom it can be disclosed (U.S. Department of Health and Human Services, n.d.). Licensure laws independently established by state licensing boards to regulate the practice of counseling in their jurisdiction are examples of state laws. Many of the ethical issues and professional judgment issues you will face as a practicing clinical mental health counselor will have legal implications as well, so it is important that you are aware of the various laws that govern your work as a mental health service provider (Remley & Herlihy, 2015).

CASE ILLUSTRATION 4.1

Although clinical mental health counselors are not directly responsible for enacting the laws and regulations governing their practice, they can play a key role in shaping the profession and how counselors are used through their advocacy efforts. A recent example is the inclusion of licensed professional counselors (LPCs) in the list of eligible service providers recognized by the federal Department of Veterans Affairs. This landmark decision provided a pathway for counselors that led to increased recognition and hiring in centers and agencies serving military personnel. Through national and state level advocacy efforts, counselors lobbied their legislative officials to support inclusion of LPCs in VA service centers. These efforts resulted in the passage of a law in 2006 that officially added LPCs to the list of professions eligible for employment with the VA provided certain educational and practice requirements were met. Although the law was enacted in 2006, the regulations allowing for the spirit of the law to take effect took another 6 years to craft. There is still room for improvement, but the efforts of thousands of practicing counselors across the country advocating for their profession and the clients they serve offer an excellent example of how counselors can impact the formulation of laws and regulations governing their practice.

Subordinate or ancillary to policies and laws are regulations. **Regulations** are used to carry out policies and implement the authority of laws. Having the same force as laws, regulations often are prescribed by a governing body with the intent of carrying out legislation enacted by elected officials. Earlier we referenced state licensure laws. In each state, these laws include regulatory language specifying the educational standards and experiential requirements a counselor needs to meet to practice. Those counselors found to be practicing in violation of these regulations are subject to fines, censorship, or other penalties. Regulations can vary from one group to another. For example, most states have laws requiring health insurance providers to cover mental illness and substance abuse treatment options. However, each state has the latitude to set its own regulations specifying what those benefits should look like and how they should be applied.

Now that you are aware of the similarities and differences among policies, laws, and regulations (see Table 4.1), we can examine examples of each that influence the practice of clinical mental health counseling. Keep in mind these policies, laws, and regulations may vary from state to state and organization to organization. As a beginning counselor, you should carefully review relevant information for the states in which you intend to practice and/or the professional organizations in which you plan to maintain membership to ensure you are compliant and maintain your good standing within the profession.

TABLE 4.1 ■ Policies, Laws, and Regulations: Similarities and Differences		
Policies	**Laws**	**Regulations**
• Aspirational	• Legal	• Organizational
• Outline goals and objectives of an organization	• Establish the provisions through which policies are put into practice	• Provide the step-by-step details related to how laws should be followed
• Created by organizational leaders or elected government officials	• Enacted by elected officials or organizational leaders	• Created by organizational leaders or elected government officials
• Cannot be enforced	• Include punishment for failure to adhere	• Include punishment for failure to adhere

GUIDED PRACTICE EXERCISE 4.1

Counselors, including counselors in training, can positively impact their profession through targeted advocacy efforts at the local, state, or national level. Identify groups advocating for professional counselors in your state. What are some of the issues for which they are advocating? How can you personally get involved in these advocacy efforts? What barriers might prevent you from getting involved?

PROFESSIONAL IDENTITY

One of the major policy issues affecting the work of mental health counselors involves the formulation of a cogent professional identity. Many of the challenges counselors face, including those discussed in this chapter, are in part influenced by the profession's struggles to effectively communicate a shared identity. For much of the past two decades, counseling organizations have attempted to address this issue and collectively unite those individuals trained as counselors and providing counseling services. Their rationale has been that the establishment of a strong professional identity that can be succinctly articulated will result in more ethical behavior among practicing counselors, a better understanding of counselor roles by providers and consumers alike, and an increased vitality for the profession (Kerwin & Doughty, 2017; Woo, Henfield, & Choi, 2014).

At the 2005 American Association of State Counseling Boards (AASCB) annual conference the topic of professional identity was discussed. From these discussions, a group of 20 counseling leaders, representing a joint effort between the AASCB and the American Counseling Association (ACA), agreed to meet for a summit to discuss advancing counselors' professional identity. The summit was called 20/20: A Vision for the Future of Counseling. Members in attendance met to discuss barriers and challenges to professional identity, identify an action plan to resolve issues impeding progress, and begin implementing action steps. Membership in the 20/20 program was expanded to include representatives from a variety of counseling-related groups and organizations. Ultimately, 31 major counseling organizations contributed to the effort.

A major deliverable that emerged from the work of the 20/20 group was a consensus definition of counseling. This was important because it provided a shared language all counselors could use in describing the work they do. With a consensus definition, advocacy and legislative lobbying efforts could be streamlined so there no longer would be mixed messages. Instead, a unified direction for what counseling is and what counselors do could be echoed. As noted in Chapter 1, the consensus definition agreed to by the representatives of the 20/20 program in 2009 defines counseling as "a professional relationship that empowers diverse individuals, families, and groups to accomplish mental health, wellness, education, and career goals" (Kaplan, Tarvydas, & Gladding, 2014; p. 368). In the years since, the consensus definition has been used to effectively communicate with clients, politicians, business leaders, professional organizations, and the public what counselors can do. The work of the 20/20 program continues as counseling leaders still strive to ensure the action plans established nearly a decade ago are enacted and the profession grows. As you read about the various regulatory and legislative issues discussed in the remainder of this chapter, keep in mind that the efforts of many counseling advocates have been aided by the work of the 20/20 program and their efforts to unify the profession.

MENTAL HEALTH PARITY

Parity, as it relates to mental health and substance abuse services, means insurers or health care service plan providers are prohibited by law from discriminating between coverage offered for mental illness, serious mental illness, substance abuse, and other physical disorders and diseases (National Conference of State Legislatures [NCSL], 2015). This includes the same freedom to choose providers, number of office visits, deductibles, copayments, facility type, geographic location, and both annual and lifetime limits. In 2008, the Paul Wellstone and Pete Domenici Mental Health Parity and Addiction Equity Act (MHPAEA) was enacted. This federal law prevents group health plans from imposing less favorable benefits for mental health and substance abuse treatment than for other health care treatment. It was proposed to reduce barriers on behavioral health use, change the formulation of behavioral health benefits, and extend parity protection to the provision of substance abuse services (Health Care Cost Institute, 2013). Protections in the MHPAEA were later expanded to include individual health plans through the Health Care and Education Reconciliation Act of 2010 (commonly referred to as the Affordable Care Act).

Despite these positive developments, access to affordable mental health care is still problematic for a significant number of individuals for a variety of reasons. First, parity does not mean health insurance plan providers are mandated to provide coverage for mental health and substance abuse care. It simply means that if they do, they must do so at a level commensurate with how they provide other health care benefits. Second, discrepancies in coverage provisions across state lines still exist. In states with stronger parity laws, health insurance providers regulated in those states must adhere to state law in lieu of federal mandates (National Alliance on Mental Illness [NAMI], 2018). Third, exemptions in both federal and state laws exist that do not require health plans to follow established federal parity laws. For example, Medicare, Medicaid fee-for-service plans, grandfathered individual and group health plans created and purchased prior to March 23, 2010, and plans whose costs increased because of parity laws are not required to equitably apply benefits to mental health, substance abuse, and other physical disorders.

Since the MHPAEA became law, some insurers and employers have voiced concerns that its implementation leads to overall larger cost increases than those found in previous studies of parity and actively lobby to have the law amended (Busch, 2012). Additionally, some health insurance plan providers still fail to offer similar benefits for mental health and substance abuse treatment. In a 2017 study, researchers found that behavioral health care was 4 to 6 times more likely to be provided out of network than medical or surgical care, and primary care providers were reimbursed for their services at a rate 20% more than for the same types of care provided by addiction and mental health care providers (Melek, Perlman, & Davenport, 2017). Consequently, the issue of parity is important for counselors to be aware of as they monitor the vitality of their practice and advocate for the increased accessibility of needed services for members experiencing myriad behavioral health and/or substance abuse–related issues.

GUIDED PRACTICE EXERCISE 4.2

Many counseling advocates have been working toward achieving parity in terms of how mental health, substance abuse, and medical conditions are viewed and treated. Although state and federal laws have been enacted to help bring about parity, they remain controversial. What advantages and disadvantages do you see in existing parity laws? How might these laws help, and in some cases hinder, clients' ability to seek the services they need to address existing mental health or substance-related issues?

LICENSURE PORTABILITY

In addition to parity, one of the more salient issues impacting clinical mental health counselors' ability to practice is licensure portability. According to the American Counseling Association (ACA, 2018), **licensure portability** "refers to the ability of a professional counselor licensed at the independent practice level to transfer their license to another state or U.S. jurisdiction when the counselor changes residence to that state or jurisdiction." Currently, no such mechanism exists for counselors to cleanly transfer their license across all state lines. Instead, professional counselors are licensed to practice at the state level only; each state licensing board independently develops its own rules and regulations based on licensure requirements codified into law by its state legislators. With the passage of the counseling licensure law in California in 2009, all 50 states plus the District of Columbia and Puerto Rico now have legislation regulating the practice of counseling, fulfilling a long-standing ACA goal.

As noted in Chapter 1, independent licensing of professional counselors at the state level has had its advantages and disadvantages. Although it has resulted in increased recognition and career options for masters-level counselors, it also has resulted in professional confusion regarding counselor preparation standards. A review of state licensing requirements depicts widespread variability in educational, training, and supervision requirements for individuals seeking to practice across the country. Specifically, there are noted disparities in the number of specified graduate credit hours (0 to 60 hours) and supervision hour requirements (500 to 4,500 hours) required for licensure, with no two scopes of practice looking the same (ACA, 2018). These differences, coupled with the complex legislative processes required to change existing statutes, have long impeded the counseling profession's efforts to implement national licensure portability (Kaplan & Gladding, 2011; Kaplan et al., 2014; Mascari & Webber, 2013). Despite these obstacles, counselors have consistently advocated on behalf of this issue and likely will continue to do so going forward (Bergman, 2013).

One of the first attempts to address the issue of licensure portability occurred in the early 2000s when a group of 31 organizations representing various segments of the counseling profession came together to work on a unified plan for promoting the needs of professional counselors from all disciplines and specialty areas. In their strategic planning sessions, the group noted the growing need for licensure portability to advance the future of professional counseling (Kaplan & Gladding, 2011). From this group, a subcommittee known as the Education Work Group (EWG) began examining educational requirements found across state licensure laws. Using a Delphi study to achieve consensus, the group sought to identify the characteristics most representative of successful practicing counselors. From the data collected, members of the EWG identified graduation from a CACREP-accredited mental health counseling or clinical mental health counseling program as the universal educational requirement for licensure. This finding eventually would form the basis of the 2013 CACREP position statement on licensure portability for professional counselors in which it was recommended graduation from a CACREP-accredited counselor training program should be a requirement for any individuals seeking licensure portability. Support for this position was mixed, with some researchers and practitioners contending that mandating graduation from a CACREP-accredited program would disenfranchise many qualified counselors whose training programs may not have been accredited for a variety of reasons. In fact, researchers examining state licensing processes concluded that many states require coursework beyond CACREP standards, and as a result, factors in addition to educational prerequisites ought to be considered by licensing boards when endorsing applicants as licensed professional counselors (Olson, Brown-Rice, & Gerodias, 2018). Consequently, further examination of licensure requirements ensued.

One of the groups consistently at the forefront of efforts to support universal licensure has been the American Association of State Counseling Boards (AASCB). For years, AASCB members have worked tirelessly to develop a seamless process for counselors to transfer their license without having to repeat application processes or be subjected to further review of educational background, supervision, and experiential hours (AASCB, 2017; Mascari & Webber, 2013). Following a thorough state-by-state analysis, the AASCB, in collaboration with the Association of Counselor Education and Supervision (ACES), American Mental Health Counselors Association (AMHCA), and National Board for Certified Counselors (NBCC), identified a series of key elements they believed to be important to include in any prospective licensure portability legislation. Based on their findings, these organizations issued a joint statement outlining a proposed pathway toward national counselor licensure endorsement. The National Counselor Licensure Endorsement Process statement, which can be found on the websites of each of the organizations contributing to its development, reads as follows:

Any counselor licensed at the highest level of licensure for independent practice available in his or her state may obtain licensure in any other state or territory of the United States if all of the following criteria are met:

- *The licensee has engaged in ethical practice, with no disciplinary sanctions, for at least five years from the date of application for licensure endorsement;*

- *The licensee has possessed the highest level of counselor licensure for independent practice for at least three years from the date of application for licensure endorsement;*

- *The licensee has completed a jurisprudence or equivalent exam if required by the state regulatory body;*

- *And the licensee complies with one of the following:*

  - *Meets all academic, exam, and postgraduate supervised experience standards as adopted by the state counseling licensure board*

  - *Holds the National Certified Counselor (NCC) credential, in good standing, as issued by NBCC*

  - *Holds a graduate-level degree from a program accredited by the Council for Accreditation of Counseling and Related Educational Programs (CACREP).*

In addition to this joint proposal, the ACA released its own licensure portability model in 2017. The ACA model states:

A counselor who is licensed at the independent practice level in their home state and who has no disciplinary record shall be eligible for licensure at the independent practice level in any state or U.S. jurisdiction in which they are seeking residence. The state to which the licensed counselor is moving may require a jurisprudence examination based on the rules and procedures of that state.

Through these initiatives, groups like the AASCB, ACA, ACES, AMHCA, CACREP, and NBCC have sought to move the counseling profession toward unified education standards, examination requirements, and years of postgraduate experience. In doing so, they believe the passage of a uniform licensure endorsement process will significantly increase public access to qualified care, establish minimum standards for safe practice, reduce administrative burdens for state regulatory boards and licensees, create consistency in licensure standards across state lines, and ensure protection of the public and the continued development of the profession.

CASE ILLUSTRATION 4.2

Throughout my career as a mental health counselor, I have held professional licenses in four states. Each time I relocated I had to reapply for my counseling license under the state guidelines for my new place of residence. Sometimes states had reciprocal agreements with other states in which my ability to verify I was licensed and in good standing in one state would allow me to obtain my license in another state. Other times I had to provide additional information related to my academic training, test scores, and supervised practice experience. The time it took to receive my license varied from 3 to 9 months. This disparity in time made it difficult to begin practicing and earn a living. Had a national licensure portability model been in place, I would have been able to relocate nationwide and transfer my license with me. This would have allowed me to apply for jobs in my new location and begin working more quickly. Further, the application process would have been more seamless because the states all would have been operating under the same eligibility criteria and licensing guidelines.

—JCW

GUIDED PRACTICE EXERCISE 4.3

In small groups, review the licensure portability models proposed by CACREP, ACA, and the AASCB/ACES/AMHCA/NBCC coalition and identify strengths and weaknesses of each. Which does your group believe to be the best model? If you were asked to develop the universal model of licensure portability for the counseling profession, what would your group identify as the key requirements? Once you have created your model, share with the rest of class and discuss any noted similarities and differences between class models.

WORKING WITH MILITARY PERSONNEL

There are approximately 2.2 million active service members and 23.4 million military veterans in the United States (SAMHSA, 2017). For many of these servicemen and women, mental health care is a valuable resource. According to a 2014 study published in *JAMA Psychiatry*, nearly one in four active-duty military members showed signs of a diagnosable mental health condition (Friedman, 2014). Further, nearly 20 veterans die by suicide each day (National Council for Behavioral Health, 2018). Despite the growing need for mental health services, large numbers of military members do not receive the help they need. Recent statistics suggest that a little more than 50% of all service members returning from deployment who need treatment for mental health conditions seek it; only half of these individuals receive adequate care (SAMHSA, 2017). As a result, removing barriers and expanding access to high-quality mental health care are fast becoming top priorities for the U.S. government.

Supporting the provision of mental health services for these individuals is Tricare. Tricare, formerly known as the Civilian Health and Medical Program of the Uniformed Services (CHAMPUS), is the government-managed health insurance program provided to all uniformed service members, retirees, and their families. All Tricare plans include coverage for medically and psychologically necessary mental health and substance use disorders using evidence-based treatments proven to be effective. However, professional counselors historically have been excluded from the Department of Defense (DoD) as eligible providers, greatly reducing the availability of needed mental health providers. When counselors became eligible to see Tricare clients, their ability to do so was limited. Unlike other mental health professions (e.g., social work, psychology), licensed professional counselors were required to first obtain a physician referral to see Tricare beneficiaries. Even with this referral, they only were able to provide services with direct supervision. This inequity was addressed through targeted advocacy work by groups such as the ACA and NBCC that have been effective in changing how professional counselors are viewed within the military health system.

In the summer of 2011, Public Law 111-383, also known as the Ike Skelton National Defense Authorization Act (NDAA), was enacted by Congress and directed the DoD to establish a set of criteria under which professional counselors would be able to independently provide care to Tricare beneficiaries and receive payment for those services. Independent practice meant counselors would no longer have to work under the supervision and referral of a physician and would now be able to engage in autonomous practice and receive third-party reimbursement for services provided. Although Congress authorized a pathway to independent practice, they instructed the DoD to develop the details as to how this change would occur. In December 2011, the DoD released its interim final rule on the matter. The interim final rule established "a transition period to phase out the requirement for physician referral and supervision for MHCs and to create a new category of allied health professionals, to be known as certified mental health counselors (CMHCs), who will be authorized to practice independently under TRICARE" (Department of Defense, 2011).

The criteria for independent practice were based on recommendations included in a study titled "Provision of Mental Health Counseling Services under Tricare" conducted by the Institute of Medicine (IOM) in 2010. In this study, funded by the DoD, government officials examined the current shortage of eligible mental health providers in the military health system and identified the skills and qualifications needed to effectively serve this population through a review of various state licensure laws and counselor training program standards. Their findings led to the establishment of a minimum criteria for counselors to be able to practice independently in Tricare (see Table 4.2).

For mental health counselors not meeting the requirements for independent practice, a 3-year period was established for them to address any unmet requirements. During this transitional period, counselors were still able to provide services to Tricare beneficiaries under the old policy in which physician referral and supervision was required. At the end of this 3-year period, counselors still not meeting the new requirements for independent practice would lose their ability to be recognized as eligible service providers by Tricare.

Although this development was certainly a step in the right direction and a significant victory for the profession, the language of the law still excluded some counselors from working with Tricare beneficiaries. Specifically, the law provided a pathway to independent practice for those individuals graduating from CACREP-accredited mental health counseling programs only. Individuals from non-CACREP-accredited programs, or who graduated from programs before they became CACREP accredited, were not eligible. Further, graduates of CACREP-accredited programs not classified as mental health programs also were not eligible. This meant that graduates of school counseling, career counseling, and college counseling and student affairs programs accredited by CACREP also were ineligible to practice independently and bill for their services under Tricare.

Advocating for its members, the ACA lobbied Congress to broaden eligibility criteria and provide pathways for a greater number of licensed professional counselors to become eligible to provide mental health care services to military personnel and their families. According to then ACA president Dr. Thelma Duffey, all members should be afforded the same recognition as other mental health professionals in the Tricare system. These efforts proved successful, for in 2015 President Barack Obama signed into law the Fiscal Year 2016 National Defense Authorization Act (Public Law 114-92) that included two significant revisions to the criteria needed for licensed professional counselors to work with Tricare. First, language was changed eliminating the need for a person to have graduated from an accredited mental health counseling program only. Instead, the regulations

TABLE 4.2 ■ IOM Recommended Criteria for CMHCs to Practice Independently in Tricare (2011)
1. Master's degree or higher in counseling from a CACREP-accredited mental health counseling program
2. State license in mental health counseling at the clinical level or the highest level available in states with a multitiered licensure system
3. Passing score on the National Clinical Mental Health Counseling examination (NCMHE)
4. Minimum of 3,000 hours of supervised clinical practice
5. Minimum of 100 hours of face-to-face supervision
6. A well-defined scope of practice

now indicate the need for an individual to hold at least a master's degree in counseling. This opens the door for counselors who specialized in areas other than mental health counseling. Second, the CACREP accreditation requirement was expanded to specify an individual's training program needed to be either CACREP accredited or regionally accredited. Both amendments apply to licensed professional counselors seeking to practice independently in the Tricare system and who apply before 2021. A complete description of the revised eligibility criteria for independent practice in the Tricare mental health system is included in Table 4.3.

With the passage of this bill into law in 2015, all licensed professional counselors meeting the new criteria would be grandfathered in the Tricare system as independent practice service providers until 2027. At that point, existing eligibility requirements could be amended or modified to accommodate any changes to professional quality and licensure standards.

EMPLOYMENT WITHIN THE DEPARTMENT OF VETERANS AFFAIRS

At the forefront of efforts to combat the mental health epidemic among active-duty and veteran military members is the Department of Veterans Affairs (VA). The VA is the federal department responsible for administering benefits for U.S. veterans, including

TABLE 4.3 ■ Amended Criteria for CMHCs to Practice Independently in Tricare (2016)
1. Master's degree (48 or 60 credit hours) or higher in counseling from an institution that is regionally accredited or has a CACREP-accredited counseling program
2. State license in mental health counseling at the clinical level or the highest level available in states with a multitiered licensure system with at least 5 years of practice in good standing
3. Passing score on the National Clinical Mental Health Counseling examination (NCMHE)
4. Minimum of 3,000 hours of supervised clinical practice
5. Minimum of 100 hours of face-to-face supervision
6. A well-defined scope of practice

GUIDED PRACTICE EXERCISE 4.4

Conduct a search for mental health jobs within the U.S. Department of Veterans Affairs in your area (www.vacareers.va.gov/careers/mental-health). What types of jobs are licensed professional counselors eligible for? What are the qualifications needed to apply for one of these jobs? Are these qualifications like those listed for available social work, psychologist, psychiatrist, and/or psychiatric nurse positions?

mental health care. Until recently, the VA did not recognize licensed professional counselors as eligible service providers despite the clear need for additional qualified mental health providers to meet growing demands for services. Working on behalf of the counseling profession, the NBCC has advocated for the increased recognition and hiring of professional counselors by the VA for over a decade. Their efforts led to positive change in December 2006 when Congress and President George W. Bush enacted legislation authorizing the VA to officially recognize licensed professional mental health counselors as employment-eligible service providers in all VA facilities (P.L. 109-461).

Despite being added to the list of professions eligible for VA employment, licensed professional counselors still faced many obstacles. It would take an additional 4 years for the VA to adopt an occupational standard for "licensed professional mental health counselors" (ACA, 2010). The new standards established categories and criteria for employment within the VA for licensed professional counselors that was comparable to the positions already in place for other providers such as clinical social workers. The specific categories established by the VA are included in Table 4.4. For each position, applicants are required to hold a minimum of a master's degree in mental health counseling or a related field from a CACREP-accredited training program. Examples of related mental health fields include addictions counseling; community counseling; gerontology counseling; marital, couple, and family counseling; and marriage and family therapy (ACA, 2010).

Counselors who complete their graduate training but who have not yet obtained state licensure can apply for positions with the VA under the GS-9 classification. Individuals hired at this level who fail to become licensed within 2 years of the date of their initial appointment will be removed from the GS-101 Licensed Professional Mental Health Counselor series and be at risk for termination of their employment. Once licensed, practicing counselors employed by the VA must maintain a valid and unrestricted license that allows them to independently practice mental health counseling and perform both diagnostic and treatment services.

In the ensuing years, continued low counselor employment led to ongoing advocacy efforts by the ACA and NBCC. These efforts resulted in several positive changes over the years. In 2012, the VA produced an addendum to their qualification standards handbook

TABLE 4.4 ■ Licensed Professional Mental Health Counselors Position Grades (GS-101 Series)	
Grade	**Title**
GS-9	Licensed professional mental health counselor (entry level for individuals with a graduate degree in counseling but who have not yet become licensed)
GS-11	Licensed professional mental health counselor
GS-12	Licensed professional mental health counselor program coordinator
GS-12	Licensed professional mental health counselor supervisor
GS-13	Licensed professional mental health counselor program manager
GS-14	Licensed professional mental health counselor program manager leadership assignments

addressing such workplace issues as credentialing, pay, advancement standards, licensing standards, and rules for employment and promotion reviews. This was followed by a 2015 ruling allowing counselors to be part of the VA's Health Professionals Trainee Program. This program was, and remains, the premier federal recruitment program for mental health service providers. Most recently, H.R. 6416, passed into law in 2016, expanded on previous legislation by providing a mechanism for the VA to begin hiring licensed professional counselors holding doctoral degrees. These milestones represent positive steps forward for the counseling profession and have helped expand the pool of qualified mental health service providers available to meet the growing mental health needs of U.S. service-men and women. Future efforts will further help address the needs of service members.

MEDICARE REIMBURSEMENT FOR LICENSED PROFESSIONAL COUNSELORS

Medicare is the federally funded health insurance program for persons 65 years of age or older, certain younger people with disabilities, and people with end-stage renal disease requiring dialysis and/or transplant. Currently, over 55 million Americans are covered under the program. Table 4.5 highlights the differences between the various parts of Medicare. Historically, Medicare has recognized psychiatrists, psychiatric nurses, and (since 1989) psychologists and licensed clinical social workers (LCSWs) as providers able to bill for outpatient mental health services provided under Part B coverage. However, Medicare does not include any provisions for LPCs to be reimbursed for services they may provide.

In recent years, Medicare reimbursement for LPCs has become the ACA's signature leg-islative priority, for it represents a significant hurdle in counseling's pursuit of professional parity. Since 2001, over 30 bills have been proposed that include language adding coun-selors to Medicare. Both the Senate (2003 and 2005) and House of Representatives (2007 and 2009) have twice passed legislation supporting the inclusion of LPCs as Medicare providers, but not at the same time. Consequently, the ability of LPCs to bill Medicare for outpatient mental health services provided remains elusive. Despite these setbacks, prog-ress has been made with additional supporters of proposed legislation coming on board.

TABLE 4.5 ■ Parts of Medicare and Coverage			
Part A	**Part B**	**Part C**	**Part D**
• Inpatient hospital stays • Care provided in a skilled nursing facility • Hospice care • Home health care	• Doctor's services • Outpatient care • Medical supplies • Preventive services	• Health Maintenance Organizations (HMOs) • Preferred Provider Organizations (PPOs) • Special Needs Plans • Medicare Medical Savings Account Plans	• Prescription drug coverage

Organizations like the ACA, AMHCA, and NBCC continue to advocate on behalf of LPCs nationwide and are optimistic their efforts will one day soon result in agreed-upon change. Though change has remained elusive, these organizations are optimistic that the winds of change are at their back and the political climate is becoming more receptive of the idea of adding licensed professional counselors as covered providers.

BECOMING INVOLVED— ADVOCATING FOR THE PROFESSION

In addition to advocating for clients, counselors also need to advocate for themselves and their colleagues. Around the country, challenges confront professional counselors who are appropriately educated, trained, and licensed and who want to practice (Yep, 2011). Counselors therefore must advocate for their profession to ensure they are able to practice their trade and provide quality services to the clients with whom they work. In recent years, the ACA has identified advocacy for the profession as one of the major calls to the counseling field (MacLeod, McMullen, Teague-Palmieri, & Veach, 2016) to address many of the issues discussed in this chapter. Specifically, counselor advocacy efforts are critical to overcoming challenges associated with gaining credibility as a mental health provider, gaining parity and recognition among third-party payers, and streamlining future efforts for licensure portability (Kerwin & Doughty, 2017; Reiner, Dobmeier, & Hernandez, 2013). To combat these challenges, counselors are called on to actively advocate for their profession and its value to society.

The term *advocacy* refers to the pleading for a cause or support of a person, group, or policy through a broad range of activities including research, education, and lobbying for the express purpose of effectuating change. According to the ACA Code of Ethics, "when appropriate, counselors advocate at individual, group, institutional, and societal levels to address potential barriers and obstacles that inhibit access and/or the growth and development of clients" (Section A.7.a, ACA, 2014). This means advocacy is more than just an extracurricular activity, it is a professional imperative especially needed now. The counseling profession faces many challenges. The struggle to gain public acceptance and increased emphasis on accreditation and credentialing standards among counselors are chief among them (Myers, Sweeney, & White, 2002). Whereas counselors are more likely to support and advocate for their clients, advocacy on behalf of the profession is often overlooked and minimally addressed. In many cases, counselors view professional advocacy to be a less desirable activity they are more apt to leave for the next person to address. However, to advocate for counseling is to promote the counseling profession (Gillig, 2003). In so doing, the work of counselors nationwide gains legitimacy and credibility, allowing counselors to become more effective agents of social change and support for their clients.

So why do counselors not participate in professional advocacy efforts? In a 2004 study by Myers and Sweeney, 71 leaders in various counseling organizations and associations were asked their thoughts on professional advocacy and what they perceive to be some of the barriers to advocacy efforts. Participants reported a number of barriers including (a) inadequate resources, (b) insufficient funding, (c) opposition by other mental health providers, (d) lack of collaboration across the profession, (e) resistance of public policy-makers, (f) lack of training in advocacy, (g) not enough time to fully engage in advocacy efforts, (h) lack of organized leadership to guide advocacy efforts, (i) lack of awareness of issues for which they should be advocating, (j) not prioritizing advocacy, (k) having little interest in advocacy efforts, and (l) not having adequate training materials to guide the process.

CASE ILLUSTRATION 4.3

In 2010 I had the privilege of serving as president of the Association for Assessment and Research in Counseling (then known as the Association for Assessment in Counseling and Education [AACE]). As president, I was able to participate in the ACA summer leadership training program along with my colleagues from other ACA divisions. During our training we visited Capitol Hill in Washington, DC, and participated in lobbying efforts by meeting with our various elected officials and advocating for the counseling profession. This was the first time I ever participated in professional advocacy efforts. Initially I was nervous, unsure what I would say to professionally represent counseling. As I met with the staff members of various congressional leaders, I found myself drawing on my passion for the profession as inspiration. The more we talked the more I felt emboldened to share why I thought counselors should be more recognized as effective mental health providers. The staff members were pleasant and listened intently to what I and my colleagues had to share. Ultimately, we left unsure whether our words were effective. However, the sense of professional pride I felt that day is what made the experience memorable to me. As a result, I strongly encourage any counselor who can do so to participate in advocacy efforts at the state or national level. Working together to share a common message is the only way we can change perceptions of the counseling profession and improve the practice conditions for ourselves and future generations of counselors.

—JCW

Fortunately, there are strategies and resources to help counselors engage in advocacy initiatives. First, it is important for counselors to have a clear understanding of who they are as a professional and what they uniquely contribute to society (Eriksen, 1997). Know what a counselor does and why that is important. In other words, help your audience (the public, legislators, third-party payers) understand what you do and how it benefits them and their interests. Once you are clear on who you are, you can begin identifying the key problems that need attention and advocacy. In the Web Resources listed at the end of this

GUIDED PRACTICE EXERCISE 4.5

Choose one of the current professional issues discussed in this chapter and research how your local state counseling association is contributing to professional advocacy efforts surrounding the issue. How can you get involved? What opportunities exist for you to make your voice heard and serve as a true agent of social change?

chapter, we included a link to the AMHCA Federal Advocacy Handbook. This is a great resource explaining how the federal government is structured, to whom requests for meetings or to share information should be addressed, and proper decorum for working with legislators and their staff. Additional resources also can be found at your state counseling association, and many sponsor annual advocacy days where counselors from across the state travel to the capital to champion a cause central to the counseling profession.

The counseling profession continues to grow, and with this growth comes some growing pains (Reiner et al., 2013). In this chapter we discussed several issues challenging the practice of counselors as the profession grows. This is by no means meant to be an exhaustive list. In fact, other challenges exist, with more likely to arise in the future. When advocating, keep your message simple and focused. Address a specific issue and its consequences. With a singular issue in hand, identify who best to advocate to and tailor your message. Speaking the language of the parties you hope to influence creates a connection that resonates with decision makers. Finally, employ various strategies to convey the point you want to make. Continual exposure to an issue, with a consistent message communicated, is key to helping others understand your position and why it would be in their best interest to respond favorably. Finally, realize that advocacy does not have to be an individual activity. Collaborate with other professionals. The voices of many are strong and likely to leave a lasting impact.

Keystones

- Parity laws help reduce barriers to mental health and substance abuse services by mandating that most health care insurance plan providers that do offer these services do so at a rate and level equal to that of other surgical and medical services. Understanding parity laws, counselors can better assist their clients in determining whether they are receiving the benefits to which they are entitled under their insurance plans at a fair and equitable rate.

- Licensure portability is an important issue for professional counselors. The establishment of a national licensure portability model will allow counselors to carry their independent practice licenses with them as they cross state lines due to relocation or in search of greater employment opportunities.

- Military service personnel remain underrepresented in terms of presentation for mental health services despite the increased prevalence of several mental disorders among this population. Although professional counselors historically have been excluded from the list of eligible service providers for military personnel, recent advocacy efforts are effectively creating new pathways for professional counselors to treat military members and bill for their services.

- National efforts to include licensed professional counselors as Medicare service providers continue despite past efforts not resulting in new legislation. The continued lobbying of the major counseling organizations provides hope that one day soon counselors will be able to treat clients who are covered under Medicare.

- With all the issues affecting the practice of counseling, the profession needs the help of each of its members to ensure it receives the recognition it deserves and clients have access to the best possible care available. As such, counselors are called on to advocate for their profession when and where possible.

- The counseling profession is greatly influenced and shaped by outside agents. Counselors are encouraged to remain up to date on the current sociopolitical landscape so that they understand how their ability to practice may be impacted.

Key Terms

Laws 79	Medicare 90	Policy 79
Licensure portability 83	Parity 81	Regulations 80

Web Resources

American Association of State Counseling Boards: Licensure and Portability (http://www.aascb.org/aws/AASCB/pt/sp/licensure)

American Counseling Association: Initial Licensure and Licensure Portability (https://www.counseling.org/knowledge-center/licensure-requirements/licensure-policies)

CACREP Position Statement on Licensure Portability for Professional Counselors (http://www.cacrep.org/wp-content/uploads/2014/02/CACREP-Policy-Position-on-State-Licensure-adopted-7.13.pdf)

Federal Advocacy Handbook for the American Mental Health Counselors Association (https://higherlogic

download.s3.amazonaws.com/AMHCA/6664039b-12a0-4d03-8199-32c785fe1687/UploadedImages/Documents/AdvocacyHandbook.pdf)

Federal Register: TRICARE Certified Mental Health Counselors (https://www.federalregister.gov/documents/2014/07/17/2014-16702/tricare-certified-mental-health-counselors)

Joint Statement on a National Counselor Licensure Endorsement Process (https://www.ftc.gov/system/files/documents/public_comments/2017/07/00009-141034.pdf)

National Board for Certified Counselors: TRICARE (http://www.nbcc.org/GovtAffairs/TRICARE)

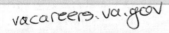
vacareers.va.gov

References

American Association of State Counseling Boards. (2017, April). Licensure and portability: Portability statement. Retrieved from http://www.aascb.org/aws/AASCB/pt/sp/licensure

American Counseling Association. (2010, October). Department of Veterans Affairs recognizes licensed professional mental health counselors. Retrieved from https://www.counseling.org/news/news-release

-archives/by-year/2010/2010/10/04/department-of
-veterans-affairs-recognizes-licensed-professional
-mental-health-counselors!

American Counseling Association. (2018). ACA
licensure portability model FAQs. Retrieved from
https://www.counseling.org/knowledge-center/
aca-licensure-portability-model-faqs

Bergman, D. M. (2013). The role of government
and lobbying in the creation of a health profession: The legal foundations of counseling.
Journal of Counseling and Development, *91*, 61–67.
doi:10.1002/j.1556-6676.1990.tb01402.x

Busch, S. H. (2012). Implications of the Mental
Health Parity and Addiction Equity Act. *American
Journal of Psychiatry*, *169*(1), 1–3. doi:10.1176/appi
.ajp.2011.11101543

Department of Defense. (2011). Tricare: Certified
mental health counselors. *Federal Register*, *76*(248),
80741. Retrieved from https://www.gpo.gov/fdsys/
pkg/FR-2011-12-27/pdf/2011-33109.pdf

Eriksen, K. (1997). *Making an impact: A handbook
on counselor advocacy.* New York, NY: Taylor &
Francis.

Friedman, M. J. (2014). Suicide risk among soldiers: Early findings from army study to assess risk
and resilience in service members (Army STARRS).
JAMA Psychiatry, *71*(5), 487–489. doi:10.1001/
jamapsychiatry.2014.24

Gillig, S. E. (2003). Counselor advocacy tips. *CSI
Exemplar*, *18*(1).

Health Care Cost Institute. (2013). The impact of the
Mental Health Parity and Addiction Equity Act on
inpatient admissions. Retrieved from http://www
.healthcostinstitute.org/files/HCCI-Mental-Health
-Parity-Issue-Brief.pdf

Kaplan, D. M., & Gladding, S. T. (2011). A vision
for the future of counseling: The 20/20 principles
for unifying and strengthening the profession.
Journal of Counseling and Development, *89*, 367–372.
doi:10.1002/j.1556-6678.2011.tb00101.x

Kaplan, D. M., Tarvydas, V. M., & Gladding, S. T.
(2014). 20/20: A vision for the future of counseling: The new consensus definition of counseling.
Journal of Counseling and Development, *92*, 366–372.
doi:10.1002/j.1556-6676.2014.00164.x

Kerwin, A. K., & Doughty, E. A. (2017). Sisters in
social justice: Do counselors and social workers advocate differently? *Journal of Counselor
Leadership and Advocacy*, *4*(2), 102–113. doi:10.1080/
2326716X.2017.1294123

MacLeod, B. P., McMullen, J. W., Teague-Palmieri,
E. B., & Veach, L. J. (2016). What does the public know about professional counseling? A study
of public knowledge and perception of professional counselors. *Journal of Counselor Leadership
and Advocacy*, *3*(2), 95–110. doi:10.1080/23267
16X.2015.1124815

Mascari, J. B., & Webber, J. (2013). CACREP
accreditation: A solution to license portability and
counselor identity problems. *Journal of Counseling
and Development*, *91*, 15–25. doi:10.1002/j.1556-6676
.2013.00066.x

Melek, S. P., Perlman, D., & Davenport, S. (2017).
Addiction and mental health vs. physical health:
Analyzing disparities in network use and pro-
vider reimbursement rates. Retrieved from http://
www.milliman.com/uploadedFiles/insight/2017/
NQTLDisparityAnalysis.pdf

Mental Health America. (2018). Policy issues.
Retrieved from http://www.mentalhealthamerica
.net/policy-issues

Myers, J. E., & Sweeney, T. J. (2004). Advocacy for the
counseling profession: Results of a national survey.
Journal of Counseling and Development, *82*(4), 466–472.
doi:10.1002/j.1556-6678.2004.tb00335.x

Myers, J. E., Sweeney, T. J., & White, V. E. (2002).
Advocacy for counseling and counselors: A professional imperative. *Journal of Counseling and
Development*, *80*(4), 394–402. doi:10.1002/j.1556-6678
.2002.tb00205.x

National Alliance on Mental Illness. (2018). What is mental health parity? Retrieved from https://www.nami.org/Find-Support/Living-with-a-Mental-Health-Condition/Understanding-Health-Insurance/What-is-Mental-Health-Parity

National Conference of State Legislatures. (2015, December). *Mental health benefits: State laws mandating or regulating*. Retrieved from http://www.ncsl.org/research/health/mental-health-benefits-state-mandates.aspx

National Council for Behavioral Health. (2018). Veterans and military. Retrieved from https://www.mentalhealthfirstaid.org/veterans-military/

Olson, S., Brown-Rice, K., & Gerodias, A. (2018). Professional counselor licensure portability: An examination of state license applications. *The Professional Counselor*, *8*(1), 88–103. doi:10.15241/so.8.1.88

Reiner, S. M., Dobmeier, R. A., & Hernandez, T. J. (2013). Perceived impact of professional counselor identity: An exploratory study. *Journal of Counseling and Development*, *91*, 174–183. doi:10.1002/j.1556-6676.2013.00084.x

Remley, T. P., & Herlihy, B. (2015). *Ethical, legal, and professional issues in counseling* (5th ed.). Upper Saddle River, NJ: Pearson.

Substance Abuse and Mental Health Services Administration. (2017, September). Veterans and military families. Retrieved from https://www.samhsa.gov/veterans-military-families

U.S. Department of Health and Human Services. (n.d.). HIPAA Privacy Rule and sharing information related to mental health. Retrieved from https://www.hhs.gov/sites/default/files/hipaa-privacy-rule-and-sharing-info-related-to-mental-health.pdf

Wheeler, A. M., & Bertram, B. (2015). *The counselor and the law: A guide to legal and ethical practice* (7th ed.). Alexandria, VA: American Counseling Association.

Woo, H., Henfield, M. S., & Choi, N. (2014). Developing a unified professional identity in counseling: A review of the literature. *Journal of Counselor Leadership and Advocacy*, *1*, 1–15. doi:10.1080/2326716X.2014.895452

Yep, R. (2011). Advocacy: Getting involved, staying involved. Retrieved from https://ct.counseling.org/2011/08/advocacy-getting-involved-staying-involved/

5

LEGAL AND ETHICAL ISSUES IN CLINICAL SETTINGS

By Julia L. Whisenhunt and Michelle Wade

Perhaps the greatest challenge of professional counseling is navigating legally and ethically ambiguous situations. Professional counselors enter this field because they have a natural desire to support people through challenging times and a willingness to be of service to humanity. It is because of our ability to think complexly about challenging situations and to see multiple dimensions to problems that causes many professional counselors to find the art of ethical decision-making challenging. Whereas the law is relatively black and white, counseling and counseling ethics are about seeing multiple shades of gray. Students often ask why the counseling ethics codes do not delineate or proscribe certain responses or types of conduct. The reason for this is that each situation is unique, and our response to each situation should involve careful and intentional consideration of the multiple dimensions of the problem. As such, although we would like to offer readers with a simple "do this" solution to each of the following types of ethical quandaries we discuss in this chapter, no such solution exists because no two ethical dilemmas are exactly the same. Rather, in this chapter, we provide two things. First, we overview the ethical decision-making process, which involves multiple essential steps. Second, we discuss some key considerations to managing each of the ethical dilemmas we cover in this chapter. In this single chapter, we are not able to address the entire code of ethics or provide a thorough review of all common ethical dilemmas; a separate course is typically devoted to ethics within most counselor education programs. Rather, we have selected a sample of ethical dilemmas that speak to the current issues in the field of clinical mental health counseling. Our review cannot be all encompassing, but we seek to provide a strong foundation from which readers can draw when presented with these types of ethical dilemmas.

LEARNING OBJECTIVES

After reading this chapter, you will be able to do the following:

- Define the six core principles that form the foundation of the American Counseling Association (2014) Code of Ethics (CACREP 2F-1-i)

- Explain the steps involved in performing an ethical decision-making model (CACREP 2F-1-i)

- Explain the key elements of professional-personal boundary conflicts related to multiple and sexual relationships (CACREP 5C-2-l)

- Explain the key elements of ethical dilemmas related to confidentiality and privileged communication (CACREP 5C-2-l)

- Explain the key elements of ethical dilemmas related to social media and professional counseling (CACREP 5C-2-l)

- Explain the key elements of ethical dilemmas related to managing interdisciplinary dynamics (CACREP 5C-2-l)

- Explain the key elements of ethical dilemmas related to managing lethality with clients who self-injure and are at risk for suicide (CACREP 5C-2-l)

GUIDED PRACTICE 5.1

Thinking of all you have learned thus far in your program, what ethical dilemmas most concern you? Consider, for instance, managing suicide or homicide risk, working with clients who are abusive toward their partner(s), reporting suspected child abuse, providing progress reports for mandated clients, addressing incompetence in a colleague, and working with clients who may be hostile toward you. These are only a few examples. Take a moment to write down the top five ethical dilemmas you think would be most challenging to address in clinical practice.

CODES OF ETHICS

There are multiple codes of ethics within the professions of professional counseling and mental health treatment. The code to which one adheres depends on one's type of license and the state in which it is held, certifications, and professional memberships. For instance, professional counselors who are members of the American Counseling Association (ACA) hold a certification as a school counselor and as national certified counselors are expected to uphold the codes established by the ACA, the American School Counselor Association (ASCA), and the National Board for Certified Counselors (NBCC). Some codes of ethics are more comprehensive than others, and professional counselors should always seek to uphold the strictest or strongest ethics codes of those to which they are expected to adhere. For most readers of this textbook, the ACA (2014) Code of Ethics will serve as the guiding force for their ethical decision-making. Accordingly, we use this code of ethics as a framework for our discussion of the eight types of ethical dilemmas we address in this chapter.

The ACA (2014) Code of Ethics is based on the following six core principles: autonomy, nonmaleficence, beneficence, justice, fidelity, and veracity. **Autonomy** is based on one's basic right to "control the direction of one's life" and the counselor's responsibility to engage the client in ways that both respect and support the client's autonomy (p. 3). In this sense, the counselor does not make decisions on behalf of the client but rather engages the client as an equal partner in the therapeutic process. **Nonmaleficence** speaks to the counselor's responsibility to avoid harming the client in any way. This includes egregious offenses that are clearly harmful, such as having a sexual relationship with a client, and unintentionally harmful offenses, such as those that occur when counselors practice outside the bounds of their competence or are multiculturally incompetent. **Beneficence** is based on the counselor's responsibility to work "for the good of the individual and society by promoting mental health and well-being" (p. 3). In this sense, counselors operate as advocates for clients, others affected by issues relevant to our practice, and the counseling profession. **Justice** involves engaging clients "equitably and fostering fairness and equality." In large part, this principle is based on accepting all clients of all diversity statuses. However, justice also involves being equitable in our policies and practices across clients and promoting systems that support the equal treatment of all clients. **Fidelity** relates to the counselor's responsibility to be true to our word, uphold our commitments and promises, and be trustworthy in our actions. Finally, **veracity** requires that professional counselors remain truthful and honest in all professional interactions. This principle is related to honor and integrity.

These fundamental principles form the foundation on which the ACA Code of Ethics is based and outline the essential prerequisites of professional counselors' conduct. Always bearing these six principles in mind, professional counselors use the individual ethics codes to guide their practice. The ACA (2014) Code of Ethics is divided into nine sections, eight of which address professional practice issues and one of which discusses the process of resolving ethical matters. Here are the eight professional practice sections addressed in the code: (1) The Counseling Relationship; (2) Confidentiality and Privacy; (3) Professional Responsibility; (4) Relationships with Other Professionals; (5) Evaluation, Assessment, and Interpretation; (6) Supervision, Training, and Teaching; (7) Research and Publication; and (8) Distance Counseling, Technology, and Social Media (p. 2). Although these codes provide a wealth of guidance regarding ethical conduct, they do not define many concrete parameters for ethical decision-making. This is due, in large part, to two considerations. First, it is impossible to define a code of ethics that addresses all possible ethical matters that may arise in professional counseling work. Second, and relatedly, professional counselors need the flexibility to weigh their ethical codes with their understanding of the unique situational factors to make decisions that align with the six fundamental principles we addressed in the preceding paragraph. This is what we call operating within the *spirit of the codes*—upholding the six fundamental principles and the values inherent to counseling for which they stand.

ETHICAL DECISION-MAKING MODEL

Using a model for ethical decision-making is a necessary process when faced with ethically or legally ambiguous or complex therapeutic matters. An ethical decision-making model provides a series of necessary steps that, when followed, can help counselors make informed and thoughtful decisions. Moreover, the completed ethical decision-making model can serve as a critical form of documentation if the counselor's judgement or behavior is brought to question. In this section, we briefly summarize the ethical decision-making process, but we refer you to other sources for a more detailed explanation of the process of making ethical decisions.

The ACA (2014) Code of Ethics section I, code 1b, Ethical Decision Making, mandates that counselors document the ethical decision-making model used when faced with an ethical dilemma. Although the ACA does not endorse a single model of ethical decision-making, numerous models of ethical decision-making are available (e.g., Corey, Corey, Corey, & Callanan, 2015; Cottone & Tarvydas, 2016; Forester-Miller & Davis, 2016; Schmit, Schmit, Henesy, Klassen, & Oliver, 2015)—but they tend to involve similar key steps. The first step is always to clearly identify the problem or dilemma and the multiple dimensions of the dilemma that influence the decision-making process. The second step involves identifying the relevant ethics codes (e.g., ACA, ASCA, NBCC) and considering the spirit of those codes, as they apply to the unique situation. The third step is very important and is one with which many professional counselors often struggle—identifying the relevant state and federal laws. Professional counselors cannot be expected to know all relevant laws by heart. Rather, counselors need to be familiar with the law and know how to access law databases to review the specific parameters of those laws. The fourth step typically involves brainstorming multiple courses of action for addressing the ethical dilemma and outlining the probable consequences for each course of action. This process is similar to a risk-benefit analysis for each course of action, wherein the counselor considers the ways in which each action could likely affect the client, other involved parties, the therapeutic relationship, the client's other relationships, and the counselor. The final step involves identifying the most appropriate course of action that most upholds the relevant ethics codes and laws. Although not always formally indicated as a step in this process, professional counselors should use supervision and consultation to help them navigate their response to ethical dilemmas. Additionally, depending on the specific model used, counselors may find an increased emphasis on social constructivist concepts and relationships (see Cottone, 2001) or multicultural factors and values (see Garcia, Cartwright, Winston, & Borzuchowska, 2003; Kocet & Herlihy, 2014). Corey et al. (2015) provide a nice overview of the ethical decision-making process and discuss all of these steps in much greater detail.

COMMON ETHICAL ISSUES IN CLINICAL MENTAL HEALTH COUNSELING

Professional-Personal Boundary Conflicts

On the surface, the topic of professional boundaries in counseling sounds rather simple: Do not have personal relationships with your clients. However, in practice, boundaries are complex, and multiple relationships are sometimes unavoidable. Moreover, there are times when multiple relationships with clients can be therapeutically beneficial and ethically appropriate (see Herlihy & Corey, 2014a). Unfortunately, the process of determining when and how to engage in multiple relationships with clients, or to otherwise blur professional boundaries, is inherently skewed by our personal biases. You may have heard of the "slippery slope" of ethics, and professional-personal boundaries is an area that exemplifies that quick and easy slide from ethically appropriate behavior to unethical behavior. For that reason, it is important for counselors in training to begin thinking about the conditions under which it would be appropriate to initiate multiple relationships with a client and those conditions under which it would be inappropriate. This preemptive preparation can help you remain alert to possible boundary crossings, avoid them when they could be detrimental to the client, minimize the impact when they occur unintentionally, and ascertain the degree to which they may be therapeutic to clients.

Let us begin by pondering on a few questions. First, what are your soft spots, or the situations in which you would be most likely to want to blur boundaries in order to assist your client? Consider a mother who cannot afford to buy clothes for her child, an older man who cannot afford his medication, or a child client who is very fond of one of your puppets and asks to take it home with him. These all can be emotionally challenging situations, and counselors can be tempted to intervene. However, doing so can open the door to some inappropriate dynamics between counselor and client. Imagine what might happen if, for instance, you gave the mother a gift card to purchase clothes for her child, and instead she bought herself a new handbag. What if the older male client began coming to you every month to assist in paying for his medication? Perhaps the little boy fails to learn that toys in the playroom must be shared with all of the children and begins requesting more toys. The important thing to remember in all these examples is that it is not the counselor's role to rescue clients; rather, our role is to support clients and, when appropriate, advocate on their behalf.

A second question to ponder is what happens when you simply cannot avoid having multiple relationships with a client. Consider a situation in which your client's child and your own child attend the same school, you schedule a service on your home and a client arrives to complete the repairs, or your new client is also the receptionist at your doctor's office—the only specialist of her kind in your area. These situations are sometimes unpredictable and unavoidable, and there may be no other option than to allow them to transpire. What can you do, though, to minimize the negative impact of these multiple relationships? Relatedly, in what types of situations would you feel having multiple relationships could be appropriate? Consider bartering for services with a client who cannot afford to pay for counseling, attending an important event for a client (e.g., wedding, funeral, graduation), or accepting a gift from an appreciative client. Indeed, there are instances when stepping slightly outside the typical professional boundaries can be beneficial to the client. Likewise, there are times when not stepping outside of the typical professional boundaries can be harmful to clients. For instance, consider the consequences of not accepting a homemade meal from a client whose culture emphasizes showing appreciation to others through sharing a meal. One of the most notable challenges of these types of situations is that there is no time to prepare a response or perform an ethical decision-making model to identify a preferred course of action; often, the counselor must respond in the moment and live with the consequences of those actions.

Finally, considering that the most liability allegations against professional counselors surround their engagement in sexually inappropriate behaviors or relationships with clients or clients' family members (CNA & Healthcare Providers Service Organization [HPSO], 2014), how do you believe counselors move from conducting themselves with professionalism to having sexual relationships with their clients? Assumedly, it is rare that counselors enter into the field with aspirations of sexually manipulating their clients. So, what might that progression look like, and how can we interrupt the process with ourselves and our peers?

These questions do not address the full scope of professional-personal boundaries in counseling, but they provide a good basis for exploring some of the most common boundary issues professional counselors face in their clinical practice. They also help to exemplify that even the best of intentions can lead to harmful consequences and professional misconduct. Having given some consideration to our automatic thoughts and feelings about this topic, let us now turn our attention to the formal codes of ethics and literature base.

What the ACA Code of Ethics Says

Sections A.5, Prohibited Noncounseling Roles and Relationships, and A.6, Managing and Maintaining Boundaries and Professional Relationships, of the ACA (2014) Code of Ethics address the topic of professional-personal boundaries in counseling. Within these two sections, 10 individual codes are meant to guide professional counselors in establishing and maintaining appropriate professional boundaries with clients. We focus on the second (A.6.b.) and third (A.6.c.) codes under Section A.6—those related to boundary extensions—and the first three codes under section A.5 (A.5.a., A.5.b., and A.5.c.)—those related to sexual relationships. The other five codes in these sections are critically important codes, and we advise you to familiarize yourself with them prior to engaging in any form of clinical interaction.

Codes A.6.b., Extending Counseling Boundaries, and A.6.c., Documenting Boundary Extensions (ACA, 2014), discuss the blurring of professional counseling boundaries and the counselor's responsibilities related to considering risks and documenting the decision-making process. These two codes make clear that professional counselors should exercise careful judgment when considering the possibility of stepping outside of their typical professional role. Part of the process of making these determinations includes seeking supervision or consultation, talking openly with the client about risks and concerns, and appropriately documenting the ethical decision-making process. Further, if there is reason to believe that the client has been harmed by the boundary extension, the professional counselor has an obligation to attempt to minimize and remedy that harm, to the degree possible.

A major concern underlying these codes is that the therapeutic relationship must not cross the line into friendship or else the counselor loses objectivity and opens the door to subsequent, and potentially progressively severe, boundary extensions. Although the therapeutic relationship is emotionally intimate, it is not a mutually reciprocal emotional intimacy. Shifting the relationship to a friendship would not honor the client's needs or permit the professional counselor to adequately assist the client. Further, when the counselor's objectivity and judgement are compromised, that counselor cannot provide appropriate intervention. Consider this example. When you are talking with your best friend about relationship difficulties that friend is having with a partner, are you able to clearly see the partner's perspective and confront your friend accordingly? Perhaps you can, but perhaps you cannot. Inherently, professional counselors are going to be slightly biased toward our clients, but we have to maintain as much objectivity as possible so that we can confront our clients and provide challenging feedback. Remember that our job is not to make the client like us. Similarly, when counselors extend boundaries with clients, we are more likely to talk ourselves into successive boundary crossings. We mentioned the slippery slope earlier, and boundary extensions are an easy way to begin sliding into unethical territory.

In an ideal situation, the professional counselor is presented with a potential boundary extension and has ample time to process the decision and consult with a supervisor or peers. However, ethical dilemmas are rarely presented under ideal circumstances, and professional counselors often have to respond in the moment to challenging requests. Although there are times during which professional counselors can simply tell their clients that they need time to consider the request, there are many situations in which counselors must make split-second decisions. It is impossible to map out all of the possible situations in which it would be acceptable to extend boundaries with a client, which is why the ACA Code of Ethics does not define which extensions would be permissible and which would not. The reason for this is that boundary extensions can sometimes be beneficial or therapeutic to the client. This may be true for situations involving major life events or celebrations, but this is never true regarding initiating a romantic or sexual relationship with clients.

Codes A.5.a., Sexual and/or Romantic Relationships Prohibited; A.5.b., Previous Sexual and/or Romantic Relationships; and A.5.c., Sexual and/or Romantic Relationships with Former Clients (ACA, 2014), prohibit professional counselors from engaging in sexual or romantic relationships with clients and their family members. These codes clearly delineate that professional counselors should not, under any circumstances, engage in, or attempt to engage in, any type of romantic or sexual relationship with clients or their family members. Although there are many gray areas in counseling and many unique circumstances, there is absolutely no defensible situation in which having a romantic or sexual relationship with a client is excusable. However, code A.5.c. allows for the possibility of entering into such a relationship at least 5 years following the end of the counseling relationship—only with careful consideration of the possibility of harm to the former client and thorough documentation of the decision-making process. In their Ethical Principles of Psychologists and Code of Conduct, the American Psychological Association (2010) also prohibits psychologists from engaging in sexual or romantic

GUIDED PRACTICE 5.2

In small groups of two to three, discuss the following questions: (a) In what instances would it be acceptable for a professional counselor to purposefully establish multiple relationships with a client? (b) How might professional counselors be able to identify when they are sliding down the slippery slope of multiple relationships in a way that could be potentially harmful to clients? (c) What do you think your policies will be regarding multiple relationships, once you start practicing?

GUIDED PRACTICE 5.3

In a small group of three, two members should role-play the following scenario, while the third member observes and provides feedback. Imagine that you are a professional counselor who is working with an attractive and intelligent client. You have frequently asked yourself why this client is unable to carry on a long-term relationship, for the client is also kind and patient. One day, at the end of your session, the client asks if it would be possible for the two of you to meet for coffee after you terminate the counseling relationship. One student plays the role of the client, while the other student plays the role of the counselor. The counselor should seek to address this question in a way that upholds the ACA Code of Ethics but also normalizes and validates the client's feelings. Remember to not be cold and rejecting, for your response could potentially leave the client feeling unlovable.

relationships with clients or their family members. The ACA and APA differ, though, in the minimum length of time following termination of services, wherein the APA requires at least 2 years to have passed prior to participating in a sexual or romantic relationship with clients or their family members. Again, the APA (2010) mandates that psychologists clearly document measures taken to avoid exploiting or harming the client.

These codes are based on the understanding that professional counseling relationships are inherently unequal in the distribution of power. Even client-centered counselors who strive diligently to minimize the power differential acknowledge that, by merit of their role, education, and licensure, they are considered the expert and are automatically given power within the therapeutic relationship. Despite best efforts to create an egalitarian relationship and share power within the relationship, it is unrealistic to expect that clients do not look to their counselors as role models or experts. Likewise, most counselors would likely argue that it is reckless for us to ignore the role of power within the therapeutic relationship. If one follows this line of reasoning, any form of sexual or romantic relationship with a client would not be fully consensual on the client's part. Further, even if a significant period of time has passed, it is likely that the power differential still exists and could affect the relationship. Consider, for instance, your favorite professor from your undergraduate program. Do you still look up to that professor and find joy in knowing that you have made that professor proud? We would venture to guess that you answered affirmatively to both parts of that question. To be sure, power does not dissolve the moment a relationship is officially terminated, and that power differential likely continues indefinitely. For that reason, pursuing a sexual or romantic relationship with a former client or that former client's family member(s) is not well advised and should involve very careful consideration of the potential for harm to the former client; an allowance for such a relationship should not be mistaken for an authorization.

What the Literature Says

Data regarding the frequency of complaints against professional counselors due to the harmful effects of multiple relationships vary. Wilkinson, Smith, and Wimberly (2016) reviewed disciplinary actions taken by U.S. state licensing boards against professional counselors and found that dual relationships with clients was the second most common cause for disciplinary action (12.32%). However, in their review of allegations made against professional counselors insured by their company, CNA and HPSO (2014), two very large and established insurers for professional liability, found that engaging in multiple relationships with clients "despite potential for client harm" accounted for 1.6% of allegations (p. 11). This difference in incidence rate could reflect the fact that CNA and HPSO collect data on only their insured counselors, whereas Wilkinson et al. reviewed cases across U.S. states. Although CNA and HPSO (2014) found that allegations of harmful multiple relationships with clients were far less frequent than allegations of sexual misconduct by professional counselors, which we discuss shortly, they reported that harmful multiple relationships with clients accounted for much higher indemnity payments than did claims of sexual misconduct (i.e., $500,000 and $89,177, respectively). These figures can be somewhat misleading, though, because the ratio of allegations of harmful multiple relationships to sexual misconduct was approximately 1:25.

Considering the risk involved, it can be anxiety-provoking to consider extending professional boundaries with clients. However, there are times when maintaining firm boundaries can be detrimental to clients and can interfere with client care. Take, for example, a situation in which a client offers you a gift of nominal value to thank you for helping the client to make it through a very challenging life experience. Similarly, consider a situation in which a client makes a dish for you so that you can share in the experience of her culture. Perhaps a child client invites you to attend his graduation—something he had not previously thought he would be able to achieve. To be sure, there are reasonable and appropriate circumstances under which professional counselors should seriously consider extending professional boundaries or establishing multiple relationships.

Ivey and Doenges (2013) explored the topic of multiple relationships for behavioral health providers who work in primary care facilities. Specifically, they proposed that denying services to a client based on a preexisting professional relationship with the person's family members or loved ones can potentially restrict them from receiving an appropriate therapeutic relationship. However, the authors emphasized the importance of approaching these multiple relationships with intentionality and sensitivity, with careful consideration of the associated ethical codes. Nickel (2004) made similar recommendations in her examination of multiple relationships in rural practice. Although not ideal, professional counselors may find themselves in situations that lend to the establishment of multiple relationships. When clients may not otherwise be able to obtain treatment, professional counselors must make a difficult decision about their ability to remain objective and to compartmentalize their work with multiple clients.

Pope and Keith-Spiegel (2008) examined this controversial topic and nine steps for professional counselors to take when trying to determine whether a boundary extension would most likely be harmful or helpful and enhance or interfere with treatment. Those nine steps are as follows: (1) consider the "best possible outcome" and the "worst possible outcome" for extending and not extending boundaries; (2) review the literature base on the topic; (3) refer to ethical codes, professional conduct rules, and relevant laws; (4) seek supervision or consultation from a trusted colleague; (5) notice and analyze your feelings and thoughts about the situation, particularly those that make you uneasy; (6) practice informed consent with the client; (7) refer clients when appropriate; (8) don't overlook blind spots in boundary extensions—even small ones; and (9) document your rationale and behaviors related to boundary extensions. These steps provide a roadmap for navigating major boundary extensions, like attending a formal ceremony for a client. However, as we mentioned earlier, counselors are sometimes presented with situations in which they must make a split-second decision. For those matters, it is important to consider now, before you enter clinical practice, what your limits are and how you may respond to different types of requests from clients. Granted, you cannot prepare for the full gamut of potential ethical dilemmas, but you can get an idea of what types of boundary extensions you would consider appropriate and those you would consider inappropriate.

Now, let us move on to a grossly inappropriate breach of ethics—sexual misconduct. Naturally, you are probably curious how often this happens. Considering the number of professional counselors in practice and the volumes of people who engage in therapy, the rates are relatively low. However, compared to other ethical violations, sexual misconduct stands out as a proportionately common issue. In their review of complaints made to state licensing boards, Wilkinson and colleagues (2016) found that sexual relationships with clients was the third most common cause for disciplinary action (8.97%). The figures reported by CNA and HPSO are much higher than those found by Wilkinson and colleagues. CNA and HPSO (2014) found that 39.7% of liability allegations involved the counselor's engagement in a romantic or sexual relationship with current clients, clients' partners, or clients' family members. By far, this form of misconduct outnumbered any other liability claims filed against CNA and HPSO insured professional counselors; the second most frequent type of claim was practicing outside of bounds of competence (15.8%). Moreover, CNA and HPSO found that the most frequent reason for suspension or termination of licenses or certifications was sexual misconduct. Although far less frequent, sexual relationships with former clients, clients' partners, or clients' family members accounted for 1.6% of liability allegations (CNA & HPSO, 2014). Combined, then, sexual misconduct accounted for 41.3% of allegations filed against CNA and HPSO insured professional counselors in 2014. To learn more about the rate of sexual misconduct complaints issued within your state, contact your state licensing board.

Barnett (2014) reviewed the topic of sexual misconduct among psychologists and proposed the following explanations for their behavior: "naivety, problems with professional competence, and character issues" (p. 176). Barnett suggested that naivety may be related to being "uneducated, uninformed, or unaware of issues relevant to boundaries, multiple relationships, sexual feelings and fantasies, the slippery slope, standards of practice, and ethical decision making" (p. 176). He further suggested that naïve professionals may not be able to accurately manage their own feelings of attraction, and they may not seek adequate support from a supervisor. Barnett defined problems with professional competence as those associated with "distress, burnout, and the impairment in professional judgment and functioning" (p. 177). Finally, Barnett (2014) talked about the probability that some people who enter into the counseling profession "choose to prey on the vulnerabilities of their clients and take advantage of them through sexually intimate behaviors" (p. 177). There are several reasons that sexual misconduct by professional counselors occurs, some of which may involve intentional manipulation and harm to clients. However, in most cases, it is likely that professional counselors ignore, rationalize, or minimize their feelings toward clients and convince themselves that they do not need to seek supervision to manage those feelings.

CASE ILLUSTRATION 5.1

Imagine you are working in a partial hospitalization program, where you have worked for a number of years. In this program, you see the real-life revolving door of mental health, wherein insurance companies pay for just enough treatment for the client to stabilize, develop some coping skills, and establish a basic sense of control prior to being discharged. There is one client, Regina, whom you have seen cycle through the program at least five times within the past 3 years. You are fond of Regina because she reminds you of your deceased aunt. Regina is a 66-year-old Latina female who, although she struggles with severe depression, is imperatively kind to you and others; it is always bittersweet to see her enter the program because you enjoy working with her, but you hate to see her in such distress. It is late November when Regina reenters the program. This time, you learn that she recently lost her son, Antony, in a tragic car accident. He was Regina's only real advocate, and he took care of her finances and helped her with all official business. Given that Regina does not read English and speaks with a thick Spanish accent, it can sometimes be difficult for her to take care of legal matters.

One day, Regina arrives to group and is visibly distressed. She tells you that her landlord plans to evict her because she has not been paying her rent. Regina explains to you that she gave her landlord cash for the rent because she does not know how to write checks. However, the landlord insists that she has not paid in 4 months—since Antony died. You further learn that her landlord has given her an eviction date of the day before Thanksgiving. It looks like Regina will be alone on Thanksgiving and homeless, for she has no other family or friends in the country. Regina says that she hates to ask you, but she needs someone to help her find a place to live. You had mentioned one time in passing that you own a small home, which your mother occupied before she passed away. Regina asks if there is any chance that she can rent the home from you. She promises to pay her bills and not mention the arrangement to anyone at the hospital.

1. What are the primary ethical issues within this case?

2. Which factors exacerbate this situation, and how do those factors relate to your ethical decision-making process?

3. How might you go about providing support to Regina without compromising your professional relationship with her?

Final Thoughts

Considering the potentially harmful and therapeutic benefits of extending counseling boundaries, and the sometimes unavoidable nature of multiple relationships, professional counselors must approach their work with an understanding that firm professional boundaries are not always possible or preferable. However, extending boundaries or developing multiple relationships must always be undertaken with the client's best interest as a priority. Further, when possible, professional counselors should perform an ethical decision-making model and seek supervision to determine the most appropriate way to manage boundary extensions and multiple relationships. Because it is not always possible to preemptively perform an ethical decision-making model, professional counselors should consider the types of boundary extensions and multiple relationships they believe are ethical and how they may navigate a variety of uncomfortable situations involving boundaries. Moreover, they should always document their rationale for engaging in boundary extensions and multiple relationships, measures they have taken to minimize client harm, and supervision they have received to help them remain objective. Failing to consider the slippery slope of blurred professional boundaries can lead to harmful consequences for both the client and the counselor—the most extreme of which is sexual misconduct.

Having feelings of attraction toward a client is not uncommon. As humans, we sometimes find ourselves attracted to others, even when that attraction is not under ideal circumstances. Moreover, attraction is something that is not able to be controlled rationally. As such, when (not if) we have feelings of attraction toward a client, it is imperative that we seek supervision accordingly. It may be that we can manage those feelings in supervision, or we may need to refer the client to another counselor. Either way, we cannot navigate that type of situation in isolation; supervision by a trusted and unbiased colleague is essential. However, if that sexual misconduct comes to pass for professional counselors, the reality is that this negligent and harmful behavior can leave lifelong emotional scars on the clients involved. Professional counselors have a responsibility to always operate in the best interest of their clients. Likewise, as colleagues, we have a responsibility to remain attuned to potential misconduct by our peers and serve as advocates for clients who may be harmed. We discuss this topic—navigating instances of supervisor misconduct—later in the chapter.

Confidentiality and Privileged Communication

Confidentiality and trust are considered foundational aspects of effective counseling (Herlihy & Corey, 2014b). Therefore, it is necessary for counselors to create appropriate boundaries and expectations regarding how confidentiality will be maintained and any possible limitations to confidentiality. Professional counselors need to consider all possible ways in which information is gathered, protected, and disseminated. One could argue that confidentiality is the concern at the forefront of every professional counselor's mind with every client. Imagine you are a practicing professional counselor who works primarily with children. How might you address situations in which the parents are overbearing and wish to know everything that transpires in counseling, especially when you sense that the child is reticent to be truthful with you due to his parents' oversight? Or maybe you work with families. Consider how you would address situations in which one family member wishes to keep a secret from another family member. Perhaps you work with court-mandated clients who wish to disclose sensitive personal history but fear their probation officer will learn of the detailed content of your sessions. Or consider situations in which a client speaks of harming self or others but then retracts those comments. All of these situations are fraught with possible confidentiality concerns. This section is geared toward helping you understand the questions and concerns you should always be evaluating related to confidentiality.

These are some of the main questions to ask yourself when confidentiality concerns appear front and center: (a) Have I addressed this situation in my informed consent? (b) How does the ACA Code of Ethics guide response to this type of situation? (c) How does my state law guide response to this type of situation? (d) To whom does confidentiality belong (e.g., child, parent)? (e) Do I have sufficient indication of risk to breach confidentiality? (f) What are the risks of not breaching confidentiality? (g) What are the risks of breaching confidentiality? (h) Are there ways to resolve this situation that do not require a breach of confidentiality? As you may notice, managing client confidentiality

GUIDED PRACTICE 5.4

Search the web and find two examples of professional counseling informed consent documents. Review each document and rate them on a scale of 0 to 10, wherein zero is poor and 10 is exceptional, in the following areas: (a) defining confidentiality and privacy, (b) explaining the limitations of confidentiality, (c) outlining the way in which client data are stored, (d) delineating policies regarding communication and online presence, and (e) establishing an emergency contact person. Using these ratings, ask yourself if, after reading this document, the client would likely have a clear idea of her rights related to confidentiality. Then, list ways you could improve the document to make the confidentiality policies clearer and more comprehensive.

is a pervasive concern for professional counselors, and ethical dilemmas related to confidentiality are frequent. They are also challenging to address, which is why we strongly encourage counselors to seek supervision and consultation when managing this type of ethical dilemma.

What the ACA Code of Ethics Says

Confidentiality is important enough to warrant an entire section within the ACA Code of Ethics. Section B, Confidentiality and Privacy, provides a framework for how to handle collecting and storing client information but also discusses possible exceptions to protecting that information. There are seven subsections to Section B: B.1, Respecting Clients' Rights; B.2, Exceptions; B.3, Information Shared with Others; B.4, Groups and Families; B.5, Clients Lacking the Ability to Give Informed Consent; B.6, Records and Documentation; and B.7, Case Consultation.

Section B.1, Respecting Clients' Rights (ACA, 2014; i.e., B.1.a. Multicultural/Diversity Considerations, B.1.b. Respect for Privacy, B.1.c. Respect for Confidentiality, and B.1.d. Explanation of Limitations), addresses how information is gathered from and protected for the client. Professional counselors are expected to understand and be sensitive toward the notion that not all clients will want their information protected in the same way. A professional counselor needs to be aware that clients hold their confidentiality, meaning they are able to decide for themselves who has access to their information and when the access happens. If a client does not wish to divulge certain information to the counselor, the counselor should seek to uphold that desire. However, there are some exceptions to maintaining confidentiality, and those limitations need to be expressly explained to the client in the beginning and throughout the counseling relationship.

Section B.2, Exceptions (ACA, 2014; i.e., B.2.a. Serious and Foreseeable Harm and Legal Requirements; B.2.b. Confidentiality Regarding End-of-Life Decisions; B.2.c. Contagious, Life-Threatening Diseases; B.2.d. Court-Ordered Disclosure; and B.2.e. Minimal Disclosure), discusses the exceptions to confidentiality, in which clients may not be able to determine if their information remains confidential. Professional counselors' primary responsibility is to promote client welfare. Therefore, the exceptions to confidentiality predominantly revolve around protecting the client. First and foremost, law supersedes ethics, and if a counselor has a legal responsibility to disclose information, the counselor must do so. This applies to court-ordered disclosure (B.2.d.) and possibly end-of-life decisions (B.2.b.). B.2.a. introduces the idea of serious and foreseeable harm. In a situation where the client, or someone else, is in danger of serious and foreseeable harm, a counselor may break confidentiality to protect those at risk. The ACA (2014) Code of Ethics defines serious and foreseeable as "when a reasonable counselor can anticipate significant and harmful possible consequences" (p. 21). Most individuals consider this section to only deal with suicidality or homicidality. However, one could argue the wording of "serious and foreseeable" allows for a number of gray areas that may benefit from walking through an ethical decision-making model and evaluating what is in the best interest of all involved parties. An example of this may include the possible transmission of a potentially fatal disease. A professional counselor should assess whether a client is intent on communicating the disease with malicious intent.

In addition, one needs to consider the word *foreseeable*. That word choice is not accidental. If harm has already occurred, the counselor does not have an ethical responsibility to breech confidentiality, however the counselor may have a legal obligation to do so. If confidentiality must be breached, B.2.e. encourages the counselor to reveal only the minimal amount of information necessary. This allows counselors to protect nonessential information while still meeting their ethical and legal obligations.

Section B.3, Information Shared With Others (ACA, 2014; i.e., B.3.a. Subordinates, B.3.b. Interdisciplinary Teams, B.3.c. Confidential Settings, B.3.d. Third-Party Payers, B.3.e. Transmitting Confidential Information, B.3.f. Deceased Clients), acknowledges most professional counselors do not exist in a bubble, and therefore, information about a client is often shared beyond the counselor to other members of the treatment team or administrative staff. Counselors discuss with clients when information is shared with others for purposes of completing job tasks, serving the client, and/or receiving reimbursement for those services rendered. Professional counselors also take precautions to transmit any confidential information in a secure and professional manner that protects the client as much as possible and in accordance with any legal mandates. Finally, unless previously agreed on, a client's information remains protected and confidential after death.

Sections B.4, Groups and Families (ACA, 2014; i.e., B.4.a. Group Work, B.4.b. Couples and Family Counseling), and B.5, Clients Lacking Capacity to Give Informed Consent (ACA, 2014; i.e., B.5.a. Responsibility to Clients, B.5.b. Responsibility to Parents and Legal Guardians, B.5.c. Release of Confidential Information), both address situations in which multiple parties are involved with the counseling process. Section B.4 explains the importance of clearly defining who the client is and everyone's role in maintaining confidentiality. Section B.5 specifically examines working with clients who cannot consent to treatment, nor consent for their information to be shared. However, professional counselors have a responsibility to clients first and foremost, as demonstrated in B.5.a. B.5.b. delineates the responsibility to the parents and legal guardians of clients who lack the capacity to give consent. In a world where a number of individuals deal with the realities of split or blended families, professional counselors must be clear in their understanding of who has the right to grant consent for the client. In addition, although the client may not be able to give consent, professional counselors attempt to receive assent from clients. Professional counselors want to engage every client in every aspect of the process, but it has to be done at developmentally appropriate levels.

Section B.6, Records and Documentation (ACA, 2014; i.e., B.6.a. Creating and Maintaining Records and Documentation, B.6.b. Confidentiality of Records and

Documentation, B.6.c. Permission to Record, B.6.d. Permission to Observe, B.6.e. Client Access, B.6.f. Assistance with Records, B.6.g. Disclosure or Transfer, B.6.h. Storage and Disposal After Termination, B.6.i. Reasonable Precautions), looks at the more concrete aspects of confidentiality. Professional counselors are ethically obligated to keep records and documentation in order to render the best possible services to clients. Those records and documents need to be protected according to legal statutes regarding private health information and only available to those permitted by the client to have access. In addition, counselors need to be aware that clients can ask to access their records at any point. If there is any information the counselor deems harmful to the client, or does not pertain to the client requesting access (e.g., information regarding another family member), the counselor can limit access. The records and documentations are protected even after termination of the client. If there is a need to dispose of the record, it is done so securely, such as shredding the file. Finally, according to B.6.i., professional counselors need to consider what will happen to their records if they are no longer capable of protecting the information. The ACA (2014) states counselors need to have a records custodian, preferably another counselor or at least another mental health professional who understands the importance of confidentiality. This individual would have the responsibility of contacting clients and/or protecting their information in the case of the counselor's incapacitation or death.

One of the most important aspects in providing quality care to clients is consulting with other professionals. Again, no professional counselor exists in a bubble, and at times, counselors may need to seek outside guidance and consult with a colleague. In those times, professional counselors are releasing confidential information about a client without permission. However, according to Section B.7, Case Consultation (ACA, 2014; i.e., B.7.a. Respect for Privacy, B.7.b. Disclosure of Confidential Information), the information is shared in such a manner as to not identify the client being discussed. It is important for professional counselors to consult with colleagues, especially regarding challenging or complex cases and making difficult ethical decisions such as breaching confidentiality. Reflecting B.2.e. and minimal disclosure, a counselor should only reveal the necessary information to provide a context and clear picture of where the dilemma resides, and the information should only be disclosed for a professional purpose.

What the Literature Says

An essential component of an effective counseling relationship is the trust clients have that their information will be protected and kept confidential (Herlihy & Corey, 2014b; Wheeler & Bertram, 2014). Herlihy and Corey argue that, whereas confidentiality is a basic ethical obligation, it is also extremely problematic. Wheeler and Bertram explain that approximately 18% of HPSO closed claims from 2003 to 2012 dealt with confidentiality, privacy, or privilege. They also state that a number of calls to the ACA Risk Management Helpline involved similar topics ranging from how to handle a subpoena, counseling minors, counseling public offenders, group counseling, and responding to requests for information after a client's death. Perhaps part of the inquiries are an attempt to understand the nuanced differences among confidentiality, privacy, and privileged communication.

Wheeler and Bertram (2014) distinguish confidentiality as the ethical obligation to protect a client's information, whereas privileged communication is legally protected information, and privacy is a basic human right for the individual to control how and what information is shared. In other words, the client determines if information is shared, unless the professional counselor is ethically or legally required to share the information. It is important to understand the client holds confidentiality because this helps the professional counselor understand that Westernized ideals of what confidentiality and privacy entail are not always culturally appropriate interpretations (Herlihy & Corey, 2014b). This fact supports the necessity of informed consent at the beginning and throughout the counseling process.

As stated earlier, effective counseling is only achievable if a client feels safe to share thoughts, feelings, and sensitive information (Herlihy & Corey, 2014b). Therefore, because there are limitations to confidentiality (both legally and ethically), counselors need to discuss these limitations and exceptions. Herlihy and Corey provide a number of examples regarding limitations of confidentiality, including the following: counseling groups, counseling minors, protecting someone from danger, or to obey court orders. If in doubt whether confidentiality should be broken, a professional counselor needs to seek consultation with other professionals and possibly an attorney (Herlihy & Corey, 2014b; Wheeler & Bertram, 2014).

Records of counseling services are documents of the counseling relationship. They can be accessed by the client, guardians, court orders, or treatment team members (Wheeler and Bertram, 2014). Wheeler and Bertram explain that psychotherapy notes, which are maintained separate from the counseling record and are only accessible to the counselor, tend to remain privileged communication even if subpoenaed. Therefore, professional counselors need to give serious consideration about how information is recorded. Remley and Herlihy (2014) argue that, although counselors should absolutely document their rationale for choices made, they should act as if the records can be accessed by anyone at any time and, therefore, limit what is documented. They also strongly suggest, as do Wheeler and Bertram, to consult with an attorney before disclosing confidential information due to a court order.

Herlihy and Corey (2014b), Remley and Herlihy (2014), and Salo (2014) explain that, once a third party is involved in the counseling process, confidentiality becomes even more complex. When working with couples or families, counselors must determine which member is the identified client and how confidentiality will be maintained (Herlihy & Corey, 2014b). Herlihy and Corey explain that views on how to handle information differ among professional counselors, but many counselors enact a "no secrets" policy to achieve successful outcomes for the couple or family. This echoes the systems approach emphasized in the ACA Code of Ethics. Counseling minors or individuals without the ability to grant consent adds the element of a third party within the counseling process, if not in the actual counseling sessions. Salo (2014) argues that professional counselors with this clientele have to straddle an ethical fence in trying to protect the client while meeting the guardian's expectations of access. States vary on whether minors can consent to treatment, and interpretations of the law are ever-changing (Salo, 2014). Therefore, it is important for counselors to understand the laws in their own state (Salo, 2014; Wheeler & Bertram, 2014). Professional counselors cannot be expected to cover all possible scenarios. Therefore, a reasonable counselor would be one who follows the ethical standards of the profession, exercises common sense, and asks what is in the client's best interest (Salo, 2014).

One of the limitations of confidentiality is when there is concern for "serious and foreseeable harm" (ACA, 2014, B.2.a.). Werth and Stroup (2014) and Wheeler and Bertram

(2014) explain there are a wide variety of behaviors that could fall into this category, from nonsuicidal self-injury to suicidality or even property damage. When a client reveals an intent to harm, professional counselors can feel trapped between wanting to make the "right decision" and protecting a client's autonomy and confidentiality (Werth & Stroup, 2014; Wheeler & Bertram, 2014). Again, law supersedes ethics, and it is vital for professional counselors to understand their professional legal obligations regarding mandated reporting (Wheeler & Bertram, 2014). Wheeler and Bertram provide examples of duty-to-report situations, such as child and/or elderly abuse or neglect, intimate partner violence, or threats to an identified third party. If a counselor is required by law to report and does not do so, the professional counselor can be held liable. This is why consultation is incredibly important when in doubt, because seeking different viewpoints on how to handle a situation allows a counselor to successfully evaluate the situation (Wheeler & Bertram, 2014).

CASE ILLUSTRATION 5.2

Miranda is a 29-year-old female who was recently sexually assaulted by a former friend. Three months ago, she and her former friend, André, had just returned from a concert, which they attended with a group of friends. All of the friends went to a bar after the concert and had a few drinks, but Miranda was the designated driver and, as such, only had one cocktail. André, however, had four mixed drinks and was slightly inebriated. André had planned to spend the night at Miranda's house so that he would not have to drive while intoxicated. After Miranda had taken all of her other friends home, Miranda and André returned to her home. She and André decided to stay up for a while and talk. One thing led to another and they began to kiss. When André started to try to take things further, Miranda refused and told André to go to sleep. Not accepting her response, André forced himself on Miranda and sexually assaulted her. In a state of confusion and disbelief, Miranda did not immediately call emergency services. However, that following Monday, she went to see her gynecologist and reported the sexual assault. Her doctor immediately referred her to counseling, which is how she came into your care.

Miranda has experienced normal, intense feelings of self-loathing and anger. Recently, though, she has started telling you about her fantasies related to Andrés death. She tells you

that she pictures herself stabbing him repeatedly and watching him die in pain. You realize that these fantasies are relatively normal among sexual assault survivors, but you also know that you have an obligation to assess the degree of risk she poses to André. You conduct a homicide risk assessment, which indicates moderate risk. However, when you directly question Miranda about her risk to André, she tells you that she just fantasizes and would never actually harm him—that would be against her religion. Something doesn't feel right to you, though, and you are not sure if you should breach confidentiality to alert André to the potential for harm.

1. What are the primary ethical issues within this case?

2. What are your state laws regarding duty to warn?

3. How can you adequately decipher the difference between risk of harm to André and Miranda's normal anger following the sexual assault?

4. What are the potential disadvantages of notifying André of the risk of harm?

5. Are there other ways to manage this risk without breaching confidentiality and notifying André?

Final Thoughts

Clients' ability to trust professional counselors comes from their understanding that counselors do not desire to share client information outside of the session. Professional counselors create a safe space in which clients should feel comfortable sharing their deepest thoughts, feelings, and behaviors without judgment and fear. However, it would be naïve of counselors to assume that confidentiality is always a guarantee. At least once in their career, counselors will have to break confidentiality and disclose information the client does not want disclosed (e.g., when a client is an imminent danger to self or in matters related to child or dependent elder abuse or neglect). This is why it is vital that counselors discuss that possibility with all clients at the beginning of the counseling relationship but also throughout the therapeutic process. Remember, clients hold confidentiality and are the masters of that information. However, at times, counselors need to remind their clients of the potential limitations to confidentiality so that clients can make informed decisions about their disclosures and treatment.

Social Media in Professional Counseling

As previously discussed, establishing professional boundaries is a vital and difficult task for professional counselors. When you add social media to the mix, it becomes an even more challenging process. Social media has created a tremendous change in our social communication systems, and professional counselors need to be conscientious about the role social media plays in their counseling practice. This section discusses the ethics of using social media from a professional boundaries standpoint. We also address relevant ethical considerations, such as confidentiality and informed consent, as they pertain to social media presence.

It is important to consider your own views on the use of social media and/or texting and how it is integrated (or not) into your own life. You may be personally aware of many social media platforms, but it is important to consider the use of those platforms from a professional perspective. Perhaps you are starting your own practice and need to advertise to build up your clientele. Or maybe you are considering writing a blog to help educate the public about mental health. In either of these situations, there are relevant concerns that must be addressed *prior* to using social media for professional purposes.

The first question to ponder as you navigate the world of social media as a professional counselor is how to maintain a personal social media presence that will not impact your professional identity. This can be a challenging endeavor, given that the privacy settings on social media platforms are forever changing and clients may have unexpected connections to you via social media. For instance, consider what you might do if a client came into session and asked about your new dog or about the concert you went to over the weekend—neither of which are pieces of information you shared with the client. You may even ask the client how he knew about the concert, and he states, "Oh, I am cousins with Katey, and she was tagged in one of your pictures." How might you respond to the client? Further, how might you navigate the conversation of maintaining professional boundaries when you find an unanticipated personal connection? To be sure, what counselors post on social media matters and can affect their professional practice.

Additionally, ask yourself whether social media is relevant to meeting your professional obligations as a counselor. Perhaps, for instance, there is an advantage to using

GUIDED PRACTICE 5.5

This exercise explores how much clients could learn from your social media page. Working with a trusted peer, exchange social media accounts (e.g., friend your peer on Facebook, follow your peer on Twitter) and make a list of everything you are able to learn about your peer from that peer's social media page. Then, highlight the personal information you think could be potentially damaging or threatening to the professional counseling relationship. Finally, exchange lists and dialogue about your findings. Although most counselors would not allow clients to follow them on social media, the point of this activity is to understand the importance of personal-professional boundaries in the use of social media.

social media to promote your practice, engage in professional advocacy, or spread awareness about mental health topics. In this sense, social media can be a tool to help counselors achieve their professional goals and participate in relevant professional activities. However, there are risks involved with social media use, even for legitimate purposes. Consider what might happen if a client were to go to the Facebook page you established for your practice and post a message about how much you have helped her. Further, what are the legal implications if a client uses social media to alert you to his suicide ideation? Some of these concerns can be addressed through installing appropriate privacy settings and through using thorough and recursive informed consent procedures, but issues may still arise, and the professional counselor must be prepared to address those issues.

Finally, consider how you may use social media to support your clinical practice. Imagine working with a millennial client who has difficulty managing stress and anxiety. The client is constantly on his phone and states that he may miss out on something important if he puts his phone down. Although you may want to help the client learn to establish boundaries with his social online presence and promote self-care, you also need to consider the culture of digital natives. Today's culture is about having access to information, and a wealth of information at that, at all times. As such, how can you use his clear preference for technology and social media to enhance treatment? There are a wealth of ways in which the counselor can "meet clients where they are," so to speak, and learn to use social media to support their therapeutic work. However, integrating social media into practice should be undertaken with intentionality and careful consideration of the risks.

What the ACA Code of Ethics Says

Regarding social media and technology-based communication (e.g., texting, e-mailing), it is imperative to review a few different ethical guidelines presented within the Code of Ethics. The 2014 revision of the ACA Code of Ethics is the first iteration that addressed social media in any way with its introduction of Section H: Distance Counseling, Technology, and Social Media. This section, as well as some ethical standards sprinkled throughout other sections, provides fairly concrete and prescribed courses of action when dealing with social media and technology-based communication. There was a deliberate and intentional choice to deviate from the more aspirational tone found in the majority of the Code of Ethics. This section covers three main topics: informed consent, confidentiality, and professional boundaries.

Social Media and Informed Consent. The first step in even being able to use social media or technology-based communication with a client is through an informed consent process. Confidentiality is the cornerstone of the counseling profession, and the informed consent process is how counselors communicate the importance of confidentiality and the expectations of the counselor-client relationship. Social media and technology-based communication add layers of depth to the informed consent process, as demonstrated in codes H.2.a., Informed Consent and Disclosure, and H.6.b., Social Media as Part of Informed Consent (ACA, 2014).

The use of technology and social media has unique informed consent considerations. When using social media or technology-based communication with clients, there needs to be a discussion about anticipated response time so that expectations are managed from the start. It is also strongly suggested that even if professional counselors are not going to engage in the use of social media or technology-based communication with clients, they still include a statement regarding their social media and technology-based communication policy. This statement allows the conversation to be had at the very beginning, rather than deep into the counseling process when the counselor-client relationship could be damaged. If the professional counselor is going to engage in the use of social media or technology-based communication professionally, the counselor needs to have a stated social media and technology-based communication policy. It needs to specifically explain risks and benefits but also the appropriateness of the use of social media and technology-based communication. Again, it is about establishing expectations from the start and thereby maintaining a true and genuine therapeutic relationship.

Confidentiality. As previously discussed, confidentiality and privacy are important aspects to our profession. Section H, Distance Counseling, Technology, and Social Media (ACA, 2014; i.e., H.2.b. Confidentiality Maintained by the Counselor, H.2.c. Acknowledgment of Limitations, H.2.d. Security, H.3. Client Verification), addresses the concept of confidentiality concerning social media and technology-based communication. Professional counselors have always been ethically responsible for protecting client information. With the rise of technology and its ever-increasing use in our society, professional counselors have to consider multiple layers of confidentiality. If a professional counselor is engaging in the use of social media or technology-based communication with clients and is accessing that information on multiple devices, the counselor has a responsibility to do his or her best to protect that information on each of the devices. Beyond that, the counselor has the additional responsibility to inform the client of who may have access to that device and how the information on that device is protected. Finally, if engaging in the use of social media, the counselor has to consider how to protect a flow of information that technically is within the public domain. It is also important to remember that the counselor is not the only one who has to protect confidentiality. The client has some responsibility as well. Therefore, the professional counselor has an ethical responsibility to have a conversation with clients about their responsibilities and what precautions they can take to protect the information and the counseling process.

Social media and technology-based communication have the ability to allow individuals to feel a sense of online disinhibition, in which they feel free to communicate thoughts, ideas, and feelings that perhaps they would not share in person. This level of anonymity makes it difficult to definitively know if the person who claims to be communicating on the other side of the social media or technology-based communication interaction is indeed the actual client. Therefore, professional counselors have an ethical responsibility to verify that they are communicating with their client. One means of doing this is through a password verification process. It is similar to a two-step verification process for an online account, where you are shown an image of your choosing that verifies this is your account. Clients have to communicate this verification code with their counselor and vice versa.

Professional Boundaries. The first codes discussed in Section H, Knowledge and Legal Considerations (ACA, 2014), specifically address potential professional boundary concerns. As stated previously, maintaining professional boundaries in the 21st century has become more difficult due to the rise of social media. Professional counselors need to be able to separate their personal social media presence from their professional social media presence. Professional counselors also need to respect the personal information clients put into the public domain through their social media presence. The ACA (2014) Code of Ethics addresses these responsibilities through three specific codes: A.5.e. Personal Virtual Relationships with Current Clients, H.6.a. Virtual Professional Presence, and H.6.c. Client Virtual Presence.

The first two codes (A.5.e. and H.6.a.) indicate that professional counselors have an ethical responsibility to maintain a professional relationship with their clients. When engaging in a social media relationship with a client, the line between professional and personal can be easily blurred. Therefore, except in rare instances, the ACA Code of Ethics specifically prohibits engaging in a personal virtual relationship with clients (i.e., do not friend or follow a client with your personal social media presence). This restriction serves as a reminder to professional counselors that their personal social media presence is just that, personal; clients should not have access to professional counselors' personal social media accounts, and counselors should actively work to ensure that access to their accounts is appropriately limited.

Although professional counselors are ethically prohibited from engaging in a virtual personal relationship with their clients, they are allowed to have a virtual professional presence, as evidenced by H.6.a. Professional counselors can have professional social media profiles that help connect them with their clients, promote mental health, educate the public, and/or advertise their services. These profiles need to be professionally based and not linked to the counselor's personal social media profile. In other words, the profiles need to be set up through different e-mail accounts or identities.

In the 21st century, it is extremely easy to access information about an individual. However, according to H.6.c., counselors respect their clients' right to privacy and clients' choice to bring into session what they choose to bring. Therefore, it is important that professional counselors respect that privacy even within the public domain.

What the Literature Says

Jencius (2014) argues the growth of technology has been dramatic within the counseling profession, and the 2014 revision of the ACA Code of Ethics had to address social media—a topic not covered in the 2005 edition. As Jencius explains, the inclusion of social media "reflects the shift from stand-alone computing, where the counselor or client works on an isolated computer, to interconnected services where the counselor and client can have access to a social world or interactions" (p. 246). Pendergast (2004) argues relationships are not limited to geographical locations; rather, society is now a "simultaneous universe." Jencius (2014) further argues that individuals feel as if they are interacting in real time with the individual at the other end of the device, and subsequently, this has led to technology interactions that feel similar to human interaction.

Before diving into research regarding the use and effectiveness of social media within the counseling realm, one needs to understand the impact social media has on society. According to Qualman (2018), a social media expert, the number of individuals using some form of social media is astronomical. To put this in context, if you were to consider the number of users reported for each of the top social media sites as representing the population of a country, they would account for seven of the 10 largest countries in the world (Qualman, 2018). Baer (2015) provides a number of interesting statistics: 56% of Americans have at least one social media profile and 22% of those Americans check their profile multiple times throughout the day. This is not a generational anomaly. Baer reports that 55% of Americans ages 45 to 54 have a social media profile.

It is evident that social media and technology-based communication are being used, but can they be used therapeutically and effectively? First, Cook and Doyle (2002) discovered that counselors could establish a strong working alliance with clients via technology that is similar to the one established face-to-face, and that relationship could actually be equitable after the third session. Coyle and Vaughn (2008) and Raacke and Bonds-Raacke (2008) argue that social media can be used as a means to form and maintain relationships. Bradley, Hendricks, Lock, Whiting, and Parr (2011) determined that e-mail communications between counselor and client enhanced the therapeutic relationship, and Alemi et al. (2007) demonstrated that e-mail contributed the most to successful treatment with substance abuse clients. As part of their research, Zabinski, Celio, Jacobs, Manwaring, and Wilfley (2003) established a counseling chat room for individuals susceptible to developing an eating disorder. Weekly discussions were had among participants on a variety of topics, and the results showed that 79% of participants preferred chatting online versus face-to-face because of the afforded anonymity and online disinhibition. To further support this trend, Merz (2010) states that texting and social media are a way to collect real-time data to assess patterns. Merz discusses a study conducted by Geddes in the United Kingdom in which bipolar clients were sent a text each morning to remind them to take their medication. He also discusses a study by Pijnenborg et al. that used texting to support clients who had a diagnosis of schizophrenia in promoting positive behaviors (e.g., medication compliance, attending scheduled sessions). Additionally, Wade (2014) discovered that counselors who engaged with their clients via texting felt the therapeutic alliance was stronger and that their clients felt more supported. Wade also reports that the amount of real-time data afforded through these exchanges helps hone the actual therapy sessions to align with established treatment goals.

If social media and technology-based communication can be used effectively and therapeutically, the next question becomes can it be done ethically and legally? First, one needs to establish a level of competency in using such technology through training, either formal or informal (Jencius, 2014). For example, one could receive training through the Telebehavioral Health Institute or by pursuing the newly minted board certified–telemental health provider (BC-TMH) credential through the Center for Credentialing and Education. Jencius also suggests attending conferences or workshops, seeking consultation, and reading peer-reviewed literature. In a more formal context, Kolmes (2012) suggests the need for social media training to be addressed in clinical training. DiLillo and Gale (2011) illustrate this concern through their research investigating whether graduate students would search the Internet for information on their client. Whereas most of the participants understood that doing so was wrong and unacceptable, 98% reported having done so. Part of training would include how to address informed consent concerns, such as a social media policy. Kolmes (2010) provides mental health professionals with an example of her social media policy and how professional counselors can use social media in their practice.

In addition to training from a use standpoint, professional counselors need to be educated on the legality of using social media and technology-based communication. Kaplan, Wade, Conteh, and Martz (2011) and Wheeler and Bertram (2014) stress the importance of knowing state licensing and federal regulations, such as the Health Insurance Portability and Accountability Act (HIPAA) and the Health Information Technology for Economic and Clinical Health Act (HITECH). These federal regulations address protected health information (PHI). Clients have the right to waive HIPAA (Person-Centered Tech, 2016), but even if waived, a professional counselor has an ethical responsibility to maintain confidentiality and establish reasonable expectations regarding the use of social media and technology-based communication.

One wants to meet clients where they are but within reason and in such a way so as to promote the clients' welfare. Person-Centered Tech (2016) developed a smartphone security guide for mental health professionals. This guide demonstrates how professional counselors can do a risk assessment on the security of their smartphones. It also provides a checklist of steps to take to protect the information on one's smartphone, such as the following: enabling encryption, having strong passwords (or fingerprint or face scanning), limiting attempts to access the phone, keeping sensitive data off of removable storage devices and the phone itself, and enabling remote wiping of the phone's memory in case the phone is lost or stolen. In other words, take the necessary precautions to protect client information. Kaplan et al. (2017), Wade (2014), and Person-Centered Tech (2016) all emphasize the importance of informed consent.

Kaplan et al. (2017) and Wade (2014) stress the importance of considering professional boundaries regarding the use of social media with clients. As Jencius (2014) explains, professional counselors will eventually encounter a client who wants to connect via social media on a personal level. Wheeler and Bertram (2014) and Kolmes (2012) caution professional counselors to carefully consider the information put forth into the public domain. As Jencius explains, one can never be certain how information will be received and processed. Therefore, the professional counselor needs to be able to separate professional life from personal life (Kaplan et al. 2017). Overall, more research needs to be conducted on the use of social media and technology-based communication within the counseling profession to critically evaluate their effectiveness and utility. However, the literature has provided a number of critical concepts to consider and prepare for when using social media and technology-based communication, whether professionally or personally.

CASE ILLUSTRATION 5.3

Carlos is an 18-year-old Latino male who is a senior in high school. He has been your client for approximately 2 weeks, and it has been difficult to establish a rapport. He is on the autism spectrum and his parents report he is a victim of bullying. He reports that he probably spends 10 to 15 hours a day on social media and online; that is where he feels most comfortable communicating. However, he tells you that his classmates are attacking him 24/7 through social media, and therefore, he is conflicted about using social media. He has not given you permission to view any of his social media profiles. He googled you and found that you have a Twitter and Facebook account. He sends a friend request through Facebook and follows you on Twitter. If you allow him access to you via social media, you could observe the activity on his accounts and learn more about the cyberbullying he is reporting. However, you have concerns about your own privacy and the ethics of having a cyberrelationship with your clients. The next time you see him in session, you ask him why he has reached out via social media. He replies, "I want to know you better so that I can trust you, and I communicate better online."

1. What are the primary ethical issues in this case?

2. What are the potential risks and benefits of establishing a cyberrelationship with this client?

3. Can social media be used in a professional way to aid Carlos's progress, and if so, how?

Final Thoughts

The ACA (2014) Code of Ethics established several guidelines regarding the use of social media and technology-based communication in counseling, such as professional counselors' responsibility to limit access to their personal social media account, to provide clear and recursive informed consent to clients regarding the rules and expectations of using social media and technology-based communication in the therapeutic relationship, to respect the privacy of clients' personal social media accounts, and to address issues of Internet and data security. However, as is true for any aspect of counseling, many situations involving social media and technology-based communication are challenging to address and potentially rooted in ethical issues. As such, it is important for professional counselors to carefully explore the role of social media and technology-based communication in their clinical practice, taking into consideration the potential legal and ethical problems that could arise. Once professional counselors have determined how they will address the topic of social media and technology-based communication in their practice, it is their responsibility to discuss the rules and expectations with their clients through the informed consent process. The most effective way to limit these challenging situations is to prepare for them. However, counselors should not be frightened away from using social media and technology-based communication in their clinical practice. Rather, with thoughtful consideration, social media and technology-based communication have the ability to support therapeutic intervention and enhance the client-counselor relationship.

Managing Interdisciplinary Dynamics

In the age of managed care and counselor advocacy, professional counselors are increasingly finding themselves working with noncounselors to provide comprehensive

GUIDED PRACTICE 5.6

Prior to your next class session, contact two licensed counselors you know and ask them about their use of an interdisciplinary care team. Using the following list, check off all types of professionals with whom the two licensed counselors consult or collaborate to manage client care. This activity should help you develop a greater appreciation for the scope of interdisciplinary collaboration within the professional counselor's everyday practice.

☐ Physician(s)

☐ Nurse(s)

☐ Psychiatric nurse(s)

☐ Administrative supervisor

☐ Clinical supervisor

☐ Utilization management expert(s)

☐ Administrative staff

☐ Data storage company

☐ Social work or community service agencies

☐ Other: _____

services for their clients. This interaction with different disciplines can bring about interesting dynamics. Professional counselors have an ethical responsibility to act in the best interest of their clients, and at times, that may be against the wishes of other team members or coworkers. Navigating these professional relationships can become complicated. Therefore, this section helps you consider the different facets of these interactions.

As you read this section, imagine you have to work with multiple individuals from multiple disciplines to help your clients achieve their goals. Perhaps you are a school counselor who has to work with administration and teachers. Or maybe you work in a hospital setting and collaborate with psychiatrists, social workers, and nurses. You are the one professional counselor in these situations.

The first question to ponder is how you uphold your professional code of ethics when working within a system of professionals who may each subscribe to a different code and have varying interpretations of those codes. Perhaps even more likely, imagine that you are working with team members who do not seem to value professional ethics to the same degree as you, even though they may not necessarily engage in illegal or unethical practice. Consider, for instance, how you might respond if a team member does not use comprehensive suicide risk assessment procedures to determine level or risk. Or perhaps a team member minimizes level of suicide risk, stating that clients need to be empowered to help themselves. Perhaps a team member believes it is acceptable to practice without supervision, even when managing major ethical dilemmas. Or maybe you work with a team member who often tells clients detailed personal stories that are irrelevant to the client's treatment. In all these scenarios, the client's care is of concern. To be sure, working within an interdisciplinary team can significantly enhance treatment because the services are more comprehensive. However, there are times when the varying perspectives held by team members can create intragroup tension and affect client care.

Let us now look at another common situation. Imagine how you might respond if a team member asks for information about a client that is not pertinent to that team member's work with the client; the questions are nosey. Technically, the team member may have access to confidential client information, but sharing that information unnecessarily would be a breach of privacy. So, how would you manage that type of conversation and the relationship dynamics that would inevitably follow?

Finally, if you are working in concert with other professional team members, do you have a responsibility to the client to explain how the team works? Because multiple professionals will have access to confidential information about the client and may talk among themselves regarding the client's treatment, the client has a right to be informed about those processes. However, for some clients, knowing too many details about the interdisciplinary team could enhance paranoia and distrust. Many clients may become anxious about the prospect of multiple people talking about them. Both scenarios could affect treatment. As such, how would you manage ensuring the client's rights are met and simultaneously working to create conditions under which therapy can be most effective? Rest assured that there are no easy answers to these questions.

What the ACA Code of Ethics Says

Section D.1, Relationships with Colleagues, Employers, and Employees, contains nine codes. The first four codes specifically address the topic of working with interdisciplinary teams. As such, those are the codes addressed in this section. The first two codes, D.1.a., Different Approaches, and D.1.b., Forming Relationships (ACA, 2014), speak to the importance of respecting colleagues and developing relationships that enhance treatment. The first code, D.1.a., highlights the importance of respecting colleagues' varying theoretical and practical approaches to treatment. Although this can certainly pertain to fundamental differences in case conceptualization and theory-driven therapeutic perspectives, this may also pertain to differences between professions. The most notable of these may surround the fact that professional counselors approach mental health from a wellness model, whereas other disciplines may approach from a medical or another philosophical framework. This code emphasizes that counselors have an ethical responsibility to respect such differences and acknowledge areas of expertise outside their own. However, when client welfare is in jeopardy, other ethics codes will take precedence over respect of interdisciplinary differences.

The second code, D.1.b., is at the heart of interdisciplinary treatment teams. Although the differences between practitioners and their professional orientations can sometimes be stark, it is critically important that professional counselors actively seek to enhance their relationships with team members. Through close, collaborative, and constructive relationships, treatment teams can best support clients. Additionally, this code pertains to instances in which counselors should seek out partnerships to enhance their services. If it is in the best interest of the client for the counselor to work with teachers, medical personnel, or any other professional, the counselor should work to establish a successful working relationship with those providers. These relationships may, at times, be challenging to establish, but they can also be entirely rewarding.

The second two codes—D.1.c., Interdisciplinary Teamwork, and D.1.d., Establishing Professional and Ethical Obligations (ACA, 2014)—focus on the counselor's responsibility to function within interdisciplinary teams while keeping the client's welfare as the priority. Additionally, let us look at B.3.b., Interdisciplinary Teams (ACA, 2014), because it discusses confidentiality within interdisciplinary teams. These three codes speak of the importance of promoting effective client care. When working in interdisciplinary teams, professional counselors' main focus is the client's welfare. Therefore, the counselor has an ethical responsibility to advocate for the client while also hearing all aspects addressed by the different team members. Due to philosophical differences and different approaches to how to best serve a client, professional counselors need to be clear about their professional and ethical obligations. The professional counselor has a responsibility to inform the client of the expectations of confidentiality within that interdisciplinary team and who has access to what information. Further, if there is a difference in opinion, the counselor should work to find a fitting compromise. If compromise is not possible, the counselor examines other ways to best address the concerns of the team and the client. In short, when client care begins to suffer as a result of poor dynamics within the treatment teams, counselors have an ethical obligation to seek to remedy those dynamics or otherwise support client care.

What the Literature Says

Minetti (2011) explains the necessity of interdisciplinary teams by stating that, through the development of knowledge from multiple sources of information, care providers are able to gather more information on recurrent patterns of behavior and, therefore, better serve patients. Greer (2012) argues that, due to the complexity of humans, collaborative practice is a moral imperative. The World Health Organization (WHO; 2010) predicts improved health outcomes for patients who have a collaborative team approach. Brown, Garber, Lash, and Schnurman-Cook (2014) explain that when collaboration is promoted, patient outcome is enhanced. Further, Brown and colleagues explain that the identification and capitalization of shared professional values leads to such collaboration. Accordingly, there is a push within health care to move toward more collaborative involvement and the formulation of interdisciplinary treatment teams (Brown et al., 2014; Greer, 2012; Minetti, 2011).

Brown and colleagues (2014) acknowledge the difficulty in collaboration due to professionals coming from different scopes of practice and philosophical frameworks. However, the Interprofessional Education Collaborative (IPEC) Expert Panel determined a number of core competencies, which include "values/ethics for collaboration, understanding of the roles and responsibilities of team members, interprofessional communication, and teams and teamwork" (Brown et al., p. 471). Brown and colleagues developed an interprofessional oath from their research to promote collaboration that then could lead to improved patient outcome. This oath builds on identifying shared professional values that can serve as a foundation for collaboration among the different philosophical viewpoints. The oath is as follows:

> We make this oath in due faith and we recognize the unique role of being a healthcare professional and the associated responsibilities which include honesty, faithfulness, compassion and collaboration. We pledge to promote health in individuals and the community rather than just treating the sick. We will protect privacy and confidentiality.
>
> The patient is the ultimate priority and focus of our care. Our role is to empower, teach and promote health in the patient, treating all persons equally and appropriately. The patient is more than a body and we will benefit the patient rather than harm.

Our care will be of the highest quality, safe, and based on evidence. We will seek to provide care within our scope of practice with ever-growing knowledge and skills.

We will work with others to provide care, recognizing the unique skills of each and we will seek to collaborate effectively on the healthcare team. (Brown et al., p. 472)

This oath acknowledges that client/patient care is the top priority and the care that professionals provide remains within their individual scopes of practice. However, team collaboration contributes to the best possible client care. Hodgson, Mendenhall, and Lamson (2013) explain that collaborative teamwork brings with it a few concerns beyond scope of practice, such as confidentiality and record keeping. As mentioned, Remley and Herlihy (2014) recommend keeping records in a manner that assumes anyone can access the information. This is extremely true within interdisciplinary teams where the client record is accessible to all team members. Although one does not want to confuse or ask the client to fill out too much paperwork, one does want to be clear in the informed consent process about who has access to what information. In addition, as a professional counselor, one could maintain separate psychotherapy notes that do not need to be accessible to the entire team because the information does not impact level of care (Wheeler & Bertram, 2014). Again, the professional counselor needs to act in the client's best interest in all respects.

CASE ILLUSTRATION 5.4

Imagine you are a newly hired counselor for an intensive inpatient eating disorder clinic. You meet with the patients individually and in groups. The nurses in the clinic have begun to ask you about what your clients talk about in sessions. They explain that the former counselor, who retired, would share her insights and notes with the nurses. This raises concerns for you about protecting the clients' confidentiality. One day in conversation, the head nurse says to you, "We need to know what is talked about because it impacts their treatment."

1. What are the primary ethical issues in this case?

2. How can you address the head nurse without compromising your clients' privacy but also respecting her needs as a collaborating partner in the clients' treatment?

Final Thoughts

When working with other disciplines, it is vital for professional counselors to constantly evaluate what is in the best interest of their clients. One common way this issue emerges is regarding different approaches to treatment and varying clinical practices. Although the professional counselor may not fully agree with a team member's perspective or actions, counselors should respect team members when, and only when, clients' treatment is not jeopardized. Further, there may be times when a client is withholding information from another team member that could interfere with or delay treatment. In those cases, professional counselors may need to share information because the client's welfare outweighs the importance of privacy. However, there may also be cases in which team members request private information out of their own personal interest. In those situations, professional counselors have a responsibility to enhance client privacy.

Working within an interdisciplinary treatment team can be challenging, but it can also help counselors to provide holistic services to clients who may not otherwise be able to access such services. Further, in consideration of the connection between physical and mental health, working in concert with professionals from other fields can help counselors to better understand issues that affect their clients and intervene from a more informed perspective. Despite the challenges, interdisciplinary treatment teams are common and can be vitally important to client care.

Managing Lethality With Clients Who Self-Injure and Are at Risk for Suicide

The intentional injuring of one's own body for the purposes of coping is often misunderstood within the lay and counseling communities alike. It can be challenging for counselors to understand the rationale for **self-injury** (SI)—the "direct and deliberate bodily harm in the absence of suicidal intent" (Nock, 2010, p. 339). Although they may seem difficult to understand, there are a number of reasons people self-injure—most of which relate to coping. It is critically important that professional counselors learn about self-injury, its treatment, and ways to discern suicide risk with clients who self-injure. This is particularly important because people who self-injure are often very secretive about their SI and may even be embarrassed or ashamed by it. As such, professional counselors must come to understand their automatic values and beliefs about SI and find ways to check those values and beliefs at the door, rather than imposing them on clients and thereby damaging the therapeutic relationship.

When you think of intentionally cutting, carving, burning, or scraping one's own skin, what feelings and adjectives come to mind? Do you find yourself scared, confused, and wondering why someone self-injures? Conversely, do you find yourself feeling sorry for those who self-injure, empathy for their suffering, and a willingness to help them? Perhaps you feel the urge to convince them why they should stop self-injuring. Or maybe you think it is a pretty common thing and should not evoke strong reactions from counselors. You may even minimize it, considering it an attention seeking behavior. All of these are relatively normal reactions, based on the counselor's own personal history and professional experience. However, some of them can be particularly harmful to clients and can seriously interfere with treatment. So, although there is no single way to personally feel or think about SI, it is critically important that we monitor our professional response to clients who self-injure. Remember that we want our clients to feel understood, valued, and respected.

Let's take this a step further. Do you believe SI is synonymous with, completely different from, indistinguishable from, or qualitatively different from suicide attempts? What do you think the relationship is, if any, between SI and suicide? Maybe you are unsure how to answer this question. If so, your reaction would fairly similarly mirror the professional literature on the topic. Although we know a lot more about SI than we did 15 years ago, there are many elements of the relationship between SI and suicide that we

GUIDED PRACTICE 5.7

Working in pairs or small groups, discuss your automatic thoughts and feelings related to self-injury. Try to avoid using your professional filter and, instead, talk about the thoughts and feelings that first come to mind when you think of someone who self-injures (remember Freudian free association?). For instance, do you feel afraid, confused, off-put, or frustrated? Please do not be afraid of stating your true feelings. It is important that you own your feelings and figure out ways to avoid imposing them on clients; disowning our feelings can lead us to inadvertently harm our clients and/or the therapeutic relationship. Next, dialogue with your peers about how you can actively work to avoid imposing your own values, beliefs, or feelings about self-injury onto the client. Develop a list of ways you can both monitor your value imposition and intervene to create a safe therapeutic climate.

do not yet fully understand. To be sure, there is a relationship, for approximately 60% of people who self-injure also have suicidal thoughts and behaviors (Whitlock et al., 2013). It may be that SI and suicide share common neural pathways and/or common factors of distress, or maybe they are different behaviors along a continuum of distress. Regardless of the relationship, it is certain that counselors must be able to assess for suicide risk with clients who self-injure. Failure to do so could have unrepairable consequences, but assuming suicide risk when none is present can also present major ethical concerns. These are just a couple of the major considerations that professional counselors should make prior to working with SI, and these constitute the focus of our discussion of SI in this chapter.

What the ACA Code of Ethics Says

There are no specific ACA ethics codes related directly to SI. There are, however, a number of ethics codes that apply to the treatment of SI (ACA, 2014; e.g., A.1.a. Primary Responsibility, A.4.b. Personal Values, B.1.c. Respect for Confidentiality, B.1.d. Explanation of Limitations [of confidentiality], B.2.e. Minimal Disclosure, C.2.a. Boundaries of Competence, and C.2.d. Monitor Effectiveness). These codes help to guide professional counselors' preparation for working with clients who self-injure, collaboration with clients' family members, and clinical practice. However, we focus on the codes that relate specifically to self-injury assessment and suicide risk assessment. The codes that apply to the process of identifying suicide risk with clients who self-injure include E.1.a., Assessment, and E.6.a., Appropriateness of Instruments (ACA, 2014). These codes speak to the importance of using assessment procedures that can improve treatment and clinical decision-making, and using assessments that are reliable and valid for their intended purposes. In this context, appropriate assessment procedures include established instruments that screen for and assess both SI and suicide; using dichotomous yes/no screening questions (e.g., Do you purposefully hurt yourself?) and/or relying on your intuition are not sufficient strategies for assessing SI and suicide.

Section B.2.a., Serious and Foreseeable Harm and Legal Requirements (ACA, 2014), states that when a client is an imminent threat to self, counselors can break confidentiality in an effort to provide appropriate support services. Not only does this code allow for the disclosure of confidential information to maintain client safety, it also requires that professional counselors consult with supervisors or peers to help determine the level of risk when there is any uncertainty related to the risk assessment.

What the Literature Says

For the purposes of this chapter, we do not provide a comprehensive overview of the risk factors for and warning signs of SI. Likewise, we do not address the functions of SI. To learn more about these topics, we refer you to the Cornell University College of Human Ecology, Self-Injury and Recovery Research and Resources website (see Web Resources). One of the foremost leaders on SI research and treatment, Dr. Janis Whitlock, and her team have developed a wealth of resources for clinicians, clients, and loved ones.

In this chapter, we focus on the process of assessment with clients who self-injure— both assessment of SI and of suicide risk. Despite common assumptions, SI is relatively common; there is an approximate lifetime prevalence rate of 18% for SI (Muehlenkamp, Claes, Havertape, & Plener, 2012). As such, it is likely that professional counselors will work with clients who self-injure; the question is whether those counselors know that their clients self-injure. To inform the assessment process, counselors can use screening items on their intake questionnaires and in their intake interviews. However, professional counselors are also urged to use established self-injury assessment instruments. There are a number of assessment instruments, all of which address different clinical needs and aspects of SI. We discuss a few of the more prominent and evidence-based instruments here.

The Deliberate Self-Harm Inventory (DSHI; Gratz, 2001) is a 17-item self-report questionnaire. It screens for the presence of SI, age of onset, duration, frequency, and severity of SI. It also asks participants to identify their means of SI. This instrument is useful for identifying SI and, when present, learning more about its severity. The Self-Injurious Thoughts and Behaviors Interview (SITBI; Nock, Holmberg, Photos, & Michel, 2007) is a 169-item structured interview (available in a 72-item short form) that measures suicidal ideation, suicide plans, suicide gestures, suicide attempts, and SI. This instrument is useful for evaluating both suicidality and SI. The Suicide Attempt Self-Injury Interview (SASII; Linehan, Comtois, Brown, Heard, & Wagner, 2006) is a 37-item structured interview that includes six scales: Suicide Intent, Interpersonal Influence, Emotion Relief, Suicide Communication, Lethality, and Rescue Likelihood. This SASII was developed, in large part, by the originator of dialectical behavior therapy, Dr. Marsha Linehan. This instrument is particularly useful when working with clients who experience both SI and suicide ideation, for it helps to identify lethality of self-injurious behaviors. The Inventory of Statements About Self-Injury (ISAS; Klonsky & Glenn, 2009) is a 46-item self-report inventory that assesses the history of and motivations for/functions of SI. It utilizes 13 SI function scales (Klonsky & Glenn, 2009). This instrument focuses largely on understanding the way SI presents for the client and the function(s) SI serves. Finally, the Non-Suicidal Self-Injury Assessment Tool (NSSI-AT; Whitlock, Exner-Cortens, & Purington, 2014) is a 39-item self-report questionnaire administered online. It addresses a range of aspects of SI, including the presence of SI, functions, recency and frequency, age of onset and cessation, locations of wounds, reasons for initially starting SI, severity, behaviors surrounding SI, habituation and the degree to which SI interferes with life, previous disclosures of SI, and treatment experiences. Like the ISAS, this instrument focuses on SI specifically, how SI started, and the effects SI has on the client's life. All of these instruments can be useful for different purposes—detecting the presence and course of SI, conducting a functional analysis of SI, and identifying risk of suicide. As you can see, though, many of them share an assumption that suicide risk may accompany SI. Indeed, this assumption is supported by the literature.

Although, as we mentioned earlier, not all clients who self-injure are suicidal, a large portion of people who self-injure also struggle with suicide—60% (Whitlock et al., 2013). A number of factors may exacerbate suicide risk among clients who self-injure. Some of these factors include, but are not limited to, the following: (a) repeated SI (Kakhnovets, Young, Purnell, Huebner, & Bishop, 2010; Wester, Ivers, Villalba, Trepal, & Henson, 2016); (b) use of multiple SI methods (Wester et al., 2016); (c) use of websites that encourage SI (Mitchell, Wells, Priebe, & Ybarra, 2014; see Lewis, Heath, Michal, & Duggan, 2012); (d) history of alcohol use, alongside current depression (Jenkins, Singer, Conner, Calhoun, & Diamond, 2014); (e) hopelessness (Chapman, Gratz, & Turner, 2014); (f) critical self-talk (Gilbert et al., 2010); (g) distorted self-image (Kerr & Muehlenkamp, 2010); (h) childhood sexual abuse (Chapman et al., 2014); and (i) for adolescents, peer victimization (see Heilbron & Prinstein, 2010). In consideration of these factors, but without assuming that clients are suicidal, professional counselors should use evidence-based suicide risk assessment procedures with clients who self-injure.

There are a number of established suicide risk assessment instruments. What follows is a brief overview of four instruments that are well established. The Suicide Probability Scale (SPS; Cull & Gill, 1988) is a 36-item self-report inventory that measures current suicide ideation, hopelessness, negative self-evaluation, and hostility. The Beck Scale for Suicide Ideation (BSI; Beck & Steer, 1991) is a 21-item self-report inventory that detects and measures current intensity of specific attitudes, behaviors, and suicidal plans within the past week. The Suicidal Behavior Questionnaire-Revised (SBQ-R; Osman et al., 2001) is a 4-item self-report inventory that assesses lifetime ideation and attempts, frequency of ideation within the past year, threat of attempt, and self-reported likelihood of future suicidal behavior. Finally, the Columbia Suicide Severity Rating Scale (C-SSRS; Posner et al., 2011) is a 6-item structured interview that examines suicidal thoughts, plans, and attempts.

Regardless of which instruments you choose to use in your clinical practice, it is imperative that they are evidence-based and that you use comprehensive procedures (i.e., multiple instruments and processes) to assess for suicide risk (see Janis & Nock, 2008). When suicide risk is present, it is important to match the level of intervention to the level of risk. This may involve developing a safety plan (see Stanley & Brown, 2012), counseling loved ones on access to lethal means (Suicide Prevention Resource Center [SPRC], n.d.), increasing the frequency of clinical sessions, voluntary hospital admission, or involuntary hospital admission. The process of determining the most appropriate level of intervention should never be made by relying on client self-report of risk (see Toprak, Cetin, Guven, Can, & Demircan, 2011) but should include consultation with supervisors or appropriately trained peers. And, naturally, counselors should document their assessment procedures, consultation or supervision, and decision-making processes as they relate to the treatment of high-risk clients.

CASE ILLUSTRATION 5.5

You work in a small outpatient treatment clinic, which is financially supported by the local medical hospital. You are new to counseling and have only been licensed for 9 months. Recently, you met with Sonequa, a 13-year-old female who was referred to you by her pediatrician due to apparent self-inflicted cuts on her inner thighs and buttocks. You have never before worked with clients who self-injure and are hesitant regarding your abilities to adequately support Sonequa, which is why you notified your clinical supervisor and arranged to increase the number of your supervision sessions while you work with Sonequa. Your supervisor instructed you to conduct a thorough suicide risk assessment during your first meeting with Sonequa, which you did. The risk assessment indicated minimal risk.

In your continued work with Sonequa, it appears that her self-injury and emotional distress are escalating. You attribute this to the work you both are doing on her early childhood trauma and the bullying she is currently experiencing at school. Your supervisor instructs you to conduct another suicide risk assessment, which indicates moderate risk. Your supervisor tells you that Sonequa needs to go into inpatient treatment, but you do not agree. Rather, you believe that inpatient treatment would amplify Sonequa's feelings of loss of control and self-derogation. Further, you believe that you can work with Sonequa's parents to manage risk on an outpatient basis. When you attempt to tell your supervisor this, she responds that you need to do as she has instructed you.

1. What are the primary ethical issues in this case?

2. Which factors exacerbate the risk Sonequa poses to herself, and how do those factors relate to your ethical decision-making process?

3. How can you respect your supervisor's expertise while also honoring your responsibility to your client?

Final Thoughts

SI is a challenging clinical issue that can be both personally and professionally taxing. It is important to remember that SI is not the primary treatment issue; SI is a symptom of underlying treatment issues, which may be related to trauma, grief, feelings of inadequacy, and a number of other sources of emotional distress. Although it can be challenging to set aside our automatic beliefs and thoughts about purposefully harming oneself, it behooves professional counselors to approach clients who self-injure with patience, understanding, and compassion. Clients who self-injure are often secretive about their SI and may have encountered negative reactions from others about their SI. As professional counselors, we must help clients who self-injure feel valued and accepted, while also remaining attuned to the level of risk associated with SI.

Without assuming that clients who self-injure are suicidal, professional counselors should practice a comprehensive and recursive suicide risk assessment process that includes the use of evidence-based assessment instruments. Because the client's level of distress can fluctuate with time and with events that transpire in counseling, it is important to remain attuned to indicators of suicide risk. Further, as in any counseling relationship, professional counselors are encouraged to revisit suicide risk periodically throughout therapy. Remember that suffering does not simply end; it waxes and wanes over time.

Finally, we encourage all professional counselors to learn more about SI and its treatment. Entering into a therapeutic relationship with a client who self-injures with the goal of ending SI as quickly as possible can have damaging and potentially fatal effects. The treatment of SI not only involves the uncovering of underlying causes of distress, but it also involves the development of effective coping skills. SI serves a purpose for those who self-injure—sometimes a life-sustaining purpose—and, therefore, it is our responsibility to help our clients develop other effective means for coping with the intolerable emotional distress they experience.

Keystones

- Professional counselors are guided by the ACA (2014) Code of Ethics but may also be required to adhere to additional codes of ethics, such as those endorsed by the NBCC and ASCA.

- All professional counselors encounter ethical dilemmas; they cannot be avoided. However, the most effective way to manage ethical dilemmas is to perform a full ethical decision-making model, which includes seeking supervision and/or consultation.

- There are times when extending counseling boundaries can be therapeutically beneficial, but the determination of when and how to extend counseling boundaries should always be made with the client's best interest in mind; professional counselors should never extend counseling boundaries for their own benefit. Moreover, professional counselors should absolutely never engage in a romantic or sexual relationship with clients.

- Confidentiality is the cornerstone upon which the counseling relationship is built. As such, counselors should actively work to maintain client confidentiality. However, limitations to confidentiality exist and, in order to provide appropriate care, counselors must sometimes breach confidentiality. When possible, counselors should work with clients to manage such situations in the least disempowering way and share as little information as possible.

- We live in a digital age, and many clients use social media daily. Although it is important to be able to meet clients where they are, so to speak, counselors should never use clients' social media accounts to learn about clients without those clients' consent. Moreover, professional counselors should keep their personal and professional social media accounts separate, so that clients are unable to access counselors' personal accounts.

- Interdisciplinary treatment teams are common practice in modern counseling. Although professional counselors may have the legal liberty to share client information with other team members, counselors should seek to uphold clients' privacy to the highest degree possible. Additionally, when counselors disagree with team members' treatment approach, counselors should continually seek to determine the course of action that is in the client's best interest.

- Self-injury is a complex treatment issue, and the relationship of self-injury to suicide is yet undetermined. As such, professional counselors who work with clients who self-injure should use established self-injury and suicide risk assessments, and conduct suicide risk assessment recursively. However, counselors should not assume that all clients who self-injure are suicidal, for doing so can be invalidating to clients and can lead counselors to overlook the underlying treatment issues.

Key Terms

Autonomy 99

Beneficence 99

Fidelity 99

Justice 99

Nonmaleficence 99

Self-injury 125

Veracity 99

Web Resources

American Counseling Association, Knowledge Center for Ethics (www.counseling.org/knowledge-center/ethics)

American Psychological Association, End-of-Life Issues and Care (www.apa.org/topics/death/end-of-life.aspx)

Center for Credentialing and Education (www.cce-global.org)

Cornell University, College of Human Ecology, Self-Injury and Recovery Research and Resources (www.selfinjury.bctr.cornell.edu)

Healthcare Providers Service Organization (www.hpso.com/individuals/professional-liability/malpractice-insurance-for-counselors)

References

Alemi, F., Haack, M. R., Nemes, S., Aughburns, R., Sinkule, J., & Neuhauser, D. (2007). Therapeutic emails. *Substance Abuse Treatment, Prevention & Policy, 2*, 7–18. doi:10.1186/1747-597X-2-7

American Counseling Association. (2014). *ACA code of ethics*. Alexandria, VA: Author.

American Psychological Association. (2010). *Ethical principles of psychologists and code of conduct*. Washington, DC: Author.

Baer, J. (2015). 11 shocking new social media statistics in America. Retrieved from http://www.convinceandconvert.com/social-media-research/11-shocking-new-social-media-statistics-in-america/

Barnett, J. E. (2014). Sexual feelings and behaviors in the psychotherapy relationship: An ethics perspective. *Journal of Clinical Psychology, 70*(2), 170–181.

Beck, A. T., & Steer, R. A. (1991). *Manual for Beck Scale for Suicidal Ideation*. New York, NY: Psychological Corporation.

Bradley, L. J., Hendricks, B., Lock, R., Whiting, P. P., & Parr, G. (2011). E-mail communication: Issues for mental health counselors. *Journal of Mental Health Counseling, 33*, 67–79.

Brown, S. S., Garber, J. S., Lash, J., & Schnurman-Crook, A. (2014). A proposed interprofessional oath. *Journal of Interprofessional Care, 28*(5), 471–472. doi:10.3109/13561820.2014.900480

Chapman, A. L., Gratz, K. L., & Turner, B. J. (2014). Risk-related and protective correlates of nonsuicidal self-injury and co-occurring suicide attempts among incarcerated women. *Suicide & Life-Threatening Behavior, 44*(2), 139–154. doi:10.1111/sltb.12058

CNA & Healthcare Providers Service Organization. (2014). Understanding counselor liability risk.

Retrieved from http://www.hpso.com/Documents/pdfs/CNA_CLS_COUNS_022814p_CF_PROD_ASIZE_online_SEC.pdf

Cook, J. E., & Doyle, C. (2002). Working alliance in online therapy as compared to face-to-face therapy: Preliminary results. *CyberPsychology & Behavior, 5,* 95–105.

Corey, G., Corey, M., Corey, C., & Callanan, P. (2015). *Issues and ethics in the helping professions* (9th ed.). Stamford, CT: Cengage Learning.

Cottone, R. R. (2001). A social constructivism model of ethical decision making in counseling. *Journal of Counseling & Development, 79,* 39–45. doi:http://dx.doi.org/10.1002/j.1556-6676.2001.tb01941.x

Cottone, R. R., & Tarvydas, V. M. (2016). *Ethics and decision making in counseling and psychotherapy* (4th ed.). New York, NY: Springer.

Coyle, C. L., & Vaughn, H. (2008). Social networking: Communication revolution or evolution? *Bell Labs Technical Journal, 13*(2), 13–18. doi:10.1002/bltj.220298

Cull, J. C., & Gill, W. S. (1988). *Suicide Probability Scale.* Los Angeles, CA: Western Psychological Services.

DiLillo, D., & Gale, E. B. (2011). To Google or not to Google: Graduate students' use of the Internet to access personal information about clients. *Training and Education in Professional Psychology, 5*(3), 160–166. doi:10.1037/a0024441

Forester-Miller, H., & Davis, T. (2016). *A practitioner's guide to ethical decision making.* Alexandria, VA: American Counseling Association.

Garcia, J. G., Cartwright, B., Winston, S. M., & Borzuchowska, B. (2003). A transcultural integrative model for ethical decision making in counseling. *Journal of Counseling & Development, 81*(3), 268–277. doi:http://dx.doi.org/10.1002/j.1556-6678.2003.tb00253.x

Gilbert, P., McEwan, K., Irons, C., Bhundia, R., Christie, R., Broomhead, C., & Rockliff, H. (2010). Self-harm in a mixed clinical population: The roles of self-criticism, shame, and social rank. *British Journal of Clinical Psychology, 49,* 563–576.

Gratz, K. L. (2001). Measurement of deliberate self-harm: Preliminary data on the Deliberate Self-Harm Inventory. *Journal of Psychopathology and Behavioral Assessment, 23*(4), 253–263.

Greer, A. G. (2012). Ethics and policy for interprofessional scopes of practice: Preparing bariatric care teams. *Bariatric Nursing and Surgical Patient Care, 7*(2), 93–96. doi:10.1089/bar.2012.9986

Heilbron, N., & Prinstein, M. J. (2010). Adolescent peer victimization, peer status, suicidal ideation, and nonsuicidal self-injury: Examining concurrent and longitudinal associations. *Merrill-Palmer Quarterly (1982-),* (3), 388.

Herlihy, B., & Corey, G. (2014a). *Boundary issues in counseling: Multiple roles and responsibilities* (3rd ed.). Alexandria, VA: American Counseling Association.

Herlihy, B. & Corey, G. (2014b). Confidentiality. In B. Herlihy & G. Corey (Eds.), *ACA ethical standards casebook* (7th ed., pp. 55–65). Alexandria, VA: American Counseling Association.

Hodgson, J., Mendenhall T., & Lamson, A. (2013). Patient and provider relationships: Consent, confidentiality, and managing mistakes in integrated primary care settings. *Families, Systems, & Health, 31*(1), 28–40. doi:10.1037/a0031771

Ivey, L. C., & Doenges, T. (2013). Resolving the dilemma of multiple relationships for primary care behavioral health providers. *Professional Psychology, Research and Practice, 44*(4), 218–224.

Janis, I. B., & Nock, M. K. (2008). Behavioral forecasts do not improve the prediction of future behavior: A prospective study of self-injury. *Journal of Clinical Psychology, 64*(10), 1164–1174. doi:10.1002/jclp.20509

Jencius, M. (2014). Technology, social media, and online counseling. In B. Herlihy & G. Corey (Eds.), *ACA ethical standards casebook* (7th ed., pp. 245–258). Alexandria, VA: American Counseling Association.

Jenkins, A. L., Singer, J., Conner, B. T., Calhoun, S., & Diamond, G. (2014). Risk for suicidal ideation and attempt among a primary care sample of adolescents engaging in nonsuicidal self-injury. *Suicide and Life-Threatening Behavior*, *44*(6), 616–628. doi:10.1111/sltb.12094

Kakhnovets, R., Young, H. L., Purnell, A. L., Huebner, E., & Bishop, C. (2010). Self-reported experience of self-injurious behavior in college students. *Journal of Mental Health Counseling*, *32*(4), 309–323.

Kaplan, D. M., Francis, P. C., Hermann, M. A., Baca, J. V., Goodnough, G. E., Hodges, S. . . . Wade, M. E. (2017). New concepts in the 2014 ACA Code of Ethics. *Journal of Counseling and Development*, *95*(1), 110–120.

Kaplan, D. M., Wade, M. E., Conteh, J. A., & Martz, E. T. (2011). Legal and ethical issues surrounding the use of social media in counseling. *Counseling and Human Development*, *48*(3), 1–6.

Kerr, P. L., & Muehlenkamp, J. (2010). Features of psychopathology in self-injuring female college students. *Journal of Mental Health Counseling*, *32*(4), 290–308.

Klonsky, E. D., & Glenn, C. R. (2009). Assessing the functions of non-suicidal self-injury: Psychometric properties of the Inventory of Statements About Self-injury (ISAS). *Journal of Psychopathology and Behavioral Assessment*, *31*, 215–219.

Kocet, M. M., & Herlihy, B. J. (2014). Addressing value-based conflicts within the counseling relationship: A decision-making model. *Journal of Counseling & Development*, *92*(2), 180–186. doi:http://dx.doi.org/10.1002/j.1556-6676.2014.00146.x

Kolmes, K. (2010). My private practice social media policy. Retrieved from http://www.drkkolmes.com/docs/socmed.pdf

Kolmes, K. (2012). Social media in the future of professional psychology. *Professional Psychology: Research and Practice*, *43*(6), 606–612. doi:10.1037/a0028678

Lewis, S. P., Heath, N. L., Michal, N. J., & Duggan, J. M. (2012). Non-suicidal self-injury, youth, and the Internet: What mental health professionals need to know. *Child and Adolescent Psychiatry and Mental Health*, *6*, 13. doi:10.1186/1753-2000-6-13

Linehan, M. M., Comtois, K. A., Brown, Z. M., Heard, H. L., & Wagner, A. (2006). Suicide Attempt Self-injury Interview (SASSI): Development, reliability, and validity of a scale to assess suicide attempts and intentional self-injury. *Psychological Assessment*, *18*, 303–312.

Merz, T. (2010). Using cell/mobile phone sms for therapeutic relationship. In K. Anthony, D. M. Nagel, & S. Goss (Eds.), *The use of technology in mental health: Applications, ethics, and practice* (pp. 29–38). Springfield, IL: Charles C. Thomas.

Minetti, A. (2011). Working together. An interdisciplinary approach to dying patients in a palliative care unit. *Journal of Medical Ethics*, *37*, 715–718. doi:10.1136/jme.2010.040980

Mitchell, K. J., Wells, M., Priebe, G., & Ybarra, M. L. (2014). Exposure to websites that encourage self-harm and suicide: Prevalence rates and association with actual thoughts of self-harm and thoughts of suicide in the United States. *Journal of Adolescence*, *37*, 1335–1344. doi:10.1016/j.adolescence.2014.09.011

Muehlenkamp, J. J., Claes, L., Havertape, L., & Plener, P. L. (2012). International prevalence of adolescent non-suicidal self-injury and deliberate self-harm. *Child and Adolescent Psychiatry and Mental Health*, *6*, 10. doi:10.1186/1753-2000-6-10

Nickel, M. (2004). Professional boundaries: The dilemma of dual and multiple relationships in rural clinical practice. *Counseling & Clinical Psychology Journal*, *1*(1), 17–22.

Nock, M. K. (2010). Self-injury. *Annual Review of Clinical Psychology*, *6*, 339–363. doi:10.1146/annurev.clinpsy.121208.131258

Nock, M. K., Holmberg, E. B., Photos, V. I., & Michel, B. D. (2007). Self-Injurious Thoughts and Behaviors Interview: Development, reliability, and validity in an adolescent sample. *Psychological Assessment*, *19*(3), 309–317. doi:10.1037/1040-3590.19.3.309

Osman, A., Bagge, C. L., Guitierrez, P. M., Konick, L. C., Kooper, B. A., & Barrios, F. X. (2001). The Suicidal Behaviors Questionnaire-Revised (SBQ-R): Validation with clinical and nonclinical samples. *Assessment*, *5*, 443–445.

Pendergast, D. (2004). Nu Xs: Is it 2 L8 4 family? *Journal of the HEIA*, *11*(2), 2–12.

Person-Centered Tech. (2016). Person-centered tech's smartphone security guide for mental health professionals. Retrieved from www.personcenteredtech.com

Pope, K. S., & Keith-Spiegel, P. (2008). A practical approach to boundaries in psychotherapy: Making decisions, bypassing blunders, and mending fences. *Journal of Clinical Psychology*, (5), 638–652.

Posner, K., Brown, G. K., Stanley, B., Brent, D. A., Yershova, K. V., Oquendo, M. A., . . . Mann, J. J. (2011). The Columbia-Suicide Severity Rating Scale: Initial validity and internal consistency findings from three multisite studies with adolescents and adults. *American Journal of Psychiatry*, *168*, 1266–1277.

Qualman, E. (2018, March 8). #Socialnomics 2018 [YouTube video]. Retrieved from https://www.youtube.com/watch?v=likKsLON2rM

Raacke, J., & Bonds-Raacke, J. (2008). Myspace and Facebook: Applying the uses and gratifications theory to exploring friend-networking sites. *CyberPsychology & Behavior*, *11*(2), 169–174. Retrieved from http://web.ebscohost.com

Remley, T. P., & Herlihy, B. (2014). *Ethical, legal, and professional issues in counseling* (4th ed.). Upper Saddle River, NJ: Pearson.

Salo, M. (2014). Counseling minor clients. In B. Herlihy & G. Corey (Eds.), *ACA ethical standards casebook* (7th ed., pp. 205–214). Alexandria, VA: American Counseling Association.

Schmit, M. K., Schmit, E. L., Henesy, R., Klassen, S., & Oliver, M. (2015). Constructing an integrated model of ethical decision making in counselor education and supervision: A case conceptualization. *VISTAS Online*. Retrieved from http://wwww.counseling.org/knowledge-center/vistas

Stanley, B., & Brown, G. K. (2012). Safety planning intervention: A brief intervention to mitigate suicide risk. *Cognitive and Behavioral Practice*, *19*, 256–264.

Suicide Prevention Resource Center. (n.d.). CALM: Counseling on Access to Lethal Means. Retrieved from https://www.sprc.org/resources-programs/calm-counseling-access-lethal-means

Toprak, S., Cetin, I., Guven, T., Can, G., & Demircan, C. (2011). Self-harm, suicidal ideation and suicide attempts among college students. *Psychiatric Research*, *187*, 140–144.

Wade, M. E. (2014). *The counselor-client relationship in a social mediated world: The counselor perspective*. Unpublished doctoral dissertation, Argosy University, Washington, DC.

Werth, J. L. Jr., & Stroup, J. (2014). Working with clients who may harm themselves. In B. Herlihy & G. Corey (Eds.), *ACA ethical standards casebook* (7th ed., pp. 231–244). Alexandria, VA: American Counseling Association.

Wester, K. L., Ivers, N., Villalba, J. A., Trepal, H. C., & Henson, R. (2016). The relationship between non-suicidal self-injury and suicidal ideation. *Journal of Counseling and Development*, *94*, 3–12. doi:10.1002/jcad.12057

Wheeler, A. N., & Bertram, B. (2014). *The counselor and the law: A guide to legal and ethical practice* (7th ed.). Washington, DC: American Counseling Association.

Whitlock, J., Exner-Cortens, D., & Purington, A. (2014). Assessment of nonsuicidal self-injury: Development and initial validation of the Non-Suicidal Self-Injury-Assessment Tool (NSSI-AT). *Psychological Assessment*, *26*(3), 935–946.

Whitlock, J., Muehlenkamp, J., Eckenrode, J., Purington, A., Baral Abrams, G., Barreira, P., & Kress, V. (2013). Nonsuicidal self-injury as a gateway to suicide in young adults. *Journal of Adolescent Health*, *52*, 486–492. doi:10.1016/j.jadohealth.2012.09.010

Wilkinson, T., Smith, D., & Wimberly, R. (2016, October). *Disciplinary trends of professional counselor licensing boards*. New Orleans, LA: Southern Association for Counselor Education and Supervision.

World Health Organization. (2010). *Mental health: Strengthening our response. Fact Sheet Number 220*. Retrieved from www.who.int/mediacentre/factsheets/fs220/en/

Zabinski, M. F., Celio, A. A., Jacobs, M. A., Manwaring, J. and Wilfley, D. E. (2003) Internet-based prevention of eating disorders. *European Eating Disorders Review*, *11*, 183–197. doi:10.1002/erv.525

DOCUMENTATION AND RECORD KEEPING IN CLINICAL SETTINGS

By Joshua C. Watson and Caroline A. Norris

In an age of legal, clinical, and fiscal accountability, documentation and record keeping are important components of professional counseling (Mitchell, 2007). In fact, state and federal laws, as well as professional best practice standards, generally require counselors to maintain timely and accurate records of the services they provide. Maintaining clinical documentation serves two primary purposes. First, it facilitates the provision of the best possible services for clients. Second, it documents that the level of care provided to a client meets the prevailing standards of care found in the counseling profession (Corey, Corey, Corey, & Callanan, 2014). When appropriately maintained, written records have the potential to enhance the counseling experience, accelerate client progress, increase access to various services, and protect both counselors and clients (Seligman, 2004). No universal standard exists for the style and format in which clinical records should be kept. As a counseling professional, it is incumbent on you to become familiar with the legal and ethical requirements for documenting clinical services provided that are relevant in your setting and jurisdiction.

Documentation and record keeping in the clinical setting are the central focus of this discussion. Our goal is to equip you with a foundation of practical knowledge to prepare you for your first real-world experiences as a counselor in training. Understanding how to document client interactions initially is challenging for many beginning counselors. Because of the legal (Health Insurance Portability and Accountability Act [HIPAA], 2007) and ethical (American Counseling Association [ACA] Code of Ethics, 2014) standards involved, many novice counselors often question what to include when writing their case notes, making reports, and logging other miscellaneous interactions with clients. This chapter is designed to demystify the process of record keeping, clarifying for you the information most relevant to include, highlighting the correct way to document in adherence with applicable legal and ethical mandates, and presenting various styles of clinical records used across clinical mental health settings.

LEARNING OBJECTIVES

After reading this chapter, you will be able to do the following:

- Understand the purpose and role of clinical documentation (CACREP 5C-1-c)

- Know the types of documentation found in clinical records

- Identify the elements of good clinical documentation (CACREP 5C-1-a)

- Understand how to maintain and secure clinical records and documentation (CACREP 5C-3-a)

- Understand client confidentiality and disclosure procedures with clinical documentation (CACREP 5C-2-l, CACREP 5C-2-m)

- Become aware of the advantages and disadvantages of electronic record keeping

PURPOSE AND ROLE OF CLINICAL DOCUMENTATION

Throughout your training program, you undoubtedly will be trained to empathize with your clients, develop a therapeutic relationship with them, build rapport, and assist them in their struggles using a variety of counseling approaches, techniques, and interventions. What often does not get as much attention in training programs is the importance of clinical documentation (Brennan, 2013). In many cases, training programs often rely on practicum and internship sites to provide this training to students. Recognizing the importance of clinical documentation in the provision of competent counseling services, we include this chapter to help prepare counselors with the knowledge needed to document their work with clients. In so doing, we thought it most appropriate to begin with clarifying what is considered clinical documentation.

Clinical documentation involves any written and/or electronic record pertaining to contact between the client and counselor and work that has occurred within the counseling relationship. The term *clinical documentation* encompasses all forms of client data. This means documentation refers to any notation counselors create related to services provided, client's role, progress achieved, new goals established, recommendations made, and the counselor's rationale for the important counseling treatment decisions made (Barnett & Johnson, 2014). As you can see, clinical documentation includes anything and everything that has been written down about the client or interactions with the client. Some examples of documentation in the clinical setting include (but are not limited to) case notes, assessment results, treatment plans, documentation of telephone or electronic communication, confidentiality agreements, consent for services, notices about business practices, or any type of billing notices. Although various sites and settings may have different documentation guidelines, counselors should strive to develop a consistent approach to record keeping and clinical documentation (Brennan, 2013; Hedberg, 2010).

Because any type of communication between a client and a counselor is considered privileged communication, a counselor is accountable for safeguarding this information. According to the Code of Ethics (ACA, 2014), counselors have an ethical obligation to create and maintain records and clinical documentation necessary to render professional services. In fact, Wheeler and Bertram (2015) have noted that a counselor's failure to maintain adequate client records violates the standard of care expected of mental health counselors and could potentially be grounds for a malpractice suit being filed against the counselor. Your ethical responsibility related to client notes and record-keeping procedures is discussed in greater detail throughout this chapter.

The purpose of record keeping and clinical documentation is to track service delivery and progress during treatment of clients receiving services in the helping profession. Record keeping allows counselors to make sure clients are receiving effective services and not experiencing further emotional distress. Ultimately, counselors are responsible for exercising beneficence and nonmaleficence, as required by the counseling profession's Code of Ethics (ACA, 2014) and must prevent harm at all cost to clients. Once the counseling relationship begins, if a service is not delivered, or services are not contributing to increased client well-being after a reasonable amount of time, record-keeping procedures can be used to safeguard the process of quality control for client care. According to Hodges (2015), one can argue that clear, concise, and effective record-keeping practices are "in the client's best interest" (p. 93).

Besides being an ethical issue, effective record-keeping practices are beneficial for practicing mental health counselors. For one, maintenance of complete clinical documentation is a way for counselors to document their clinical assessment and evaluate potential diagnoses they believe to be a fit for their clients. In the current era of managed care, being able to document specifically why a diagnosis was given and how counseling will function to address said diagnosis is important for counselors to receive third-party reimbursement for their services. Client files are a great place to record information related to signs and symptoms either reported or observed that support the counselor's clinical judgment.

Another reason counselors keep written records of their work is to track client progress. Detailed records capturing what takes place each session allow counselors to see whether clients are improving and closing in on achieving their stated treatment goals. Additionally, clear documentation allows counselors to see what specific interventions appear to be working and which might not be as effective. In future sessions, time can be saved by focusing efforts on those interventions that have demonstrated effectiveness. Documentation also can include details related to why an intervention worked or did not work, what issues it was applied to, and how the client responded to it. In situations where counselors may be unsure of how to proceed, consultation may need to be sought. In working with consultants, information in a client's record may need to be shared to give the consultant a better understanding of the case and what dynamics may be in play (Carney & Jefferson, 2014). Additionally, consultation efforts themselves should be noted in the client's case file, regardless of whether the counselor incorporates any of the consultant's recommendations in subsequent treatment.

Also, clinical documentation can serve as a memory aid (Cameron & Turtle-Song, 2002). Some counselors, particularly those working in mental health agencies serving a large segment of the population, may carry extensive client loads. Staffing a caseload of more than 50 clients is not uncommon in these types of settings. When working with so many clients, it may become a challenge for counselors to remember all that has been going on in session and separate individual cases. Being able to quickly glance through a client's record and review previous documentation is a great way for counselors to remind themselves about the client they are about to see and what the focus of treatment has been over the past few sessions.

Case notes also facilitate communication among treatment professionals and promote continuity of care (Wheeler & Bertram, 2015). As many mental health centers become multidisciplinary treatment settings, and integrated behavioral health care (see Chapter 10) becomes the norm, case notes will be essential to ensuring all providers who work with a client are on the same page and aware of what is occurring for the client. For example, a client may have a medication review appointment with his psychiatrist. During this meeting, the client reports feeling more depressed recently. The psychiatrist may or may not make alterations to the client's medication regimen (i.e., raise the dosage, increase frequency of use, change medication entirely). Without documenting the client's verbalization of increased feelings of depression, the counselor working with this client may not know this was an issue and thus not be able to address the feelings in subsequent counseling sessions. Similarly, when a counselor documents changes in client mood, behavior, affect, and thought processes, the psychiatrist can note these changes and possibly make medication adjustments designed to help the client.

Clearly, there are many good reasons for counselors to keep clinical records on the clients they see. The previous examples are but a few of the helpful ways documentation facilitates the therapeutic process. Now that you appreciate the importance of clinical documentation, let's look at some of the types of documentation you typically include in a client's record. Across each of these types of documentation your records should be consistent with best practice standards endorsed by the counseling profession, clear and concise, aligned with professional ethical codes, and auditable.

GUIDED PRACTICE EXERCISE 6.1

In small groups of two to three students, discuss whether you believe the following scenario is ethical. A counselor at a local clinical mental health center is carrying a busy caseload. He typically sees eight to ten clients per day. With little time between sessions to document, he often brings client files home and adds case notes from the day's sessions. Occasionally, he forgets which client said what and often finds himself guessing when it comes to documenting in a file. He rationalizes that they all basically were seeking help for the same issues so it is really not that big of a deal.

TYPES OF DOCUMENTATION FOUND IN CLINICAL RECORDS

Several different documents may be found in a client's record (Wheeler & Bertram, 2015). Where you work and the type of work you do largely influence how a client file will look and the documents included. Some of the items you likely will be expected to document in your case files include the following:

- Client identification information (e.g., name, age, gender, relationship status)

- Informed consent documents

- Financial arrangements (e.g., insurance information, self-pay, sliding-scale agreements, employee assistance program participation)

- Psychosocial assessment

- Mental status examination results

- Release of information

- Ancillary information (e.g., test results; medical records; past clinical records or letters from service providers; communication from third parties such as parents, employers, spouses, or teachers)

- Treatment plans

- Case notes

Client Identification Information

The first document typically found in a client's file is a listing of demographic information about the client. Here is where you document information related to the client's age, gender, race, ethnicity, relationship status, sexual orientation, and employment status among other variables. This information is helpful when attempting to identify treatments potentially useful for the client. Additionally, this information allows ancillary health care providers to gain familiarity with a client they may not have interacted with previously. Identification information also may include contact information for the client such as a home mailing address, preferred contact number, and/or e-mail address.

Informed Consent Documents

Respecting client autonomy, informed consent should be sought before services are provided to a client. **Informed consent documents** include a variety of information describing what the counseling process will look like, what the client can expect from the counselor, what the client will be expected to do, how services will be arranged and how they will be paid for, and what recourse the client has should the services provided be deemed inappropriate or ineffective (see Figure 6.1). **Consent** is sought from individuals who are legally able to provide it. In most cases, this means individuals over the age of 18 who are competent to make their own decisions. For children or adults with diminished

FIGURE 6.1 ■ Sample Informed Consent Document

CONSENT TO TREATMENT

I, _____, the undersigned, hereby attest that I have voluntarily entered into treatment, or give my consent for the minor or person under my legal guardianship mentioned above, at MidState Behavioral Health Services, hereby referred as the Center. Further, I consent to have treatment provided by a psychiatrist, counselor, psychologist, social worker, or intern in collaboration with his/her supervisor. The rights, risks and benefits associated with the treatment have been explained to me. I understand that the therapy may be discontinued at any time by either party. The clinic encourages that this decision be discussed with the treating therapist. This will help facilitate a more appropriate plan for discharge.

Recipient's Rights: I certify that I have received the Recipient's Rights pamphlet and certify that I have read and understand its content. I understand that as a recipient of services, I may get more information from the Recipient's Rights Advisor.

Non-Voluntary Discharge from Treatment: A client may be terminated from the Center non-voluntarily, if: A) the client exhibits physical violence, verbal abuse, carries weapons, or engages in illegal acts at the clinic, and/or B) the client refuses to comply with stipulated program rules, refuses to comply with treatment recommendations, or does not make payment or payment arrangements in a timely manner. The client will be notified of the non-voluntary discharge by letter. The client may appeal this decision with the Clinic Director or request to re-apply for services at a later date.

Client Notice of Confidentiality: The confidentiality of patient records maintained by the Center is protected by Federal and/or State law and regulations. Generally, the Center may not say to a person outside the Center that a patient attends the program or disclose any information identifying a patient as an alcohol or drug abuser unless: 1) the patient consents in writing, 2) the disclosure is allowed by a court order, or 3) the disclosure is made to medical personnel in a medical emergency, or to qualified personnel for research, audit, or program evaluation.

Violation of Federal and/or State law and regulations by a treatment facility or provider is a crime. Suspected violations may be reported to appropriate authorities. Federal and/or State law and regulations do not protect any information about a crime committed by a patient either at the Center, against any person who works for the program, or about any threat to commit such a crime. Federal law and regulations do not protect any information about suspected child (or vulnerable adult) abuse or neglect, or adult abuse from being reported under Federal and/or State law to appropriate State or Local authorities. Health care professionals are required to report admitted prenatal exposure to controlled substances that are potentially harmful. It is the Center's duty to warn any potential victim, when a significant threat of harm has been made. In the event of a client's death, the spouse or parents of a deceased client have a right to access their child's or spouse's records. Professional misconduct by a health care professional must be reported by other health care professionals, in which related client records may be released to substantiate disciplinary concerns. Parents or legal guardians of non-emancipated minor clients have the right to access the client's records. When fees are not paid in a timely manner, a collection agency will be given appropriate billing and financial information about client, not clinical information. My signature below indicates that I have been given a copy of my rights regarding confidentiality. I permit a copy of this authorization to be used in place of the original. Client data of clinical outcomes may be used for program evaluation purposes, but individual results will not be disclosed to outside sources.

I consent to treatment and agree to abide by the above stated policies and agreements with MidState Behavioral Health Services.

_____   _____
Signature of Client/Legal Guardian   Date
(In a case where a client is under 18 years of age, a legally
responsible adult acting on his/her behalf)

_____   _____
Witness   Date

Source: MidState Behavioral Health Services (MBHS) © 2007

cognitive abilities, informed consent is obtained from parents, guardians, or legal powers of attorney. Copies of any documentation related to transferred rights to make decisions for others should be kept in the case file.

When working with children and minors, counselors sometimes will document assent among these clients. **Assent** refers to the personal agreement to engage in therapeutic activities with the counselor. Although the parents or guardians provide the legal informed consent, asking children themselves if they want to participate is a good step toward building rapport and facilitating client buy-in. Consent and assent form formats vary from site to site. Counselors in private practice settings get the opportunity to create their own forms. Several resources are available to assist counselors in creating their own documentation of a client's consent and assent (Hedberg, 2010; Wiger, 2010, 2011).

Financial Arrangements

Let's face it, despite our best intentions to want to help clients, there is a business component to the services counselors provide. Documentation of the financial aspects of client care should be included in a client's case file. For clients who have private insurance, copies of their insurance cards and contact information for the mental health portion of their benefits should be documented. Additionally, information related to whether preauthorization is required for services should be noted along with the number to call to gain authorization. Clients receiving services who do not have private insurance may elect to pay for services themselves. In cases such as these, the financial agreement struck between the counselor and client should be documented and agreed to (via signature) by all relevant parties. This documentation should include the fees associated with various services (e.g., individual sessions, group sessions, testing and assessment, medication management) and when payment is expected. In some settings, a sliding-scale fee structure is established for clients who may not be able to afford the services they need. If a reduced fee is negotiated with a client, the counselor should document the agreed-upon fee structure in the case file.

Psychosocial Assessment

A **psychosocial assessment** is a comprehensive evaluation of a client's mental health, well-being, and social functioning. Psychosocial assessments allow counselors to collect client information, both current and historical, that allows for a better understanding of what may be going on with the client and related to the presenting problem. Through a series of structured questions, counselors gain a complete picture of client functioning and are better equipped to establish individualized treatment goals. Many mental health centers have their own formatted psychosocial assessment. However, in some settings, counselors may be asked to create their own. Across formats, there are some common sections included. (See Figure 6.2.)

The first section of a psychosocial assessment usually addresses the client's presenting problem. Using as many of the client's own words as possible, counselors document the reason for seeking counseling. This section also can include information related to who might have initiated the treatment. For example, the client may have been court-ordered, brought in by parents, or seeking treatment as part of a couple or family. Knowing why a client is seeking treatment and whose idea it was to get help are important in understanding client motivation and willingness to participate in the therapeutic process.

FIGURE 6.2 ■ Sample Psychosocial Assessment Document

MidState
Behavioral Health Services

ADULT PSYCHOSOCIAL ASSESSMENT
INTAKE INTERVIEW

Counselor: _____ Date: _____

Client Name: _____ SS#: _____

Date of Birth: _____ Age: _____ Race: _____ Gender: _____

Next of Kin: _____ Relationship to client: _____

Address: _____ Telephone: _____

Information obtained from: □ Client   □ Family Member   □ Parent/Spouse   □ Employer

INITIAL REASON FOR SEEKING TREATMENT (PRESENTING PROBLEM):

_____

_____

_____

_____

PRECIPITATING FACTORS:

_____

_____

_____

_____

CURRENT SYMPTOMS: *(mark all that apply)*

□ abnormal thoughts	□ elevated mood	□ mania	□ self-injurious behavior
□ anger or aggressiveness	□ euphoria	□ missing school / work	□ severe mood swings
□ anxiety	□ hallucinations	□ obsessions / compulsions	□ sleep disturbances
□ appetite disturbance	□ hopelessness / helplessness	□ oppositional	□ substance abuse (current)
□ cognitive impairment	□ hyperactivity	□ orientation / memory	□ substance abuse (past)
□ decreased energy	□ grief	□ panic attacks	□ tearfulness
□ delusions	□ guilt	□ paranoia	□ treatment noncompliance
□ depression	□ impulsivity	□ poor concentration	□ withdrawal symptoms
□ disruption of thoughts	□ poor	□ pressured speech	□ worthlessness
□ dissociative states	□ irritability	□ problems with ADLs	□ other

FUNCTIONAL IMPAIRMENTS: *(specify severity and note any recent changes)*

_____

_____

_____

TREATMENT HISTORY:

Have you had previous counseling/therapy experience? ☐ Yes ☐ No Psychiatric hospitalization? ☐ Yes ☐ No

If yes, please indicate when: _____ therapist's name: _____

What types of therapy/counseling have you experienced? _____

_____

_____

Has a helping professional ever recommended you take medications? ☐ Yes ☐ No Did you take them? ☐ Yes ☐ No

What medications were recommended and who made the recommendation? _____

_____

Do you believe that the medication was helpful? ☐ Yes ☐ No If no, why not? _____

DEVELOPMENTAL HISTORY:

How old was mother when you were born? _____ Were there labor and delivery problems? ☐ Yes ☐ No

Were you born: ☐ early ☐ on time ☐ late ☐ don't know What was your birth weight? _____

Were there any problems with language development? _____

Were developmental milestones achieved at the appropriate ages? _____

Any difficulties encountered during development? _____

FAMILY HISTORY:

Family of Origin:

Parents' marital status: ☐ married ☐ separated ☐ divorced ☐ widowed

Relationship with mother: _____

Relationship with father: _____

Siblings:

Name	Sex	Age	Current Relationship with Client

Marital Status:

☐ single/never married ☐ married ☐ separated ☐ divorced ☐ widowed

Age when married: _____ Number of years married: _____ Number of years separated/divorced: _____

(Continued)

FIGURE 6.2 ■ (Continued)

Children:

Name	Sex	Age	Residing at home?

Type of dwelling family resides in: (house, apartment, etc., include # of bedrooms): _____

Is there a history of mental illness in the family?   □ Yes   □ No   If yes, specify: _____

Are any family members deceased: □ Yes □ No   If yes, specify: _____

EDUCATIONAL HISTORY:

Highest grade completed in school: _____   Year graduated: _____

Type of student: _____

_____

Did client have any school-related problems?   □ Yes   □ No   If yes, please explain: _____

Was client ever suspended (at-home or in-school)?   □ Yes   □ No   If yes, please explain: _____

EMPLOYMENT HISTORY:

Is client currently employed?   Yes / No   If yes, name of employer: _____

Describe job duties: _____

Number of years at current job:_____   Satisfaction with job: □ Excellent □ Good □ Fair □ Poor

Does client find it difficult to maintain employment? _____

MEDICAL HISTORY:

Have you ever had any serious illnesses, injuries, or surgery? (Please specify) _____

_____

Please list all current medications you are taking: (prescribed or over-the-counter) _____

_____

Who prescribes your medication for you?_____

Doctor's telephone number: _____   Office address: _____

Do you have any known allergies? □ Yes □ No   If yes, please list: _____

Have you ever been pregnant? _____   Have you ever had a miscarriage? _____

RISK ASSESSMENT:

Have you ever had any involvement with legal authorities? ☐ Yes ☐ No If yes, please explain: _____

Do you have any pending legal issues (probations, upcoming hearings, etc.)? _____

Have you ever been abused: ☐ physically ☐ emotionally ☐ mentally ☐ other ☐ no abuse

If yes to any of the above, please describe: _____

_____

Are you sexually active? ☐ Yes ☐ No   If yes, at what age did you become active? _____

How many partners have you had? _____ Do you practice safe sex or use birth control? ☐ Yes ☐ No

Have you ever used drugs or alcohol? ☐ Yes ☐ No If yes, at what age did you start using? _____

Substance:	Amt:	Freq:	How long using:

Do your parents drink or use drugs? ☐ Yes, current use ☐ No, never ☐ Previous usage ☐ Not Sure

Do your friends drink or use drugs? ☐ Yes, current use ☐ No, never ☐ Previous usage ☐ Not Sure

INTERPERSONAL HISTORY:

Social Relationships:

How easy is it for you to make friends?   ☐ very easy   ☐ about average   ☐ very difficult

How easy is it for you to keep friends?   ☐ very easy   ☐ about average   ☐ very difficult

How many close friends do you have? _____

Leisure Activities:

How do you like to spend your free time? _____

_____

What are your hobbies, interests? _____

Spiritual/Religious Beliefs:

Do you practice a particular religion? ☐ Yes ☐ No If yes, what is your religious affiliation? _____

Strengths or support: _____

Problems or weakness: _____

Any recent changes: _____

(Continued)

FIGURE 6.2 ■ (Continued)

SELF ASSESSMENT

What do you see as your greatest strengths or characteristics? _____

_____

_____

What are the areas that you would most like to improve about yourself? _____

_____

_____

Who will be your greatest supports or allies throughout your counseling experience? _____

_____

_____

_____	_____	_____
Counselor Signature	*Credentials*	*Date*
_____	_____	_____
Counselor Signature	*Credentials*	*Date*
_____	_____	_____
Psychiatrist Signature	*Credentials*	*Date*

Source: MidState Behavioral Health Services (MBHS) © 2007

The second section, although this might be combined with the previous section, looks at the client's history with the presenting concern. Questions asked in this section look at how long the current issue has been problematic for the client, what changes in issue severity or intensity have been observed, how the client has attempted to manage the issue in the past, and what has been successful or not helpful. Information gathered in this section can help jump-start treatment by avoiding interventions or approaches the client readily identifies as having been tried in the past with little success. Knowing about previous treatment history could prove beneficial should the counselor need to consult with past providers in caring for the client.

Following these first two sections, many sections could be included in the psychosocial assessment in various orders. One of these sections relates to family history. This section accomplishes two goals. First, it allows the counselor to gather information about the client's family including individuals' relationship to the client, age, and marital status. This section also includes questions related to a history of mental health concerns among family members. Many of the mental disorders you are learning about in your training program have strong genetic components to them. Knowing who in a client's immediate and extended family has struggled with mental health issues might offer clues related to the client's presenting issues.

Mental Status Examination

A **mental status examination** (MSE) is a structured assessment of a client's behavioral and cognitive functioning (Martin, 1990). It is typically used to develop a baseline understanding of a client's presentation and aid in conceptualizing a potential diagnosis. Although the MSE follows a standardized protocol, it remains a largely subjective tool, with clinicians making their own determinations of a client's speech, appearance, and cognitive state. Typically, an MSE is conducted by a psychiatrist or psychologist, but there are times when counselors may participate in the process of evaluation. In any event, counselors should be familiar with the contents of the MSE and know how that information can be useful in goal setting and treatment planning with their clients. The components of an MSE are included in Table 6.1.

TABLE 6.1 ■ Components of the Mental Status Examination (MSE)	
Appearance	How does the client look? Is the client dressed appropriately and properly groomed?
Level of alertness	Is the client conscious? Can the client focus on the conversation? Is the client alert and attentive?
Speech	Is the client's speech normal in tone, volume, and quantity?
Behavior	Is the client pleasant? Cooperative? Agitated? Distressed?
Awareness of surroundings	Does the client know where he or she is? Is the client able to identify date, time, and place?
Mood	How does the client feel? Is the client's mood appropriate for the situation?

(Continued)

TABLE 6.1 ■ (Continued)	
Affect	How does the client appear? Does the client appear flat or excited?
Thought process	Are the client's thoughts logical and coherent?
Thought content	Are the client's thoughts rational and appropriate?
Memory	Does the client have a functioning short-term memory and long-term memory?
Ability to perform calculations	Can the client perform simple mathematical computations (e.g., addition, subtraction)?
Judgment	When given a common scenario, can the client discern what the most appropriate course of action would be (e.g., finding a lost wallet on the subway)?
Higher functioning and reasoning	Can the client identify the meaning of common phrases or expressions (e.g., treat others as you would want to be treated)?

GUIDED PRACTICE EXERCISE 6.2

Prompt: Becky is a junior in college and is seeking counseling to address some anxiety-related issues she began having this fall. Becky is a nursing student and recently found out her parents are no longer able to help her financially with a portion of her rent and tuition. Working more hours to get her basic financial needs met is an idea her parents recommended that Becky believes will be a detriment to her academic success. Becky uses rapid speech, is constantly fidgeting during the session, and seems generally fearful about her situation.

Role-play: Invite two students to role-play a brief counseling session in front of the class, or have students break up into pairs and role-play with each other. One student will take on the role of the counselor and the other the client.

Write: Using Table 6.1 as a guide, write down short responses for each of the components listed in the table as part of the MSE.

Example:

Appearance	Appears well groomed, appears tired
Level of alertness	Alert
Speech	Rapid speech
Behavior	Biting her nails, playing with hair, constantly moving during session
Awareness of surroundings	Oriented x 4 This term means the client is aware of (1) who they are, (2) where they are, (3) what day it is, and (4) the situation they are in.
Mood	Anxious, fearful, stressed

Affect	Normal
Thought process	Mostly coherent
Thought content	Some irrational; dichotomous thinking; appropriate
Memory	Normal functioning
Ability to perform calculations	Not observed
Judgment	Good
Higher functioning and reasoning	Good, may be slightly impaired

Several formats of case notes are presented in this chapter. Which seems to make the most sense for you and how you envision your work with clients? What might be some of the advantages and disadvantages of using this approach over the others presented? Share your thoughts with the class when finished.

Release of Information

Clients maintain legal ownership of their case files. Any sharing of information in a client's record must be approved by the client unless there is an urgent need to reveal information for the safety of the client or others. The Health Insurance Portability and Accountability Act of 1996 (HIPAA) establishes data privacy and security provisions for the safeguarding of medical information, including mental health records. Because clients maintain ownership of their records, they can authorize their release to other parties. A client's record will typically include documentation of such release authorizations. On these release forms, clients indicate to whom information can be released, what information can be released, and for what stated purpose. Clients may choose to release information to parents, spouses, employers, primary care physicians, or other medical or mental health providers. If documentation is not included in the client's record, permission must be sought before releasing any information. Many agencies and counseling centers have their own standard versions of release forms. Becoming familiar with these forms is important for beginning counselors.

Ancillary Information

Clients may be receiving additional services apart from counseling from a service provider. For example, a client may be seeing a counselor as well as a psychiatrist at a local mental health clinic. The psychiatrist may include medical history and medication regimen information in the client's file. Additionally, results of lab work conducted or assessments administered may appear in a client's file.

A client's file also may include documentation from third parties that may relate to the client's presentation or potential diagnosis. For example, a letter from a professional school counselor or teacher may document how a child is behaving in school and what problems are being observed. Or a court order indicating mandated counseling for a client could be found in the file. These items may or may not be useful to the counselor, depending on the issues being discussed with the client.

Treatment Plans

Treatment plans are a synopsis of a counselor's work with a client. They include a description of the client's presenting problem or issue, any potential diagnosis that may apply, goals established, and strategies or interventions planned to help reach those goals. Simply stated, treatment plans are designed to serve as a guideline for achieving a client's stated goals (Parsons & Zhang, 2014). As counselors develop treatment plans for their clients, they should include three primary features: an overview, a listing of long-term goals, and a listing of short-term goals (Berman, 2015). The *overview* should be a brief recap of why the client is presenting for services, the salient issues or symptoms experienced, how the problem is currently being experienced, and how the problem has been addressed or treated in the past. *Long-term goals* should directly relate to the goals established. Using a solution-focused perspective, these goals should represent where a client would like to be by the end of counseling. Supplementing these long-term goals are short-term goals. *Short-term goals* should represent progressive steps toward achieving a long-term goal. For example, an adolescent working toward a goal of independence may set short-term goals focusing on taking charge of small segments of life such as setting one's own schedule or making one's own meals. When writing treatment plans, keep in mind they are designed to be actively used by the counselor and client. As such, they should be written in easy-to-understand language and avoid technical jargon. Goals also should be stated in a way that allows them to be assessed to determine progress. We include a sample treatment plan for you to follow.

Sample Treatment Plan

The following treatment plan was constructed with guidance from Jongsma, A. E., Peterson, L. M., & Bruce, T. J. (2014). The Complete Adult Psychotherapy Treatment Planner. *Hoboken, NJ: Wiley.*

Overview. Client, 32, is attending services to learn to manage the anxiety symptoms she is experiencing; she frequently worries about adequately performing at her job and details related to her future. Client reports she feels out of control related to her worrying, which has occurred more days than not, for the past 9 months. Client describes shortness of breath, racing thoughts, restlessness, and difficulty falling asleep as symptoms related to her anxiety. Client has no previous treatment and is not taking any prescribed medication. She reports she has only tried to alleviate her worry with increased time at the office, which she believes has instead escalated the anxiety she is experiencing.

Diagnosis. F41.1 generalized anxiety disorder

Long-Term Goals.

1. Learn and implement coping skills that stabilize and reduce the anxiety.
2. Resolve core conflict that is the source of the anxiety.

Short-Term Goals.

1. Describe situations, thoughts, feelings, and actions associated with frequent worry and assess their impact on her daily functioning.

2. Learn and implement calming skills to reduce and manage anxiety symptoms.

3. Identify, challenge, and replace unhelpful self-talk with positive and empowering self-talk.

4. Learn and implement personal and interpersonal skills to reduce anxiety and improve interpersonal relationships.

5. Identify major life conflicts that may contribute to current experience with anxiety.

Interventions.

1. While building rapport, use empathy and encouragement to help the client feel safe in describing her anxiety-related symptoms.

2. Ask the client to share her experiences of anxiety and how they have impacted her both personally and professionally.

3. Teach the client calming and relaxation skills (e.g., mindful breathing, self-soothing, progressive muscle relaxation) and assign daily practice.

4. Use cognitive-behavioral therapy techniques to explore the client's self-talk patterns that contribute to anxious feelings.

5. Use modeling and role-play to build the client's conflict resolution skills and assign the client to implement these skills into her personal and professional relationships.

6. Evaluate progress with implementation and provide feedback as needed until competency with conflict resolution skills is verbalized by the client.

7. Explore with the client any critical unresolved life conflicts and begin work to resolve them.

Case Notes

Case notes are the session-to-session archives counselors keep about their work with clients. They document what was discussed in session, the outcome of these discussions, and any plans for future sessions originating from these discussions. In writing case notes, be *clear, concise,* and *accurate.* Only the most significant information from counseling sessions should be included (Luepker, 2012). The goal of case note writing is to document the most meaningful aspects of the session and summarize what was reported by the client and observations of the client made by the counselor while protecting the client's confidentiality rights. For ethical reasons, what occurs in the therapeutic relationship and any actions the counselor takes that may have ethical implications are imperative to include (Brennan, 2013). Case notes serve to track the delivery of services, as well as track client progress. Writing case notes is a learned skill and will become easier for beginning counselors the more client interactions they have and the more they develop their case conceptualization skills.

When deciding what to include in a case note, the counselor must maintain a delicate balance between documenting only the most relevant information to preserve the client's confidentiality and not leaving out pertinent information (Luepker, 2012). It is common for new counselors to want to offer a play-by-play of the entire counseling session, often from their view of what took place. Case notes come in many formats. A SOAP note is an excellent format for new counselors to assist with documenting the most relevant information about the session. SOAP stands for subjective-objective assessment plan. The SOAP note was developed by Weed in 1964 to improve the continuity of service delivery to clients among health care professionals (Cameron & Turtle-Song, 2002). It is a good format that includes the relevant information needed to document what occurred in session, what the counselor assessed, and how counseling will proceed from here. Table 6.2 provides an example of a clear, concise, and accurate SOAP note. Keep in mind that the SOAP note is one of many different note-taking styles used by counseling professionals. Certain settings may require a specific style to maintain consistency across client records. Counselors are

TABLE 6.2 ■ Example of a SOAP Note	
Subjective	What does the client report? What does the client report regarding symptoms and progress since the last session? This section pertains to information voiced directly to the counselor, so it is important to include the client's thoughts, feelings, problems, symptoms, and progress toward achieving desired goals (Cameron & Turtle-Song, 2002).
	Include five to seven brief statements.
	E.g. Client reported she was fired from her job this past week and stated she felt both "frustrated" and "disappointed."
Objective	What do you observe? Describe the client's affect, attitude, level of participation, and noteworthy behavior. Because this portion is focused on factual and quantifiable terms, when recording observations, it is important for the counselor to refrain from using language that uses labels, personal judgement, or opinions (Cameron & Turtle-Song, 2002).
	E.g. Client monopolized much of the time in session. Client was oriented to the date, time, place, and her own identity. Client was agitated, anxious, and tearful.
Assessment	Summarize the counselor's critical thoughts about the session. Synthesize the subjective and objective observations. Include diagnosis or impressions.
	E.g. Client seems to be improving, despite the challenge of the circumstance. Client is appropriately applying coping skills and has become more open to discussing her feelings about the event in a deeper way than in previous sessions.
Plan	Describe the parameters of treatment. Include an action plan (e.g., homework, next session) as well as prognosis.
	E.g. Continue to challenge client's thoughts and beliefs about self and encourage the client to seek social support. Client will complete a daily thought record once per day over this next week.

encouraged to learn how records should be kept at their setting and become familiar with the preferred style.

Another type of case note counselors may use is a STIPS (signs and symptoms, topics of discussion, interventions, progress and plan, special issues) note. The STIPS format was developed by Prieto and Scheel (2002) to assist beginning counselors in accomplishing seven general cognitive-developmental goals:

1. To acquire relevant facts about the client and case

2. To form diagnoses or a clinical understanding of the client's presenting problems

3. To form meaningful and effective treatment plans and goals that directly relate to a client's presenting problems

4. To understand within-session processes when working with clients and the relevant domains to track regarding a client's problems and within-session goals

5. To understand the counseling process across sessions with clients and how to longitudinally track a client's problems and overall progress in treatment

6. To evaluate and adjust, in an ongoing manner, their treatment interventions to best serve a client's needs

7. To use relevant criteria to evaluate the usefulness of counseling for clients at the end of treatment and to understand how their counseling interventions have led to a particular outcome in treatment for this specific client

The specific information counselors should document in a STIPS note is described in Table 6.3. As a beginning counselor, the depth and breadth provided by this style of note may help you better understand your role in the counseling process and how you are impacting client functioning and progress.

A third type of case note format is known as DAP. A DAP note includes three key components: describe, assess, and plan. In the describe (D) section, the counselor documents how the client presented, what was discussed in session, what the primary focus of the session was, and any observations the counselor may wish to record. Items in the describe section should represent a combination of subjective and objective data. For example, the counselor may record that the client was visibly shaken and crying (objective) and feeling saddened by the recent loss in her life (subjective). The (A) section is for assessment. Here is where the counselor documents clinical impressions and hypotheses to test in subsequent sessions. Counselors address the question of *why* in terms of how a client is feeling, thinking, or acting. Assessment also includes notation of progress made toward established treatment goals. The final section is called plan (P) and details next steps based on the events that transpired in the current session. Counselors record what they believe should be done next to help clients reach their goals.

Regardless of the format used, when documenting counselors should limit as much as possible identifying information of people and places where the client interacts. For example, if the client states he has been attending Alcoholics Anonymous meetings at the local community recreation center, the counselor might want to leave out the location to reserve the anonymity of the group. The case note would report: *Client reported*

TABLE 6.3 ■ Example of a STIPS Note	
Signs and symptoms	Document the client's current level of functioning, clinical signs and symptoms experienced, and any significant changes from previous levels of functioning; observable client behaviors. *E.g. Client appeared for session visibly distressed. Client had difficulty maintaining eye contact and was tearful and emotional in describing current feelings.*
Topics of discussion	Document all major issues discussed in the session and provide updates on progress, or lack thereof, on issues discussed in previous sessions. *E.g. Client discussed plans for summer break once the current semester ends. She plans to visit friends in California and research possible intern sites there as well. Client reports having had productive conversations with her parents this past week regarding her career plans after school.*
Interventions	Document specific counseling interventions implemented in session, linking each intervention to a specified goal or treatment objective. *E.g. This session we had client construct a family genogram to examine why she may not have strong relationships with her cousins.*
Progress and plan	Document a summary of the client's progress toward established treatment goals and the outcomes of any interventions that have occurred. *E.g. This session client was able to reconcile feelings toward her sister and begin process of forgiveness. We completed an empty chair technique that proved to be quite cathartic for her, allowing her to express feelings she has kept bottled up for some time.*
Special issues	Document newly developed or ongoing critical clinical issues that should be tracked and updated. *E.g. Client was recently placed on a new medication and is worried whether it will be as effective as her previous medication. Will need to continue checking in on medication compliance and client experiences taking it.*

attending AA meetings twice this past week. Often it is a good idea to use clients' own words by writing them verbatim in quotation marks when something they said represents a particularly meaningful point. Verbatim client phrases, however, should be kept to a minimum to ensure clarity when reviewing notes later to search for client themes and to track the effectiveness of therapeutic interventions (Cameron & Turtle-Song, 2002). Additionally, when quotations are used Cameron and Turtle-Song (2002) recommend to "use only key words or a very brief phrase" (p. 287). Using direct quotes from a client will also be beneficial for counselors documenting clients' declarations of harm to self. Including quotation marks to describe a metaphor the client used to describe feelings of depression can help remind counselors of important phrases clients have used in previous sessions and allow for the counselor to be more impactful by reflecting the client's own words in future sessions. For example, a client expressing feelings of sadness may describe a "dark cloud hovering over her." This metaphor has power and meaning to the client. Recording it in the case notes will allow the counselor to come back to this imagery in future sessions. The counselor could use the same language to assess current feelings by asking, "Does it still feel like that dark cloud is hovering over you?" or "Have there been any breaks in the dark clouds you experience above you?" Following the tips included in Table 6.4 will help you write effective case notes.

TABLE 6.4 ■ Tips for Writing Effective Case Notes
Be clear. Use simple language that specifically describes what the client is experiencing without including too much technical jargon. This will aid with clarity and help with continuity of care throughout the managed care arena to ensure that if necessary, individuals from a variety of health practices can understand the pertinent content of the notes if the client were to legally release their session notes into the hands of another health care provider.
Be concise. Report only the necessary information needed to help describe treatment progress. Information should pertain to the issues or reasons why the client is seeking treatment and how it relates to his or her goal attainment. To protect client confidentiality, omit any identifying information unless absolutely needed. It is important to be concise due to the open nature of managed care, and it is possible this information could be released to other health care professionals and paraprofessionals (Cameron & Turtle-Song, 2002). You simultaneously serve as your client's counselor and confidentiality advocate.
Be accurate. Report what actually happens in session. Do not offer conjecture or your opinion as to what the client may have been thinking or feeling. The goal of case note writing is to provide a factual representation of what occurred during session, so a counselor's opinion or attitude about what happened or how the session went is inappropriate to include, even when providing observation. The best way to think about it: Stick to the facts!
When appropriate, use the client's own words. Make sure to document specific analogies, metaphors, or illustrations clients use to describe their situation. Referring to these in subsequent sessions is a good way to build rapport and track client progress, if integrated into session notes and used occasionally. Cameron & Turtle-Song (2002) recommend using client quotations minimally, because if overused they can make certain client themes and progress toward goals difficult to track. It is important to include quotations when documenting sessions where suicidal or homicidal ideation, or a shift in overall well-being, is discussed. Case notes should include what the client reported regarding counseling-related concerns and goals rather than verbatim recollection of what was said (Cameron & Turtle-Song, 2002).
Use active voice. Write in the first-person active voice. State what you the counselor are doing or saying and what the client is doing or saying. Often novice counselors tend to write in the way they are remembering: "The client reports she is frustrated with being the provider in her family and is feeling really unappreciated." Unlike passive voice, active voice suggests the client is the "doer" and can act upon forces in her life, as opposed to life acting upon her. An example of rephrasing in active voice: "The client reported she is frustrated with providing for her family, and expressed she felt unappreciated." Not only is it active voice, but it reflects *what happened* in session, not *what is happening*.

GUIDED PRACTICE EXERCISE 6.3

Imagine you are starting a private practice. As the sole proprietor, you are responsible for creating the documentation used in your practice. What sort of information would you most want to collect from your clients at the onset of treatment? How would you go about acquiring this information from the client so that it is most useful in shaping treatment?

GUIDED PRACTICE EXERCISE 6.4

Prompt: A client is seeking counseling and is coming in for her second session. The counselor has already completed the psychosocial intake and knows that the client is looking to use counseling as a supportive resource as she transitions through a divorce. The client is 43 years old and her spouse 4 months ago asked her for a divorce. The client was not expecting this. The client and her spouse have one child together who is middle school age. The client recently has increased her alcohol intake, is struggling to get up for work on time, and has taken 8 sick days over the past 4 months because of the difficulty she is having getting up for work.

Role-play: Invite two students to volunteer to role-play a brief counseling session in front of the class, or have students break up into pairs and role-play with each other. One student will take on the role of the counselor and the other the client.

Write: Using the SOAP note example to guide you, as if this client were truly a part of your caseload, write down five to seven statements of what you might want to include in the subjective portion of the SOAP note. Hint: See Table 6.4 for case note writing tips.

Example:

Subjective: Client reported since the recent separation from her spouse she is having difficulty getting out of bed in the mornings for work and has taken more sick days in the past few months than she has taken in the past few years. Client reported that on nights her son is staying with her spouse she notices she has started to increase her alcohol intake. Client expressed feeling "down," having low energy, and not enjoying the things she used to love about her life less and less. Client stated she wants to reconcile with her spouse but is fearful he will not be open to resolving their issues. Client stated she wants to use counseling to help her "get through this" and become "stronger as a parent and wife." Client stated she has not had any thoughts of self-harm or ending her life.

ELEMENTS OF GOOD CLINICAL DOCUMENTATION

Knowing how to create good clinical documentation is not inherent and is often learned through experience. However, knowing the elements of good clinical documentation can provide beginning counselors with a helpful foundation of practical knowledge. Essentially, good clinical documentation is purposeful, ethical, and comprehensible. There are many ways to write case notes, and we examined some of the more common types and formats in this chapter. We now focus on some common elements to include in a client's case file.

When writing in a client's file, the client's welfare is an ethical priority. The Code of Ethics (ACA, 2014) acknowledges the ethical duty of counselors to create, maintain, and keep client records safe and out of the hands of those the information is not meant for. Records must be created in a sufficient and timely manner to enable appropriate and continuous care. Luepker (2012) argues that counselors should write progress notes promptly after each session and states that this is why the "50-minute hour" emerged, referring to how most counseling sessions are structured to last 50 minutes, so the counselor has a 10-minute window to write down the most salient aspects from session and

TABLE 6.5 ■ Time-Sensitive Documentation	
Child Protective Services (CPS) reporting	The report must be created no later than 48 hours after there is belief that a child has suffered abuse or neglect.
Adult Protective Services (APS) reporting	The report must be made immediately upon becoming aware of abuse, neglect, or exploitation.
Case notes	No specified time frame; however, it is best and most ethical practice to write all case notes within a 24 hours so the practitioner can document the most accurate information.

Regulations may vary based on state-to-state differences in protocol. Please check the guidelines for mandated reporters in the state your counseling program is located and in any state you intend to practice.

squeeze in some brief self-care (p. 24). In certain circumstances, there is an allotted time frame for creating certain clinical documents, like suspected child abuse reports and case notes from client interactions. In some cases, there is not a specific time in which certain documentation must be created; however, keeping client records as up to date as possible is an ethical responsibility that must not be taken lightly to ensure the accuracy of the information included. Examples of time-sensitive client information counselors may be asked to document are included in Table 6.5.

CASE ILLUSTRATION 6.1

Vignette: Documentation to Ensure the Safety of Minors

Mary is a student counselor working with Jenna, a 12-year-old girl, whose father has brought her to counseling after learning she has been making complaints about being bullied at school to her principal. Mary uses a lot of play therapy–based techniques when working with children, for she believes it helps children become more comfortable. Today in session Jenna disclosed that her father sometimes hits her repeatedly with a metal cooking spatula when upset with her. When the session ended, Mary approached her supervisor to describe what Jenna had disclosed in session. Mary struggled believing Jenna's remarks, stating she believed the father was too caring to harm Jenna and that Jenna's statements could have been "make-believe." After a discussion over CPS reporting, Mary's supervisor assisted her in appropriate documentation in her case notes and helped Mary with a CPS report. Mary felt like she betrayed the father of her client. The supervisor reminded Mary that Jenna is her client, and her father is not. Keeping Jenna safe was Mary's priority, and she was legally and ethically obligated to include this information in the case notes and report the harm for further investigation to the appropriate authorities.

Conditions for Releasing Notes

Although a counselor and client engage in a professional relationship that encompasses confidentiality, if subpoenaed by a judge, the counselor is legally obligated to comply by releasing the specific clinical documentation requested (ACA, 2013). The legal system often brings counselors and client records into courtrooms because under certain circumstances documentation is needed to protect child welfare, involuntarily hospitalize individuals who are dangerous to self or others, and for other situations that might involve the client behaving unethically (Mitchell, 2007). The ACA (2014) Code of Ethics specifically outlines codes related to respect for confidentiality as it pertains to clinical documentation and court-ordered disclosure and recommends that if information must be disclosed, "only essential information is revealed" (B.1.c., B.2.d., &, B.2.e., p. 7). Case notes can be released under the following conditions:

- A judge (not just any legal or government personnel) subpoenas the counselor and specifically requests the counselor provide case notes for the client (ACA, 2013). Additionally, the ACA (2013) advises counselors to seek legal advice if subpoenaed to provide client records. Additionally, if the records pertain to multiple individuals, such as records subpoenaed for a couple (for a situation such as child custody or a divorce hearing), you will need both individuals to authorize the release of records before you can comply.

- The client has signed a document often called "Consent for Release of Information," a contract that specifically outlines to whom and for what purposes information can be shared, along with what can be shared. In order for the counselor to talk to anyone, he or she must get permission to share anything related to their counseling relationship prior to the release of the information. It is common for individuals to share aspects of counseling such as attendance records with employers, probation officers, and educational personnel.

GUIDED PRACTICE EXERCISE 6.5

Ms. Jackson left the counseling office after her son Anthony's appointment in a hurry and forgot to get a note stating her son attended counseling services today. When returning her son to school, Ms. Jackson realized she forgot the note and got a very judgmental reaction from the school administrator when she showed up without his appointment verification document. The school counselor happened to pass by and noticed that Ms. Jackson seemed stressed out and offered to help her with the situation.

You are Anthony's counselor. You receive a call from a woman named Eva, who states she is the school counselor at a school where you know Anthony attends. She informs you of the situation and asks if you will verbally verify or e-mail her the document Ms. Jackson forgot. You do not have a release on file that gives you permission to discuss your counseling relationship with Anthony with anyone else. *What do you do?*

Solution: The most ethical way to handle the situation is not to provide Eva, the school counselor, or anyone else who is not Ms. Jackson or Anthony any information because you do not have legal consent to. Now aware of the situation, you could call Ms. Jackson and explain to her that you would be more than happy to give the information to the school but that you need her to come back to your office and give her written permission to speak with certain individuals at her son's school first. This way you will have maintained your client's confidentiality and avoided disclosing records you do not yet have permission to share. Verbal permission is not a permissible reason to breach confidentiality; it absolutely must be in writing.

Why are clinical documentation and record keeping so important? The short response to this question is *for the sake of both the client and the counselor*. As a counselor, documentation serves as personal proof of ethical service delivery. Case notes "tell the story" of what happened through the course of service delivery. If a counselor were to be accused of unethical practice, having documentation of following ethical procedures serves as evidence for ethical practice. This is imperative, for counselors will be held responsible for the welfare of the client, which stands true for both intended and unintended harm that may occur. A counselor will have to endure both legal and ethical consequences should any harm occur, which may result in malpractice lawsuits or even having a professional license revoked.

Because clients seek counseling for a variety of personal reasons, counselors must recognize that a power differential exists between client and counselor. In the counseling relationship, the client is the seeker of services, and the counselor is the service provider. This dynamic puts clients in a vulnerable position and counselors in a position of authority. This is true regardless of the therapeutic approach chosen. A counselor using a person-centered approach may see the counseling relationship as two humans interacting; however, the power differential still exists. Justly, the counselor is responsible for the client's welfare for the duration of the counseling relationship. Counselors have an ethical duty to aspire to help their clients become autonomous human beings, as described in the ACA Code of Ethics that promotes the core value of autonomy. Consequently, record keeping is the counselor's way of documenting the intentionality behind each interaction and a place to justify therapeutic decisions made to ensure the welfare of the client during the counseling relationship.

CASE ILLUSTRATION 6.2

Vignette: Case Worker Custody Case

A counselor who self-contracts with various agencies was given the opportunity to conduct family therapy in the home of the Garcia and Ross family. Ms. Garcia disclosed that the reason she was seeking counseling services for her family involved a new living arrangement where she and her two sons were blending families with her boyfriend and his two daughters. The counselor met with Ms. Garcia and Mr. Ross first to receive legal consent to speak with their children after discussing their primary concerns and goals for the family. The counselor decided it could be helpful to meet with the children privately after the consent was signed and confidentiality was reviewed to the kids in a way they understood.

The counselor explained to the children what family counseling is and why sometimes it can be helpful to families who are going through various transitions. In the first few minutes of the meeting with the children, Ms. Garcia's oldest son disclosed that his mother told him she wanted the family to do family counseling so they could take away their father's custody rights. Immediately the counselor felt uneasy, for this was not brought up prior to agreement to work with the family. If this was the case, the counselor might have to submit all clinical documentation from services with the family to a judge, if subpoenaed, and possibly even testify on the family's behalf.

A good rule of thumb with ethical record keeping is *if you didn't document it, it never happened*. Counselors must ensure client records accurately reflect client progress and the services provided. The Code of Ethics (ACA, 2014) generously accommodates creating new methods of documentation, such as electronic or digital record keeping methods, which are discussed later in this chapter. Despite the legal and ethical importance of clinical record keeping, uniform standards as to what should be included in case files do not exist. Standards vary from setting to setting and across states. Information required at a clinical mental health clinic may not be as important for a counselor working in private practice. Individuals should make sure they are familiar with the standards adopted by their setting and document accordingly. Although not consistent across all settings, there are some common elements you can expect to see in a client's record. These elements are highlighted in Table 6.6.

TABLE 6.6 ■ Relevant Information to Document

Client interactions	Phone calls, e-mails, voice mails, or mail correspondence between client and counselor
Client attendance	What days did the client attend services, and for what duration? When specifically did the client cancel? Did the client miss the session, without canceling?
Formal diagnosis and diagnostic impressions (Luepker, 2012)	Do you have access to previous formal diagnoses? Can you justify the course of chosen treatment with the given diagnostic impression?
Medication (current and historical) (Luepker, 2012)	Is the client taking any prescribed medication? How long has the client been taking this medication? Is the client taking the medication as prescribed? Has the medication prescription changed over the course of treatment? Has the client been previously prescribed other medications?
Types of services delivered	Individual counseling, family counseling, couples counseling, group counseling
Treatment plans (ACA, 2014, A.1.c.)	What is the client's presenting problem? What goals are you currently working on? What progress has been made? Is there a specific way progress is being tracked? What therapeutic interventions are being incorporated into treatment?
Plans to prevent self-harm or harm to others	Was there recently suicidal or homicidal intent? Is the client currently suicidal or homicidal? How intense are these thoughts? How frequent are these thoughts? Has the client previously attempted to harm self or others? Include any referral information, such as suicide hotlines, local hospitals, and other community resources to assist the client when you are unavailable.
Client billing information (Luepker, 2012)	Insurance information, payment information, late or missed payments

GUIDED PRACTICE EXERCISE 6.6

Pair up with another student in class and role-play. One student portrays the role of the counselor and the other the client. In this role-play, the client is having suicidal ideations and the counselor is tasked with assessing the severity of these thoughts. At the end of the role-play, the counselor is to document what occurred in a case note. Together, discuss what was recorded and what else the counselor may have wanted to document.

All clinical documentation should include information such as the date, time, and *purpose* for the interaction (Luepker, 2012). This seems obvious; however, this information is fundamental to creating purposeful clinical documentation. Perhaps a counselor calls a client to cancel a session because she is ill and will not come to the office as previously planned. When the counselor calls the client to cancel, the counselor should document specifically *when* the interaction took place. It will also be important for the counselor to document *who* initiated the cancellation and *why* services were cancelled. This information is necessary when documenting because it creates an accurate description of contact between the client and the counselor to be included in client records.

To illustrate our point, consider a situation where a client has cancelled on a counselor three consecutive times at a clinic where an attendance policy is in place that asserts a counseling relationship can be terminated after three consecutive cancellations. When reviewing this client's records, it will be important to know that the client repeatedly chose not to receive services and initiated the cancellations. Now, picture a scenario where a counselor cancels on a client for three consecutive sessions with no reason mentioned. For ethical reasons, it will be important to know the counselor chose not to provide services repeatedly for the client. The reasons for knowing some of the details surrounding these various situations are all essential to understanding if a counselor is engaging with clients ethically. These two examples demonstrate a situation where a counselor can appropriately terminate a counseling relationship and a situation with possible client abandonment. These examples highlight the relevance for creating purposeful documentation that includes all necessary information.

A second element of good clinical documentation is that it is *ethical*. This concept has already been interwoven throughout this chapter. Although the ethical element of good clinical documentation has been mentioned before, it is an element that deserves the utmost clarity. The counselor must create accurate documentation (ACA, 2014). Because clinical documentation is how the profession safeguards service delivery and quality control of counseling services, records need to accurately reflect a client's situation. A counselor should not manipulate information in any way and must document information in the truest sense. Counselors should be careful to avoid falsifying records to make clients seem like they are making progress when they are not or that they are in contact with a client more often than they are. The counselor should document how the client is doing in the present, while differentiating the client's prognosis from the client's here-and-now experience.

Counselors are cautioned to be careful about what is included in their case notes (Cameron & Turtle-Song, 2002). They should be mindful of what may intentionally be included or excluded and the reasons for inserting or leaving out certain information. Ethically, case notes should not be manipulated to protect a client. Deliberately omitted information that intentionally or unintentionally could cause harm to others could put counselors at risk for sanctions up to and including losing their professional licenses. A key task for clinical supervisors involves the obligation to "monitor client welfare" and "services provided by the supervisee" (ACA, 2014, p. 12), which can pertain to providing support for understanding the ethics behind certain components and processes related to record keeping. New counselors should request consultation when they first begin to write case notes. Seeking consultation with a more experienced counselor or supervisor ensures the clinical documentation created meets the ethical standards of the profession and is not placing the counselor in a position of liability. Supervisors also can help new counselors process their experiences with their clients to help them understand what absolutely needs to be included in the record and what may be more conjecture.

Third, good clinical documentation is *comprehensible*. Counselors summarize when documenting client interactions, giving only necessary details in a way that is logical and coherent. Because the counselor is chiefly concerned with reflecting accurate information while protecting a client's right to confidentiality, the counselor will only include the most relevant and important information (Luepker, 2012). A key reason for doing so is counselors are ethically responsible to "protect the confidential information of prospective and current clients" (ACA, 2014, p. 7). Case notes, for example, create a succinct summary of counseling sessions. The counselor wants to describe what is most significant to include from the session. Often the content of a session note is based on treatment objectives. For a client who is experiencing anxiety, describing how the client reported having two panic attacks over this past week would be more relevant than stating the client reported having "an okay week." Typically, a case note will include five to seven brief statements about the overall session. The case note typically serves as documentation of the interaction but additionally serves as a reminder for the counselor. Documenting a limited amount of information from the interaction will both serve to protect the client's confidentiality and help the counselor remember key aspects of interactions with clients.

CASE ILLUSTRATION 6.3

Vignette: Using Direct Quotes

Marie reports she has been having trouble sleeping and has recently suffered from a poor appetite since her youngest child moved off to college.

Marie expressed feeling sad and depressed and described her feelings "like a dark cloud lives above me."

However, there are times when a counselor should bypass a succinct summary of the session and provide greater detail. This would be the case when the counselor determines the safety of the client or the safety of someone the client knows is in jeopardy. In instances where a client has expressed either suicidal or homicidal ideation, the counselor should include more detailed information in the case note and include components such as any preventative action taken by the counselor and suicide warning signs (Luepker,

2012). A documented risk assessment is usually the most appropriate course of action in these circumstances. Details in this situation demonstrate the counselor is doing the required due diligence to understand the extent of the client's situation to immediately offer the most effective help. Because harm to self (suicide) or others constitutes a breach in confidentiality, the counselor needs to document all relevant details to understand the safety of all individuals involved in the situation and the reasons why acting on these client disclosures was warranted. A listing of key suicide risk assessment questions is included in Table 6.7.

MAINTAINING AND SECURING CLINICAL RECORDS AND DOCUMENTATION

To ensure an individual's health and medical information are kept private and protected, a federal law known as the Health Insurance Portability and Accountability Act (HIPAA, 1996) establishes rules for who can look at, receive, and use this personal information as well as measures health care providers must take to protect the confidentiality, integrity,

TABLE 6.7 ■ Key Suicide Risk Assessment Questions to Ask and Document	
Suicidal ideation	Have you had thoughts of harming yourself or ending your life? What has been going on in your life to make you have thoughts like this?
Suicidal planning (means)	If you decided to try to end your life, how would you do it? Can you tell me about any plans you may have already made?
Access to means	You mentioned that if you were to hurt yourself, you'd probably do it by [describe method]. How easy would it be for you to do this?
Protective factors	What are some reasons that would stop you or prevent you from trying to hurt yourself? What holds you back from actually doing it?
Past experiences	What have been your past experiences of attempting to hurt yourself? What other people do you know who have tried to or have ended their own life?
Future expectations	What are some of the things happening in your life or likely to happen in your life right now that would make you more or less likely to want to hurt yourself? How do you think people who know you would react if you killed yourself? What would they say, think, or feel?

GUIDED PRACTICE EXERCISE 6.7

Digital record keeping is becoming more popular among counselors and practice settings. However, many clients remain apprehensive about its use and potential data breaches. How would you explain to a client the safety of this format should you work at a setting that uses such a system?

and security of the information. Included in this act are two specific rules. The HIPAA Privacy Rule establishes national standards for how individually identifiable information is to be protected and kept private. Within this rule, the term **confidentiality** refers to ensuring client information only be disclosed to authorized individuals. The HIPAA Security Rule sets national standards for securing personal health information (PHI) recorded electronically. Specifically, counseling providers must take reasonable measures to maintain appropriate administrative, technical, and physical safeguards for protecting PHI. These include the following:

1. Ensuring the confidentiality, integrity, and availability of all PHI personally created, received, maintained, or transmitted

2. Identifying and protecting against reasonably anticipated threats to the security or integrity of the PHI

3. Protecting against reasonably anticipated, impermissible (unauthorized) uses or disclosures

4. Ensuring compliance by other mental health professionals with access to the client's record and PHI

One step counselors can take to help protect client confidentiality is deidentifying the client in the case file. **Deidentification** is a process used to prevent a client's identity from relating to information found in a case file. One approach to deidentifying a case file is known as the *safe harbor* method. Using this approach, the counselor ensures that personally identifying information is expunged from the client file. This relates to information about the client or the client's immediate family. According to federal guidelines, 18 pieces of information classified as identifying information would need to be removed. This information is listed in Table 6.8.

TABLE 6.8 ■ Identifying Information to Remove From Client File Using the Safe Harbor Method

Name	Address	Dates (birth, admission, treatment, discharge)
Telephone numbers	Vehicle identification numbers or license plate numbers	Fax numbers
Device identifiers or serial numbers	E-mail addresses	Website URLs
Social security number	Internet protocol (IP) addresses	Medical record numbers
Biometric identifiers (fingerprints, voice recordings)	Health plan beneficiary numbers	Photographs or videos
Account numbers or client file record numbers	Certificate or license numbers	Code numbers

Although case files may still be kept in hard-copy format, many counselors are now using digital records in their practice. This new technology has afforded counselors great flexibility and in many ways facilitated the delivery of counseling services. However, challenges also exist in using this medium. The following section talks more about the growing use of electronic digital records in counseling practice.

ELECTRONIC DIGITAL RECORD KEEPING

The counseling field is one of the most progressive professions in adapting to the influence of emergent technology. This means counselors must be flexible to adapting to newer and potentially more effective ways of keeping up with client data digitally. Historically (and still in some settings today), client documentation and records were created with pen and paper (in some cases electronic word documents that are printed), stored in individual files, and often secured in locked filing cabinets. When clients are terminated, the client file is relocated somewhere else to be stored with the load of other documentation and records from previous clients, often left to take up space and collect dust. Counselors are legally and ethically required to maintain records for several years depending on the client's age and to ensure clients have access to their records for a certain amount of time. Over time, technology has created a way for counselors to create secure paperless systems that are easier to access and conserve physical space.

Electronic record keeping involves the use of many different mediums to improve the accuracy and efficiency of creating and storing client records. Most electronic record-keeping software can be easily downloaded onto any type of computer and involves storage onto cloud-like digital platforms with certain security settings in place. A number of software programs for electronic record keeping have been created specifically for professional counselors, designed to meet the unique needs of the profession. Some formats presently used are Yellow Schedule, Therapy Notes, and the Care Logic Enterprise. Electronic record-keeping software varies in capabilities, so the counselor should research the software options before committing to purchase.

Types of Electronic Record-Keeping Software

Most commonly, users pay a monthly or annual fee for software that can be easily downloaded onto any type of computer. Software features vary but often include the ability to create case notes, schedule clients, and assist with billing.

Yellow Schedule

This software uses Google Calendar and a network based on a cloud that syncs to a computer, tablet, or other mobile devices. Yellow Schedule allows the counselor to schedule appointments, process payments, create client notes, and schedule automated reminders. Yellow Schedule encrypts, backs up, and stores all data in a HIPAA compliant manner. This software has demonstrated the ability to increase revenue and to reduce the amount of times clients miss a session without cancelling. Clients can confirm appointment attendance within seconds after receiving a text or e-mail reminder. Individual and group rates are available, starting at $29.95 per month.

Therapy Notes

This software can be easily downloaded to any web browser and allows the counselor to schedule appointments and keep up with a professional to-do list. Other capabilities of this software include a system that allows the counselor to create progress notes and treatment plans conveniently and in little time. Therapy Notes also includes electronic billing and a patient portal. The patient portal allows clients and the counselor to communicate in a HIPAA friendly online environment that has been deemed secure. Therapy Notes also regularly backs up all digital data. Unlimited technical support, by phone or e-mail, is also available. This software can be purchased for $59 per month when purchased individually.

Care Logic Enterprise

Created by the company Qualifacts, the Care Logic Enterprise is a HIPAA compliant software built for larger health care providers. This software also is a program downloaded onto a cloud-like structure known as a single enterprise platform. Some of the key features of this software include the ability to share information across a large system of employees, compare performance among peers, track short- and long-term progress of an agency, and track client progress over time. The main appeal of this software is the ability to share information among mental health professionals with administrators when many clients are involved. This program is built to an agency's customized needs and offers a pay-as-you-go plan, as opposed to a flat rate per month. Qualifacts offers in-person training, as well as live online training and webinars to Care Logic Enterprise users.

Encryption and Data Backup

According to the Code of Ethics (ACA, 2014), counselors are held ethically responsible for securing client records and documentation in any medium and must ensure that only authorized persons have access to this information. Although ethical standards acknowledge counselors must keep files away from unauthorized individuals, and clients must be informed about third-party companies that have access to client data for purposes like billing, the Code of Ethics has not specifically acknowledged that devices must be encrypted.

HIPAA (2007) states digital records must be secured so individuals who have access to the files (like tech support or other individuals who work for the software company) cannot share or modify client data. Encryption through password-protected data storage is commonly recommended to be HIPAA compliant. Encrypted flash drives and computers with individual user passwords are ways this criterion can be met.

Because the counselor must ensure that clients have access to their records upon request and must secure and maintain client records, it is also in the counselor's best interest to have some type of backup system to ensure that digital records can be revived if technology were to ever unpredictably delete client data. Most software programs for electronic record keeping have varying degrees of encryption when automatic backups take place. Counselors must remain extremely cautious when choosing a software program to make sure the company doesn't share information with third parties when backing up information. Dropbox (2011), for example, has a clause letting users know it will share information with others if it finds it "reasonably necessary" to disclose the information to law enforcement or other authorities. However, if the counselor encrypts all client data before backing the data up, most backup systems will not be able to decrypt the data. It is in the counselor's best interest to carefully select electronic record-keeping software and become well acquainted with the program of choice to ensure data are efficiently encrypted and backed up appropriately.

Advantages to Electronic Record Keeping

There are many advantages to using electronic record keeping as a counselor. Electronic record keeping has streamlined the way records are kept and maintained by the counselor. A major advantage of electronic record-keeping systems is that they free up more of the counselor's time. Insurance companies typically only reimburse the counselor for time spent with the client, meaning the counselor does not get paid for the time spent preparing for session or in record keeping. When use of electronic record-keeping software frees up more of the counselor's time, the counselor can increase the number of hours spent with clients. This allows the counselor to extend services to other clients and can increase a counselor's overall revenue.

Electronic record keeping allows the counselor to access client records quickly and conveniently. In the managed care system, counselors often work with other professionals like psychiatrists or case managers. A digital system may provide individuals with access to the most up-to-date information, thus increasing the overall quality of client care and decreasing barriers to communication among health care professionals as well as the counselor with insurance companies.

Another advantage to electronic record keeping is the conservation of space. Regardless of the setting, whether it's a small private practice or a large behavioral health agency, with paper-based systems the counselor must allocate portions of revenue to maintaining enough space to store and access client data. This could mean having to allocate entire rooms or floors for storage at an agency; an individual with a private practice may have to pay for private storage in paper-based systems. Hard drives and flash drives are exponentially smaller when compared with endless shelves of client records. With cloud-like storage structures in place on the Internet, data storage can be virtual. Electronic methods essentially have the potential to decrease operating costs if the counselor or agency doesn't need as much space to store data.

Disadvantages to Electronic Record Keeping

Technology has created many major enhancements for clinical record keeping; however, technology is not immune to error. One major disadvantage of electronic record keeping involves data loss, which may occur if the technology, such as a USB flash drive or computer hard drive, becomes physically damaged. Counselors will be held liable for any damaged information and must keep records and allow clients access to them to maintain their license to practice. Another serious disadvantage involves the risk of a breach in confidentiality, which can occur if a software program is not fully secure. The Code of Ethics (ACA, 2014) does not specifically outline the measures a counselor needs to take to ensure data is secure. Despite these ambiguous terms, the counselor must adhere to the ethical standard in place, meaning the counselor must make an educated decision about the best way to meet the standards set forth by the Code of Ethics. The counselor is responsible for protecting all digital data and securely backing up all data stored electronically.

Electronic record keeping also may be time-consuming during the set-up phase or conversion from paper record-keeping methods. Although many software programs aim at saving the counselor time through a streamlined process, the counselor may need to spend time selecting a program, for maintaining client confidentiality is crucial to ethical practice. The counselor will also need to spend time becoming familiar with the software's features to learn how to effectively use it. Another issue for counselors to be aware of involves the marketing of "HIPAA compliant" software programs. No official certification is required for software manufacturers to make this claim, so the buyer is ultimately responsible if the software company markets its software this way but does not meet current HIPAA (2007) standards.

Whether counselors use digital or hard-copy records, maintaining client welfare is of utmost importance. In this chapter we discussed several elements of clinical record keeping and best practices to help you maintain ethical and effective case files.

Keystones

- Clinical record keeping is part of a counselor's ethical responsibility and duty to clients served. Every effort should be made to ensure client welfare is maintained.

- Client records include various information. Counselors should be familiar with the methods of collecting this information and be able to understand and incorporate it into the counseling process.

- Confidentiality is important in keeping client records. Counselors must actively work to protect the identities of their clients and the unauthorized use or release of their personal health information (PHI).

- Electronic digital record keeping is becoming a more common part of counseling practice. The use of electronic records has both its advantages and disadvantages. Counselors should be familiar with both and make informed decisions whether to use based on the best interests of their clients and counseling practice.

Key Terms

Assent 141

Case notes 151

Confidentiality 164

Consent 139

Deidentification 164

Informed consent
   documents 139

Mental status examination 147

Psychosocial assessment 141

Treatment plans 150

Web Resources

APA Mental Health Progress Note Templates (https://www.apadivisions.org/division-31/publications/records/progress.aspx)

TheraNest: Free Note Templates and Intake Forms (https://www.theranest.com/resources/counseling-note-templates/)

References

American Counseling Association. (2013). De-identified composite call made to the ACA sponsored risk management helpline. Retrieved from https://www.counseling.org/docs/default-source/risk-management/august_13_subpoenas.pdf

American Counseling Association. (2014). *ACA code of ethics*. Alexandria, VA: Author.

Barnett, J. E., & Johnson, B. W. (2014). *Ethics desk reference for counselors* (2nd ed.). New York, NY: Wiley.

Berman, P. S. (2015). *Case conceptualization and treatment planning: Integrating theory with clinical practice* (3rd ed.). Thousand Oaks, CA: Sage.

Brennan, C. (2013). Ensuring ethical practice: Guidelines for mental health counselors in private practice. *Journal of Mental Health Counseling, 35*(3), 245–261. doi:10.17744/mehc.35.3.9706313j4t313397

Cameron, S., & Turtle-Song, I. (2002). Learning to write case notes using the SOAP format. *Journal of Counseling & Development, 80*(3), 286–292. doi:10.1002/j.1556-6678.2002.tb00193.x

Carney, J. M., & Jefferson, J. F. (2014). Consultation for mental health counselors: Opportunities and guidelines for private practice. *Journal of Mental Health Counseling, 36*(4), 302–314. doi:10.17744/mehc.36.4.821133r0414u37v7

Corey, G., Corey, M. S., Corey, C., & Callanan, P. (2014). *Issues and ethics in the helping professions with 2014 ACA codes*. Stamford, CT: Cengage Learning.

Dropbox. (2011, July). Dropbox privacy policy. Retrieved from http://www.dropbox.com/privacy

Health Insurance Portability and Accountability Act. (2007). Retrieved from http://www.access.gpo.gov/nara/cfr/waisidx_07/45cfr164_07.html

Hedberg, A. (2010). *Forms for the therapist*. New York, NY: Academic Press.

Hodges, S. (2015). *The counseling practicum and internship manual: A resource for graduate counseling students* (2nd ed.). New York, NY: Springer.

Luepker, E. T. (2012). *Record keeping in psychotherapy and counseling: Protecting confidentiality and the professional relationship* (2nd ed.) New York, NY: Routledge.

Martin, D. C. (1990). The mental status examination. In H. K. Walker, W. D. Hall, & J. W. Hurst (Eds.), *Clinical methods: The history, physical, and laboratory examinations*. (3rd ed.). Boston, MA: Butterworths.

Mitchell, R. W. (2007). *Documentation in counseling records: An overview of ethical, legal, and clinical issues* (3rd ed.). Alexandria, VA: American Counseling Association.

Parsons, R. D., & Zhang, N. (2014). *Becoming a skilled counselor*. Thousand Oaks, CA: Sage.

Prieto, L. R., & Scheel, K. R. (2002). Using case documentation to strengthen counselor trainees' case conceptualization skills. *Journal of Counseling & Development, 80*(1), 11–21. doi:10.1002/j.1556-6678.2002.tb00161.x

Seligman, L. (2004). *Diagnosis and treatment planning in counseling* (3rd ed.). New York, NY: Springer.

United States. (1996). The Health Insurance Portability and Accountability Act (HIPAA). Washington, D.C.: U.S. Dept. of Labor, Employee Benefits Security Administration.

Weed, L. L. (1964). Medical records, patient care and medical evaluation. *Irish Journal of Medicine, 278*, 593–600, 652–657.

Wheeler, A. M., & Bertram, B. (2015). *The counselor and the law: A guide to legal and ethical practice* (7th ed.). Alexandria, VA: American Counseling Association.

Wiger, D. E. (2010). *The clinical documentation sourcebook* (4th ed.). New York, NY: Wiley.

Wiger, D. E. (2011). *The psychotherapy documentation primer* (3rd ed.). New York, NY: Wiley.

WORKING WITH MANAGED CARE AND THIRD-PARTY REIMBURSEMENT AGENCIES

Whether directly billing third-party payers for counseling services rendered or prospective clients asking if you accept their type of insurance, dealing with managed care and insurance companies is an ever-present reality for the 21st-century mental health counselor. A common reaction by newer counselors navigating the myriad rules and regulations stipulated by managed care is one of frustration and surprise. However, much of the strife associated with managed care comes from counselors' lack of knowledge and preparation with how it directly impacts their practice. This is not to say that managed care does not have its challenges, and many seasoned counselors would advise those entering the profession to avoid accepting insurance payments altogether. Although their expressions of caution are not unwarranted, they are certainly incomplete. Therefore, it is prudent for counselors who plan to accept insurance to familiarize themselves with managed care—way in advance. As you begin exploring what managed care entails, consider the benefits of accepting third-party payments for counselors: a consistent referral source, a low-cost form of advertisement, a continuous revenue stream, and an opportunity to build a reputation, just to name a few.

As you will see in this chapter, the prominence of managed care in the 21st century continues to be a major determinant in how clinical mental health counselors practice. We begin this chapter by exploring exactly what managed care is and the types of health maintenance organizations available. Next, we explore the concept of provider panel status for clinical mental counselors. Then, we jump into selecting appropriate treatment approaches covered under managed care. Finally, we finish with how to file claims and document treatment efforts and shed light on claim disputes and the appeals process in managed care.

LEARNING OBJECTIVES

After reading this chapter, you will be able to do the following:

- Differentiate between the various types of managed care organizations relevant to clinical mental health counselors

- Identify the practice and management issues associated with managed care that affect clinical mental health counselors (CACREP 5C-2-m)

- Identify and describe the two major legislative policies affecting clinical mental health counselors working in managed care systems (CACREP 5C-2-i)

- Demonstrate appropriate record-keeping strategies that document treatment efforts in managed care and third-party payer systems (CACREP 5C-2-m)

- Describe the claim filing, disputation, and appeals process for third-party payer systems (CACREP 5C-2-m)

Provision of health care services in the United States has drastically changed since the 1980s. Then, physicians were sole decision-makers of patients' care, determining the type, frequency, and intensity of treatment interventions using a fee-for-service system of payment. A **fee-for-service system** is a payment model that itemizes each service component, which maximizes the quantity of services provided. Pharmaceutical companies targeted physicians who had discretion in deciding which medications to prescribe their patients (Carson, 1997). As you might recognize, in this unregulated fee-for-service system, physicians and pharmaceutical companies were quite profitable, often at the expense of employers and patients. One solution to the rise in health care costs was the advent of managed care.

The passage of the Health Maintenance Organization Act in 1973 spurred the promotion and development of health maintenance organizations (HMOs) as a mechanism to control the rising costs of health care in the United States. This federal statue, which challenged the status quo of unregulated fee-for-service systems, created opportunities for alternatives. To support development of HMOs, the federal government provided qualified HMOs access to funding, indemnity from state laws, and greater access to employer-based health insurance. Although mental health counseling was not at the forefront of the managed care revolution, its effects are well evident in how clinical mental health counselors provide counseling services today.

HMOs, PPOs, POS, AND EPOs

So, what exactly is managed care? **Managed care** is an umbrella term used to describe a practice or set of practices that provides oversight in the delivery of health care services. The philosophy behind managed care is to provide cost-effective services while ensuring the appropriateness and quality of those services. More specifically, managed care systems have agreements with certain hospitals, care providers, and health care practitioners (e.g., physicians, psychiatrists, counselors) to provide a defined set of services to their members at an agreed-on price. Although opinions differ as to whether managed care has benefited the U.S. health care system, some considerations to keep in mind are that managed care (a) reduces health care costs, (b) creates a network of readily available providers, (c) expedites information among in-network providers, and (d) provides access to affordable health care services. Conversely, criticisms of managed care include its (a) restricted access to services and providers of care, (b) exclusionary practices based on preexisting conditions, and (c) quality of services provided.

So, why is it important for clinical mental health counselors to be familiar with managed care? Managed care guidelines determine if counselors are eligible to provide services and stipulate how those services should be provided and whether they are reimbursable (Braun & Cox, 2005). With passage of the Patient Protection and Affordable Care Act in 2010, commonly referred to as the Affordable Care Act (ACA), health care coverage expanded for millions of Americans in both the private and public health care systems. The greatest benefit of the ACA occurred primarily through eligibility for and expansion of Medicaid programs at the state level. The act also prohibited existing health plans from placing dollar limits on lifetime coverage of services, which includes counseling and many others (American Counseling Association, 2012). As a result, millions of Americans not previously covered under any health care insurance or previously limited by their current health plans now have greater access to mental health and substance abuse services. As you can imagine, having a working knowledge of managed care is important for clinical mental health counselors who rely on insurance reimbursement for services they provide. Let's continue our conversation by exploring the four major types of managed care programs counselors often encounter: HMOs, PPOs, POS, and EPOs.

HMOs

Health maintenance organization (HMO) plans are a type of managed care that focuses on preventative care and utilization management. **Utilization management** is defined as "a set of techniques used by or on behalf of purchasers of health care benefits to manage health care costs by influencing patient care decision-making through case-by-case assessments of the appropriateness of care prior to its provision" (Committee on Utilization Management by Third Parties & Institute of Medicine, 1989, p. 17). In other words, utilization management mitigates unnecessary health care costs by ensuring services are medically necessary. HMOs not only finance medical care, they also provide it and include doctors, hospitals, specialists, clinics, and insurers.

In HMO plans, primary care physicians (PCPs) serve as the first point of contact for all medical care. They are often identified as "gatekeepers" because members of an HMO must first choose their PCP; the PCP offers both general medical care and referrals for specialist services, if deemed necessary. A key cost-saving feature of HMOs is that medical services are provided on a prepaid basis because HMOs use only contracted doctors and other service providers or entities that are part of the HMO network. As a result, policyholders are only allowed to seek medical care with in-network providers, which can vary in size depending on the HMO. Some advantages of HMOs include low out-of-pocket cost, stability in price over time, and a focus on preventative care. Another advantage is policyholders pay a set price each month for the HMO plan, and there are no limits placed on how often medical care services can be used. Some disadvantages of HMOs include challenges in receiving specialized care, no coverage for out-of-network services, and limited to no freedom of choice.

PPOs

Similar to HMOs, preferred provider organizations (PPOs) contract with doctors, hospitals, clinics, and so forth to create a network of providers. The in-network providers, known as "preferred providers," have agreed with insurers to provide health care services at a reduced rate. PPO policyholders who seek providers in network are often charged a low copayment; monthly premiums are generally paid for by sponsors or employers on behalf of policyholders. Sponsors or employers in contract with PPOs increase patient volume, which can reduce both deductibles and copayments, although amounts vary depending on the sponsor or employer.

Unlike HMOs, PPOs offer more flexibility in selecting providers. A PCP referral in most PPO plans is unnecessary for specialist care. For instance, a person with a PPO plan can choose to receive services with an in-network provider at the established copayment, without a referral if specialized care is sought. However, the same person can choose to seek services from an out-of-network provider, without a referral, and the PPO will cover the expense, although not at the lower in-network price. Because the out-of-network provider has not agreed to a discounted rate for medical services, the additional cost is passed on to the policyholder. Thus, policyholders who stay in network receive care at a lower price than those whose choose to receive care out of network. The major advantage of PPOs and significant difference from HMOs is freer choice in choosing health care providers, although usually at a higher cost. The major disadvantage of PPOs is the substantial cost associated with out-of-network providers.

POS

Point-of-service (POS) plans have characteristics of both HMOs and PPOs. As with HMOs, policyholders must first choose a PCP from a predetermined list of in-network providers and pay minimal copayments for each visit without a deductible. The PCP serves as the "point of service" person who acts as gatekeeper. If policyholders seek specialist services, in or out of network, they must first get a referral from their PCP. Like PPOs, POS plans provide coverage for out-of-network services but usually at a higher cost when compared to in-network providers. However, POS plans tend to pay more toward out-of-network services if referred by a PCP. If an out-of-network provider is chosen, a referral from a PCP is not required, although substantial out-of-pocket costs can be expected. Some advantages of POS plans include maximum freedom of choice, smaller copayments, no deductible when in-network providers are used, and omission of the gatekeeper function for chosen out-of-network providers. Some disadvantages include significant copayments for out-of-network services (especially without a PCP referral), deductibles that must be met before insurance pays for out-of-network services, and the gatekeeper for reduced out-of-network costs.

EPOs

In exclusive provider organizations (EPOs), in-network service providers are used exclusively. The managing entities of EPOs contract exclusively with doctors, psychiatrists, specialists, hospitals, and so forth to form a provider network only accessible to its members. Because policyholders can only choose from in-network providers, referrals for specialist services are not necessary. Some advantages of EPOs include (a) lower premiums as compared to HMOs and PPOs and (b) no need for specialist referrals. A major disadvantage of EPOs is that any service received out of network is completely at the expense of the policyholder. Hence, EPOs may be ideal for the individual who does not foresee major medical expenses or uses medical services infrequently.

Managed care was developed in response to rising health care costs. Some managed care organizations (MCOs) (e.g., EPOs and HMOs) attempt to limit health care costs by restricting policyholders' freedom of choice in service providers, although a significant benefit to having limited provider options is lower premiums. MCOs such as PPOs and POS plans give policyholders more flexibility in seeking out-of-network care, although this comes at a higher cost in the form of premiums, deductibles, and copayments. So how does all this apply to the counselor? Well, given how managed care is rooted in the U.S. health care system, it behooves counselors to become approved providers in MCO networks. This is discussed further in the next section.

CASE ILLUSTRATION 7.1

Jodi, a recently licensed professional counselor, is opening a private practice and debating whether to accept cash payments, insurance, or both. Although Jodi is not familiar with managed care, she decides to research the strengths and weakness of each organization to make an informed decision of which insurance panels to join. She targets HMO, PPO, POS, and EPO plans in her area. After reviewing the health insurance plans, she discovers that each has its strengths and limitations. For instance, HMO and POS plans will require Jodi's potential clients to obtain a referral before she can provide counseling. Likewise, HMOs may offer lower reimbursement rates for her counseling services. However, should she choose to become paneled on POS plans, her potential clients would have more flexibility in in-network and out-of-network providers and maximum choice in deciding if Jodi is the right counselor for them. Should Jodi decide to become credentialed in POS plans, she may receive lower reimbursement rates, but her caseload may steadily increase if her reputation precedes her because of clients' freedom of choice. She also considers PPOs, which tend to pay higher reimbursements but usually require policyholders to pay higher copays. With PPOs, a PCP referral is unnecessary for her services. Thus, potential clients only have to walk through the door and request her services. Upon completing her research, Jodi determines that being credentialed with local HMO and PPO plans offers her the best reimbursement-to-client-volume ratio. Furthermore, Jodi discovered that most of her community members were insured through HMOs.

GUIDED PRACTICE EXERCISE 7.1

In class, in groups of four, each student takes ownership of a managed care organization (POS, HMO, PPO, EPO) and debates with their partners reasons why their managed care organization is superior. Some areas to focus on include provider network, cost, and freedom of choice. Once the debate ends, as a group, identify any limitations of each managed care organization.

CLINICAL MENTAL HEALTH COUNSELORS AND PROVIDER PANEL STATUS

Imagine working in private practice. You start slow, accepting clients on a cash-only basis, limiting the number of clients on your caseload. Months into it, you realize that your break-even point is far higher than the earnings you bring in based on your cash-only clientele. So you decide to accept more clients, but the majority of them have health insurance and are unwilling to pay cash for counseling services already covered by their insurance plan. You have limited options: continue to see clients who pay cash or begin taking insurance. The first option, as you currently are experiencing, is limiting your clientele because the majority have health insurance and are unwilling to pay cash for services already covered by their health plan. The second option will allow you to accept more clients, which is necessary to successfully continue your counseling practice. Although hesitant, you choose the second option but are unsure of how to start and what steps are required to begin accepting insurance. The first step is to receive provider status from each MCO you are considering.

What Is Provider Status?

Provider status, better known as credentialing, designates a health care provider as being approved by an insurance company or MCO to provide a specific service. In other words, MCOs vet their providers to ensure they meet certain standards before receiving approval status. Without this status, counselors can be denied access to the marketplace, and policyholders may experience limited options when choosing qualified mental health counselors (Hinkle, 1999). Although requirements for provider status vary from one insurance entity to the next, counselors are generally required to be independently licensed to practice in their respected state, have malpractice insurance, and have no disciplinary actions against them. However, just because an ethical or legal infraction exists against the counselor does not automatically bar that counselor from becoming credentialed. Rather, applicants with infractions are further scrutinized by a special committee to determine eligibility.

Not everyone is eligible to become credentialed. Even if you are working toward a degree in counseling, most insurance panels have strict rules against nonlicensed individuals and provider status. This is not to say that licensed professional counselor interns (LPC interns) are not eligible to work with all insurance companies—but doing so often occurs only under special circumstances. The majority of private insurance companies (e.g., Blue Cross Blue Shield, Cigna, United Health) have stricter guidelines than state-regulated insurance plans, which may consider enrolling LPC interns under supervision on insurance panels if a significant provider shortage exists. However, this exception varies across states and insurance plans. Now that you have a general understanding of provider status and the importance of receiving it, let's explore the necessary steps to obtain it.

Obtaining Provider Status

Credentialing can be a time-consuming and task-oriented process, seemingly requiring counselors to "jump through hoops" to have their name and/or practice recognized as an approved provider. Again, it is important to recognize that the credentialing processes may vary by insurance company. Here are some general steps counselors can take to obtain provider status in their state (see Table 7.1 for quick reference): (a) preplan and prepare, (b) obtain an employer identification number, (c) obtain malpractice insurance, (d) familiarize yourself with the taxonomy code, (e) obtain an NPI number, (f) create a profile in CAQH, and (g) review and submit application.

Preplan and Prepare

Although this may sound like a no-brainer, it is important to know what you are getting yourself into. Ask seasoned counselors who have been through the credentialing process. Find out what was most challenging for them, mistakes they made, things they thought went really well, and if they have any tips or suggestions they are willing to share. Given the quasi-standardized process of credentialing, why attempt to reinvent the wheel; rather, seek out wisdom from those who have successfully obtained credentialing. Furthermore, investigate each insurance company for whom you are considering becoming an approved provider. Some important things to consider are reimbursements rates, the claims process, and the service disputes and appeals process. Knowing these things ahead of time can save you major headaches in the future. Finally, you should know your clientele well enough to determine which insurance panels to consider. If you are new to the area, ask other counselors. You may be surprised at how helpful they can be.

TABLE 7.1 ■ Quick Reference: Seven General Steps to Obtaining Provider Status

1. Preplan and prepare

2. Obtain an employer identification number

3. Obtain malpractice insurance

4. Familiarize yourself with the taxonomy code

5. Obtain an NPI number

6. Create a profile in CAQH

7. Review and submit application

Obtain an Employer Identification Number

An employer identification number (EIN) is a nine-digit number used by the Internal Revenue Service to identify your company and is required when submitting an application for credentialing. Most applications also ask for your tax identification number, which is simply your social security number. There are four common ways to apply for an EIN: online or by mail, fax, or telephone, each with varying timetables. The fastest method is online, which usually takes 24 hours. Should you choose to apply by mail, it can take up to 4 weeks. Here are some additional things to consider before applying for your EIN: consider the name of your business, the type of entity it is (e.g., sole proprietor, partnership, limited liability company), and where it is located. Knowing this information simplifies the process.

Obtain Malpractice Insurance

Although most practicing counselors, especially those in private practice, carry malpractice insurance, it may be a good time to consider if your current coverage is enough. However, if you are starting a practice or agency, one of your first steps is to obtain malpractice insurance, a requirement if you are considering becoming an approved provider. The amount of malpractice insurance required may vary depending on the insurance panel you are considering. Important to know about malpractice insurance are the occurrence limit and aggregate limit. The **occurrence limit** is the maximum amount an insurer is willing to pay for any one claim. Similarly, the **aggregate limit** is the maximum amount an insurer is willing to pay for the lifetime of the policy, which is renewed annually.

Familiarize Yourself With the Taxonomy Code

Mental health counselors should familiarize themselves with the health care provider taxonomy code before applying for an NPI number. The taxonomy code is a HIPAA-standard code set and the only code allowed to report HIPAA-standard transactions related to the type, classification, and specialization of health care providers (Centers for Medicare & Medicaid Services, 2018). Counselors submitting for credentialing must identify these codes when submitting their application for an NPI number. Obtaining an NPI number is discussed further in the next section. The taxonomy code is a unique alphanumeric code made up of 10 characters, designed to be used electronically. Each code uniquely identifies a specific type of provider. The code is updated twice a year and is available from Washington Publishing Company (see Web Resources).

Obtain an NPI Number

A national provider identifier (NPI) is a 10-digit identifier used for administrative and financial transactions under the Health Insurance Portability and Accountability Act (HIPAA) issued to care providers. This number is used by federal programs (e.g., Medicare, Medicaid), private health care insurers, and health care providers to file claims, bill insurance, and facilitate communication among providers. Obtaining an NPI is fairly simple. It can be done online, only takes a few minutes, and is free. Or one can simply call the National Provider Identifier Enumerator at 1-800-465-3203 to request an application. There are two types of NPIs: Entity Type 1 and Entity Type 2. An Entity

Type 1 is designated for sole proprietorships (e.g., private practice). An Entity Type 2 is designated for partnerships and corporations (e.g., hospital) separate from the individual occurring at the organizational level. A helpful consideration is once you have completed your NPI application online, do not forget to print and save your confirmation page; it has your NPI number on it.

Create a Profile in CAQH

Because most MCOs have their own criteria for approving health care providers, counselors would have to submit an application to each insurance company for which they seek provider status. Not only is this time-consuming, it can become expensive if one seeks out multiple health insurance companies. More recent advancements in data collection and information sharing have streamlined this process. The Council for Affordable Quality Healthcare (CAQH), a nonprofit, allows health care providers to create profiles that can be shared with health care organizations. CAQH ProView has more than 1.4 million providers and approximately 900 health care organizations participating in the exchange (CAQH Solutions, n.d.). However, not all health care organizations use CAQH, which may require counselors to submit a separate application to each entity for which they wish to receive provider status.

Review and Submit Application

The final step is to review and submit your application. Although this step may sound unnecessary, it is important to ensure that you have addressed everything correctly before submitting your application. A simple mistake can result in months of delays in credentialing. Consider the amount of energy and effort put into gathering information, obtaining an EIN and NPI number, reviewing taxonomy codes, and creating a profile on CAQH, your application deserves a thorough once-over before submission.

Pros and Cons of Provider Status

Regardless of whether you work in an agency, hospital, or private practice setting, provider status on insurance panels is something you may want to consider. Most counselors

GUIDED PRACTICE EXERCISE 7.2

In class, with a partner, explore the steps to obtaining provider status. Use the Web Resources located at the end of this chapter to deepen your exploration. Once complete, answer the following questions.

1. What are some challenges and barriers that would prevent counselors from becoming credentialed?

2. Would you or your partner consider becoming credentialed upon receiving a license to independently practice? Why or why not?

3. What is something you learned as a result of your exploration concerning provider status that you may not have known before? It does not have to be something explicitly stated in the chapter.

working in these settings practice under the private practice's, agency's, or hospital's panel status. If that is the case, you are not actually an approved provider. Counselors considering joining insurance panels should carefully weigh the pros and cons before deciding on any course of action. Obtaining provider status has its advantages. Even if you work in an agency or hospital setting, having provider status gives you flexibility in the future. Alternatively, it creates an opportunity for you to see clients privately, independent of your current employer. Another advantage of obtaining provider status is the built-in referral source. Having a consistent referral source through insurance has its own advantage. Clients channeled through insurance in which you have provider status may simplify the claims process and safeguard against inappropriate counselor-policyholder compatibility. And being an approved provider of insurance panels is a wonderful way to advertise your counseling services. Finally, when counselors choose to become an approved provider they increase policyholders' options in choosing counselors by increasing the provider marketplace.

Just as there are many advantages to obtaining provider status, there are many disadvantages. As you may have already noticed, the process of obtaining provider status is arduous and time-consuming. Counselors can invest a lot of time and energy seeking advice and consultation, gathering data, and filling out forms even before completing the actual application for provider status. And what if a mistake is made? For some, the cost-to-benefit payoff may not warrant engaging in the challenging process of obtaining provider status. Others may learn that their sought-after insurance panel is full and unwilling to accept new providers. Likewise, counselors concerned about their clientele's privacy may think twice about obtaining provider status. Although HIPAA compliance is mandated on behalf of counselors, and there is no exception under provider status, by default there is one more set of eyes privy to personal client data (e.g., diagnosis, clinical case notes). Finally, health insurance companies implement strict rules and regulations for providers under their marketplace. For instance, they determine reimbursement rates, types of services allowed, when and if claims will be paid, and what sanctions occur if errors of omission or commission are made.

SELECTING COVERED TREATMENT APPROACHES

Counter to the counseling profession's ideologies of wellness, well-being, and quality of life (Kaplan, Tarvydas, & Gladding, 2014), managed care has challenged the professional identities of many counselors. What some would consider valid reasons for counseling, such as learning new skills to deal with life's ever-changing circumstances, guidance in how to make difficult decisions, and prevention of mental illness, do not seem to resonate with managed care and the medical necessity of treatment for mental illness. The term **medical necessity** in managed care is important in determining whether services or procedures are necessary for health and treatment. According to Medicare.com (2018), medical necessity can be defined as services, procedures, or supplies used to treat and diagnosis health conditions that are justifiable and meet accepted standards of medicine. For counselors, this means that services provided must be justified and for a specific, identifiable purpose; without such treatment, more serve health consequences and higher future costs could result. Essentially, managed care has forced counselors who bill insurance companies to think and operate from a pathology mind-set—something must be wrong before counseling services will be authorized for reimbursement.

Preauthorization for Services

MCOs are well known for their rules and regulations, outlining requirements for service providers to be reimbursed for counseling services they provide to policyholders. Although what specifically is required by each insurance company may vary, depending on if it is federal, private, or state insurance, some general guidelines exist. One of the more central themes among MCOs is the concept of preauthorization. **Preauthorization**, or simply prior authorization, is the determination of whether prescriptions, procedures, or services are medically necessary and appropriate prior to beginning. For example, Jacob wants to seek counseling for his symptoms of depression. Depending on his type of insurance and whether his chosen counselor is an approved provider, Jacob may need preauthorization from the insurance company before counseling will be covered. If he fails to receive prior authorization or the insurance company denies him and determines counseling is not the most appropriate treatment, he is responsible for any financial responsibilities related to counseling sought out on his own. Some insurance plans require preauthorization for all specialist services, whereas others do not. Some may not require prior authorization up to a certain number of sessions, whereas others require preauthorization for out-of-network services. Thus, it is important that counselors be familiar with insurance companies in their communities and especially those in which they have provider status.

Policyholders can contact their insurance company to inquire if prior authorization is necessary before seeking counseling-related services. However, it is common practice for service providers (e.g., counselors, physicians, physical therapists) to request prior authorization on behalf of policyholders. Some insurance companies even place the responsibility of prior authorization on the policyholder but do make concessions for both family members and service providers. Prior authorization can be achieved in three general ways. Providers and/or policyholders can call to speak with a representative in the prior authorization department, submit a request for prior authorization online, or fax a prior authorization form. Note that prior authorizations are only valid for a certain period (e.g., 30 days). Each health insurance plan may request certain evidence that supports the medical necessity of counseling or counseling-related services, and it begins with a mental health diagnosis.

Required Diagnosis

Often the first criteria required to obtain preauthorization for behavioral health services is a mental health diagnosis. Most health insurance plans such as Humana, Aetna, Cigna, and so forth require a diagnostic impression consistent with either the *Diagnostic and Statistical Manual of Mental Disorders* (*DSM-5*; American Psychiatric Association, 2013) or the *International Classification of Diseases* (*ICD-10*; World Health Organization, 1992) standards. Numerous authors throughout the profession literature have raised ethical concerns about diagnosing and managed care. For instance, Danzinger and Welfel (2001) identified the challenge mental health professionals experience when client diagnoses do not align with insurance companies' reimbursement guidelines. Thus, mental health professionals many find themselves in a difficult position of either maintaining an accurate diagnosis stance with reimbursement or altering clients' diagnostic criterion to gain reimbursement. Wylie (1995) referred to this as "diagnosing for dollars" (p. 22). When counselors give clients with less severe problems a more severe problem classification, this is known as **upcoding** (Cooper & Gottlieb, 2000). Conversely, when counselors give clients with more severe problems a less severe problem classification, this is known as **downcoding** (Cooper & Gottlieb, 2000, p. 199). Both practices are used to gain clients access to services and counselors access to reimbursement. However, both are deceptive, unethical, and could potentially have legal ramifications.

In addition to the diagnostic impression, care providers must demonstrate the need for services. Fortunately, counselors in both outpatient and inpatient settings have mechanisms in place in the form of documentation. Surveys, screening tools, risk assessments, and symptom severity scales are common forms of documentation that may be used to obtain preauthorization for mental health services. For services that require inpatient care, additional evidence such as admitting physicians' documentation, psychiatric evaluations, and medical records may be required. The key takeaway is that documentation evidence needs to indicate that services requested are appropriate and medically necessary.

CASE ILLUSTRATION 7.2

Natalie has been in private practice for over 6 years working with children and adolescents and their families. She is an exceptional counselor and truly cares about her clients. Although not a novel experience for Natalie, she has struggled with insurance companies where she is credentialed because only certain diagnoses are covered, and family counseling is not. She has always played by the rules, but her practice is struggling. She just turned away three clients this week for the exact reasons mentioned previously. Frustrated with insurance companies, she decides that this cannot continue. The next day, Natalie meets with a child who is having behavioral issues at school; she reports that she is bullied almost every day. In session, Natalie notices how anxious the client seems. Upon completion of the diagnostic assessment, biopsychosocial assessment, and anxiety inventory, Natalie's client did not fit the criteria of any *DSM-5* diagnosis. However, the family insisted that their child needed counseling

services and requested that she see Natalie. In order to be reimbursed for her services, Natalie decides to diagnosis the child with conduct disorder, which is reimbursed by insurance. However, the client's family is fearful that a diagnosis of conduct disorder is too severe and worry about the negative implications of such a diagnosis. As a result, Natalie decides to render a diagnosis of adjustment disorder, which is also covered by the insurance. Looking at both instances, when Natalie gave the client a diagnosis of conduct disorder, she engaged in upcoding, giving a client with less severe problems a more severe problem classification. When Natalie changed the diagnosis of conduct disorder to adjustment disorder to appease her client's family, Natalie engaged in downcoding, giving a client with a more severe problem a less severe problem classification. At this point, Natalie is "diagnosing for dollars," a deceptive and unethical practice that could have legal ramifications.

GUIDED PRACTICE EXERCISE 7.3

This exercise is intended to expand your current thought processes without judgment in a safe environment. In class, with a partner, discuss your position on diagnosing. How does diagnosing fit or not fit with your theoretical orientation? How does your position on diagnosing fit with managed care? When finished, explore the concepts of upcoding and downcoding. If you were to engage in this type of practice, what would be your justification in so doing? Discuss any moral, ethical, and legal ramifications you foresee.

Covered Treatments

Although third-party payers do not explicitly state which therapeutic approaches are covered under their insurance plans, they certainly outline which behavioral health services are covered, state whether preauthorization is required, and set limits on the number of visits allowed annually and over a lifetime. For example, Medicaid, the largest payer for mental health services in the United States (Medicaid.gov, n.d.), outlines services for both inpatient and outpatient care; psychiatric evaluation and testing; medication and case management; individual, group, and family therapy; alcohol and substance abuse treatment; and many others in addition to physician services. Medicaid also limits the number of visits (e.g., 30 visits per calendar year) allowed under certain procedures and stipulates which *DSM-5* diagnoses are covered. If providers recommend continued treatment beyond Medicaid's annual limit, preauthorization is required. Medicaid's comprehensive coverage of mental health services often exceeds that of most private health insurance companies. Generally speaking, federal and private insurance companies will not reimburse for treatments of hypnotherapy, biofeedback, experimental therapies, and services provided by nonlicensed individuals.

Preauthorization of services does not guarantee payment for services. Most MCOs implement a retroactive review process once claims are filed to determine the appropriateness of services provided and evidence of medical necessity. Again, health insurance companies do stipulate which therapeutic approaches are covered; however, certain theories and models of clinical mental health counseling better align with managed care. For a review of five common models found in clinical mental health counseling, see Chapter 3.

FILING CLAIMS AND DOCUMENTING TREATMENT EFFORTS

Similar to obtaining provider status, filing claims for reimbursement of services can be long and tedious, dividing a counselor's time between seeing clients and billing insurance companies. Counselors working in larger practice settings such as an agency or hospital are often not tasked with filing claims. Larger clinical settings have claim or billing specialists whose sole function is to bill insurance. For independent practitioners, the burden of filing claims falls solely on them, although third-party billing companies are available at an additional cost. However, most private practitioners' overhead does not allow for such a luxury. Therefore, it seems prudent that counselors who may find themselves in this role be well versed in the claim filing process.

Claims Process

Once services have been rendered it is time to seek payment. In managed care this is known as filing a claim. Counselors filing claims should be aware of the policies and procedures for doing so, which vary depending on the insurance company. Some important policies and procedures to be aware of include how claims should be submitted, the time frame in which claims can be filed (e.g., 60 days for Magellan), how and when claim payments are administered, what constitutes a complete or clean claim, why claims may be denied, and who to contact should questions arise during the claim filing process. Now that you have a firm understanding of the policies and procedures it is time to begin the claim filing process.

An important first step is to ensure that preauthorization was obtained for services requiring prior authorization. Remember, not all mental health or substance abuse services require prior authorization; this varies by MCO and insurance company. As a reminder, insurance companies will not reimburse for services that require preauthorization when it was not obtained. The next step is completing a claim form, of which there are different versions. For instance, Magellan has two claim forms, one for outpatient services (CMS-1500) and the other for inpatient (UB-04). Note that both are standard forms approved by the Centers for Medicare and Medicaid Services and the National Uniform Billing Committee. Some insurance companies recognize that expediency is of the essence and offer the option of electronic claims submission. Sections to be completed on claim forms include patient demographic and insurance information; provider's information, including provider ID number and EIN; date and place of service; diagnostic and procedure codes; individual charge for services rendered; unit(s) of services provided; and the provider's signature.

To prevent a claim's denial or delayed payment, counselors should carefully review their claim forms before submission. Some things to keep in mind are to use the appropriate claim form, ensure it is sent to the right place (if mailed), and service dates fall within appropriate authorization periods. Once your claim is prepared, it is time to submit for payment. Claims are usually paid within 30 business days. For claims not paid within 30 business days, providers can inquire as to the payment status of the claim.

Periodically, insurance companies will conduct audits to ensure quality, utilization, and practice management. As an approved provider filing claims on behalf of policyholders, you agreed to maintain quality records of behavioral health services. This pertains to appointment books, payment records, and clinical case notes. Although each record is an important source of data in an audit process, clinical case notes are used to document treatment effort and are discussed next.

Clinical Case Notes

In compliance with the American Counseling Association's (2014) Code of Ethics and applicable federal and state statutes, clinical mental health counselors are required to maintain accurate clinical case notes documenting the occurrence and details of treatment. Managed care has created a problem-evidence-treatment paradigm in which providers must sufficiently and continuously document appropriateness and medical necessity of treatment. Treatment efforts must align with objectives identified in service plans and correspond to mental health diagnoses. As you may have noticed, clinical case notes are important in professional practice and serve to communicate vital information to third-party payers. Let's focus the reminder of our attention on what constitutes an appropriate case that sufficiently documents treatment effects in managed care.

Clinical case notes vary (e.g., SOAP, DARP) in structure and format; however, elements reported remain relatively consistent. For instance, case notes include both client and counselor subjective and objective data, an evaluation or assessment of progress toward goals and objectives, and a plan for future sessions. Client and counselor subjective data is what is said in session by counselor and client; objective data is what counselors identify with their five senses. In other words, objective data is what can be seen, heard, smelled, felt, and tasted, as it relates to treatment, in session. As a disclaimer, the last two senses, feel and taste, are not common elements reported in case notes. Evaluations and assessments toward treatment goals can occur through subjective or objective means. For instance, a counselor can obtain qualitative data in the form of verbal descriptors from clients. Likewise, counselors can use objective measures such as a depression inventory to periodically measure depression symptomology. The last component of effective case notes is the plan for the future. It should explore the client's current response to counseling services, specific goals or objectives addressed in the current session, and what will occur next.

Periodically, health insurance companies conduct audits on paneled providers or agencies. Audits can take place in person or be initiated by letter. Audits can occur for many reasons, such as being a new business, reoccurring claim errors, and a sudden increase in claim submissions. Third-party payers don't need a reason to conduct an audit. They are in the business of saving money where it counts. Therefore, providers should not wait to be audited before developing their own internal audit procedures. Procedures should focus on retaining appropriate evidence such as sign-in logs, treatment plans, administrative documents, billing and claim receipts, and regularly maintained health records. A final suggestion is that documentation should occur immediately after services are provided. Waiting too long could result in inaccurate reporting, omission of critical details, and simply forgetting to complete a case note.

MANAGED CARE DISPUTES AND APPEALS PROCESS

Claim disputes between providers and health insurance companies can be a major headache. It is not uncommon for service providers to receive denials or rejections of claims they submit. There are many valid reasons why claims are denied or rejected. Some common reasons include an expired filing time limit, wrong claim form used, incorrect EIN or TIN, diagnosis and procedure codes not matching authorization, no prior authorization, simple billing errors and missing information, not verifying policyholder coverage, duplicate billing, upcoding and downcoding, poor documentation, and providing two services to the same person in one day. However, a clear difference exists between a denied claim and a rejected one. A rejected claim results from errors. Once the errors have been amended, it can be resubmitted for processing. A denied claim is one that has been determined by the insurance company as unpayable. Should you find yourself in a position where your claim is denied, all insurance companies have an appeals process.

Appeals Process

If an insurance company refuses to pay a claim, as a provider, you have the right to appeal the decision. An **appeal** is an action taken by you the provider regarding a payment decision made by an insurance company. It is important to recognize when a claim is being denied. Most insurance companies will not print the word *denied* on claims; rather, the reimbursement amount will show zero dollars, along with a reason and remark code. Both codes can be found by looking on Washington Publishing Company's website (see Web Resources). It is also important not to sit on denied claims because time is of the essence. For instance, Blue Cross Blue Shield of Texas (BCBSTX) allows claim reviews for audit payments within 30 days, overpayments within 45 days, and claim disputes within 180 days. Additionally, BCBSTX has two levels of claim disputes. The first claim review will be completed within 45 days and a provider will receive a claim review determination. If the provider is dissatisfied, a second claim review is possible so long as it occurs within 15 days following the written claim determination of your first claim. BCBSTX will complete the second claim review within 30 days along with a final claim determination. Most insurance companies follow a similar procedure. As you may have noticed, time is of the essence in appealing a claim.

Providers should understand why their claim was denied in the first place. Following insurance companies' procedures when filing a claim can prevent additional wasted time. Most insurance companies have a claim review form that asks for the original claim number, group number, provider identification numbers, client demographic and insurance information, and detailed information about the claim review request. This last section is very important and may require providers to make a case as to why the claim should be paid. This narrative should be a professional written statement that directly addresses the reasons why the claim was denied in the first place. Also, be aware that further supporting documentation may be necessary. Once the claim form is complete, review it for errors and send it to the correct mailing address. This address can be found on most insurance companies' websites or by calling the company directly. Most insurance companies have an online claim form that can be submitted electronically. Should you decide to go this route, gather your resources ahead of time. Finally, do not forget to make copies for your records.

Some helpful recommendations to consider when filing a claim include not overrating, knowing your limits, and learning from your mistakes. It is common, at least initially, to be angry at insurance companies that deny your claims. Shouting loudly that you will take legal action should be your last step, not your first. Being familiar with insurance companies' policies and procedures can certainly mitigate claim denial; however, if you are new to receiving third-party payments, trial and error can serve its purpose. As you have already noticed, appealing a denied claim is time-consuming, especially when trying to juggle seeing clients and filing new claims. Know where to invest your time when submitting an appeal. You may want to ask yourself if fighting for $20 is worth it when you have already invested 10 hours of your time on the first two appeals. Striking the right balance at first may require making mistakes, but in the end you have to be willing to take a step back and see the bigger picture. Finally, claims are denied for valid reasons, and rather than take it personally or as something negative, try to think of it as a learning experience. Your first denial will not be your last, but with experience comes a wealth of knowledge if you learn and grow from past mistakes.

GUIDED PRACTICE EXERCISE 7.4

On your own, explore each step of the appeals process. Now imagine if one of your colleagues came to you for advice about filing an appeal for a denied claim. What information would you share, and why? The very same colleague is now asking you how she should proceed. What information or recommendation(s) can you provide to assist her in making an informed decision?

Keystones

- *Managed care* is an umbrella term used to describe a practice or set of practices that provides oversight in the delivery of health care services. The philosophy behind managed care is to provide cost-effective services while ensuring the appropriateness and quality of those services. More specifically, managed care systems have agreements with certain hospitals, care providers, and health care practitioners (e.g., physicians, psychiatrists, counselors) to provide a defined set of services to its members at an agreed-on price. Throughout U.S. health care systems are four main types of managed care organizations: point-of-service plans, health maintenance organizations, preferred provider organizations, and exclusive provider organizations, each with its own strengths and weaknesses.

- Provider panel status, simply known as credentialing, designates a health care provider as being approved by an insurance company or MCO to provide a specific service. Without this status, counselors can be denied access to the marketplace, and policyholders may experience limited options when choosing qualified mental health counselors. Provider status varies from one insurance entity to the next. Generally speaking, counselors are required to be independently licensed, have malpractice insurance, and have no disciplinary actions against them. However, ethical or legal infractions against counselors do not automatically disbar them from becoming credentialed.

- Credentialing to be an approved provider is time-consuming and tedious. However, with careful planning by counselors, they can become approved providers in a reasonable amount of time. These steps require the counselor to preplan and prepare, obtain an employer identification number, obtain malpractice insurance, familiarize oneself with the taxonomy code, obtain an NPI number, create a profile in CAQH, and review and submit one's application.

- Preauthorization is the determination of whether prescriptions, procedures, or services are medically necessary and appropriate prior to starting. Many managed care organizations require prior authorization before certain services will be reimbursed whereas others do not. Both providers and policyholders can contact the policyholder's insurance company to inquire if prior authorization is required. Preauthorization of services does not guarantee payment for services.

- Although third-party payers do not explicitly state which therapeutic approaches are covered under their insurance plans, they outline which behavioral health services are covered, note if preauthorization is required, and set limits on the number of visits allowed annually and over a lifetime. However, certain models of clinical mental health counseling (e.g., cognitive-behavioral based) lend themselves well to managed care.

- Clinical case notes communicate vital information to third-party payers by presenting evidence of continued appropriateness and medical necessity of counseling services.

Although clinical case notes vary in structure and format, they generally consist of three main parts: both client and counselor subjective and objective data, an evaluation or assessment of progress toward goals and objectives, and a plan for future sessions. Counselors billing insurance companies for services should implement good documentation habits early on because it is not a matter of if but when they will be audited.

Key Terms

Aggregate limit 178
Appeal 186
Downcoding 182
Fee-for-service system 172

Managed care 172
Medical necessity 180
Occurrence limit 178
Preauthorization 181

Provider status 176
Upcoding 182
Utilization management 173

Web Resources

Credentialing.com FAQ (https://credentialing.com/faq)

Medicaid: Behavioral Health Services (www.medicaid.gov/medicaid/benefits/bhs/index.html)

NPI Online Application (https://nppes.cms.hhs.gov/NPPES/StaticForward.do?forward=static.instructions)

Practice of the Practice: How Do I Fill Out an Insurance Claim Form? (www.practiceofthepractice.com/how-do-i-fill-out-an-insurance-claim-form)

Washington Publishing Company's Health Care Code List (www.wpc-edi.com/reference)

References

American Counseling Association. (2012). The Affordable Care Act: What counselors should know. Retrieved from https://www.counseling.org/PublicPolicy/PDF/What_counselors_should_know-the_Affordable_Care_Act_12-12.pdf

American Counseling Association. (2014). *ACA Code of Ethics*. Alexandria, VA: Author

American Psychiatric Association. (2013). *Diagnostic and statistical manual of mental disorders* (5th ed.). Arlington, VA: Author.

Braun, S. A., & Cox, J. A. (2005). Managed mental health care: Intentional misdiagnosis of mental disorders. *Journal of Counseling & Development, 83*, 425–433. doi:10.1002/j.1556-6678.2005.tb00364.x

CAQH Solutions. (n.d.). ProView: More provider data. Less redundant paperwork. Retrieved from https://www.caqh.org/sites/default/files/solutions/proview/CAQH_ProView_FINAL_4.7.15_final.pdf?token=4-8cNh4E

Carson, C. B. (1997). The effect of managed care on the pharmaceutical industry. Retrieved from http://nrs.harvard.edu/urn-3:HUL.InstRepos:8965565

Centers for Medicare & Medicaid Services. (2018). Taxonomy. Retrieved from https://www.cms.gov/Medicare/Provider-Enrollment-and-Certification/MedicareProviderSupEnroll/Taxonomy.html

Committee on Utilization Management by Third Parties & Institute of Medicine. (1989). *Controlling costs and changing patient care? The role of utilization management*. Washington, DC: National Academies Press.

Cooper, C. C., & Gottlieb, M. C. (2000). Ethical issues with managed care: Challenges facing counseling psychology. *The Counseling Psychologist, 28*, 179–236.

Danzinger, P. R., & Welfel, E. R. (2001). The impact of managed care on mental health counselors: A survey of perceptions, practices, and compliance with ethical standards. *Journal of Mental Health Counseling, 23*, 137–150.

Hinkle, J. S. (1999). *Promoting optimum mental health through counseling: An overview*. Greensboro, NC: CAPS.

Kaplan, D. M., Tarvydas, V. M., & Gladding, S. T. (2014). 20/20: A vision for the future of counseling: The new consensus definition of counseling. *Journal of Counseling & Development, 92*, 366–372. doi:10.002/j.1556-6676.2014.00164.x

Medicaid.gov. (n.d.). Behavioral health services. Retrieved from https://www.medicaid.gov/medicaid/benefits/bhs/index.html

Medicare.com. (2018). What "medically necessary" means and how it affects your Medicare coverage. Retrieved from https://medicare.com/resources/what-medically-necessary-means-and-how-it-affects-your-medicare-coverage/

World Health Organization. (1992). *The ICD-10 classification of mental and behavioural disorders: Clinical descriptions and diagnostic guidelines*. Geneva, Switzerland: Author.

Wylie, M. S. (1995, May/June). The power of the DSM-IV: Diagnosing for dollars. *Family Therapy Networker*, pp. 22–32.

MODELS OF CLINICAL SUPERVISION

By Rochelle Cade and Justin Tauscher

Chandra is enrolled in a clinical mental health counseling program and about to begin her practicum experience. In practicum she will see her first clients at the university counseling and training clinic. As part of the practicum course requirements, Chandra is expected to participate in individual supervision with the clinic director and group supervision with her practicum course instructor. She is excited to begin seeing clients and observe her classmates' counseling sessions at the clinic. However, Chandra also feels unsure of what to expect in supervision and is nervous about supervisors observing her counseling skills. She hopes her supervisors offer a combination of constructive feedback to help improve her skills and support and guidance as she continues growing as a counselor in training. Chandra is curious as to how supervision and the supervisory relationship will be different from relationships with which she is familiar like coaching, mentoring, teaching, or counseling. Although Chandra fully expects supervision to be a positive experience, she is unsure of what to expect.

Can you relate to Chandra? Perhaps you too are curious as to what supervision will be like and how it will foster your development as a clinical mental health counselor. In this chapter, you will learn about the basic elements of supervision in professional counseling. By its conclusion, you should have a greater appreciation for the unique role supervision plays in counseling for both counselors in training and experienced practitioners. Further, you should find yourself better prepared to engage in future supervisory relationships as both supervisee and supervisor.

LEARNING OBJECTIVES

After reading this chapter, you will be able to do the following:

- Describe the nature and purpose of clinical supervision (CACREP 2F-1-m)
- Discuss theoretical frameworks and models of clinical supervision

- Summarize the qualities of effective clinical supervisors
- Examine supervision techniques and interventions
- Identify how technology can be used to assist in the delivery of supervision services (CACREP 2F-1-j)

NATURE AND PURPOSE OF CLINICAL SUPERVISION

Clinical supervision plays an essential role in the development of counselors in training and continued professional development of experienced clinical mental health counselors. Specifically, supervision facilitates the process of learning how to competently practice and the acquisition of professional attitudes foundational to ethical practice throughout a counselor's career (Falender, Shafranske, & Ofek, 2014). For many beginning counselors, supervision is the place where clinical reasoning, ethical decision-making, application of knowledge and skills, and development of the values of our profession are modeled, developed, reinforced, and enhanced (Barnett, 2014). And that just scratches the surface! Supervision also helps you better understand yourself and how your values, ideas, and beliefs shape the way you practice. So, as you can see, supervision clearly plays a critical role in helping you become an effective clinical mental health counselor.

If you were to take the time to review the professional counseling literature, you would find several definitions of supervision expressed. In the American Counseling Association (ACA; 2014) Code of Ethics, supervision is defined as a process in which the supervisor engages in a collaborative relationship with a supervisee to promote the growth and development of the supervisee, protect the welfare of the clients seen by the supervisee, and evaluate the performance of the supervisee. Further clarifying the role of both **supervisor** and **supervisee**, Bernard and Goodyear (2014) defined supervision as an intervention provided by a senior member of a profession to a more junior member in a relationship that extends over time. The relationship is evaluative, aims to enhance the professional services and functioning of the junior member, and ensures the fitness of the supervisee to enter the counseling profession. Similar to Bernard and Goodyear's definition of supervision, White and Winstanley (2014) described supervision as a formal relationship–based system of support. These definitions speak more to the relational aspect of supervision, but others define the process and what should be addressed in supervision.

According to the American Association of State Counseling Boards (AASCB; 2007), clinical supervision includes, but is not limited to, the supervisor's participation in evaluation, diagnosis, development of treatment, clinical documentation, appropriate referral, adherence to legal and ethical practice, and nurturing the counseling process. These are just a few definitions, and there are certainly many more in the counseling profession as well as other helping professions like social work or psychology. Examining the commonalities in these definitions, you can see that **clinical supervision** is a relational experience between an experienced senior counselor and a less experienced junior counselor designed to facilitate development of the skills, abilities, and personal attributes the junior counselor needs to be an effective clinician. It is important to recognize that both supervisor and supervisee are clinically responsible for the welfare of the clients being served by the supervisee. However, when ethical, professional, and even some legal issues arise, the responsibility falls on the clinical supervisor for professional activities carried out by the supervisee while engaged in the supervisory relationship (AASCB, 2007).

Purpose of Supervision

In the counseling profession, clinical supervisors have two primary purposes in supervision: to support the growth and development of the supervisee and protect the welfare of clients receiving services from the supervisee. To achieve the first purpose, the supervisor must create a safe holding environment (Barnett & Molzon, 2014). A **holding environment** is a place for supervisees to share their experiences as counselors including their knowledge, skills, fears, struggles, difficulties, and successes. The holding environment is supported by the structure, format, and frequency of supervision and is insulated with core conditions essential to the supervisory relationship. As a result, counselors feel safe sharing their concerns without fear of being judged or viewed negatively.

The second purpose, to protect the welfare of the client, is an ethical and professional obligation of the supervisor. Although the supervisor and supervisee are both clinically responsible for the care of the client, ultimately the supervisor bears full ethical and professional responsibility for the services provided (AASCB, 2007). Part of how supervisors protect clients is by monitoring and evaluating supervisees to ensure they're fit for practice under supervision and for independent practice. This evaluation often involves both formal and informal methods of assessment, and it should be developmental. As novice counselors, it is not expected that you will know the correct action to take in every situation. In fact, even the most seasoned counselors will tell you that they still encounter client situations in which they need to seek advice to best understand.

Clinical supervision is an intensive relationship-based process that supports and facilitates the supervisee's professional development and clinical competence over time. The supervisory relationship is complex, with tension between the purposes of ensuring, promoting, and monitoring the development of supervisees' competence and the duty to protect clients (Falender & Shafranske, 2014).

CASE ILLUSTRATION 8.1

What Would Counseling Be Without Supervision?

Imagine if Jorge, a counseling student in practicum, was meeting with his client, Maya, at the counseling training clinic on campus. Maya, a 34-year-old Hispanic female, is from the community seeking treatment for childhood sexual abuse. Even though this was their first session, Jorge seemed very hesitant to engage Maya in conversation as to why she sought out counseling services in the first place. In fact, Maya verbalized that her traumatic memories have resulted in her contemplating suicide. Jorge, although he has taken the crisis class and knows how to conduct a suicide assessment, fails to attend to Maya's disclosure of suicide and instead asks Maya to tell him about her career. As the session progresses, Jorge begins to feel more comfortable in session and recognizes that he has made a huge misstep by not assessing Maya's risk for suicide. Perceiving that his client is doing better in session now than at the beginning, Jorge decides that it is not necessary to bring up Maya's mention of suicide. In fact, Jorge feels pretty good about his session with Maya. The session ends, and Maya exits the counseling training clinic. As you quickly notice, without supervision, many errors of omission or commission made by Jorge go unaddressed. Without a supervisor Maya's verbalization of suicide and Jorge's failure to attend to Maya in session would have been missed. As a result, Maya may feel that her needs were ignored by Jorge and end up deciding to end her life despite her seeking help. Or she may decide that counseling is a waste of time and never seek it out again. Likewise, Jorge would never recognize the mistakes he made in session—and could potentially continue to make the same ones over and over again—while perceiving that he was doing well as a counselor in training. Although this scenario is severe, clinical supervision serves to protect clients, supervisees, and the counseling profession.

SUPERVISION MODELS, PRACTICES, AND PROCESSES

A model is a methodical way in which supervision is applied or practiced. Supervision models provide direction for where and how the supervisor and supervisee navigate the supervisory process. Best practices suggest supervisors should share their model of supervision in the first supervision session for this communicates to the supervisee what to expect in supervision sessions. There are many models of supervision, including developmental models, orientation- or theory-driven models, and integrative models. Like in the counseling relationship, the choice of which model to use should be dictated by the individual supervisee and his or her specific needs from supervision. To help familiarize you with some of the more common supervision models, a description of each follows.

Developmental Models

Developmental models of supervision are based on the idea that supervisees develop counseling knowledge, skills, and competence over time and their needs in supervision will be related to their developmental level. Consequently, supervisors match the style and structure of supervision to the supervisee's developmental level. An example is the *integrated developmental model* developed by Stoltenberg, McNeill, and Delworth (1998). This model contains four counselor levels (see Table 8.1), and the supervisor is tasked with noting the strengths and needs of the supervisee and the evolution of skills that mark the transition from one developmental level to another.

In the first level, the supervisee is uncertain of, and lacks confidence in, his or her counseling skills. Without certainty or confidence in their own skills, supervisees operating at this level rely on the supervisor for advice and direction for counseling sessions. Supervisors respond to this need by not only providing helpful structure and support but also encouraging autonomy and risk taking in the counseling session. In the second level, the supervisee experiences a conflict between the continued dependence from the first level and a budding sense of autonomy. Supervisees begin to rely less on the supervisor, trust their own thoughts and feelings, and experiment with how these thoughts and

TABLE 8.1 ■	The Integrated Developmental Model
Level 1	Supervisees at this level are highly motivated to participate. They are focused primarily on themselves and how they will perform as a counselor. Often, the supervisee has limited self-awareness primarily due to inexperience.
Level 2	Supervisees at this level begin to function more independently. Rather than focusing on themselves, the supervisee is more concerned with the experiences of the client. Motivation fluctuates at this stage from a great need for supervision to little perceived need.
Level 3	Supervisees at this level have gained experience and are now focused on developing a strong professional identity. They remain consistently motivated to participate in supervision because of the opportunity it provides to grow as a person and professional.
Level 4	Supervisees at this stage have benefited greatly from previous supervision and clinical experience. They have developed an individualized approach to counseling that fits them personally and are now at a stage where they can begin thinking about serving as supervisors themselves.

feelings inform their work with clients. Supervisors support and encourage the autonomy and experimentation of the supervisee and remain empathetic to the supervisee's need for instruction and advice from the supervisor. Level three is characterized by the supervisee's budding identity development as a counselor and professional. With increased autonomy, confidence, and a growing sense of identity in counseling, the supervisee can relate more as a peer with the supervisor. In the fourth and final level, the supervisee is able to practice independently and can begin shifting to a new role as a supervisor for other less experienced counselors.

Orientation-Specific Models

Counselors practice from a particular theoretical orientation (e.g., psychoanalytic, narrative, cognitive-behavioral therapy) when working with their clients. Often, this same theoretical orientation informs their work as a supervisor. Orientation-specific supervision operates from a counseling theory framework and typically focuses on the supervisee's adherence or fidelity to the theory in counseling sessions. According to Leddick (1994), orientation-specific models can be viewed as being analogous to the sports enthusiast who believes the best future coach would be a person who excelled in the same sport. In other words, these supervisors truly practice what they preach. However, just because a supervisor adheres to a particular theoretical model or paradigm does not mean his or her supervisees have to follow the same approach. Orientation-specific supervision also can be used to encourage and support the development of a supervisee choosing a different theoretical orientation than the supervisor.

Orientation models include Adlerian, cognitive, cognitive-behavioral, experiential, feminist, multimodal, narrative, psychodynamic, person-centered, solution-focused, and systemic. A complete review of each model is beyond the scope of this section; however, the following section provides a brief description of four orientation-specific models of supervision.

Person-Centered

The person-centered model of supervision is based on the person-centered theory of counseling developed by Carl Rogers (1951). Similar to the counseling relationship, the core conditions of empathy, congruence, and unconditional positive regard are the foundation for the supervisory relationship. Supervisors operating from this perspective believe supervisees have both the capacity and resources within them for growth as a person and as a clinician. Supported by a deep trust in the supervisee, the supervisory relationship, and the process, the supervisor allows the supervisee to direct the supervision sessions in this model. The supervisee chooses what needs he or she would like met in a supervisor and brings these issues to the forefront.

Cognitive-Behavioral

Cognitive-behavioral supervision is based on the cognitive-behavioral model of counseling combining both cognitive and behavioral therapies. Supervisors operating from this perspective view cognitions or thoughts as the driving force behind a supervisee's beliefs, feelings, and behaviors. In supervision, supervisees are encouraged to use cognitive techniques on themselves. They examine their own cognitions and how these inform their work with clients. For example, a supervisee may be led to examine why she may be fearful of addressing a particular issue with a client or unsure of her ability to be helpful to her clients. This experience also gives the supervisee an understanding of how the model can work with clients. Based on a collaborative relationship between supervisor and supervisee, the supervisor jointly structures the supervision session with the supervisee by developing an agenda for the session, creating strategies to accomplish the agenda in session and between sessions and monitoring supervisee progress from session to session.

Psychodynamic

Psychodynamic models of supervision have a lengthy history in comparison to other models of supervision. This model focuses on the client's resistance, defense mechanisms, transference, and countertransference between client and counselor. However, the model also can be used to focus on the supervisees' resistance, defense mechanisms, transference, and countertransference between supervisee and supervisor. In the psychodynamic model, supervisors operate as an expert or authority who can facilitate the supervisee's exploration and understanding of his or her own psychological processes. Like the previous models described, the use of psychodynamic techniques in supervision models for the supervisee how these same techniques can be used in the counseling relationship by providing direct experiences. For example, attending to dreams might be employed as a learning strategy in supervision.

Narrative

Narrative models of supervision assume that people are natural storytellers and have generated a story about themselves. Stories emerge from personal experiences and play an important role in defining a person's identity. In supervision, attention is focused on these stories, the characters populating the stories, and how stories are edited or revised.

In this approach, supervisors maintain a position of curiosity and pose questions to the supervisee that help to write the story of who and how they are as a counselor. The supervisee serves as editor of the story and rewrites or adds chapters to the story throughout supervision. These stories help supervisees better understand their perceptions regarding their ability to do their work well and to discover new ways to address challenging circumstances emerging in their work with clients.

Integrative Models

Supervisors may find operating from a single orientation model to be restrictive or limiting and choose to operate from an integrative model. An integrative model is when more than one distinct model of counseling or supervision are combined. Or an integrative model may be a combination of supervisory approaches or interventions without full endorsement of the theories or models that inform those approaches. This type of integrative model is called technical eclecticism. Two examples of integrative models, the discrimination model and microskills supervision, are discussed next.

The discrimination model, developed by Bernard in the 1970s, is an atheoretical model of supervision based on technical eclecticism (Bernard & Goodyear, 2014). It is called a discrimination model because the supervisor individualizes his or her responses, in other words discriminates, to meet the needs of the supervisee. Instead of being derived from a single theory or model, skills, techniques, and interventions from a variety of theoretical approaches are used based on current supervisory roles and supervisee skills. Supervisors employing the discrimination model focus on their roles as teacher, counselor, and consultant and on three areas of supervisee skills, process, conceptualization, and personalization, rather than focusing on the internal experiences or psychological processes of the supervisee. Let's first examine the counselor roles.

The three roles the supervisor can assume in the supervision process include those of a *teacher, counselor*, and *consultant*. The teacher role emerges when there is a need to train or further develop a supervisee's skills. Operating from this perspective, the supervisor helps the supervisee learn new skills and practice implementing them. A second role supervisors can assume is that of a counselor. Many times in supervision, the supervisee may present with a need to discuss what is occurring in the counseling sessions and how it is affecting him or her personally. Here, the supervisor responds to the supervisee using basic attending skills and tries to actively listen. Finally, supervisors also can assume the role of a consultant. As a consultant, the supervisor works with the supervisee to evaluate various courses of action that can be taken and select the best case based on the needs of the client in a given situation. Although these different roles can emerge at any time in the supervision process, they typically appear in relation to one of three primary focal areas: process, conceptualization, or personalization.

Process skills include greeting the client, pacing the counseling, and closing the session. *Conceptualization* skills include the supervisee's ability to navigate content provided by the client to identify client themes or patterns and case conceptualize. The third skill, *personalization* skills, comprises the unique elements the supervisee brings to the counseling session. Personalization includes the supervisee's personality, culture, values, beliefs, and theoretical orientation. Supervisors use their roles to facilitate the supervisee's skill development.

The microcounseling supervision model (MSM), introduced by Russell-Chapin and Ivey in 2004, is another example of an integrative model of supervision. This model can be used by supervisors working from various models or theoretical orientations. Microcounseling skills, or *microskills*, are the basic and foundational skills used by counselors in session. Examples of microskills include open questions, closed questions, reflection of feeling, reflection of content, paraphrasing, and summarizing. Like other models, there are three stages: reviewing microskills with intention, classifying skills with mastery, and processing supervisory needs. In the first stage, the supervisor defines each microskill and ensures the supervisee's understanding of these skills. The supervisor uses the Counseling Interview Rating Form (CIRF) that provides a format for baseline and follow-up evaluation of the supervisee's use of microskills in session. In the second stage, the CIRF is used to identify the microskills the supervisee has demonstrated or mastered in the counseling session. In the final stage, the supervisor summarizes the skills that have been demonstrated and those that have been mastered in review of counseling sessions and scores on the CIRF. Supervisees are invited to discuss their questions or concerns and reflect on how the supervision session informs their work with the client.

There are a variety of supervision models from which a supervisor may operate. Supervisors may choose among the models based on consistency with their theoretical orientation in counseling or another preference. Regardless of the model chosen by the supervisor, all aim to enhance the competence of the counselor (Falender et al., 2014).

CASE ILLUSTRATION 8.2

The Case of Natalya

Models of supervision provide structure and direction and guide supervisors to work competently with their supervisees. Let's see what happens when supervision lacks structure and direction by examining the case of Natalya. Natalya, a licensed professional counselor-supervisor, provides group supervision to six supervisees each week. Natalya describes her supervision style as free-flowing and open. Most supervision sessions begin with each supervisee sharing a concern about his or her client or clinical skill. Each supervisee wants to improve his or her skills but is often faced with Natalya attending to less important things about her supervisees' clients (i.e., details unrelated to supervision). Natalya rarely is able to keep on task and jumps between being a counselor and supervisor, which creates confusion among her supervisees. To make matters worse, Natalya provides wonderful suggestions, but they seem to go above her supervisees' level of competence. Her supervisees think the world of Natalya and believe she could be an excellent supervisor if she incorporated some structure and direction in her supervision style of practice. If Natalya is going to succeed as a supervisor, she needs to ground herself in a supervision model of practice. Her supervisees want structure and guidance that is realistic and tangible, which is something a model of supervision would provide. Finally, Natalya seems to have many of the qualities of a supervisor, and by adopting a model of supervision practice, she will be able to offer her supervisees better guidance and suggestions on how to competently work with clients. As you can see, a model of supervision benefits both Natalya and her supervisees.

GUIDED PRACTICE EXERCISE 8.1

In reviewing the various models of supervision, which could you imagine being supervised from? Detail two specific reasons why you chose that particular model. How does the chosen supervision model align with your theoretical counseling orientation, style of counseling, and personal values and beliefs?

Practices

Best practices are a set of techniques, methods, or guidelines that represent the most efficient or prudent course of action. Best practices are set forth by an authority like a professional organization or association. The Association for Counselor Education and Supervision (ACES) appointed a taskforce that authored best practices for clinical supervision. Borders et al. (2014) identified the best practices in clinical supervision based on a comprehensive review of literature and research, existing theory, and legal precedents. The following is a discussion of these practices.

Clinical supervision is a relational process, and the supervisor's first task is to develop the supervisory relationship. Supervisors understand, respect, and appreciate multicultural considerations in the creation and maintenance of the professional relationship with the supervisee. An effective supervisor is one who addresses diversity at the onset of the supervisor-supervisee relationship. This can mean supervisors simply asking supervisees if they perceive, experience, or recognize any differences (e.g., gender, race, values) within the supervisory relationship. Likewise, strong supervisors are not hesitant to address diversity issues brought forth by the supervisee in supervision—even if they challenge the supervisor's own competence. Hence, supervisors model for supervisees appropriate methods for addressing diversity issues in supervision, with the intended effect of supervisees doing the same in their counselor practice.

At the onset of supervision, the supervisor engages in an informed consent process similar to informed consent in counseling. This may include a supervision contract or agreement that provides the supervisee with information about what to expect in the supervisory process. The contract outlines the roles and responsibilities of the supervisor and supervisee, supervisor's model or approach to supervision, scheduling and duration of supervision, measurement and evaluation of the supervisee's skills, documentation and record keeping, confidentiality, and expectations for when and how the supervisee should contact the supervisor in crisis or emergency situations. Post-master's supervision contracts will have additional content (e.g., termination of supervision, fees). The contract or agreement should be signed and dated by both parties and the supervisee should be provided with a copy.

Supervisors should collaborate with the supervisee in identifying goals; this may comprise goals for each supervision session and goals to be achieved by the end of the supervision process. Supervisees should not be unsure or surprised by the methods or timing of evaluation of their progress toward identified goals or counselor preparation program standards. Supervisors should provide regular and ongoing feedback to supervisees regarding their performance. This feedback may be informed by collecting data from multiple sources and collaborating with additional supervisors with whom the supervisee may be working. Supervisors should provide balanced feedback to supervisees that includes the supervisee's strengths and growth areas.

It is the supervisor's responsibility to ensure that both the supervisor and supervisee adhere to relevant ethical codes and professional standards. This includes the supervision provided to the supervisee by the supervisor and the counseling provided to the client by the supervisee. Though supervisors are not working directly with the clients, they are tasked with ensuring the welfare of the clients seen by the supervisee. Supervisors are also tasked with ensuring the welfare of the supervisee. **Gatekeeping** is the term used to describe the supervisor's responsibility to intervene with supervisees who are clinically impaired on engage in conduct that would be detrimental to client. Supervisors also monitor their own conduct for signs of burnout, impairment, or other deficiencies. Engaging in reflection, seeking consultation, supervision, mentoring, counseling and professional development are all methods supervisors use to enhance their effectiveness and competence in clinical supervision.

Processes

Supervision is a complex relationship that involves both dyadic systems and a triadic system. There are two dyads. The first dyad is the client and the counselor. Supervisors typically do not directly participate in this dyad nor do they interact with the client. The second dyad is the counselor/supervisee and the supervisor. Similarly, the client does not participate in this dyad. In addition to the dyads, there is a triadic system of the client, counselor/supervisee, and supervisor. In other words, the supervisor and supervisee have a relationship centered around the supervisee's relationship with the client. Within the triadic system, parallel processes and isomorphism can occur.

Parallel Processes

The concept of **parallel processes** is rooted in the psychoanalytic concepts of transference and countertransference. Transference refers to the client's unconscious reenactment of his or her unresolved needs with the counselor. In supervision, transference occurs when counselors/supervisees reenact with their supervisors what their clients have enacted with them. This occurs outside the supervisee's awareness. Countertransference happens when the supervisor then responds to the supervisee/counselor similarly to the way the counselor responds to the client. More simply stated, the supervision session parallels the counseling session.

Parallel processes can occur in supervision in a variety of ways. For example, a client may become withdrawn in session when the counselor confronts the client's behavior and actions that are inconsistent with the client's goal. The counselor then enters supervision and becomes withdrawn when the supervisor provides feedback. As stated in the previous paragraph, the counselor is not aware that he or she is reenacting in supervision what the client brought to the counseling session.

Supervisees early in their counseling experience may find exploring parallel processes confusing or anxiety provoking. Supervisors use their judgement on when it is appropriate to discuss their observations of parallel processes with supervisees. When addressing it in supervision, it can be helpful to give examples of when and how the parallel process is observed and frame the experience as an opportunity for learning and increasing supervisee self-awareness. Supervisees with more counseling experience may have a greater ability to recognize the parallel processes when they occur during supervision and discuss how this awareness can be used to inform counseling sessions.

Isomorphism

Isomorphism has its roots in mathematics and systems theory. In mathematics, morphism refers to the mapping of one mathematical structure to another mathematical structure. Maps equal in form are isomorphic. Similarly, systems theory "maps" the interrelational similarities of counseling and supervision. In other words, the map of supervision is equal in form to the map of counseling. Isomorphism used here combines the mapping element from mathematics and the interrelational element from systems theory. Koltz, Odegard, Feit, Provost, and Smith (2012) described isomorphism as a repeated, bidirectional relational pattern that occurs in counseling or supervision. An example of the relational pattern repeating from counseling to supervision follows to help illustrate the concept. A counselor/supervisee had a counseling session with a couple feeling forlorn and contemplating divorce. The couple seeks the counselor/supervisee's direction in deciding if they should remain married or seek a divorce. The counselor/supervisee then enters the supervision session feeling forlorn and seeks direction from the supervisor.

Concepts of parallel processes and isomorphism can be confusing and particularly challenging to distinguish. Key differences are in their origins and focus. The parallel process originates from psychoanalytic theory and thus operates outside of one's awareness. Isomorphism originates in part from systems theory. It focuses on the repeated or recurrent relational patterns or similar dynamics that occur in supervision (between supervisor and supervisee) and counseling (between counselor and client). In contrast, the parallel process focus is intrapsychic.

Triangles

A triangle is a way to conceptualize relationships and has its origins in Bowenian family therapy. Within the three-person triangle, two persons are likely to be in coalition with each other leaving the third person on the peripheral, alienated, or excluded. When the coalition has conflict or tension, the third person can be recruited to take sides or form a new coalition. If this occurs, one member of the original coalition becomes the third party. One indicator of a coalition is when two members collude or secretly discuss the third member of the triangle. However, it is important to note that triangles have useful and positive purposes, as is the case in supervision.

In supervision, the triangle includes the client, counselor/supervisee, and supervisor and is a dynamic inherent in the supervisory process. In this triangle, two parties, the supervisee and the supervisor, meet regularly to discuss the third party, the client. These two members of the triangle collaborate to help the third member of the triangle achieve counseling goals. Supervisors need to be aware that collaboration with a supervisee for the benefit of the client can shift into collusion with the supervisee against the client. It is also possible for the client and counselor to discuss the supervisor, collaborating or colluding with the supervisor becoming the third party.

This section discussed the models, practices, and processes of clinical supervision. Supervisors use models of supervision to provide direction for navigating the supervisory process and are adept at recognizing the parallels occurring between the client and counselor and the supervisee and supervisor. Best practices in clinical supervision aid supervisors in improving and ensuring the effectiveness of the supervision they provide.

QUALITIES OF EFFECTIVE SUPERVISORS

Your experience in supervision will likely begin in one of your clinical courses (e.g., practicum or internship) and continue after graduation as you are supervised for licensure. Once licensed to practice independently and throughout your career, you will still seek out supervision for new or complex clinical issues. As you can see, the setting in which and person from whom you receive supervision will change. Much has been written on effective supervisory qualities or characteristics. Carifio and Hess (1987) described effective supervisors as those who exhibit high levels of empathy, understanding, unconditional positive regard, flexibility, concern, attention, investment, curiosity, and openness. Each of these qualities serves to create and maintain a supervisory relationship in which the supervisee feels safe to share successes and struggles. In addition to these, a sense of humor is a desirable characteristic of a supervisor. Humor can help the supervisor and supervisee find amusement and light-hearted moments that provoke laughter throughout supervision. This can offset the anxiety, stress, and emotional toll that come with counseling, particularly for counselors in training seeing clients for the first time. Respect for individual differences among supervisees and appreciation of diversity are also important characteristics of a supervisor. The supervisor needs to be able to operate within the supervisee's assumptive world, understand his or her values and beliefs, and consider the supervisee's culture. These personal characteristics of the supervisor can foster a meaningful supervisory relationship in which the tasks of supervision are completed.

In addition to the qualities or characteristics of supervisors, supervisory tasks or behaviors are indicative of a good supervisor. Abiddin (2008) outlined tasks that included appropriately structuring supervision; providing clear, direct, and constructive feedback; evaluating fairly and on agreed-upon criteria; navigating among roles such as teacher and counselor; accessing a variety of supervisory interventions; and adapting to individual differences in supervisees. Good supervisors tailor supervision to match the needs of the supervisee (Barnett & Molzon, 2014) by varying the amount of structure, direction, support, challenge, and collaboration in supervision sessions (Borders, 2014). Practicing and modeling self-care and supporting the self-care of the supervisee are also important attitudes and tasks of the supervisor (Barnett & Molzon, 2014).

Finally, effective supervisors are competent in the clinical areas to be supervised (e.g., play therapy, substance abuse treatment) and in clinical supervision (Barnett & Molzon, 2014). Supervisor competence can be captured in nine themes: ethics and professional practice, knowledge of the profession, diversity, reflective practice, supervisory alliance, structuring supervision, supervision research/theory, learning, and evaluation (Olds & Hawkins, 2014). Part of how supervisors gain competence in these areas is to engage in meta-competence, the ability to assess what one knows and does not know (Falender & Shafranske, 2014). In other words, good supervisors obtain continuing education;

engage in consultation and supervision; use feedback from mentors, other supervisors, colleagues, supervisees, and clients; and reflect on continued learning and effectiveness as a clinical supervisor.

Effective clinical supervisors impart knowledge, enhance skills, and help prepare the supervisee for success (Barnett & Molzon, 2014). Supervisors have a number of personal characteristics that support and maintain a supervisory relationship with supervisees similar to those that support a counseling relationship with clients. Through this relationship, good supervisors intentionally select interventions and techniques that meet the needs of supervisees and facilitate their growth. Effective supervisors examine their own effectiveness and actively seek opportunities to learn and grow as clinical supervisors.

CASE ILLUSTRATION 8.3

Joel the Ineffective Supervisor

Joel has been providing supervision for years in his clinical practice. He certainly has the knowledge and skills to provide supervision, but he lacks many of the necessary relational skills to develop a strong supervisor-supervisee relationship. In fact, many of his current supervisees find him rude and condescending and not very attentive toward their needs. One supervisee reported that Joel is so focused on the business side of things that he has lost touch with the purpose of providing supervision. She further stated that when he actually attempts to provide supervision, he just tells supervisees to do what he says in their next session rather than discussing the client/supervisee issue before collaboratively coming to a solution. Joel seems to have forgotten the purpose of counseling and is twice removed from the purpose of supervision. He has lost his connection to counseling and seems more concerned with the financial side of things. This is why Joel is considered an ineffective supervisor.

SUPERVISION TECHNIQUES AND INTERVENTIONS

A technique or intervention is a method or skill used by the supervisor to produce a desired result in supervision. A supervisor may choose a technique to help a supervisee gain insight or awareness or to consider an alternative perspective. Clinical supervisors use a variety of supervision techniques and interventions and intentionally select among them based on the form and format of supervision and the supervisee's needs.

GUIDED PRACTICE EXERCISE 8.2

After reading the Qualities of Effective Supervisors section, list additional qualities and characteristics of effective supervisors not discussed in the chapter. How do those qualities and characteristics align with your personal values and theoretical counseling orientation? When finished, find an in-class partner and share what you have identified and discovered.

Forms of Supervision

Supervision can simultaneously occur within the counseling session or it can occur retrospectively by digital, video, or audio recording or supervisee recall after the counseling session. A discussion of each of these and their advantages and disadvantages follows.

Live Supervision

In live supervision, the supervisee is the counselor in session and the supervisor observes the session. Depending on the setting and resources, the supervisor can observe the supervisee through a one-way mirror or a live feed in a viewing room or the supervisor's office. Counselors under supervision reveal this to their clients during the initial informed consent process. Clients must agree to this arrangement before it can occur. An advantage of live supervision is that the supervisor can intervene and offer the supervisee immediate feedback to apply within the counseling session. Supervisors can phone into the session, enter the counseling session, or talk to the supervisee in session through a wireless device worn by the supervisee. A disadvantage of this format is the logistics or scheduling needed. For live supervision to happen, the client and counselor must attend the session, and the supervisor must be available to observe the session. This can become challenging for supervisees when clients cancel or reschedule supervision. Similarly, it can be a challenge for supervisors with multiple supervisees to observe.

Recordings

Digital or video recordings of counseling sessions capture both the sound and picture of the counseling session and are played during the supervision session. These recordings allow the supervisor to provide feedback on the content, process, and nonverbal skills of the supervisee. An advantage of using recordings in supervision is that they can be paused, rewound, or fast-forwarded in the supervision session. Although audio recordings do not capture the picture, they are particularly useful when counseling sites do not allow for other forms of recording. A disadvantage to this form of supervision is the many ways in which recordings or the technology can fail. Examples include a supervisee forgetting to record the session, dead batteries, recording over sessions, and inaudible sounds on the part of the client or counselor. Even if supervisees are well prepared and the technology works properly, events outside the control of the supervisor or supervisee

GUIDED PRACTICE EXERCISE 8.3

Assume you are the supervisee in the mowing scenario described on the next page. You have entered supervision with the goal of watching and listening to a recorded session with your supervisor for feedback and you cannot hear anything said in session over the sound of the lawnmower. How might you adjust your goal and receive feedback on this session with just video (absence of audio)? In other words, what would be the new focus of supervision?

can cause problems. In one summer session, the first author supervised an internship student whose counseling sessions with a particular client could be watched but not heard because of the physical plant personnel mowing the grass outside the counseling and training clinic at the time of the counseling session.

Recall Supervision

Recall supervision occurs when a supervisee recalls a counseling session that has already occurred. It has a long history as a widely used format of supervision for it predates the introduction and evolution of recording capabilities and technology. Supervisors can direct the supervisee as to the important elements of the counseling session to recall for supervision purposes. For example, a supervisor may choose to focus on the supervisee's recall of the skills he or she used in session. Or a supervisor may focus on the supervisee's recall of his or her internal processes from the counseling session. Advantages of this type of supervision are that it is free, can be used by supervisees in a variety of practice settings, and does not rely on technology. It can also serve as a backup when issues occur in live supervision or in recording counseling sessions. A notable disadvantage of recall supervision is its reliance on observation, memory, and accurate self-report of the supervisee. As the amount of time from the counseling session to the supervision session increases, the ability of the supervisee to recall the session diminishes. Supervisees can keep their case notes and treatment plans updated to aid in their recall of the content and process of counseling sessions.

Formats of Supervision

Supervision can occur in several formats: individual, triadic, group, or team. It is common for supervisees to participate in both individual and group supervision for it is a Council for Accreditation of Counseling and Related Educational Programs (CACREP) requirement (CACREP, 2016). These are not the only formats of supervision, and it is likely a supervisee will participate in one of the other formats before being licensed to practice independently. A brief description of supervision formats follows.

Individual Supervision

Supervision that occurs with one supervisor and one supervisee is called individual supervision. Supervisees may participate in individual supervision with a faculty member, supervisor of an external clinical site, or post-master's supervisor. Similar to the description of Chandra at the start of the chapter, supervisees entering individual supervision for the first time can be unsure of what to expect.

Triadic Supervision

Triadic supervision includes a supervisory relationship between one supervisor and two supervisees. Supervisees benefit from the exchange of feedback with another supervisee and the supervisor. Having three perspectives in supervision can allow for new ideas that would not occur in individual supervision. Essential to the effectiveness of triadic supervision is the supervisor's thoughtful and intentional selection of the two supervisees.

Group Supervision

This format of supervision includes a supervisory relationship between more than two supervisees. Counselor preparation programs frequently use their practicum and internship class time for group supervision. Supervisees benefit from hearing the counseling experiences of their classmates. This can decrease supervisee anxiety and normalize their concerns related to confidence and competence. Group supervision also provides a safe environment in which supervisees can test their assumptions, try out new behaviors, and give and receive feedback.

Team Supervision

As the name suggests, this format includes a team, typically comprised of the supervisee's peers and a supervisor. A reflecting team, created by Tom Anderson, is an example of team supervision for working with families. The reflecting team observes a counselor working with a family. After observing, the reflecting team begins a respectful discussion of the family counseling session while the family observes. The family then shares their responses to the reflecting team's discussion. In this format, the reflecting team members and the family are actively involved in the counseling process.

Peer Supervision

This format includes a group of peers who meet regularly for mutual benefit to discuss and receive feedback on their cases, counseling skills, and professional difficulties or challenges. Peer supervision occurs in group but should not be confused with group supervision. A key difference between the two is that peer supervision does not have a defined or designated leader.

Supervisees may experience a variety of forms, formats, and interventions as they matriculate through a counselor preparation program and post-master's supervision until licensure for independent practice. Each offers the supervisee an opportunity to receive feedback that can inform and enhance their work with clients.

TECHNOLOGY-ASSISTED SUPERVISION

In recent years, there has been a dramatic rise in the use of technology for health care delivery. The field of behavioral health has not been immune from this trend, with the advent of technology-based innovations for all phases of counseling practice including screening, assessment, therapeutic intervention, and documentation (Berrouiguet, Baca-García, Brandt, Walter, & Courtet 2016; Ben-Zeev, 2012; Kay-Lambkin, Baker, Lewin, & Carr, 2009; Marsch, 2012; Marsch & Ben-Zeev, 2012). As technology is increasingly being integrated into the care delivery process, considering how new technologies can augment or enhance the practice of supervision becomes important. This section provides an overview of technology use in supervision and outline issues to consider when deciding to incorporate it into supervision practice.

What Does It Mean to Use Technology for Supervision?

Technology is an incredibly broad term with probably as many interpretations as there are people in the world. To some, having steady access to a telephone line constitutes a technological advance. To others, interpreting a client's sleep habits from sensor data gathered from a mobile phone and entered into an electronic health record could be an innovative solution best suited for their setting or practice. Different approaches solve different issues, making it important to always match a chosen technology to the settings and individuals with whom it will be used. However, when choosing to use technology, supervisors should remember that the most advanced technology is not always the best technology for a given environment. Feasibility of implementing a new technology often hinges on many factors including cost and complexity of the intervention, characteristics of individuals who will use the tools, and the setting in which the tools will be used (Damschroder et al., 2009). When thinking about how to apply technology to the supervision process, consider if you need a solution for "in the moment" support or if you are looking to enhance less immediate communication between a supervisor and supervisee.

Synchronous Versus Asynchronous Technology Models

A good way to think about the types of technology available for helping in the supervisory relationship is whether they help facilitate direct or indirect communication. **Synchronous technology** products allow for back-and-forth interaction between supervisees and their supervisor in *real time*. An example of synchronous technology is a video call where the supervisor and supervisee interact with little to no delay in response. In contrast, **asynchronous technology** involves a *delay in response time* between the initiation of contact and a reply (Chapman, Baker, Nassar-McMillan, & Gerler, 2011). Examples of supervision provided via asynchronous technology include a counselor asking a question to a supervisor via text or e-mail. Table 8.2 provides further examples of synchronous and asynchronous technologies.

When thinking about synchronous and asynchronous technologies, one is neither inherently better nor worse than the other. Both types have situations ideally suited for their application. Counselors and their supervisors should discuss and identify what types of interaction are appropriate for each form of technology prior to implementing a new strategy. Asynchronous technology can be highly effective in situations such as providing administrative supervision, asking questions about case conceptualizations, or getting delayed feedback on recorded sessions. On the other hand, synchronous technologies are ideal for situations that benefit from in-the-moment processing or reflection. Developing initial case conceptualizations, reviewing crisis responses, and working through transference or countertransference issues are all examples of supervision tasks that may be best suited toward a synchronous technology.

Whereas some situations are best suited for either asynchronous or synchronous technologies, other situations are typically less appropriate for certain modalities. One would not want to use asynchronous technology in a situation where an

TABLE 8.2 ■ Examples of Synchronous and Asynchronous Technology for Supervision		
Modality of Technology	**Examples**	**Best Use Cases**
Synchronous	• Telephone • Video/webcam conferencing • Instant messaging/chat rooms • "Bug" in the ear/live observation via webcam • Virtual environments (e.g., "Second Life")	• Crisis or when urgent response is needed • More in-depth client conceptualization • Exploration of complex transference/countertransference issues
Asynchronous	• Text messaging • E-mail • Social networking • Session recordings • Cloud-based document sharing • Electronic health record review	• Noncrisis communication • Scheduling • Brief, concrete questions • Documentation review and feedback • Sharing resources and training materials

Note: All communications, synchronous or asynchronous, should always take place using a secure and encrypted HIPAA-compliant platform.

immediate response might be necessary, such as in a crisis or other time-sensitive scenario. With limited ability to ensure communication has transmitted through an asynchronous mechanism, synchronous technology or live communication is best suited to support these scenarios. For this reason, it is incredibly important for the supervisor and counselor to be on the same page with expectations about response time when using asynchronous technology. For example, if a supervisor does not check e-mail after-hours, it is important for a counselor to know this and have another plan in place for seeking support should he or she need it. Synchronous technologies also require a degree of communication and planning before implementation so that support may continue even if there is a problem with technology. Consider a scenario where a counselor is meeting with his supervisor via video conference and the audio stops working. In this case, it would be important to have a backup phone number established to reduce frustration or anxiety or cancellation of the session altogether. Establishing backup plans for technology-related problems should be done early in a supervisory relationship, before the use of a technology platform is introduced.

There are many options for incorporating technology into the supervision process. Individuals may explore technology as an augment to traditional, in-person supervision, or they may use technology to access supervisors who live in a different location, thus replacing an in-person relationship but perhaps expanding access to a critical support service. When thinking about adding technology to a supervisory relationship, reflect on the gap that needs filling. Is there a need for increased administrative oversight of files by a supervisor? Perhaps a HIPAA-compliant online file sharing program may help with this goal. Is there a desire for in-the-moment observation of counseling sessions? A video conference solution might best fit this need. It is important to pair a technology intervention with an identified need in a supervisory relationship. Although it can be overwhelming to consider the breadth of possibilities for applying technology to supervision, thoughtful reflection on the potential benefits of using technology and having a plan to mitigate risk will likely help individuals feel better about the practice of using something new.

Benefits and Risks of Technology-Enhanced Supervision

Although there is a growing amount of research on technology-based clinical interventions, less research exists about the prevalence and application of technology in supervision. Understandably, this might give some pause about becoming an early adopter of technology in supervision practice. When weighing this consideration, it is important to reflect on how technology will benefit the relationship and what can be done to mitigate risks associated with using technology.

Benefits of Technology-Enhanced Supervision

One of the biggest benefits seen when technology is integrated into health care delivery systems is more individuals able to access services (Marsch & Lord, 2015). With the benefit of technology, clients may seek services at more convenient times, from more specialized providers, and remain in a location more comfortable for them. These benefits apply to the practice of enhancing supervision with technology. Counselors are able to seek out more specialized supervisors and access supervision at times or in places that are more convenient for them. Some counselors unable to receive supervision due to a rural location or lack of area resources may be able to find supervision that would not otherwise be accessible. Similar to what is seen when clients use technology-enhanced care delivery and show higher disclosure and satisfaction, supervisees also show more self-disclosure and satisfaction in their supervision experience when using technology-enhanced methods (Cummings, 2002; Xavier, Shepherd, & Goldstein, 2007). This is in large part due to the convenience of supervision contact, individualization of supervision feedback, and increased safety associated with communicating via a technology platform. Interestingly, similar to the benefits clients see through a technology-facilitated treatment

GUIDED PRACTICE EXERCISE 8.4

List scenarios where technology might enhance supervision. Ask yourself what type of technology might best help in these scenarios. In a hypothetical scenario, think of a problem that might occur and develop a backup plan.

intervention (Clarke et al., 2016), technology-enhanced supervision also preserves the working relationship between participants (Reese et al., 2009). Although technology-enhanced supervision allows for greater access to support and maintains the critical features of a positive supervisory relationship, it remains important to be aware of risks associated with technology-enhanced supervision.

Risks of Technology-Enhanced Supervision

Incorporating technology into the supervisory relationship can also bring communication complications (Vaccaro & Lambie, 2007). Messages exchanged between a supervisor and counselor via e-mail, text, or other asynchronous method not only run the risk of not transmitting in a timely manner but also being interpreted in a way other than intended. Perhaps a question was not asked clearly (making one appear to know less than one does) or a response was briefer than desired (making it sound curt or aggressive). For this reason, it is often best to keep asynchronous communications short and task oriented (e.g., setting up an appointment, focusing on administrative tasks, sharing resources) rather than focused on more complex processing issues. Supervision participants should agree ahead of time that if supervisors feel something is best handled via an in-person or synchronous method of communication, then this will be communicated in response to the asynchronous contact.

Working with a supervisor who lives far away or is unfamiliar with your area presents risks or challenges as well. Most states have laws specific to them and may be different in other places. This may influence components of the supervisory relationship including, but not limited to, professional development (e.g., supervisor unfamiliar with licensing laws in a given state) and clinical response (e.g., supervisor unfamiliar with laws around involuntary commitment in a given state). It is imperative that supervisors be educated about the laws in states in which they provide supervision and also prudent for counselors to seek supervision from individuals in their own state (or familiar with state law) whenever possible, even if using technology.

A further risk to consider is less about the communication between a counselor and supervisor and more about the platform selection. The counseling profession has clearly identified laws (e.g., HIPAA, 42 CFR, part 2) and ethical codes guiding the way a professional should interact with personal health information. When selecting a technology platform for use in supervision, it is imperative that counselors and supervisors consider these laws and ethical codes. Although it might be convenient to use a popular social networking site to facilitate supervision, it likely is not the best choice. Even though all parties may have access and the platform may have the desired functionality of text, voice, video, and document sharing it still is likely not appropriate for use. Technology must be HIPAA compliant for it to be appropriate for most types of clinical supervision. Non-HIPAA-compliant services can be ideal for training, education, and some administrative tasks (such as scheduling or canceling a supervision appointment) but are not suited for transmitting, storing, or viewing personal health information associated with client files. Individuals should inquire with the vendor of a particular service about HIPAA compliance. This information changes often and must be confirmed regularly. Just because a device or program was HIPAA compliant once does not mean it will remain that way.

CASE ILLUSTRATION 8.4

The Challenge With Technology in Supervision

Have you ever misinterpreted a text message or e-mail from a friend? Perhaps something was not communicated clearly or an emotion was projected other than what was intended by the sender. Sending a well-intended message to your supervisor to inform him or her that you are running late to supervision can easily be interpreted as being inconsiderate of your supervisor's time. Likewise, your supervisor informing you that supervision has been cancelled via e-mail rather than calling you by phone may send an unintended message. Just like with counselors who use electronic communication with their clients, there is always the risk of communicating unintended messages; even more dangerous is the possibility of the recipient of your message not being the intended receiver.

Is Technology Right for Me?

After considering the problems technology might help solve, the products available, the benefits of incorporating technology, and complications resulting from technology use in supervision, it is important to think about how to implement these interventions in practice. Just because something seems like a good fit, is the newest technology, or has been successful somewhere else does not mean it will be feasible to implement in a given setting or supervisory relationship. Individuals thinking of implementing technology into their practice should consider who will be using the technology, where it will be used, and what resources and knowledge will be needed to start using these tools. If a setting has poor Internet speed or lacks computer hardware, implementing a technology product might not be a good fit. If your setting has ample access to resources but low self-efficacy among staff tasked with using technology, selecting a tool with a simple interface or fewer steps for use would be most ideal. If you have an enthusiastic supervisor and counselor, access to resources, and clearly identified tools to help the process, it is *still* prudent to show restraint when implementing. Try picking one new tool at a time so as not to overwhelm the supervision process with new procedures. Keeping an implementation plan simple will also help you understand what might not be working if something goes wrong and aid in more easily coming up with a solution.

Supervision is a complex process that relies on a strong relationship between supervisor and supervisee. Technology not only has the potential to make that connection more accessible, it might even strengthen it by allowing for more interaction at more convenient times. Making decisions about using technology can be overwhelming. Choose technology products that fit an identified gap in the supervision process and make sense in the context of a given service setting. Although technology has been shown to maintain feelings of alliance and enhance satisfaction by counselors, technology-assisted supervision is not unlike traditional supervision. If someone feels unsure about what to do, ask for the help needed from a supervisor, no matter if in person or online.

Supervisors have the dual responsibilities of promoting the supervisee's professional growth and development and protecting the interests and welfare of the clients with whom the supervisee counsels. Supervisors rely on supervision models to help them navigate these responsibilities. Techniques and interventions, including those that incorporate technology, are intentionally selected by supervisors to facilitate the supervisee's professional growth as a counselor and clinical competence.

Keystones

- *Supervision* has many definitions and is a term broadly used in a variety of professions. In counseling, the term *clinical supervision* is used to describe an intensive relationship-based process that supports and facilitates the supervisee's professional development and clinical competence over time while ensuring the welfare of the supervisee's clients.

- There are a variety of supervision models from which a supervisor may practice. In this chapter, developmental models, orientation or theory-driven models, and integrative models were described. A commonality of the models is that they all aim to enhance the clinical competence of the supervisee.

- A number of qualities and behaviors are indicative of an effective supervisor. Good supervisors exhibit some of the same qualities as effective counselors, including empathy, understanding, unconditional positive regard, flexibility, and patience. They also tailor supervision sessions to meet the needs of the supervisee and ensure that supervision sessions prepare the supervisee for success.

- Techniques and interventions in supervision vary according to supervisor preference or personality and theoretical orientation. Despite this variance, the techniques or interventions used are all intentionally selected by the supervisor to meet the unique needs of the supervisee.

- Technology shows promise for enhancing the supervision practice. Matching the type of technology selected with how it will benefit the practice and planning for complications associated with technology use are keys for success. Aligning a technology with the setting and individual characteristics of those using it will best predict success when implementing new technology in practice.

Key Terms

Asynchronous technology 206

Clinical supervision 191

Gatekeeping 199

Holding environment 192

Isomorphism 200

Parallel processes 199

Supervisee 191

Supervisor 191

Synchronous technology 206

Triadic supervision 204

Web Resources

Approved Clinical Supervisor Code of Ethics (www .ncblpc.org/Assets/LawsAndCodes/ACS_Code_ of_Ethics(forSupervisors).pdf)

Association for Counselor Education and Supervision (www.acesonline.net)

Association for Counselor Education and Supervision Standards for Counselor Supervisors (www.acesonline.net/sites/default/files/aces_ stds_for_counseling_supervisors_jcdv69n1-1.pdf)

National Board for Certified Counselors (www.nbcc.org)

References

Abiddin, N. Z. (2008). Exploring clinical supervision to facilitate the creative process of supervision. *Journal of International Social Research, 1/3*, 13–33.

American Association of State Counseling Boards. (2007). *Approved supervisor model.* Retrieved from http://www.aascb.org/aws/AASCB/asset_manager/get_file/37297

American Counseling Association. (2014). *Code of ethics.* Alexandria, VA: Author.

Barnett, J. E. (2014). Introduction: The (hopefully) essential primer on clinical supervision. *Journal of Clinical Psychology: In Session, 70*(11), 1023–1029. doi:10.1002/jclp.22123

Barnett, J. E., & Molzon, C. H. (2014). Clinical supervision of psychotherapy: Essential ethics issues for supervisors and supervisees. *Journal of Clinical Psychology: In Session, 70*(11), 1051–1061. doi:10.1002/jclp.22126

Ben-Zeev, D. (2012). Mobile technologies in the study, assessment, and treatment of schizophrenia. *Schizophrenia Bulletin, 38*, 384–385.

Bernard, J. M., & Goodyear, R. K. (2014). *Fundamentals of clinical supervision* (5th ed.). Upper Saddle River, NJ: Pearson.

Berrouiguet, S., Baca-García, E., Brandt, S., Walter, M., & Courtet, P. (2016). Fundamentals for future mobile-health (mHealth): A systematic review of mobile phone and web-based text messaging in mental health. *Journal of Medical Internet Research, 18*(6), e135.

Borders, L. D. (2014). Best practices in clinical supervision: Another step in delineating effective supervision practice. *American Journal of Psychotherapy, 68*(2), 151–162.

Borders, L. D., Glosoff, H. L., Welfare, L. E., Hays, D. G., DeKruyf, L., Fernando, D. M., & Page, B. (2014). Best practices in clinical supervision: Evolution of a counseling specialty. *The Clinical Supervisor, 33*(1), 26–44. doi:10.1080/07325223.2014.905225

Carifio, M. S., & Hess, A. K. (1987). Who is the ideal supervisor? *Professional Psychology, 18*, 244–250.

Chapman, R. A., Baker, S. B., Nassar-McMillan, S. C., & Gerler, E. R. (2011). Cybersupervision: Further examination of synchronous and asynchronous modalities in counseling practicum supervision. *Counselor Education and Supervision, 50*(5), 298–313.

Clarke, J., Proudfoot, J., Whitton, A., Birch, M. R., Boyd, M., Parker, G., . . . & Fogarty, A. (2016). Therapeutic alliance with a fully automated mobile phone and web-based intervention: Secondary analysis of a randomized controlled trial. *JMIR Mental Health, 3*(1), e10. doi:10.2196/mental.4656

Council for Accreditation of Counseling and Related Educational Programs. (2016). *2016 CACREP standards.* Alexander, VA: Author.

Cummings, P. (2002). Cybervision: Virtual peer group counselling supervision—Hindrance or help? *Counselling and Psychotherapy Research, 2*(4), 223–229.

Damschroder, L. J., Aron, D. C., Keith, R. E., Kirsh, S. R., Alexander, J. A., & Lowery, J. C. (2009). Fostering implementation of health services research findings into practice: A consolidated framework for advancing implementation science. *Implementation Science, 4*(1), 1. doi:10.1186/1748-5908-4-50

Falender, C. A., & Shafranske, E. P. (2014). Clinical supervision: The state of the art. *Journal of Clinical Psychology: In Session, 70*(11), 1030–1041. doi:10.1002/jclp.22124

Falender, C. A., Shafranske, E. P., & Ofek, A. (2014). Competent clinical supervision: Emerging effective practices. *Counselling Psychology Quarterly, 27*(4), 393–408. doi:10.1080/09515070.2014.934785

Kay-Lambkin, F. J., Baker, A. L., Lewin, T. J., & Carr, V. J. (2009). Computer-based psychological treatment for comorbid depression and problematic alcohol and/or cannabis use: A randomized controlled trial of clinical efficacy. *Addiction, 104*(3), 378–388.

Koltz, R. L., Odegard, M. A., Feit, S. S., Provost, K., & Smith, T. (2012). Parallel process and isomorphism: A model for decision making in the supervisory triad. *Family Journal*, *20*(3), 232–238. doi:10.1177/1066480712448788

Leddick, G. R. (1994). Models of clinical supervision. *ERIC Digest*. Retrieved from https://www.counseling.org/resources/library/ERIC%20Digests/94-08.pdf

Marsch, L. A. (2012). Leveraging technology to enhance addiction treatment and recovery. *Journal of Addictive Diseases*, *31*(3), 313–318.

Marsch, L. A., & Ben-Zeev, D. (2012). Technology-based assessments and interventions targeting psychiatric and substance use disorders: Innovations and opportunities. *Journal of Dual Diagnosis*, *8*(4), 259–261.

Marsch, L. A., & Lord, S. (2015). Applying technology to the assessment, prevention, treatment, and recovery support of substance use disorders. *Textbook of Addiction Treatment: International Perspectives*, 1085–1092.

Olds, K., & Hawkins, R. (2014). Precursors to measuring outcomes in clinical supervision: A thematic analysis. *Training and Education in Professional Psychology*, *8*, 158–164.

Reese, R. J., Usher, E. L., Bowman, D. C., Norsworthy, L. A., Halstead, J. L., Rowlands, S. R., &

Chisholm, R. R. (2009). Using client feedback in psychotherapy training: An analysis of its influence on supervision and counselor self-efficacy. *Training and Education in Professional Psychology*, *3*(3), 157–168.

Rogers, C. (1951). *Client-centered therapy: Its current practice, implications and theory*. London, England: Constable.

Stoltenberg, C. D., McNeill, B., & Delworth, U. (1998). *IDM supervision: An integrated developmental model for supervising counselors and therapists*. San Francisco, CA: Jossey-Bass.

Vaccaro, N., & Lambie, G. W. (2007). Computer-based counselor-in-training supervision: Ethical and practical implications for counselor educators and supervisors. *Counselor Education and Supervision*, *47*(1), 46–57. doi:10.1002/j.1556-6978.2007.tb00037x

White, E., & Winstanley, J. (2014). Clinical supervision and the helping professions: An interpretation of history. *The Clinical Supervisor*, *33*, 3–25. doi:10.1080/07325223.2014.905226

Xavier, K., Shepherd, L., & Goldstein, D. (2007). Clinical supervision and education via videoconference: A feasibility project. *Journal of Telemedicine and Telecare*, *13*(4), 206–209.

CURRENT AND EMERGING TRENDS IN CLINICAL MENTAL HEALTH COUNSELING

SECTION II

9

INCORPORATING EVIDENCE-BASED PRACTICES IN THE TREATMENT OF MENTAL DISORDERS

At this point in your training as a professional counselor, your instructors have undoubtedly introduced you to a multitude of theories, techniques, and interventions available for use with your clients. Each seemingly holds promise for helping clients achieve their counseling goals and benefiting positively from the experience. Additionally, you likely will continually be exposed to new theories throughout your career as a professional counselor. With so many options, several questions have likely arisen in your mind. *Which approach should I use? How do I know if this is the right choice for my client? Will this approach be effective? If so, how will I know?* These questions are perfectly natural for beginning counselors. In fact, experienced counselors routinely ask themselves these same questions from time to time throughout their careers. So what is a counselor to do? Although you should make decisions related to the direction and approach used in your counseling work based on the unique needs of each client and your own clinical intuition, there are guidelines available to help in your selection process. This chapter introduces you to the concept of evidence-based practice (EBP). EBP refers to the intentional selection of therapeutic approaches or modalities that have been rigorously examined using various research methodologies to document their effectiveness with diverse clients and a range of presenting issues and concerns.

Incorporating the best available research into clinical practice is one of the core components of EBP. Among mental health professionals, this practice has become the accepted standard in most facilities and agency settings (Baker, 2012). Although this approach to treatment may seem like a recent advancement, interest in developing an evidence base supporting the efficacy and effectiveness of the work counselors do dates to the early 1970s. Since then, researchers have been collecting, aggregating, and synthesizing data collected from scores of studies to provide a snapshot of what seems to work in counseling. Although not a guarantee that these approaches will be effective with every client with whom you interact, the research supports the general utility of these approaches when used in the way designed. As such, counselors who integrate these approaches into their work with clients are said to be practicing in an evidence-based manner. In this chapter, you will learn more about EBP, including the advantages and disadvantages of incorporating EBP into your routine interactions with clients and best practices for evidence-informed decision-making. Armed with this new knowledge, you will be better equipped to answer some of those questions mentioned earlier.

LEARNING OBJECTIVES

After reading this chapter, you will be able to do the following:

- Define evidence-based practice (EBP)

- Articulate the importance of EBP in contemporary counseling practice

- Describe the process for identifying and selecting appropriate empirically supported treatments (ESTs) to employ in your clinical work with clients (CACREP 5C-2-m)

- Evaluate the effectiveness of therapeutic approaches identified as ESTs

- Implement ESTs in various clinical settings (CACREP 5C-2-c)

- Identify ESTs currently practiced in clinical mental health settings (CACREP 5C-3-b)

EVIDENCE-BASED PRACTICE DEFINED

The use of research to guide clinical practice has existed in psychology since the 1800s. However, the formalization of this concept is a relatively new development (Norcross, Beutler, & Levant, 2006). In 2005, a Presidential Task Force was commissioned by the American Psychological Association to study the growing interest in evidence-based practice. Based on a review of existing literature and group deliberations, the task force reached consensus on a definition of **evidence-based practice** (EBP) as "the integration of the best available research with clinical expertise in the context of patient characteristics, culture, and preferences" (APA Presidential Task Force on EBP, 2006, p. 273). Shortly thereafter, this new training paradigm spread to other health care–related fields, and the term *evidence-based practice* began appearing in nursing, social work, and counseling journals as well (Rahman & Applebaum, 2010). References to the use of EBP in counseling practice can be found in the latest versions of both the American Counseling

Association (ACA) Code of Ethics and the Council for the Accreditation of Counseling and Related Educational Programs (CACREP) standards. As a result, counselors are being tasked with moving their practice in this direction.

As research supporting clinical practice continues, counselors will become increasingly responsible for combining this scientific evidence with their own clinical expertise and client preferences in promotion of EBP (Aarons, Wells, Zagursky, Fettes, & Palinkas, 2009). In recognition of this shift in practice, the APA task force's definition directly speaks to the combination of three perspectives when choosing interventions for working with clients. First, counselors should evaluate available interventions, especially interventions supported by research, and discern what the research indicates about the efficacy of these interventions. When reviewing the research literature, it is important to recognize that the utility of established evidence is directly related to the questions needing to be addressed (Sackett & Wennberg, 1997). Is the counselor more interested in the etiology, pathogenesis, or prognosis of a disorder among a population? If so, **longitudinal studies** (where observational data are gathered repeatedly over time) that track clients over an extended period would be more useful. On the other hand, if the counselor was more interested in learning about the proven efficacy and/or effectiveness of a specific treatment, **randomized control trials** (studies where separate groups created by chance are used to compare treatments or interventions) should be sought. These designs are the least prone to error and often seen as the ideal research design. Research designs are further discussed later in this chapter.

Second, counselors should consider their own clinical experience and expertise, realizing that intuition educated by years of experience is beneficial in understanding a client's presenting problem. Of the three perspectives, this one is the most challenging to comprehend. Clinical intuition is largely an ambiguous term and varies across counselors. Additionally, it is hard to explain how and when one develops such intuition. Is it an innate characteristic or one we can be trained to develop? What does seem to be known is that clinical experience supports stronger decision-making. The more experience you have working with a variety of clients, the more you are able to understand potential precursors to identified problems and conceptualize your clients at a deeper level. Further, a significant body of literature exists supporting the fact that nonspecific therapeutic factors often contribute the most to positive outcomes in counseling (Ilardi & Craighead, 1994). As a result, counselors should try to integrate their in vivo experiences with what the research suggests.

Finally, clinicians should account for the unique experience of their clients and how the worldview of these clients is impacted by their culture, values, beliefs, and preferences. Counseling, however practiced, will only be effective when client buy-in is achieved. When clients are not invested in the process, little progress is made. In your training program you have been taught that counseling should be a co-constructed activity. This includes mapping out treatment options and potential interventions to use. Clients should be regular contributors to the decision-making process. Soliciting clients' thoughts and opinions on various interventions can help you maximize the time spent in session by attempting approaches that will be well received. Much of this may be covered in the informed consent to treatment you discuss with your clients at the onset of counseling, but the process should not end there. Routinely check in with your clients to ensure the approaches being attempted resonate with them, are consistent with their needs, and do not impose external values they themselves may not endorse. In their text *Clinician's Guide to Evidence-Based Practices: Mental Health and the Addictions*, Norcross, Hogan, and Koocher (2008) outline a number of client characteristics and values counselors should consider when making treatment decisions, including presenting concerns, comorbidity, age, stage of life, developmental history, gender, gender identity, ethnicity, social class, race, religion, employment status, capability, sexual orientation, and worldview.

Collectively, these perspectives are often referred to as the three legs of the EBP stool (see Figure 9.1; Spring, 2007; Yates, 2013). This problem-solving approach to the delivery of care serves as a way for counselors to reconcile the humanistic core values on which the counseling profession is based with the emerging demands placed on using scientific research in practice (Lister & Moody, 2017).

Related Terminology

Essentially, EBP assists counselors by enhancing the quality of services they deliver and improving client outcomes. Among mental health professionals, EBP has gradually become the standard form of practice for health services planning and delivery (Altin, Passon, Kautz-Freimuth, Berger, & Stock, 2015; Baker, 2012). Despite calls for EBP to become an integral part of the counseling profession (Hays, 2010; Shapiro, 2009), a fair amount of uncertainty and confusion remains among counseling professionals as to what constitutes EBP and how counselors transition to this approach for routine client care (Yates, 2013). To help you, the beginning counselor, develop a working understanding of EBP it is important to differentiate the term from similar concepts.

A term commonly mistaken as being synonymous with EBP is **empirically supported treatment** (EST). Whereas EST refers to a *specific* technique, intervention, or treatment shown to be efficacious in previous research, EBP refers more broadly to the overall process of making data-informed clinical decisions related to client care (Bloom, Fischer, & Orme, 2009). The decision to use an EST with a client is an example of a counselor demonstrating EBP. Traditionally, treatments and interventions used in counseling have not been based on evidence of efficacy or effectiveness (Hoagwood & Olin, 2002).

FIGURE 9.1 ■ Evidence-Based Practice Stool

Available Research

Clinical Expertise   Client Values/Beliefs

GUIDED PRACTICE EXERCISE 9.1

Think about your favorite counseling approach. Perhaps it is one you have used successfully in your work with a client. Or it could be an approach you have learned about that seems to resonate with you in some meaningful way. Is this approach considered an EST? Conduct a brief review of the literature and see if you can locate at least three research-based articles in which the approach is evidenced to work.

However, in nearly all clinical mental health settings, counselors are now being expected to adhere to EBP for doing so often relates to the ability to get paid for the services they provide (see Chapter 7 for more on EBP and managed care). Later in this chapter we describe the process of identifying and implementing ESTs in your clinical work with a variety of clients.

Another term often used incorrectly as a synonym of EBP is **practice-based evidence** (PBE). With PBE, counselors' firsthand clinical experiences with their clients are used to inform research. Rather than implementing established ESTs as part of informed EBP, counselors using PBE gather their own data from clients through observation, assessment, and monitoring progress made toward established treatment goals. This information is then compared to an existing model or standard of care. For example, a counselor may be working with a couple who are experiencing marital discord due to poor communication skills by both partners. The counselor, after gathering enough information about the couple and their presenting problem, identifies CBT as a therapeutic approach that might be effective. During counseling, the counselor compares the progress made by his clients with what the research indicates should be expected using CBT in this manner. By comparing actual experiences to an identified benchmark, counselors can see what is working, what is not working, and what modifications may need to be made (Barkham, Hardy, & Mellor-Clark, 2010; Laska, Gurman, & Wampold, 2014).

IMPORTANCE OF EVIDENCE-BASED PRACTICE TO CONTEMPORARY COUNSELING PRACTICE

Evidence-based practice is significant for counselors seeking to work in contemporary clinical mental health settings. Not only does EBP represent current best practice in the field, its use also has ethical and legal implications.

Ethical Implications

Adopting an EBP approach aids counselors in adhering to the ethical standards and responsibilities enforced and established by the American Counseling Association (2014) in its Code of Ethics. For instance, ethical code A.4.a., Avoiding Harm (p. 4), delineates that counselors must not harm clients, trainees, or research participants. If harm is unavoidable or unanticipated, counselors must seek to minimize and provide remediation for said harm. Evidence-based practice assists counselors in avoiding harm by prompting them to consider their own expertise as well as their clients' experiences and needs when evaluating approaches and techniques to use. Another example relates to ethical code C.2.a., Boundaries of Competence (p. 8), which explains that counselors must only practice within the bounds of their competence, while continuing to seek greater competence in working with diverse populations. Evidence-based practice lends itself well to this specific ethical code because one of its main components is meant to account for counselor expertise, otherwise referred to as competence. One last particularly relevant ethical code is F.7.h., Innovative Theories and Techniques (p. 14). Whereas this code refers to counselor educators, it essentially emphasizes the promotion of approaches and techniques based in empirical evidence. This ethical code is like the focus EBP has on using approaches and techniques empirically proven to be effective in recent research.

Legal Implications

Evidence-based practice also has legal implications for counselors. Specifically, the appropriate use of EBP may help counselors avoid legal issues. To do so, it is important to consider the three legs of the EBP stool. For example, most civil suits brought against counselors relate to malpractice. Malpractice suits encompass several issues that relate to EBP. For instance, one malpractice issue relates to a counselor's use of a theory or technique that is not commonly practiced in the field. A counselor properly employing EBP is perhaps less likely to encounter such an issue brought against him or her due to the *available research* and *client values/beliefs* components of EBP. By using empirically supported approaches and techniques, while also considering client values and beliefs, counselors are obligated to use accepted treatment approaches that fit with their clients' presenting needs and are consistent with their values and worldview (Wheeler & Bertram, 2012; Yates, 2013).

Another common cause for malpractice claims is when counselors practice a procedure or technique for which they have not been adequately trained. In this situation, the use of EBP also would aid in preventing a malpractice suit. This is due to the EBP components of *clinical expertise* and seeking out research on empirically proven techniques relevant to the *client values/beliefs*. When choosing treatment options, counselors following an EBP approach are to consider the boundaries of their competence. Depending on the context, counselors may discover options regarding empirically proven procedures and techniques that fit with their scope of practice and training. Conversely, counselors also may discover that no options exist within their realm of competence, prompting them to explore ways to gain competence with that procedure or technique (APA Presidential Task Force, 2006; Spring, 2007; Wheeler & Bertram, 2012; Yates, 2013).

A third potential malpractice issue relates to not using a potentially more helpful technique. The application of EBP may assist counselors in avoiding this malpractice suit as well. Here all three legs of the EBP stool come into play. In this situation, counselors would actively employ the most helpful approaches and techniques within their competence by accounting for client needs as well as counselor expertise and subsequently seeking out relevant empirically established approaches and techniques (APA Presidential Task Force, 2006; Spring, 2007; Wheeler & Bertram, 2012; Yates, 2013).

IDENTIFYING EMPIRICALLY SUPPORTED TREATMENTS SUPPORTING EVIDENCE-BASED PRACTICE

A common misconception is the belief that all research found in counseling journals is considered evidence-supported treatment. However, EST research is far less common and often difficult to find. For an intervention to be considered an EST and thus a part of EBP, it must be included in the National Registry of Evidence-Based Programs and Practices (NREPP). The NREPP is a SAMHSA-maintained searchable online registry of mental health and substance abuse interventions thoroughly reviewed and rated by independent reviewers. NREPP submission guidelines delineate four criteria that must be met for an intervention to be eligible for review and possible inclusion in the registry. Each is listed with explanation and examples.

1. ***The intervention has produced one or more positive behavioral outcomes ($p \leq .05$) in mental health, mental disorders, substance abuse, or substance use disorders among individuals, communities, or populations with significant differences between groups over time being demonstrated for each outcome.***

In conducting research, investigators make statistical inferences by generalizing results drawn from a sample to the larger population with some calculated degree of certainty. These statistical inferences are made using a process called null hypothesis statistical testing (NHST) where an observation is tested against a hypothesis of no effect or no relationship. For example, a researcher may want to see if dialectical behavior therapy (DBT) positively impacts treatment outcomes with adolescent clients who are depressed. The null hypothesis would be that there is no relationship between DBT and client outcome. In other words, the treatment is no better than any other approach a counselor might use. To test this hypothesis, the researcher might choose to assess the client at various points during the course of treatment by administering a depression screening inventory. The client's scores would then be compared to see if differences exist and, if so, whether they are statistically significant. If they are ($p \leq .05$), the researcher would reject the null hypothesis and conclude that DBT *does* in fact make a difference in treatment outcomes for adolescents dealing with depression.

CASE ILLUSTRATION 9.1

Statistical Versus Clinical Significance

One of the standards for inclusion in the NREPP database is the existence of at least one study where statistical significance has been found with a p value $\leq .05$. But what does this value really mean? The p value is associated with a statistical concept known as null hypothesis statistical testing (NHST). In NHST, the probability (p value) of obtaining a test statistic value (e.g., t, F, χ^2) is calculated and compared to an arbitrarily selected alpha level (usually $\alpha = .05$) before the study is conducted (Watson, Lenz, Schmit, & Schmit, 2016). When the computed p value is less than or equal to the chosen alpha level, the null hypothesis is rejected, and the observed pattern of data is said to be sufficiently unlikely given the null being true resulting in a claim of statistical significance. However, NHST only tells us what the probability of obtaining data as extreme or greater would be *if* the null hypothesis were true, not whether the null hypothesis *is* true. In other words, all we can take from NHST is the percentage of the time we should expect similar results if the null hypothesis were in fact true. As a result, taking this approach is often regarded as somewhat superficial and uninformative. Results from a statistical test may indicate a noteworthy (i.e., statistical) difference yet fail to describe whether the results are of clinical significance or pertain to the population of interest (Thompson, 2002). Current best practices in research direct researchers to also report on the clinical significance of findings. Clinical significance addresses the extent to which results make a difference for clients and infer both the magnitude and directionality of an effect. As a counselor engaged in EBP, being knowledgeable of the differences between statistical and clinical significance will help in determining whether a treatment should be used with a client.

2. *Evidence of the positive behavioral outcomes has been demonstrated in at least one study using an experimental or quasi-experimental design. Experimental designs are to include random assignment of participants, a control or comparison group in addition to the intervention group, and pre- and posttest assessments. Quasi-experimental designs include a control or comparison group and pre- and posttest assessments but do not use random assignment.*

Quasi-experimental designs are used to validate treatment methods or to establish potential associations between variables. Using our previous example, the researcher could create two sets of adolescents. One group would be treated using a DBT approach whereas the other group would be treated using a cognitive-behavioral therapeutic (CBT) approach. Like before, the researcher assesses adolescents at various points in the treatment process to see if differences in depression screening scores exist. Now, instead of looking at differences over time across only a single group (the DBT group), the researcher can look to see if there is a difference between scores (DBT and CBT groups). Doing so allows the researcher to make conclusions that one approach may be preferable over the other. Because quasi-experimental designs do not include random assignment of participants, it is impossible to determine whether the groups were in fact equal at baseline (i.e., equally depressed based on screening inventory scores). To truly make a causal inference, experimental designs where random assignment is used would be the preferred approach.

3. *The results of these studies have been published in a peer-reviewed journal or other professional publication (e.g., a book volume) or documented in a comprehensive evaluation report. Comprehensive evaluation reports must include the following sections or their equivalent: a review of the literature, theoretical framework, purpose, methodology, findings/results (with statistical analysis and* **p** *values for significant outcomes), discussion, and conclusions.*

Evidence supporting a treatment is only useful if it can be accessed by others. Researchers seek to share their findings with the professional community by publishing their work. With the advent of the Internet, the ability to publish anything, anywhere, anytime now exists. A search query of virtually any term results in thousands of hits on the Internet. With so much information available, knowing what to trust could be challenging for counselors seeking information to aid in their work with clients. To contribute to the evidence base of a treatment, research must appear in a reputable source. In most cases, this means a peer-reviewed journal. Peer review is a process through which professionals review each other's work, assessing its merit based on the identified need for the study, its rationale, execution, results, and contributions to the profession. During this process, a blind review is used so evaluators are unaware of the author and therefore commenting solely on the research and not the status or reputation of the researcher. The blinded peer-review process is often viewed as a gold standard in the profession and a testament to the quality of the work being published.

4. *Implementation materials, training and support resources, and quality assurance procedures have been developed and are ready for use by the public (SAMHSA, 2018).*

Building on our previous example, let's say you are tasked with implementing a new program at your mental health facility for adolescents diagnosed with depression. You search the literature and find several studies in which the researchers indicate DBT to be an effective treatment option. Excitedly, you decide that DBT will be the theoretical foundation of the program you are developing. However, for you to reasonably expect to see similar results as those found in previous studies, you will need to implement the treatment in the exact same way as was done in these studies. Because of the importance of precise replication, a fourth criterion for ESTs is a documented protocol for implementation. In your DBT group, you would want to use the published standardized protocol for DBT that was used in these studies.

CASE ILLUSTRATION 9.2

In my career as a mental health counselor, I have had an opportunity to become familiar with the importance of EBP. For nearly 3 years, I was in private practice. For the first time, I was solely responsible for the billing of my services. This meant routine communication with various managed care companies with which I was paneled. Previously, I worked in clinical settings where administrative support staff handled these tasks. What I quickly found was that I would need to change my approach to counseling. Now I was being required to select interventions not only based on the perceived fit for the client but also on the available evidence supporting a given intervention. I became more versed in the professional literature. As I read research, I considered how the participants in these studies compared to the clients I was seeing. I reflected on my professional training, and where deficient, I sought to gain new skills, so I could implement these EST approaches I was reading about. In time, I began to realize that the focus on EBP was less a burden and more a blessing. Knowing that I was using approaches found to be effective increased my confidence and optimism for positive results. This optimism was shared by my clients as well. As I shared with them the research supporting the interventions I thought we should try, I saw hope emerge. Although you might be hesitant to incorporate EST in your work with clients, I encourage you to try. You too may find it to be a helpful tool in delivering quality care to your clients.

EVALUATION STANDARDS

With the amount of research being conducted on therapeutic practice, the number of ESTs is expected to grow exponentially. However, not all research produces evidence of the effectiveness of a treatment. Further, whereas a treatment may be evidenced to work with one population, the same may not hold true for your individual client. As you begin searching through the literature on ESTs, you may find yourself becoming confused by all the possibilities available. In fact, the sheer volume of research often dissuades counselors from adopting EBP. Fortunately, you do not have to let confusion stand in the way of providing your clients with the best possible care. Criteria exist to help counselors wade through existing research and interpret the findings reported. Specifically, the interpretation of evidence should be based on three criteria: the quality, robustness, and relevance of the evidence (Claes, van Loon, Vandevelde, & Schalock, 2015).

Quality

To appropriately evaluate the quality of evidence supporting a treatment or intervention, you should keep in mind what is meant by the term *evidence.* When we speak of **evidence**, we are referring to available facts and information supporting the truth and validity of a belief or proposition. In this case, do the data support this treatment working? Using this definition, you can begin to see that not all research is the same. The true value of research findings lies in the methods used to obtain said data. A hierarchical categorization of evidence-supported treatments exists based on the research methodologies employed to gather evidence data (see Figure 9.2).

At the top of this hierarchy are A-level practices. A-level practices are supported by the combined research findings of meta-analyses and meta-syntheses. Meta-analyses aggregate data collected across multiple randomized and controlled studies whereas

FIGURE 9.2 ■ EST Evidence Hierarchy

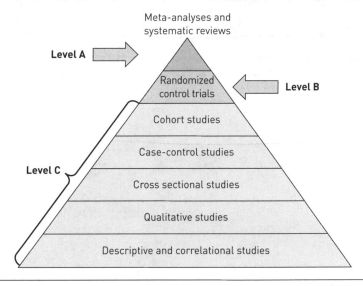

Meta-analyses and systematic reviews

Level A

Randomized control trials — Level B

Cohort studies

Case-control studies

Level C

Cross sectional studies

Qualitative studies

Descriptive and correlational studies

meta-syntheses combine qualitative data collected across studies to form a new interpretation of the phenomena being examined. Bringing together data across multiple studies sheds light on the true effect of an intervention and strengthens the evidence for its continued use in client care. Right below A-level practices are B-level practices. B-level practices are supported by individual effectiveness studies employing either experimental or quasi-experimental designs. Unlike the evidence supporting A-level practices, evidence supporting B-level practices is limited by lack of control over variables, number of sessions, clearly defined therapeutic method, and delimited problems (Shean, 2015). As a result, these studies should be interpreted considering the parameters in which the study was conducted. Finally, there are C-level practices. C-level practices are supported by evidence collected from studies that do not meet the rigor and requirements noted for level-B practices. Data supporting level-C practices originate from qualitative studies, case-controlled studies, cohort studies, descriptive studies, correlational studies, and integrated reviews of studies producing inconsistent findings. Although this information is indeed useful, the lack of control in these studies makes generalizability difficult. Counselors making treatment decisions using any of these three levels of practice are cautioned to consider the advantages and disadvantages of each while remaining cognizant of the needs of the client to whom these decisions will apply.

In addition to determining what level of research was conducted to produce data evidencing the efficacy and/or effectiveness of a treatment, counselors also should look to see that certain elements associated with quality research are included in the published works they reference. The National Research Council (Shavelson & Towne, 2002) identified a series of standards for use in assessing research quality (see Table 9.1). Although there is no benchmark or magic number for how many standards must be met to establish quality research, the general understanding is that the more aligned a research study is with these standards, the higher its quality (National Center for the Dissemination of Disability Research [NCDDR], 2005). Using this checklist is a great way for counselors to compare research findings and determine which may be a more accurate representation of treatment outcome.

GUIDED PRACTICE EXERCISE 9.2

In groups of three to four students, discuss the merits of each evidence level. How could you make a case for the use of B-level or C-level practices as a part of EBP? When you are finished, have your group share its ideas with the rest of the class.

GUIDED PRACTICE EXERCISE 9.3

Locate a research article related to a construct you are interested in. Using the EBP checklist presented in this chapter, determine the quality of the evidence reported in the article. Based on your findings, would this be a treatment you would feel comfortable using with clients, or would you look to find additional research to support your treatment decisions?

TABLE 9.1 ■ Standards for Assessing the Quality of Published Research
• Does the researcher include a significant, important question that can be investigated empirically and that contributes to the existing knowledge base?
• Does the researcher include test questions that are linked to relevant theory?
• Does the researcher apply methods best addressing the research questions of interest?
• Is the research based on clear chains of inferential reasoning supported by a thorough review of the extant professional literature?
• Does the researcher include a description of all pertinent information necessary to reproduce or replicate the study?
• Does the researcher include a description of all study design, methods, and procedures using language that is independent, fair, and balanced?
• Does the researcher include a description of the sample, interventions, and use of any comparisons groups?
• Does the researcher use appropriate and reliable conceptualization and measurement of variables?
• Does the researcher evaluate alternative explanations of any findings?
• Does the researcher assess and account for the potential impact of systematic bias?
• Has the research been vetted through the peer-review process?
• Does the researcher adhere to quality standards for data reporting?

Robustness

Robustness is a method for evaluating incongruent evidence. As you dive into the counseling research, you likely will find studies in which the results appear to contradict one another. In one study, an author may recommend a treatment whereas in another that author may deem the treatment to be ineffective. In cases such as this one, it is important to look at the robustness of the research results. Several characteristics contribute to the robustness of research. The first relates to the sample used in the study. Samples should be of enough size to allow for true effects to be found. With small samples, outlying scores are more influential and thus likely to skew findings. The larger the sample the more stable the findings. If you were taking a poll of students at your university, you would have more confidence in your findings being generalizable to the entire campus population were you to survey 1,000 students rather than 10 students. Another aspect of the sample to consider is its diversity. A good sample should be representative of the population from which it was drawn. The sample should be normally distributed and include representation from all subgroups that may comprise the population of interest to the researcher.

Robustness also can be assessed through reporting of the magnitude of the observed effect. In quantitative studies, knowing *how* a treatment works rather than simply *that it works is important*. Estimations of **effect size** provide a standardization of their findings across measures, variables, and populations (Lipsey & Wilson, 2001) that are readily understandable by counselors who may not have advanced statistical training (Trusty, Thompson, & Petrocelli, 2004). These effects are typically categorized as being small, medium, or large and relate to a percentage of one standard deviation unit change in the outcome variable (see Table 9.2). For example, an effect size estimate of .50 would be indicative of a difference equivalent to one half of a standard deviation. If a measure has a mean of 50 and a standard deviation of 10, an effect size estimate of .50 means scores on this measure can be expected to change by 5 points (half of 10) following exposure to a specific treatment. Several different effect size measures exist and can be grouped into two classes: those that represent differences within and between groups, the *d* family, and those that depict association between variables, the *r* family (Watson et al., 2016). Becoming familiar with various effect size estimates will help you in understanding the research you read and the quality of the evidence reported in it.

A final way to assess robustness is to observe the number of sources used to collect data. Robust studies acquire data from multiple sources using various means to do so. By drawing information from several sources, the researcher seeks to eliminate confirmation bias and offset any potential errors in design or study implementation. Further, these sources may have differing perspectives and capture the true efficacy or effectiveness of a treatment that alternative methods may not be equipped to detect.

Relevance

The **relevance** of evidence relates to its purpose and use of practices (Claes et al., 2015). Relevant evidence has the potential to make an impact either at the individual client, organizational, or systemic level. When counselors read research, they should look in the discussion sections of these articles for implications. Implications can

TABLE 9.2 ■ Evaluation of Effect Size Measures			
	Effect Size Estimate		
Family	Small	Medium	Large
r-family effects	.10	.30	.50
d-family effects	.20	.50	.80

GUIDED PRACTICE EXERCISE 9.4

Quantitative and qualitative research represent two ways of knowing. Each addresses a different type of research question and approaches data collecting from a unique perspective. There are advantages and disadvantages to each approach. Based on your experiences, what do you perceive to be the strengths and limitations of each approach? How might the two complement each other in building an evidence base for a counseling intervention or therapeutic approach?

be included that relate to service delivery or public policy. Evaluating the relevance of evidence is contextual. Counselors should consider the questions being asked in the research they review, what treatments are found to be effective for a presenting issue or disorder, and for whom these treatments are most likely to work (Bouffard & Reid, 2012). Comparing the answers to these questions to their own situations, counselors can best determine whether the research is relevant to their practice or client population.

The relevance of evidence also can be established by looking at its stimulation value. In other words, new research should add value to the existing knowledge base. The work should generate follow-up research that either seeks to replicate or expand on current findings. Relevant research causes the profession to take notice and challenges existing practice methods. For this to occur, research needs to be seen. One way the research community gauges the stimulation value of published research is to look at a metric known as impact factor. **Impact factor** is a calculation of the number of citations received by a journal from other journals catalogued in the Web of Science database. The higher the number, the stronger the impact the journal has within its subject category. Articles published in journals with high impact factors are highly visible and often cited in other works, thereby stimulating the advancement of knowledge. Figure 9.3 depicts how journal impact factor scores are calculated.

Now that you are familiar with the techniques and procedures used for evaluating the evidence supporting various counseling techniques and interventions, you should have the basic skills needed to begin implementing them with your clients and engaging in EBP. Over time, and with continued practice, these skills will further develop and your practice will flourish.

IMPLEMENTING EMPIRICALLY SUPPORTED TREATMENTS IN CLINICAL SETTINGS

Implementing best available research evidence into clinical practice is one of the core components of evidence-based practices, and the ability to introduce various ESTs in sessions with clients requires the counselor's expertise. In addition to clinical expertise and best

---

FIGURE 9.3 ■ Calculating Impact Factor Scores

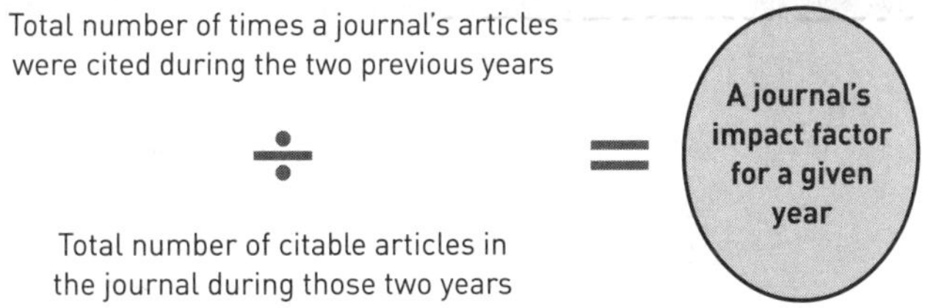

Total number of times a journal's articles were cited during the two previous years

÷

Total number of citable articles in the journal during those two years

=

A journal's impact factor for a given year

available research, the preference of the client is important when introducing ESTs into the therapeutic relationship (Drisko, 2014). Incorporating ESTs into counseling requires several steps between the counselor and client, for it is an interactive process aimed at promoting client feedback and input. Using a decision-making process can help counselors identify the specific needs of a client and bring more awareness to client values and preferences. As stated by Drisko and Grady (2012), there are six steps for counselors to follow in the EBP decision-making process:

1. Drawing on client needs, and circumstances learned in a thorough assessment, identify answerable practice questions and related research information needs.

2. Efficiently locate relevant research knowledge.

3. Critically appraise the quality and applicability of this knowledge to the client's needs and situation.

4. Discuss the research results with the client to determine how likely effective options fit with the client's values and goals.

5. Synthesize the client's clinical needs and circumstances with the relevant research and develop a shared plan of intervention collaboratively with the client.

6. Implement the intervention.

In the EBP decision-making process, the integration of applicable research and a thorough understanding of the client and the client's needs is needed to make informed clinical decisions supporting EBP (see Figure 9.4). Addressing these questions, counselors should be able to select the best course of action when it comes to selecting diagnostic assessments, exploring the etiology of disorders, planning treatment, and evaluating client progress toward the goals established for treatment (Carpenter, Bernacchio, & Burker, 2013; Drisko, 2014). Further, involving the client in the decision-making process is a great way to foster buy-in and treatment compliance. When clients believe they have some control over the process and can decide their own outcomes, they invest more in the counseling process because they believe you both will be working together to solve their unique problems and not simply applying a generic approach to a presenting problem that does not include individual context.

FIGURE 9.4   ■   Integration of Research and Client Needs

CASE ILLUSTRATION 9.3

The Case of Mateo

Mateo is a 34-year-old Hispanic male who recently presented for counseling at the community mental health clinic. He is married and has two children ages 12 and 9. Mateo works at a local oil refinery and has been there since graduating high school. The company has been experiencing a decline in profit and has begun reducing its workforce. Mateo is worried he might lose his job and not be able to support his family. His worries have intensified recently and are having a significant impact on his life. He is unable to sleep and has been arguing with his wife a lot more. Further, he reports an increase in alcohol consumption to the point where he states he now drinks six to eight beers a night just to try to calm down and get some rest. Although he has not been given any indication his job is at risk, and by all accounts he is a strong employee, he still cannot seem to stop worrying. He mentions at intake that if he loses his job he feels like life will hardly be worth living. Friends and family have tried to help him snap out of this funk, but so far nothing has seemed to work.

GUIDED PRACTICE EXERCISE 9.5

Review the case of Mateo in Case Illustration 9.3. Using the EBP decision-making process discussed in this chapter, outline how you would go about working with Mateo in counseling from an EBP perspective.

Implementation Barriers

Despite counselors increasingly being tasked with implementing treatments that have demonstrated the strongest impact in high-quality research analyses (APA, 2006; Burkhardt, Schröter, Magura, Means, & Coryn, 2015), institutional and individual practitioner barriers exist limiting their usage. An understanding of these barriers is vital to ensuring successful execution of ESTs (Becker & Jensen-Doss, 2013) in counseling practice. These implementation barriers exist at numerous levels. In a qualitative study in which 11 counselors engaged in EBP were interviewed, several barriers at the intervention, client, counselor, organization, and system level were identified (Powell & Hausmann-Stabile, 2013). Some of these barriers are included in Table 9.2. When faced with these barriers, counselors are encouraged to seek consultation and identify potential avenues for removing barriers whether it be through increased education and training, refined practice dynamics, or advocating for systemic change in the delivery of counseling services to diverse client populations. Change may not be immediate, but persistence should be practiced.

TABLE 9.2 ■ Barriers to Implementing EBP in Clinical Settings
Intervention-Level Barriers
• Proprietary nature of ESTs (cost-prohibitive to use)
• Less convenient and more difficult than treatment as usual
• Confusing implementation protocols
Client-Level Barriers
• Lack of buy-in and support
• Resistance to treatment efforts
• Cultural barriers
Counselor-Level Barriers
• Lack of consistency with previous education and/or training
• Lack of time/poor time management
• Lack of incentive to use (personal, professional, financial)
Organization-Level Barriers
• Inadequate infrastructure and administrative support
• Lack of qualified supervision
• Limited resources to fully implement
System-Level Barriers
• Differing values and priorities across treatment settings
• Paperwork and/or other administrative burdens
• Nonrecovery-based model of care

IDENTIFYING EMPIRICALLY SUPPORTED TREATMENTS PRACTICED IN CLINICAL MENTAL HEALTH SETTINGS

Now that you have learned how to evaluate ESTs and implement them in your clinical work with clients, the question remains of where you find research supporting ESTs. There are a number of sites you can visit as you conduct your research. This section briefly introduces a few sites and search methods with which you should become familiar. The URLs for these sites are included in the Web Resources at the end of this chapter.

Library Databases

One of the first places you can look for research to bolster your EBP is in your library's online database. There you can conduct search queries on several topics in a targeted manner. When conducting a search, make sure you choose the option to give you only results appearing in peer-reviewed journals. These articles have been vetted and deemed representative of quality research. Although other sources you find online may also represent quality research, using peer-reviewed articles ensures a level of quality the beginning researcher may favor.

Additionally, limit your search to only the most recent findings. The counseling profession is constantly changing as new research emerges. What counselors once may have considered best practice may no longer hold relevance for contemporary practice. A good rule to follow is to look at research published in the last 5 years. Anything longer and you run the risk of potentially relying on outdated data to make informed clinical decisions.

American Counseling Association

Another great source of information is the American Counseling Association. On their website, a database of *Practice Briefs* is housed. These briefs are research-based summaries of best practices, evidence-based practices, and research-based approaches used to address several client-presenting issues and counseling topics. Counselors can search by disorder or presenting problem and get a snapshot of some of the current approaches being used in the treatment of that issue, including the advantages and disadvantages of each. In many of the papers, the authors include best practices for all stages of counseling, including assessment, diagnosis, and evaluating treatment progress. What's great about these briefs is that they are concise and written in practitioner-friendly language free of a lot of the technical jargon included in research articles. Basically, they share what works and why it should be used.

Substance Abuse and Mental Health Service Administration (SAMHSA)

The SAMHSA website holds a wealth of knowledge related to evidence-based practices. As mentioned earlier in this chapter, the National Registry for Evidence-Based Practices and Programs (NREPP) is a searchable database of existing treatment modalities for which empirical support of their efficacy and effectiveness exist. The database is searchable by key word, so counselors can look specifically for the issues salient to the client populations with whom they are working. In addition to the NREPP, SAMSHA also publishes a web guide to evidence-based practices. The web guide features research findings and details about EBP used to prevent and treat a variety of mental and substance use disorders. Stakeholders throughout the behavioral health field can use the EBP web guide to promote awareness of current intervention research and to increase the implementation and availability of EBPs (SAMHSA, 2018).

Evidence-based practice is a trend in the counseling profession that appears to have staying power. With the potential to benefit clients, counselors, and the counseling profession as a whole, there is great appeal in the approach. For counselors, EBP allows

GUIDED PRACTICE EXERCISE 9.6

In the American Counseling Association's *Practice Briefs* database, search for a counseling topic of interest to you. What research exists supporting specific strategies and interventions for discussing this topic in counseling? Are you currently using the identified ESTs? If not, what are some of the barriers preventing you from doing so?

them to engage in practices that have been empirically proven, providing some level of assurance to themselves, their clients, and the managed care partners who may be funding treatment that the approaches and techniques used work effectively. For clients, EBP provides assurance they will be receiving the most effective treatment available in a manner that meets their individual needs and considers their unique set of values and beliefs. As you continue your training, looking to integrate EBP will be a worthwhile investment of your time and energy.

Keystones

- Incorporating best available research into clinical practice is one of the core components of evidence-based practice. Among mental health professionals, this practice has become the accepted standard of practice in most facility and agency settings.

- When reviewing the research literature, counselors should remain cognizant of the fact that the utility of established evidence is directly related to the questions needing to be addressed and should be evaluated accordingly.

- Evidence-based practice incorporates the use of existing research, counselor expertise, and consideration of clients' values and beliefs in all decision-making processes related to client care and treatment planning.

- Adopting an EBP approach to counseling is a great way for counselors to ensure they practice in a legal, ethical, and beneficent manner with each and every one of their clients.

- When evaluating research evidence, counselors should consider several factors to determine its appropriateness. Included in their consideration should be the quality, robustness, and relevance of the evidence reviewed.

- When implementing empirically supported treatments in counseling, counselors are encouraged to follow the six-step EBP decision-making process model to ensure informed decisions are made in the best interests of the client.

- Several barriers may impede a counselor's ability to employ EBP. Awareness of these barriers can help counselors proactively find ways to overcome them and successfully practice from an EBP perspective.

Key Terms

Effect size 227

Empirically supported
    treatment 219

Evidence 225

Evidence-based practice 217

Impact factor 229

Longitudinal studies 218

Practice-based evidence 220

Randomized control trials 218

Relevance 228

Robustness 227

Web Resources

American Counseling Association (ACA) Center for Counseling Practice, Policy, and Research *Practice Briefs* (www.counseling.org/knowledge-center/practice-briefs)

American Psychological Association (APA) Evidence-Based Practice in Psychology (www.apa.org/practice/resources/evidence)

Substance Abuse and Mental Health Services Administration (SAMHSA) Evidence-Based Practices Web Guide (www.samhsa.gov/ebp-web-guide)

Substance Abuse and Mental Health Services Administration (SAMHSA) National Registry of Evidence-Based Programs and Practices (www.samhsa.gov/nrepp)

References

Aarons, G. A., Wells, R. S., Zagursky, K., Fettes, D. L., & Palinkas, L. A. (2009). Implementing evidence-based practice in community mental health agencies: A multiple stakeholder analysis. *American Journal of Public Health, 99*(11), 2087–2095.

Altin, S., Passon, A., Kautz-Freimuth, S., Berger, B., & Stock, S. (2015). A qualitative study on barriers to evidence-based practice in patient counseling and advocacy in Germany. *BMC Health Services Research, 15*, 317. doi:10.1186/s12913-015-0979-9

American Counseling Association. (2014). *ACA code of ethics.* Alexandria, VA: Author.

APA Presidential Task Force on Evidence-Based Practice. (2006). Evidence-based practice in psychology. *American Psychologist, 61*(4), 271–285. doi:10.1037/0003-066X.61.4.271

Baker, S. B. (2012). A new view of evidence-based practice. *Counseling Today, 12.* Retrieved from http://ct.counseling.org/2012/12/a-new-view-of-evidence-based-practice/

Barkham, M., Hardy, G. E., & Mellor-Clark, J. (2010). Improving practice and enhancing evidence. In M. Barkham, G. E. Hardy, & J. Mellor-Clark (Eds.), *Developing and delivering practice-based evidence: A guide for psychological therapies* (pp. 329–353). New York, NY: Wiley.

Becker, E. M., & Jensen-Doss, A. (2013). Computer-assisted therapies: Examination of therapist-level barriers to their use. *Behavior Therapy, 44*(4), 614–624. doi:10.1016/j.beth.2013.05.002

Bloom, M., Fischer, J., & Orme, J. G. (2009). *Evaluating practice: Guidelines for the accountable professional* (6th ed.). Columbus, OH: Pearson.

Bouffard, M., & Reid, G. (2012). The good, the bad, and the ugly of evidence-based practice. *Adapted Physical Activity Quarterly, 29*(1), 1–24. doi:10.1111/j.1365-2753.2010.01408.x

Burkhart, J. T., Schröter, D. C., Magura, S., Means, S. N., & Coryn, C. L. (2015). An overview of evidence-based program registers (EBPRs) for behavioral health. *Evaluation and Program Planning*, *48*, 92–99. doi:10.1016/j.evalprogplan.2014.09.006

Carpenter, V. R., Bernacchio, C., & Burker, E. J. (2013). Use of evidence-based practice in rehabilitation counseling: Facilitating recovery and community integration for persons with schizophrenia. *Journal of Applied Rehabilitation Counseling*, *44*, 11–22.

Claes, C., van Loon, J., Vandevelde, S., & Schalock, R. (2015). An integrative approach to evidence based practices. *Evaluation and Program Planning*, *48*, 132–136. doi:10.1016/j.evalprogplan.2014.08.002

Drisko, J. W. (2014). Research evidence and social work practice: The place of evidence-based practice. *Clinical Social Work Journal*, *42*, 123–133. doi:10.1007/s10615-013-0459-9

Drisko, J. W., & Grady, M. D. (2012). *Evidence-based practice in clinical social work*. New York, NY: Springer.

Hays, D. (2010). Introduction to counseling outcome research and evaluation. *Counseling Outcome Research and Evaluation*, *1*, 1–7. doi:10.1177/2150137 809360006

Hoagwood, K., & Olin, S. S. (2002). The NIMH blueprint for change report: Research priorities in child and adolescent mental health. *Journal of the American Academy of Child & Adolescent Psychiatry*, *41*(7), 760–767. doi:10.1097/00004583-200207000-00006

Ilardi, S. S., & Craighead, W. E. (1994). The role of nonspecific factors in cognitive-behavior therapy for depression. *Clinical Psychology Science and Practice*, *1*(2), 138–155. doi:10.1111/j.1468-2850.1994.tb00016.x

Laska, K. M., Gurman, A. S., & Wampold, B. E. (2014). Expanding the lens of evidence-based practice in psychotherapy: A common factors perspective. *Psychotherapy*, *51*(4), 467–481. doi:10.1037/a0034332

Lipsey, M. W., & Wilson, D. B. (2001). *Practical meta-analysis*. Thousand Oaks, CA: Sage.

Lister, K. E., & Moody, S. J. (2017). Cutting the profession's Gordian knot: A call for evidence-based practice in counseling. *Journal of Counselor Leadership and Advocacy*, *4*(2), 137–146. doi:10.1080/2326716X.2017.1322930

National Center for the Dissemination of Disability Research. (2005). What are the standards for quality research? Retrieved from http://ktdrr.org/ktlibrary/articles_pubs/ncddrwork/focus/focus9/Focus9.pdf

Norcross, J. C., Beutler, L. E., & Levant, R. F. (2006). *Evidence-based practices in mental health: Debate and dialogue on the fundamental questions*. Washington, DC: American Psychological Association.

Norcross, J. C., Hogan, T. P., & Koocher, G. P. (2008). *Clinician's guide to evidence-based practices: Mental health and the addictions*. New York, NY: Oxford University Press.

Powell, B. J., & Hausmann-Stabile, C. (2013). Mental health clinicians' experiences of implementing evidence-based treatments. *Journal of Evidence-Based Social Work*, *10*, 396–409. doi:10.1080/15433714.2012.664062

Rahman, A., & Applebaum, R. (2010). What's all this about evidence-based practice? The roots, the controversies, and why it matters. *Generations*, *34*(1), 6–12.

Sackett, D. L., & Wennberg, J. E. (1997). Choosing the best research design for each question. *BMJ: British Medical Journal*, *315*(7123), 1633–1634.

Shapiro, J. P. (2009). Integrating outcome research and clinical reasoning in psychotherapy planning. *Professional Psychology: Research and Practice*, *40*, 46–53. doi:10.1037/a0012596

Shavelson, R. J., & Towne, L. (2002). *Scientific research in education*. Washington, DC: National Research Council, National Academy Press.

Shean, G. D. (2015). Some methodological and epistemic limitations of evidence-based therapies.

Psychoanalytic Psychology, 32(3), 500–516. doi:10.1037/a0035518

Spring, B. (2007). Evidence-based practice in clinical psychology: What it is, why it matters, what you need to know. *Journal of Clinical Psychology, 63*(7), 611–631. doi:10.1002/jclp.20373

Substance Abuse and Mental Health Service Administration. (2018). Evidence-based practices web guide. Retrieved from https://www.samhsa.gov/ebp-web-guide

Thompson, B. (2002). "Statistical," "practical," and "clinical": How many kinds of significance do counselors need to consider? *Journal of Counseling & Development, 80*, 64–71. doi:10.1002/j.1556-6678.2002.tb00167.x

Trusty, J., Thompson, B., & Petrocelli, J. V. (2004). Practical guide to reporting effect size in quantitative research in the Journal of Counseling and Development. *Journal of Counseling and Development, 82*, 107–110. doi:10.1002/j.1556-6678.2004.tb00291.x

Watson, J. C., Lenz, A. S., Schmit, M. K., & Schmit, E. L. (2016). Calculating and reporting estimates of effect size in counseling outcome research. *Counseling Outcome Research and Evaluation, 7*(2), 111–123. doi:10.1177/2150137816660584

Wheeler, A. M., & Bertram, B. (2012). Civil malpractice liability and licensure board complaints. In *The counselor and the law* (6th ed., pp. 43–76). Alexandria, VA: American Counseling Association.

Yates, C. (2013). Evidence-based practice. The components, history, and process. *Counseling Outcome Research and Evaluation, 4*, 41–54. doi:10.1177/2150137812472193

10

BEHAVIORAL MEDICINE

A Holistic Look at
Health and Illness

In recent years, the mortality rate among the mental health population has sky-rocketed, beyond that of the general population, as a result of primary medical conditions that go unmitigated (Brown, Bennett, Li, & Bellack, 2011; Felker, Yazel, & Short, 1996; Harris & Barraclough, 1998). In fact, Barnett et al. (2012) and Kessler et al. (2005) hypothesized that nearly 50% of clients with mental illness have at least one comorbid chronic medical disease (e.g., diabetes, hypertension, high cholesterol, stroke, asthma, cardiovascular and pulmonary disease). In response to this health care crisis, clinical mental health settings have begun to integrate primary health care services into their existing paradigm of service delivery. This shift in treatment delivery has profound implications for clinical mental health counselors in the 21st century, requiring them to have specialized knowledge, training, and skills (Council for Accreditation of Counseling and Related Educational Programs [CACREP], 2016). Thus, counselors employed in these integrated settings work well using a team-based approach, are effective communicators and coordinators of services, and have knowledge that spans across the helping disciplines (e.g., counseling, medicine, psychology, psychiatry, sociology).

We begin by shedding light on what behavioral medicine is. Next, we explore a practical application of the behavioral medicine approach in managing mental and behavioral issues in medical clients. Then we transition into how counselors can effectively communicate with both clients and providers in an integrated system of care, as well as transfer those skills when conducting client interviews. Finally, we conclude with how to motivate medical clients to engage in and sustain behavioral change across the life span.

LEARNING OBJECTIVES

After reading this chapter, you will be able to do the following:

- Describe the major tenets of the behavioral medicine approach for medical clients with comorbid behavioral and mental health disorders (CACREP 5C-1-b)

- Identify and describe the three mechanisms of the biopsychosocial model, along with their interactions, to the contribution of disease formation and illness prevention (CACREP 5C-2-g)

- Demonstrate appropriate strategies for effectively communicating with clients and providers in an integrated system of care (CACREP 5C-3-d)

- Identify and apply a systematic approach to conducting interviews with clients diagnosed with comorbid disorders (CACREP 5C-3-a)

- Contrast the differing roles and responsibilities clinical mental health counselors experience in an integrated system of care (CACREP 5C-2-a)

- Describe the significance of self-regulation and its impact on motivating behavioral change among medical clients with comorbid behavioral and mental health disorders

BEHAVIORAL MEDICINE APPROACH

Understanding how behaviors directly impact a person's overall health is at the foundation of the behavioral medicine approach. The word *behavioral* in behavioral medicine can be misleading and is best understood from a broader context of the whole person and the impact on the entire health system, and less in terms of the manifestation of a specific behavior. Counselors applying this approach develop interventions designed to target a specific behavior or set of behaviors in hopes of managing the debilitating effects of an illness, preventing a new illness, and improving a person's overall health and quality of life (Society of Behavioral Medicine, 2016). To help visualize the behavioral medicine approach in practice, let us examine the case of Sarah described in Case Illustration 10.1.

CASE ILLUSTRATION 10.1

Sarah is a 55-year-old Caucasian female who identifies herself as lower-middle class. She was recently widowed, has no children, and lives alone. She reports her major problem as feeling depressed all the time. During the third counseling session, she reports that her husband died a

(Continued)

(Continued)

few years ago in a tragic car accident. Over the years, Sarah has gained a significant amount of weight that results in her using a wheelchair, although not all the time. She was clinically diagnosed as obese and has other health-related illness (e.g., body pains and aches, headaches, low energy, loss of interest in activities) not present prior to the death of her husband. During the initial patient interview, Sarah disclosed that she has a family history of diabetes, obesity, and other heart-related issues. Sarah and her counselor Bennett collaboratively established goals of managing her weight, increasing her physical activity, and improving her mood. Bennett worked with Sarah for 1 year on a variety of personal issues, including developing a diet and exercise regimen and managing her depression, concurrently. Sarah also met with the agency's psychiatrist and primary care physician to manage her symptoms of depression and address her medical concerns. Sarah is very sensitive about her weight; thus, the suggestion that she exercise and better manage her diet was met with resistance. Knowing this, Bennett had to approach her in a unique way. He started simple. He began with education on how healthy eating does not necessarily mean "tasteless eating."

He went grocery shopping with Sarah, taking note of how she shopped and what she bought. He observed how Sarah "doctored up" her coffee before their sessions. He noted times when she walked instead of using the wheelchair. Through learning more about Sarah's habits, Bennett offered simple suggestions such as using milk versus heavy cream and a sugar substitute instead of sugar in her coffee. On their shopping trips, Bennett suggested that Sarah buy fresh fruits and vegetables instead of frozen, knowing that it would force her to be more active in the cooking process versus her simply heating the food in a microwave. Bennett often encouraged Sarah to walk with him around the office building prior to their sessions. Individually, these suggestions of behavioral change seemed small, but in the long run, they had profound effects. At the end of Sarah and Bennett's counseling relationship, Sarah was down 15 pounds, cooked most of her meals using fresh ingredients, relied less on her wheelchair, and reported feeling significantly less depressed over the 1-year period. Sarah still has a long road ahead of her; however, it was these small changes in behavior that not only impacted her physical health but also improved her mental well-being.

Counselors adhering to the behavioral medicine approach recognize most chronic diseases as having a behavioral component that can be targeted to improve overall health, which is the focus of this chapter. To fully appreciate the behavioral medicine approach, we must first understand its development.

Origin and History of Behavioral Medicine

Behavioral medicine, as we understand it today, first emerged in the 1970s in response to the biomedical model, the dominantly held ideology at the time. Research laboratories established at the University of Pennsylvania and Stanford University provided both medical and mental health researchers and practitioners the opportunity to develop the field of behavioral medicine. Additionally, publications like Leo Birk's 1973 book *Biofeedback: Behavioral Medicine* and journals such as the *Journal of Behavioral Medicine* and *Annals of Behavioral Medicine* shed light on the growing field of behavioral medicine and provided outlets for new research to be disseminated.

Aided by the growing body of research supporting behavioral medicine, the 1990s saw the formation of professional societies and federal agencies focused primarily on the field of behavioral medicine. In 1990, the International Society of Behavioral Medicine (ISBM) was created to serve the needs of vested disciplines interested in behavioral medicine issues; and in 1995, the National Institute of Health (NIH) created the Office of Behavioral and Social Science Research (OBSSR) to focus solely on behavioral and social constructs specific to mental and physical health and foster collaboration and cooperation among researchers and practitioners across various disciplines of study. More recent influences that have contributed to the continual development of behavioral medicine include the evidence-based practice movement beginning in the early 2000s, advances in technology promoting behavior change, developments in epidemiology in identifying risk factors, and growing concerns in health care cost efficiency (Keefe, 2011).

So What Exactly Is Behavioral Medicine?

The first definition of behavioral medicine was established by behavioral and biomedical experts at the Yale Conference on Behavioral Medicine (Schwartz & Weiss, 1977, p. 379):

> Behavioral Medicine is the field concerned with the development of behavioral-science knowledge and techniques relevant to the understanding of physical health and illness and the application of this knowledge and these techniques to diagnosis, prevention, treatment and rehabilitation. Psychosis, neurosis and substance abuse are included only insofar as they contribute to physical disorders as an end point.

As a result of Schwartz and Weiss's experience at this very same conference, they expanded on the original definition:

> Behavioral Medicine is the interdisciplinary field concerned with the development and integration of behavioral and biomedical science knowledge and techniques relevant to health and illness and the application of this knowledge and these techniques to prevention, diagnosis, treatment, and rehabilitation. (Schwartz & Weiss, 1978, p. 249)

In 1979, Pomerleau and Brady, recognizing the contributions of behavior in health and illness, offered the following definition:

> Behavioral medicine can be defined as (a) the clinical use of techniques derived from the experimental analysis of behavior—behavior therapy and behavior modification—for the evaluation, prevention, management, or treatment of disease or physiological dysfunction; and (b) the conduct of research contributing to the functional analysis and understanding of behavior associated with medical disorders and problems in health care. (p. xii)

A more contemporary definition provided by the ISBM (n.d.) described behavioral medicine as "the interdisciplinary field concerned with the development and integration of psychosocial, behavioral and biomedical knowledge relevant to health and illness and the application of this knowledge to prevention, etiology, diagnosis, treatment and rehabilitation" (para. 1).

As you can see from the rapid evolution of the field of behavioral medicine, certain tenets have persisted. For the purposes of our discussion, **behavioral medicine** is defined as a multidisciplinary science that integrates knowledge from various fields related to health and illness and applies that knowledge to the treatment and prevention of illness through the use of behavioral interventions. From this perspective, chronic illnesses such as obesity, substance use, depression, and hypertension are understood to occur from the interaction between genetic factors, social and cultural influences, and state of psychological well-being that lead to particular lifestyle choices. It is these amendable risk factors (behaviors) such as smoking, poor dietary habits, limited physical activity, and high levels of stress that can potentially exacerbate current illnesses and further compromise overall health that most concern practitioners. As you saw from Sarah's experience described earlier in this chapter, many factors contributed to her state of health and well-being. As such, clinical mental health counselors practicing from the behavioral medicine approach must have a firm theoretical understanding of how biological, psychological, and social factors contribute to illness formation and health persistence. This is best explained by the biopsychosocial model.

Biopsychosocial Model

The biopsychosocial model was first introduced by George Engel in 1977 as an alternative to the biomedical model, which has dominated the field of medicine since the mid-20th century. The application of the **biomedical model** is the manner in which health professionals diagnosis and treat disease, focusing primarily on biology while disregarding psychological and social factors that contribute to disease and illness (Engel, 1977). In other words, disease and illness are the result of viruses, gene expression, and physical abnormalities, in absence of other contributing factors such as living conditions, substance use, dietary habits, and so forth. Despite the dominance of the biomedical model and its support observed in both medicine and psychiatry, proponents (Borrell-Carrió, Suchman, & Epstein, 2004; Engel, 1977, 1980; Epstein & Borrell-Carrió, 2005) of the biopsychosocial model often criticized the biomedical model for many reasons. The most notable reasons summarized by Engel included the dualistic separation of person and illness; the reductionistic viewpoint, that is, if something could not be reduced or explained in its simplest form it was ignored; and finally, the objective observer who remained distant and separated from the client (Borrell-Carrió et al., 2004).

The **biopsychosocial model** is best thought of as a philosophy of client care and an approach to clinical practice in treating disease and illness. From this perspective, causes of disease and illness are the result of interactions among biological (e.g., genetic, sex), psychological (e.g., personality, self-esteem), and social factors (e.g., culture, peers). In its simplest form, the biopsychosocial model signifies the mind-body connection. To better understanding this model and interacting factors and their impact on health and illness, please refer to Figure 10.1.

As you can see in Figure 10.1, the biopsychosocial model is made up of three factors: (A) biological, (B) psychological, and (C) social. No single (A, B, or C) factor is more important than the other; however, understanding that each factor interacts with the other, regardless of whether the outcome is positive or negative, is critical to understanding illness formation and health persistence. Notice the overlapping area, represented by a darker shade of gray, among the three factors. The shared areas between A and B, B and C, and A and C can be thought of as characteristics, traits, or dynamics representative of the interaction between two factors that do not explain the cause of disease or illness but contribute to its existence. For example, being overweight (Biological [A]) and having a low socioeconomic status (Social [C]) may contribute to a low rate of glucose metabolism (gray shaded area between A and C). Likewise, low socioeconomic status (Social [C]) and poor coping skills (Psychological [B]) may contribute to the experience of trauma (gray shaded area between C and B). Being overweight (Biological [A]) and poor coping skills (Psychological [B]) may contribute to an introverted personality type (gray shaded area between A and B).

In each of these examples, a possible outcome for the interaction between two factors is described, but according to the biopsychosocial model, it is the interaction among *all* factors that best explains health determination and illness formation. Therefore, let us reexamine the previous examples from a holistic view, as intended by the biopsychosocial model, to include the respective third missing factor and the interaction among factors.

> Considering all factors together, being overweight (A), low socioeconomic status (C), poor coping skills (B), low metabolism (A and C), adverse experience to trauma (C and B), and an introverted personality type (A and B) may collectively explain obesity, diabetes, hypertension, depression, and post-traumatic stress disorder (A and B and C).

FIGURE 10.1 ■ **The biopsychosocial model is composed of three interacting factors: biological, psychological, and social, providing a theoretical framework to understanding illness formation and health persistence.**

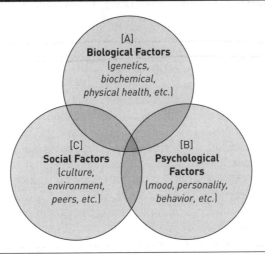

As clinical mental health counselors, it is important to understand that the interaction among factors (center of Figure 10.1) collectively describes the cause of illness. Further, altering one or more factors may contribute to a different prognosis, and a similar factor composition between two persons may result in a different disease or illness diagnosis. Although our conversation regarding the biopsychosocial model has so far consisted of describing the causes of illness, the same model can be used to inform health promotion and disease prevention. If disease and illness are the product of interactions among biological, psychological, and social factors, then it makes sense that interventions must align with this ideology. In the next section, we begin to see the practical application of the behavioral medicine approach in managing mental and behavioral issues in medical clients in a service delivery approach known as integrated care.

MANAGING MENTAL AND BEHAVIORAL ISSUES IN MEDICAL CLIENTS

Managing mental and behavioral issues in medical clients poses its own set of challenges. As counselors, should we focus on mental and behavioral issues only and ignore medical concerns? Is it necessary to address medical issues before attending to mental and behavioral problems? Are mental and behavioral disorders best explained by medical conditions? These are some of the concerns clinical mental health counselors face when working with medical clients who have comorbid mental and behavioral health disorders.

Of the many challenges faced by medical clients with comorbid mental and behavioral issues, access to and navigating the array of necessary services (Barnett et al., 2012; Brekke et al., 2013) is one of the more prevalent, especially for novice counselors. Rarely does a single entity or organization offer every service possible to persons with chronic illnesses. Instead, clients often must navigate through what is known as a continuum of care. A **continuum of care** (CoC) is "a system that guides and tracks clients over time through a comprehensive array of health services spanning all levels and intensity of care" (Healthcare Information and Management Systems Society, 2014, para. 1). Although not a formal system of care delivery, CoC can be thought of as a collection of service providers in varying levels of communication with one another. And with advances in secure technologies and electronic health records (EHRs), mutual sharing of information is becoming more and more of a reality between health care providers.

Nonetheless, challenges such as funding, compatibility among EHRs systems, and agreement between providers on what type of information should be shared persists. To address these challenges, most, if not all, health care organizations have designated workers (e.g., CoC coordinators or specialists) who specialize in tracking clients from one entity to the next and ensure a continuum of care through maintaining appropriate relationships, management and sharing of vital health information, and advocating for client services when necessary (Haggerty et al., 2003; Reid & Wagner, 2008). Despite the advances in CoC practices, clients unfortunately do fall through the cracks as a result of errors made by health care providers and clients not fully committing to the treatment process. One solution to circumvent these gaps in care is the resurgence of integrated care treatment in the 21st century, especially in clinical mental health settings.

Integrated Care Treatment

Integrated care treatment is grounded in the behavioral medicine approach, focusing on the holistic self to improve health and treat illness. **Integrated care treatment** is "the systematic coordination of general and behavioral healthcare" (Substance Abuse and Mental Health Services Administration-Health Resource and Service Administration, Center for Integrated Health Solutions [SAMHSA-HRSA, CIHS], n.d., para. 3). From this perspective, treatments are designed to address complex health care issues such as mental illness, physical illness, and substance use, concurrently, in recognition of the parallel effects between the mind and body. Since the early 1980s, researchers (e.g., Caton, 1981; Regier et al., 1990) have found higher prevalence of substance use among persons with mental illness, a trend continuing into the 21st century (Chow, 2013). A more recent concern for health care professionals is a higher mortality rate among persons with mental health illness. These persons are dying 15 to 20 years sooner than persons from the general population with similar primary health conditions (Thornicroft, 2011). Many factors contribute to early death in this population, such as a sedentary lifestyle, poor diet, smoking and consumption of illicit substances, disparities in accessing primary health care services, difficulties in navigating the health care system, and stigma associated with mental illness.

To combat this phenomenon, SAMHSA, in 2009, awarded funding to 100 behavioral health agencies across the United States for the purpose of integrating primary health care services into clinical mental health settings (Scharf et al., 2013). Many primary health care settings have integrated mental health services within their paradigm of treatment. Regardless of the direction of integration (behavioral and mental health into primary care or primary care into behavioral and mental health), the care that results from these multidisciplinary teams made up of behavioral and mental health and primary health care practitioners is the strength behind integrated care treatment. Interdisciplinary teams' level of interaction and method of communication varies depending on where they fall on the continuum of service integration.

Continuum of Service Integration

Blount (2003) described service integration between behavioral health and primary health care entities along a continuum (see Figure 10.2). At one end of the continuum,

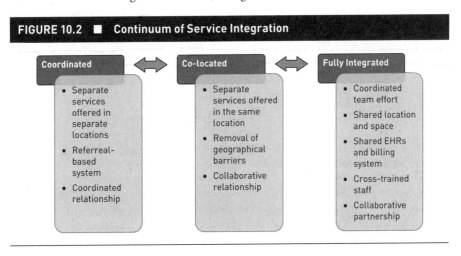

FIGURE 10.2 ■ Continuum of Service Integration

Coordinated
- Separate services offered in separate locations
- Referreal-based system
- Coordinated relationship

Co-located
- Separate services offered in the same location
- Removal of geographical barriers
- Collaborative relationship

Fully Integrated
- Coordinated team effort
- Shared location and space
- Shared EHRs and billing system
- Cross-trained staff
- Collaborative partnership

services are identified as *coordinated*. Coordinated services are those rendered in two or more locations by two or more different health care professionals. However, each professional and entity are connected through a referral-based system (Westheimer, Steinley-Bumgarner, & Brownson, 2008). For example, a client discharging from an inpatient psychiatric hospital might receive referrals to a community mental health agency, a primary care physician, and a marriage counselor. In most instances, the referring hospital has some degree of relationship with the outside entities that is best characterized as coordinated. The referral-based system depends on the resources available in the community or nearby communities and poses a significant challenge for rural and underserved geographical settings. Directly in the middle of the continuum is service coordinating identified as co-located. Co-located services are highlighted by providers that are distinctly separate (i.e., specialized in mental health or primary health but not both); however, the providers of those services exist in the same location. In most instances, providers of care share the same building space. On one side of the building is behavioral and mental health services and on the other side is primary health. Having different providers in the same location benefits client care and allows for more opportunities to collaborate and coordinate among health care professionals. A medical professional only needs to walk across the building to consult with a behavioral health professional concerning a client's compliance with treatment and coordinate future services.

On the other side of the continuum, opposite from coordinated, is *fully integrated*. Service provision identified as fully integrated is based on a coordinated partnership. In other words, differing health care professionals work together in teams. They share the same location and in most instances the same office space. It is not uncommon for a fully integrated entity to have the same support staff interacting with every client (e.g., greeting them, assisting with paperwork, managing behavioral and medical appointments). Furthermore, a fully integrated system of care shares the same EHRs, billing department, and treatment plan and meets regularly as a treatment team (Blount, 2003; Westheimer et al., 2008). Despite the specific characterizations of each—coordinated, co-located, and fully integrated—most organizations and entities that offer integrated services occur along the continuum of service delivery. This is true for many reasons: (a) budgetary constraints, (b) limited physical space, (c) lack of available health professionals, (d) geographical isolation, and (e) health care needs. What is important to understand is that service integration (i.e., coordinated, co-located, fully integrated) offers a stringent approach to managing behavioral and mental illness in medical clients by mitigating many of the barriers experienced by clients navigating the continuum of care.

GUIDED PRACTICE EXERCISE 10.1

In class, in groups of three, each student will take ownership of an integrated model along the service continuum (coordinated, co-located, or fully integrated). Describe to your partners the strengths and limitations of your selected model regarding client care, coordination of services, and communication among providers. How do you foresee your selected model of service integration circumventing many of the perceived and actual barriers that clients experience?

Interventions Implemented in Integrated Care Treatment

Integrated care treatment encompasses a vast array of services individualized to the person and his or her needs. Although degrees of consistency exist among mental and primary health disease (e.g., symptomology), the behavioral medicine approach recognizes that no two persons are the same. Thus, no two treatment approaches are the same. Treatment is highly specialized to the individual; treatment goals are created collaboratively and have the following characteristics: specific, measurable, realistic, and meaningful to the person. In an integrated system of care, interventions include psychiatric services, medical services, medication management, individual and group counseling, case management, social support services, and psychoeducation. Although a team approach is used and roles and responsibilities tend to blend between health care professionals, clinical mental health counselors' primary roles and responsibilities are to provide individual and group counseling; facilitate psychoeducational sessions; design, develop, and implement individualized behavioral interventions; conduct diagnostic assessments; and assist in providing crisis services. Regardless of roles and responsibilities, health care professionals in an integrated care treatment recognize that behaviors and lifestyle choices are at the center of disease and illness formation. Fisher et al. (2011) supported this ideology, stating that behavior is fundamental to "prevention, treatment, and management of the preventable manifestations of diseases and health conditions" (p. e15). In others words, interventions are designed to target specific behaviors contributing to disease and illness formation. To better understand this ideology, let us explore two common primary health diseases (i.e., obesity, diabetes) found in the mental health population, as well as common behavioral interventions clinical mental health counselors can implement in community mental health settings.

Obesity is a primary medical disease characterized by an excessive accumulation of body fat, often a contributing factor to other health disorders (Mayo Clinic, 1998-2016). Since the early 1980s, obesity has been on the rise in both the general and mental health population and strongly associated with the rise in diabetes (Brown et al., 2011). Obesity and diabetes both have a behavioral-health linkage (Fisher et al., 2011), and amendable risk factors such as poor diet, sedentary lifestyle, excessive alcohol consumption and substance use, cigarette smoking, and unaddressed behavioral and primary health disorders contribute to the development and progression of these diseases (Sharma, 2007). To combat these diseases, counselors and other health care professionals focus their efforts on designing, implementing, evaluating, and then redesigning interventions that target overall health by focusing on behaviors such as diet, nutrition, and weight loss; physical activity and weight loss; tobacco use; alcohol and substance use; and mental illness, concurrently.

Table 10.1 provides an example of various interventions designed collaboratively by both the counselor and client to synchronously manage comorbid illnesses. However, successful client outcomes rest on more than just a concurrent delivery of services. They also require providers to effectively communicate with their clients and among each other.

TABLE 10.1 ■ Concurrent Interventions Used in an Integrated Treatment Approach				
Diet, Nutrition, and Weight Loss	**Physical Activity and Weight Loss**	**Tobacco Use**	**Alcohol and Substance Use**	**Mental Illness**
Preplanning meals weekly or monthly	Low-impact exercises such as Chair Zumba and swimming	Clinician-assisted tobacco cessation program	Cognitive-behavioral therapy to help clients recognize, avoid, and cope with stressors associated with using alcohol and other substances	Medication management
Creating grocery list prior to shopping; Clinician-assisted grocery shopping	Weight-training exercises; using a trainer	Nicotine replacement therapy	Medication management	Individual and group counseling
Healthy cooking classes	Daily group walking exercise	Support group	Individual and group counseling	Case management
Use of a food tracker app	Use of an exercise monitoring app	Use of a cessation app	Support group	Life skills group
Food pyramid education	Benefits of physical activity education	Harmful effects of tobacco usage education	Education on the cycle of addiction and stages of change	Education on mental illness

Note: Table 10.1 describes possible interventions implemented for clients with comorbid behavioral and mental illnesses and primary health disorders. Interventions are provided concurrently and tailored to the individual client.

COMMUNICATING WITH CLIENTS AND PROVIDERS

Navigating the continuum of care for the novice clinical mental health counselor can be challenging and at times seem overwhelming. Providers of care are, although not intentional, not as forthcoming with information as one would hope (Durbin et al., 2012). This can occur for many reasons, but the most notable are related to concerns with confidentiality and the Health Insurance Portability and Accountability Act (HIPAA) of 1996, differences in professional language, geographical barriers, and imperfect relationships between providers (Clochesy, Dolansky, Hickman Jr., & Gittner, 2015; Erickson & Millar, 2005; Forster et al., 2004). Likewise, clients often under- or overreport health information, making it challenging to ascertain an accurate and complete picture of what is really going on.

It is not uncommon for clients to present for service with certain symptoms and underreport others—which can occur for many reasons. A few of those reasons identified in the literature include the stigma associated with mental and physical illness, negative experiences with previous health care providers, cultural differences between client and provider, and cause-and-effect of symptoms associated with their mental illness and compromised physical health (Bradford, Coleman, & Cunningham, 2007; Cohen & Krauss, 2003; Dickey, Normand, Weiss, Drake & Azeni, 2002). Therefore, it may not be until the initial screening or intake process that clients are made aware of these "unknowns" and/or additional issues. Client issues are expansive and can range from emotional distress to severe and persistent mental health disorders to personality disorders, which are often confounded with primary medical illnesses and/or substance use problems. Thus, the 21st-century clinical mental health counselor is effective in communicating with other health care providers and their clients in identifying and treating complex health care issues. This begins with developing and nurturing the therapeutic alliance.

Therapeutic Alliance

The concept of the therapeutic alliance can be traced back to Freud's (1913) work and the development of the concept of transference. However, many researchers (e.g., Bordin, 1979; Bowlby, 1988; Greenson, 1965; Horwitz, 1974; Rogers, 1951; Zetzel, 1956) have conceptualized the therapeutic alliance differently than Freud. In fact, most noted that the therapeutic alliance was something that is present focused. Rogers (1951) identified three components of the therapeutic alliance: congruence, empathy, and unconditional positive regard, which are artifacts of the counselor and essential in developing and fostering a relationship. Likewise, Luborsky (1976) conceptualized the alliance into two components along the therapy continuum. In early therapy, the therapeutic alliance was understood as the client's perception of the counselor as being supportive; in later therapy, the alliance was characterized as the collaborative partnership between client and counselor. Bordin (1979) operationalized the therapeutic alliance by outlining specific qualifiers, to include agreement on goals, agreement on tasks, and an establishment of a bond between client and counselor. Despite differences in how therapeutic alliance is conceptualized from one author to the next, certain commonalities exist.

First, the therapeutic alliance is attended to in the present. Effective counselors are constantly monitoring and evaluating the quality of the client-counselor relationship. They note times when the relationship is strong and times when it is not so strong to facilitate the counseling process and assist clients in reaching their desired goals. Second, the therapeutic alliance is constantly in flux. Just because the last session was productive does not mean the next one will be. Clients' perceptions of the counselor are ever changing, and a positive perception can be easily thwarted from one moment to the next, especially with persons with complex health care issues. Therefore, it is not uncommon for the therapeutic alliance to ebb and flow throughout the counseling process, especially at the onset of the counseling relationship. Finally, the therapeutic alliance describes the relationship dynamics between client and counselor, one that significantly contributes to successful client outcomes (Lambert & Barley, 2001).

Up to this point, we have discussed the therapeutic alliance in terms of client and counselor; however, rarely does a person have just a single provider. As we have seen in the previous section, clients often traverse the continuum of care, meeting with many different health care providers. Therefore, in contemporary clinical mental health settings offering integrated services, the therapeutic alliance extends beyond the counselor and client and includes the relationship between the client and all providers in the continuum of care, as well as the relationships between all practitioners who provide care to the client.

To help visualize this proposed relationship dynamic, let's take a look at Figure 10.3. In this figure the client is positioned at the topic of the diagram with an array of health care providers in the client's continuum of care listed below. The client is served by a counselor, psychiatrist, primary care physician, and social worker. Note that the left side of the diagram represents the relationship between the client and the various providers in the continuum of care whereas the right side of the diagram denotes the relationships between the client's providers of care. No single dyad is considered more important than the other; rather, it is the synergistic effect of all relationships that contributes to the greatest client outcomes. Let us examine the case of David, a client seeking services for the first time (see Case Illustration 10.2).

CASE ILLUSTRATION 10.2

David is a 24-year-old male who self-identifies as multiracial. He is married with two children and works as a financial planner. He is a very positive person with a good attitude about life. Over the past 6 months, David reports that he has experienced some weird sensations—it was difficult to explain—and he was hearing and seeing strange things not previously experienced. David called three private counselors to seek out help and received little reassurance that they could assist him. David was hesitant to contact the local community mental health agency because of how others portrayed it, yet this was his only option. David eventually called because he needed to seek out help and gain some answers as to what was going on. David spoke with a counselor on the phone who conducted a screening assessment. The counselor on the phone was very direct and to the point, but David had so many questions and was concerned about what was going on. He did not feel like he was being helped at that moment, but the counselor was able to get him an intake appointment. David's interaction with the intake counselor was no more successful than with the counselor he spoke to on the phone.

After completing the intake assessment, David was scheduled to meet with the agency's psychiatrist and primary care physician later in the week to address additional concerns indicated by David and the intake counselor. However, David is unsure if this is the right approach for him. His initial experiences during the screening and intake made him more anxious and unsure about following through with the next two appointments. He is starting to think he made a huge mistake. Within a continuum of care, and especially when using an integrated care treatment approach, clients like David need to feel safe and supported by the counselors they work with. David's feelings surrounding his interactions with the first counselor carried over to the intake counselor. It was unfortunate that he had a similar experience during the intake assessment, and now he is considering discontinuing services altogether. Practitioners working in a coordinated system of care (e.g., integrated care treatment approach) need to be cognizant of how the therapeutic alliance extends to all practitioners in that system. Imagine what would have happened if David had the opposite experience.

FIGURE 10.3 ■ **The Therapeutic Alliance in an Integrated System of Care**

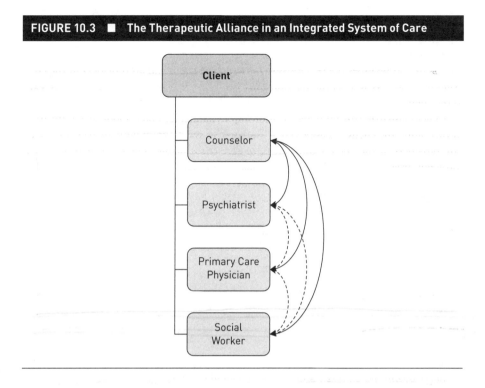

One model that emulates the importance of these relationships dynamics necessary for effective communication in an integrated system of care is the client-centered care paradigm.

Client-Centered Care

Client-centered care, although not a novel approach, has been consistently misunderstood by health care providers due to the lack of agreement of what it actually entails (Hughes, 2011; Robinson, Callister, Berry, & Dearing, 2008). In 2001, the Committee on Quality of Health Care in America and Institute of Medicine defined **client-centered care** as "providing care that is respectful of and responsive to individual client preferences, needs, and values and ensuring that client values guide all clinical decisions" (p. 40). Over the years, numerous models and frameworks have been constructed to depict what client-centered care should look like (Shaller, 2007). In fact, Cronin (2004) was commissioned by the National Health Council to systematically review nine differing models of client-centered care and synthesize elements of consensus and divergence. Her work yielded 45 concepts embedded in descriptors of what client-centered care entails. Six elements consistently appeared in three or more definitions: "(a) education and shared knowledge, (b) involvement of family and friends, (c) collaboration and team management, (d) sensitivity to nonmedical and spiritual dimensions of care, (e) respect for client needs and preferences, and (f) free flow and accessibility of information" (Shaller, 2007, pp. 4–5).

Provider-to-Provider Communication in an Integrated System of Care

In an integrated care treatment approach, effective communication among providers is critical when using a team-based approach (Lardieri, Lasky, & Raney, 2014). Thus, a culture shift is often required for any clinical mental health settings that integrate new areas of health care (i.e., behavioral or medical), as well as for the providers of those new areas of health care. The previously held ideology of a single specialty of care (i.e., behavioral health only or medical health only) is no longer feasible in an integrated system of care. The infusion of medical and behavioral health professionals, each with their own specific skill set and areas of expertise, can pose certain provider-to-provider challenges such as boundary crossing, diffusion of roles and responsibilities, and professional language differences. Despite these challenges, health care professionals in an integrated system of care must collaborate and coexist to deliver comprehensive and effective services. Because provider-to-provider communication primarily involves the exchange of information, it must be effective and efficient across various services and settings (Gulmans, Vollenbroek-Hutten, Van Gemert-Pijnen, & Harten, 2007). Here are four simple considerations to facilitate effective communication between providers: (a) respect, (b) integrative use of language, (c) clarification of roles and responsibilities, and (d) cross-training.

Respect

Respect for other professionals within an integrated system of care can translate into higher quality of care for clients. For instance, respect can create avenues of easier access to vital information, facilitate a smoother exchange of information, and improve relationships between providers. Further, respect communicates a level of professionalism that increases the likelihood other providers will be willing to interact with you in the future.

Integrative Use of Language

Language is our primary method of communicating from one provider to the next. It can occur in written form such as clinical case notes, consultation reports, and medical charts, or it can be spoken between two or more professionals. Communication difficulties occur when professionals have a specific language they use in their discipline of practice and are unable to use or comprehend the vernacular or jargon used by other disciplines. For instance, doctors and nurses write in shorthand, using medical symbols or abbreviations. Counselors speak in terms of prevention, personal strengths, and wellness and highlight the counseling relationship to facilitate change. Psychologists may reference scores obtained from a battery of assessments in their consultation report. Each individual believes he or she is contributing valuable information to be used in treating the client. However, the differences in professional language create an unnecessary barrier, keeping those on the inside informed and everyone else on the outside looking in. Therefore, health care providers in an integrated system of care should become familiar with the common verbiage used and incorporate that when writing and speaking to professionals in disciplines other than their own.

GUIDED PRACTICE EXERCISE 10.2

In class, with a partner, identify the potential shared roles and responsibilities practitioners (e.g., doctors, nurses, counselors, social workers, psychologists) may undertake in an integrated care treatment approach. Also consider the unique role of each practitioner. For example, a psychiatrist's unique function is to treat mental illness by prescribing psychotropic medications. Counselors do not prescribe medications but instead implement counseling interventions to treat symptoms of mental illness. However, both the psychiatrist and the counselor may offer clients' medication and symptom management and share the responsibility of ensuring clients' health and well-being.

Clarification of Roles and Responsibilities

In an integrated system of care, it is extremely important to clarify each person's role and responsibility (Lardieri et al., 2014). Confusion over who does what can easily get convoluted in a team-based approach. Each provider in an integrated system of care serves a unique purpose in the pathway to care; however, each member also serves to bridge the gaps in care through shared roles and responsibilities. Therefore, it is critical to identify, at the onset, each provider's unique role and responsibilities as well as the shared roles and responsibilities. For instance, a counselor's role might be to implement behavioral interventions that promote weight loss and increased physical activity, and a doctor's role might be to prescribe medications to manage diseases of diabetes and hypertension. Despite the different role of each professional, they share the responsibilities of ensuring client compliance with treatment interventions, providing referrals when necessary, and sharing vital health information.

Cross-Training

The idea of cross-training might seem unnecessary to some and overwhelming to others, but understanding what others do in an integrated system of care is critical in a team-based approach. Cross-training gets professionals to interact, create opportunities to talk using a shared language, model how they practice, and facilitate the formation of working relationships (Lardieri et al., 2014). Cross-training can take the form of counselors demonstrating how they deescalate crisis situations, medical doctors providing education on common primary medical diseases occurring in mental health clients, or psychiatrists describing their assessment process when meeting with a client for the first time. The goal of cross-training is to get everyone on the same page to create an efficient and effective system of care.

Provider-to-Client Communication in an Integrated System of Care

Interpersonal communication between provider and client is critical to client satisfaction, compliance with treatment, and successful client outcomes (de Negri, Brown, Hernandez, Rosenbaum, & Roter, n.d.; Flickinger et al., 2016). Within an integrated system of care are numerous contact points for clients, beginning with checking in with support staff to meeting with a counselor for screening or intake to the first visit with a psychiatrist and/or medical doctors. Although each interaction may occur independently, depending on the model of integration implemented, the effects of each interaction reverberate from one contact to the next. Therefore, as a future provider of care it is paramount to engage in effective communication practices. Four simple considerations to facilitate effective communication between provider and client are: (a) respect, (b) creating a caring environment, (c) engaging in conversation, and (d) effectively using verbal and nonverbal communication.

Respect

Just like the respect described in provider-to-provider communication, counselors and other providers need to respect their clients, and clients need to perceive that they are respected. This occurs through establishing a therapeutic alliance. Respect for clients can translate into fewer no-show appointments, compliance with medications, a willingness to try new interventions, and better client outcomes.

Creating a Caring Environment

Empathy, compassion, and respect can go a long way in creating an environment that helps clients feel safe and secure. This begins the minute they are greeted and continues until the appointment is finished. Be thoughtful in how you communicate messages and remain present the entire time. Also, do not be afraid to incorporate a visually pleasing décor. Think about it for a moment. How many times have you been to a bland doctor's office or met with a colleague in their unflattering office? Did you feel welcomed or uncomfortable? Remember, a little can go a long way in creating a sense of security for clients who may have reservations about being there in the first place.

Engaging in Conversation

Effective communication is a two-way process. In its simplest form, information is communicated in a clear and understandable manner. Next, that information is received, comprehended, and acknowledged. In an integrated system of care, both the client and provider have the opportunity to speak, ask questions, express similar or disagreeing opinions, and come to a mutual understanding of what was discussed (de Negri et al., n.d.).

Effectively Using Verbal and Nonverbal Communication

Both spoken words and body language send messages that can be perceived positively or negatively by clients. Usually, clients do not seek out services under the most ideal conditions. A pleasant vocal tone and a positive attitude can go a long way with persons seeking health care services. Also, language in itself can be complex and difficult for persons from different cultural backgrounds to speak and understand. It behooves practitioners to use simplistic and common words and phrases and avoid professional jargon when communicating with clients. Procedures should be explained in easy-to-follow language, and opportunities to ask questions should be extended to the client.

CONDUCTING CLIENT INTERVIEWS

As one of the most critical phases in the treatment process, client interviewing takes center stage. Think of it as the point of origination or the phase of possible termination, depending on the client's experience. In early medicine and psychiatry, the perspective held by the majority of practitioners was the biomedical approach (Engel, 1977). The primary clinical focus was on disease, better understood as a biological deviation from what was considered normal. Information obtained under this paradigm consisted of symptomology, medical history, and findings from diagnostic assessments (Lyles, Dwamena, Lein, & Smith, 2001). In other words, any biological information that could be reduced to its simplest measurable form was obtained. Despite this dominantly held ideology, George Engel (1977) insisted that to truly understand the problems or issues of the human condition, practitioners must consider the holistic self, to include not only biomedical characteristics but also the inherent psychological and social aspects. Therefore, client interviewing not only focuses on what type of data to obtain but also considers the method by which data are obtained. In other words, the "how" of obtaining the "what" are not mutually exclusive. As a result, clinical mental health counselors need to have basic competencies to be effective in the interviewing process. This section focuses on the skills and processes required for the client interview. We begin by exploring the basic interviewing skills counselors must possess. Next, we explore the general stages and processes of the client interview. Finally, we discuss unforeseen incidents that may arise during the interview process.

Basic Interviewing Skills

Basic interviewing skills facilitate communication of vital information between practitioner and client. Within the client-centered care model, the therapeutic alliance rests on the practitioner's ability to initiate and foster a relationship, and this begins in the initial interview. A negative experience during the initial interview could result in the client generalizing that experience to all providers within the integrated system of care, creating additional unnecessary barriers to health and wellness. Therefore, clinical mental health counselors are proficient in the skills of active listening, expressing empathy, appropriate use of open and closed questions, and awareness and monitoring of nonverbal body language.

Active Listening

A method of both intentional listening and responding, **active listening** better facilitates mutual understanding between two persons. Active listening is not passive listening—simply hearing what has been said. Rather, active listening is a process constantly occurring throughout the interviewing process. Bodie (2011) and Drollinger, Comer, and Warrington (2006) characterized active listening as a process that involves three stages: sensing, processing, and responding.

The stage of *sensing* relates to listening behaviors that demonstrate attention to information and signal to the other individual that they are present-focused (Vickery, Keaton, & Bodie, 2015). Sensing behaviors include appropriate eye contact, a nonjudgement facial expression, engagement in silence, and well-placed minimal encouragers (e.g., head nodding, one or two word utterances such as *um-hm, hmm, I see, yes*). *Processing* relates to listening behaviors that allow for remembering, synthesization, and reconstruction of information (Vickery et al., 2015). Processing behaviors include engaging in silence and reflecting on content said before responding. The last stage, *responding*, is characterized by listening behaviors that ensure continuity of information exchange (Vickery et al., 2015). Responding is not reacting to information. Rather, it is the appropriate exchange of information facilitated by open- and closed-ended questions and nonverbal body language to encourage additional information and to clarify misunderstood information. However, a skilled clinician would respond not only by using open- and closed-ended questions but also by reflecting content and feeling.

Reflection of content is the process of stating back to the client the essence of what was said in a nonjudgmental or leading manner. It is not parroting word for word what the client said but rather uses different words to communicate back the meaning of what was said. Reflection of content takes two forms: paraphrasing and summarizing. Paraphrasing is a succinct restatement of what was said, thereby keeping the original meaning but using different words. For example, suppose a client states, "I am constantly tired, even when I wake up from 8 or 10 hours of uninterrupted sleep." The counselor may state, "You're tired no matter how much sleep you get." Summarizing is similar to paraphrasing, however, it involves more information verbalized by the client. Summarizing is often used at the end of an interview, when finishing a specific topic, or when changing a topic.

Reflection of feeling is similar to reflection of content; however, there is an explicit identification of feelings, and feeling words are included in the statement. For example, a client may state, "I thought earning my bachelor's degree was going to help me get a job. Instead, I have been to five interviews and no one has called me back. My rent is due in a few weeks and I am almost out of savings. I am not sure what I am going to do." The counselor may state, "You are under a lot of pressure to find a job, and it is causing you to feel stressed." Open- and closed-ended questions, appropriate nonverbal body language, and reflection of content and feeling are all appropriate methods of responding in the skill of active listening. They communicate to clients that you hear and understand what is being said, express empathy, and facilitate development of the therapeutic alliance.

Empathy

Carl Rogers (1959) defined **empathy** as "the ability to perceive the internal frame of reference of another with accuracy, and with the emotional components and meanings . . . as if one were the other person" (p. 210). In other words, empathy is the counselors' ability to put themselves in the other person's shoes, without losing their own cognitive and emotional self, and the ability to engage in dialogue that reflects this. For clients presenting with both mental health and medical-related issues, there might be a great deal of anxiety or trepidation. Here, empathy plays an important role in strengthening the counselor-client relationship.

Open-Ended Questions

These questions are structured in a manner that continues a conversation and are not sufficiently answered with a simple yes or no response. Usually **open-ended questions** begin with "what" and "how" and avoiding using "why" to encourage clients to speak without reservation throughout the interview process. Open questions also encourage elaboration and provide additional information that may prove to be invaluable in later phases of the interview. Some examples of open-ended questions are "How are you feeling today?" or "What brings you into my office today?" The word *describe* can be powerful in the interview process. For instance, "Describe your reaction to the medication for me."

Closed-Ended Questions

These questions limit a client's response to usually a one-word yes or no response. **Closed-ended questions** are designed to tailor a conversation to a specific point or event. For example, "Are you taking your medications as prescribed?" or "Is this the first time you have sought out counseling services?" Notice that both questions can be answered with either a yes or no response and direct the interview to a specific event. Closed-ended questions are not incorrect or "bad." Rather, they by design lend little additional information to the counselor.

Nonverbal Body Language

Nonverbal body language is everything other than words that communicates messages to the client. This includes facial expressions, body posture, vocal tone, gestures, eye movements, and attitude. Although most counselors' intent with nonverbal body language is harmless, clients often interpret these messages and decipher their own meaning throughout the interview. Additionally, be aware of how cultural differences and background may inform how clients perceive nonverbal body language. What may have been intended to communicate one message may be interpreted to mean something completely different. In situations like this, counselors should regularly check in with their clients to make sure their messages are being received as intended.

GUIDED PRACTICE EXERCISE 10.3

The basic counseling skills of active listening that include reflection of content and reflection of feeling, open- and closed-ended questions, and management of nonverbal body language are critical to successful client interviews. In groups of three, role-play the interview process. One student will play the role of the client, the second student will play the role of the interviewer, and the third student will be the process observer. The goal of this role-play is to practice basic interviewing skills. Each student in the triad should have the opportunity to play every role.

Use the following guidelines in setting up your role-play: (a) this is the client's first time seeking out integrated care treatment, (b) the client has both behavioral and medical health care concerns, and (c) the client is unsure of whether seeking help is the right step. Attempt to use as many of the basic counseling skills as possible. The process observer's job is to provide an outside perspective on the skills used by the counselor. Remember that this is practice; do not be afraid to attempt any of the basic counseling skills, and finally, have some fun with this activity.

Stages and Processes of the Client Interview

Using a behavioral medicine approach, the client interview can span many facets of a person's life. Areas covered generally consist of the presenting problem and other additional problems, history of the presenting problem and other additional problems, medical and mental health history, assessment of basic needs, family history, alcohol and illicit substance use, criminal history, mental status exam, social history, medication history, physical examination, assessment of suicidality, history of hospitalizations, and identification of personal strengths. This list is not exhaustive of the type of information that can be collected during the interview, and it often depends on the setting and scope of the agency of where the client seeks services. Regardless of the type of information collected, a good interview is a systematic process that occurs in stages and relies on the basic interview skills. Generally speaking, client interviews occur across the following six stages:

Stage 1: Do your homework (counselor)

Stage 2: Establish the environment

Stage 3: Identity major problem(s) and any additional pressing problem(s)

Stage 4: Develop a mutual understanding of the problem(s)

Stage 5: Collaboratively plan and identify next steps

Stage 6: Termination

Stage 1: Do Your Homework

Bickley (2013) stressed the importance of preparing for the interview session. Accessing and reviewing available information (e.g., medical charts, clinician case notes, referral forms) prior to the interview can assist the interviewer during the interview. Knowing prior diagnoses, medication history, and treatment history is always useful. When possible, consult with the client's previous providers of care (with proper consent of course). In a fully integrated system of care, a client's consent is applicable to all providers of treatment within that system, allowing for easier sharing of vital health care information.

Stage 2: Establish the Environment

Do you remember how you felt when meeting with your doctor or dentist for the first time? Was it pleasant? What made it pleasing? If not, what could have been done differently that would have made it more pleasurable for you? Remember that not all clients are excited to seek health care services, and this is never more apparent than during the initial interview. Therefore, take the time to establish the working environment and build the therapeutic alliance. Introduce yourself and explain your role as the interviewer, identify the purpose of the interview, be inviting and pleasant, attend to your nonverbal body language, remain open to casual conversation, and address any initial concerns the client may have. Try limiting your questions during this stage, for it may make the client feel interrogated in later stages of the interview. The goal of this stage is to create an environment highlighted by feelings of trust and safety. Using the basic skills of active listening and reflection of content is helpful in building rapport early in the interview.

Stage 3: Identity Major Problem(s) and Any Additional Pressing Problem(s)

This is the information-gathering phase. Both Bickley (2013) and Smith (2003) recommend establishing the agenda early on in this stage for two reasons. First, it helps to ensure that both the client and the interviewer achieve their goals for the interview. Second, it assists with time management. Interviews can be time-consuming and exhausting for both the client and the interviewer. Setting the agenda assists with time constraints and errors of omission. In identifying problems, clients often use a story format. Usually it is loaded with important information that needs to be distilled through further conversation and appropriate use of closed-ended questions. At other times, the interviewer needs to ask open-ended questions to draw out and clarify what was said. Skilled interviewers integrate both questions and reflection of content and feeling to facilitate a deeper level of understanding. Similarly, it is not uncommon for clients to become emotional during this stage. As you and the client collaboratively explore their problems, sudden feelings of anger, sadness, frustration, and so forth are embedded within the context of what is said. It is important, as the interviewer, to acknowledge those feelings by reflecting feeling. This demonstrates effective listening on your behalf and validates what the client is currently feeling.

Stage 4: Develop a Mutual Understanding of the Problem(s)

Once the problem or problems have been identified, it is important that you and the client agree as to what they actually are and share a common understanding of how they developed. This can be challenging, especially if you and the client disagree as to what the problems are and how they originated. Remember that being correct is not more important than being collaborative. Therefore, a careful review of what has been discussed is warranted. During this stage, it is important for the interviewer to engage in paraphrasing and summarization skills. It is recommended that after paraphrasing or summarizing critical information, the interviewer conduct a check-in with the client. Examples of check-ins are "Does that sound right to you?," "Have I summed up everything correctly?," or "Are we on the same page?" Getting the client to agree or disagree helps to ensure accuracy of information and provides opportunities for clarifying any misunderstandings.

Stage 5: Collaboratively Plan and Identify Next Steps

Now that the major problems have been identified and agreed on, it is time to establish a plan to approach those problems. This usually means referral to services within or outside the system of care and additional in-depth assessments (e.g., health, medical, substance use, basic needs, suicidality). Planning occurs collaboratively; however, the client takes the lead in identifying which problem or set of problems they wish to address first. Even with a collaborative approach to planning, some clients may feel hesitant or overwhelmed with deciding on what problem to address first, or they may feel they have to take on every problem right away. Both situations have their pitfalls and could result in clients experiencing minimal success or maximum failure. The skills of paraphrasing and open- and closed-ended questions are helpful in navigating these types of outcomes. Once the plan is established and mutually agreed on, it is important that the interviewer be transparent in what will happen next, outlining clients' responsibilities and ensuring they have access to the necessary information to be successful in carrying out their plan (e.g., referrals in hand, dates and times of their next appointment, linked with appropriate health care providers).

Stage 6: Termination

The final stage of the interview process is termination. Unexperienced interviewers may find it challenging to end an interview session, especially with clients who are talkative and continuously asking questions. Likewise, clients may have a hard time with feeling abandoned or experience a sense of remorse for sharing so much about their lives in such a short period. It is important to address clients' concerns of remorse and feeling abandoned. The basic skills of reflecting feelings and content, expressing empathy, and relying on the established rapport can be effective with clients who seem ambivalent about termination. Interviewers who find it difficult to terminate should always prepare themselves and their clients for termination. Indirectly remind clients that interviews are time limited. For instance, inform them that there is only 10 minutes left in the interview and that the two of you need to begin the process of termination. Because the process of termination is more than just saying goodbye, take the time to provide a brief review of the plan, answer any final questions the client may have, and ensure the client has the necessary information in hand before leaving the interview.

Unanticipated Incidents During the Interview

A primary task of clinical mental health counselors is to conduct client interviews. Even though a systematic process ensues, which spans from the beginning to middle to end, unexpected events or situations may occur that can challenge the most skilled counselor and ultimately end the interview process. These unforeseen incidents are broken down into three categories based on severity, each requiring a differing level of action on behalf of the interviewer. The first category is *minor incidents* and includes situations or behaviors such as a client refusing to answer questions, getting up and leaving the interview, or being disruptive. The second category is *intermediate incidents* and includes situations or behaviors such as a client who is actively psychotic, engaged in deception, or has a physical or cognitive disability. The last category is *major incidents* and includes situations or behaviors such as a client expressing suicidality or being under the influence of drugs or alcohol.

Minor Incidents

Minor incidents of a client refusing to answer questions, getting up to leave, or being disruptive can certainly challenge the interview process. Not all clients are receptive to health care services and may even be against the idea of some stranger asking them questions about their personal life. Interviews are designed to identify sensitive information, which may cause an unexpected reaction of someone refusing to answer your questions or even go as far as someone suddenly leaving the interview. Do not fret. There are a few things you can do to avoid these unexpected reactions. First, prepare clients ahead of time and inform them that you will be asking questions regarding personal and sensitive information. It is also helpful to remind them they are the architect of the interview and you are just the facilitator. In other words, empower them and help them realize that they are in control. Also, remind them of confidentially (as well as limits to confidentiality) and how information will remain private.

Even with planning, it may be impossible to avoid disruption in the interviewing environment. Often clients bring family members, their children, and others to the interview. Or the client's cell phone rings, or the interviewer is paged across the loudspeaker. Remaining open and flexible is key in addressing these minor disruptions. Politely ask that children wait in the play area (most clinical settings now have a supervised play area). Remind clients that the interview can be a lengthy process and distractions could result in the interview taking longer than necessary. Ask clients to set their phone to silent prior to starting the interview and silence your own phone, which avoids the potential distraction all together; inform support staff to hold all your phone calls until you have finished the interview. Regardless of the type of minor incidents that could occur, careful planning, remaining flexile and open, and being polite can have a profound impact on the interview process.

Intermediate Incidents

Intermediate incidents pose a greater challenge to the interview process. Depending on the type of incident that occurs, a client or the interviewer could decide one of two things: adapt and continue or end the interview. Situations or behavior such as a client being actively psychotic, engaging in deception, or having a physical disability all warrant a differing level of response. For clients that are actively psychotic, the interviewer needs to evaluate the safety of the individuals, the accuracy of information obtained, and the overall effectiveness of the interview process. If the client's baseline (normal functioning) is identified as psychotic and the client is safe to self and others and willing to participate, then the interview can continue. However, if those parameters are not in place, the interview should probably be discontinued and the person's needs attended to.

Likewise, a person being deceptive or unwilling to participate makes for one difficult interview. This could result in the interviewer determining the information to be inaccurate or the process to be ineffective and may result in termination of the interview. However, if the client is committed to seek help, perhaps more time and attention are needed to build rapport. If you perceive your client to be deceptive or providing incongruent statements, consider the following: Often clients live with severe and persistent conditions that they become desensitized to, resulting in a failure to report a problem as a problem, even though it may be obvious to you; clients with an extensive history of mental illness and/or physical health disorders, especially when untreated, may be poor historians of their own life events. The key is to not react by jumping to conclusions but rather respond using the basic interviewing skills learned previously, which can assist in identifying if a client is truly being deceptive.

A final intermediate incident relates to disabilities and the challenges they may pose to the interview process. It is not uncommon for clients seeking mental and/or primary health care services to have a physical or cognitive disability. Generally speaking, disabilities include intellectual and cognitive disorders; visual, vocal, and auditory impairments; and mobility constraints. The impairment from any one disability varies from person to person and therefore should be addressed early in the interview process and approached with sensitivity and respect for the person.

Even though it may be impossible to plan for a person with disabilities, there are some general action steps you can take. First, when clients call to schedule an interview appointment, ask them if they have any physical or cognitive impairments. It is better to be prepared versus being ill-equipped to handle what comes your way. Second, for clients with visual, vocal, and auditory disabilities, be sure to provide images and text in a large font size. Be flexible in how you deliver and receive information; not everything has to be spoken. Use visual aids and other formats when presenting information. On a similar note, language barriers can pose additional challenges to both the interviewer and interviewee. Language differences can lead to misunderstanding, recording false information, and a negative interview experience. Most, if not all, clinical mental health settings are contracted with a language interpretive service (e.g., Language Line) that is free to the client. However, these interpretative services require some preplanning on behalf of the interviewer.

Major Incidents

Major incidents pose an even greater challenge to the interviewing process. Incidents such as clients stating they are suicidal or who appear to be intoxicated or under the influence of illicit substances warrant your immediate attention. This usually requires counselors to stop the interview to address the client's current needs, often involving crisis services (e.g., crisis assessment and intervention, coordinating acute hospitalization or detoxification services). Having a client verbalize suicidality can be anxiety provoking. But to ignore these expressions for help is even more disconcerting. Likewise, interviewing a client who is intoxicated or under the influence of drugs can lead to uncooperative behaviors and become a safety issue for both the client and interviewer. Due to the limited cooperation and potential safety issues that arise from being under the influence of substances, it may be best practice to terminate the interview and reschedule it (Kabale, Nkombua, Matthews, & Offiong, 2013). Remember, your first priority is to ensure your clients' safety and your own; regardless of the incident that arises, nothing beats being prepared.

GUIDED PRACTICE EXERCISE 10.4

On your own, consider additional unanticipated incidents not previously mentioned that you think would impact the interview process. Once identified, answer the following questions:

1. How would I classify the incident (i.e., minor, intermediate, or major)?

2. What evidence indicates that it is a minor, intermediate, or major incident?

3. How would you address the incident, if termination of the interview was not necessary?

4. What basic interviewing skills would be helpful for each incident identified?

MOTIVATING BEHAVIOR CHANGE IN MEDICAL CLIENTS

Change can be difficult for anyone, especially if what needs changing has become habitual and highly rewarding (Bouton, 2014). It is not uncommon to cringe at the thought of change and even feel anxious or trepidatious when considering it. Imagine if you could no longer have your morning cup of coffee or drink carbonated beverages with your afternoon meal. What if you were told you had to quit smoking cigarettes or drinking alcohol because of health reasons? For some of you reading this, you might be thinking, *that doesn't sound too difficult* or *I could easily give up drinking sodas* or *that's a no-brainer for me*. Others may have a deeper insight into how difficult halting a behavior such as drinking caffeine or smoking cigarettes can actually seem. It might be like crossing the Sahara with only a single bottle of water—nearly impossible. Persons who hold this perspective regarding behavior change would rather have others or the environment adapt to them. This type of mentality is what makes sustaining behavioral changes across the life span so difficult. That is because behavioral change is a continuous lifestyle choice (Westenhoefer, 2001). So, how do clinical mental health counselors motivate behavioral change in medical clients? To answer this question, we begin by briefly exploring the stages of change. Next, we examine two sources of motivation for change that counselors can impact through their therapeutic work with clients presenting with comorbid behavioral and mental health disorders.

Transtheoretical Model of Behavioral Change

Behavioral change is as much a process of cognitive fortitude as it is behavioral action (Lenio, n.d.). When a client decides to eat healthier and commit to exercise to improve health, rarely does this occur as a single event but rather as a series of events. It requires awareness, decision-making, and a commitment to change. Prochaska and DiClemente (1983) originally described behavioral change as occurring across five stages: precontemplation, contemplation, preparation, action, and maintenance. These stages contain 10 processes that persons experience as they enter into change: consciousness raising, dramatic relief, self-reevaluation, environmental reevaluation, self-liberation, social liberation, counterconditioning, stimulus control, contingency management, and helping relationship. In 1997, Prochaska and Velicer introduced a sixth stage, termination. The termination stage is best theorized as maintaining total self-efficacy and having no temptation to revert to an original behavior (Prochaska & Velicer, 1997). For clients with comorbid disorders, helping them understand the process of change and identifying where they are in the process can be a powerful first step. For future clinical mental health counselors such as yourselves, having a general understanding of the transtheoretical model of behavioral change serves as a great resource for identifying appropriate interventions to motivate and sustain change. To dive fully into the transtheoretical model of behavioral change is beyond the scope of this section; however, a brief review of its six stages follows. To learn more, see the Web Resources section at the end of the chapter and the original sources (Prochaska & DiClemente, 1983; Prochaska & Velicer, 1997).

Behavioral change begins with the stage of *precontemplation*. Clients must first be aware that a behavior is even a problem. For medical clients with a comorbid disorder, they must accept that behaviors such as eating fatty food, having a sedentary lifestyle, or drinking alcohol in excess is negatively affecting their health. Likewise, clients who are aware of behaviors that negatively impact their health, yet refuse to change those behaviors, are also in the precontemplation stage of change. Counselors need to prepare themselves for clients who may have no intention of changing their behaviors. However, educating clients on how behaviors can impact health and illness can be powerful in this stage, as well as education on how the stages of change can help normalize clients' feelings regarding the process. Sometimes you have to prepare the soil even before planting a seed.

The second stage is *contemplation*. Clients at this stage are thinking about change but have not yet begun the process. They are often ambivalent and weighing the pros and cons of change. An example of a client in the contemplation stage is one who knows he may need to lose weight for health reasons but does not feel he can truly commit to the dietary changes and increased physical activity such a goal would require. Counselors can be effective by developing clients' pros and cons concretely and identifying barriers to pros and supports for cons.

The third stage is *preparation*. Clients in this stage are ready to take action but have not acted. They may engage in what is known as preaction, the first step before actual action. This can take the form of marking a start date on the calendar, scheduling an appointment, or informing others that they plan to change. Counselors can be effective by providing support and encouragement and assisting clients in engaging in as many preaction steps as necessary. This builds client confidence and develops their self-efficacy.

The fourth stage is *action*. In this stage, clients are actively engaged in work. Whether that is no longer smoking or drinking alcohol, actively participating in physical exercise, or getting involved in a support group, clients are expending energy that directly relates to the changed behavior. Counselors can help clients commit to the change process through teaching them how to monitor their progress, set realistic goals, and establish pathways to prevent reverting to the old behavior.

The fifth stage, *maintenance*, is characterized by a state of equilibrium. Clients have not engaged in the previous behavior for a period greater than 6 months. Clients at this stage have reached a huge milestone. Counselors can assist clients in establishing a relapse prevention plan. A **relapse prevention plan** outlines step by step a client's possible triggers (e.g., stimuli, persons, situations, events, environmental settings) and a systematic course of action if a client is faced with a potential relapse; successful plans are detail oriented, specific, and realistic. Furthermore, clients in this stage should have a well-developed repertoire of coping skills and be able to implement them with a high degree of self-efficacy. Finally, although not a stage, *relapse* is often identified when discussing stages of change. Relapse occurs when clients revert to a previous stage and engage in a previously stopped behavior. Relapse is not the end of the world; however, clients can easily feel as though it is. Counselors can be most effective when relapse occurs by normalizing it but not sanctioning it and helping clients to identify the trigger(s) that caused relapse and strengthen their coping skills. Although the transtheoretical model of behavioral change can serve as a wonderful educational tool in understanding the processes (see Prochaska & DiClemente, 1983; Prochaska & Velicer, 1997, for a detailed discussion on the 10 processes of change) and stages of change, we need to understand the internal and external motivational factors that contribute to clients' self-regulation.

Internal Self-Regulation

To truly understand human behavior, you must first identify what motivates it (Spiegler, 2016). Intrinsic motivators are factors internal to a person and can either occur out of necessity (e.g., the need to connect with others, desire to satisfy sexual urges) or be learned (Seifert, Chapman, Hart, & Perez, 2012); they are refined by personal values, beliefs, and cultural background (U.S. National Research Council Committee on Aging Frontiers in Social Psychology, Personality, and Adult Developmental Psychology, 2006). When working with clients with comorbid disorders, it is important to understand the internal constructs that influence motivation. These include decision-making processes, perceived self-efficacy, attitude regarding change, and the ability to project oneself into the future (Bandura, 2001; Gollwitzer, Fujita, & Oettingen, 2004). Sawyer, Miller-Lewis, Searle, Sawyer, and Lynch (2015) collectively identified these internal processes as a person's capacity to self-regulate, that is, the ability to control thoughts, behaviors, and emotions in response to the perceived environment. Self-regulation is a developmental phenomenon and begins early in childhood; it paves the way for observed behaviors in adulthood (Choe, Olson, & Sameroff, 2013). For clients with comorbid disorders, failure to self-regulate results in dire consequences, such as exacerbated symptoms associated with mental illness, engagement in risky behaviors, and early death. Counselors can assist clients in identifying their current methods of internal self-regulation and modify those that result in unhealthy behaviors. More specifically, counselors can help clients identify how they respond to environmental stressors, develop strategies for emotion regulation and self-control, and reframe negative thought orientation. Researchers have identified cognitive, behavioral, and combined cognitive-behavioral therapy (e.g., Beck & Fernandez, 1998a, 1998b; Emmelkamp, 1994; Hollon & Beck, 1994); rational-emotive behavioral therapy (e.g., Pychyl & Flett, 2012); and dialectical-behavioral therapy (Sampl, Wakai, Trestman, & Keeney, 2008) as effective approaches in assisting clients in modifying internal methods of self-regulation. However, evidence indicates that once a behavior is enacted it becomes more difficult to intervene due to gratification (Beck & Fernandez, 1998a, 1998b). Thus, to fully understand self-regulation, we need to explore external motivators that impact it.

External Self-Regulation

External factors that influence motivation occur outside the person (Ryan & Deci, 2000). These include rewards (e.g., money, promotion at work), punishments (threats that result from a behavior), and social factors that influence self-regulation. Some clients with comorbid disorders may have no desire to change a particular behavior (zero intrinsic motivation) unless external forces are involved. For example, clients with little motivation to quit smoking are less likely to do so when barriers stand in their way such as being surrounded by others who smoke, being unable to afford smoking cessation treatment, and fear of gaining weight. Likewise, to offer clients a reward- or punishment-based system of motivation is not only unfeasible and potentially harmful, it often results in a process known as overjustification. **Overjustification** occurs when the external source of motivation diminishes the internal source of self-regulation. This could result in clients engaging in a behavior as a result of an incentive or threat of punishment; however, once the external force is removed the behavior often stops. So, how can counselors effectively promote external self-regulation? Case Illustration 10.3 explores the case of Henry.

CASE ILLUSTRATION 10.3

Henry is a single 37-year-old male who self-identifies as Hispanic. He comes from a well-to-do family and graduated from a prestigious university. He recently broke up with his girlfriend of 5 years, which is causing him to experience bouts of sadness and depression. To cope, Henry has previously engaged in risky behaviors (i.e., occasional drug use, unprotected sex with strangers) but reports that this is no longer an issue. Henry's most recent concern is that he continues to feel sad and depressed and is unable to control his eating and excessive weight gain. He has tried to lose weight on his own but has not been successful, causing him to feel even more depressed. He is beginning to isolate from friends and family, lacks motivation to exercise, continues to eat fattening foods, and has very little insight into how his depression and weight gain are linked. Henry seems to lack any mechanism for self-regulation. Internally, his decision-making skills regarding his eating habits are poor, he has limited self-efficacy to engage in exercise, and he is unable to recognize how his current behaviors are exacerbating his symptoms of depression and

his outlook on life. Henry's external motivators of wanting to manage his depression and control his weight are not greater than the gratification he receives from eating fatty foods and isolating from others. In fact, those behaviors diminish the value of his external motivators to self-regulate and serve as barriers to change. In working with Henry, counselors would be most effective by removing those unnecessary barriers. Assisting Henry in understanding the link between his depression and eating and developing a realistic exercise regimen and diet plan could strengthen his external motivation for wanting to feel less depressed and get in shape. This goal is to improve Henry's source of external self-regulation through removing barriers that may thwart his decision to engage in healthy behaviors. In doing so, Henry will begin to make healthier eating choices, exercise more often, and feel less depressed. By removing these barriers, Henry's external sources of self-regulation will improve and, over time, so will his internal sources of self-regulation (i.e., self-efficacy, decision-making abilities, attitude, and foresight into the future).

Although we have discussed internal and external mechanisms of self-regulation as if they occur exclusively from one another, the exact opposite is true. At the onset of treatment, clients with comorbid disorders may verbalize the desire to change but show little action in doing so. This is because numerous perceived barriers stand in their way and moderate their external sources of self-regulation (e.g., desire to lose weight, seek help for depression). Counselors can be most effective in teaching clients how to overcome those barriers and in doing so, strengthen clients' ability to externally self-regulate, which ultimately advances their internal ability (i.e., decision-making ability, self-efficacy in completing tasks, having foresight into the future, attitude) to do the same. Remembering that internal and external motivators to self-regulation work in tandem and are what promotes and sustains behavioral change across the life span is vital to the success clinical mental health counselors experience with their clients.

Keystones

- Behavioral medicine is a multidisciplinary science that integrates knowledge from various fields related to health and illness; practitioners apply this knowledge in the treatment and prevention of illness through targeting behaviors that impact overall health and well-being. The behavioral medicine approach is grounded in the philosophical principles of the biopsychosocial model. Illness formation and health promotion is best conceptualized as the product of three interacting factors: biological, psychological, and social. A practical application of the behavioral medicine approach can be observed in integrated care treatments.

- To better manage behavioral and mental illness in medical clients, many clinical mental health settings have begun to offer integrated care treatment. Integrated care treatment is the systematic approach to treating both behavioral and primary health care needs concurrently. The strength of integrated care treatment results from the level of service integration between providers from both behavioral and primary health care settings. Service integration occurs along a continuum: coordinated, co-located, and fully integrated.

- The therapeutic alliance conceptualized from the integrated care treatment approach includes the relationship between counselor and client but also hinges on the relationship between the client and all providers in the continuum of care, as well as the relationship between all providers. Effective communication with clients and between providers occurs when the therapeutic alliance is attended to throughout the treatment process. Among providers, effective communication is facilitated when

providers show respect for one another, integrate others' professional language when communicating, have a clear understanding of their and others' roles and responsibilities, and partake in cross-training. Effective communication is facilitated between clients and providers when providers respect their client, create a caring environment, engage in conversation with clients, and effectively use verbal and nonverbal communication skills.

- Successful client interviews require counselors to be competent in using the basic interview skills: active listening, empathy, open- and closed-ended questions, and attending to nonverbal body language. Client interviews follow a systematic approach, which generally occurs across six stages. Although a systematic approach to interviewing is used, counselors need to be aware of unanticipated incidents that may arise during the interview process.

- Motivating medical clients with comorbid behavioral and mental illness to engage in and sustain behavioral change can be challenging. Remember that behavioral change is a temporal process, and by educating clients on the stages of change, counselors can mitigate many of the barriers (e.g., lack of awareness, resistance, relapse) clients may experience as they proceed to alter deep-rooted behaviors. Effective self-regulation is critical to clients sustaining behavioral change across the life span. Counselors need to work with clients in identifying the processes of both internal (i.e., decision-making process, perceived self-efficacy, attitude, forethought) and external (i.e., rewards, punishments, social factors) mechanisms of motivation. Effective motivation removes immediate barriers inhibiting behavioral change but does not diminish a client's internal self-regulation.

Key Terms

Active listening 255

Behavioral medicine 242

Biomedical model 242

Biopsychosocial model 242

Client-centered care 251

Closed-ended questions 257

Continuum of care 244

Empathy 256

Integrated care treatment 245

Nonverbal body language 257

Open-ended questions 256

Overjustification 265

Reflection of content 256

Reflection of feeling 256

Relapse prevention plan 264

Web Resources

Aims Center: Evidence-Based Behavioral Interventions in Primary Care (https://aims.uw.edu/evidence-based-behavioral-interventions-primary-care)

International Society of Behavioral Medicine (www.isbm.info)

National Institutes of Health, Office of Behavioral and Social Sciences Research (https://obssr.od.nih.gov)

Society of Behavioral Medicine (www.sbm.org)

Substance Abuse and Mental Health Services Administration: Integrated Care (www.integration.samhsa.gov)

Transtheoretical Model of Behavioral Change (www.health.gov.au/internet/publications/publishing.nsf/Content/drugtreat-pubs-front9-wk-toc~drugtreat-pubs-front9-wk-secb~drugtreat-pubs-front9-wk-secb-3~drugtreat-pubs-front9-wk-secb-3-3*and* http://mdquit.org/health-behavior-models/transtheoretical-model-ttm)

References

Bandura, A. (2001). Social cognitive theory: An agentic perspective. *Annual Review of Psychology*, *52*, 1–26.

Barnett, K., Mercer, S. W., Norbury, M., Watt, G., Wyke, S., & Guthrie, B. (2012). Epidemiology of multi-morbidity and implications for health care, research, and medical education: A cross-sectional study. *Lancet*, *380*(9836), 37–43. doi:10.1016/S0140-6736

Beck, R., & Fernandez, E. (1998a). Cognitive-behavioral self-regulation of the frequency, duration, and intensity of anger. *Journal of Psychopathology and Behavioral Assessment*, *20*, 217–229. doi:10.1023/A:1023063201318

Beck, R., & Fernandez, E. (1998b). Cognitive-behavioral therapy in the treatment of anger: A meta-analysis. *Cognitive Therapy and Research*, *22*, 63–74.

Bickley, L. S. (2013). *Bates' guide to physical examination and history-taking* (11th ed.). Philadelphia, PA: Lippincott Williams & Wilkins.

Birk, L. (1973). *Biofeedback: Behavioral medicine*. New York, NY: Grune & Stratton.

Blount, A. (2003). Integrated primary care: Organizing the evidence. *Family Systems & Health*, *21*, 121–133. doi:10.1037/1091-7527.21.2.121

Bodie, G. D. (2011). The Active-Empathic Listening Scale (AELS): Conceptualization and evidence of validity within the interpersonal domain. *Communication Quarterly*, *59*, 277–295. doi:10.1080=01463373.2011.583495

Bordin, E. S. (1979). The generalizability of the psychoanalytic concept of the working alliance. *Psychotherapy, 16*, 252–260.

Borrell-Carrió, F., Suchman, A. L., & Epstein, R. M. (2004). The biopsychosocial model 25 years later: Principles, practice, and scientific inquiry. *Annuals of Family Medicine, 2*(6), 576–582. doi:10.1370/afm.245

Bouton, M. E. (2014). Why behavior change is difficult to sustain. *Preventative Medicine, 68*, 29–36. doi:10.1016/j.ypmed.2014.06.010

Bowlby J. (1988). *A secure base: Clinical applications of attachment theory.* London, England: Routledge.

Bradford, J. B., Coleman, S., & Cunningham, W. (2007). HIV system navigation: An emerging model to improve HIV care access. *AIDS clients care and STDs, 21*(Suppl. 1), S49–S58. doi:10.1089/apc.2007.9987

Brekke, J. S., Siantz, E., Pahwa, R., Kelly, E., Tallen, L., & Fulginiti, A. (2013). Reducing health disparities for people with serious mental illness: Development and feasibility of a peer health navigation intervention. *Best Practices in Mental Health, 9*, 62–82.

Brown, C. H., Bennett, M. E., Li, L., & Bellack, A. S. (2011). Predictors of initiation and engagement in substance abuse treatment among individuals with co-occurring serious mental illness and substance use disorders. *Addictive Behaviors, 36*(5), 439–447. doi:10.1016/j.addbeh.2010.12.001

Caton, C. L. M. (1981). The new chronic client and the system of community care. *Hospital and Community Psychiatry, 32*, 475–478. doi:10.1176/ps.32.7.475

Choe, D. E., Olson, S. L., & Sameroff, A. J. (2013). Effects of early maternal distress and parenting on the development of children's self-regulation and externalizing behavior. *Development and Psychopathology, 25*, 437–453. doi:10.1017/S0954579412001162

Chow, C. M. (2013). Mission impossible: Treating serious mental illness and substance use co-occurring disorder with integrated treatment: a meta-analysis. *Mental Health and Substance Use, 6*(2), 150–168. doi:10.1080/17523281.2012.693130

Clochesy, J. M., Dolansky, M. A., Hickman, R. L. Jr., & Gittner, L. S. (2015). Enhancing communication between clients and healthcare providers: SBAR3. *Journal of Health and Human Service Administration, 38*(2), 237–252.

Cohen, J. W., & Krauss, N. A. (2003). Spending and service use among people with fifteen most costly medical conditions. *Health Affairs, 22*(2), 129–138. doi:10.1377/hlthaff.22.2.129

Committee on Quality of Health Care in America, & Institute of Medicine. (2001). *Crossing the quality chasm: A new health system for the 21st century.* Washington, DC: National Academy Press.

Council for Accreditation of Counseling and Related Educational Programs. (2016). *2016 CACREP standards.* Alexander, VA: Author.

Cronin, C. (2004). *Client-centered care: An overview of definitions and concepts.* Washington, DC: National Health Council.

de Negri, B., Brown, L. D., Hernandez, O., Rosenbaum, J., & Roter, D. (n.d.). Improving interpersonal communication between health care providers and clients. Retrieved from http://pdf.usaid.gov/pdf_docs/Pnace294.pdf

Dickey, B., Normand, S. T., Weiss, R. D., Drake, R. E., & Azeni, H. (2002). Medical morbidity, mental illness, and substance use disorder. *Medical Illness and Severe Mental Illness, 53*(7), 861–867. doi:10.1176/appi.ps.53.7.861

Drollinger, T., Comer, L. B., & Warrington, P. T. (2006). Development and validation of the active empathetic listening scale. *Psychology & Marketing, 23*, 161–180. doi:10.1002=mar.20105

Durbin, J., Barnsley, J., Finlayson, B., Jaakkimainen, L., Lin, E., Berta, W., & McMurray, J. (2012). Quality of communication between primary health care and mental health care: An examination of referral and discharge letters. *Journal of Behavioral Health Services & Research, 39*(4), 445–461. doi:10.1007/s11414-012-9288-9

Emmelkamp, P. M. G. (1994). Behavior therapy with adults. In A. E. Bergin & S. L. Garfield (Eds.), *Handbook of psychotherapy and behavior change* (pp. 379–427). New York, NY: Wiley.

Engel, G. (1977). The need for a new medical model: A challenge for biomedicine. *Science, 196*(4286), 129–136.

Engel, G. (1980). The clinical application of the bio-psychosocial model. *American Journal Psychiatry, 137*(5), 535–544.

Epstein, R. M., & Borrell-Carrió, F. (2005). The biopsychosocial model: Exploring six impossible things. *Families, Systems, & Health, 23*(4), 426–431. doi:10.1037/1091-7527.23.4.426

Erickson, J., & Millar, S. (2005). Caring for clients while respecting their privacy: Renewing our commitment. *Online Journal of Issues in Nursing, 10*(2), Manuscript 1. doi:10.3912/OJIN.Vol10No02Man01

Felker, B., Yazel, J. J., & Short, D. (1996). Mortality and medical comorbidity among psychiatric clients: A review. *Psychiatric Services, 47*(12), 1356–1363. doi:10.1176/ps.47.12.1356

Fisher, E. B., Fitzgibbon, M. L., Glasgow, R. E., Haire-Joshu, D., Hayman, L. L., Kaplan, R. M., . . . Ockene, J. K. (2011). Behavior matters. *American Journal of Preventative Medicine, 40*(5), e15–e30. doi:10.1016/j.amepre.2010.12.031

Flickinger, T. E., Saha, S., Roter, D., Korthuis, P. T., Sharp, V., Cohn, J., . . . Beach, M. C. (2016). Communication study: Respecting clients is associated with more client-centered communication behaviors in clinical encounters. *Client Education and Counseling, 99*(2), 250–255. doi:10.1016/j.pec.2015.08.020

Forster, A. J., Clark, H. D., Menard, A., Dupuis, N., Chernish, R., Chandok, N., . . . van Walraven, C. (2004). Adverse events among medical clients after discharge from hospital. *Canadian Medical Association Journal, 170*(3), 345–349.

Freud, S. (1913). On beginning the treatment: Further recommendations on the technique of psychoanalysis. *In Standard Edition, 12*, 122–144.

Gollwitzer, P., Fujita, K., & Oettingen, G. (2004). Planning and implementation of goals. In R. F. Baumeister & K. D. Vohs (Eds.), *Handbook of self-regulation: Research, theory, and applications* (pp. 211–228). New York, NY: Guilford Press.

Greenson, R. R. (1965). The working alliance and the transference neurosis. *Psychoanalysis Quarterly, 34*, 155–179.

Gulmans, J., Vollenbroek-Hutten, M. M. R., Van Gemert-Pijnen, J. E. W. C., & Van Harten, W. H. (2007). Evaluating quality of client care communication in integrated care settings: A mixed method approach. *International Journal for Quality in Health Care, 19*(5), 281–288. doi:10.1093/intqhc/mzm029

Haggerty, J. L., Reid, R. J., Freeman, G. K., Starfield, B. H., Adair, C. E., & McKendry, R. (2003). Continuity of care: A multidisciplinary review. *British Medical Journal, 327*(7425), 1219–1221. doi:10.1136/bmj.327.7425.1219

Harris, E. C., & Barraclough, B. (1998). Excess mortality of mental disorder. *British Journal of Psychiatry, 173*, 11–53. doi:10.1192/bjp.173.1.11

Health Insurance Portability and Accountability Act of 1996, Pub. L. §§ 104-191 (1996).

Healthcare Information and Management Systems Society. (2014). Definition: Continuum of care. Retrieved from http://www.himss.org/definition-continuum-care?ItemNumber=30272

Hollon, S. D., & Beck, A. T. (1994). Cognitive and cognitive-behavioral therapies. In A. E. Bergin & S. L. Garfield (Eds.), *Handbook of psychotherapy and behavior change* (pp. 428–466). New York, NY: Wiley.

Horwitz, L. (1974). Clinical prediction in psychotherapy. Northvale, NJ: Jason Aronson.

Hughes, R. (2011). Overview and summary: Client-centered care: Challenges and rewards. *Online Journal of Issues in Nursing, 16*(2). doi:10.3912/OJIN.Vol16No02ManOS

International Society of Behavioral Medicine. (n.d.). About ISBM. Retrieved from https://www.isbm.info/about-isbm/

Kabale, B. M. I., Nkombua, L., Matthews, P., & Offiong, B. E. (2013). Healthcare professionals' perceptions of alcohol-intoxicated trauma clients: Implications for healthcare delivery at South Rand Hospital Emergency Department. *South African Family Practice, 55*(4), 398–402. doi:10.1080/207862 04.2013.10874383

Keefe, F. J. (2011). Behavioral medicine: A voyage to the future. *Annuals of Behavioral Medicine, 41,* 141–151. doi:10.1007/s12160-010-9239-8

Kessler, R. C., Demler, O., Frank, R. G., Olfson, M., Pincus, H. A., Walters, E. E., . . . Zaslavsky, A. M. (2005). Prevalence and treatment of mental disorders, 1990 to 2003. *New England Journal of Medicine, 352*(25), 15–23. doi:10.1056/NEJMsa043266

Lambert, M. J., & Barley, D. E. (2001). Research summary on the therapeutic relationship and psychotherapy outcome. *Psychotherapy Theory Research & Practice, 38*(4), 357–361. doi:10.1037/0033-3204 .38.4.357

Lardieri, M. R., Lasky, G. B., & Raney, L. (2014). *Essential elements of effective integrated primary care and behavioral health teams.* Washington, DC: SAMHSA-HRSA Center for Integrated Health Solutions.

Lenio, J. A. (n.d.). Analysis of the transtheoretical model of behavior change. *Journal of Student Research,* 73–83. Retrieved from http://www2 .uwstout.edu/content/rs/2006/14lenio.pdf

Luborsky, L. (1976). Helping alliances in psychotherapy: The groundwork for a study of their relationship to its outcome. In J. L. Cleghorn (Ed.), *Successful psychotherapy* (pp. 92–116). New York, NY: Brunner/Mazel.

Lyles, J. S., Dwamena, F. C., Lein, C., & Smith, R. C. (2001). Evidence-based client-centered interviewing. *Journal of Clinical Outcomes Measurement, 8*(7), 28–34.

Mayo Clinic. (1998–2016). Disease and condition: Obesity. Retrieved from http://www.mayoclinic .org/diseases-conditions/obesity

Pomerleau, O. F., & Brady, J. P. (1979). *Behavioral medicine: Theory and practice.* Baltimore, MD: Williams & Wilkins.

Prochaska, J., & DiClemente, C. (1983). Stages and processes of self-change of smoking: Toward an integrative model of change. *Journal of Consulting and Clinical Psychology, 51*(3), 390–395.

Prochaska, J., & Velicer, W. (1997). The transtheoretical model of health behavior change. *American Journal of Health Promotion, 12*(1), 38–48.

Pychyl, T. A., & Flett, G. L. (2012). Procrastination and self-regulatory failure: An introduction to the special issue. *Journal of Rational-Emotive Cognitive-Behavioral Therapy, 30,* 203–212. doi:10.1007/ s10942-012-0149-5

Regier, D. A., Farmer, M. E., Rae, D. S., Locke, B. Z., Keith S. J., Judd, L. L., & Goodwin, F. K. (1990). Comorbidity of mental disorders with alcohol and other drug abuse. *Journal of the American Medical Association, 264,* 2511–2518. doi:10.1001/ jama.264.19.2511

Reid, R. J., & Wagner, E. H. (2008). Strengthening primary care with better transfer of information. *Canadian Medical Association Journal, 179*(10), 987–988.

Robinson, J. H., Callister, L. C., Berry, J. A., & Dearing, K. A. (2008). Client-centered care and adherence: Definitions and applications to improve outcomes. *Journal of the American Academy of Nurse Practitioners, 20*(12), 600–607. doi:10.1111/j.1745-7599.2008.00360.x

Rogers, C. R. (1951). Client-centered therapy. Boston, MA: Houghton Mifflin.

Rogers, C. R. (1959). A theory of therapy, personality and interpersonal relationships as developed in the client-centered framework. In S. Koch (Ed.), *Psychology: A study of a science* (3rd ed., pp. 184–256). New York, NY: McGraw-Hill.

Ryan, R. M., & Deci, E. L. (2000). Self-determination theory and the facilitation of intrinsic motivation, social development, and well-being. *American Psychologist, 55*(1), 68–78. doi:10.1037/0003-066X.55.1.68.

Sampl, S., Wakai, S., Trestman, R., & Keeney, E. M. (2008). Functional analysis of behavior in corrections: Empowering inmates in skills training groups. *Journal of Behavior Analysis of Offender and Victim: Treatment and Prevention*, *1*(4), 42–51.

Sawyer, A. C. P., Miller-Lewis, L. R., Searle, A. K., Sawyer, M. G., & Lynch, J. W. (2015). Is greater improvement in early self-regulation associated with fewer behavioral problems later in childhood? *Developmental Psychology*, *51*(12), 1740–1755. doi:10.1037/a0039829

Scharf, D. M., Eberhart, N. K., Schmidt, N., Vaughan, C. A., Dutta, T., Pincus, H. A., & Burnam, M. A. (2013). Integrating primary care into community behavioral health settings: Programs and early implementation experiences. *Psychiatric Services*, *64*(7), 660–665. doi:10.1176/appi.ps.201200269

Schwartz, G. E., & Weiss, S. M. (1977). Editorial: What is behavioral medicine? *Psychosomatic Medicine*, *39*, 377–381.

Schwartz, G. E., & Weiss, S. M. (1978). Behavioral medicine revisited: An amended definition. *Journal of Behavioral Medicine*, *1*(3), 249–251.

Seifert, C. M., Chapman, L. S., Hart, J. K., & Perez, P. (2012). Enhancing intrinsic motivation in health promotion and wellness. *American Journal of Health Promotion*, *26*(3), 1–10.

Shaller, D. (2007). *Client-centered care: What does it take?* New York, NY: The Commonwealth Fund.

Sharma, M. (2007). Behavioural interventions for preventing and treating obesity in adults. *Obesity Reviews*, *8*(5), 441–449.

Smith, R. C. (2003). An evidence-based infrastructure for client-centered interviewing. In R. M. Frankel, T. E. Quill, & S. H. McDaniel (Eds.), *The biopsychosocial approach: Past, present, future* (pp. 148–163). Rochester, NY: University of Rochester Press.

Society of Behavioral Medicine. (2016). About: Society for Behavioral Medicine. Retrieved from http://www.sbm.org/about

Spiegler, M. D. (2016). *Contemporary behavior therapy* (6th ed.). Boston, MA: Cengage.

Substance Abuse and Mental Health Services Administration-Health Resource and Service Administration, Center for Integrated Health Solutions. (n.d.). What is integrated care? Retrieved from http://www.integration.samhsa.gov/about-us/what-is-integrated-care

Thornicroft, G. (2011). Physical health disparities and mental illness: The scandal of premature mortality. *British Journal of Psychiatry*, *199*(6), 441–442. doi:10.1192/bjp.bp.111.092718

U.S. National Research Council Committee on Aging Frontiers in Social Psychology, Personality, and Adult Developmental Psychology. (2006). Motivation and behavioral change. In L. L. Carstensen & C. R. Hartel (Eds.), *When I'm 64*. Washington, DC: National Academies Press. Retrieved from http://www.ncbi.nlm.nih.gov/books/NBK83771/

Vickery, A. J., Keaton, S. A., & Bodie, G. D. (2015). Intrapersonal communication and listening goals: An examination of attributes and functions of imagined interactions and active-empathic listening behaviors. *Southern Communication Journal*, *80*(1), 20–38, doi:10.1080/1041794X.2014.939295

Westenhoefer, J. (2001). The therapeutic challenge: Behavioral changes for long-term weight maintenance. *International Journal of Obesity*, *25*(Suppl. 1), S85–S88.

Westheimer, J. M., Steinley-Bumgarner, M., & Brownson, C. (2008). Primary care providers' perceptions of and experiences with an integrated healthcare model. *Journal of American College Health*, *57*(1), 101–108. doi:10.3200/JACH.57.1.101-108

Zetzel, E. R. (1956). Current concepts of transference. *International Journal of Psychoanalysis*, *37*, 369–375.

PSYCHOPHARMACOLOGY FOR THE NONMEDICAL MENTAL HEALTH PROFESSIONAL

Prescription drug use has steadily increased in the United States. Statistics from the Mayo Clinic's Rochester Epidemiology Project indicate that nearly 70% of Americans are on at least one prescription drug (Mayo Clinic, 2013). The rise in popularity and ubiquitous nature of prescription drugs in America has been attributed to several factors, including declining health, the growth of third-party insurance, increased drug marketing to physicians and consumers, an aging population, and greater social acceptance of usage. Clearly more than just a passing fad, the use of prescription drugs is likely to continue to play a major role in health care into the foreseeable future (Kaut, 2011), especially when used to treat psychological and behavioral disorders.

Since 2001, the number of individuals being prescribed medications to treat psychological and behavioral disorders has increased dramatically. As of 2010, more than 20% of adults and 6% of children and adolescents were being prescribed psychotropic medications (Medco Health Solutions, 2011). As a result, clinical mental health counselors can expect to interact with a growing number of clients either taking prescription medications as part of their treatment or seeking to begin doing so. Although the practice of prescribing medications is most commonly outside the purview of most mental health professionals (Noggle, 2009), having knowledge in this area can be an asset. According to King and Anderson (2004), proper training in basic psychopharmacology is needed for clinicians to effectively counsel these individuals, provide comprehensive treatment planning, ensure client well-being, and minimize instances of professional liability. In this chapter, foundational principles of psychopharmacology, reasons why different drugs are prescribed and how they influence client presentation, suggestions for effectively communicating with prescribing doctors, and strategies to successfully implement drug therapy into client treatment planning are discussed. With this information, you will be able to more competently and ethically work with your clients.

LEARNING OBJECTIVES

After reading this chapter, you will be able to do the following:

- Identify the parts of a nerve cell and the basic neurotransmitters commonly associated with psychotropic medications

- Describe how nerve cells in the brain communicate with one another and share information that directs our thoughts, feelings, and behaviors

- Differentiate between pharmacokinetics and pharmacodynamics

- Explain the neurobiological and medical foundation and etiology of addiction and co-occurring disorders (CACREP 5C-1-d)

- Identify the classifications, indications, and contraindications of commonly prescribed psychopharmacological medications for appropriate medical referral and consultation (CACREP 5C-2-h)

- Employ effective strategies for cross-disciplinary interfacing with integrated behavioral health care professionals (CACREP 5C-3-d)

HOW THE BRAIN WORKS: NERVE CELLS AND NEUROTRANSMITTERS

Without a doubt the brain is the most complex organ in the human body. It serves as the command center for our entire central nervous system. Despite volumes of research, there is still much we do not know about the brain and how it works. However, what we do know has led to some significant advances in our understanding of human functioning as well as the development of various psychotropic agents (i.e., medications). For example, we now know that the human brain serves two primary functions. The first is to coordinate the relaying of information between the various organs (e.g., stomach, kidneys) and systems (e.g., digestive system, cardiovascular system) in the body. Think about the last meal you ate. How did you know when to stop eating? If you are like most people, you stopped eating when you began to feel full. This feeling of satiation is produced in your brain in response to incoming signals it receives from your stomach and digestive system. They alert the brain when enough nourishment has been consumed and the current behavior (eating) can be stopped. The second function is to manage the production of our most basic human conditions: thoughts, emotions, and behaviors. In the example of eating a meal, the brain responds to the incoming signals from the stomach indicating satiation and initiates an appropriate behavior in response—to stop eating! When functioning correctly, the process of relaying information between the regions of the brain and throughout the entire body occurs effortlessly and instantaneously. However, problems can arise that may cause this process to not function as designed. When problems occur, the result is usually the manifestation of the various signs and symptoms with which our clients present for treatment. As mental health counselors, knowing the physiological reasons why clients think, feel, and act the way they do helps us develop more client-adaptive treatment plans. To gain a better idea of what this process looks like, let's examine the structure of nerve cells and how they transmit impulses to one another.

The entire human body is comprised of trillions of microscopic units known as cells. These cells form the basis of all living organisms. One specific kind of cell is the nerve cell. **Nerve cells** (also called **neurons**) represent the core components of our brain, spinal cord, and peripheral nervous system. In the human brain alone, there are approximately 100 billion nerve cells, each with thousands of synaptic connections to other nerve cells (see Figure 11.1). To put this number into perspective, if you were to count nerve cells at a rate of one cell per second, it would take you 3,171 years to reach 100 billion. Quite a long time for sure! These cells' primary responsibility is to relay information and guide human functioning through electrochemical signaling. Several types of neurons (e.g., sensory and motor neurons) manage the multitude of stimuli we

FIGURE 11.1 ■ Estimated Number of Neurons in the Brain and Spinal Cord

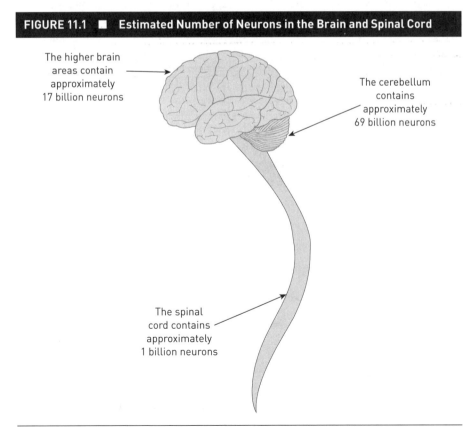

The higher brain areas contain approximately 17 billion neurons

The cerebellum contains approximately 69 billion neurons

The spinal cord contains approximately 1 billion neurons

meet daily. These neurons come in a variety of shapes and sizes, but they all share a common structure.

In each neuron we find the same four fundamental parts: cell body, dendrites, axons, and terminal buttons (see Figure 11.2 for an illustration of the structure of a neuron). At the center of each neuron is the **cell body** (or **soma**). The cell body contains several parts, the most important of which is the cell nucleus. The nucleus is important because it contains all the genetic material that allows the cell to perform its designated function. It is here in the cell nucleus that information is both processed and acted on. The cell body also contains several other organelles and mitochondria responsible for cell growth and regeneration. When it is not busy processing incoming messages from other cells, the neuron operates in a relaxed state. In this relaxed state, the amount of available electrical charge is greater outside the cell than it is within. This state of relaxation is known as the **resting potential**.

The resting potential of a neuron changes when neighboring neurons release messages. When the availability of a new message is detected, the receiving neuron quickly becomes electrically charged and springs into action. This includes an activation of the cell dendrites. The **dendrites** are branch-like structures that act as receptors and help the neuron receive messages from other neurons. The average neuron has from 2,000 to 3,000 receptor cells. Each dendrite is programmed to receive a specific type of transmitted message. Incoming messages can be classified as either *excitatory* or *inhibitory* (Tripp & Eliasmith, 2016). Excitatory messages increase the likelihood that the message will be forwarded on to other neurons, and inhibitory messages decrease that likelihood. Once a message has been received and transported to the cell body by way of the dendrites, the cell nucleus begins preparing for the appropriate cellular activity. The response of the cell is predicated by the state of the message it receives. When more excitatory signals are received, the result is the neuron entering into an energized state. This stimulation fundamentally changes the electrical state of the neuron and leads to the production of a nerve impulse called an **action potential**.

FIGURE 11.2 ■ Structure of a Neuron

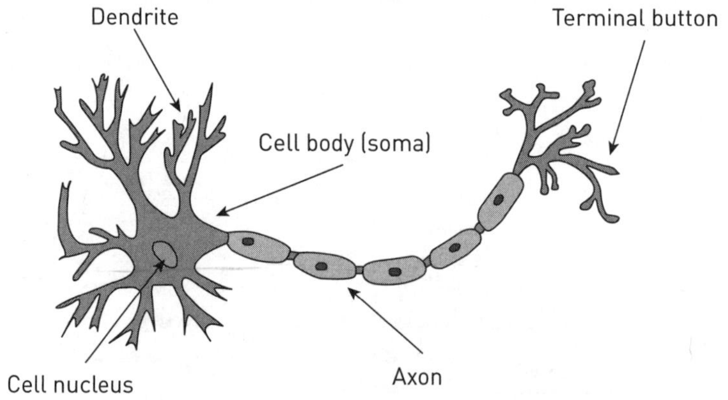

Once the neuron has been sufficiently stimulated, it prepares to transfer the action potential on to the next neuron. This process is then repeated continually as the nerve impulse travels to distant parts of the brain and body delivering its message to the appropriate recipients.

When the neuron is ready to transmit an action potential impulse to another neuron, its message is sent out away from the cell body through a long, slender tube known as an **axon**. Although each neuron may have several axons, they typically have only one that extends a considerable distance from the cell body. This axon serves as the main conduit for message transmission. At the end of the axon branch is a vesicle known as a terminal button. **Terminal buttons** serve as the storage center for a set of chemicals called **neurotransmitters** that help facilitate impulse transmission. Each of these neurotransmitters functions in its own way and works to relay certain types of impulse messages. According to Kolb and Whishaw (2009), a substance may be considered a neurotransmitter if it meets the following four characteristics:

- The chemical must be synthesized in the neuron or otherwise be present in it.

- When the neuron is active, the chemical must be released and produce a response in some target cell.

- The same response (excitatory or inhibitory) must be obtained when the chemical is experimentally placed on the target.

- A mechanism must exist for deactivating or removing the chemical from its site of action after its work is done.

Several hundred types of chemical messengers meet the criteria for neurotransmitters. These substances can be classified into three major categories: biogenic amine neurotransmitters, amino acid transmitters, and peptide neurotransmitters (Bear, Connors, & Paradiso, 2007). *Biogenic amine neurotransmitters* (also known as monoamines) are responsible for terminating the action of released transmitters in the synaptic gap and then recycling unused neurotransmitters for future use. These neurotransmitters are best understood in terms of their relationship to psychological disturbances. Six of the best-known biogenic amine neurotransmitters are serotonin, norepinephrine, epinephrine, dopamine, histamine, and acetylcholine. *Amino acid neurotransmitters* are primarily designed as building blocks for proteins and serve as the primary agents in the neurotransmission process. The two primary amino acid neurotransmitters are gamma-aminobutyric acid (GABA) and glutamate. The final category, *peptide neurotransmitters*, consists of substances associated with mediation of the perception of pain, appetite stimulation, and mood regulation among other functions. An example of this category is cholecystokinin (CCK). Scientists have been able to positively identify a dozen unique neurotransmitters that play a role in most brain activity. Of the 12 or so neurotransmitters identified, seven are commonly involved in the actions of psychotropic medications: glutamate, gamma-aminobutyric acid, acetylcholine, dopamine, norepinephrine, epinephrine, and serotonin (Ingersoll & Rak, 2016). A brief description of each is provided in Table 11.1.

Neurotransmitter	Description
Glutamate (Glu)	Glutamate is an amino acid that functions as the main excitatory neurotransmitter by lowering the threshold for neural excitation and encouraging neural firing to send signals between nerve cells. Under normal conditions, glutamate has been shown to play a major role in learning and memory.
Gamma-aminobutyric acid (GABA)	GABA is an amino acid that functions as an inhibitory neurotransmitter. It reduces neural firing and prevents overexcitation of neurons, leading to greater stability in the brain. Along with glutamate, GABA is one of the most abundant neurotransmitters in the CNS.
Acetylcholine (Ach)	One of the first major neurotransmitters to be identified, acetylcholine can be found in both the peripheral and central nervous systems. In the PNS acetylcholine is found in the synapse between axons and skeletal muscles and regulates muscle contraction. In the CNS it is thought to play a role in memory, learning, attention, behavioral arousal, and mood regulation.
Dopamine (DA)	Dopamine is a neurotransmitter that has both excitatory and inhibitory effects. In addition to aiding in the control of the brain's reward and pleasure centers, dopamine has been shown to play a role in movement, learning, attention, and emotions.
Norepinephrine (NE)	Primarily an excitatory neurotransmitter, it is usually produced by the cell bodies of neurons in the brain stem. Wakefulness and alertness are two of the primary functions of norepinephrine. Additionally, norepinephrine has been shown to play a major role in the onset and progression of depressive symptoms.
Epinephrine (Epi)	Also known as *adrenalin*, epinephrine is more common in the PNS than the CNS. It is produced by the adrenal gland and plays a central role in the body's fight or flight response. Epinephrine serves as the conduit for transferring messages to the brain that typically require an immediate response (e.g., moving your hand off of a hot stove burner).
Serotonin (5-HT)	Serotonin is one of the more active neurotransmitters in the CNS. It is involved in the inhibition of activity and behavior. It also is active in mood regulation, control of eating, pain regulation, and both sleep and arousal. Less understood is the apparent connection between serotonin and the presence of anxiety.

TABLE 11.1 ■ Neurotransmitters Commonly Targeted by Psychotropic Medications

CHEMICAL NEUROTRANSMISSION PROCESS

Nerve cells are not directly connected with one another. A gap, known as a **synapse**, exists between them. The most common synaptic gap is an *axodendritic synapse*. In this type of synapse, intracellular communication occurs via the transmitting of neurotransmitters from the terminal button of one neuron to the receiving dendrites of another. For each neuron, approximately 10,000 synaptic connections can potentially be made. By themselves, action potentials do not have enough electrical charge to cross these synapses on their own. Instead, they must rely on the neuron's available neurotransmitters to provide the boost required to clear the synaptic gap. As the action potential travels through the axon the cell enters a state of exocytosis. During this stage, the terminal buttons are activated, and they begin releasing molecules of their various neurotransmitter substances that lie in wait for the soon-to-be-arriving nerve impulse. When the impulse reaches the terminal button of the transmitting (presynaptic) neuron it attaches itself to the available neurotransmitter molecules and is released out into the synapse ready to be received by neighboring (postsynaptic) neurons. As these neighboring neurons recognize that a new impulse has been released they begin activating their own dendrites to receive the message (see Figure 11.3). Remember, each dendrite is designed to interact with only one type of neurotransmitter. So, whereas there may be thousands of receptor cells, only a percentage of them will be active to receive the available action potential.

When the action potential impulse initially makes contact with the receiving dendrite it quickly relays this information to the cell body so that the neuron learns what type of message (excitatory or inhibitory) is being sent and which neurotransmitters are being used to accomplish this task. The information gained during this initial binding helps determine how polarized the neuron will become and how strong the action potential will be when released. This process of preparing the neuron for signal reception is known as the **first messenger effect**. This first phase provides the neuron with a sneak preview of what it is about to receive. In anticipation of the impulse's arrival, it can begin making appropriate preparations (think about how you might dip your toes into a pool to gauge the temperature before jumping in completely). Once the neuron has been primed for the type of message it is about to receive, the **second messenger effect** takes over. In the second messenger effect the exact state of the incoming message is confirmed, and the cell nucleus begins to actively increase or decrease receptor cell production depending on the state of the message received. When receptor cell production is decreased the neuron becomes less sensitive (a process known as *downward regulation*). The less sensitive the neuron, the less impact the incoming message will have on the cell and its ultimate functionality. When receptor cell production is increased the neuron becomes more sensitive (a process known as *upward regulation*) and more of the incoming message carried in the action potential is

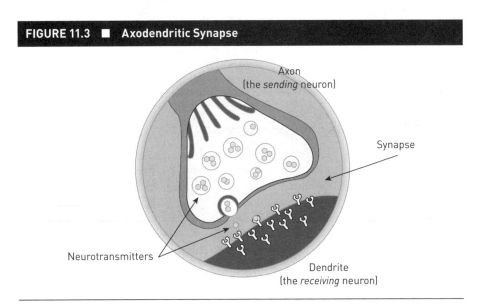

FIGURE 11.3 ■ Axodendritic Synapse

Axon
(the *sending* neuron)

Synapse

Neurotransmitters

Dendrite
(the *receiving* neuron)

received by the neuron. Prior research has shown that this increased flow is strongly related to many of the side effects often reported by individuals taking prescription medications.

Once the action potential has been accurately transmitted, the presynaptic neuron acts quickly to retrieve any unused neurotransmitters and recycles them for future use. This retrieval process is called **reuptake**. In addition to facilitating the recycling of unused neurotransmitters, the reuptake process also regulates neurotransmitter levels and dictates how long a nerve impulse or signal will last. Sometimes the reuptake process fails, and unused neurotransmitters remain in the synaptic gap. To prevent this clutter from building up, the brain releases specific enzymes (monoamine oxidase) into the synapse to dissolve all the residual neurotransmitters regardless of what they are or their function. This cleansing process allows for a clear channel to be available for future impulses when they are ready to be sent and released into the synapse.

All tasks executed by the brain rely on the smooth and efficient release of neurotransmitters (see Figure 11.4). However, the normal neural transmission process on occasion breaks down and problems arise. As mentioned earlier, these problems can lead to many of the changes in mood and affect we see in clients as well as the emergence of several psychiatric disorders. To simplify the discussion, we can group the possible neurotransmission problems into three main categories. The first involves a malfunctioning of the presynaptic neuron. In this case, the neuron transmitting the impulse is not producing an adequate number of neurotransmitter molecules. Because these neurotransmitters provide the charge needed to move an impulse message into the synapse, a decrease in their number means less possibility for the message to be picked up by neighboring receptor cells. The second problem occurs when the postsynaptic neuron has too few receptor cells (dendrites). When there are an insufficient number of receptor cells the probability of the

FIGURE 11.4 ■ Synaptic Regulating Activity

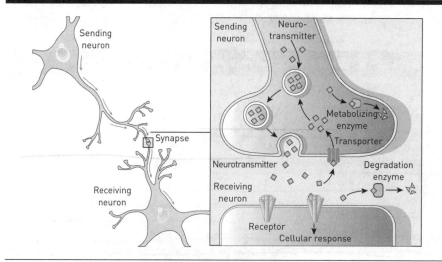

Generic Neurotransmitter System. Date 16 March 2011

Source: https://www.flickr.com/photos/nida-nih/7875022602/in/photolist-cZTxRL

Author NIDA(NIH) https://commons.wikimedia.org/wiki/File:Generic_Neurotransmitter_System.jpg This material is in public domain.

message being accurately relayed diminishes. The receiving neuron may misinterpret the message or not pick it up at all. In either case, the incoming message does not register strong enough to excite the neuron into transmitting the impulse on to the next cell. As a result, the message fails to continue. Finally, the third problem involves issues with the proper cleaning out of the synaptic gap. When the synapse is not cleared after each transmission it makes it becomes increasingly more difficult for future transmissions to occur. As a result, messages are not relayed. This overflow of the synapse can be related to either a deficient reuptake process or diminished enzyme production. In both cases, excess neurotransmitters do not find their way back into the presynaptic neuron and simply remain in between the neuron gap.

Hopefully you now have a better understanding of how messages are relayed between nerve cells. Our discussion so far has focused on how the neurotransmission process occurs under natural circumstances. However, this process can be influenced by external sources like medications or drugs. So, what is a drug? A **drug** can be operationally defined as "any substance that brings about a change in biological function through its chemical actions" (Katzung, 2001, p. 3). Drugs help our body maintain a preferred state of homeostasis or stability through one or more of the following mechanisms:

- Increasing the amount of neurotransmitters produced by presynaptic neurons and released into a synapse

- Blocking the reuptake of a neurotransmitter from the synapse

- Binding to the receptor site on the postsynaptic neuron, disabling the activity of the neurotransmitter present in the synapse

- Inhibiting the enzymes that break down neurotransmitters

- Changing the sensitivity of postsynaptic neurons to neurotransmitters (Patterson, Albala, McCahill, & Edwards, 2009)

In the following sections we examine how drugs can be administered to influence human functioning and look at a pair of psychopharmacological principles: pharmacokinetics and pharmacodynamics.

CASE ILLUSTRATION 11.1

In my experience I have found that several clients get confused with the seemingly endless number of names given to the medications they are being prescribed. This confusion stems from the fact that different treatment providers appear to be using a different language to describe the same medication. Doctors and pharmacists may refer to medications by their chemical or generic names.

The advanced knowledge in pharmacology these professionals have allows them to speak clearly with one another using these terms. For some clients, these drugs may best be known by their brand names. The endless ads on television with their catchy jingles and slogans help solidify brand recognition. For others, drugs may best be known based on their street names or a description of the

(Continued)

(Continued)

pill's purpose, color, or shape. Several times I have had clients report to me that they are taking "nerve pills" or that they forgot to take their "little white triangular pill" that morning.

To effectively function in settings where most clients being seen also were on a medication regimen, it became imperative that I gained fluency across all of these different "languages." My advice to you is to become familiar with the common medications prescribed to clients in your work setting. This includes knowing the chemical composition or generic name, the brand name, and the street names of the drugs. Also, knowing what the pills look like will be a plus. To help you, there are several resources you can purchase and keep with you as a handy reference. With advances in technology, there now are smartphone apps that provide you all the information needed to identify a particular medication and communicate with the various parties (clients, families, psychiatrists, case managers) with whom you likely will interact.

PHARMACOKINETICS: INTRODUCING DRUGS INTO THE BODY

The term **pharmacokinetics** refers to the in vivo (occurring inside the body) drug processes and includes the administration, absorption, distribution, metabolism, and excretion of drugs (Sinacola & Peters-Strickland, 2012). In other words, pharmacokinetics deals with how a drug is introduced into our system and makes its way throughout the body. To help your understanding, we spend some time further discussing each of these processes. For visual learners, Figure 11.5 illustrates the pharmacokinetic process. As a mental health counselor, it may be important for you to understand how drugs work, so you are more informed when working with medicated clients. This knowledge will assist you in understanding what you are seeing in terms of client presentation and communicating with clients what they should expect or experience when taking psychotropic medications.

Administration

For medications to be effective they need to be introduced to the human body. Several methods are available for administering drugs (see Table 11.2). The most common is oral administration. Drugs can be administered orally by one of three ways: liquid, tablet, or capsule. Of the three, liquids typically produce some of the quickest therapeutic

GUIDED PRACTICE EXERCISE 11.1

Partner up with two to three classmates in a small group. As a group, discuss what you believe the impact of increased access to psychotropic drugs has been on the practice of counseling. Do clients seem less invested in the process and more interested in the "quick fix" they believe medication provides? As counselors, how can we help clients see the value of counseling in addressing their problems and experiencing the change they desire?

TABLE 11.2 ■ Drug Administration Methods	
Type	**Description**
Oral	Medication is taken by mouth in a liquid, tablet, or capsule form.
Intravenous	Medication is administered via injection directly into the bloodstream. This is the quickest way to reach a therapeutic effect.
Buccal	Medication is placed between the cheek and gums and allowed to dissolve. It diffuses into the bloodstream by way of the mucous membranes of the inner cheek.
Sublingual	Medication is placed under the tongue and allowed to dissolve. It diffuses into the bloodstream by way of tissues beneath the tongue.
Rectal	Medication is administered anally in the form of a suppository. It is most often used in patients who have digestive tract difficulties.
Intramuscular	Medication is administered via injection into the muscle tissue. The medication is then slowly absorbed into the bloodstream resulting in the need for fewer doses.
Transdermal	Medication is administered as an adhesive patch that is placed on the body and diffused through the skin.
Subcutaneous	Medication is administered via injection just below the surface of the skin and is diffused into the bloodstream through the blood vessels.
Inhalation	Medication is administered in the form of a gas or aerosol that is to be breathed in and absorbed through the lungs.
Topical	Medication is applied to a specific part of the body as a lotion, cream, or gel. The absorption process occurs through the skin or mucous membranes.

effects. Because of the varying chemical properties of individual drugs, they are often administered at different dosing schedules. Prescriptions for drugs that should be taken intermittently are often written with specific dosing schedules. Some frequently used dosing schedules are 4 times a day (q.i.d.), 3 times a day (t.i.d.), twice a day (b.i.d.), once daily (qd), in the morning (am), in the evening (pm), at bedtime (hs), before meals (ac), and after meals (pc). In addition, some drugs may need to be administered continuously (e.g., IVs).

CASE ILLUSTRATION 11.2

For many people, especially those suffering from mental illness, remembering to take medications can be challenging. In my work with clients I find it helpful to try to tie the taking of medication to other activities so as not to forget. For example, with some clients I have suggested they place their medications near the coffee pot so when they go to grab a cup in the morning they see the

(Continued)

(Continued)

bottle and remember to take their morning medication. With others, we developed a plan to pack meals ahead of time and include the pills to be taken in small pouches in the package. This way, when the client sits down for lunch at work, the pills that may need to be taken with that meal are right there. With younger clients, I find that tying the taking of medications to activities they enjoy works well. In this form of operant conditioning, children are "rewarded" for remembering to take their medication with a snack, television time, or the ability to play a video game. Pairing the medication with a pleasurable activity helps overcome the tendency to avoid the medication because of how it tastes, the dislike of taking pills, or not liking how they feel afterward.

As you begin working with clients, I encourage you to experiment with simple strategies such as these that might work for you and your clients. When clients remain medication compliant, it greatly enhances the therapeutic process and allows you to focus more on the root cause of problems rather than the in-the-moment experiencing of symptoms. Overall, this is a simple strategy, but it seems to really work for me and my clients.

The processes occurring after a drug has been administered can be separated into four distinct areas collectively known by the acronym ADME:

- Absorption
- Distribution
- Metabolism
- Excretion (or elimination)

Absorption

Absorption refers to the process by which exogenous drugs enter the bloodstream and begin circulating throughout the body. When ingested orally, absorption typically occurs in the stomach or small intestines. With the other methods described, absorption takes place at the site of administration. The speed at which the drug is absorbed impacts the amount of time required for a drug to reach an appropriate concentration level in the bloodstream. Several factors can influence the rate at which a drug is absorbed into the bloodstream. These include the chemical composition of the drug, the site of absorption, whether it is taken with food or fluids, and its interaction with gastrointestinal acids.

Although drugs that absorb slowly require longer periods of time before therapeutic effects are felt, they typically are associated with fewer side effects. The factor that dictates when an individual will begin feeling the therapeutic effect of an ingested drug is its concentration level. When a drug concentration produces a desired response, it is called a *therapeutic dose*. When the drug concentration begins producing uncomfortable side effects it is referred to as a *toxic dose*. The difference between the therapeutic dose and toxic dose is known as the **therapeutic index**. Ideally, we want drugs to have a high therapeutic index. This means that when taken at the level prescribed, an individual will receive a desired effect with little chance of experiencing any side effects.

Distribution and Metabolism

After the drug has been absorbed into the bloodstream it is transported throughout the body by way of the circulatory system. The first stop for most drugs, especially those administered orally, is the liver. Here in the liver the drug's active ingredients are transformed into metabolites and prepared for transmission to the target area of the body. For psychotropic medications, this target area is the brain. This process of metabolism accomplishes two primary objectives: (a) it makes the drug more water soluble so that it can travel through the bloodstream more fluidly, and (b) it chemically transforms the drug so that it can be excreted from the body once it has enacted its therapeutic effect.

Throughout the distribution process, several factors can influence the amount of the drug that reaches the brain. The first is protein binding. *Protein binding* occurs when drug molecules bind irreversibly with plasma proteins in the bloodstream. This process decreases the ability of the drug to both metabolize and be excreted from the body. In other words, instead of reaching the brain and producing a therapeutic effect, the drug molecules instead remain in the bloodstream. To counteract this occurrence, some drugs may be prescribed with higher loading (initial) doses so that the probability of the drug reaching the brain is increased. In this instance, the physician or psychiatrist may instruct the patient to take an elevated dose at first to overload the body's initial response to fend off the foreign substance. By increasing the initial dosage, a still therapeutic amount of the drug will remain in the system after the body begins metabolizing the substance and preparing for its elimination.

The second factor deals with the drug's half-life. The **half-life** of a drug describes the amount of time it takes the body to eliminate 50% of the drug from the body. Half-lives vary in length from drug to drug. Drugs with longer half-lives tend to remain in the body for greater periods of time and usually are more available to be transported to the brain. As a result, less of a drug is needed to maintain an appropriate therapeutic level. After an initially elevated loading dose, medications with longer half-lives may be moved to a more intermittent dosing schedule. On average, approximately six half-lives are needed to completely eliminate a drug from the body.

Finally, the distribution of a drug is affected by the drug's steady state. The **steady state** of a drug refers to the amount of time required for a drug to reach a stable concentration level in the bloodstream. A stable concentration is achieved when the amount of the drug entering the body matches the amount exiting the body. At this point the drug is said to be present at a level sufficient enough to produce optimal results (therapeutic index). When the therapeutic index is reached, individuals will still benefit from the positive effects of the medication even when it is not being administered (between dosage periods). For most drugs, the steady state can be reached in five half-lives. In other words, if a drug has a half-life of 12 hours it will take almost 2.5 days (60 hours) to reach a steady state.

Excretion

Excretion refers to the elimination of a substance from the human body. As we earlier mentioned, the body prepares to eliminate foreign substances by metabolizing the drug molecules so that they can more easily pass through the body. This process occurs primarily in the liver and kidneys, with urine serving as the main route of elimination for most of the metabolites produced and unprocessed drug residual. Most of the drugs produced today are eliminated from the body at a rate proportional to the amount of the drug left in the bloodstream. In other words, the body eliminates a percentage of the drug that is roughly equal to the new amount of the drug absorbed with each new dosage taken. This allows patients to maintain the presence of a drug in their system at a steady therapeutic level.

The flow chart provided in Figure 11.5 provides you with an overview of the pharmacokinetic process. To further your understanding, there are a few additional terms you will likely see when discussing the distribution and metabolism of a drug (adapted from Ingersoll & Rak, 2016). The first is loading dose. A **loading dose** is an amount of a drug initially given that is typically higher than what will be subsequently prescribed. A loading dose may be prescribed so that the client can achieve the recommended therapeutic level of a drug more rapidly. A second term that you should be familiar with is maintenance dose. The **maintenance dose** is the regular dose of the medication that maintains the steady state plasma concentration in the therapeutic range. Maintenance doses usually begin after an individual has been on a medication for 1 to 3 weeks, depending on the severity of the client's symptoms and the medication prescribed. And finally, you will often see the word *titration* when discussing medication regimens. **Titration** refers to the art and science involved with balancing a drug dose against the client's symptoms. There are two types of titration, upward and downward. Upward titration is when a dosage is

---

FIGURE 11.5 ■ Pharmacokinetic Process

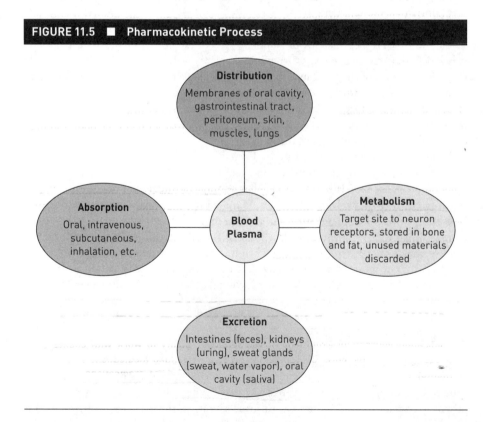

Distribution
Membranes of oral cavity, gastrointestinal tract, peritoneum, skin, muscles, lungs

Absorption
Oral, intravenous, subcutaneous, inhalation, etc.

Blood Plasma

Metabolism
Target site to neuron receptors, stored in bone and fat, unused materials discarded

Excretion
Intestines (feces), kidneys (uring), sweat glands (sweat, water vapor), oral cavity (saliva)

gradually increased, and downward titration is when the dosage is gradually decreased. Counselors, with knowledge of their clients, can greatly assist the prescribing physician in titrating a medication to find the correct dosage. Now that we have examined how drugs are processed by the human body, we turn our attention toward examining what drugs do to our bodies once entered into the system.

PHARMACODYNAMICS: HOW DRUGS AFFECT THE BODY

The term **pharmacodynamics** refers to the study of the processes by which drugs affect the mind and body. When discussing pharmacodynamics, we are primarily talking about the observable outcomes of drugs acting on the body and interacting with neurotransmitters involved in the various neurotransmission processes. How drugs accomplish these tasks is influenced by several factors. One of the most important is the intended use of the specific drug. Drugs can be classified into four broad categories based on their intended purpose.

The first category includes those drugs prescribed to produce a desired effect. In other words, these drugs help ensure that a client experiences a desired result. An example of this type of drug is aspirin. We take *aspirin* when we experience pain (e.g., headaches, joint pain, muscle tension). It is our hope that by taking the aspirin the pain symptoms we are experiencing will dissipate. The lessening of our pain is the desired result. The second category includes those drugs that are prescribed to replace normal functions that are either absent or insufficiently present in the body. An example of this type of drug is *insulin*. Insulin is used by diabetics to help regulate blood sugar levels when the body is not able to produce enough insulin on its own. A third usage of drugs is to mimic normal presentations in the body. These drugs are used when we want to experience an otherwise natural sensation on command. A prime example is *caffeine*. Caffeine mimics the effects of epinephrine (also known as adrenaline) in that it excites the body and produces a euphoric rush sensation. It is not surprising that many people routinely turn to caffeinated beverages (coffee and colas) when they feel sluggish and need a pick-me-up to get going. The fourth and final category includes those drugs that alter the current functioning of the body. *Laxatives* are a good example of this type of medication. When one is constipated and having intestinal discomfort one may take a laxative to help alleviate some of the pressure experienced. Laxatives loosen the bowels so that elimination becomes much easier. In this example, the active ingredients in the laxative work to alter the body's current state of functioning.

GUIDED PRACTICE EXERCISE 11.2

Think about yourself for a moment. Do you believe drugs permanently cure or temporarily solve mental health issues? Where does this belief come from? What impact does it have on your ability to work with clients who either present wanting medications or are currently taking one or more medications as part of their treatment regimen?

Another factor influencing the effect of a drug is the intended duration of its use. Doctors prescribe medications for all types of problems. Some can be cured in a relatively short period of time, whereas others may require lifelong attention. Medications prescribed for acute treatments are typically fast acting and have a relatively short half-life. The active chemicals in these medications do not build up in the body and often are quickly metabolized. An example of an acute treatment would be an antibiotic that a doctor prescribes when you are sick. Drugs intended to be taken for longer intervals are often prescribed as part of a medical maintenance treatment. These are drugs one may need to continue taking to help regulate a condition or prevent further complications from occurring. Individuals taking medications for hypertension or high cholesterol do so as part of a maintenance program. The expected duration of usage influences how much of a drug is prescribed and how often it should be taken, two factors important in regulating a therapeutic dosage for clients.

In addition to the biological functions discussed, drugs also play a role in the neurotransmission process. Psychotropic drugs are routinely prescribed because of their ability to alter the production, function, and elimination of neurotransmitters in the brain. Regardless of which neurotransmitters they effect, all psychotropic drugs fall into one of two categories: agonists or antagonists. Agonist drugs help increase the body's normal responses whereas antagonist drugs block these normal responses. The duality of these drugs is best explained using a lock and key analogy. As we mentioned earlier when describing the neurotransmission process, sometimes nerve impulses (action potentials) are not able to successfully move from neuron to neuron. When this is the case, messages get delayed and the body fails to produce an appropriate response. Agonist drugs can aid this process by acting like keys. They help open up the neural pathways to allow message flow to once again occur smoothly. On the other hand, we also mentioned situations where too much information is passing between nerve cells. In this case the message becomes muddled as the receiving neurons have too much action potential to try to decipher. Again, this results in poor message transmission and delayed, or in some cases no, response. This is where antagonist drugs are prescribed. They act as the lock that closes down the neural pathways, restricting the amount of information flowing through the synapse. They allow enough of the message to pass for the receiving neuron to pick up the signal but do not allow the synaptic gap to become flooded with excess neurotransmitters. It has been this author's experience that the lock and key analogy is an effective way to help work through client ambivalence toward starting a medication regimen, for it facilitates clients understanding in simple terms why taking a medication is going to help change the various thoughts and emotions they are experiencing.

The preceding examples represent just a few of the ways that drugs influence human functioning. Of course, everyone is different, and responses to particular medications can vary considerably. The sheer number of medications available for every type of ailment or illness is evidence to this fact. In my clinical experience, I have found that many of the questions and concerns clients have about the drugs they are prescribed deal with how the drug will make them feel and what they can expect. Your best course of action in these types of situations is to refer clients to discuss these questions with their doctor or psychiatrist, but there are some factors you could discuss with your clients that may help them understand what to expect when starting a medication regimen. This information can help clients as they monitor their usage to determine whether the medication is successfully accomplishing its intended purposes. The factors you should discuss with your clients are listed in Table 11.3.

TABLE 11.3 ■ Factors Influencing a Drug's Effect	
Amount ingested	The amount of a drug taken has an impact on the effect it has on a body. Some drugs require higher loading dosages to get the active ingredients in the drug in the body at a sufficient level to produce a desired effect. These typically result in clients feeling the results of their usage much quicker.
Time since last ingestion	The period of time between dosages deals with the half-life of the drug. Drugs with shorter half-lives are more quickly metabolized by the body and eliminated. This results in having to take more frequent doses to maintain a steady state of the drug in the bloodstream.
Frequency of ingestion	How often one takes a drug also relates to the therapeutic index. Depending on how quickly the drug metabolizes in one's system, taking a drug too frequently may lead to toxic levels that can be extremely dangerous and lead to an overdose.
Setting of ingestion	In our discussion of pharmacokinetics, we talked about the varying speeds with which a medication enters the bloodstream based on how the drug was ingested. You should recall that intravenous and oral administrations lead to the quickest therapeutic effect.
Set of the person	The effects of a drug will vary based on the gender, size, build, and weight of an individual. The same dosage of a medication may be toxic for a petite woman but have relatively little effect on a large man.

Knowing what the body does to a drug (pharmacokinetics) and what a drug does to the body (pharmacodynamics), we now can begin looking at the role drug therapy plays in the treatment of mental illness. Since the 1950s, when the antipsychotic effects of *Thorazine* were discovered by chance, psychotropic medications have contributed to the effective treatment of various mental illnesses (Farmer, 2014). Today, psychotropic medications are routinely prescribed to individuals to treat a variety of mental health issues impairing their healthy functioning and well-being. According to statistics compiled by the National Institute of Mental Health (NIMH; 2013), approximately one in four adults in the United States experiences mental illness in a given year, a percentage equating to nearly 61.5 million individuals. As noted in the introduction to this chapter, more than 20% of adults and 6% of children and adolescents are prescribed psychotropic medications to treat their mental illness (Medco Health Solutions, 2011). Given the ubiquity of psychotropic medications, mental health counselors would be wise to become familiar

GUIDED PRACTICE EXERCISE 11.3

The set of a person (age, gender, height, weight) plays an important role in determining the proper dosage for a medication to be administered. That said, how do these factors impact medications prescribed to children? What additional factors should be considered before exploring the possibility of medicating children for mental health–related issues?

with the more commonly prescribed medications, so they can detect signs and symptoms related to the use of a drug and intelligently converse with their clients regarding their prescribed drug therapy regimen. In the following section, the primary categories of psychotropic medications are introduced, and the drugs most commonly prescribed in each category are highlighted.

PSYCHOTROPIC DRUGS AND MENTAL ILLNESS

Psychotropic medications can be grouped into five categories based on the various psychological and behavioral disorders they are designed to address: antidepressants, anti-anxiety agents, antipsychotics, mood stabilizers, and stimulants. Again, although you will not be in a position to prescribe medications to your clients, having a basic understanding of medications, why they are prescribed, and how they may affect a client's presentation will assist you in understanding more about your clients over the course of therapy.

Antidepressants

Antidepressants are a broad category of psychotropic drugs used to treat depressive disorders. Initially developed in the 1950s, the use of antidepressants has become more common in recent years as their efficacy in alleviating symptoms has increased. According to a National Center for Health Statistics report (Pratt, Brody, & Gu, 2011), nearly 1 in 10 persons over the age of 12 in the United States is prescribed an antidepressant. From 1998 to 2008, the rate of antidepressant usage in the United States for persons of all ages rose nearly 400%. Several classes of antidepressants exist. These classes are commonly grouped based on their introduction to the market.

First-Generation Antidepressants

This class includes both monoamine oxidase inhibitors (MAOIs) and tricyclic antidepressants. MAOIs are the oldest class of antidepressants. Developed in the 1950s, MAOIs elevate levels of norepinephrine, serotonin, and dopamine in the brain by inhibiting the monoamine oxidase enzyme that breaks down these neurotransmitters. MAOIs fell out of favor because of numerous drug interactions and the strict dietary restrictions to which individuals taking the drug needed to adhere. When mixed with food or drink containing tyramine, dangerous spikes in blood pressure can occur. Although not used all that frequently today, some people do benefit from their use. Examples of MAOIs include phenelzine (*Nardil*), tranylcypromine (*Parnate*), isocarboxazid (*Marplan*), and selegiline (*Emsam*).

Tricyclics represent the second class of first-generation antidepressants. Developed to replace MAOIs, **tricyclics** work by inhibiting the reuptake of serotonin, norepinephrine, and to a lesser extent dopamine. Because these drugs lack selectivity and affect several different neurotransmitters, they carry several adverse side effects including weight gain, loss of sex drive, dizziness and nausea, difficulty urinating, increased heart rate, and disorientation or confusion. Amitryptyline (*Elavil*), clomipramine (*Anafranil*), desipramine (*Norpramin*), and nortriptyline (*Pamelor*) are all names of tricyclic drugs you might see prescribed to your clients.

Second-Generation Antidepressants

First developed in the 1980s, these classes of drugs benefited from advances in science and medicine. The most popular type of second-generation antidepressants are called **selective serotonin reuptake inhibitors** (**SSRIs**). As their name implies, SSRIs help to alleviate depressive symptoms by blocking the reabsorption of serotonin—a neurotransmitter associated with mood. By inhibiting the reuptake of serotonin, more of the chemical is available to be taken up by the other nerve cells. The popularity of SSRIs is due largely to their lack of severe adverse effects. Common adverse effects noted by individuals who have taken SSRIs include nausea, vomiting, diarrhea, sexual dysfunction, headaches, anxiety, dizziness, dry mouth, weight gain or loss, drowsiness, and difficulty sleeping. Additionally, like other antidepressants, an increase in suicidal thoughts and behaviors may occur. To reach full therapeutic effect, SSRIs should be taken for 2 to 8 weeks depending on medication. Once symptoms begin to subside, the normal course of treatment calls for usage to continue for an additional 6 months at which time use should be discontinued gradually for serious withdrawal symptoms can occur. SSRIs include drugs such as fluoxetine (*Prozac*), fluvoxamine (*Luvox*), sertraline (*Zoloft*), paroxetine (*Paxil*), escitalopram (*Lexapro*), and citalopram (*Celexa*).

Third-Generation Antidepressants

The result of increased research due to the steady popularity of SSRIs, third-generation antidepressants, also called atypicals, exhibit a range of actions in addition to serotonin reuptake inhibition (Ingersoll & Rak, 2016). One example of a third-generation antidepressant is **selective norepinephrine reuptake inhibitors** (**SNRIs**). Like SSRIs, these drugs retard the reuptake process and increase the amount of the targeted chemical in the brain, in this case norepinephrine. Popular SNRI drugs include venlafaxine (*Effexor*), desvenlafaxine (*Pristiq*), and duloxetine (*Cymbalta*). Another atypical third-generation antidepressant separate from SNRIs is bupropion (*Wellbutrin*). Bupropion is a norepinephrine and dopamine inhibitor that appears to produce the same results as SSRIs or SNRIs. The benefit of bupropion is that it holds fewer adverse side effects, increasing the likelihood that clients will better adhere to their prescribed dosing regimen.

For clients prescribed antidepressants, mental health counselors should ensure they understand how the medication works. Unfortunately, medication treatment does not provide a quick fix. Most clients will not begin experiencing the full effect of the medication they are taking for 10 to 12 weeks. Although some of the newer classes of antidepressants (SSRIs and SNRIs) are faster-acting, they still may take at least 3 to 4 weeks to reach full therapeutic effect. Additionally, clients should be reminded that they likely will be on a prescribed medication for a period before they can begin phasing it out. Most prescribing physicians look to keep clients on an antidepressant protocol for at least 6 months before exploring the possibility of discontinuation.

Anti-Anxiety Agents

Anti-anxiety agents (commonly referred to as *anxiolytics*) are medications that reduce the symptoms of anxiety such as panic attacks, extreme fear, and worry. The most common drugs prescribed for the treatment of anxiety are benzodiazepines (also known as tranquilizers). First made available in the 1960s, benzodiazepines remain a popular option for physicians to prescribe their clients because they are fast-acting and have relatively few side effects. Benzodiazepines work by facilitating the binding of GABA, a neurotransmitter found to play an important role in decreasing the effects of anxiety, to GABA receptors. Essentially, benzodiazepines slow down the nervous system and help calm the body and mind. Commonly prescribed benzodiazepines include alprazolam (*Xanax*), clonazepam (*Klonopin*), diazepam (*Valium*), and lorazepam (*Ativan*).

Caution is needed when prescribing benzodiazepines to children, the elderly, and persons with developmental disabilities because sometimes paradoxical reactions may occur resulting in anxiety symptoms becoming exacerbated. Examples of paradoxical reactions include increased anxiety, agitation, hostility, impulsive behavior, and manic episodes. Additionally, caution should be given when clients continue taking benzodiazepines for an extended period. Ideally, these drugs are best suited for short-term usage, but that does not always end up being the case. Clients prescribed these medications for an extended length of time will eventually develop a tolerance to the drug, resulting in the need for higher doses of the drug to get the same therapeutic effect. When this occurs, a physical dependence may develop. When the decision is made to discontinue benzodiazepine treatment, clients should be encouraged to follow their physician's instructions for tapering off the drug because the withdrawal from benzodiazepines is often unpleasant and difficult.

In addition to benzodiazepines, certain antidepressants also may be prescribed to treat the symptoms of anxiety. The most widely used antidepressants are SSRIs such as fluoxetine (*Prozac*), sertraline (*Zoloft*), paroxetine (*Paxil*), escitalopram (*Lexapro*), and citalopram (*Celexa*). Certain advantages and disadvantages accompany the use of SSRI antidepressants in the treatment of anxiety. An advantage is that the risk for dependence and potential abuse is much lower. For clients worrying about becoming addicted to a medication and hesitant to start a treatment regimen, these drugs may be a good starting point. However, a disadvantage is the fact that these drugs take at least 3 to 4 weeks before full therapeutic effect is felt. It would be unlikely that clients experiencing panic attacks would benefit from these drugs because they are not designed to be taken "as needed." They are more commonly used in the treatment of more long-term, chronic conditions such as obsessive-compulsive disorder, post-traumatic stress disorder, social anxiety disorder, and generalized anxiety disorder.

Antipsychotics

Antipsychotic medications are most commonly prescribed to treat illnesses such as schizophrenia and mania caused by bipolar disorder. In these cases, they diminish the positive symptoms of schizophrenia and prevent relapses, often within 2 weeks of first usage. To a lesser extent, antipsychotics also can be used to treat severe cases of anxiety or depression. Antipsychotic medications can be categorized into two groups: first-generation antipsychotics and second-generation antipsychotics.

First-Generation Antipsychotics

First-generation antipsychotics were developed in the 1950s and are still used today. These drugs primarily function as dopamine D2 antagonists, but the exact role they play in treating psychotic symptoms remains unknown. For some people, taking these medications greatly reduces, and in some cases eliminates, many of their symptoms of schizophrenia. For others, their effect is negligible. Some examples of first-generation antipsychotics commonly used include chlorpromazine (*Thorazine*), haloperidol (*Haldol*), and thioridazine (*Mellaril*). A drawback to this class of antipsychotics is the high rate of extrapyramidal side effects such as muscle rigidity, bradykinesia (slowness of movement), dystonias (involuntary muscle contractions), tremors, and akathisia (agitation or restlessness) they have been known to cause. However, for many clients, the benefits of the drug far outweigh the side effects they experience. Additionally, many individuals report side effects dissipating over time with continued use of these first-generation antipsychotics. Counselors should discuss with their clients the pros and cons of using these drugs to determine whether continued usage is most appropriate.

Second-Generation Antipsychotics

Also referred to as atypical antipsychotics, this newer class of antipsychotics was developed in the 1970s. These second-generation antipsychotics differ from first-generation drugs in that they have a different mechanism of action and produce significantly fewer extrapyramidal symptoms (Meltzer, 2004). Although the reduction in undesirable side effects is a plus, researchers note that the overall efficacy of second-generation antipsychotics compared to the earlier first-generation antipsychotics is negligible for most individuals (Leucht et al., 2013). Nonetheless, they have become a popular drug of choice for most medical professionals looking to treat positive psychotic symptoms. According to the U.S Food and Drug Administration (2016), 11 atypical (second-generation) antipsychotics are currently approved for use: aripiprazole (*Abilify*), clozapine (*Clozaril*), olanzapine (*Zyprexa*), quetiapine (*Seroquel*), risperidone (*Risperdal*), ziprasidone (*Geodon*), asenapine (*Saphris*), iloperidone (*Fanapt*), paliperidone (*Invega*), lurasidone (*Latuda*), and olanzapine/fluoxetine (*Symbyax*).

Mood Stabilizers

Mood stabilizers regulate brain chemistry and help control emotional states and behavior. They prevent the extreme highs (manic or hypomanic episodes) and lows (depressive episodes) clients experience. Mood stabilizers work to keep clients' moods within parameters clinically described as normal (Ingersoll & Rak, 2016). The first FDA-approved mood stabilizer was lithium. Prescribed since the 1970s, lithium remains a popular and effective option for the treatment of bipolar disorder. According to Hauser (2016), approximately 50% of persons prescribed lithium will notice improvement in their condition, and an additional 40% to 50% will improve when lithium is taken concurrently with another medication. In addition to effectively treating mania and depression, lithium remains the only medication proven to reduce the risk of suicide in clients diagnosed with bipolar disorder (Fink, 2013). Common side effects include stomach problems, weight gain, frequent urination, kidney damage, liver damage, fatigue, and memory loss. Although most of these side effects can be reduced or eliminated with dosing adjustments or secondary drugs, the more concerning issue with the use of lithium is the need to maintain blood concentration levels within a very narrow range. A fine line exists between therapeutic and toxic levels of lithium. Counselors working with clients prescribed lithium should periodically check in to make sure they are taking their medication exactly as prescribed and following up with their prescribing doctor for regular blood tests to check their lithium levels.

In addition to lithium, anticonvulsants also have been used to stabilize mood in clients diagnosed with bipolar disorder. Anticonvulsants work by calming hyperactivity in the brain and are typically prescribed to individuals who rapidly cycle between manic and depressive episodes. Examples of anticonvulsants you might see clients being prescribed include valproic acid (*Depakote*), lamotrigine (*Lamictal*), and carbamazepine (*Tegretol*). Each of these anticonvulsants has a different mechanism of action. Whereas Depakote and Tegretol seem to be more effective in treating mania than depression, Lamictal appears to be more effective in treating mania than it is in treating depression. Clearly describing the symptoms experienced helps ensure clients will be prescribed the correct medications for their conditions.

Stimulants

Stimulants are used to treat symptoms of attention deficit hyperactivity disorder (ADHD) by managing symptoms related to hyperactivity, impulsive behavior, and diminished attention spans. Stimulants are quite effective, with 70% of adults and 70% to 80% of children reporting decreased ADHD symptoms when used as prescribed. Stimulants come in many forms, with variations available for short-acting, intermediate-acting and long-acting use (see Table 11.4). Short-acting medications are typically taken multiple times a day and are helpful in maintaining therapeutic levels of the drug in the bloodstream. For clients who have a hard time remembering to take medications and follow administration guidelines, long-acting medications may be the better option.

By themselves, stimulants are not habit-forming. However, these drugs are often the subject of abuse and addiction. As a result, they should not be prescribed to individuals with a history of addiction or substance abuse–related issues. For those clients who do find themselves becoming addicted to stimulants, withdrawal should be medically

TABLE 11.4 ■ Short-Acting, Intermediate-Acting, and Long-Acting Stimulants Prescribed to Treat ADHD		
Short-Acting	**Intermediate-Acting**	**Long-Acting**
Adderall	Evekeo	Focalin XR
Dexedrine	Ritalin SR	Adderall XR
Focalin	Metadate SR	Vyvanse
Ritalin	Methylin SR	Concerta
		Ritalin LA

managed and medication use tapered. There are no FDA-approved medications for treating stimulant addiction, so a detoxification protocol typically includes counselors using some form of behavioral therapy to address the triggers and causes of abusive usage.

TALKING MEDICATION WITH CLIENTS

By now you should recognize that there are a multitude of medications available for all types of mental illness and disorders. Table 11.5 provides you with a list of some of the more commonly prescribed psychotropic medications, including their generic (nonproprietary) name, brand (trade) name, and specified usage. Now that you have a better understanding of how psychotropic medications fit into the overall treatment plan for many mental health clients, we discuss how you can use this newfound knowledge in your direct work with clients and their families. Although you will not be prescribing medications, you will be able to serve as an advocate for your clients taking medications as part of their treatment protocol.

TABLE 11.5 ■ Commonly Prescribed Psychotropic Medications		
Generic Name	**Brand Name**	**Prescribed Usage**
Alprazolam	Xanax	Anxiety, panic
Amitriptyline	Elavil	Depression
Amoxapine	Asendin	Psychotic depression
Amphetamine	Adderall	ADHD
Aripiprazole	Abilify	Schizophrenia
Bupropion	Wellbutrin	Depression, ADHD
Buspirone	BuSpar	Anxiety
Carbamazepine	Tegretol	Bipolar disorder
Chlordiazepoxide	Librium	Anxiety
Chlorpromazine	Thorazine	Schizophrenia
Citalopram hydrobromide	Celexa	Depression
Clomipramine	Anafranil	Depression, OCD
Clonazepam	Klonopin	Anxiety
Clorazepate	Tranxene	Anxiety
Clozapine	Clozaril	Schizophrenia

(Continued)

TABLE 11.5 ■ (Continued)

Generic Name	Brand Name	Prescribed Usage
Desipramine	Norpramin	Depression, ADHD
Dextroamphetamine	Dexedrine	ADHD
Diazepam	Valium	Anxiety
Divalproex sodium	Depakote	Bipolar disorder
Doxepin	Adapin, Sinequan	Depression
Escitalopram	Lexapro	Depression, anxiety
Fluoxetine	Prozac	Depression, OCD, panic
Fluphenazine	Prolixin	Schizophrenia
Fluvoxamine	Luvox	Depression, OCD
Haloperidol	Haldol	Schizophrenia
Hydroxyzine	Vistaril	Anxiety, sleep
Imipramine	Tofranil	Depression, panic
Lamotrigine	Lamictal	Mood stabilizer
Lithium carbonate	Eskalith, Lithobid	Bipolar disorder
Lithium citrate	Cibalith-S	Bipolar disorder
Lorazepam	Ativan	Anxiety
Lurasidone	Latuda	Antipsychotic, mood stabilizer
Maprotiline	Loxitane	Schizophrenia
Mesoridazine	Ludiomil	Depression
Methylphenidate	Ritalin	ADHD
Mirtazapine	Remeron	Depression
Molindone	Moban	Schizophrenia
Nefazodone	Serzone	Depression
Nortriptyline	Pamelor	Depression
Olanzapine	Zyprexa	Schizophrenia, mood stabilizer
Oxazepam	Serax	Anxiety

Generic Name	Brand Name	Prescribed Usage
Paroxetine	Paxil	Depression
Pemoline	Cylert	ADHD
Perphenazine	Trilafon	Schizophrenia
Phenelzine	Nardil	Depression
Prazepam	Centrax	Anxiety
Prochlorperazine	Compazine	Schizophrenia
Quetiapine	Seroquel	Schizophrenia
Risperidone	Risperdal	Schizophrenia
Sertraline	Zoloft	Depression
Temazepam	Restoril	Sleep, anxiety, panic
Thioridazine	Mellaril	Schizophrenia
Thiothixene	Navane	Schizophrenia
Tranylcypromine Sulfate	Prarnate	Depression
Trazodone	Desyrel	Depression
Trifluoperazine	Vesprin	Schizophrenia
Trimipramine	Surmontil	Depression
Valproic acid	Depakene	Bipolar disorder
Venlafaxine	Effexor	Depression
Zolpidem	Ambien	Anxiety, sleep

Addressing Drug Compliance With Clients

Regardless of how effective a medication, its therapeutic benefits will remain limited if the client does not follow the prescribed treatment protocol. To help ensure clients receive the full benefit of taking a drug, there are several strategies you can employ when working with your clients to promote drug compliance. The following are two strategies designed to help you make your clients feel comfortable with the level of care they are about to receive.

The first strategy involves educating your clients. Although public understanding of the benefits and risks of psychotropic drug treatment appears to have increased, marked suspiciousness about safety and efficacy is still common (Angermeyer & Matschinger, 2004).

This chapter has provided you with the information needed to make more informed decisions about clients and the medication protocols they follow. In many cases, clients too can benefit from additional knowledge about what taking medication will be like and how it will affect their daily living. A stigma associated with seeking mental health services remains, especially those involving the need for medication. As a result, many clients may be leery about even entertaining the thought of starting to take medication. As a clinical mental health counselor, one of your initial goals should be to discuss some of the concerns your clients may have about taking medications. Although each client will have his or her own reasons for not wanting to take medications, the following are some of the reasons most commonly given:

- It's addicting; I don't want to become an addict.

- I am stronger if I don't need medicine.

- If I need medication it means I am weak and unable to handle my problems on my own.

- Medications won't (never) work for me.

- If I don't take medication it means I am not crazy.

- I can't stand the side effects associated with taking medications.

- I'll never get off the medication once I start.

- I only need to take medication on "bad days."

Addressing these concerns individually, you can help dispel some of the myths and rumors your clients may have heard about various medications and their effects on every-day functioning. One way to begin a discussion of medication usage with your clients is by explaining what medications are and how they differ from drugs. In addition to those clients who fear who they might become on medications there are others who view medication as a panacea that will completely cure all of their ills and resolve all of their problems. The true purpose of medication probably lies somewhere in between. Share with your clients that medications, like all other therapeutic interventions we employ, are a tool constituting only one part of a more comprehensive treatment plan. Clients should not expect miracles because they take medications, nor should they become too discouraged if the prescribed medication does not appear to be helping them. Many times, the process of medicating a client includes a period of trial and error in which several medications may need to be tried before the right drug, dosage, and administration protocol is determined.

A second strategy involves reviewing with your clients the importance of following the medication protocol exactly as prescribed. This seems straightforward, but many individuals deviate from their prescribed medication regimen. To illustrate this point, take a moment and ask yourself the following questions:

- Have you ever not taken a medication as directed?

- Have you ever taken more than your prescribed dosage?

- Have you ever taken less than your prescribed dosage?

- Have you ever stopped taking a medication prematurely because you were feeling better?

- Have you ever resumed taking a medication you had left over later?

If you are being honest with yourself, your answer to at least one of these questions was yes. Now consider the fact that you are the trained professional! Imagine how your clients, who might not have the same knowledge and insight as you, are managing their medication usage. To help keep clients engaged in their treatment you should discuss with them the importance of adhering to a prescribed medication schedule. **Adherence** refers to the extent to which a client takes his or her prescribed medication at the exact time and in the correct dosage. This differs from compliance, a term often mistaken for being synonymous with adherence. **Compliance** refers to the overall extent to which a client takes the medication as prescribed. Clients who are drug compliant are generally following their medication schedules as prescribed, but they may occasionally miss or skip a dosage, take only half a pill, or change the times they take their medication. Occasional deviations are to be expected; however, we want to ensure that they are kept to a minimum. When compliance begins to wane clients may no longer experience the full effect of the medication and their symptoms may return. Table 11.6 highlights information you might choose to share with your clients in hopes of promoting their adherence to a prescribed medication schedule.

Addressing Drug Usage for Members of Special Groups

Psychotropic medications are prescribed to treat psychological and behavioral disorders with great success for all types of individuals. However, for some special groups of

TABLE 11.6 ■ Promoting Drug Adherence Through Education
Counselors should make sure their clients know the following information about any medications prescribed
1) Brand name and generic name
2) What the pill looks like
3) The reasons why the drug is being prescribed and what it is supposed to help
4) The correct dosage and when and how (e.g., with meals) it should be taken
5) How long the drug should be taken (i.e., acute care or maintenance care)
6) Potential side effects
7) How the drug might interact with other medications they might be taking or considering
8) Whether the medication acts as a supplement or a replacement therapy
9) The appropriate storage requirements for this medication (i.e., temperature)
10) Where to acquire additional reliable information about the prescribed drug

GUIDED PRACTICE EXERCISE 11.4

You recently completed an assessment of a client referred to you by a local physician. The client informs you that the doctor has prescribed an antidepressant, but the client has not yet filled the prescription. The client indicates feeling ambivalent toward taking the antidepressant because he does not want to be crazy or unstable. How would you discuss these feelings with the client and help him better reach an informed decision?

individuals additional precautions need to be taken when medication becomes a part of their recommended treatment plan. Special groups for which care and attention are needed when medications are prescribed include children and adolescents, older adults, and women who are pregnant or may become pregnant. Among children and adolescents, prescribing psychotropic drugs has traditionally been challenging due to a lack of knowledge as to how these chemicals would affect the developing brain. This trend though seems to be changing. According to the American Academy of Child and Adolescent Psychiatry (2012), the use of psychotropic medications in children and adolescents has steadily increased in popularity over the past 20 years as evidence supporting the effectiveness of these medications when used appropriately has emerged. Today, a number of medications used to treat children and adolescents have been deemed safe and effective. That said, children (especially those age 6 and under) and adolescents need to be closely monitored when taking medications. Mental health counselors should inquire about drug regimens each time they meet with a client, making sure to determine whether the client is benefiting from the medication's therapeutic effects or suffering from any adverse effects or reactions.

Similarly, when working with elderly clients, it is important to discuss potential issues that may arise from use of psychotropic medications. For one, many elderly clients may be taking prescription medications for other health-related issues or ailments. The use of psychotropic medications might interact with these other medications to produce adverse effects or even mitigate their effectiveness. These clients should be encouraged to talk with their doctor and share all medications currently being prescribed. They also should be reminded to closely follow prescribed treatment regimens and take their medications in the correct dosage and at the correct time. A second issue related to psychotropic drug use among elderly clients is the fact that many age-related changes may exacerbate the side effects associated with many of these medications (Masand, 2000). For example, among elderly clients taking antipsychotic drugs, anticholinergic reactions, tardive dyskinesia, heart arrhythmias, reduced bone density, sedation, and cognitive slowing all are serious concerns. Clients, as well as their families and caregivers, should be made aware of these issues so their presence can be understood and properly communicated to the prescribing physician.

For women with mental health concerns, pregnancy can be an especially challenging time. Approximately 500,000 pregnancies each year involve women with an emerging or already present psychiatric illness (JPS Foundation, 2014). Although many of the medications used to treat mental illnesses such as anxiety, depression, bipolar disorder, and schizophrenia are evidenced to be safe and effective for women who are pregnant, a conversation with expectant mothers should focus on potential issues associated with their use of psychotropic medications while pregnant. Some medications used while pregnant can result in problems with the normal prenatal growth and development of the fetus, harm to the womb that might put the baby's life at risk, early delivery, birth defects, and even miscarriage. Depending on the stage of pregnancy, the drugs taken, ingestion method, and dosage all may need to be regulated and carefully monitored. These conversations are best had by the expectant mother and her doctor, but mental health counselors can serve as a source of education, support, and encouragement for mothers along the way.

TALKING MEDICATION WITH OTHER TREATMENT PROVIDERS

Understanding brain functioning is an area of intense and active research. As mental health counselors, you certainly are not expected to be experts in this area; however, a cursory knowledge of neuroanatomy can lead to better conceptualization of your clients and their presenting issues. In addition, the foundational knowledge will let you more fully participate in multidisciplinary treatment teams when client care is discussed. This section offers some tips for communicating with other treatment providers who may be involved in the care of your clients.

Sometimes when communicating with other treatment providers your role is that of an informant. As the client's counselor, it is likely you are the professional with whom he or she spends the most time. Psychiatrists or psychologists may spend as little as 5 to 10 minutes periodically checking in with the client to see how treatment is going or determine if adjustments to medications might be needed. However, you spend 50 to 60 minutes working with your client on a daily, weekly, or monthly basis depending on the level of care provided. Information clients share with you or observations you make can be helpful to prescribing physicians as they work to calibrate the correct medication regimen for a client. In these situations, share with the doctor gains you see being made, areas still needing to be addressed, and side effects emerging. Having this information helps in making informed decisions on what medications to prescribe.

Other times you will need to advocate for your client with other treatment providers. Some clients may feel they are unable to question a doctor because they view that person as an authority figure. The doctor also may be the one who determines whether they remain in treatment or are discharged from care, so caution may be exhibited in what is shared in conversations with the doctor. As your client's advocate, you can speak to the doctor and suggest when you see clients having difficulty or why following a treatment regimen may create undue stress on a client (e.g., financial cost of obtaining medications, strict dietary requirements, unmanageable side effects). By the nature of their training, doctors work to alleviate symptoms and address presenting problems. As counselors, our developmental and holistic training allows us to see how medication fits into the broader context of clients' lives. When possible, helping doctors to see the bigger picture helps our clients and improves the likelihood that they will remain treatment compliant. With the knowledge gained in this chapter, you now can have these conversations and feel confident in your ability to best contribute to the treatment of your clients.

GUIDED PRACTICE EXERCISE 11.5

Imagine that you are working as a mental health counselor in an inpatient treatment facility. A new client was recently admitted and added to your caseload. During your interactions with the client, he shares with you some side effects he is having because of taking a medication he was prescribed upon admission to the facility. He is uncomfortable with these side effects and has not been 100% compliant with his treatment. What would you say to the client regarding his inconsistent dosing, and what would you say to the attending physician who prescribed the client the medication in the first place?

Keystones

- The flow of information from nerve cell to nerve cell via neural pathways allows our brain to both send and receive information from all parts of the body and respond appropriately.

- Breakdowns in the transmission process are responsible for the signs and symptoms of psychological and behavioral disorders clients report experiencing.

- Drugs are exogenous substances that can be used to help regulate the transmission process by either exciting or inhibiting select neurotransmitters.

- Pharmacokinetics refers to the set of processes that describe what the human body does to a drug once it enters the system. Pharmacodynamics describes what drugs do to the human body once ingested.

- Different classes of drugs exist for different types of disorders and can be used to treat the symptoms of depression, anxiety, bipolar disorder, schizophrenia, and ADHD among other disorders.

- When taking drugs as part of a treatment regimen, it is important to be aware of not only the intended treatment effect but also the adverse and side effects of taking a particular drug.

- The effectiveness of a drug depends on a number of factors, and the needs of each client should be evaluated on a case-by-case basis.

- Although not able to prescribe medications, mental health counselors can play an important role in drug therapy by educating clients, communicating with prescribing physicians and psychiatrists, and advocating for clients and their overall health and well-being.

Key Terms

Action potential 276

Adherence 299

Axon 277

Cell body (soma) 276

Compliance 299

Dendrites 276

Drug 281

First messenger effect 279

Half-life 285

Loading dose 286

Maintenance dose 286

Nerve cells (neurons) 275

Neurotransmitters 277

Pharmacodynamics 287

Pharmacokinetics 282

Resting potential 276

Reuptake 280

Second messenger effect 279

Web Resources

Medication and Counseling Treatment (www.samhsa .gov/medication-assisted-treatment/treatment)

Psychiatric Times (www.psychiatrictimes.com/psycho pharmacology)

References

American Academy of Child and Adolescent Psychiatry. (2012). Best principles for integration of child psychiatry into the pediatric health home. Retrieved from https://www.aacap.org/App_Themes/ AACAP/docs/clinical_practice_center/systems_ of_care/best_principles_for_integration_of_child_ psychiatry_into_the_pediatric_health_home_2012.pdf

Angermeyer, M. C., & Matschinger, H. (2004). Public attitudes toward psychotropic drugs: Have there been any changes in recent years? *Pharmacopsychiatry*, *37*(4), 152–156. doi:10.1055/s-2004-827169

Bear, M. F., Connors, B. W., & Paradiso, M. A. (2007). *Neuroscience: Exploring the brain* (3rd ed.). Philadelphia, PA: Lippincott Williams & Wilkins.

Farmer, R. L. (2014). Interface between psychotropic medications, neurobiology, and mental illnesses. *Smith College Studies in Social Work*, *84*(2–3), 255–272. doi:10.1080/00377317.2014.923640

Fink, C. (2013). Bipolar medication spotlight: Lithium. *Psych Central*. Retrieved from http://blogs .psychcentral.com/bipolar/2008/07/bipolar -medication-spotlight-lithium/

Hauser, J. (2016). Mood stabilizers for bipolar disorder. *Psych Central*. Retrieved from http://psychcentral .com/lib/mood-stabilizers-for-bipolar-disorder/

Ingersoll, R. E., & Rak, C. F. (2016). *Psychopharmacology for mental health professionals: An integrative approach* (2nd ed.). Boston, MA: Cengage Learning.

JPS Foundation. (2014, May). *Psychiatric medication use during pregnancy and breastfeeding*. Retrieved from https://www.jpshealthnet.org/sites/default/ files/psych_meds_and_pregnancy_e-resource_-_ may_2014.pdf

Katzung, B. G. (2001). Basic principles. In B. G. Katzung (Ed.), *Basic and clinical pharmacology* (pp. 1–74). New York, NY: McGraw-Hill.

Kaut, K. P. (2011). Psychopharmacology and mental health practice: An important alliance. *Journal of Mental Health Counseling*, *33*(3), 196–222. doi:10.17744/mehc.33.3.u357803u508r4070

King, J. H., & Anderson, S. M. (2004). Therapeutic implications of pharmacotherapy: Current trends and ethical issues. *Journal of Counseling and Development*, *82*(4), 329–336. doi:10.1002/j.1556-6678.2004.tb00318.x

Kolb, B., & Whishaw, I. Q. (2009). *Fundamentals of human neuropsychology* (6th ed.). New York, NY: Worth.

Leucht, S., Cipriani, A., Spinelli, L., Mavridis, D., Orey, D., Richter, F., . . . Davis, J. M. (2013). Comparative efficacy and tolerability of 15 antipsychotic drugs in schizophrenia: A multiple-treatments meta-analysis. *Lancet*, *382*(9896), 951–962. doi:10.16/S0140-6736 (13)60733-3

Masand, P. S. (2000). Side effects of antipsychotics in the elderly. *Journal of Clinical Psychiatry*, *61*(Suppl. 8), 43–49.

Mayo Clinic. (2013, June 19). Nearly 7 in 10 Americans are on prescription drugs. *ScienceDaily*. Retrieved from www.sciencedaily.com/releases/2013/06/13061 9132352.htm

Medco Health Solutions. (2011). America's state of mind. Retrieved from http://apps.who.int/ medicinedocs/documents/s19032en/s19032en.pdf

Meltzer, H. Y. (2004). What's atypical about atypical antipsychotic drugs? *Current Opinion in Pharmacology*, *4*(1), 53–57. doi:10.1016/j.coph.2003.09.010

National Institute of Mental Health. (2013). Statistics: Any disorder among adults. Retrieved from http:// www.nimh.nih.gov/statistics/1ANYDIS_ADULT.shtml

Noggle, C. A. (2009). Future trends in the application and impact of psychopharmacology within the school setting. *Psychology in the Schools*, *46*(9), 915–917. doi:10.1002/pis.20433

Patterson, J., Albala, A. A., McCahill, M. E., & Edwards, T. M. (2009). *The therapist's guide to psychopharmacology, revised edition: Working with patients, families, and physicians to optimize care.* New York, NY: Guilford Press.

Pratt, L. A., Brody, D. J., & Gu, Q. (2011). *Antidepressant use in persons aged 12 and over: United States, 2005–2008.* NCHS data brief, no. 76. Hyattsville, MD: National Center for Health Statistics.

Sinacola, R. S., & Peters-Strickland, T. (2012). *Basic psychopharmacology for counselors and psychotherapists* (2nd ed.). Columbus, OH: Pearson Merrill.

Tripp, B., & Eliasmith, C. (2016). Function approximation in inhibitory networks. *Neural Networks*, *77*, 95–106. doi:10.1016/j.neunet.2016.01.010

U.S. Food and Drug Administration. (2016). Atypical antipsychotic drugs information. Retrieved from http://www.fda.gov/Drugs/DrugSafety/Postmarket DrugSafetyInformationforPatientsandProviders/ ucm094303.htm

12

NEUROSCIENCE AND THE BRAIN

What Mental Health Counselors Need to Know

By Lori A. Russell-Chapin and Theodore J. Chapin

As highly trained and experienced mental health practitioners, we have worked diligently to apply current knowledge and skills in providing our clients the best counseling experience we could offer. Most clients would improve, some would need periodic booster sessions, but a few just didn't seem to get better. Of course, these clients often had more serious, chronic problems such as trauma, addiction, or personality disorders. Despite our efforts in giving them the best professional help we could, they continued to struggle with little to no appreciable improvement. This caused us to ask ourselves two very important questions. What are we missing, and what else could we do for these clients? The answers to both were basic and unexpected. We needed to better understand the biological basis of behavior and learn how to harness its potential for our clients' benefit.

Thus began our journey into the world of neurofeedback, neuroscience, and neurocounseling. With much trepidation, we began what would become several years of intense study, new skill building, and practice. Some 7 years later, we feel like we have a newfound appreciation for the physiological aspects of behavior. We've come to understand the importance of healthy neurological functioning in the restoration, maintenance, and optimization of clients' mental health. We've been astounded at the progress that even clients with more moderate to severe emotionally and physiologically debilitating conditions have been able to experience. We've become much more knowledgeable, expanded our skills, and fundamentally changed the way we do therapy. In this chapter we share some of what we've learned and offer several physiologically based interventional strategies. It is our hope that this knowledge helps mental health counselors become more effective in their work with all of their clients, especially those who struggle with particularly difficult, challenging, chronic, or debilitating conditions.

LEARNING OBJECTIVES

After reading this chapter, you will be able to do the following:

- Understand basic neurogenesis and neuroplasticity concepts
- Recognize the impact of biological and neurological mechanisms on mental health (CACREP 5C-2-g)
- Identify necessary brain correlates to counseling skills
- Integrate neuroscience and neurocounseling into counseling practice
- Employ techniques and interventions for prevention and treatment of a broad range of mental health issues (CACREP 5C-3-b)

NEUROPLASTICITY AND NEUROGENESIS

It has long been held that the brain and its number of neurons were largely fixed by adulthood and that these neurons could not be replaced or regenerated when they died (Cajal, 1913–1914). Even before this, there was a strong scientific bias toward what was called **localizationism** (brain function was fixed to certain physicals regions of the brain) and **lateralization** (brain functioning was specialized to either hemisphere of the brain) when a surgeon named Paul Broca (1861) dissected a speech-impaired stroke patient's brain and discovered damage to the left frontal lobe, assigning the function of speech to that part of the brain. This set research on a course of mapping the functions of the human brain and reinforced the presumption that brain functions were hardwired, localized, and lateralized. Lateralized functions included speech and mathematical ability wired to the left hemisphere and emotional and spatial reasoning to the right. Many of these findings remain useful today; however, more current research in neuroplasticity suggests brain function is not necessarily limited to certain prescribed locations or even hemispheres of the brain.

Although in later work the role of learning and memory was acknowledged as capable of changing the brain, until recently, most neuronal growth was thought to occur in the first few years of life and to conclude by early adulthood (Conel, 1939). Today, with advances in research and brain imaging technology, through both animal and human studies, we now know this is not the case (Doidge, 2007, 2016). Remarkably, the functions of the human brain have been found to be much more dynamic, flexible, and open to incredible change throughout the life span.

William James (1890) is generally credited with presenting the first theory of brain plasticity in his book, *Principles of Psychology*. In it, he described changes in nervous paths associated with the establishment of habits. The term *neuroplasticity*, defined in the next section, was first used by a Polish neuroscientist named Jerzy Konorski (1948) who suggested that over time, neurons in the vicinity of a firing neuron also would activate, creating plastic changes in the brain. Donald Hebb (1949), a Canadian psychologist who wrote extensively about learning theory, explained that when one cell (neuron) fires near enough to another, and repeatedly or persistently does so, a growth process or metabolic change takes place in one or both cells that increases the efficiency of the association. This idea has become known as Hebb's law. Today we express it as "neurons that fire together, wire together." Of course, the opposite also can be true. Neurons that do not fire together, and are not wired together, adhere to the "use it or lose it" principle (Doidge, 2007). However, learned associations, of course, are not always for the good. Neuroplasticity also can lead to rigidity and repetition in the brain, as is the case in anxiety and obsessive-compulsive disorder.

CASE ILLUSTRATION 12.1

Captivatingly, Pascual-Leone (Pascual-Leone, Amedi, Fregni, & Merabet, 2005) provided a metaphor to explain the process of neuroplasticity. He suggested the plastic brain was like sledding down a snowy hill in the winter. The first time down, we navigate the terrain and steer the sled, ending up at the bottom of the hill. He likened the terrain to our genes, a given, and the path we take to our variety of possible choices. When we go down the hill the second time, he explained, we will likely take a path some way or another related to the first path. However, after a day of sledding, some paths will likely have been used a lot and others very little. The paths that have been used a lot will become very difficult to get out of. These he described as mental tracks or neuronal pathways, which once laid down become speedy and efficient for both healthy and unhealthy behavior.

Types of Neuroplasticity

In their description of the dynamic and ever-changing nature of the brain, Kay, Hurley, and Taber (2012) simply defined **neuroplasticity** as the processes by which the brain is remodeled in response to both internal metabolic conditions and external environmental factors. These processes include changes to the individual neuron, changes in the connections or synapses between neurons, neuronal pruning, and neurogenesis or creation of new neurons. In Chapter 11, you learned about the basic structure of the neuron. This knowledge will come in handy as we describe the concept of neuroplasticity. Neuroplasticity at the neuronal level involves changes to the neuronal structure that include axonal sprouting and dendritic remodeling to strengthen or increase synaptic connections or dendritic shrinking or retraction and pruning of axons that weaken or decrease synaptic connections (Kay et al., 2012). When the brain is faced with change or challenge, it can adapt by altering its existing connections to meet the challenge or dispose of unnecessary neuronal capacity.

Neuronal pruning, the natural process of removing unnecessary or degraded synapses, is as essential as neuronal growth, a process termed **neurogenesis**. Developmentally, we are born with many more neurons than we need. In early childhood many of these are pruned away. When we pass from childhood to teenage years, even more neurons become unnecessary and are pruned away (Conel, 1939). Each night when we sleep, glia cells within our spinal fluid perform a sort of neurological house cleaning, destroying toxins and clearing away the debris from obsolete connections that are no longer of use (Xie et al., 2013). After injury by stroke, high fever, anoxia (oxygen deprivation), or traumatic head injury, neuronal pruning also serves to remove damaged or destroyed axonal and dendritic material (Kay et al., 2012). This allows the brain to more efficiently use its vital resources of oxygen, blood flow, and nutrients to better serve its healthy and necessary neuronal needs.

In a summary of research on neurogenesis, Kay et al. (2012) noted that it is generally accepted that the creation, migration, maturation, and integration of new neurons in the adult mammalian and human brain occur in two primary locations. These locations are the subventricular zone of the caudate that is incorporated into the olfactory bulb (involved in the filtering and detection of odors) and the subgranular zone of the dentate gyrus that is incorporated into the hippocampus (involved in memory formation, organization, and storage). Both functions have direct bearing on the limbic system, involved in emotional regulation, and may play an important role in alert, processing, and reaction to potential threat. Evidence of neurogenesis in other ventricular regions incorporated into the cerebral cortex also was noted. Perhaps most exciting is the potential use of **neural stem cells** (see Figure 12.1), cells that are capable of self-renewal (neurons) and differentiation into other cells (glia cells), to repair damaged brain areas as in the case of stroke, traumatic brain injury, or neurological degenerative diseases (Sawada & Sawamoto, 2013).

Not all newly generated cells survive and become neurons. Many become glial cells that play an important role in supporting and regulating the development of new neurons. Other factors also affect the process of neurogenesis, including the presence of a brain-derived neurotropic factor, vascular endothelial growth factor, and insulin-like growth factor (Kay et al., 2012). In addition, the presence of injury, negative aversive stress, depression, and illness have been found to suppress neurogenesis. So, both internal metabolic conditions and external environmental factors can either promote or inhibit neurogenesis.

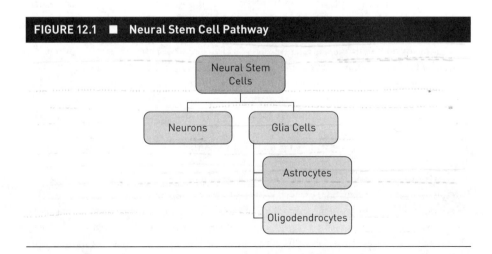

FIGURE 12.1   ■   Neural Stem Cell Pathway

CASE ILLUSTRATION 12.2

Charlie was recently involved in a car accident that resulted in a severe brain injury. Both his physical and cognitive functioning were impaired, with only mild improvements after surgery and medication. This outcome is not uncommon for persons with a severe brain injury, which is associated with loss of cells due to tissue destruction. With the advances in research on neural stem cells, it is possible that one day persons like Charlie may have additional treatment options to repair the damaged parts of their brain. This is because neural stem cells have the amazing ability to develop into new neurons or supporting cells for neuronal growth, which may help repair damaged brain tissue and ultimately give persons back a level of functioning previously lost.

Finally, perhaps even more amazing are the neuroplastic processes that Doidge (2016) presented in his book, *The Brain's Way of Healing*. Defying the presumptions of localizationism and lateralization, Doidge cited the work of many pioneers in the application of neuroplastic techniques. This work found that brain maps, which identified previously intact cortical areas and related functions lost due to injury or disease, could be expanded and rewired to other cortical areas, including cross hemisphere adaptation. These efforts have been applied in areas of chronic pain, degenerative disorders, paralysis after stroke, blindness, phantom pain, and severe head injury.

Strategies to Increase Neuroplasticity and Neurogenesis

Research on the brain's ability to reorganize itself physically and functionally has led to several strategies to increase neuroplasticity and neurogenesis. Some of these strategies include exercise, enriched or novel environments, learning, attention, mental practice, massive physical practice, medication, transcranial stimulation, meditation, and talk therapy (Doidge, 2007, 2016; Kay et al., 2012).

GUIDED PRACTICE EXERCISE 12.1

Independently, define and describe the processes of neuroplasticity, neurogenesis, and neuronal pruning. Once finished, find an in-class partner and share your thoughts on these concepts.

GUIDED PRACTICE EXERCISE 12.2

With an in-class partner, using Figure 12.1 and information from the text, describe neural stem cells in your own words. What purpose do neural stem cells serve in the process of creating new neurons?

Exercise

Exercise has been found to increase blood flow and the production of brain-derived neurotropic factor (BDNF), which stimulates the nucleus basalis, the part of the brain that allows us to focus attention and to remember what we are experiencing (Kilgard & Merzenich, 1998). This puts the brain in an extremely plastic state that has been found to not only increase cardiorespiratory fitness but to also increase gray matter volume in the prefrontal cortex and hippocampus (Erickson, Leckie, & Weinstein, 2014), enhancing executive function and memory.

Enriched Environments

Research on enriched and novel environments, initially studied in animal research, found that mice living with toys, balls, and tubes resulted in a fivefold increase in hippocampal neurons (Kempermann, Gast, & Gage, 2002). This work was later extended to humans, where it was found that cognitively challenging leisure activities such as playing a musical instrument, board games, reading, dancing, bowling, babysitting, and golfing were all associated with lower risks of dementia (Verghese et al., 2003). As we now understand, it is important to stay cognitively challenged, physically active, and socially engaged to maintain healthy neuroplasticity.

Learning

Learning has long been held as a mechanism of brain change. However, it wasn't until the work of Kandel (2003, 2006), studying giant marine snails with unusually large neurons, that the neurological mechanisms of learning became better understood. He found that individual neurons altered their structure and strength of synaptic connections, following the release of a protein called kinase A. It is kinase A that turns on the gene to make a protein that alters the structure of the neuron to grow new connections to others neurons. For example, when a lone neuron develops a long-term memory for sensitization, its number of synaptic connections has been found to increase from 1,300 to 2,700, a huge amount of synaptic change. The implication of his work for long-term memory is that spacing of learned material is critical with moderate exposure (10 times a day) across a longer period of time (several days) being superior to heavy exposure (40 times a day) across a shorter period of time (1 day) (Kandel, Schwartz, & Jessel, 2000). Repeated exposure over time allows more opportunities for the metabolic mechanisms of synaptic growth to occur.

Attention

As mental health counselors, better understanding the underlying brain mechanisms of attention is imperative in our efforts to best help the clients we serve. We use attention throughout the process of counseling, and attention is a skill taught to clients during counseling sessions. Before the plasticity of learning can be effectively harnessed, the brain must be brought to a state of focused attention. There are three components to attention: alerting, orienting, and self-regulating (Ivey, Ivey, & Zalaquett, 2016).

The *alerting* response begins when the entire brain and body send signals through the senses (visual, auditory, touch, olfactory, gustatory) and the gut/brain axis. Any "wake-up" call goes to the brainstem to produce necessary norepinephrine for the next phase of orientation. *Orienting* and trying to decide what to do with the alerting response require navigation using bidirectionality of either bottom-up or top-down communication through the body and brain. This navigational system assists with the final phase of attention, *self-regulating*, by determining what action is needed next. What goal or direction is needed to be able to focus and attend? This self-regulation process requires many different brain connections as well as some local, regional, and global communications in the brain. The prefrontal cortex may be required for executive functioning and decision-making. The insula may be needed for assisting with homeostasis, and the cingulate cortex is needed for executive functioning in the anterior portion, cognitive processes in the dorsal regions, and emotional regulations in the ventral regions. However, without being able to calm down and self-regulate, attention is difficult to achieve.

Once attention is achieved, the neuroplasticity concepts of novelty, mood, and challenge are needed even more to engage the brain. Then the use of intentional active listening skills becomes extremely important to the counseling process and maintenance of focused attention. For example, researchers using fMRI studies have discovered that active listening actually "lights up" or activates the brain (Kawamichi et al., 2015). The use of attending behaviors activates the ventral striatum that is part of the brain's reward system (Ivey et al., 2016). Summarizations are associated with the default mode network (DMN) needed for reflection of self and others. Using immediacy questions and statements about being present in the here-and-now involves executive functions, limbic HPA hormones, the amygdala, and memory in the hippocampus (Ivey et al., 2016). Fan, Duncan, de Greck, & Northoff (2011) conducted a meta-analysis of reflection skills and discovered the insula became activated, strengthening emotional and even consciousness needs. Engen and Singer (2013) also showed affective empathy with increased activity in the insula, again an important structure for bodily homeostasis needs.

Probably most fascinating was the work of Sinha, Lacadie, Constable, and Seo (2016) who underscored the importance of reframing and reappraisal skills when building adaptability and coping strategies. In their fMRI research, resiliency was activated in the ventral medial prefrontal cortex (vmPFC). Using all of these intentional attending skills in counseling is effective for the listening and change process to occur, but these same micro- and macrocounseling skills also activate certain brain structures and functions and assist in building new neuronal growth and plasticity. Now counselors better understand that selecting a particular intentional skill may gain a particular response from a client, but it also assists in focused attention and brain growth.

Mental Practice

The mechanisms of mental practice employ imagination and repetition, and were first proposed by Cajal (1904). He suggested that well-directed mental practice (repeated thoughts) must create and strengthen neuronal connections. Later, Pascual-Leone et al. (1995) using transcranial magnetic stimulation (TMS) brain mapping technology found that mental practice alone (2 hours a day for 5 days in a row) resulted in motor signal change equivalent to those who physically practiced playing the piano. However, their actual performance was not equivalent to the physical practice group until the mental practice group had at least one day of physical practice. Today, mental practice or mental rehearsal is a commonly applied strategy in sports psychology for athletes with preestablished skill and training. It's impossible to watch a basketball game without seeing players who visualize their free throw before taking the shot or watch a golf tournament without seeing a golfer visualize a swing before making a putt.

Massive Physical Practice

Massive physical practice has been studied and employed in the rehabilitation of lost physiological functioning from stroke, including paralysis and aphasia. In both animal and human studies, massive physical practice has been found to expand neuronal maps and restore physiological functioning. Taub (1980), using deafferentation experiments, cut off the nerves to the spines of monkeys who could then not use their arms. In time he observed that these animals somehow began using their arms and hands to eat. He concluded that independent motor programs in the brain must have initiated voluntary movement, even though the neuronal messages were blocked. In generalizing this observation to humans with motor, speech, or sensory damage from stroke, he hypothesized that "learned nonuse" may occur during the several months of cortical shock following a stroke. He further reasoned that the brain's neuroplastic capacity and the use of massive physical practice may combine to help rewire the lost functioning.

Using an exhausting, incremental shaping schedule of 12 tasks a day, performed 10 times each for 6 hours a day over 15 days straight, 80% of the stroke patients who had lost arm function saw substantial improvement. Even those who began the work 4 years after their stroke saw significant improvement. More recently Taub observed that 3 hours of training a day, with an increasing number of movements per hour, may be best. He also cautioned that because half of the area in the affected brain map is shrunk by a stroke, even after treatment, rewiring will not be perfect. However, both musculature and neuronal functioning can benefit from rehabilitation after a stroke. Taub's principles have been applied to other problems, including aphasia and visual processing. Later, in investigating the extent of the neurological change produced by these procedures, Merzenich et al. (1984) using brain mapping technology found 1 to 2 millimeters of neuronal growth in the finger maps and 14 millimeters to a half an inch of growth in the arm maps. Even more interesting, they noted that the monkeys' facial map, located near the arm map, had taken over functions of the arm map. They concluded that not only can surviving healthy neurons grow more neuronal branches, but even more astounding, reorganization can extend across large sectors of the brain map.

Medication

Medication, specifically antidepressants, has been found to increase neuroplasticity in both animals and humans. Magnetic resonance imaging (MRI) studies have reported smaller hippocampal volume in post-traumatic stress disorder (Bremner, Elzinga, Schmal, & Vermetten, 2008) and major depressive disorder (Malykhin, Carter, Seres, & Coupland, 2010). This is likely due to the effect of glucocorticoids (stress hormones), which are elevated in the blood of stressed and depressed individuals (Oomen, Mayer, DeKloet, Jous & Lucassen, 2007). Antidepressant medication has been found to activate the glucocorticoid receptors, reducing the effects of chronic stress and increasing hippocampal neurogenesis. Once administered, antidepressant medications have been found to reverse hippocampal volume deficits in both PTSD and depression. It is important to note that the hippocampus is not losing or gaining neurons but rather, the decrease and increase is due to changes in dendritic and synaptic density (Bennett, 2011).

Transcranial Stimulation

Several types of transcranial stimulation have been found to increase neuroplasticity. These may stimulate the brain focally or generally. These include electroconvulsive therapy (ECT), transcranial magnetic stimulation (TMS), and cranial electrical stimulation (CES) and the portable modulation stimulator (PoNS). Electroconvulsive therapy is a general stimulation technique that has been found to increase hippocampal volume (Nordanskog et al., 2010) and levels of brain-derived neurotropic factor (BDNF) (Martinotti et al., 2011). Transcranial magnetic stimulation, or deep brain stimulation, has been used to increase or decrease the neuronal activity related to various conditions and their related functions (Cramer et al., 2011). Cranial electrical stimulation (Kirsch & Nichols, 2013) uses a weak electrical current, less than 4 milliamps, to reduce cortical activation producing a state of relaxation, reduced fatigue, and decreased ruminative thoughts. It also has been found to increase blood plasma levels of endorphins, adrenocorticotropic hormone, serotonin, melatonin, norepinephrine, and cholinesterase and to decrease serum cortisol levels; it is frequently used to treat anxiety, depression, and insomnia. The portable neuromodulation stimulator (PoNS) developed by Yuri Danilov targets part of the brain stem called the pons, delivering a weak electrical signal that reportedly modifies and corrects how the neurons are firing (Danilov, Kaczmarek, Skinner, & Tyler, 2015). It is placed on the tongue because the tongue has 48 kinds of sensory receptors, with 15,000 to 50,000 nerve fibers that pass information directly on to the brain. After 400 to 600 milliseconds, an electroencephalogram recording indicates the brain's electrical activity has stabilized and all parts of the brain start to react and fire together, correcting any dysregulation related to symptomatic behavior. It has been used to help reduce the symptoms related to such neurodegenerative illnesses as Parkinson's and multiple sclerosis as well as impaired functioning related to stroke, head injury, and chronic pain.

Neurofeedback

Neurofeedback is a form of biofeedback and neuromodulation that uses electroencephalogram and computer technology to form a brain-computer interface (BCI) that allows for real-time monitoring and change of brain wave activity as it is being shaped (increased or decreased) through the principles of operant and classical conditioning (Chapin & Russell-Chapin, 2014). Dysregulation in the brain's electrical activity has been correlated with many behavioral, psychological, emotional, cognitive, and physical health problems. The efficacy of neurofeedback in the treatment of such problems as ADHD, anxiety, depression, emotional trauma, insomnia, epilepsy, chronic pain, substance abuse, traumatic brain injury, learning disabilities, autistic spectrum, and personality disorders has been well demonstrated (Myers & Young, 2012). Many clients who begin neurofeedback and are taking prescription medication to help manage their condition find that they can reduce, and in some cases eliminate, the need for continued medication. In addition, neurofeedback's ability to help reregulate the brain's electrical activity helps potentiate its corresponding neurological functions and enables clients to enjoy a much more efficient, creative, and successful life. Today, neurofeedback has become widely available and is not only used to treat clinical problems but has found growing application in peak performance. Professional athletes, CEOs, artists, surgeons, and anyone interested in achieving optimal cognitive, emotional, and physical performance can use neurofeedback to help achieve their goals.

Meditation

Meditation involves a variety of practices that include relaxation, focused attention on a chosen object, and a nonreactive open monitoring of experience from one moment to the next to achieve a sense of well-being or enlightenment (Davidson & Lutz, 2008). Many studies have found neuroplastic changes through meditation. These include increased cortical thickness (Lazar et al., 2005), increased gray matter density in the brain stem (Vestergaard-Poulsen et al., 2009), and larger hippocampal and frontal gray matter volume (Luders, Toga, Lepore, & Gaser, 2009). Still other research has found changes in the brain's electrical activity indicating high amplitude of gamma synchrony (Lutz, Greischar, Rawlings, Ricard, & Davidson, 2004). Gamma synchrony is thought to reflect a unity of consciousness, sense of satisfaction from insight or learning, or happiness. Brain activity has also been shown to vary by meditative experience (Davidson & Lutz, 2008) with novice meditators showing much more activation in multiple attentional, monitoring, and orienting areas, including the amygdala, and less gamma wave synchrony than more experienced or expert meditators. Meditation has been found to have many other beneficial effects on anxiety, stress reduction, and general health. A recent example combining the benefits of meditation and aerobic exercise found a significant reduction in depression and rumination among individuals with major depressive disorder as well as enhanced synchronized brain activity (Alderman, Olsen, Brush, & Shors, 2016).

Talk Therapy

In the first demonstration that talk therapy can affect the brain, Schwartz and Beyette (1996) applied neuroplastic strategies to the treatment of obsessive-compulsive disorder (OCD). Their therapy was devised by comparing the positron emission tomography (PET) brain scans of persons with and without OCD. Clients were first taught to relabel what was happening to them as an episode of OCD and not an attack of germs, AIDS, or some other aversive trigger. This was intended to help them get some distance from the trigger. Clients also were reminded that OCD attacks do not immediately go away because they set off a deeply established, faulty brain circuit that results in automatic compulsive behavior. Next, clients were instructed to refocus their attention on a positive, pleasure-giving activity at the moment of the attack. This could be gardening, helping someone, engaging in a hobby, playing an instrument, or working out. The focus was not to be on how they felt during the exercise but rather on what they did. Then, by engaging in massive practice, that is, concentrating on the new behavior for 30 minutes after each episode, new neuropathways had an opportunity to develop. In other words, clients were given the opportunity to "delink" from the OCD behavior and "link" to a healthier response. Schwartz and Beyette (1996) reported that 80% of clients got better when

GUIDED PRACTICE EXERCISE 12.3

With an in-class partner, consider the strategies you have previously engaged or currently engage in to increase neuroplasticity and neurogenesis. What strategies would you recommend or not recommend to your future clients? Discuss reasons why and why not.

they used this method in combination with a prescribed antidepressant such as Prozac or Anafranil. They suggested the medication functioned like training wheels, providing an opportunity for new neuropathways to become strengthened.

Of course, there are many kinds of talk therapy. Some use more obvious neuroplastic strategies such as mental imagery, hypnosis, neurolinguistics programming, eye movement desensitization and reprocessing (EMDR), and brain spotting, paired with externally observed and internally experienced reflexive responses, that access deep, physiologically held emotional experience in memory form (Grand, 2013). According to Doidge (2007, 2016), talk therapy in all of its forms is a neurological intervention. By getting clients to talk about their various conflicts and issues, therapists are able to access relevant circuitry that is involved in the problem. Then by encouraging clients to focus on alternative behavior, perspectives, and feelings, clients are provided the opportunity to remodel their brain activity and neurological functioning.

Rick Hanson (2013) in his work on the negativity bias and contemplative practice noted that negative neural pathways have a powerful, evolutionary prerogative to protect us from threat. They have been so vital to our historic survival that they are quickly learned (within a few seconds), deeply embedded, and easily reaccessed when the prospect of actual or perceived threat emerges. For persons with emotional and behavioral disorders, negative neuronal pathways tend to dominate their psychological and behavioral landscape. To rewire this dysregulation and hardwire happiness, he suggested we have to consciously engage clients in their positive experience and repeatedly hold them there for a minimum of 10 to 20 seconds, allowing a positive neural pathway to become established. Once established, healthier behavior and emotional experience can emerge. Talk therapy is clearly a tremendous vehicle for such neurological transformation, but of course as most mental health counselors know, effective talk therapy requires a skilled clinician and a committed client willing to persevere to realize its full benefit.

Implications for Mental Health Counselors

With the burgeoning research on neuroplasticity and the popular press's tendency to uncritically extol its benefits, much has become misunderstood, oversimplified, and perhaps even exaggerated, in its ease of application for personal change. Michael Merzenich (2013), a pioneer in neuroplasticity and active engineer of neuroscience into clinical practice, noted that the work requires the capacity for focused attention, dogged determination, a commitment to hard work, and ongoing maintenance of an overall healthy brain. Mental health counselors are well advised to better understand the underlying neuroscience, but they must also appreciate the challenge of integrating this knowledge into more effective therapy. The following implications are presented to help summarize the key principles of neuroplasticity and to guide mental health counselors in its realistic application with their clients.

1. Neuroplasticity can work both for and against a client. Neurologically speaking, problem states involve deeply ingrained neural pathways that are all too easily triggered, automatically replay, and become strengthened with each repeated episode. To alter and reconstruct such patterns with a more positive and healthier neuropathway is difficult but not impossible.

2. The brain is capable of incredible change across the life span, but it is not easy. Significant change takes a lot of effort. Clients must be able to be alert, engaged, motivated, and ready for action to stimulate the necessary neurochemicals for neuroplastic change.

3. Certain conditions make neuroplastic change more likely. These involve the brain's current overall physiological health and include such factors as sleep, diet, and exercise, as well as the presence and consequences of past overwhelming psychosocial stress, trauma, or depression. Of course, the effects of aging, substance abuse, physical injury to the brain, and chronic debilitating health conditions can also conspire to make neuroplastic change more difficult. Clients' overall wellness matters.

4. Learning is an associative process and involves incremental and progressive change that continually modifies and corrects previous neural pathways. Less efficient behavioral patterns take time to weaken and become replaced with more efficient patterns before mastery can be achieved. Trial and error, repetition of new behavior, and reinforcement of positive outcomes all help strengthen more positive pathways.

5. Early change is fragile and fleeting if not followed up with massive practice, refinement, and significantly experienced positive emotional states. Negative experience is quickly learned and easily retriggered, within a few seconds. Positive states require reflection, reverence, and time to soak in (10 to 20 seconds) the enjoyable experience. This helps consolidate learning and change and reinforces the likelihood of its reoccurrence. Otherwise, the brain will be inclined to simply cast off what was learned and remain stuck in the negative pathway.

6. Mental rehearsal is as useful for meaningful neurological change as actual external, physical experience. This gives recognition to many established and new perceptually oriented counseling approaches such as mental imagery, hypnosis, neurolinguistic programming, EMDR, brain spotting, role-playing, active imagination, and dream work. Because the brain does not completely differentiate the internal from the external, this can be harnessed in the clinician's office for the client's potential benefit.

7. Talk therapy is brain therapy! When therapists interact with their clients they are accessing and activating both negative and positive neural pathways. Simple listening without active, intentional, alternative, positive intervention risks

strengthening the negative pathways that clients want to change. This suggests that mental health counselors must appreciate the importance and risk of prolonged assessment and focus on the problem and must develop a repertoire of neurologically positive interventional strategies to be implemented to a significant extent in every counseling session. It is only this way that clients may realize the benefits of positive neuroplasticity.

THE NEUROSCIENCE OF WELLNESS AND ITS IMPERATIVE AS THE BEHAVIORAL FOUNDATION FOR POSITIVE NEUROPLASTICITY

The roots of wellness extend back to the work of Halbert Dunn (1961) who challenged the prevailing focus on health being the absence of disease and infirmity. Instead, he proposed that true health was a state of complete physical, mental, and social well-being. This notion took some time to take hold, and it wasn't until Donald Ardell (1976), some 15 years later, that the concept of high-level wellness really became understood as the absence of disease with conscious intentional effort toward healthy functioning in all aspects of life. Later, Hettler (1984) outlined six dimensions of wellness: occupational, physical, social, intellectual, spiritual, and emotional aspects of life. Although different wellness models may relabel these original dimensions, all six areas are typically incorporated into wellness assessment (Becker et al., 2009; Chapin, 2016) and educational programs (Travis & Ryan, 2004).

Unfortunately, as noted in a recent research report by the Global Wellness Institute (Young & Johnston, 2016) on the future of wellness at work, only 9% of the global workforce has access to a workplace wellness program, and these have been found to have low participation. In addition, they are usually coordinated through the human resources department and are primarily focused on fixing health problems such as smoking, obesity, diabetes, and stress. Although obviously important work, these efforts do not come near fulfilling the promise of wellness as a multidimensional state of intentional healthy functioning.

The neurological basis of wellness is presented in this section, with specific attention to the importance of a healthy lifestyle (sleep, diet, and exercise), emotional balance (stress management and meditation), social connection (interpersonal relationships and the social engagement system), lifelong cognitive challenge, and meaning and purpose in life. Through intentional encouragement of these behaviors, mental health counselors can help their clients more fully realize the promise of wellness by strengthening their resiliency and creating positive neuroplastic change. This section closes with a brief but important discussion of how to facilitate such change with clients.

Healthy Lifestyle

All meaningful change is only possible with a healthy lifestyle. Of course, many factors contribute to a healthy lifestyle. Some of these are beyond the scope of this chapter but are nonetheless important to consider in the development of a successful wellness plan. These include maintenance of good general health, limited use of medication and illegal substances, and judicious use of technology. When the body is ill and fighting disease, many of its resources are rerouted to survival and recovery. Although necessary, the healing process can easily overwhelm and undermine the physiological and psychological mechanisms of a healthy lifestyle. Who can exercise, eat right, and sleep well when they are stressed or fatigued in a fight against an attacking disease? In the same way, substance abuse and chronic overreliance on medication can undermine the body's ability to self-regulate its physiological and neurological functions. In addition, in today's world, with ever-increasing technology use in work, school, and leisure, growing evidence has demonstrated that overuse (more than 2 hours a day beyond work or school) can result in significant dysregulation of the brain's electrical activity to the same levels as seen in ADHD, marijuana dependence, and dementia (Swingle, 2015). These factors cannot be ignored. Teaching the following therapeutic lifestyle changes (TLC) to clients is essential for efficacious counseling practice, but it is also an ethical responsibility to educate on what research has demonstrated (Ivey, Ivey, & Zalaquett, 2014).

Sleep

Most important of all lifestyle factors is sleep. It lays the foundation for both healthy neurological functioning and physiological recovery. During good-quality sleep, glial cells make their way through cerebrospinal fluid and flush out toxins, including beta-amyloid proteins, the same substance implicated in the formation of beta-amyloid plaque associated with Alzheimer's disease. The sustained unconscious state of sleep is thought to allow more room for the movement of the glial cells to remove the waste from the brain (Xie et al., 2013). Poor or inadequate sleep results in weakened synaptic potentiation (functioning) and inefficient memory processing (Abel, Havenkes, Saletin, & Walker, 2013) that can impair many neurological functions including reasoning, problem-solving, and attention to detail. Chronic decreased sleep has also been linked to increases in obesity, diabetes, and cancer. Good-quality sleep, as recommended by the National Sleep Foundation (see Table 12.1), is essential for optimal daily functioning (Hirshkowitz et al., 2015). Mental health counselors should also be aware that many clients do not have good sleep hygiene (sleep habits), which can significantly limit the duration and quality of their sleep (Chen, Kuo, & Chueh, 2010). Good sleep hygiene includes but is not limited to creating a conducive sleep environment, following a regular and relaxing bedtime routine, limiting exercise and intake of food or drink before bedtime, and knowing how to handle common sleep problems. Melatonin supplementation, neurofeedback training for insomnia, and 10-minute naps (Tietzel & Lack, 2002) are safe and effective interventions for problem sleep.

Diet

The American diet has been heavily criticized for its excess of genetically modified foods; use of herbicides, pesticides, and growth hormones; and heavy saturation of processed food (Hill & Castro, 2009). These factors have resulted in nutritional deficiency, neurotoxicity, and obesity. Diet is important for its nutritional value, neurological production of neurotransmitters and healthy functioning of the microbiome, and the stomach's digestive environment (which has been found to have significant

TABLE 12.1 ■ National Sleep Foundation–Endorsed Quality Sleep Needs for Various Age Groups	
Age Range	**Recommended Hours of Quality Sleep**
6–11 years of age	9–11 hours per night
12–17 years of age	8–10 hours per night
18–25 years of age	7–9 hours per night
26 years of age or older	7–9 hours per night

implications for mental health) (Deans, 2016). The gut/brain axis is often called the *sixth sense*, and keeping this microbiome healthy though foods and even a prebiotic and probiotic is recommended. Sharing with clients that 95% of all serotonin, as well as many other neurotransmitters, is created in the gut makes healthy eating a more understandable need (Ivey et al., 2016). The best diet, according to Amen (2001), is one that includes protein (lean meat, fish, organic dairy, and nuts), complex carbohydrates (vegetables and fruit), and both saturated (animal, dairy, and coconut oil) and monoun-saturated fats (omega-3 and olive oil)—this is commonly known as the Mediterranean diet. Diets including simple carbohydrates (sugar, pasta, and other white foods such as potatoes, flour, and white rice) have been found to have a toxic effect on the brain's neurological functioning, impairing memory and neuroplasticity (Molteni, Barnard, Ying, Roberts, & Gomez-Pinella, 2002) and lead to an increased risk for metabolic disease, cardiovascular disease, obesity and type 2 diabetes (Stanhope, Schwartz, & Havel, 2013). More recently, researchers have found that the Mediterranean diet, with its micronutrients (trace minerals) and macronutrients (carbohydrates and proteins), is associated with larger frontal, parietal, and occipital cortical thickness, whereas a diet higher in carbohydrates and sugar was associated with lower entorhinal cortical thickness (hub of memory and navigation between the hippocampus and neocortex) (Staubo et al., 2017).

Also important in the discussion of diet is the benefit of dietary supplements. Although healthy nutrition can supply most of what the brain needs, selective use of dietary sup-plements can improve neurological and immunological functioning (Balch, 2010). It has been well established that inflammation, the immune system's normal response to injury or disease, if left unchecked, can interfere with the brain's optimal functioning. Some commonly suggested dietary supplements include omega-3s (found in fish oil), turmeric, and vitamin D. Both omega-3s and turmeric are anti-inflammatory and as such, can aid in the reduction of oxidative stress caused by various neurological injury and disease processes (Ghosh, Banerjee, & Sil, 2015). Vitamin D, usually obtained from exposure to sunlight, has been found to help promote immune functioning and general physical and mental health (Aranow, 2011). Although many other food supplements have been found to have beneficial effects on a variety of mental and physical health conditions (Balch, 2010), omega-3s, turmeric, and vitamin D are likely to help all clients maintain healthy brain functioning.

GUIDED PRACTICE EXERCISE 12.4

In groups of three to four, create a wellness plan that includes emotional, behavioral, and physiological self-regulation strategies, using the following case study. Include rationales as to why those strategies were chosen using evidence from the case study. Be sure to reference the wellness healthy lifestyle strategies specifically and the material in this section.

Case study: A self-employed, 21-year-old female store owner with a high school education and 1 year of college presented with a history of anxiety, depression, mild OCD, possible ADHD, and trauma. She was an average student and reported being bullied during middle and high school. At that time she said she also struggled with the loss of her grandparents and a relationship with a boyfriend she described as emotionally abusive. At age 19 she became suicidal and was hospitalized. Her presenting issue involved anxiety about her first pregnancy, very difficult morning sickness, and worry that ceasing her antidepressant medication would cause her to slide into a serious depressive episode.

Her psychosocial medical history noted a family history of maternal anxiety and depression, a paternal cousin with addiction issues, a paternal aunt with bipolar disorder, and a sister diagnosed with ADHD. Possible birth trauma was noted in being born by C-section and suction. She also noted repeated episodes of childhood strep infection and reported two head injuries: the first at age 3, to the front of her head, and the second at age 16, reportedly caused by a mild whiplash injury following a car accident. Since becoming pregnant, the client reports ceasing both alcohol use of four or five drinks a week and one to two daily caffeinated beverages. Her technology use has significantly increased from an average of 4 hours a day to 10 to 12 hours a day. Her prepregnancy sleep pattern also changed; she is unable to get to sleep until 3:00 a.m. but still gets 8 to 9 hours of sleep each night. Her morning sickness has been severe, with repeated hospitalizations for dehydration.

Her neurotherapy assessment found moderate trauma, severe anxiety, mild depression, a tendency toward overfocused ADHD, and a significant auditory attention problem (inattention and impulsivity). The top 10 problems noted on her symptom checklist were becoming annoyed and irritated, sleep onset, negative self-talk, chronic pain, emotional trauma, frequently ill, depression, stubbornness, fretting, and stuck on the negative.

Exercise

Daily aerobic exercise is an easy, inexpensive, and effective way to maintain wellness and optimal neuroplasticity (Chapin & Chapin-Russell, 2014). It is essential in the maintenance of general physical health but also promotes neurological, cognitive, and physical health. Forty minutes of aerobic exercise 3 times a week stimulates the production of brain-derived neurotropic factor (BDNF), an important neuronal protein metabolite that calls the brain to focused attention for optimal learning and neuroplastic change (Ratey, 2008). Described as "miracle grow" for the brain, it provides energy by activating glutamate, increasing antioxidant production, and growing new brain cells to enable synaptic plasticity. Exercise has also been found to reduce depression (Blumenthal et al., 1999) and to improve memory and hippocampal growth (Erickson et al., 2011). More recent research and human clinical trials have linked exercise and diet to the battle of inevitable cognitive decline and impairment in older adults (Jackson et al., 2016). This work has found that exercise and a healthy diet serve to reduce oxidative stress and inflammation that hampers cerebral blood flow, increasing both cerebrovascular and cognitive reserve and preserving cognitive function.

In addition to aerobic exercise, resistance or strength training (weight lifting) has been found to improve memory and executive function, decrease depression and chronic fatigue, improve quality of sleep and cognition, reduce anxiety, and improve self-esteem (O'Conner, Herring, & Carvalho, 2010). The mechanisms of change from resistance training involve neural adaptation, new nerve cell generation in the brain, an increase in neurotransmitters, and increased blood flow for more efficient oxygen delivery and waste product removal.

Although exercise is obviously a great of source of physical and neurological health, not all clients are able to overcome the emotional obstacles in implementing an ongoing exercise routine. For some, psychological stress impedes their ability to engage in physical activity (Stults-Kolehmainen & Sinha, 2014). Therefore, combining a stress management program with an exercise intervention may help to reduce this obstacle and allow more clients to enjoy the multiple benefits of exercise.

Emotional Balance

When stress mounts, the brain's central and peripheral nervous system kicks in to manage the perceived threat. The sympathetic (fight or flight) response becomes activated by the amygdala, the brain's emotional processing center. This engages the hypothalamus, pituitary and adrenal glands (HPA axis) that release the adrenal hormones (epinephrine and norepinephrine), and glucocorticoid hormone (cortisol) to increase energy availability to meet the oncoming threat. Once the threat is resolved, the parasympathetic (rest and digest) response is engaged, releasing acetylcholine to restore baseline functioning. Of course, problems can occur at either end of the process. Some examples of problems associated with chronic sympathetic overactivation include cardiovascular disease, hypertension, digestive disorders, and eventually depression. Examples of problems associated with chronic parasympathetic overactivation include low blood pressure, low heart rate, anxiety, chronic fatigue, and chronic pain (Thompson & Thompson, 2015). Under normal conditions, the parasympathetic response dominates and promotes a physiological state of calm-recovery, with healthy immune system functioning that successfully wards off the effects of disease and heals injury. However, when stress and excessive inflammation with its oxidative stress overwhelm the immune system, the impact of disease, injury, and inflammation can cause significant physiological and neurological damage.

Even mild stress can affect the brain and its cognitive functioning. Arnsten, Mazure, and Sinha (2012) noted that the neural circuits responsible for self-control are "highly vulnerable" to mild stress. The prefrontal cortex, responsible for executive functioning (concentration, planning, decision-making, insight, judgment, and ability to retrieve memories), becomes weakened, and older areas of the brain, such as the hypothalamus (homeostatic regulation), take over, causing paralyzing anxiety or excessive indulgence in food, drink, drugs, or spending. When stressful events increase, a concept described as cumulative adversity, the risk of adverse health outcomes, also increases. This is associated with several neurological changes including stress-induced activity in the lateral prefrontal cortex (behavioral control), insula (emotional control), striatum (executive planning of movement), amygdala (emotional regulation), hippocampus (memory), and temporal lobe (perceptual integration) areas (Seo, Tsou, Ansell, Potenza & Sinha, 2014). In terms of behavioral health, Felitti and Anda (2010) found that four or more adverse childhood experiences can predispose that child to a 390% increased risk for adult pulmonary lung disease, a 240% increased risk for hepatitis, a 460% increased risk for depression, and a 1,220% increased risk for suicide attempt.

In a more recent study, a neurological strategy was identified that promoted "neuroflexibility" and resiliency in the face of stress (Sinha et al., 2016). This involved a change in the response of the ventromedial prefrontal cortex (learned associations between context, location, event, emotional and adaptive responses) that initially showed decreased activation and maladaptive coping, followed by increased activation and active resilient coping. Other adaptive behavioral strategies for stress management and emotional balance that mental health counselors can use with their clients include peripheral skin temperature, heart rate variability, and meditation training. All three teach clients how to self-regulate their physiological and neurological responses.

Peripheral skin temperature training is a biofeedback technique that involves the use of a digital thermometer attached to the finger of the non-dominant hand. When the peripheral skin temperature is low (84 degrees or lower), the client's muscle tension is high and blood flow to the periphery is impeded, lowering the temperature and reflecting a higher state of stress. When the temperature is high (90 degrees and above), muscle tension is minimal and peripheral blood flow is unimpeded, reflecting a state a relaxation (Demos, 2005). Heart rate variability training is another biofeedback technique that uses a plethysmograph (device to monitor blood flow) and slow, diaphragmatic breathing to elicit a parasympathetic response of calm recovery (McCraty, Atkinson, & Tomasino, 2001). Both peripheral skin temperature and heart rate variability training have been found to facilitate alpha brain wave states of calm and focus.

Meditation in its many forms typically involves a quiet environment, comfortable posture, focused attention, and an open reflective attitude. It has been associated with many beneficial outcomes including decreased anxiety, depression, and pain; improved stress and mental health–related quality of life; reduced blood pressure, symptoms of irritable bowel syndrome, flare-ups of ulcerative colitis, and incidence of acute respiratory illness; reduced loneliness; and increased empathy and social connectedness (Goyal et al., 2014). Two recent meta-analyses of magnetic resonance imaging research on meditation (Boccia, Piccardi, & Guariglia, 2015; Fox et al., 2014) found numerous changes in the brain structure including in the rostrolateral prefrontal cortex (meta-awareness, introspection, and complex processing), sensory cortices and the insular cortex (tactile information, conscious proprioception, and body awareness), hippocampus (memory formation and emotional processing), anterior cingulate cortex and midcingulate cortex (attention, self-control, and self-regulation), and the superior longitudinal fasciculus and corpus callosum (network communication pathways within and across the hemispheres of the brain). In addition, it may slow age-related neurological degeneration (Luders, 2013), improve overall immune system functioning, and increase activation of the default mode network (Xu et al., 2014) which is important in attention, retrieval of episodic memory, and emotional processing. Meditation is clearly a valuable therapeutic tool for reflective, internal processing of external life experiences that can promote understanding, problem-solving, and flexibility in response to life's challenging events.

Social Connection

Human beings are social creatures. As mammals, procreation and survival depend on our ability to form social bonds. Evolution from our reptilian ancestry has deeply integrated social attachment mechanisms in our biological and neurological substrates (Porges, 2011). These mechanisms serve to compel and support our friendship, family, work, and community relationships and help us live longer, more satisfying, and happier lives. Robert Sapolsky (2004) in discussing the effects of social support and social isolation on stress and life expectancy noted that people with the fewest social connections have about a 2.5 times greater chance of dying early those with the most social connections. He suggested this may be due to the "psychoneuroimmune route" that begins with socially isolated people experiencing more stress, that stress leading to overactivation of the stress response, which then causes immune suppression, and results in more debilitating consequences from infectious disease. Still other research that followed 1,000 older, community-dwelling people without dementia but who reported "feeling alone" and "being alone" found more rapid (40%) motor decline and a 50% a year increase in risk of death (Buchman et al., 2010). The authors concluded that with the pain of loneliness and isolation may come increasing disinterest in physical interaction, mobility, exercise, and healthy eating, leading to hastened death.

Lieberman (2013) in his work on social connections explained why our brains are wired to connect and used functional magnetic resonance imaging (fMRI) research to demonstrate the neural mechanisms of social connection involving the dorsal anterior cingulate cortex (rapid reward-based decision-making), anterior insula (self-awareness and interpersonal experience), and somatosensory cortex (reception and interpretation of sensory information). He also referenced earlier work (Kross, Berman, Mischel, Smith, & Wager, 2011) noting that social rejection shares the same neural circuitry as pain and suggested this may explain why social rejection is so painful. Lieberman (2013) further illustrated the implications of these findings, noting research that found Tylenol reduces the brain's response to social pain, individuals who were rejected scored 15% lower on intelligence tests, employees recognized for high praise were willing to give up almost $30,000 in yearly pay, and employees who saw how their work was helping others had twice the productivity as those who did not. Clearly, social connection is a highly motivating factor in human interaction and its absence or loss painful (Lieberman & Eisenberer, 2009) and even injurious to health and behavior.

Writing about the "social engagement system," Porges (2011) described the importance of *interoception* as the ongoing neurological and interpersonal process of monitoring and evaluating interpersonal safety. He proposed that the primary mechanisms involved in safety included calm prosodic speech, soft facial expression, and inviting social gaze. Critical or angry vocal tone, tense facial musculature, and avoidance of eye contact signal danger that activates the fight or flight response and in cases of extreme threat a dissociative or freeze response. Most mental health counselors are familiar with the facilitative effects of positive attending and empathy, as well as the debilitative effects of interpersonal conflict, verbal and physical abuse, and trauma. Healthy social connection creates a sense of safety, positive attachment, and interpersonal recognition.

Lifelong Cognitive Challenge

As previously noted in this chapter, an enriched environment with ample opportunity for cognitive challenge is an established strategy for enhancing neuroplasticity (Verghese et al., 2003). The quality of the cognitive challenge matters, and reading, playing board games and musical instruments, and dancing were all associated with a reduced risk of dementia. The sooner one engages in cognitive challenge the better. A study on the effects of lifelong bilingualism found a significant delay (4.3 years) in the onset of dementia and its symptoms (5.1 years) as compared to a group of lifelong monolingual patients (Craik, Bialystok, & Freedman, 2010). Another study found a group of older healthy adults with at least 10 years of musical experience had better performance in nonverbal memory, naming, and executive processing skills, as compared to nonmusicians (Hanna-Pladdy & McKay, 2011). The study found a strong predictive effect of high musical activity throughout the life span on preserved cognitive functioning in advanced age. In addition, a more recent investigation (McDonough, Haber, Bischof, & Park, 2015) found that other mentally challenging activities that required new learning and sustained mental effort, such as quilting and digital photography, also helped maintain cognitive vitality. This functional magnetic resonance imaging (fMRI) study found increased activity in the medial frontal, lateral temporal, and parietal cortex, associated with attention and semantic processing, in those who engaged in such challenging activities. Other tasks such as socializing, activities such as travel and cooking with no learning component, listening to music, playing simple games, or watching classic movies did not result in these changes.

Early research on the effects of cognitive challenge on cognitive functioning was done with mice bred to develop Alzheimer's dementia (Cracchiolo et al., 2007). This work found a complete enrichment environment (with social, physical, and novel play) was superior to impoverished, social, and even social and physically challenging environments in protecting the mice from cognitive impairment, increased brain beta-amyloid deposits, and increased hippocampal immunoreactivity (inflammation). An explanation for the neurological benefit of cognitive challenge has been proposed in the concepts of "cognitive reserve and metabolic reserve" (Stranahan & Mattson, 2012). Cognitive reserve is the brain's ability to compensate for neuropathology by more effective engagement or recruitment of the healthy neurons. Metabolic reserve focuses instead on the neuronal circuits and suggests stronger cellular and somatic energy metabolism that better potentiates the functioning of the neuron itself. In other words, critical behavioral factors such as exercise, reduced caloric intake, and type of diet may offer neuroprotective benefits that preserve cognitive function. For mental health counselors the conclusion is clear. Lifelong cognitive challenge is neuroprotective and helps to mitigate the onset and degree of mild cognitive impairment and Alzheimer's dementia.

CASE ILLUSTRATION 12.3

Mia, a 65-year-old South Korean woman who immigrated to the United States in her late 30s, is experiencing symptoms of forgetfulness and memory loss. She is having difficulty performing familiar tasks and finding the right words and does not seem to always be oriented to time and place. During her intake interview, Mia reports that she spent most of her childhood and early adult life working in the rice fields and helping her family with farming in South Korea. Education was never a priority for her or her family. She further states that her family was not wealthy, so additional resources for education were not available. Mia's earlier life environment provided ample opportunity for physical and some social challenge but very little cognitive challenge. It wasn't until her older adult life that Mia began taking an interest in learning. Although she is socially engaged with friends and enjoys cooking and watching television, those activities offer little cognitive challenge. Mia's cognitive decline may be best explained by the limited cognitive challenge her environment provided early on in life. Mia's neurons never built associations with other neurons, and as a result, her brain now lacks the plasticity needed to circumvent the cognitive impairments she is currently experiencing. Remember the concept of Hebb's law discussed earlier. In Mia's case, the lack of plasticity in her neurons equates to the "use it or lose it" principle.

Meaning and Purpose in Life

The search for meaning and purpose in life has a long history that has evolved from the original work on self-actualization (self-fulfillment through personal growth) by Abraham Maslow (1943) and man's search for meaning (motivational striving) by Victor Frankl (2006) to its more modern form in today's positive psychology movement, represented by work on creative flow (complete mental immersion in an activity) by Mihaly Csikszentmihalyi (1990), authentic happiness (reaching one's potential for lasting fulfillment) by Martin Seligman (2002), and hardiness (applying control, commitment, and challenge to life purpose) by Salvatore Maddi (2004). These writers emphasized human motivation based on a deep drive toward self-fulfillment, but how do mental health counselors help their clients find purpose in life?

Patrick McKnight (McKnight & Kashdan, 2009) described life purpose as a central, self-organizing aim that becomes a predominant theme of identity, provides a framework for systematic patterns in daily life, and harnesses resources directed toward meaningful goals. He further suggested that acceptance and mindfulness-based cognitive-behavioral interventions may provide clarification and commitment to life purpose. To test this out he studied people diagnosed with social anxiety disorder (SAD) and compared their reports on measures of life purpose, effort and progress on life purpose, and ratings of well-being with a healthy control group (Kashdan & McKnight, 2013). He found that people with SAD reported significant boosts in well-being on the days characterized by strong effort or progress toward their life purpose. He concluded that commitment to a purpose can enrich the lives of people with SAD. However, is a meaningful life a happy life?

In a summary of research on the key differences between a happy and meaningful life, Baumeister, Vohs, Aaker, and Garninsky (2013) concluded that happy people tend to satisfy their wants and needs for health, wealth, and ease in life, but this did not create a sense of meaning. Happiness was more present oriented and fleeting, whereas meaningfulness involved integration of the past, present, and future and was longer lasting. Happiness seemed to involve good social connections but was more focused on what people gave to you (taking), whereas meaningfulness came more from what you gave to others (giving). Meaningfulness was also more stressful, challenging, and self-expressive than happiness. Overall the authors found that being happy and finding meaning in life overlapped, but meaningfulness seemed to involve a deeper and more altruistic motivation. When happiness comes from meaningfulness, people have stronger immune system functioning, less reactivity to stress, less chance of developing diabetes, better cholesterol levels, better sleep, and decreased depression.

In a more detailed summary of research on the health benefits of having a purpose-driven life, Kaplin and Anzaldi (2015) noted a 50% decreased risk of developing Alzheimer's disease, slower rate of age-related cognitive impairment, and better cognitive function even with significant deposits of beta amyloid plaque in the brain. They also found a reduced risk for stroke (22% less risk for each standard deviation increase in purpose in life), lower risk of heart attack (27% less risk of a heart attack within 2 years for each 1 point improvement on a 6-point scale of purpose in life), and a reduced risk of death (72% less risk of death from stroke, 44% less risk from cardiovascular disease, and 48% less risk from any cause). They further noted that persons with a higher purpose in life also had less neurological inflammation associated with neurodegenerative disease. They had a less than expected impact from psychosocial stress than persons with low life purpose and more "chronic calming," likely reflecting a more optimally functioning immune system. Finally, they noted that people with high life purpose had less depression and a stronger self-concept. Somewhat surprising was their conclusion that purpose in life and religion were independent phenomena and not related.

In a review of research on religion, Azar (2010) found that religion, rather than being a path to purpose in life, may be instead a social manifestation of how the brain works. More specifically she noted that the brain wants to see patterns, find meaning, and attribute control to a higher authority, especially in times of uncertainty and strife. She also noted that the counterintuitive (turn the other cheek) or supernatural elements (the angel came down from heaven) often presented in religious stories makes them more memorable, and the sense of social community and safety that comes from shared virtues, rules of conduct, rituals, and sense of affiliation protects us from the "different other." She also noted research (Kapogiannis et al., 2009) that has essentially rejected the notion of the "God spot" in the brain and replaced it with the "theory of mind" concept that better explains the neurological activation involved in the deciphering of others' emotions and intentions, whether they be God, parents, or some other authority. None of these findings should be construed to say there are no neurological, health, or social benefits from religion. There are indeed many. These include security in the midst of larger groups, greater activation of attentional centers, less self-focus, increased calmness, less depression and anxiety, greater longevity, less alcohol and drug use, greater health care use, and increased prosocial and charitable behavior.

So if religion may not provide a path to greater purpose and meaning, what does? Mihaly Csikszentmihalyi (1990) explained the concept of flow in his work on the psychology of optimal experience and described flow as a mental state of being completely immersed in an activity that provides a genuine sense of satisfaction. Steven Kotler (2014) applied the concept of flow to creativity and the development of life purpose. He defined flow as an optimal state of consciousness with laser focus and heightened, creative performance. He explained how flow states can be induced artificially with transcranial magnetic stimulation and cited research indicating that flow states do not just heighten creativity in the moment but also train the brain to be more creative beyond the moment. He also described three neurological changes associated with flow states. These included a change from fast beta waves (active problem-solving) to slower alpha-theta waves (calm, imaginative focus); an increase in transient hypofrontality (deactivation of the prefrontal cortex) that quiets the higher executive functions and sense of self; and a release of various neurotransmitters (synaptic chemical messengers) that creates a sense of pleasure, imaginative reflection, quiet focus, pattern recognition, and lateral thinking. This results in effortless information processing that quiets the higher cognitive function of the frontal and medial temporal lobes and activates the skill-based knowledge supported by the basal ganglia (Dietrich, 2004).

Kotler (2014) outlined 17 triggers of flow organized in four categories: psychological (internal strategies that drive attention into the now), environmental (novel qualities in the environment that drive people deeper into the zone), social (interpersonal conditions and communication style that produces more group interaction), and creativity (effort at pattern recognition and risk taking). Creative flow can be triggered across a variety of activities including problem-solving, athletic performance, writing, creative arts, professional skills, learning, and business.

WORKING WITH CLIENTS TO DEVELOP AN EFFECTIVE WELLNESS PLAN: AN OVERVIEW

Although counselors have been approaching counseling from a wellness and holistic perspective for many years, the integration of neurocounseling is a relatively new approach to wellness. There are seven major steps to creating an effective neurocounseling wellness plan.

1. Obtain a thorough psychosocial and neurological history including birth weight, Apgar scores, and birthing history. Be sure to assess attention capacity and cognitive efficiency levels. Ask about concussions and brain traumas. The use of customized inventories may be necessary and important to the success of each counseling treatment from self-report inventories to standardized personality instruments to quantitative EEG assessments. Also take baseline measurements of breathing patterns, skin temperature, and heart rate variability to offer unique and quantifiable measurements to the treatment plan.

2. Use a positive asset search (Ivey et al., 2014) to gain valuable available resources for clients.

3. Create a wellness plan that includes emotional, behavioral, and physiological self-regulation strategies. Use the wellness lifestyle strategies discussed earlier for goal direction.

4. Develop counseling goals that are measurable and achievable.

5. Keep a journal of the progress through symptoms checklists and client and counselor notes.

6. Every third or fifth session, share the results of the journals and checklists.

7. Evaluate and reassess counseling goals.

Keystones

- It has long been held that the brain and its number of neurons were largely fixed by adulthood and these neurons could not be replaced or regenerated when they died. Even before this, there was a strong scientific bias toward what was called localizationism and lateralization; however, more current research in neuroplasticity suggests brain function is not necessarily limited to certain prescribed locations or even hemispheres of the brain.

- Neuroplasticity is the processes by which the brain is remodeled in response to both internal metabolic conditions and external environmental factors. At the neuronal level, neuroplasticity involves changes to the neuronal structure that include axonal sprouting and dendritic remodeling to strengthen or increase synaptic connections or dendritic shrinking or retraction and pruning of axons that weaken or decrease synaptic connections.

- Neuronal pruning, the natural process of removing unnecessary or degraded synapses, is essential to healthy brain development and functioning. People are born with many more neurons than they need, and in early childhood many of these are pruned away. Glia cells within our

spinal fluid perform a sort of neurological house cleaning, destroying toxins and clearing away the debris from obsolete connections no longer of use. This allows the brain to more efficiently use its vital resources of oxygen, blood flow, and nutrients to better serve its healthy and necessary neuronal needs.

- Strategies to increase neuroplasticity and neurogenesis include exercise, enriched environments, learning, attention, mental practice, massive physical practice, medication, transcranial stimulation, neurofeedback, meditation, and talk therapy.

- Implications for mental health counselors concerning neuroplasticity include (a) neuroplasticity can work both for and against a client; (b) the brain is capable of incredible change across the full life span, but it is not easy; (c) certain conditions make neuroplastic change more likely; (d) learning is an associative process and involves incremental and progressive change across neural pathways; (e) early change is fragile and fleeting if not followed up with massive practice, refinement, and significantly experienced positive emotional states; (f) mental rehearsal is as useful for meaningful neurological change as actual external, physical experience; and (g) talk therapy is brain therapy.

- The neurological basis of wellness includes a healthy lifestyle (sleep, diet, and exercise), emotional balance (stress management and meditation), social connection (interpersonal relationships and the social engagement system), lifelong cognitive challenge, and meaning and purpose in life.

- There are seven major steps to creating an effective neurocounseling wellness plan.

Step 1: Obtain a thorough psychosocial/neurological history. Step 2: Use a positive asset search to gain valuable available resources for clients. Step 3: Create a wellness plan that includes emotional, behavioral, and physiological self-regulation strategies. Step 4: Develop counseling goals that are measurable and achievable. Step 5: Keep a journal of the progress through symptoms checklists and client and counselor notes. Step 6: Every third or fifth session, share the results of the journals and checklists. Step 7: Evaluate and reassess counseling goals.

Key Terms

Lateralization 306

Localizationism 306

Neural stem cells 308

Neurogenesis 307

Neuronal pruning 307

Neuroplasticity 307

Web Resources

Biofeedback Certification International Alliance (www.bcia.org/i4a/pages/index.cfm?pageid=1)

Counseling Today: Counseling and Neuroscience: The Cutting Edge of the Coming Decade (https://ct.counseling.org/2009/12/reader-viewpoint-counseling-and-neuroscience-the-cutting-edge-of-the-coming-decade)

Neurocounseling Interest Network (www.neurocounselinginterestnetwork.com)

Neuroplasticity: The 10 Fundamentals of Rewiring Your Brain (http://reset.me/story/neuroplasticity-the-10-fundamentals-of-rewiring-your-brain)

Neuroplasticity: You Can Teach an Old Brain New Tricks (https://bigthink.com/think-tank/brain-exercise)

Neuroscience: A Collection of TED Talks on the Topic of Neuroscience (www.ted.com/topics/neuroscience)

Neuroscience and Counseling (www.neuropsychotherapist.com/neuroscience-and-counselling)

Psychology Today: Neurofeedback: A Remarkable Counseling Tool (www.psychologytoday.com/us/blog/brain-waves/201608/neurofeedback-remarkable-counseling-tool)

Society for Neuroscience (www.sfn.org)

References

Abel, T., Havekes, R., Saletin, J., & Walker, M. (2013). Sleep, plasticity, and memory form molecules to whole-brain networks. *Current Biology*, *23*(17), 774–788.

Alderman, B. L., Olson, R. L. Brush, C. J., & Shors, T. J. (2016). MAP training: Combining meditation and aerobic exercise reduces depression and rumination while enhancing synchronized brain activity. *Translational Psychiatry*, *6*, 726.

Amen, D. (2001). *Healing ADD*. New York, NY: Putnam.

Aranow, C. (2011). Vitamin D and the immune system. *Journal of Investigative Medicine*, *59*(6), 881–886.

Ardell, D. (1976). High level wellness: An alternative to doctors, drugs, and disease. Emmaus, PA: Rodale.

Arnsten, A., Mazure, C., & Sinha, R. (2012). Neural circuits responsible for conscious self-control are highly vulnerable to even mild stress. When they shut down, primal impulses go unchecked and mental paralysis sets in. *Scientific American*, *306*(4), 48–53.

Azar, B. (2010). A reason to believe. *Monitor on Psychology*, *41*(11), 52.

Balch, P. (2010). *Prescription for nutritional healing*. New York, NY: Avery.

Baumeister, R., Vohs, K., Aaker, J., & Garbinsky, E. (2013). Some key differences between a happy life and a meaningful life. *Journal of Positive Psychology*, *8*(6), 505–516.

Becker, C., Moore, J., Whetstone, L., Glascoff, M., Chaney, E., Felts, M., & Anderson, L. (2009). Validity evidence for the salutogenic wellness promotion scale (SWPS). *American Journal of Health Behavior*, *33*(4), 455–465.

Bennett, M. R. (2011). The pre-frontal-limbic network in depression: A core pathology of synapse regression. *Progress in Neurobiology*, *93*, 457–467.

Blumenthal, J., Babyak, M., Moore, K., Craighead, W., Herman, S., Khatri, P., & Ranga Krishnan, K. (1999). Effects of exercise training on older adults with major depression. *Archives of Internal Medicine*, *19*(159), 2349–2356.

Boccia, M., Piccardi, L., & Guarigilia, P. (2015). The meditative mind: A comprehensive meta-analysis of MRI studies. *BioMed Research International*. doi:10.1155/2015/419808

Bremner, J. D., Elzinga, B., Schmahl, C., & Vermetten, E. (2008). Structural and functional plasticity of the human brain in posttraumatic stress disorder. *Progress in Brain Research*, *167*, 171–186.

Broca, P. P. (1861). Loss of speech, chronic softening and partial destruction of the anterior left lobe. *Bullitn de la Societs Anthropologique*, *2*, 235–238. Transcribed by C. D. Green, 2003.

Buchman, A., Boyle, P., Wilson, R., James, B., Leurgans, S., Arnold, S., & Bennett, D. (2010). Loneliness and the rate of motor decline in old age: The rush memory and aging project, a community cohort-based study. *BioMed Central Geriatrics*, *10*, 77.

Cajal, S. R. (1904). Textura del sistema nervioso del hombre y de los seretebrados. In R. Zatorre & I. Peretz (Eds.), *The biological foundations of music* (pp. 315–329). New York, NY: Annals of New York Academy of Sciences.

Cajal, S. R. (1913–1914). *Degeneration and regeneration of the nervous system* (R. M. May, Trans.). London, England: Oxford University Press.

Chapin, T. J. (2016). The lifestyle assessment inventory. In L. Russell-Chapin, N. Sherman, & A. Ivey (Eds.), *Your supervised practicum and internship: Field resources for turning theory into practice*. New York, NY: Routledge.

Chapin, T. J., & Russell-Chapin, L. (2014). Neurotherapy and neurofeedback: Brain-based treatment for psychological and behavioral problems. New York, NY: Routledge.

Chen, P., Kuo, H., & Chueh, K. (2010). Sleep hygiene education: Efficacy on sleep quality in working women. *Journal of Nursing Research*, *18*(4), 282–289.

Conel, J. L. (1939). The postnatal development of the human cerebral cortex (Vols. *1–6*). Cambridge, MA: Harvard University Press.

Cracchiolo, J., Mori, T., Naxian, S., Tan, J., Potter, H., & Arendash, G. (2007). Enhanced cognitive over-activity and above social or physical activity is required to protect Alzheimer's mice against cognitive impairment, reduce Abeta deposition, and increase synaptic immunoreactivity. *Neurobiology of Learning and Memory*, *88*(3), 277–294.

Craik, F., Bialystok, E., & Freedman, M. (2010). Delaying the onset of Alzheimer's disease: Bilingualism as a form of cognitive reserve. *Neurology*, *75*(19), 1726–1729.

Cramer, S. C., Sur, M., Dobkin, B. H., O'Brien, C., Sanger, T. D., Trojanowski, J. Q. . . . Vinogradov, S. (2011). Harnessing neuroplasticity for clinical applications. *Brain*, *134*(6), 1591–1609. doi:1093/brain/awr039

Csikszentmihalyi, M. (1990). *Flow: The psychology of optimal experience*. New York, NY: Harper and Row.

Danilov, Y., Kaczmarek, K., Skinner, K., & Tyler, M. (2015). Cranial nerve noninvasive neuromodulation: New approach to neurorehabilitation. In F. H. Kobeissey (Ed.), *Brain neurotrauma: Molecular, neurophysiology and rehabilitation aspects* (Ch. 44). Boca Raton, FL: CRC Press/Taylor and Francis.

Davidson, R., & Lutz, A. (2008). Buddha's brain: Neuroplasticity and meditation. *Signal Processing Magazine*, *25*(1), 174–176.

Deans, E. (2016). Microbiome and mental health in the modern environment. *Journal of Physiological Anthropology*, *36*(1), 1.

Demos, J. (2005). *Getting started with neurofeedback*. New York, NY: Norton.

Dietrich, A. (2004). Neurocognitive mechanisms underlying the experience of flow. *Conscious Cognition*, *13*(4), 746–761.

Doidge, N. (2007). *The brain that changes itself*. New York, NY: Penguin Group.

Doidge, N. (2016). *The brain's way of healing*. New York, NY: Penguin Group.

Dunn, H. (1961). *High level wellness*. Arlington, VA: Beatty.

Engen, H. G., & Singer, T. (2013). Empathy circuits. *Current Opinion in Neurobiology*, *23*, 275–282. doi:10.1016/j.conb.2012.11.003

Erickson, K., Leckie, R., & Weinstein, A. (2014). Physical activity, fitness and gray matter volume. *Neurobiology of Aging*, *35*, 520–528.

Erickson, K., Voss, M., Prakash, R., Basak, C., Szabo, A., Chaddock, L. . . . Kramer, A. (2011). Exercise training increases size of hippocampus and improves memory. *Proceedings of the National Academy of Sciences*, *108*(7), 3017–3022.

Fan, Y., Duncan, N., de Greck, M., & Northoff, G. (2011). Is there a core neural network in empathy? An fMRI based quantitative meta-analysis. *Neuroscience and Biobehavioral Reviews*, *35*, 903–911.

Felitti, V. J., & Anda, R. F. (2010). The relationship of adverse childhood experiences to adult health, well-being, social function and healthcare. In R. Lanius, E. Vermetten, & C. Pain (Eds.), *The impact of early life trauma on health and disease: The hidden epidemic* (pp. 77–87). New York, NY: Cambridge University Press.

Fox, K. C., Nijeboer, S., Dixon, M. L., Floman, J. L., Ellamil, M., Rumak, S. P., Sedlmeier, P., & Christoff, K. (2014). Is meditation associated with altered brain structure? A systematic review and meta-analysis of morphometric neuroimaging in meditation practitioners. *Neuroscience Biobehavior Review*, *43*, 48–73.

Frankl, V. (2006). *Man's search for meaning*. Boston, MA: Beacon Press.

Ghosh, S., Benerjee, S., & Sil, P. (2015). The beneficial role of curcumin on inflammation, diabetes and neurogenerative disease: A recent update. *Food Chemical Toxicology, 83*, 111–124.

Goyal, M., Singh, S., Snlings, E., Gould, N., Rowland-Seymour, A., Sharma, R. . . . Haythornthwaite, J. (2014). Meditation programs for psychological stress and well-being: A systematic review and meta-analysis. *Journal of American Medical Association, 174*(3), 357–386.

Grand, D. (2013). Brainspotting: The revolutionary new therapy for rapid and effective change. Boulder, CO: Sounds True.

Hanna-Pladdy, B., & MacKay, A. (2011). The relation between instrumental musical activity and cognitive aging. *Neuropsychology, 25*(3), 378–386.

Hanson, R, (2013). Hardwiring happiness: The new brain science of contentment, calm and confidence. New York, NY: Penguin/Random House.

Hebb, D. O. (1949). *The organization of behavior.* New York, NY: Wiley.

Hettler, B. (1984). Wellness: encouraging a lifetime of pursuit of excellence. *Health Values, 8*(4), 13–17.

Hill, R., & Castro, E. (2009). *Healing young brain.* Charlottesville, VA: Hampton Roads.

Hirshkowitz, M., Whiton, K., Albert, S., Alessi, C., Bruni, O., DonCarlos, L. . . . Catesby Ware, J. (2015). National Sleep Foundation's updated sleep duration recommendations: Final report. *Sleep Health, 1*(4), 233–243.

Ivey, A. E., Ivey, M. B., & Zalaquett, C. (2014). Intentional interviewing and counseling: Facilitating client development in a multicultural society. Belmont, CA: Brooks/Cole.

Ivey, A. E., Ivey, M. B., & Zalaquett, C. (2016). The neuroscience of listening, empathy, and microskills. *Counseling Today, 59*(2), 18–21. Alexandria, VA: American Counseling Association.

Jackson, P. A., Pialoux, V., Corbett, D., Drogos, L., Erickson, K. I., Eskes, G. A., & Poulin, M. J. (2016).

Promoting brain health through exercise and diet in older adults: A physiological perspective. *Journal of Physiology, 594*(15), 4485–4498.

James, W. (1890). *Principles of psychology*: Vol 1. New York, NY: Henry Holt.

Kandel, E. (2003). The molecular biology of memory storage: A dialogue between genes and synapses. In H. Jornvall (Ed.), *Nobel lectures, physiology or medicine, 1996–2000.* Singapore: World Scientific.

Kandel, E. (2006). In search of memory: The emergence of a new science of mind. New York, NY: W. W. Norton.

Kandel, E., Schwartz, J., & Jessel, T. (2000). *Principles of neural science* (4th ed.). New York, NY: McGraw-Hill.

Kaplin, A., & Anzaldi, L. (2015). New movement in neuroscience: A purpose-driven life. *Cerebrum, 7.*

Kapogiannis, D., Barbey, A., Su, M., Zamboni, G., Kruger, F., Grafman, J., & Raichle, M. (2009). Cognitive and neural foundations of religious belief. *Proceedings of the National Academy of Sciences, 106*(12), 4876–4881.

Kashdan, T., & McKnight, P. (2013). Commitment to a purpose in life: An antidote to the suffering by individuals with social anxiety disorder. *Emotion, 13*(6), 1150–1159.

Kawamichi, H., Yoshihara, K., Sasaki, A. T., Sugawara, S. K., Tanabe, H. C., Shinohara R. . . . Sadato, N. (2015). Perceiving active listening activates the reward system and improves the impression of relevant experiences. *Social Neuroscience, 10*(1), 16–26. doi:10.1080/17470919.2014.954732

Kay, J., Hurley, R., & Taber, K. (2012). The dynamic brain: Neuroplasticity and mental health. *Journal of Psychiatry and Clinical Neuroscience, 24*(2), 119–121.

Kempermann, D., Gast, D., & Gage, F. (2002). Neuroplasticity in old age: Sustained fivefold induction of hippocampal neurogenesis by long-term environmental enrichment. *Annals of Neurology, 52*, 135–143.

Kilgard, M., & Merzenich, M. (1998). Cortical map reorganization enabled nucleus basalis activity. *Science*, *279*, 1714–1718.

Kirsch, D. L., & Nichols, F. (2013). Cranial electrotherapy stimulation for treatment of anxiety, depression and insomnia. *Psychiatric Clinics of North America*, *36*,169–176.

Konorski, J. (1948). *Conditioned reflexes and neuron organisation*. New York, NY: Cambridge University Press.

Kotler, S. (2014). *The rise of Superman*. New York, NY: Houghton Mifflin Harcourt.

Kross, E., Berman, M., Mischel, W., Smith, E., & Wager, T. (2011). Social rejection shares somatosensory representation with physical pain. *Proceedings of the National Academy of Sciences*, *108*(15), 6270–6275.

Lazar, S., Kerr, C., Wasserman, R., Gray, J., Greve, D., Tradway, M. T. … Fischi, B. (2005). Meditation experience is associated with increased cortical thickness. *NeuroReport*, *16*(17), 1893–1897.

Lieberman, M. (2013). Social connection: Why our brains are wired to connect. New York, NY: Crown.

Lieberman, M., & Eisenberger, N. (2009). Neuroscience pain and pleasure of social life. *Science*, *323*(5916), 890–891.

Luders, E. (2013). Exploring age-related brain degeneration in meditation practitioners. *Annals of the New York Academy of Science*, *1307*, 62–72.

Luders, E., Toga, A. W., Lepore, N., & Gaser, C. (2008). The underlying anatomical correlates of long-term meditation: Larger hippocampal and frontal volumes of gray matter. *NeuroImage*, *45*(3), 672–678.

Lutz, A., Greischler, L. L., Rawlings, N. B., Ricard, M., & Davidson, R. J. (2004). Long-term meditators, self-induced high amplitude gamma synchrony during mental practice. *Proceedings of National Academy of Sciences*, *101*(46), 16369–16373.

Maddi, S. (2004). Hardiness: An operationalization of existential change. *Journal of Humanistic Psychology*, *44*(3), 279–298.

Martinotti, G., Ricci, V., Di Nicola, M., Caltagironi, C., Bria, P., & Angelucci, F. (2011). Brain derived neurotropic factor and electroconvulsive therapy in a schizophrenic patient with treatment-resistant paranoid-hallucinatory symptoms. *Journal of Electroconvulsive Therapy*, *27*, 44–46.

Maslow, A. (1943). A theory of human motivation. *Psychological Review*, *50*(4), 370–396.

McCraty, R., Atkinson, M., & Tomasino, D. (2001). *Science of heartmath: Exploring the role of the heart in human performance*. Boulder Creek, CO: Institute of HeartMath.

McDonough, I., Haber, S., Bischof, G., & Park, D. (2015). The synapse project: Engagement in mentally challenging activities enhances neural efficiency. *Restorative Neurology and Neuroscience*, *33*(6), 865.

McKnight, P., & Kashdan, T. (2009). Purpose in life as a system that creates and sustains health and well-being: An integrative, testable theory. *Review of General Psychology*, *13*, 242–251.

Merzenich, M. (2013). Soft-wired: How the new science of brain plasticity can change your life. San Francisco, CA: Parnassus.

Merzenich, M., Nelson, R., Stryker, M., Cynader, M., Scheppmann, A., & Zook, J. (1984). Somatosensory cortical map changes following digit amputation in adult monkeys. *Journal of Comparative Neurology*, *224*(4), 591–605.

Malykhin, N. V., Carter, R., Seres, P., & Coupland, N. J. (2010). Structural changes in the hippocampus in major depressive disorder: Contributions of disease and treatment. *Journal of Psychiatry and Neuroscience*, *35*, 337–343.

Molteni, R., Barnard, R., Ying, Z., Roberts, C., & Gomez-Pinilla, F. (2002). A high-fat, refined sugar diet reduces hippocampal brain derived neurotropic factor, neuronal plasticity and learning. *Neuroscience*, *112*(4), 803–814.

Myers, J. E., & Young, J. S. (2012). Brain wave biofeedback: Benefits of integrating neurofeedback in counseling. *Journal of Counseling and Development*, *90*(1), 20–28.

Nordanskog, P., Dahlstrand, R., Larsson, M. R., Larsson, E. M., Knutsson, L., & Johanson, A. (2010). Increase in hippocampal volume after electroconvulsive therapy in patients with depression: A volumetric magnetic resonance imagery study. *Journal of Electroconvulsive Therapy*, *26*, 62–67.

O'Connor, P., Herring, M., & Carvalho, A. (2010). Mental health benefits of strength training in adults. *American Journal of Lifestyle Medicine*, *4*(5), 377–396.

Oomen, C. A., Mayer, J. L., De Kloet, E. R. Jous, M., & Lucassen, P. L. (2007). Brief treatment with the glucocorticoid receptor antagonist mifepristone normalizes the reduction in neurogenesis after chronic stress. *European Journal of Neuroscience*, *25*(12), 3395–3401.

Pascual-Leone, A., Amedi, A., Fregni, F., & Merabet, L. B. (2005). The plastic brain cortex. *Annual Review of Neuroscience*, *28*, 377–401.

Pascual-Leone, A., Nguyet, D., Cohen, L., Brasil-Neto, J., Cammarota, A., & Hallet, M. (1995). Modulation of muscle responses evoked by transcranial magnetic stimulation during the acquisition of new fine motor skills. *Journal of Neurophysiology*, *74*(3), 1035–1037.

Porges, S. (2011). The polyvagal theory: Neurological foundations of emotions, attachment, communication and self-regulation. New York, NY: Norton.

Ratey, J. (2008). Spark: The revolutionary new science of exercise and the brain. New York, NY: Little Brown.

Sapolsky, R. (2004). *Why zebras don't get ulcers*. New York, NY: Holt.

Sawada, M., & Sawamoto, K. (2013). Mechanisms of neurogenesis in the normal and injured adult brain. *Journal of Medicine*, *62*, 13–28.

Schwartz, J., & Beyette, B. (1996). *Brain lock: Free yourself from obsessive and compulsive behavior*. New York, NY: Regan Books/Harper Collins.

Seligman, M. (2002). Authentic happiness: Using the new positive psychology to realize your potential for lasting fulfillment. New York, NY: Free Press.

Seo, D., Tsou, K., Ansell, E., Potenza, M., & Sinha, R. (2014). Cumulative adversity sensitizes neural response to acute stress: Association with health problems. *Neuropsychopharmacology*, *39*(3), 670–680.

Sinha, R., Lacadie, C., Constable, R. T., & Seo, D. (2016). Dynamic neuronal activity during stress signals resilient coping. *Proceedings of the National Academy of Sciences*, *113*(31), 8837–8842.

Stanhope, K., Swarz, J., & Havel, P. (2013). Adverse metabolic effects of dietary fructose: Results from the recent epidemiological, clinical and mechanistic studies. *Current Opinions in Lipidology*, *24*, 14–21.

Staubo, S. C., Aakre, J. A., Vemuri, P., Syrjanen, J. A., Mielke, M. M., Geda, Y. E. ... Roberts, R. O. (2017). Mediterranean diet, micronutrients and macronutrients, and MRI measure of cortical thickness. *Alzheimer's Dementia*, *13*(2), 168–177.

Stranahan, A., & Mattson, M. (2012). Metabolic reserve as a determinant of cognitive aging. *Journal of Alzheimer's Disease*, *30*(2), 5–13.

Stultz-Kolehmainen, M. A., & Sinha, R. (2014). The effects of stress on physical activity and exercise. *Sports Medicine*, *44*(1), 81–121.

Swingle, M. K. (2015). I-mind: How cell phones, computers, gaming, and social media are changing our brains, our behavior, and the evolution of our species. Portland, OR: Inkwater Press.

Taub, E. (1980). Somatosensory deafferentation research with monkeys: Implications for rehabilitation medicine. In L. P. Ince (Ed.), *Behavioral psychology in rehabilitation medicine: Clinical applications* (pp. 371–401). Baltimore, MD: Williams & Wilkins.

Thompson, M., & Thompson, L. (2015). *The neurofeedback book: An introduction to basic concepts in applied psychophysiology* (2nd ed). Wheat Ridge, CO: Association for Applied Psychophysiology.

Tietzel, A. J., & Lack, L. C. (2002). The recuperative value of brief and ultra-brief naps on alertness and cognitive performance. *Journal of Sleep Research*, *11*(3), 213–218.

Travis, J., & Ryan, R. (2004). The wellness workbook: How to achieve enduring health and vitality (3rd ed.). New York, NY: Ten Speed.

Verghese, J., Lipton, M., Katz, C., Hall, C., Derby, G., Kuslansky, A. . . . Buschke, H. (2003). Leisure activities and risk of dementia in the elderly. *New England Journal of Medicine*, *348*(25), 2508–2516.

Vestergaard-Poulsenm P., van Beck, M., Skewes, J., Bjarkam, J., Carsten, R., Stubberup, M. . . . Roepstorff, A. (2009). Long-term mediation is associated with increased gray matter density in the brain stem. *NeuroReport*, *20*(2), 170–174.

Xie, L., Kang, H., XX, Q., Chen, M., Liao, Y., Thiyagarajan, M. . . . Nedergaard, M. (2013). Sleep drives metabolite clearance from adult brain. *Science*, *342*, 373–377.

Xu, J., Vik, A., Groote, I., Lapopoulos, J., Holen, A., Ellingsen, O., Haberg, A., & Davenger, S. (2014). Nondirective meditation activates default mode network and areas associated with memory retrieval and emotional processing. *Frontiers in Neuroscience*, *8*, 86.

Young, O., & Johnston, K. (2016). *The future of wellness*. Miami, FL: Global Wellness Institute.

TRAUMATOLOGY, BEREAVEMENT, AND CRISIS INTERVENTION

By Karisse A. Callender, Samantha Klassen-Bolding, and Erika L. Schmit

Trauma, bereavement, and crisis intervention are three specific and important aspects of clinical mental health counseling. According to the Substance Abuse and Mental Health Services Administration (SAMHSA; 2015), trauma is extensive in the United States and can have a lasting effect on individuals, families, and communities. In fact, trauma is the leading cause of death for individuals ages 1 to 46 (Rhee et al., 2014) and the third leading cause of death across other age groups (National Center for Injury Prevention and Control, 2016). Copeland, Keeler, Angold, and Costello (2007) estimate that two thirds of children experience at least one traumatic event by the age of 16. Similarly, in a well-known earlier study on adverse childhood experiences (ACEs) Felitti et al. (1998) identified that 28% of minor participants experienced physical abuse, and 21% experienced sexual abuse. In addition, the majority of participants experienced at least one ACE, and roughly 20% experienced three or more ACEs. As you can imagine, trauma affects every aspect of the person (physical, emotional, psychological, and spiritual), regardless of age, and should be understood in that context by clinical mental health counselors.

Like trauma, bereavement, or the loss of a loved one (Crunk, Burke, & Robinson, 2017), may result in individuals experiencing grief, a psychological response, over their loss—which can result in post-traumatic stress symptoms (Kristensen, Elklit, & Karstoft, 2012). In recent years, researchers have discussed what is known as complicated grief, in which the individual experiences severe distress over the loss and finds it difficult to cope with everyday life situations. This loss may be the result of a crisis or traumatic event, given the alarming rates of crises and traumas in the United States. As such, it is not uncommon for clinical mental health counselors to feel challenged when working through client issues of trauma, bereavement, and crisis, for they are often intertwined and further complicated by already existing mental health concerns. Yet for counselors to work effectively with this population, they must consider all facets of their clients, working from a holistic perspective, to promote health and recovery that respects and honors the cultural needs of their clients.

Samantha, Erika, and I have experience with trauma-based work in both inpatient and outpatient community settings. Our experiences include work with diverse children, adolescents, adults, couples, and families who experienced both direct and indirect effects of trauma and crisis. We are excited to share this information with you and hope that you find the material informative and helpful as you learn to navigate the intricacies of trauma-based work.

We first discuss crisis and the impact it may have on an individual diagnosed with serious mental illness. Next, we look into trauma-informed counseling models and discuss the counseling process with individuals who have experienced trauma. Then we discuss disasters and how these events, both predictable and unpredictable, may impact individuals and the communities in which they live and work. Finally, we examine counseling strategies, techniques, and interventions that may be effective with this population.

LEARNING OBJECTIVES

After reading this chapter, you will be able to do the following:

- Identify differing mental health diagnoses and crises and their impact on each other (CACREP 2F-3-g, CACREP 5C-2-f)

- Describe trauma-informed counseling models (CACREP 2F-5-a)

- Explain the counseling process from intervention through recovery

- Identify how disasters may impact individuals and the community (CACREP 2F-3-g)

- Employ effective counseling strategies, techniques, and interventions with individuals experiencing trauma (CACREP 2F-3-m)

IMPACT OF CRISES ON INDIVIDUALS WITH MENTAL HEALTH DIAGNOSES

To begin, we want to share a little about our professional experience working with individuals in crisis who have been diagnosed with a serious mental illness. **Serious mental illness**, as it is defined in the literature, describes a classification of mental health diagnoses of major depression, bipolar, and schizophrenia (Schmit, 2016). Our clients were diagnosed with what is colloquially described as "the Big Three" in mental health. As you can imagine, working with individuals in crises can be chaotic, which forced us (as counselors) to think quickly on our feet. Our clients were not only in a state of crisis; they were also a danger to either themselves or others. This was especially the case for us because we worked predominantly in an acute care, inpatient behavioral hospital and an inpatient substance abuse and mental health facility. These individuals experienced many stressors in their lives: trauma; substance use; physical, sexual, and emotional abuse; limited family support systems; and homelessness. The goal in this and many other settings seemed simple: to stabilize. However, working in the hospital setting, for example, includes a myriad of other things not commonly known by other helping professionals. Our responsibilities were many. We provided individual, family, and group counseling; referral services; education sessions; and crisis intervention. Working with these individuals was hard at times but extremely rewarding, and our hope for you (as a future counselor) is to become educated about mental health and how this may affect a person in crisis or who has experienced trauma.

It can be challenging to determine the prevalence of crises in the United States because there are many types of trauma. And sometimes individuals experience several traumas in their lifetime, which is referred to as having complex trauma. Suicide rates have increased in both males and females over the past 10 years and are one of the leading causes of death in the United States (National Institute of Mental Health, 2016). Crises also come in the form of natural disasters (e.g., earthquakes, hurricanes, tsunamis), and we have experienced the deadliest in history during the 2000s alone. Crises can have a major impact on one's mental health, especially for those already experiencing a serious mental illness. For instance, Jordan was consistently abused by his father as a small child. He, along with his three siblings, was put in the custody of Child Protective Services (CPS). Jordan had severe behavioral issues as an adolescent while in foster care. He ran away from home on several occasions, made failing grades in school, fought his siblings, and threw his classroom desk regularly while cursing. Now, imagine Jordan as an adult. What do you think he experiences? How might a counselor have worked with Jordan as a child to help with these issues?

Understanding how crises may affect the individual is crucial in the mental health field. The term **crisis** can be defined as a sudden event that may impact a person's life and can lead to a detrimental situation. This can range from losing a job, to loss of a friendship or dissolution of a marriage, to witnessing a loved one being abused or, even worse, murdered. A crisis only has to be perceived by the individual and does not need to be directly witnessed or experienced. This is known as **secondary trauma**, or "second-hand exposure," to an event (Shannonhouse, Barden, Jones, Gonzalez, & Murphy, 2016, p. 202). Examples of secondary trauma include witnessing a death resulting from a car crash or hearing a traumatic story being told by a client. In these situations, as you can imagine, individuals may experience a negative impact on their well-being and mental health.

Many types of crises can happen in an individual's lifetime: economic, interpersonal, mental health, medical, and natural disasters, just to name a few. In addition, crises can be immediate, short-term, or long-term and put into three categories: situational, developmental, and social. A **situational crisis** is unanticipated. For example, a family of four returns home after having dinner in the city only to realize that their house had caught fire. In contrast, a **developmental crisis** may be expected as part of an individual's development cycle. These types of crises, though anxiety provoking, are generally anticipated: for example, a marriage, birth of a child, changing one's career, and transition to old age. Finally, a **social crisis** involves an uncontrollable cultural event. For instance, experiencing a robbery on your way to the car or being sexually assaulted at party. The impact of any of these can be experienced on an immediate (i.e., not allowing for planning), short-term (i.e., less than a month), or long-term basis (i.e., longer than a month).

The impact of crises on individuals can have a huge influence on their everyday lives (Dass-Brailsford, 2010). Think about a major natural disaster such as Hurricane Katrina. How did this impact those living in New Orleans? What about the thousands of people who could not afford to pack up and leave their homes? How might a mental health issue compound these issues?

Mental Health and Diagnoses Classification

Mental health is something counselors talk about often. But what does mental health really mean, and can we simply define something that is inherently so complex? The World Health Organization (WHO; 2014) defines **mental health** as "a state of well-being." A person's mental health refers to the state of their psychological and emotional wellness. Mental health is experienced on a continuum throughout the individual's life span and can be affected by circumstances. For an individual to be officially diagnosed with a mental health disorder, he or she must seek treatment from a mental health provider (e.g., licensed professional counselor, social worker, psychiatrist) who will determine a diagnosis by using the *Diagnostic and Statistical Manual of Mental Disorders* (*DSM-5*) (American Psychiatric Association [APA], 2013).

Mental illness fails to discriminate and can affect anyone regardless of race, ethnicity, class, age, religion, and so forth. Take a moment and consider your current state of mental well-being. What comes to your attention immediately? Describe any emotional and physical responses you may have had. If you had to compare your current mental health with previous experiences in your life, what would the outcome be? Think about the last time you considered the state of your mental health. We do not typically take time throughout the day to consider the state of our mental health, and we may be surprised about our thoughts and feelings when we set time aside to do so.

According to the *DSM-5* (APA, 2013), mental health diagnoses of major depression, bipolar disorder, and schizophrenia are commonly associated with traumatic experiences. It is difficult to pinpoint trauma as the driving force behind these mental illnesses or that persons with these diagnoses are less prepared to address and integrate traumatic events into their sense of self. Imagine that you have experienced the loss of a loved one. What would that be like for you? It is conceivable that a person could fall into a spiral of sadness and experience fluctuations in mood states. Similarly, a person could avoid others and become psychologically distant from family and friends. Likewise, a person diagnosed with bipolar disorder experiences pervasive mood states characterized by periods of mania and depression. Given the behaviors associated with either mood state, you can imagine that an individual with bipolar disorder could be more susceptible to deleterious effects of a traumatic event.

Crises and Mental Health

Experiencing a crisis for an average, healthy individual is difficult; however, this can be catastrophic for those who suffer from mental illness. Some of the common symptoms after enduring a crisis include psychological distress (e.g., depression, fear, anxiety), relational disturbances (e.g., detachment), cognitive impairment (e.g., lack of concentration), somatic grievances (e.g., inability to sleep, headaches, stomachaches), and changes in daily functioning (e.g., inability to work or complete common life tasks). Now, consider the impact of crises on an individual experiencing mental illness. For instance, reflect on the case of Kelly.

Kelly is a 38-year-old female who has suffered from depression for 5 years. She feels sad most of the day, has trouble sleeping every night, and cannot seem to find pleasure in any activity. Two weeks ago, Kelly witnessed the death of her mother from an unexpected heart attack. How might this affect Kelly, who is already experiencing depression? Kelly may reach a darker place than before, may feel an immense amount of guilt and pain, and may even consider attempting suicide.

Crises may impact an individual with mental illness in different ways, which may be classified into four categories: physical, emotional, psychological, and spiritual. **Physical symptoms** may include headaches, loss of appetite, pain, and fatigue. Physical symptoms can be considered the body's response to a traumatic experience. They are the most readily visible symptoms and may be easily noticed. **Emotional symptoms** may include feelings of deep sadness or anger. **Psychological symptoms** may include depression and anxiety. Both emotional and psychological symptoms may be seen through a person's inability to engage in or complete simple life tasks (e.g., getting dressed in the morning, taking the children to school, preparing meals) or lashing out to others as in the case of Jordan described earlier. Finally, **spiritual symptoms** may include a lack of a sense of meaning. Individuals experiencing spiritual symptoms may have difficulty finding purpose in life. In the case of religious clients, they may question the existence of their higher spiritual power or begin to think of that power as cruel or uncaring. These symptoms often precipitate depression and can sometimes lead to suicidal ideation and suicide attempts (Hazler & Mellin, 2004; McCarthy & Dobroshi, 2014). Consider Kelly's case. What kinds of symptoms might she be experiencing?

Counselors can make a huge difference in those lives affected by crises. To effectively support individuals who have experienced trauma or crisis, counselors must possess core skills. These skills include active listening (Rogers, 1961), cultural competence (Rosen, Greene, Young, & Norris, 2010), the ability to express empathy, and the ability to ask the appropriate questions in the moment. In addition to these basic skills, counselors who receive education in crisis counseling related to rape (Westmarland & Alderson, 2013), financial crises (Giorgi, Arcangeli, Mucci, & Cupello, 2015), suicide prevention and intervention, telephone crisis counseling (Rogers & Lester, 2012), federal government responses (Dodgen & Meed, 2010), coping skills related to crises (Balkin, 2013; Schmit, 2015), and advocacy (Mellin, 2009) will be especially prepared to work with individuals experiencing trauma or crisis.

GUIDED PRACTICE EXERCISE 13.1

In groups of three, develop a short case study outlining an individual experiencing a crisis. Next, develop a crisis plan for how you would handle this situation. Consider the following questions:

1. Specifically, what type of crisis is this individual experiencing?

2. What types of mental health issues might you expect?

3. Imagine yourself as a counselor. How would you handle this situation?

TRAUMA-INFORMED COUNSELING MODELS

Although a number of therapeutic modalities may be employed in the treatment of trauma (e.g., constructivist, humanistic, psychodynamic, cognitive-behavioral), trauma-specific counseling models have been created to address the cognitive, behavioral, and emotional symptoms reflective of the trauma response. These models are primarily associated with the cognitive-behavioral paradigm; they have shown a strong evidence base in randomized clinical trials and thus are considered frontline treatment when working with clients with trauma.

Trauma-Focused Cognitive-Behavioral Therapy

Trauma-focused cognitive-behavioral therapy (TF-CBT) is an evidence-based treatment developed by Cohen, Mannarino, and Deblinger (2006) to assist children and adolescents in recovering after a traumatic event. The approach is structured, short-term (e.g., lasting from 8 to 25 sessions), and capable of positively impacting trauma-related outcomes associated with affective, cognitive, and behavioral functioning. The guiding principle behind TF-CBT is gradual exposure to trauma using a variety of cognitive and behavioral interventions delivered individually with children and conjointly with parents. Children, adolescents, and caregivers participating in TF-CBT gradually progress from reviewing psychoeducational materials into practicing relaxation skills, learning affective coping skills, and using cognitive reframing strategies. Treatment culminates in the creation of a trauma narrative that is shared with important others in the child's life, followed by in vivo exposure to triggers to reduce avoidance behaviors that interfere with the child's daily functioning. The acronym **PRACTICE** is used to describe the progression of treatment, with stages of intervention incorporating **p**sychoeducation and **p**arenting strategies, **r**elaxation, **a**ffect modulation, **c**ognitive coping, **t**rauma narrative, **c**ognitive processing, and in vivo **e**xposure.

Therapy begins by educating parents and children about the basics of trauma responses in order to normalize the child's reactions; reduce self-blame; and describe the structure, goals, and mechanisms of change in TF-CBT. The therapist works closely with the child's caregiver to teach strategies for strengthening the parent-child relationship, managing difficult or inappropriate behaviors, and reinforcing skills the youth will use to cope with the trauma. The TF-CBT therapist begins individual sessions with the child or adolescent by teaching relaxation skills for managing distress (e.g., mindfulness, progressive muscle relaxation, deep breathing, guided imagery), creating a "toolbox" to access when encountering triggers in day-to-day life, creating the trauma narrative, and taking part in vivo exposure exercises.

After the individual is comfortable using a variety of relaxation exercises, the therapist teaches the client how to recognize and modulate different affective states by educating the client about the cognitive triangle, describing the association between different life situations and his or her thoughts, feelings, and behaviors. The next component of treatment involves cognitive coping, wherein the individual learns to evaluate his or her thoughts and change them when patterns of thinking are unhelpful or inaccurate, both within and outside the context of trauma-related experiences. At this point in therapy, the individual and his or her caregiver should have learned and consistently practiced a variety of strategies for managing emotions and modifying thoughts when needed. The next stage in treatment involves creating a trauma narrative, where the individual tells the story of his or her trauma using a creative medium (e.g., chapter book, comic strip, collage, drawing, song, poem). Throughout this process, the therapist and client use cognitive processing strategies to identify and correct faulty or unhelpful beliefs the youth experiences in relationship to the trauma, ultimately creating an accurate, hopeful view of the self and the youth's family, world, and future.

Kira, Ashby, Omidy, and Lewandowski (2015) recommended modifications to the TF-CBT protocol to address current, continuous, or cumulative trauma experiences (CCC-TF-CBT) when individuals experience complex psychological responses due to the cumulative effects associated with exposure to a number of interpersonal, intergroup, and systemic traumas. The CCC-TF-CBT model incorporates eight precognitive, cognitive, behavioral, and social interventions. Treatment begins by prioritizing safety and addressing the potential for self-harm by teaching the client behavioral skills for regulating personal and group-based emotional experiences. Clinicians help clients stimulate the will to live by identifying the client's positive qualities and empowering them to rely on these aspects of their identity to foster hope, resilience, and personal growth. After the client experiences stabilization and a sense of safety, clinicians begin the traditional work associated with TF-CBT (e.g., psychoeducation, stress inoculation, and trauma narration). After the client moves through these phases of therapy, the CCC-TF-CBT therapist engages in social interventions related to advocacy and social justice, empowering the client to reconnect with his or her social network. Although outcome research does not yet exist using the CCC-TF-CBT model, this approach may provide additional benefits for clients who experience multiple traumas.

Outcome Research Using TF-CBT

Lenz and Hollenbaugh (2015) conducted a meta-analysis of TF-CBT for treating PTSD and co-occurring depression among children and adolescents. This meta-analysis included 21 peer-reviewed studies, and findings reflected that TF-CBT was exceptionally superior to no treatment or wait-list comparisons. Additionally, TF-CBT was found to be moderately more effective than alternative treatments regardless of ethnic identity or the type of trauma the individual had experienced. The researchers found variable effect sizes for co-occurring depression when compared with alternative treatment modalities, though TF-CBT was considerably more effective than wait-list or no treatment conditions for reducing depressive symptoms. Beyond individual treatment, initial research into TF-CBT delivered in group format has shown positive outcomes. Group TF-CBT may be especially useful as an alternative to individual delivery formats when large numbers of children and caregivers are in need of trauma-focused treatment, such as in response to natural disasters, in war-affected areas, or when resources for individual therapy are especially limited (Deblinger, Pollio, & Dorsey, 2016).

Cognitive Processing Therapy

Cognitive processing therapy (CPT) is an evidence-based treatment for PTSD and related symptomatology that consists of 12 weekly sessions delivered in group, individual, or combined group and individual formats. This approach was originally developed by

Patricia Resick, Candice Monson, and Kathleen Chard for veteran and military populations and is commonly used by the U.S. Department of Veterans Affairs (VA) health care system to treat PTSD in soldiers (Chard, Ricksecker, Healy, Karlin, & Resick, 2012). Cognitive processing therapy is built on the assumption that clients must activate and reexperience traumatic memories in the present to correct maladaptive, dysfunctional attributions and expectations. The CPT practitioner provides a supportive, safe environment and helps clients identify and modify irrational thoughts or avoidance behaviors that prevent healing and maintain dysfunction (Lenz, Bruijn, Serman, & Bailey, 2014).

Regardless of the format of delivery, therapy proceeds in an organized, structured manner, building on information covered during previous sessions to gradually help clients reprocess traumatic events. During the first four sessions, clients are educated about the theory behind CPT. The CPT therapist helps clients explore their beliefs about the meaning associated with their trauma and recognize how the trauma has impacted their beliefs about self, others, and the world. Clients learn about the connections among thoughts, feelings, and behaviors and identify "stuck points" in their thinking, particularly as they relate to their interpretations of the traumatic event (Chard et al., 2012). This portion of therapy concludes with clients writing detailed narratives about the most traumatic portion of their experiences, including sensory details, thoughts, and feelings. Therapy proceeds with clients learning core cognitive therapy skills in sessions five through seven. During this phase of therapy, clients practice examining and challenging thoughts by looking at the evidence for or against their beliefs, critically examining the context in which the belief was formed and learning to identify cognitive distortions or unhelpful patterns of thinking. The therapist uses handouts such as the Challenging Questions Worksheet, Patterns of Problematic Thinking Worksheet, and the Challenging Beliefs Worksheet to provide clients with tools to solidify understanding and use for between-session practice (Chard et al., 2012).

In sessions 8 through 12, the client and therapist focus heavily on examining and challenging unrealistic, unhelpful, or self-defeating beliefs in five key areas: safety, trust, power/control, esteem, and intimacy. The therapist uses cognitive techniques such as Socratic questioning to help the client critically examine, evaluate, and modify these beliefs when they contribute to or maintain distress. Therapy culminates with the client rewriting the initial trauma narrative and impact statement, comparing this new statement with the initial narrative completed during the fourth session of therapy. This reauthoring and comparison process allows the client to recognize changes in thoughts, feelings, and behaviors that have occurred over the course of therapy. Therapists also help clients plan for relapse prevention by identifying areas that may continue to be problematic or represent possible stumbling blocks in the future (Chard et al., 2012).

Outcome Research Using CPT

Lenz et al. (2014) conducted a meta-analytic review to determine the efficacy of CPT for treating PTSD and co-occurring depression. The researchers included studies that used a between-groups quantitative research design whose participants completed standardized assessments before treatment and at termination. Studies were restricted to those that used CPT as the primary therapeutic modality and whose participants had been diagnosed with PTSD by a formally trained mental health professional. After analyzing 11 studies that fit these criteria, Lenz and colleagues (2014) discovered large to very large effect sizes for CPT versus wait list, and medium to large effect sizes for CPT when compared with alternative treatments.

Monson and colleagues (2012) investigated whether CPT could positively impact adjustment across life domains (e.g., social, leisure, family, work, and income) following a course of CPT for veterans diagnosed with PTSD. The researchers determined that CPT significantly improved social adjustment, the quality of extended-family relationships, and housework completion following the end of therapy when compared with individuals who were on a wait list. Additionally, clients experienced reduced symptoms related to reexperiencing the traumatic event, avoiding situations or circumstances that reminded them of their trauma, emotional numbing, and hyperarousal.

Eye Movement Desensitization and Reprocessing

Eye movement desensitization and reprocessing (EMDR) was created by Francine Shapiro after she experienced relief from distressing thoughts and emotions while engaging in a particular pattern of saccadic eye movements. Shapiro became interested in understanding whether others would also experience the benefits of using saccadic eye movements to dispel the negative thoughts and emotions associated with traumatic or distressing memories (Luber & Shapiro, 2009). EMDR is an exposure-based therapy that involves incorporating physiological aspects with the psychological components of trauma-based treatments (Shapiro, 2001). EMDR practitioners view posttraumatic issues in functioning as a combination of visual, kinesthetic, and auditory reminders of traumatic events. Clients who are "stuck" may have perpetually negative beliefs about the traumatic event, themselves, others, and the world, ultimately reflecting an arrested state of memory processing. EMDR practitioners help clients move past these arrested states of memory by bringing up mental images associated with traumatic events, exploring the negative thoughts they experience in these moments, and visually tracking an external stimulus often provided by the clinician, who may guide the client in a pattern of eye movements using an object. Clients are also taught to self-monitor, recognizing the triggers that may cause trauma-related thoughts and feelings to surface (Shapiro, 2001). Practitioners who use EMDR believe clients can process through traumatic memories using a combination of cognitive, affective, and physiological activities using rapid eye movements that mimic REM sleep (Shapiro, 2001).

Outcome Research Using EMDR

Chen and colleagues (2014) conducted a meta-analysis to determine the efficacy of EMDR for individuals diagnosed with post-traumatic stress disorder. The authors used a sample of randomized controlled trials that used EMDR and outcome measures associated with PTSD, including depression, anxiety, and subjective distress, and found that EMDR significantly reduced symptoms associated with each measure. Additionally, EMDR appears to produce psychophysiological changes accompanied with reductions in PTSD symptomatology, including decreased heart rate and parasympathetic tone in reaction to individualized trauma scripts over time (Sack, Hoffman, Wizelman, & Lempa, 2008). These benefits appear to extend to children and adolescents as well as adult clients, although additional randomized clinical trials are needed to determine whether the degree of change is promising and long-lasting (Greyber, Dulmus, & Cristalli, 2012).

GUIDED PRACTICE EXERCISE 13.2

Read the following client vignette and respond to the guided practice questions. You may want to discuss the vignette with classmates in small groups after you have recorded your responses.

George is a 35-year-old combat veteran who recently retired from the military, returning to his home in Virginia with his wife, Georgia, who is a nurse. He did three tours in the Middle East and had the most difficult time during his most recent deployment, wherein he experienced significant distress after witnessing an IED explode near a local school, killing and injuring numerous children. He was referred to the counseling clinic at the Department of Veterans Affairs after a recent check-in with his primary care physician during which he complained of tension, racing heartbeat, and trouble breathing. After meeting with the intake counselor, George went on to describe additional trauma-related symptoms, including frequent nightmares about the event, flashbacks when driving past school campuses, and intrusive thoughts throughout the day.

1) Which of the three trauma-informed counseling approaches discussed would you consider using with this client? Why?

2) How would you conceptualize this client's response in relationship to the information you reviewed earlier in the chapter?

3) Who else, if anyone, would you involve in this client's treatment?

COUNSELING SURVIVORS FROM INTERVENTION THROUGH RECOVERY

A description of specific trauma interventions is found later in this chapter. However, this section gives you an idea about how treatment would begin, progress, and culminate when working with individuals who have survived one or more traumatic events. A narrative of this process follows and is summarized in Table 13.1.

TABLE 13.1 ■ Counseling Survivors From Intervention Through Recovery	
Stage of Treatment	**Associated Processes**
One: Identification of trauma	Informal assessment
	• Clinical interviews
	Formal assessment
	• CAPS
	• TESI
	• LEC-5
	• CAPS-CA
	• CPSS

(Continued)

TABLE 13.1 ■ (Continued)	
Stage of Treatment	**Associated Processes**
Two: Recovery planning	Will vary depending on setting
	Should be a collaborative process
	Create a sense of safety
	Empower clients and families
	Create goals, objectives, interventions
Three: Therapeutic intervention	Will vary depending on chosen modality
	May include "treatment agnostic" skills
	• Psychological first aid
	• Grounding
	• Prolonged exposure
	• Safety skills
	• Trauma narration
	• Cognitive processing
	• Stress inoculation training
	• Emotion regulation strategies
Four: Treatment consolidation and relapse prevention	Clients have progressed, are reaching goals
	May use formalized assessments to demonstrate measurable change
	Should include safety planning
	• Warning signs
	• Internal coping strategies
	• External resources
	Discuss relapse prevention strategies
	• "Flagging the minefield" exercise

Stage 1: Identification of Trauma

The first step in treatment for any concern is identification and assessment. The clinician may become aware of issues with traumatization during the clinical interview or may begin to suspect concerns with traumatization a few sessions in. It is important to be sensitive, empathic, and intentional in your approach to identification and assessment. It is imperative to create a safe, secure, therapeutic environment in which the client feels empowered and in control of the discussion (Seligman & Reichenberg, 2012). Extra attention should be paid to building rapport and assessing developmental milestones when working with youth with trauma or with adults who may have a cognitive delay or intellectual impairment. A number of instruments can assist in assessing PTSD and other trauma-related symptoms in both adults and youth, including the Clinician-Administered PTSD Scale (CAPS), the Traumatic Events Screening Inventory (TESI), the Life Events Checklist for DSM-5 (LEC-5), the Clinician-Administered PTSD Scale for Children and Adolescents (CAPS-CA), and the Child PTSD Symptom scale (CPSS) Child Behavior Checklist (Lenz & Klassen, 2016; Seligman & Reichenberg, 2012; Weathers et al., 2013). This list is certainly not exhaustive, but it may be useful to incorporate a formalized assessment in addition to the clinical interview to determine the frequency and severity of reported symptoms. Clients may present with more than one clinically significant concern, and it is common to have acute stress disorder (ASD) or post-traumatic stress disorder (PTSD) and a comorbid disorder such as depression, alcohol or drug abuse problems, and panic disorder (APA, 2013).

Stage 2: Recovery Planning

Treatment and recovery planning should be a collaborative, empowering process wherein the clinician, client, and important stakeholders such as parents, family members, or spouses meet to determine the goals, outcomes, and interventions incorporated to support the client's recovery. Creating a sense of safety and **empowerment** is especially important for individuals who have experienced one or multiple traumatic events, for a loss of control and sense of disenfranchisement can be particularly salient with these individuals (Seligman & Reichenberg, 2012). Procedures and forms involved in treatment and recovery planning are likely to vary depending on the clinician's setting, as are the number of sessions allotted, the frequency with which sessions occur, the types of services that may be incorporated into the treatment plan, and the level of collaboration between the clinician and other members of the client's treatment team (e.g., case managers, group counselors, psychiatrists).

Regardless of the form that treatment and recovery planning takes, it is imperative that the counselor help the client obtain a sense of personal responsibility and control within the context of determining goals, outcomes, and interventions. Goals should be stated in the client's language and positively worded, giving the individual something to work toward rather than against. For example, "I want to be able to cope with what happened to me and be able to manage my reactions to achieve some sense of normalcy again." Objectives should be specific, measurable, attainable, realistic, and time-limited. For example, "Helena will reduce the number of days per week she experiences avoidance behaviors (e.g., refusing to attend school, avoiding situations and conversations that remind her of her grandfather, requesting to have another person with her at all times) from 7 days per week to 3 or 4 days per week over the next 90 days." Interventions should be specific and entail what the clinician or other members of the client's treatment team will do to help clients reach their goals. For example, "Alex will provide manualized TF-CBT treatment 4 times monthly to Helena and her mother Louisa to assist Helena in coping with the cognitive, emotional, and behavioral aspects of her PTSD and returning to a level of pretrauma functioning."

Stage 3: Therapeutic Intervention

Therapeutic intervention may occur using one of the specific treatment modalities discussed earlier in the chapter. However, a number of so-called treatment-agnostic approaches may be incorporated into another therapeutic modality to support recovery when clients have experienced trauma alongside another mental health diagnosis. For example, clinicians may incorporate psychological first aid, grounding, prolonged exposure, safety skills, trauma narration, emotion regulation strategies, relaxation skills, cognitive processing, stress inoculation training, and trauma systems work into the client's treatment plan. A more detailed explanation of many of these interventions is found later in the chapter.

Stage 4: Treatment Consolidation and Relapse Prevention

Whereas formal assessment occurs at the onset of therapy to determine an appropriate course of action based on the client's individual needs, effective therapy necessitates ongoing evaluation to determine client progress toward reaching the goals and objectives identified at the beginning of treatment. Treatment consolidation refers to knowing when clients have reached a point in therapy where they have learned how to manage the cognitive, emotional, and behavioral symptoms associated with their unique mental health needs. This may involve the use of formal assessments to determine change on particular scales associated with their symptomatology, or it may simply involve a conversation using clients' treatment plan to help them determine whether they believe they have reached their goals.

Relapse prevention includes discussing strategies reviewed over the course of therapy and engaging in a "flagging the minefield" exercise to help clients anticipate future challenges and understand how the strategies they learned in therapy can help them overcome difficulties in these specific situations (Erford, 2014). Safety planning is another important component of relapse prevention, for it gives clients an immediate plan for coping when their personal resources are stretched too thin or when they experience a particularly significant trigger. Safety plans typically include warning signs that problems may be developing again, internal coping strategies for managing difficult emotions during times of distress or dysregulation, external sources of support (e.g., both individual people and particular groups that may be supportive) to turn to in times of need, and the names and numbers of crisis hotlines and counseling agencies they may return to if and when clinically significant problems arise.

CASE ILLUSTRATION 13.1

Helena is a 10-year-old Hispanic girl who was referred for counseling after experiencing the traumatic loss of her grandfather, whom she witnessed being shot during an invasion of their home 2 months prior. Helena lives with her mother, Louisa, and younger brother, Alberto, in low-income public housing, and this was not the first shooting to occur in their community. The family moved to another housing unit after the incident occurred, although the unit was still within sight of their previous residence. Louisa decided to take Helena to counseling after noticing she had begun wetting the bed, having frequent nightmares about her grandfather's death, showing an intense fear response when friends or neighbors knocked on the door, and avoiding windows that faced their former apartment. She began refusing to go anywhere alone, panicking if she were left by herself in a particular area of the home. Helena also experienced times wherein she would "space out" and when prompted to listen or reengage by her mother or teacher at school, would become easily startled and emotional.

Louisa brought Helena to a local mental health agency and was informed that she qualified for routine case management, psychiatric services, and counseling based on her history, needs, diagnosis, and associated level of care. Helena was assigned to begin seeing Alex, a trauma-focused cognitive-behavioral therapist. During their first session, Alex met with both Louisa and Helena to provide psychoeducation about the trauma response, explain the process of working through trauma from a cognitive-behavioral perspective, describe the parameters of treatment and different modules of TF-CBT, and highlight the need to meet regularly with Louisa to review items covered in Helena's sessions to ensure she felt prepared to support between-session practice and to process her own reactions to the family's traumatic loss.

During the first phase of treatment, Alex helped Helena learn stress management skills; strategies for recognizing and modulating her emotions; and ways of interrupting negative, unhelpful cognitions using thought-stopping exercises. Helena also learned about the cognitive triangle, developing an understanding of the connection between different life situations and her thoughts, feelings, and emotions. She learned to engage in positive self-talk, use affirmations, and critically examine and modify her thoughts when they were not true

or helpful. At this phase in treatment, Helena was coping effectively with her emotions, demonstrating less hypervigilance and emotional reactivity, and engaging in fewer avoidance behaviors. Helena and Louisa met with Alex to discuss her progress and determine whether Helena felt prepared to begin creating her trauma narrative. Both Helena and Louisa expressed reluctance and worry, nervous that beginning the narrative would "open up a can of worms" and send Helena backsliding. Alex reiterated the rationale behind creating the narrative and retelling the story to desensitize Helena to its effects, ultimately helping her move past the traumatic loss at a pace where she felt comfortable.

Helena began her trauma narrative by creating a storybook about what had happened to her grandfather, gradually shifting her cognitive perspective from one that was self-blaming and responsible for his death (e.g., "I should have made sure the door was locked. The world is a scary place, and I can't trust anyone") to one of self-acceptance and understanding (e.g., "It wasn't my fault; there are a few bad people out there, but it's okay to trust other people to not hurt you"). This process spanned several weeks, and Alex was careful to move at Helena's pace to avoid retraumatizing her and to ensure she was able to cope effectively with each aspect of her story. Before Helena shared her storybook with her mother, Alex met with Louisa to help prepare her to hear the narrative and respond in a helpful, supportive manner to the content within. After Helena shared her trauma narrative in a joint session with her mother, Helena met with Alex a few more times to ensure she had made lasting progress in cognitively processing the event and had not returned to a self-blaming narrative.

IMPACT OF DISASTERS ON INDIVIDUALS AND COMMUNITIES

At the beginning of this chapter, you learned about the impact of disasters on individuals with mental health diagnoses, and now you have the opportunity to learn more about how disasters impact individuals and communities. When responding to crises, traumatic events, or disasters, it is important to understand and remember some key words: **Stress** refers to any tension or pressure individuals experience, **trauma** can result from single or multiple incidents happening over a short or long period as a result of actual or perceived threat, **coping** is the cognitive or behavioral actions individuals use to deal with stressors, **adaptation** is the degree to which your client's level of functioning has changed, and **resiliency** is the individual's ability to bounce back from adversity or stressors. These are all terms to take into consideration, and look for, when working with individuals impacted by disasters.

When establishing a plan for dealing with crises in the community, be aware of these questions: (a) What are the immediate needs of the community members? (b) Who is affected? (c) What are cultural factors to consider? (d) Are the needs of the community better met by a gender-specific crisis team? (d) How long will you be in the community? (e) How can you incorporate the collective strengths of members in the community? (f) What referral agencies are important?

Individual Impact

Clients experiencing a disaster, crisis, or traumatic event can be impacted either directly or indirectly. Direct impact refers to the effects of the disaster on your client whereas indirect impact refers to the effects of the disaster on family members, friends, and others in the community. Disasters can affect individuals on a scale from subtle to extreme, and the way your clients respond to these events, whether they were one-time or long-lasting, depends on a few factors: their level of resilience and development, the meaning attached to the event, environmental factors, and the details of the event, among other traits. In addition, clients' response to these events may be complicated or enhanced by their experiences, access to support from the community and loved ones, and basic coping skills.

According to the World Health Organization (WHO), a disaster occurs when there is a serious disruption in the normal functioning of a community where there is widespread loss exceeding the abilities of the community. Disasters come in various forms: tornadoes, earthquakes, hurricanes, flooding, landslides, and fires. During these events, individuals can become separated from their homes, loved ones, pets, and resources. Individuals may also experience grief, loss, trauma, or severe injury that may impact their normal life functioning. Individuals may use healthy or unhealthy ways of coping with their emotions and reactions to disasters.

Some examples of healthy coping include seeking counseling, connecting with loved ones, reaching out to other community members for support, incorporating spirituality or religious beliefs, and engaging in problem-solving with others. As mentioned, not all of your clients will handle these situations the same way, so you may have some who isolate, refuse counseling, encourage chaos, reject resources or help from officials, and turn to drugs or alcohol as a way to cope. These clients will need your help to recover so they can learn to restore their lives after the disruption caused by the disaster.

Another indication of how individuals may be affected is in the way they react and respond to the disaster and traumatic events. These reactions are reflected in two diagnostic criteria: acute stress disorder (ASD) and post-traumatic stress disorder (PTSD). Both diagnoses necessitate exposure to a traumatic event (direct or indirect) and a response that reflects reexperiencing the event, avoiding or numbing reminders of the event, and hypervigilance. One of the main differences between these diagnoses is that ASD is diagnosed when symptoms last from 3 days to a month postevent, whereas a PTSD diagnosis is warranted when symptoms last more than a month, usually occurring during the first 3 months, postevent (APA, 2013).

Community Impact

Disasters also impact the whole community. The social and psychological impact of disasters may result in long-term adjustment and consequences, and community members may change their perception of their surroundings. Communities may experience mass casualties, displacement of community members, intense strain on resources, structural damage to important landmarks, disconnection from other communities, and a general sense of panic within the affected area. When this happens, communities can either join together to collaborate, or they can become fragmented and isolated, creating further tension and conflict in the midst of disaster. Within the initial period postdisaster, communities may be overwhelmed with shock, fear, panic, anger, and confusion. It is crucial to reduce chaos and connect with loved ones and pets (McGlothlin, 2014). In addition, local agencies and organizations should seek financial or government support. Agencies such as the American Red Cross and the Federal Emergency Management Agency (FEMA) and local counseling personnel can support communities during this time by providing manpower, rescue efforts, resources, and crisis intervention strategies.

CASE ILLUSTRATION 13.2

We recommend a person-centered approach to treatment planning, which involves seeing clients from a holistic perspective and determining their strengths and resources in addition to areas of need and growth. In our experience, you will gain valuable information by beginning the treatment plan by asking clients about their perspective on their mental health needs, determining how their concerns have impacted their lives, and deciphering how important others might describe their concerns at this time. Incorporating questions related to physical health and substance use will help you determine whether there are comorbid issues that may need to be addressed. Additionally, asking about client strengths and resources in terms of their recovery may help you identify important stakeholders in clients' lives that will support their adjustment over time.

CASE ILLUSTRATION 13.3

As you begin your work with clients, you will notice that in addition to working with individuals, there are a lot of couples and families who need help dealing with trauma-related issues. In our work with clients, we find that sometimes we have to play the role of case manager as we help our clients recover. One important thing to remember is that trauma and crisis management requires

(Continued)

(Continued)

a lot from you and your clients, and we want to reassure you that this is okay. Be aware that sometimes you are the only person these clients have helping them, so it may mean you have to do the case management on your own. However, you should continue to collaborate with other agencies and supportive systems in your community and seek supervision to be sure you are maintaining ethical practices. From a practitioner's standpoint, collaboration is not only beneficial for you as a professional, it is also important for rebuilding a sense of safety and connectedness in the community, especially after a disaster or major crisis.

You want to be sure you find out from your clients what they believe they need help with before you start listing what you think should be done. Do they need resources to help them relocate? Did they lose their job and need information on a job center? Do they need a referral to a psychiatrist? What about availability of food? Do they need information about a local food pantry? If medical care is needed and they do not have insurance or money, can you provide them with information about a free clinic at a local hospital? Some family members may need babysitting or day care services as they recover from the disaster or traumatic event. Is there a school or community agency you can refer them to? Do they need directions to a local agency that may have free clothing for adults and children?

Flourishing and Posttraumatic Growth

Although we have extensively discussed the negative impacts of disasters on individuals and communities, many individuals experience posttraumatic growth and flourish in the face of adversity. **Posttraumatic growth** (PTG; Calhoun & Tedeschi, 2006) occurs when individuals who have endured some form of trauma experience positive change. We want to be clear that this does not mean that they are not affected in any way by the disaster. However, we must impress upon you the fact that some persons experience some form of growth and learning as a result of disasters or traumatic events. Communities may also flourish after a disaster by supporting one another and using the resources available (such as disaster recovery centers and emergency relief supplies) while promoting holistic recovery from the disaster.

GUIDED PRACTICE EXERCISE 13.3

Around 2:00 a.m. your small town is hit by an unexpected gas explosion from a nearby oil refinery. The explosion causes severe damage to homes and properties and results in mass casualties. There are children crying, adults screaming, and families trying to reconnect. Get together with your classmates and discuss how this disaster impacted the community. What might you expect to see from individuals in your community as they deal with the aftermath of the explosion? How might you be helpful in your role as a counselor? Who might you collaborate with to help this community recover from this disaster? What might you be experiencing on a personal level as you try to help members of your community?

EFFECTIVE COUNSELING STRATEGIES, TECHNIQUES, AND INTERVENTIONS

Earlier in this chapter, you learned about trauma-informed counseling models, how to counsel survivors from intervention through recovery, and the impact of disasters on an individual and community level. Next, you will learn about effective **counseling strategies**, techniques, and interventions that can be used with children, adolescents, and adults. Because there are several interventions for trauma, bereavement, and crises, especially when working with children and youth, this chapter does not offer an exhaustive list. To complement our discussion, we have added additional intervention resources in the Web Resources at the end of this chapter.

Techniques and interventions are an important part of treatment planning and client care. However, treatment planning requirements are likely to vary depending on your setting, including your practicum and internship sites. A clear collaborative plan when addressing trauma, bereavement, and crisis is an essential component of client care and involves the use of interventions that are closely connected to goals, objectives, and treatment outcomes. Remember, techniques and interventions are what you, as the counselor, are going to use to help your client achieve his or her goals, objectives, and treatment outcomes.

Now that you have an understanding of trauma-informed counseling models such as TF-CBT, CPT, and EMDR, we focus on strategies, techniques, and interventions for children, adolescents, and adults. It is important that these techniques and interventions make sense for diverse clients. We recommend that you are intentional with the strategies, techniques, and interventions you select based on your theoretical approach and the age, nature of the presenting concerns, and cultural background of your clients (Lenz, Haktanir, & Callender, 2016). Be sure to take time to explain how these techniques and interventions will be helpful to your clients and why they are important as they process trauma, grief, and crises.

Psychological First Aid

This is an evidence-based approach to helping children and adults immediately after a disaster or traumatic event. This approach may also be used with **first responders** and disaster relief workers. Right after a disaster or traumatic event, your clients may display signs of acute stress, including disorientation, panic, agitation, and exceeding worry. Psychological first aid can be used to reduce initial distress and symptoms of acute stress, support short-term and long-term adaptive coping skills, and improve overall functioning. Techniques in psychological first aid follow four basic standards: techniques are consistent with research on risk and resilience for posttraumatic events, delivered in a culturally informed and flexible manner, age and developmental level appropriate, and practical and applicable in field settings.

Grounding

Grounding is used to help your clients detach from emotional pain. Various circumstances can cause emotional pain, such as a lack of impulse control, sadness, substance use, and nightmares. Grounding can help to distract clients from their inner pain and focus on their external world though mental, physical, and self-soothing techniques. If you decide to use grounding with your clients, there are a few important things to remember. Grounding can be done in a variety of settings and doesn't have to be done in public. Your clients can use grounding when they want to center themselves or as a distraction from their emotional pain. However, grounding is not the same as relaxation. A few examples of grounding exercises include counting to 10, repeating the alphabet, stretching, focusing on breathing, touching various objects, using positive affirmations, holding ice cubes, remembering a safe space, and thinking of favorite hobbies.

Grounding may not work with all of your clients because this is a new skill that takes practice. If grounding seems difficult for your clients, remind them to practice this new skill as often as they can. You might encourage them to list their favorite grounding methods and even have someone help them as they practice. In addition, clients can make an audio recording of their preferred grounding method to play at any time or even adjust the grounding method to suit their personal style. One of the most important roles you will play is to encourage your client not to give up.

Prolonged Exposure

Prolonged exposure (PE; Foa, Hembree, & Rothbaum, 2007) is a frontline, behaviorally oriented intervention that helps clients to progressively engage in exposure to feared stimuli until the intensity of their emotions decreases. Prolonged exposure is a 10- to 12-session manualized treatment intervention that targets and mitigates PTSD symptoms through image exposure, psychoeducation, in vivo exposure to traumatic situations, and breath retraining. One of the advantages of PE is that this intervention is efficacious across a variety of traumas (Gurak, Freund, & Ironson, 2016).

Seeking Safety

Seeking safety (Najavits, 2002) is a manualized therapeutic intervention designed for treating individuals with active co-occurring PTSD and substance use. Central ideas in seeking safety include using coping skills to replace substance use, self-respect, staying safe, trust, persistence in the face of adversity, identifying safe and helpful people, remaining substance-free while healing from PTSD, and trying something different. In addition, seeking safety focuses on case management and behavioral, cognitive, and interpersonal areas. The manual consists of 25 sessions that can be completed in any order. However, some essential lessons to cover if you do not have the opportunity to conduct all 25 sessions are Safety, Detaching From Emotional Pain, PTSD: Taking Back Your Power, Asking for Help, and When Substances Control

You. Seeking-safety interventions may be more effective when other supportive services are integrated such as Alcoholics Anonymous (AA) or other self-help groups (Lenz, Henesy, & Callender, 2016).

Trauma Narrative

The trauma narrative, or gradual exposure, has been used with children who have experienced single episodes of trauma in the form of physical, sexual, and emotional abuse; exposure to community violence; traumatic grief and loss; or interpersonal crises or disasters such as break-ins, natural disasters, and parental separation. Trauma narratives help children disconnect the reminders, thoughts, or discussions of the traumatic event from intense emotions such as shame, rage, horror, extreme helplessness, or terror. When using trauma narratives over the course of several sessions, clinicians encourage the child or adult to describe in detail what occurred before, during, and after the traumatic events.

Clinicians should also elicit and seek to understand the thoughts and feelings the client experienced during the trauma. This must be done carefully and in regulated increments to help the client talk and write about upsetting aspects of the trauma. This process occurs over several sessions, with each step a little more challenging than the previous one. Trauma narratives help the child to become more comfortable with talking about the thoughts and feelings about the trauma with his or her parents or primary caregivers (Cohen et al., 2006). As in TF-CBT, trauma narratives may be shared with important others in the child's or adult's life, particularly when caregivers are involved and need additional information about the individual's traumatic experience to help him or her cope more effectively.

Stress Inoculation Training (SIT)

Stress inoculation training (SIT; Meichenbaum, 1985) is designed to teach individuals nurturing and coping skills. SIT is not a single technique. Rather, SIT is a generic term used to refer to a combination of interventions such as Socratic questioning, rehearsal, cognitive restructuring, problem-solving, relaxation training, and self-monitoring. There are three phases of SIT: building rapport and conceptualization of the problem, acquiring skills and rehearsing them, and application and follow-through of skills. These phases help clients learn the nature of stress and coping, monitor maladaptive thoughts and behaviors, and gain adequate knowledge about coping skills to facilitate a healthier way to deal with unexpected stressors.

Trauma Affect Regulation: Guide for Education and Therapy (TARGET)

Trauma affect regulation: guide for education and therapy (TARGET) is a strengths-based educational intervention for trauma survivors who seek a practical and safe approach to their recovery (Ford & Russo, 2006). The goal of TARGET is to help survivors to understand how trauma impacts their brain and body's response to stress, deescalate and regulate extreme emotions, and manage intrusive thoughts from the trauma though a single sequential skill set. This skill set is based on research that suggests that affect regulation involves recognizing, regulating, and recovering from unhelpful emotional states. The acronym **FREEDOM** refers to the 7-step approach used in TARGET to change the PTSD response into a positive approach that can promote long-term recovery from trauma. The following are the steps to FREEDOM:

- **F**ocus: slowing down, orienting one's self to what is going on and doing a self-check

- **R**ecognize: process the trauma by learning to recognize triggers and stressors

- **E**motion: identify one of the main emotions

- **E**valuate: evaluate one primary thought

- **D**efine: identify one main personal goal

- **O**ptions: recognize and identify the healthy options for positive choices

- **M**ake a contribution: learn to make a difference in the world

Trauma Systems Therapy

Trauma systems therapy (TST; Saxe, Ellis, & Brown, 2015) is a model used with traumatized children that includes interventions that address the trauma system. This trauma system includes survival-in-the-moment states, where the child experiences trauma in a specific moment and the environment or primary care system (e.g., family, friends, school) is unable to help the child regulate such states. The TST approach assesses whether there is a fit between the way the child regulates his or her emotions and the adequacy of the community or primary care system to help the child. The clinician implements interventions based on the outcome of these assessments. This intervention is appropriate for children with plausible trauma histories or who have difficulty regulating their emotions.

Cognitive-Behavioral Play Therapy

Children affected by trauma may experience a variety of impairments in behavioral and emotional self-regulation, difficulties with interpersonal relationships, and cognitive distortions about other people in their lives and the world around them. Because play is a natural activity for children to direct creative and personal expression, integrating play into trauma treatment should be considered (Lenz & Klassen, 2016). Clinicians can use play as a way to build the therapeutic relationship with children, support other assessments, and support engagement in therapy for trauma-related issues. When play is combined with cognitive-behavioral interventions, children can process the impact of traumatic events without the burden of using only talk therapy, for children can have

GUIDED PRACTICE EXERCISE 13.4

Your clients are a young couple, John and Mary, who recently experienced a stillbirth after 3 miscarriages. John and Mary desperately wanted a baby and were excited about the upcoming birth of their daughter. Mary was very ill during her pregnancy and had to stop working so she could be on strict bedrest. Mary experienced complications and had to be rushed to the hospital where she experienced the stillbirth. John reported that Mary is no longer eating, gets up during the night from nightmares, and states that she can hear the baby crying. Identify which strategy or intervention may be best for Mary. What are some important issues you should consider during her therapy? Who should you consult with? What impact do you think this has on John?

difficulty thinking clearly when overwhelmed by emotions (Hansen & Saxe, 2009). Play is especially suited for younger children who have experienced trauma because children ages 3 to 5 may not have developed the ability to express themselves in terms that allow them to explain the nature of the trauma and their subsequent responses (Lenz & Klassen, 2016).

Homework

You can assign homework to your clients as a way to enhance your counseling sessions as you work through the impact of trauma and crises. Homework gives the client something to practice or complete in between sessions. Assignments should be directed toward symptom improvement, be used to monitor client progress, help to master skills learned in counseling, and create opportunities for your clients to develop more structure and focus on achieving counseling goals. By assigning homework, your clients have something to look forward to, and it creates a sense of empowerment as they take personal responsibility for their growth and progress (no matter how small). Some examples of homework assignments are journaling, thought records, and other worksheets based on your intervention. Be sure you are familiar with the homework you assign. So, if it's a worksheet, you should probably try completing it yourself. Review the homework assignments with your clients when they show up to the next session. If your clients struggle to complete the assignments, you can discuss the material in session for it may indicate that you are moving too fast, that they did not fully understand what to do, or that they are not ready to move on to a new task (Callender, 2017).

After reading this chapter, we hope that you feel more knowledgeable and confident when working with clients who have experienced trauma, crisis, or bereavement. It may seem like a lot to know, and it honestly is a lot to learn. However, with practice, the right training, and your determination, you can work successfully with these clients. We also hope that this chapter sparks conversations with your classmates and professors about trauma, crisis, and bereavement and how best you can contribute to your future clients' empowerment, development, and recovery.

CASE ILLUSTRATION 13.4

We know there are several considerations for choosing the right intervention with your clients after they experience a traumatic event or crisis. We thought it might be helpful to list these considerations for you. These are not necessarily to be done in a specific order; however, it will be good for you to be familiar with these points when you meet with your clients. Our intention here is to help you think of your clients from a trauma-informed perspective and to understand that you may have to revisit these items at some point in your counseling services.

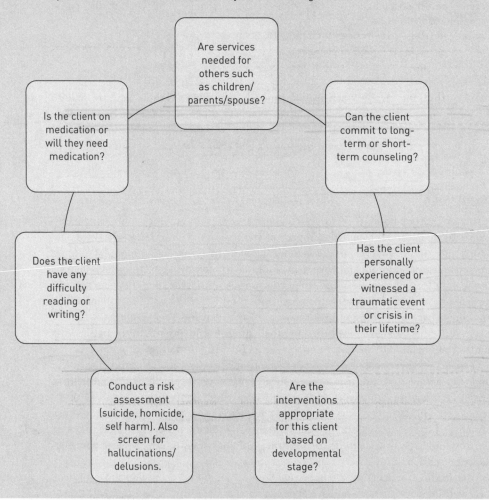

Are services needed for others such as children/parents/spouse?

Is the client on medication or will they need medication?

Can the client commit to long-term or short-term counseling?

Does the client have any difficulty reading or writing?

Has the client personally experienced or witnessed a traumatic event or crisis in their lifetime?

Conduct a risk assessment (suicide, homicide, self harm). Also screen for hallucinations/delusions.

Are the interventions appropriate for this client based on developmental stage?

Keystones

- Trauma, bereavement, and crisis are important aspects of clinical mental health counseling and consist of an intricate dynamic of client care, case management, healing, and empowerment.

- Individuals may experience one or multiple traumatic events over their life span that can affect the mental, physical, emotional, environmental, and financial domains of their lives.

- There are two ways individuals can be impacted by a traumatic event: directly (where they experience the event themselves) or indirectly (where they observe or learn about the event happening to others).

- Three trauma-informed models are well-evidenced in the professional literature:

trauma-focused cognitive behavioral therapy (TF-CBT), cognitive processing therapy (CPT), and eye movement desensitization and reprocessing (EMDR).

- Counselors can use several techniques, interventions, and strategies with clients affected by trauma or crisis; however, the counselor should consider the age of the client, the traumatic event that occurred, and resources available to the client.

Key Terms

Adaptation 350

Cognitive processing
    therapy (CPT) 342

Coping 350

Counseling strategies 353

Crisis 338

Developmental crisis 338

Emotional symptoms 340

Empowerment 347

Eye movement desensitization
    and reprocessing (EMDR) 344

First responders 353

FREEDOM 356

Grounding 354

Mental health 339

Physical symptoms 340

Posttraumatic growth
    (PTG) 352

PRACTICE 341

Psychological symptoms 340

Resiliency 350

Secondary trauma 338

Serious mental illness 337

Situational crisis 338

Social crisis 338

Spiritual symptoms 340

Stress 350

Trauma 350

Trauma-focused cognitive
    behavioral therapy
    (TF-CBT) 341

Web Resources

American Counseling Association: Trauma and Disaster Mental Health (www.counseling.org/knowledge-center/trauma-disaster)

Crisis Prevention Institute (www.crisisprevention.com)

Disaster Assistance (www.disasterassistance.gov)

International Association of Trauma Professionals (www.traumapro.net)

National Alliance on Mental Illness (NAMI): Crisis Intervention Team (CIT) Programs (www.nami.org/Law-Enforcement-and-Mental-Health/What-Is-CIT)

National Child Traumatic Stress Network (www.nctsn.org)

Substance Abuse and Mental Health Services Administration (SAMHSA): Trauma-Informed Approach and Trauma-Specific Interventions (www.samhsa.gov/nctic/trauma-interventions)

Trauma Center at Justice Resource Institute (www.traumacenter.org)

Trauma-Focused Cognitive Behavioral Therapy (https://tfcbt.org)

Trauma Institute & Child Trauma Institute: Certificate Program (www.childtrauma.com/training/certificate-program)

U.S. Department of Veterans Affairs: PTSD: National Center for PTSD (www.ptsd.va.gov/professional/treatment/early/early-intervention-for-trauma.asp)

References

American Psychiatric Association. (2013). *Diagnostic and statistical manual of mental disorders: DSM-5*. Washington, DC: Author.

Balkin, R. S. (2013). Validation of the goal attainment scale of stabilization. *Measurement and Evaluation in Counseling and Development*, 46(4), 261–269. doi:10.1177/0748175613497040

Calhoun, L. G., & Tedeschi, R. G. (2006). The foundations of posttraumatic growth: An expanded framework. In L. G. Calhoun & R. G. Tedeschi (Eds.), *Handbook of posttraumatic growth: Research and practice* (pp. 3–23). New York, NY: Routledge, Taylor & Francis.

Callender, K. A. (2017). Homework assignments in therapy. In J. Carlson & S. Dermer (Eds.), *The SAGE encyclopedia of marriage, family, and couples counseling*. Thousand Oaks, CA: Sage.

Chard, K. M., Ricksecker, E. G., Healy, E. T., Karlin, B. E., & Resick, P. A. (2012). Dissemination and experience with cognitive processing therapy. *Journal of Rehabilitation Research & Development*, 49, 667–678.

Chen, Y., Hung, K., Tsai, J., Chu, H., Chung, M., Chen, S. . . . Chou, K. (2014). Efficacy of eye movement desensitization and reprocessing for patients with posttraumatic stress disorder: A meta-analysis of randomized controlled trials. *PLOS ONE*, 9, 1–17.

Cohen, J. A., Mannarino, A. P., & Deblinger, E. (2006). *Treating trauma and traumatic grief in children and adolescents*. New York, NY: Guilford Press.

Copeland, W. E., Keeler G., Angold, A., & Costello, E. J. (2007). Traumatic events and posttraumatic stress in childhood. *Archives of General Psychiatry*, 64, 577–584.

Crunk, A. E., Burke, L. A., & Robinson, E. M. (2017). Complicated grief: An evolving theoretical landscape. *Journal of Counseling & Development*, 95, 226–233. doi:10.1002/jcad.12134

Dass-Brailsford, P. (2010). *Crisis and disaster counseling: Lessons learned from Hurricane Katrina and other disasters*. Los Angeles, CA: Sage.

Deblinger, E., Pollio, E., & Dorsey, S. (2016). Applying trauma-focused cognitive-behavioral therapy in group format. *Child Maltreatment, 21*, 59–73. doi:10.1177/1077559515620668

Dodgen, D., & Meed, J. (2010). The federal government in disaster mental health response: An ever-evolving role. In P. Dass-Brailsford (Ed.), *Crisis and disaster counseling: Lessons learned from Hurricane Katrina and other disasters* (pp. 181–196). Los Angeles, CA: Sage.

Erford, B. (2014). *40 techniques every counselor should know*. New York, NY: Pearson.

Felitti, V. J., Anda, R. F., Nordenberg, D., Williamson, D. F., Spitz, A. M., Edwards, V. . . . Marks, J. S. (1998). Relationship of childhood abuse and household dysfunction to many of the leading causes of death in adults: The adverse childhood experiences (ACE) study. *American Journal of Preventive Medicine, 14*(4), 245–258. doi:10.1016/S0749-3797(98)00017-8

Foa, E. B., Hembree, E. A., & Rothbaum, B. O. (2007). Prolonged exposure therapy for PTSD: Emotional processing of traumatic experiences – Therapist guide. New York, NY: Oxford University Press.

Ford, J. D., & Russo, E. (2006). A trauma-focused, present centered, emotion self-regulation approach to integrated treatment for PTSD and addiction. *American Journal of Psychotherapy, 60,* 335–355.

Giorgi, G., Arcangeli, G., Mucci, N., & Cupelli, V. (2015). Economic stress in the workplace: The impact of fear of the crisis on mental health. *Work, 51,* 135–142. doi:10.3233/WOR-141844

Greyber, L. R., Dulmus, C. N., & Crisalli, M. E. (2012). Eye movement desensitization reprocessing, post-traumatic stress disorder, and trauma: A review of randomized controlled trials with children and adolescents. *Child & Adolescent Social Work Journal, 29,* 409–425. doi:10.1007/s10560-012-0266-0

Gurak, K. K., Freund, B., & Ironson, G. (2016). The use of both prolonged exposure and cognitive processing therapy in the treatment of a person with PTSD, multiple traumas, depression, and suicidality. *Clinical Case Studies, 15,* 295–312. doi:10.1177/1534650116641214

Hansen, S., & Saxe, G. (2009). Trauma systems therapy: A replication of the model, integrating cognitive behavioral play therapy into child and family treatment. In A. A. Drewes (Ed.), *Blending play therapy with cognitive behavioral therapy: Evidence-based and other effective treatments and techniques* (pp. 139–164). Hoboken, NJ: Wiley.

Hazler, R. J., & Mellin, E. A. (2004). The developmental origins and treatment needs of female adolescents with depression. *Journal of Counseling & Development, 82,* 18–24. doi:10.1002/j.1556-6678.2004.tb00281.x

Kira, I. A., Ashby, J. S., Omidy, A. Z., & Lewandowski, L. (2015). Current, continuous, and cumulative trauma-focused cognitive behavior therapy: A new model of trauma counseling. *Journal of Mental Health Counseling, 37,* 323–340.

Kristensen, T. E., Elklit, A., & Karstoft, K. I. (2012). Posttraumatic stress disorder after bereavement: Early psychological sequelae of losing a close relative due to terminal cancer. *Journal of Loss and Trauma, 17,* 508–521.

Lenz, A. S., Bruijn, B., Serman, N. S., & Bailey, L. (2014). Effectiveness of cognitive processing therapy for treating posttraumatic stress disorder. *Journal of Mental Health Counseling, 36,* 360–376.

Lenz, A. S., Haktanir, A., & Callender, K. (2016). Meta-analysis of trauma-focused therapies for treating posttraumatic stress disorder. Manuscript submitted for publication.

Lenz, A. S., Henesy, R., & Callender, K. (2016). Effects of seeking safety for co-occurring posttraumatic stress disorder and substance use. *Journal of Counseling and Development, 94,* 51–61. doi:10.1002/jcad.12061

Lenz, A. S., & Hollenbaugh, K. M. (2015). Meta-analysis of trauma-focused cognitive behavioral therapy for treating PTSD and co-occurring depression among children and adolescents. *Counseling Outcome and Research Evaluation, 6,* 18–32. doi:10.1177/2150137815573790

Lenz, A. S., & Klassen, S. (2016). Posttraumatic stress in children and adolescents. *ACA Practice Brief.* Retrieved from https://www.counseling.org/knowledge-center/practicebriefs

Luber, M., & Shapiro, F. (2009). Interview with Francine Shapiro: Historical overview, present issues, and future directions of EMDR. *Journal of EMDR Practice and Research, 3,* 217–231. doi:10.1891/1933-3196.3.4.217

McCarthy, J. B., & Dobroshi, Z. (2014). Major depression, bipolar disorder, and psychosis in children. *Journal of Infant, Child, and Adolescent Psychotherapy, 13,* 249–261. doi:10.1080/15289168.2014.937984

McGlothlin, G. (2014). Emergency preparedness and response in the community and workplace. In L. R. Jackson-Cherry & B. T. Erford (Eds.), *Crisis assessment, intervention, and prevention* (pp. 245–266). Boston, MA: Pearson.

Meichenbaum, D. (1985). *Stress inoculation training.* New York, NY: Pergamon Press.

Mellin, E. A. (2009). Responding to the crisis in children's mental health: Potential roles for the counseling profession. *Journal of Counseling and Development, 87,* 501–506.

Monson, C. M., Macdonald, A., Vorstenbosch, V., Shnaider, P., Golsdstein, E. S. R., Gerrier-Auerbach, A. G., & Mocciola, K. E. (2012). Changes in social adjustment with cognitive processing therapy: Effects of treatment and associated with PTSD symptom change. *Journal of Traumatic Stress, 25,* 519–526. doi:10.1002/jts.21735

Najavits, L. M. (2002). *Seeking safety: A treatment manual for PTSD and substance abuse.* New York, NY: Guilford Press.

National Center for Injury Prevention and Control. (2016). 10 leading causes of death by age group, United States – 2016. Retrieved from https://www.cdc.gov/injury/wisqars/pdf/leading_causes_of_death_by_age_group_2016-508.pdf

National Institute of Mental Health. (2016). Suicide. Retrieved from https://www.nimh.nih.gov/health/statistics/suicide/index.shtml

Rhee, P., Joseph, B., Pandit, V., Aziz, H., Vercruysse, G., Kulvatunyou, N., & Friese, R. S. (2014). Increasing trauma deaths in the United States. *Annals of Surgery, 260,* 13–21.

Rogers, C. R. (1961). *On becoming a person.* Cambridge, MA: Riverside Press.

Rogers, J. R., & Lester, D. (2012). Crisis intervention and counseling by telephone and the Internet (3rd ed.). Springfield, IL: Charles C Thomas.

Rosen, C. S., Greene, C. J., Young, H. E., & Norris, F. H. (2010). Tailoring disaster mental health services to diverse needs: An analysis of 36 crisis counseling projects. *Health & Social Work, 35,* 211–220.

Sack, M., Hofmann, A., Wizelman, L., & Lempa, W. (2008). Psychophysiological changes during EMDR and treatment outcome. *Journal of EMDR Practice and Research, 2,* 239–246. doi:10.1891/1933-3196.2.4.239

Saxe, G. N., Ellis, B. H., & Brown, A. D. (2015). *Trauma systems therapy for children and teens* (2nd ed.). New York, NY: Guilford Press.

Schmit, E. L. (2015). The relationship between working alliance and therapeutic goal attainment in an adolescent inpatient, acute care behavioral hospital. Doctoral dissertation, available from ProQuest Dissertations and Theses database.

Schmit, M. K. (2016). Integrated behavioral and primary healthcare: Comparing the effectiveness of treatment modalities on holistic client functioning. Doctoral dissertation, available from ProQuest Dissertations and Theses database. (Accession Order No. 10104371)

Seligman, L., & Reichenberg, L. (2012). Selecting effective treatments: A comprehensive, systematic guide for treating mental disorders (4th ed). San Francisco, CA: Jossey-Bass.

Shannonhouse, L., Barden, S., Jones, E., Gonzalez, L., & Murphy, A. (2016). Secondary traumatic stress for trauma researchers: A mixed methods research design. *Journal of Mental Health Counseling, 38,* 201–216. doi:10.774/mehc.38.3.02

Shapiro, F. (2001). *Eye movement desensitization and reprocessing (EMDR): Basic principles, protocols and procedures* (2nd ed.). New York, NY: Guilford Press.

Substance Abuse and Mental Health Services Administration. (2015). Trauma and violence. Retrieved from http://www.samhsa.gov/trauma-violence

Weathers, F. W., Blake, D. D., Schnurr, P. P., Kaloupek, D. G., Marx, B. P., & Keane, T. M. (2013). *The Life Events Checklist for DSM-5 (LEC-5).* Instrument available from the National Center for PTSD at www.ptsd.va.gov

Westmarland, N., & Alderson, S. (2013). The health, mental health, and well-being benefits of rape crises counseling. *Journal of Interpersonal Violence, 28,* 3265–3282. doi:10.1177/0886260513496899

World Health Organization. (2014). Mental health: A state of well-being. Retrieved from http://www.who.int/features/factfiles/mental_health/en/

14

CLINICALLY BASED ASSESSMENT, DIAGNOSIS, AND TREATMENT PLANNING

Clinical assessment, diagnosis, and treatment planning are best thought of as a tripartite practice, inseparable from one another, occurring in clinical mental health counseling. That is, clinical assessment guides the diagnostic process that ultimately informs treatment planning. Although described here in a linear fashion, it actually occurs more dynamically (see Figure 14.1). As you can see, rendering a diagnosis of major depression is based on a collection of evidence, to include clinical assessment information such as the Beck Depression Inventory-II (BDI-II; Beck, Steer, & Brown, 1996), Columbia-Suicide Severity Rating Scale (C-SSRS; Posner et al., 2011), Mental Status Exam (MSE), and a clinical interview, which informs both treatment

FIGURE 14.1 ■ A diagram of the tripartite practice of clinical assessment, diagnosis, and treatment planning found in clinical mental health counseling, highlighting the dynamic interactions among each process.

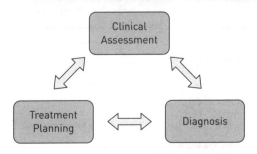

goals and objectives of learning new coping skills and establishing a safe environment and interventions of individual and group counseling, psychopharmacology, and physical exercise. Likewise, data obtained from reoccurring assessment moderates treatment goals and objectives, which in turn may alter the dimensionality of a major depression diagnosis. Within the context of the counseling relationship, assessment, diagnosis, and treatment planning are fluid constructs, modified across time in response to client needs and goal obtainment. As you may now notice, 21st-century counselors working in clinical mental health settings possess specialized knowledge, training, and skill in clinically based assessment, diagnosis, and treatment planning (Council for Accreditation of Counseling and Related Educational Programs [CACREP], 2016).

The role and purpose assessment serves in clinical mental health counseling is examined in this chapter. Next, both formal and informal assessment strategies found in clinical mental health counseling are explored. After, readers dive into the emergence of cross-cutting dimensional assessments and how they are used. Then we discuss how counselors can effectively use assessment data to accurately diagnose clients using current diagnostic systems (i.e., *DSM-5, ICD-10*). The chapter concludes with how to put all the pieces together, that is, using both assessment data and diagnosis to inform development of a comprehensive treatment plan.

LEARNING OBJECTIVES

After reading this chapter, you will be able to do the following:

- Identify the role and purpose of psychological tests and assessment in clinical mental health counseling (CACREP 5C-1-e)

- Describe formal and informal assessment strategies

- Identify common assessments used by counselors found in various clinical mental health settings

- Differentiate between concepts of reliability, validity, and test bias as they relate to selecting, administering, and scoring tests, assessments, and rating scales

- Apply a diagnostic process, including differential diagnosis and the use of current diagnostic classification systems, including the *Diagnostic and Statistical Manual of Mental Disorders* (*DSM*) and the *International Classification of Diseases* (*ICD*; CACREP 5C-2-d)

- Describe and conduct an intake interview, mental status evaluation, biopsychosocial history, mental health history, and psychological assessment for treatment planning (CACREP C5-3-a)

- Develop a treatment plan using a five-step approach

ASSESSMENT IN CLINICAL MENTAL HEALTH SETTINGS

Assessment in counseling, if not careful, can quickly turn into a means-to-an-end practice of justifying clinical necessity. Although not an incorrect practice, it is best thought of as an incomplete one that teeters on the edge of a slippery slope that may negatively impact the counselor-client relationship. Reasons found throughout the professional literature that may explain this less-than-favorable practice include settings that embody a medical model of practice, counselor burnout, muddled counselor identity, job-related stress, high client loads, inadequate training and preparation, and so forth. As a counselor in training, you have an ethical responsibility to promote client welfare (American Counseling Association [ACA], 2014, E.1.b.) through appropriate assessment and evaluation procedures that require competence in the purpose, selection, administration, and scoring of assessments (ACA, 2014, E.2.b.), and you are responsible for the decisions made, on behalf of clients, based on assessment results (ACA, 2014, E.2.c.). Likewise, competent counselors recognize how multicultural variables (e.g., age, ethnicity, gender, religion, disability, language) impact the process of assessment and minimize potential biases though appropriate selection of instruments and by using culturally informed assessment practices (ACA, 2014, E.8). As you may notice, assessment is an in-depth dynamic process that begins at the onset of counseling and continues throughout the counseling experience—facilitated by the counselor-client relationship. To better understand the dimensionality of assessment in clinical mental health counseling, readers should explore what assessment is, its role and purpose in counseling, and who is qualified to administer assessments.

What Is Assessment?

Before going any further, we need to define assessment because it will shape our discussion going forward. According to Watson and Flamez (2015), **assessment** "is the process by which counselors gather the information they need to form a holistic view of their client and the problems with which they present" (p. 4). Likewise, Balkin and Juhnke (2018) identified the practice of assessment as "the collection of information in order to identify, analyze, evaluate, and address the problems, issues, and circumstances of clients in the counseling relationship" (p. 2). As you may notice, both definitions of assessment are broad, highlighting both the process and content of gathering information needed to comprehensively identify issues of concern. The *process* of assessment is facilitated by the counselor-client relationship and is ongoing throughout the counseling process. The *content* of assessment are the data obtained from direct or indirect sources using formal and informal assessment strategies, discussed further in the next section, used by both the counselor and client to make informed decisions about treatment.

The terms *assessment* and *test* are often used synonymously with one another in clinical practice; however, subtle differences do exist. An assessment is a comprehensive process of gathering information about a client and may include data from a psychological test. A **psychological test**, often referred to simply as a test, is an instrument used to measure a latent construct of interest, such as depression, anxiety, wellness, or job satisfaction. The term **latent construct**, commonly referenced as construct, is theoretical, that is, a concept that is not directly measurable. How a latent construct is described is based on how it is operationally defined. An **operational definition** is a clear and concise statement or set of statements, known as facets, of how something is measured. A theorist or researcher develops a test based on the operational definition of the construct of interest. The facets are directly observable and measurable and relate to the construct of interest. Although this may seem confusing at first, remember that how something is measured is based on how it is defined. For instance, how would you measure happiness? Is it based on need fulfillment, frequency of positive emotions, or reaching one's potential? Well, it depends on how it is operationally defined. An important takeaway from this section is your ability to recognize that assessment is the process of gathering client data; a test may be one aspect of data acquired during an assessment.

Role and Purpose of Assessment

Imagine meeting a client for the first time. During this interaction, you notice his disheveled appearance, how quickly he folded his arms when sitting down, his aggressive tone of voice when answering your first question, how his eyes appear to be bloodshot, and how he smells of alcohol every time he speaks. In this moment, you are gathering information about your client. The assessment process has already begun. It is important to recognize that the client data previously described are not sufficient on its own to make clinical decisions pertaining to treatment. Rather, it is one tiny piece of the story, tangential evidence that may be used to formulate questions for deeper inquiry. Skilled counselors use their trained senses, clinical intuition, and knowledge and expertise to gather, evaluate, analyze, and organize information, even before a formal assessment takes place.

As such, the role and purpose of assessment is multifaceted. An assessment often initiates the formation of a counselor-client relationship, commonly occurring at the initial screening phase. Obtaining information such as demographics (e.g., name, address, phone number, sex), health history, current mental health diagnosis, prior and current medications, reasons for seeking out counseling services, and so forth asks clients to share sensitive and often private information. Therefore, clinical mental health counselors must be skilled in the manner in which questions are asked and be able to listen and empathize in nonjudgmental ways. Exceptional counselors are those who continuously use their basic counseling skills throughout the counseling process.

Assessment also serves to gather information about your client to reach a desired outcome. Without identifying a problem or concern, how will the counselor and client know what to address in counseling, which direction they should take, and when they have reached their final destination? Likewise, assessment can also be used to identify client strengths and resources that may prove useful in future counseling sessions. As such, assessment information obtained at the onset of counseling informs the direction and focus of future counseling processes (e.g., diagnosis, treatment planning). Assessment includes screening, intake interviews, tests, observations, and information gathered from a secondary source (e.g., partner, family, friend, health professional). Assessment is not a means-to-an-end process; rather, it begins at the onset of counseling and continues throughout. In the next section, we discuss both formal and informal assessment strategies and then overview three clinical interviewing strategies commonly found in clinical mental health counseling.

CASE ILLUSTRATION 14.1

Why assessment is important in counseling.

Imagine a client walking into your office for the first time. You notice his appearance, listen to his concerns, and begin exchanging information about the counseling process. He informs you that he is willing to pay cash for sessions. Although this sounds really enticing, you know nothing about this client or his presenting concerns. How would you know if counseling is even appropriate for the client? Let's pretend, even for a second, that you enrolled this person as one of your clients. What would be the purpose of counseling? How would you know what issues to focus on? How would you evaluate the client's progress and your effectiveness? As you can tell, the purpose of assessment in counseling is multifaceted and critically important to the entire counseling process. Without assessing the client and his or her concerns, counseling can result in harm to the client and be dangerous to the counselor from both an ethical and a legal perspective. As such, assessment is the backbone of counseling, always there to support both counselor and client throughout the counseling process.

GUIDED PRACTICE EXERCISE 14.1

What is assessment, and what is its purpose?

Using the chapter as a reference, how would you describe to an imaginary client what assessment is and its purpose in the counseling process?

FORMAL AND INFORMAL ASSESSMENT STRATEGIES

Assessment sheds light on a client's perspective through both formal and informal strategies. Remember the imaginative example of the counselor who met a client for the first time. The counselor relied on sensory data to understand the client's perspective through informal means. Early on in the counseling process, counselors attempt to understand a client's experience as it relates to both the client and presenting issues. These experiences often center around intra- and interpersonal dynamics; cognitive, behavioral, or emotional dysregulation; and/or wellness, life satisfaction, or functioning concerns. Depending on a counselor's theoretical orientation, he or she may choose to focus on one or more aspects of the client experience through the counseling process.

As you will see, numerous assessment strategies are available and used by counselors to understand the client experience. Assessment strategies can include both formal and informal methods such as observations, interviews, standardized and nonstandardized tests, projective tests, performance-based tests, self-assessments, and inventories. **Formal assessment strategies** follow a specific, standardized set of procedures that yield quantifiable data that can be compared to a normative population (Cohen & Swerdlik, 2005). Examples of formal assessment include standardized tests and inventories and rating scales. On the other hand, counselors using **informal assessment strategies** do not follow a strict set of procedures and are not concerned with comparing results to a normative sample. Rather, informal assessment methods seek out client subjective data and tend to be more inclusive of the entire client experience. Examples of informal assessment strategies include interviews, open-ended questions, and nonstandardized instruments. Projective tests are also an informal assessment strategy.

Throughout the professional literature, the terms *formal assessment* and *informal assessment* are used interchangeably with *standardized assessment* and *nonstandardized assessment*, respectively, and in this chapter, no distinction is made between them. Regardless of whether formal or informal strategies are used, assessment is a client-driven process based on the counselor-client relationship. In continuing our discussion of assessment strategies, it is important to recognize that both formal and informal assessment strategies can be found in assessment practices performed by a clinical mental health counselor. This is never more apparent than during the clinical interview.

Clinical Interview in Mental Health Counseling

The clinical interview is one of the best methods to gather client information, using both formal and informal strategies, that can be used throughout the counseling process (i.e., diagnosis, treatment planning). A ubiquitous intervention among health care providers (e.g., counselors, social workers, physicians), the **clinical interview** is "an action-oriented intervention in which a counselor solicits information about a client and the client's past using a series of questions, assesses the client's verbal and nonverbal responses to those questions, and uses that information to formulate a diagnosis for the client" (Watson & Flamez, 2015, p. 396). In addition to formulating a diagnosis, the information obtained from the clinical interview is used to inform treatment planning, treatment and intervention selection, and identification of client strengths. Depending on the counselor's theoretical orientation and personal counseling style, and the treatment setting and population served (i.e., multicultural considerations), clinical interviews can range from structured to semistructured to unstructured, and anywhere in between, depending on the purpose of the interview.

Structured Interviews

In a structured interview the counselor uses a specific set of protocols when interacting and communicating with clients. Structured interviews follow a standardized procedure, that is, counselors with similar backgrounds and training would consistently obtain similar information during the interview. Other qualities of structured interviews include predetermined content areas and questions, stipulations in how questions are asked, and whether a follow-up question is appropriate; generally speaking, questions asked lean more toward being closed-ended. Structured interviews have many advantages in the assessment process. For instance, direct questions provide counselors a clearer picture of the presenting problem, and data obtained during the interview tend to be reliable, quantifiable, and comparable to populations of interest. Conversely, structured interviews have pitfalls such as the lack of flexibility on behalf of the counselor. Thus, counselors must follow the interview schedule and protocol. When answers from a structured interview lack detail, such as the reasons why a client indicated severe depression, the counselor must adhere to the standardized interviewing procedures. Additional challenges include clients perceiving the counselor to be distant, impersonal, or nonempathetic; difficulty in obtaining meaningful client responses with persons who are less verbal; and time-consuming instruments used.

Semistructured Interviews

Similar to structured interviews regarding predetermined questions being used, counselors using semistructured interviews are able to alter the order and adjust the wording of questions to accommodate the client (Power, Campbell, Kitcoyne, Kitchener, & Waterman, 2010). An interviewing format such as this provides counselors with flexibility when asking questions and allows clients to provide more detailed responses. Semistructured interviews are common in clinical mental health settings due to the partial structure and flexibility they offer both counselor and client. An example of a semistructured interview question might be "Have you engaged in any self-harming behaviors in the past 2 weeks?" Depending of the client's response, a follow-up question may address specifically the type of self-harming behaviors (e.g., cutting, reckless driving, excessing alcohol consumption or substance use). If the client stated no, then follow-up questions would be unnecessary. Advantages of semistructured interviews include counselors having flexibility in adapting questions, clients being free to provide as much detail as they wish, and a less formal environment. Some disadvantages of semistructured interviews include time constraints similar to that of structured interviews, client responses limited in comparability and generalizability due to the adapted questions asked, and potential for miscommunication on behalf of both counselor and client.

Unstructured Interviews

Unstructured interviews are the most widely used clinical assessment method by counselors (Craighead & Nemeroff, 2004) and preferred over other methods by many health professionals (Peterson, 2004; Sattler, 2002). Unstructured interviews lack predefined content areas or questions and do not adhere to any procedural steps. Counselors using this more conversational approach may ask a series of both open- and closed-ended questions depending on the purpose of the interview. This provides clients maximum opportunity to share details. For instance, a counselor might ask the client to describe the symptoms he or she is experiencing. Depending on how the client responds, the counselor may continue with a more open-ended question: "What do you mean by stress?" Or the counselor might choose a closed-ended question: "Does this occur more than 6 times per week?"

Although it may seem as if questions are unorganized, this is not the case. Counselors using an unstructured interview format are skilled in question formulation, recognize thematic patterns within and across client narratives, and are proficient in recognizing diagnostic criteria associated with frequently occurring mental health disorders. There are many advantages to using an unstructured interview format: questions are flexible and adaptable, deviations in the interview schedule are acceptable, client information obtained is often rich and descriptive, counselors can target specific areas in client narratives, and clients may perceive the interviewer to be more empathetic and the environment to be safer. Some disadvantages of unstructured interviews: interviews are

GUIDED PRACTICE EXERCISE 14.2

Differentiating between clinical interview formats.

In groups of three, differentiate between each clinical interview format (i.e., structured, semistructured, and unstructured). Each partner will take ownership of a clinical interview format and develop a brief four-question protocol. In a counselor-client role-play, administer your interview protocol to a partner. The partner not directly involved as client or counselor will serve as an observer. That person's role is to provide feedback to the dyad once the role-play is over. Continue to engage in this role-play until everyone has had a chance to administer their protocol. At the end of this exercise, the course instructor can review the class experience as a whole.

time-consuming, client data can be difficult to interpret, and interviewers must be skilled in question formulation and recognize when to probe deeper.

Regardless of the format used by counselors, clinical interviews are the main assessment strategy used. The clinical interview is not a static intervention; rather, it is a comprehensive, dynamic method that often includes an intake interview, symptom-specific assessment, mental status examination, and suicide risk assessment. Each of these processes is discussed in more detail later in the chapter. Let's continue our discussion of assessment by briefly exploring some common tests, assessments, and rating scales used by clinical mental health counselors.

COMMON TESTS, ASSESSMENTS, AND RATING SCALES USED BY CLINICAL MENTAL HEALTH COUNSELORS

Depending on the information obtained during the intake session, clinical mental health counselors may use symptom-specific, disorder-specific, or purpose-specific tests, assessments, or rating scales to better understanding a client's presenting issue. Instruments fitting this description are often quantitative and standardized, that is, emphasis is placed on numbers and following specific procedures. Results obtained from these instruments are consistent across clients with similar demographics and faithfully valid. Before diving into specific tests, assessments, and rating scales, let's briefly review the statistical concepts of reliability and validity.

According to Watson and Flamez (2015), **reliability** is "the ability of test scores to be interpreted in a consistent and dependable manner across multiple test administrations" (p. 62).

Consider the example of a counselor who administers the Beck Depression Inventory-II (BDI-II) to a client diagnosed with major depression. Upon initial assessment, the client's BDI-II total score was 34, which indicates severe depression. Two weeks later, the counselor again administers the BDI-II, and the client's total score was 11, which indicates minimum depression. Given the short time span between administrations of the BDI-II, a 23-point difference, from severe to minimal depressive symptomatology, should be concerning. Although the score of the second administration of the BDI-II was lower, a 23-point difference from pre- to posttest is unrealistic and not representative of the disorder of major depression. Thus, the counselor should proceed with extreme caution and conclude that the scores are not reliable. Conversely, if subsequent administration of the BDI-II yielded a total score of 32 after a 2-week period, a counselor could assert that the scores appear to be reliable.

Another concept related to reliability is validity. When an anxiety scale demonstrates consistency in scores across administrations for persons with anxiety disorder, one can conclude that the scores demonstrate evidence of validity, that is, the scale accurately measures the same construct from one administration to the next. As such, reliability is an inherent property of validity, meaning scores that are valid are also reliable. According to the *Standards for Educational and Psychological Testing*, **validity** is "the degree to which evidence and theory support the interpretations of test scores entailed by proposed uses of test" (American Educational Research Association, American Psychological Association, & National Council on Measurement in Education, 1999, p. 9). Hence, scores considered valid accurately measure the construct being assessed. For instance, the Addiction Severity Index (ASI; McLellan, Luborsky, O'Brien, & Woody, 1980) has been shown to be effective in identifying the severity level among persons abusing drugs and alcohol. However, it is not effective in predicting the likelihood of a person completing alcohol and drug treatment. Thus, counselors should ensure that tests, assessments, and rating scales chosen as part of the clinical interview process are both reliable and valid.

A final concept to keep in mind with respect to tests, assessments, and rating scales is that of bias, commonly referred to as test bias. **Test bias** occurs when scores of one group are significantly different from scores of another group based solely on group membership. For instance, say you want to determine the average IQ among a group of fifth graders using an available IQ test. Upon analyzing your data, you noticed that White students' IQ scores were significantly higher than non-White students'. Based on this finding, the scores from the IQ test demonstrate evidence of bias based on group membership: White versus non-White students. Three types of test bias exist: construct bias, method bias, and item bias (van de Vijver & Tanzer, 2004). **Construct bias** occurs when a construct being measured (e.g., IQ, depression, despair, satisfaction) is conceptualized or understood differently across groups. **Method bias** occurs when differences in scores are the result of factors surrounding the test administration (e.g., environment, length of test) rather than the construct of interest being measured. **Item bias** occurs when poorly worded or ambiguous items result in differences in scores among groups. Test bias is usually the result of some type of cultural bias (difference in scores based on cultural factors; van de Vijver & Tanzer, 2004). As a result, persons belonging to culturally or linguistically diverse backgrounds could easily be misrepresented in the assessment, diagnosis, and treatment processes of counseling. Therefore, counselors should carefully consider the appropriateness, limitations, and psychometric properties of any tests, assessments, and rating scales prior to administering them to their clients (ACA, 2014, E.6.a.).

Now that the concepts of reliability, validity, and test bias are fresh in your mind, let's briefly explore common tests, assessments, and instruments used in clinical mental health counseling. Be aware that the tests, assessments, and rating scales discussed are not exhaustive; rather, they are examples of instruments that demonstrate evidence of reliability and validity, are simple to administer and score, and are widely available.

Alcohol and Substance Use–Specific Instruments

Alcohol Use Disorder Identification Test (AUDIT)

AUDIT (Babor, Higgins-Biddle, Suanders, & Monteiro, 2011) is a 10-item questionnaire used to screen adults for person at risk of alcohol problems as a result of hazardous alcohol consumption. Each question has a set of responses, and responses are anchored with a range of possible scores, from 0 to 4. The response score for each item can be added to yield a total score. Total scores range from 0 to 40, with a score of 8 or more indicating harmful drinking behaviors that warrant further assessment. See the Web Resources section at the end of this chapter to find the second edition of AUDIT online.

CAGE-AID

CAGE-AID, originally adapted from CAGE to include an assessment of drug use, is a four-item assessment tool used to screen alcohol- and drug-related problems among adults. The tool by itself is insufficient to diagnose for alcohol- or substance-related disorder but is designed to detect the presence of a problem. Each item on CAGE-AID is scored as either 0 = *No* or 1 = *Yes*, with a total score range of 0 to 4. A total score of 2 or greater is considered significant and warrants further inquiry during the clinical interview. See the Web Resources section at the end of this chapter to find a version of CAGE-AID online.

Mental Health–Specific Instruments

Patient Health Questionnaire (PHQ-9)

The PHQ-9 (Kroenke, Spitzer, & Williams, 2001) is a self-administered assessment used to screen for the presence and severity of depression among adults. Developed originally from the Primary Care Evaluation of Mental Disorders (PRIME-MD), the PHQ-9 is commonly used in primary care settings. The nine-item assessment is quick to administer and score. Each item has a possible range of scores from 0 to 3, with 0 = *Not at all* and 3 = *Nearly every day*. The score from each of the nine items is added together to form a total score. Total scores range from 0 to 27. The severity level of depressive symptomatology can be interpreted from the total score: 1–4 = *minimal*, 5–9 = *mild*, 10–14 = *moderate*, 15–19 = *moderately severe*, and 20–27 = *severe*. See the Web Resources section at the end of this chapter to find a version of the PHQ-9 online.

General Anxiety Disorder-7 (GAD-7)

The GAD-7 (Spitzer, Kroenke, Williams, & Lowe, 2006) is a self-report assessment used for screening and determining severity of generalized anxiety disorder. Commonly found in outpatient and primary care settings, the GAD-7 assess persons across seven items. Clients are asked to reflect on the past 2 weeks to assess the frequency and severity of symptoms present. Each item is scored based on the following: 0 = *Not at all*, 1 = *Several days*, 2 = *More than half the days*, and 3 = *Nearly every day*. Total scores range from 0 to 21. The severity level of anxiety symptomatology can be interpreted from the total score: 5–9 = *Mild*, 10–14 = *Moderate*, and >15 = *Severe*. See the Web Resources section at the end of this chapter to find a version of the GAD-7 online.

The PTSD Checklist (PCL)

The PCL (Blanchard, Jones-Alexander, Buckley, & Forneris, 1996; Weathers, Litz, Herman, Huska, & Keane, 1993) is a self-report assessment corresponding to symptomatology associated with post-traumatic stress disorder (PTSD). The PCL aids in both screening and diagnosing PTSD and can be used to monitor changes in severity of PTSD symptoms. The PCL assesses clients across 17 items and only takes approximately 5 to 10 minutes to complete. Each item is scored based on the following: 1 = *Not at all*, 2 = *A little bit*, 3 = *Moderately*, 4 = *Quite a bit*, and 5 = *Extremely*. Total scores range from 17 to 85. Higher total scores indicate greater severity, and lower total scores indicate the opposite. See the Web Resources section at the end of this chapter to find a version of the PCL online.

Suicide Risk–Specific Instrument

Columbia-Suicide Severity Rating Scale (C-SSRS)

The C-SSRS (Posner et al., 2011) is a clinician-administered assessment tool used to detect the presence of suicidal ideations and behaviors. Questions from the C-SSRS are asked in interview format and concentrate on two main areas: suicidal ideation and suicidal behavior. Questions are answered with a yes or no response. If a response of yes is provided, the interviewer will prompt the client to describe the response in detail. Depending on how a client responds to certain items, the counselor determines which items to explore next. The C-SSRS provides a foundation from which exploration for suicidal ideations and behaviors may take place; however, determining suicidality is a function of clinical judgment. See the Web Resources section at the end of this chapter to find a version of the C-SSRS online.

The instruments previously discussed are by no means exhaustive. Rather, our intent is to provide you a snapshot of the varieties of instruments available, as part of the clinical interview, to better understand clients' presenting issues and aid in the process of diagnosis and treatment planning. With proper training, counselors have a plethora of tests, assessments, and rating scales at their disposal. However, this does not suggest that counselors are qualified to administer, score, and interpret any instrument they choose.

Test User Qualifications

The ACA (2014) Code of Ethics is clear that counselors only provide testing and assessment services in which they are trained and competent (E.2.a.). Although professional organizations (e.g., ACA) provide guidelines on education and ethical practices related to testing and assessment, licensure boards define counselors' scope of practice, to include testing and assessment. The purpose of limiting users for certain tests is to ensure both responsible testing practices and protection of the public welfare. Thus, only those who have the appropriate knowledge, training, skill, experience, and credentials are able to administer and score certain tests. In fact, many test publishers limit the access to certain tests by requiring evidence of proper training and credentials in order to purchase. Most test publishers (e.g., Pearson, SIGMA) use a tier or level system that outlines who is qualified to purchase which tests.

For instance, SIGMA (2018) has three qualification levels: A, B, and C. Level *A* tests and assessments require a bachelor's degree, equivalent training in assessment, professional membership in organizations that require training and experience in assessment, certification from an organization that requires training and experience in assessment, or practical experience in using tests and assessment. Level *B* tests and assessments require a minimum of a master's degree and training specific to psychological testing or equivalent training focused on psychological testing from a professional organization. Level *C* tests and assessments require a doctoral degree in psychology or closely related field or may be administered under direct supervision by a qualified psychologist or professional. It is important to remember the ethical obligation counselors have to their clients regarding appropriate use of tests and assessments and how those results are used in the diagnosis and treatment processes. One final consideration to keep in mind regarding tests and assessments is culture. Counselors should carefully consider their clients' culture and background before administering any test or assessment to ensure appropriateness of fit and when interpreting and reporting findings.

DIAGNOSING CLIENTS USING CURRENT DIAGNOSTIC SYSTEMS

The *Diagnostic and Statistical Manual of Mental Disorders* (*DSM*) and the *International Classification of Diseases* (*ICD*) are two methods for classification of diseases used in clinical mental health counseling. The *DSM* is strictly used for mental disorders such as depression, schizophrenia, eating disorders, neurocognitive disorders, and so forth. Although the *ICD* includes the same mental health disorders as the *DSM*, it also comprises other diseases and health-related conditions not found in the *DSM*. For instance, atherosclerosis, a narrowing of arteries caused by excess plague buildup that can lead to stroke or heart attack, can be found in the *ICD* but not the *DSM*. So what is the point of having two classification systems when one, the *ICD*, seems to be inclusive of the disorders found in the other, the *DSM*? It may seem logical to abandon the *DSM* altogether in support of using the *ICD* classification system. Although this may make sense, put a pin in that particular train of thought until after further exploring each classification system.

DSM-5

In its fifth revision, the *DSM-5*, published by the American Psychiatric Association (APA), is the primary diagnostic tool used by physicians, psychiatrists, psychologists, clinical social workers, and licensed professional counselors to classify mental and psychological disorders in the United States. Since its first edition in 1952, the *DSM* has relied on a categorical classification system, that is, whether the symptomatology associated with a particular disorder is present in a client. A significant change in the *DSM-5*, when compared to previous editions, was the addition of dimensional assessments to the categorical diagnoses. With the addition of the dimensional approach to diagnosis, diagnostic categories could be assessed across not only their presence or absence but also across the dimensions of frequency, duration, sensitivity, and severity. Dimensional assessments are rating scales used to assist health practitioners in the diagnosis and treatment planning phases.

Now to address the question posed earlier about abandoning the *DSM* in favor of the *ICD* classification system. First, the *DSM* provides users with criteria and definitions and offers a thorough description of each diagnosis included in the manual. This diagnostic tool helps guide counselors in rendering more accurate diagnosis and thereby ensuring that clients receive only the services they need. In addition, the *DSM* allows for standardization of both diagnosis and language for practitioners and third-party payers. Imagine if every counselor in the United States had his or her own system of diagnosing. There is no telling how many unique ways the diagnosis of bipolar disorder, for instance, would be defined and subsequently assessed. As you may have noticed, the *DSM* is an important tool used for diagnosis and treatment by clinical mental health counselors. Before switching gears to the *ICD* classification system, let's spend a few minutes discussing an emerging trend in diagnosis. With the *DSM-5*, the APA introduced a variety of emerging measures (see Web Resources). These include disorder-specific severity measures, disability measures, personality inventories, early development and home background assessments, and cross-cutting assessments. Of particular interest to counselors is the purpose and application of cross-cutting assessments in support of both clinical interview and monitoring outcomes.

Cross-Cutting Assessment

The *DSM-5* features a novel assessment strategy known as cross-cutting assessment. In support of the dimensional approach to diagnosis, developers of the of the *DSM-5* introduced **cross-cutting assessments** that measure symptomatology common across diagnoses. With the advent of cross-cutting assessment, counselors have the ability to assess symptomatology, irrespective of diagnosis, for children, adolescents, and adults. Based on the information obtained, counselors can choose a subsequent assessment that assists in specifying severity across particular symptoms. A distinct advantage of using a cross-cutting assessment is that it is designed to capture a range of symptoms prior to identifying any particular diagnosis. Information obtained from this assessment method may better assist counselors in being more efficient in the diagnosis and treatment planning phases. You may be wondering how these cross-cutting assessments work.

First, the APA (2014) has developed cross-cutting assessments specific to age: adults (self-rated), children 6 to 17 years of age (parent/guardian-rated), and children 11 to 17 years of age (self-rated). The Level 1 assessment is more generalized, containing symptom domains that "cut" across diagnoses (e.g., anger, anxiety, depression). The evaluation period for a Level 1 assessment ranges from 1 week (adults) to 2 weeks (child), and individuals are assessed across 13 domains for adults or 12 domains for children. If any Level 1 domain is rated as clinically significant, the counselor would follow up with a Level 2 assessment.

Level 2 assessments are more comprehensive, that is, they measure specificity and severity level across a narrower time span. For instance, based on a Level 1 assessment for adults, the score for the depression domain exceeded the threshold and warrants further exploration using the Level 2, Depression, Adult (PROMIS Emotional Distress, Depression, Short Form). This particular assessment evaluates symptoms associated with depression (e.g., helplessness, hopelessness, mood) occurring within the past 7 days, across eight items, using a Likert-type rating scale. Although this type of assessment may seem promising to counselors during the initial assessment phase, Schmit and Balkin (2014) encourage counselors to use caution when using these types of assessments. In their evaluation of cross-cutting assessments, they noted that many of the measures failed to meet evidence of reliability and validity, and symptomatology assessed (e.g., anger, hopelessness, helplessness) may correspond to many diagnoses but are themselves not *DSM-5* diagnoses. Hence, counselors should never render a diagnosis based on a single piece of evidence, such as results from a Level 1 and Level 2 assessment, but on a collection of evidence obtained from the clinical interview. If interested in learning more about Level 1 and Level 2 assessments, see the APA's Assessment Measures located in the Web Resources section.

ICD-10

Another classification system clinical mental health counselors should be familiar with is the *International Classification of Diseases* (*ICD*), currently in its 10th revision, developed by the World Health Organization. The 10th revision expanded the number of possible codes and specifiers beyond the *ICD-9* and is used not only by health practitioners but also coders, IT professionals, insurance organizations, government entities, and others who document disease in health records and bill health insurance plans. In the United States, two versions of the *ICD* are commonly used: *ICD-10-CM* (clinical modification) and *ICD-10-PCS* (procedure coding system). The *ICD-10-CM* is used by practitioners for diagnostic coding purposes, whereas the *ICD-10-PCS* is used by practitioners for procedural purposes in inpatient hospitals. For instance, a counselor may render the *DSM-5* diagnosis of bipolar disorder, current episode hypomanic, which corresponds to the *ICD-10-CM* code of F31.0. Procedure codes such as G9857 or T1502, for instance, indicate an action taken by a health care provider or entity such as "patient admitted to hospice" or "administration of oral, intramuscular and/or subcutaneous medication by health care agency/professional, per visit," respectively.

Counselors need to document in client records the appropriate diagnosis using the *DSM*. When submitting claims to third-party payers, counselors use the *ICD-10* codes to document diagnosis and type of services provided. In fact, any electronic transaction that includes client-protected health information (e.g., diagnosis, health services, claims, referrals, payments) must use an *ICD-10* code between parties. Hence, *ICD-10* codes are HIPAA compliant, that is, follow the Health Insurance Portability and Accountability Act (HIPAA), a U.S. law designed to protect health information. From a practice standpoint, the *DSM-5* conveniently includes *ICD-10* codes, but counselors should be aware that not all *ICD-10-CM* codes are included in the *DSM-5*. However, counselors are by no means required to memorize codes from the *ICD-10-CM* or *ICD-10-PCS*. If a code is required, there are numerous websites to assist counselors with code lookups (see the Web Resources section). Now that you have a general understanding of the current diagnostic systems used by clinical mental health counselors in the United States, let's continue our conversation of assessment by diving into the process of diagnosis.

Process of Diagnosis

Although you may not realize it, the process of diagnosis has already begun. For counselors to accurately diagnose, they need to obtain information from their client, through assessment, as to why the client warrants counseling services. The initial contact, often called a screening, can take place over the phone or in person and is used to ensure that counseling services are a good fit. If results from the screening and the counselor's clinical intuition indicate that counseling may be a viable option, then an intake interview is conducted. After the intake interview, the counselor should assess a client's level of functioning using the Mental Status Exam (MSE) before rendering a diagnosis. Let's review each of these components in more detail.

Screening

Often considered the initial contact with a client and possibly the most important step in the clinical interview process is the screening assessment. A screening assessment can be a simple questionnaire that is effective at identifying whether a person is at risk and in need of counseling services. Although screening assessments may vary, depending on their purpose, they generally include demographic information, reasons for seeking counseling services, previous and current mental health diagnoses, living situation, current risk behaviors, suicidality, and referrals (see Table 14.1). The goal of a screening is to obtain a snapshot of both the client and presenting issues. Based on the information provided, counselors, along with the client, can make informed decisions as to whether counseling services are fitting or even necessary. Counseling is not a recommended service for everyone and every presenting issue. For instance, say an adult male walks into your office and mentions that he hasn't eaten in the past 3 days and he has no desire to seek out counseling services, at least now. Although counseling may seem appropriate in this situation, it will not address his major concern: meeting his basic need of food. Based on your screening results, counseling does not seem like a good fit; instead a referral to a local food pantry or homeless shelter seems most appropriate. If the screening assessment indicated that counseling was appropriate, then the next step is the intake interview.

Intake Interview

A common assessment strategy found to occur in assessment is the intake interview, which can occur in structured, semistructured, or unstructured formats. According to Watson and Flamez (2015), an **intake interview** is "an assessment technique that provides counselors with information about clients' past functioning and how it relates to their current situation and the problems they are facing" (p. 394). Based on this definition, an intake interview is comprehensive and assesses biopsychosocial factors relevant to the client and presenting issues. Although areas of exploration during the intake interview vary depending on setting, specialization of practice, client demographics (e.g., age), and so forth, there are common core areas found across intake interviews. In fact, intake interviews tend to expand on content areas found in the initial screening assessment. Using

TABLE 14.1 ■ Example of Screening Assessment
1. Demographic information: age, ethnicity, race, gender, marital status, employment, education
2. What concerns, problems, or issues bring you into counseling?
3. Have you received counseling in the past?
4. Have you noticed any recent changes in mood? If so, please describe the changes.
5. Have you ever been diagnosed with a mental health disorder?
6. Have you used alcohol or illicit substances within the past 30 days?
7. Any previous history of alcohol or substance use?
8. Have you ever had thoughts of suicide?
9. Have you ever attempted suicide?
10. Do you have a family history of mental illness or suicide? If yes, please describe.
11. Are you currently taking any medications? If so, please list and include dosage and last use.
12. Describe your current living situation.
13. Are you in need of any referrals? If so, please detail your needs.

Note: Items can be easily modified to fit a particular setting or population.

both open- and closed-ended questions, counselors may seek out the following information during an intake interview (Watson & Flamez, 2015):

- Client demographic information: (e.g., age, race, gender, ethnicity, employment status, current living situation).

- Reasons why the client is seeking out counseling services.

- Presenting concerns or problems: The identified problem or concern is explicitly stated by the client and mutually understood by both counselor and client. During this portion of the intake interview, the counselor attempts to understand the depth and scope of the presenting concern, assisting clients in developing concrete statements of what is presently occurring.

- Previous counseling experience: A history of previous counseling experience may prove useful in the counseling process. Information obtained, with prior consent, from previous treatment providers may better inform the diagnosis and treatment planning processes.

- Family and developmental history: An exploration of family dynamic, family constellation, family history of mental illness, and noteworthy personal developmental milestones may shed light on current functioning and prove beneficial during treatment.

- Medical history: Information sought includes previous and current medical and mental health diagnoses, previous and current medications taken, known drug allergies, medical procedures, and so forth.

- Education and vocational history: Information sought includes highest grade level completed, history of employment, name of current employer (if applicable), employment and educational goals, and so forth.

- Previous and current risk behaviors: Information sought includes identification of risk behaviors such as substance use, alcohol use, self-harming behaviors, risky sexual behaviors, history of suicide, previous and current suicidal ideations, and so forth.

Within the context of a helping relationship, both counselor and client may come to the conclusion that secondary source information from the client's family members, friends, partner, physician, or other health professionals, with consent, may prove useful during the clinical interview. Sometimes clients have a difficult time remembering information or are not willing to share details they find difficult to discuss. Likewise, counselors may find it worthwhile to seek secondary source information to fill in the gaps or confirm information obtained during the intake interview. Remember that secondary source information is just one piece of informal evidence obtained during the assessment process, used to better understand the client's perspective, and should never serve as the sole determinate in making decisions about client treatment.

Perhaps most important to consider during the intake interview is understanding clients from their cultural background. Hence, considerations of diversity and culture are not separate processes from the intake interview itself. Rather, effective counselors consider the multicultural factors of their clients throughout the interview by asking culturally informed questions or how questions are perceived or understood. Using this approach can lead to less bias in the information obtained and better assist counselors in understanding client data within context. A helpful tool to assist counselors in developing culturally informed interview protocols or when conducting culturally informed intake assessments is the Cultural Formulation Interview (CFI), adopted by the APA in the *DSM-5*, which is available for free download (see Web Resources section). The CFI provides counselors an outline of how to integrate culturally relevant information into the clinical assessment process. Cultural areas for consideration include defining the problem, cause of the problem and current supports, previous methods of coping, and current and previous help-seeking behaviors, each explored with respect to a client's culture and background.

Mental Status Exam. The Mental Status Examination (MSE) is a clinician-administered assessment used to obtain information about the client's level of functioning and self-presentation during the clinical interview (Seligman, 1986). Often conducted informally, the counselor may ask a series of questions related to some or all areas of the MSE. Additionally, the counselor, through conversation, is able to observe and experience the client's self-presentation as well as assess daily functioning. Similar to the screening and intake interview, the MSE alone should not be used to determine a diagnosis or treatment interventions; rather, it serves as another piece of evidence in an attempt to understand the client's perspective. Data from the MSE can easily be reported as a

GUIDED PRACTICE EXERCISE 14.3

Developing you own intake interview protocol.

Using the information in this section, develop your own intake interview protocol. Begin by identifying domains (e.g., demographic information, employment history, medical history, current and previous substance use) you consider important. Consider how your chosen domains will benefit the diagnosis, treatment planning, and treatment process. Also consider how many items you would include and which interview format to use: structured, semistructured, or unstructured. After addressing these factors, develop your intake interview protocol. Once complete, switch with an in-class partner and offer each other feedback. Keep this protocol as a resource for when you begin independent practice as a licensed professional counselor.

brief one- to two-paragraph narrative describing the counselor's observations and the client's self-report of information assessed across six domains: (1) appearance, attitude, and activity; (2) mood and affect; (3) speech and language; (4) thought process, thought content, and perception; (5) cognitive; and (6) insight and judgment. See Table 14.2 for a brief description of each domain. For more detailed information on the MSE,

TABLE 14.2 ■ Summary of the Mental Status Examination Domains

Domain	Description
Appearance, attitude, and activity	*Appearance*: physical characteristics, manner of dress and grooming, level of consciousness, posture, apparent age *Attitude*: how the client approached the interview and interacted with the interviewer *Activity*: voluntary and involuntary physical movements during interview
Mood and affect	*Mood*: client's self-report of internal feeling state *Affect*: observable changes in mood state noted by the counselor as expressed by the client
Speech and language	The rate, rhythm, and volume of speech; the quality of word selection used to formulate a sentence
Thought process, thought content, and perception	*Thought process*: the rate at which thoughts flow and the degree to which they are organized and connected *Thought content*: substance or themes of thoughts *Perception*: how the client perceives self, others, and the external world across the five senses
Cognitive	Client's ability to think, reason, and use logic; intellectual level, memory, and higher functioning
Insight and judgment	*Insight*: self and other awareness *Judgment*: ability to make sound judgments after considering internal and external information

Note: Information adapted from Polanski and Hinkle (2000) and Trzepacz and Baker (1993).

consider reviewing Polanski and Hinkle's (2000) article in the *Journal of Counseling & Development* (see reference list for full citation).

Information obtained from each of the six domains of the MSE provides counselors with both subjective and objective information that can be used in determining a diagnosis. At this point in the clinical interview, data have been collected from three sources: the screening assessment, intake interview, and MSE, which can be used as a compass to guide counselors on the path of determining an appropriate *DSM-5* diagnosis. As a best practice, consider using a symptom-specific measure or cross-cutting assessment prior to rendering a final diagnosis. As a result, two things have been established: the severity level of symptoms and a baseline score. Both will prove useful when determining a specifier for the diagnosis and establishing objectives during treatment planning. In the next section we present a six-step process to diagnosis, referred to as differential diagnosis.

Differential Diagnosis

The similarity of symptoms across diagnoses can be a challenge even for the most seasoned counselors. Likewise, rendering a diagnostic impression without giving it a second thought or only relying on minimal evidence to draw a conclusion is just as erroneous. Although not a novel approach, what if counselors tackled diagnosis from a multiple-diagnoses perspective? Based on a preponderance of evidence collected from the clinical interview, counselors judiciously rule out diagnoses that fail to explain symptoms and conditions present. This method of diagnosing is known as differential diagnosis. Simply put, **differential diagnosis** is a systematic process of ruling out competing diagnoses, using

GUIDED PRACTICE EXERCISE 14.4

Case conceptualization practice.

Develop a case conceptualization based on the following case scenario. Consider Neukrug and Schmitzer's (2006) three-phase model—(a) evaluate information, (b) organize information, and (c) interpret information from a theoretical orientation—and a counseling theory you identify with.

Case scenario: Sylvia, a 27-year-old divorcee, arrives early to her first session of counseling. Sylvia describes herself as being physically and psychologically well most of her life until 8 months ago. Sylvia is a night cashier at a local convenience store and was recently held up at gunpoint. Although she continues to work the nightshift, she feels anxious while tending the register. She finds herself always looking over her shoulder at work and in her personal life. One afternoon, her heart began to pound, she perspired profusely, and she experienced shortness of breath. She felt as though she was dying. Sylvia reported that she is fearful to leave her house most days but needs to keep her job because of family responsibilities. Sylvia has lived with a roommate for the past 3 years after her divorce.

To help guide the process of case conceptualization, use the following prompts:

What stands out to you?

What cultural or contextual considerations are present?

Are there any patterns or themes?

Is there enough information to conceptualize Sylvia's case? If not, what information would you need (hint: consider your theoretical orientation)?

prior evidence, that share common symptomatology. The systematic process of differential diagnosis includes six steps:

1. Consider the validity of symptoms.
2. Consider if symptoms are caused by a medical condition.
3. Consider if symptoms are caused by substance or alcohol use.
4. Consider if symptoms are situational.
5. Consider no diagnosis at all.
6. Render diagnosis.

Step 1: Consider the Validity of Symptoms

Using evidence from the clinical interview, counselors should first assess the validly of symptoms present. Ask yourself this question: Do these symptoms actually exist? Although not common, clients may present with factitious symptoms. Factitious symptoms may occur on the conscious level (e.g., malingering, factitious disorder) or unconsciously (e.g., somatoform disorder, somatization disorder, conversion disorder). Counselors who have conducted a thorough clinical interview, that is, used multiple sources to collect client information, should be able to address this step accurately. Likewise, circumventing this step may prove troublesome during the treatment planning and intervention stages.

Step 2: Consider If Symptoms Are Caused by a Medical Condition

In the next step of differential diagnosis, counselors should consider whether symptoms presented are better explained by a medical condition. Again, using data from the clinical interview, can a medical condition explain the root cause of symptomatology? Counselors may ask themselves this question: Is the anxiety symptom, for instance, the result of another medical condition? If the anxiety is caused by other medical conditions such as heart disease, diabetes, thyroid probes, or a side effect of medication, consultation with the client's medical provider is an important step. Likewise, if the anxiety symptom is the result of a medical condition and is causing the client to experience clinically significant distress, an adjustment disorder may be appropriate. For most diagnoses under consideration, the *DSM-5* provides counselors with suggested medical conditions to rule out during the diagnostic process.

Step 3: Consider If Symptoms Are Caused by Substance or Alcohol Use

A common misstep by many counselors is overlooking substance use as the root cause of symptom presentation. Counselors should *always* consider whether substance or alcohol use better explains the presentation of symptoms. For instance, immediate use of hallucinogens or stimulants can explain symptoms of paranoia and psychosis. Similarly, withdrawal from alcohol and substances can mimic symptoms of depression, hallucinations, anxiety, and suicidal ideations. Essentially, substance and alcohol use have the potential to mimic many psychiatric symptoms associated with a variety of mental health disorders. Moral of the story: Assess everyone for substance and alcohol use when using differential diagnosis.

Step 4: Consider If Symptoms Are Situational

In this step, counselors need to consider if symptoms are situational rather than rooted in a psychological disorder. For instance, divorce, loss of job, or death of a loved one can result in emotional and behavior responses of anxiety, depression, anger, isolation, and so forth. Thus, counselors must be prudent when determining if symptoms are a reaction to a situation or event. If so, a diagnosis of adjustment disorder better explains symptom presentation versus depressive disorder or anxiety disorder. Counselors should consider the onset and duration of symptoms. Symptom onset for adjustment disorder occurs within 3 months and generally persists for no more than 6 months.

Step 5: Consider No Diagnosis at All

Although this step may sound counterintuitive, counselors can feel compelled by clients and health organizations to offer a diagnosis, even if one does not fit. The *DSM-5* offers a range of V- and Z-Codes that may better explain a person's health status, reason for visit, presentation of emotions and behaviors, and so forth than a mental health diagnosis. Much of the information needed to render a V- or Z-Code is obtained during the intake interview. Something to keep in mind when using V- or Z-Codes is the source of distress. Is it internal or external to the person? If the source is external, the use of a V- or Z-Code is favorable. Pages 715–727 of the *DSM-5* provide counselors with a list of V- and Z-Codes as well as their description.

Step 6: Render Diagnosis

After systematically addressing the validity of symptoms, ruling out substance and alcohol use and medical conditions, and determining whether symptoms are situational or better explained by V- and Z-Codes, it is time to render a diagnosis. Consider which symptoms are most salient. Using the *DSM-5*, select a disorder that fits the most salient symptoms identified. You may want to start broadly by selecting a chapter first (e.g., Depressive Disorders, Obsessive-Compulsive and Related Disorder) and narrowing your options as you peruse diagnoses within the selected chapter. Next, when you have narrowed your options to a single diagnosis, find evidence to support each criterion of the disorder. If you find yourself heading down the wrong path, it is perfectly okay to backtrack and choose another disorder that aligns with the evidence. Sometimes evidence aligns perfectly with diagnostic criteria, and other times it can be challenging. If the latter happens to be true, consider whether evidence was simply missed during the clinical interview but can be inferred using the preponderance of evidence collected. If not, there is a high likelihood that criterion and diagnosis do not fit. Although this may seem like a sticky situation, counselors should not forget their secret weapon: clinical judgment. If you follow these six steps, relying on the evidence collected during the clinical interview before moving onto the next step, and use your clinical judgment, you should feel more than confident in the diagnosis rendered.

CASE ILLUSTRATION 14.2

Why differential diagnosis is important.

Jennifer is a 37-year-old Hispanic woman with an extensive history of substance use and depression, multiple suicide attempts, and a pervious diagnosis of major depression. Jennifer identifies as a chain-smoker and does not take into consideration her physical health. Her diet consists of fast food, and she rarely engages in physical exercise. She has a family history of diabetes, heart disease, and lung cancer. Within the past month, Jennifer has experienced depressed mood, hyperactivity and impulsivity, rapid speech, periods of grandiosity and euphoria, suicidal thoughts, and countless nights of insomnia. She reported experiencing similar symptoms a few months ago. Given the plethora of information provided by Jennifer, a counselor needs to carefully consider all possible diagnoses using the differential diagnosis approach.

Although Jennifer has received a previous diagnosis of major depressive disorder, the validity of that diagnosis may no longer be true. Likewise, given her lifestyle choices and family medical history, numerous medical conditions may attribute to her more recent symptomatology presentation. Also, substance withdrawal may contribute to symptoms experienced. As you may notice, rendering a diagnosis based on Jennifer's case scenario can be challenging. Thus, using a differential diagnosis approach allows counselors to carefully consider all presenting factors, ruling out those deemed unrelated to the current symptom presentation systematically. Based on Jennifer's history and after ruling out current substance use and medical concerns, the evidence points to a diagnosis of bipolar disorder.

INTEGRATING ASSESSMENT DATA INTO THE TREATMENT PLANNING PROCESS

Now that evidence has been collected and distilled, a diagnosis rendered, and building blocks of a helping relationship laid, the counselor is tasked with organizing this information in a way that makes sense. To facilitate this process, the counselor relies on formulating a hypothesis that attempts to explain the client's perspective. You may be asking yourself how one develops a hypothesis explaining the client and presenting issues. Well, hypotheses emerge from the counselor's theoretical orientation. As you may already know, numerous theoretical frameworks (e.g., psychoanalysis, Adlerian, behavioral, person-centered) guide counselors in the development of a working hypothesis. In counseling, this working hypothesis is better known as case conceptualization.

Case Conceptualization

According to Neukrug and Schwitzer (2006), **case conceptualization** is a clinical tool used by counselors to organize client information—behaviors, thoughts, feelings, and physiology—in a manner that explains the client's perspective from the counselor's theoretical orientation. In other words, explaining why a client engages in self-harm behaviors or consumes alcohol in excess provides counselors a framework from which to work. Although numerous models of case conceptualization exist (e.g., Kress & Paylo,

2015; Sperry & Sperry, 2012), Neukrug and Schmitzer (2006) purposed a three-phase model: (1) evaluate information, (2) organize information, and (3) interpret information from a theoretical orientation.

In the first step, counselors should evaluate the presenting concerns through observations, assessments, and behavioral measurements. The goal of this step is to obtain all relevant information, past and present, that accurately explains the present concern. This is accomplished during the clinical assessment phase. In the second step, the counselor should organize the information obtained from observing, assessing, and measuring the presenting concern into patterns and themes. This is much like putting a puzzle together. First, identify the boundaries of the presenting concerns and then fill in the middle to better understand the concerns within the context of the client's perspective. In the last step, the counselor, from his or her theoretical orientation, should interpret and explain the patterns and themes that have emerged. Using the counselor's theoretical approach, information is filtered in a way that makes sense to the counselor.

Which information gets filtered depends on the counselor's theoretical orientation. For instance, a humanistic counselor's conceptualization is distinct from a cognitive counselor's, yet they both explain client phenomena in a systematic manner that explains the "what" and "why" of the presenting issue and begins to shed light on "how" to solve the issue. Without case conceptualization, counselors would be shooting from the hip, so to speak, aimlessly trying to figure out the best course of action. Thus, case conceptualization gives counselors tangible context to client issues that creates a pathway from which treatment can be developed.

Developing Client Treatment Plans

The importance of establishing treatment plans in the delivery of mental health services cannot be overstated (Jongsma & Peterson, 2014). Clinical mental health counselors are expected to have the knowledge and skills to develop sound treatment from case conceptualization, which relies on methodically integrated data from both clinical assessment and diagnosis. So, what exactly is a treatment plan, and what does it entail? According to Seligman (1996), a *treatment plan* comprises

> plotting out the counseling process so that both counselor and client have a road map that delineates how they will proceed from their point of origin (the client's presenting concerns and underlying difficulties) to their destination, alleviation of troubling and dysfunctional symptoms and patterns, and establishment of improved coping. (p. 157)

As you may have already noticed from this definition, treatment planning is a collaborative process between the counselor and client. Counselors should keep in mind that treatment plans are collaborative and strength-based and represent clients' best interests. Likewise, treatment plans help counselors stay on task, keep counseling sessions organized, and allow monitoring of treatment outcomes. To help beginning counselors formulate a well-developed treatment plan, here is a simple five-step model applicable to most clinical mental health settings: (1) define the problem, (2) establish treatment goals or objectives, (3) determine counseling interventions, (4) evaluate client progress, and (5) revise the treatment plan.

Define the Problem

Throughout the clinical assessment phase, counselor and client systematically organize information to determine the presenting issue. It is not uncommon for numerous problems to emerge, some proposed by the client and others from the counselor. Thus, counselor and client need to mutually agree on what problems are most important and where treatment should begin. Sometimes the client does not agree with the counselor's synopsis of the problem. This may be the result of a poor therapeutic alliance, a symptom of the client's mental illness, or a combination of the two. In this case, counselors should exercise good clinical judgment when collaboratively establishing the problems. Some situations that warrant counselors' clinical judgment when prioritizing problems include suicide and homicide, self-harm and other dangerous behaviors, substance and alcohol use, deterioration in functioning, and concern with meeting basic needs.

Sometimes the words chosen to frame the problem are another reason why counselors face resistance when defining the problem. Imagine if a counselor identified the problem as "you drink too much" or "you're depressed all the time." How do you think a client would feel in this situation? Is there a better way to formulate the problem? In these types of situations, remember that treatment planning is a collaborative process. Do not be afraid to elicit the client's help in this situation. How would the client articulate the problem? This process may seem stress-inducing for beginning counselors, but remember, sometimes it is the lack of understanding clients' perspective (i.e., empathy) that gets in the way. Here are some tips to help counselors define the problem: (a) use kind language that matches the client's verbiage, (b) problems should align with the client's needs, (c) prioritize problems using a hierarchy, and (d) be collaborative. Once the problem has been defined and mutually understood by both the counselor and client, it is time to establish treatment goals and objectives.

CASE ILLUSTRATION 14.3

Defining the problem.

A critical step in treatment planning is defining the problem. Sometimes clients may not know how to contextualize the problem, and other times counselors have their own assumptions as to what the problem might be. Both pathways can lead to a difficult treatment process and poor outcomes. Imagine if the counselor never fully explored the client's problem, questioned the validity of information presented during the clinical interview, or just relied on his or her assumptions without ever checking in with the client. A likely outcome would be that 3 weeks into treatment, the counselor notices a pattern of the client showing up late, never completing homework, and resisting the therapeutic process. It turns out that the identified problem of sexual dissatisfaction in his marriage reported by the client actually emerged in session when he shared his experience of guilt and shame from engaging in adultery. It is imperative that the identified problem be clearly understood and mutually agreed on by both counselor and client because it sets the tone for establishing goals and objectives that in turn informs intervention selection and methods of evaluation.

Establish Treatment Goals or Objectives

Often the terms *goals* and *objectives* are used interchangeably in treatment planning. However, goals are distinct from objectives. Treatment goals are more global and represent the bigger picture. For instance, a goal of improved mood is common for a person with major depression. Objectives are the measurable steps of how a client will achieve a specific goal. Continuing with the depression example, objectives may include developing strategies for thought distraction, getting a full night's rest, reporting feeling more positive about self and situation, and establishing a daily routine. Each objective is directly related to the overall goal and provides a pathway for the client to be successful in achieving the goal of creating an improved mood.

Goals and objectives need to be realistic; that is, they have to be specific and meaningful to clients and something they are committed to doing. Additionally, strong objectives are measurable in some way. Using the previous objective of getting a full night's rest, how often should this occur? How will it be measured? How will you keep the client accountable? These are some of the challenges beginning counselors face when creating objectives. A better way of writing the previous objective is to be specific and measurable. For instance, the client will get 7 to 8 hours of sleep, 3 times per week, for 6 months, as evidenced by client self-report and sleep journal. Client's mood will be evaluated each month using the BDI-II for comparison. When comparing the initial objective, getting a full night's rest, to the subsequent objective, 7 to 8 hours of sleep, what stands out? Which of the two seems more measurable? Creating effective goals and objectives can be challenging for counselors. Remember, quality goals and objectives are meaningful, realistic, concise, and measurable; they hold the client accountable.

Determine Counseling Interventions

Once treatment goals and objectives have been established, it is time to select interventions to support clients in achieving their objectives and goals. Similar to how objectives hold the client accountable, interventions are the micro-steps the counselor employees to support clients in achieving their objectives. Interventions emerge from counselors' theoretical orientation and align with the client's objectives, goals, and needs. Although many theories provide counselors with strategies and interventions to employ (e.g., cognitive, behaviorism, CBT), many do not (e.g., person-centered, existentialism), at least in the traditional sense of how an intervention is understood. Thus, counselors must merge their theoretical orientation with the evidence base for a particular problem.

Refer to our previous objective: client will get 7 to 8 hours of sleep, 3 times per week, for 6 months, as evidenced by client self-report and sleep journal. Counselors, using evidence-based practices and their theoretical orientation, need to determine an appropriate intervention. Some things to consider are the level of care (e.g., inpatient, outpatient), treatment modality (e.g., individual counseling, group counseling), frequency of the intervention, and the number of sessions. Additionally, counselors need to seek research evidence, if available, shown to be effective in meeting the objectives and goal and consider how their theoretical orientation informs establishing an intervention. Using our previous objective and a CBT framework, an appropriate intervention might include outpatient, weekly individual counseling for 6 months. Using CBT, the counselor will emphasize emerging automatic thoughts that prevent sleep and use stress inoculation training to improve the client's sleep patterns. Finally, a strong intervention can be measured. In other words, you know when the intervention is effective. One method is to assess the client's depression symptomatology using the BDI-II every 2 months. An improvement in the client's mood across a 2-month treatment period would be a positive indicator of intervention effectiveness. Alternatively, the counselor could rely on the client's self-report of current mood states using an open- and closed-ended question format. Regardless of evaluation method, counselors should consider, throughout treatment planning, how they will measure client progress and intervention effectiveness.

As you may have noticed, when developing an intervention, the counselor has a lot of moving parts that need to be considered. Here are some helpful questions to keep in mind: (a) Does the intervention align with the treatment goal and objectives? (b) Does the research evidence support the intervention? (c) Is the intervention realistic and obtainable? (d) Does the intervention fit within the counselor's theoretical orientation? (e) Is the intervention effective, and is the client making progress toward stated goals and objectives?

Evaluate Client Progress

Throughout the treatment planning process, counselors should carefully consider how they will evaluate client progress. In the steps of establishing treatment goals and objectives and determining counseling interventions, methods for evaluation were already included. Treatment planning in this manner places monitoring of client progress and intervention effectiveness at the forefront. From a practice standpoint, being able to document client progress and intervention effectiveness is paramount to receive reimbursement from third-party payers.

Counselors have numerous methods at their disposal to evaluate both client and intervention outcomes. For instance, counselors can employ an informal questionnaire, ask open-ended or scaling questions, rely on client self-reports, administer a rating scale, or observe behavioral change. These types of strategies should sound familiar. Similar to formal and informal assessment strategies are formative and summative evaluation methods. **Formative evaluation methods** are strategies used to assess the client's experience in real time (Watson & Flamez, 2015). For instance, during the counseling session the counselor may ask the client how helpful an intervention was or what aspects of the intervention were most helpful. Formative evaluation methods take the form of open-ended questions, scaling questions, role-plays, and client self-reports and often reflect qualitative types of data. **Summative evaluation methods** are strategies used at set time points (e.g., every 2 weeks, once a month) throughout the counseling process (Watson & Flamez, 2015). For instance, at the end of the counseling experience the counselor again administers the Beck Anxiety Inventory (BAI) to compare to previously collected BAI scores. Summative evaluation methods are often rating scales, structured assessments, or other formal assessment strategies. Information obtained from both evaluation methods can be used to shape treatment and interventions, as well as monitor client progress toward objectives and goals.

Revise the Treatment Plan

A final step in treatment planning is to ensure that current treatment goals and objectives are still relevant and useful to the client and the presenting problem. Like most things in life, situations change. The same holds true in counseling and treatment planning. Think of a treatment plan as a living document, designed to be edited, adjusted, or revised in consultation with your client. What was once an established goal or objective may no longer be. Perhaps the client has achieved the goal or objective already, no longer values a particular goal, or the client's life has taken a significant downswing. As such, the counselor should be prepared to adjust treatment plans when necessary, relying on both formative and summative data collected throughout treatment.

Keystones

- Clinical assessment, diagnosis, and treatment planning are best thought of as a tripartite practice, inseparable from one another, occurring in clinical mental health counseling. As a reflexive process, clinical assessment guides the diagnostic process that ultimately informs treatment planning.

- Assessment is more than a means-to-an-end practice. It is the relational process by which counselors gather the information they need to form a holistic view of their clients and the problems with which they present.

- Assessment strategies can include both formal and informal methods. Formal assessment strategies follow a specific, standardized set of procedures that yield quantifiable data that can be compared to a normative population. Informal assessment strategies do not follow a strict set of procedures and are not concerned with comparing results to a normative sample. Rather, informal assessment methods seek out client subjective data and tend to be more inclusive of the entire client experience.

- Reliability is the ability of test scores to be interpreted in a consistent and dependable manner across multiple test administrations. Validity is the degree to which evidence and theory support the interpretations of test scores. Test bias occurs when scores of one group are significantly different from scores of another group based solely on group membership.

- The clinical interview is an action-oriented intervention in which a counselor solicits information about a client and the client's past using a series of questions, assesses the client's verbal and nonverbal responses to those questions, and uses that information to formulate a diagnosis for the client. Clinical interviews can be structured, semistructured, or unstructured.

- The process of diagnosis encompasses different assessment strategies, both formal and informal, and commonly includes a screening assessment, an intake assessment, and a mental status examination as a means to collect information about the client and presenting issue before a diagnosis is rendered.

- Differential diagnosis is the systematic process of ruling out competing diagnoses, using prior evidence, that share common symptomatology criteria. The systematic process of differential diagnosis includes six steps: (1) consider the validity of symptoms, (2) consider if symptoms are caused by medical conditions, (3) consider if symptoms are caused by substance or alcohol use, (4) consider if symptoms are situational, (5) consider no diagnosis at all, and (6) render diagnosis.

- Treatment planning is a five-step process that involves (1) defining the problem, (2) establishing treatment goals/objective, (3) determining counseling interventions, (4) evaluating client progress, and (5) revising the treatment plan.

Key Terms

Assessment 365

Case conceptualization 384

Clinical interview 368

Construct bias 371

Cross-cutting assessments 375

Differential diagnosis 381

Formal assessment
   strategies 367

Formative evaluation
   methods 388

Informal assessment
   strategies 368

Intake interview 377

Item bias 371

Latent construct 365

Method bias 371

Operational definition 366

Psychological test 365

Reliability 370

Summative evaluation
   methods 388

Test bias 371

Validity 371

Web Resources

Alcohol Use Disorders Identification Test (AUDIT) (www.integration.samhsa.gov/AUDIT_screener_for_alcohol.pdf)

APA Cultural Formulation Interview (www.psychiatry.org/File%20Library/Psychiatrists/Practice/DSM/APA_DSM5_Cultural-Formulation-Interview-Supplementary-Modules.pdf)

APA Online Assessment Measures (www.psychiatry.org/psychiatrists/practice/dsm/educational-resources/assessment-measures)

CAGE and CAGE-AID Introduction and Scoring (www.magellanproviderfocus.com/media/379891/aod_cage_cage-aid_screening.pdf)

Centers for Medicare and Medicaid Services: ICD-10-CM Code Lookup (https://www.cms.gov/medicare-coverage-database/staticpages/icd-10-code-lookup.aspx)

Columbia-Suicide Severity Rating Scale (C-SSRS) (www.integration.samhsa.gov/clinical-practice/Columbia_Suicide_Severity_Rating_Scale.pdf)

Find-a-Code: ICD-10-PCS Code Lookup (www.findacode.com/icd-10-pcs/icd-10-pcs-procedure-codes-set.html)

GAD-7 (www.integration.samhsa.gov/clinical-practice/GAD708.19.08Cartwright.pdf)

Good Therapy: Treatment Plan (www.goodtherapy.org/blog/psychpedia/treatment-plan)

Patient Health Questionnaire (PHQ-9) (www.integration.samhsa.gov/images/res/PHQ%20-%20Questions.pdf)

Pearson Clinical Psychology Qualifications Policy (www.pearsonclinical.com/psychology/qualifications.html)

PTSD Checklist: Civilian Version (PCL-C) (www.mirecc.va.gov/docs/visn6/3_ptsd_checklist_and_scoring.pdf)

SAMHSA Screening Tools (www.integration.samhsa.gov/clinical-practice/screening-tools#suicide)

References

American Counseling Association. (2014). *ACA code of ethics*. Alexandria, VA: Author.

American Educational Research Association, American Psychological Association, and National Council on Measurement in Education. (1999). *Standards for educational and psychological testing*. Washington, DC: American Psychological Association.

American Psychiatric Association. (2013). *Diagnostic and statistical manual of mental disorders* (5th ed.). Arlington, VA: Author.

Babor, T. F., Higgins-Biddle, J. C., Suanders, J. B., & Monteiro, M. G. (2001). *The Alcohol Use Disorders Identification Test: Guidelines for use in primary care* (2nd ed.). World Health Organization.

Balkin, R. S., & Juhnke, G. A. (2018). *Assessment in counseling: Practice and applications*. New York, NY: Oxford University Press.

Beck, A. T., Steer, R. A., & Brown, G. K. (1996). *Manual for the Beck Depression Inventory-II*. San Antonio, TX: Psychological Corporation.

Blanchard, E. B., Jones-Alexander, J., Buckley, T. C., & Forneris, C. A. (1996). Psychometric properties of the PTSD Checklist (PCL). *Behaviour Research and Therapy, 34*, 669–673. doi:10.1016/0005-7967(96)00033-2

Cohen, R. J., & Swerdlik, M. E. (2005). Psychological testing and assessment: An introduction to tests and measurement (6th ed.). Boston, MA: McGraw Hill.

Council for Accreditation of Counseling and Related Educational Programs. (2016). *2016 CACREP standards*. Alexander, VA: Author.

Craighead, W. E., & Nemeroff, C. B. (2004). *The concise Corsini encyclopedia of psychology and behavioral science* (3rd ed.). Hoboken, NJ: Wiley.

Jongsma, A. J., & Peterson, L. M. (2014). *The complete adult psychotherapy treatment planner* (5th ed). Hoboken, NJ: Wiley.

Kress, V. E., & Paylo, M. J. (2015). *Treating those with mental disorders: A comprehensive approach to case conceptualization and treatment*. Boston, MA: Pearson Education.

Kroenke, K., Spitzer, R. L., & Williams, J. B. W. (2001). The PHQ-9 validity of a brief depression severity measure. *Journal of General Internal Medicine, 16*, 606–613. doi:10.1046/j.1525-1497.2001.016009606.x

McLellan, A. T., Luborsky, L., Woody, G. E., & O'Brien, C. P. (1980). An improved diagnostic evaluation instrument for substance abuse patients. The Addiction Severity Index. *Journal of Nervous and Mental Disease, 168*(1), 26–33.

Neukrug, E. S., & Schwitzer, A. (2006). Skills and tools for today's professional counselors and psychotherapists: From natural helping to professional counseling. Belmont, CA: Brooks/Cole.

Peterson, D. R. (2004). Science, scientism, and professional responsibility. *Clinical Psychological: Science and Practice, 11*, 196–210.

Polanski, P. J., & Hinkle, J. S. (2000). The mental status examination: Its use by professional counselors. *Journal of Counseling & Development, 78*(3), 357–364. doi:10.1002/j.1556-6676.2000.tb01918.x

Posner, K., Brown, G. K., Stanley, B., Brent, D. A., Yershova, K. V., Oquendo, M. A., . . . Mann, J. J. (2011). The Columbia-Suicide Severity Rating Scale: Initial validity and internal consistency findings from three multisite studies with adolescents and adults. *American Journal of Psychiatry, 168*, 1266–1277.

Power, Z., Campbell, M., Kitcoyne, P., Kitchener, H., & Waterman, H. (2010). The hyperemesis impact of symptoms questionnaire: Development and validation of a clinical tool. *International Journal of Nursing Studies, 47*, 67–77. doi:10.1016/j.ijnurstu.2009.06.012

Research Foundation for Mental Hygiene, Columbia Lighthouse Project. (2008). Columbia-Suicide Severity Rating Scale. Retrieved from http://cssrs.columbia.edu/

Sattler, J. M. (2002). Assessment of children: Behavioral and clinical applications (4th ed.). La Mesa, CA: Sattler.

Schmit, E. L., & Balkin, R. S. (2014). Evaluating emerging measures in the *DSM-5* for counseling practice. *The Professional Counselor, 4,* 216–231. doi:10.15241/els.4.3.216

Seligman, L. (1986). *Diagnosis and treatment planning in counseling.* New York, NY: Human Science Press.

SIGMA. (2018). Testing qualification levels. Retrieved from http://www.sigmaassessmentsystems.com/place-an-order/testing-qualifications/

Sperry, L., & Sperry, J. (2012). *Case conceptualization: Mastering this competency with ease and confidence.* New York, NY: Routledge.

Spitzer, R. L., Kroenke, K., Williams, J. B. W., & Lowe, B. (2006). A brief measure for assessing generalized anxiety disorder. *Archives of Internal Medicine, 166,* 1092–1097.

Trzepacz, P. T., & Baker, R. W. (1993). *The psychiatric mental status examination.* Oxford, England: Oxford University Press.

van de Vijver, F., & Tanzer, N. K. (2004). Bias and equivalence in cross-cultural assessment: An overview. *European Review of Applied Psychology, 54,* 119–135.

Watson, J. C., & Flamez, B. (2015). *Counseling assessment and evaluation: Fundamentals of applied practice.* Thousand Oaks, CA: Sage.

Weathers, F. W., Litz, B. T., Herman, D. S., Huska, J. A., & Keane, T. M. (1993, October). *The PTSD checklist: Reliability, validity, and diagnostic utility.* Paper presented at the Annual Meeting of the International Society for Traumatic Stress Studies, San Antonio, TX.

15

STRATEGIES FOR WORKING WITH SPECIFIC CLIENT POPULATIONS

The diversity of clients served by clinical mental health counselors is endless. In response to the everchanging sociopolitical landscape in the United States and personal life circumstances, many populations have unique needs that require special considerations beyond that of the general population. Although numerous factors contribute to the disparities experienced among specific client populations—ranging from personal choice to historical oppression and racism to politics and religion to biological and sociological factors, among many others—it is clear that 21st-century counselors must be culturally component and aware of the diverse needs of those they serve. Imagine counseling an incarcerated client for the first time. Did you know that persons from this specific population can pose challenges of reluctance and resistance in counseling? That is, they may perceive counseling as useless and you, the counselor, as someone who cannot be trusted. Other considerations you may not be aware of regarding incarcerated clients include that most have an extensive history of trauma and a dismal outlook on life after release; and they are more likely than persons from the general population to experience mental illness and substance use issues (Gonzalez & Connell, 2014; Substance Abuse and Mental Health Services Administration [SAMHSA], n.d.). To further complicate matters, the likelihood of recidivism among formerly incarcerated persons is approximately 68% (Durose, Cooper, & Snyder, 2014), and the rate of recidivism among those with mental health illness is 50% to 230% higher than those without (Baillargeon, Binswanger, Penn, Williams, & Murray, 2009). Knowing this information about persons formerly incarcerated prior to establishing a counseling relationship may better facilitate multicultural sensitivity by the counselor as well as provide the opportunity to challenge any unaddressed biases.

Clinical mental health counselors must take into consideration the diverse needs and special circumstances of specific populations when providing counseling services. Although this chapter identifies certain populations, it is in no way inclusive of every population or every circumstance or strategy. Rather, this chapter serves as a gentle reminder of the diversity of clients served and the important role counselors play in working with clients from diverse backgrounds. To assist beginning-level counselors in their training and preparation, this chapter overviews special considerations and circumstances and various strategies for effectively working with specific populations. We encourage those reading this chapter to deepen their interest and knowledge of the specific populations mentioned by exploring the Web Resources available at the end of this chapter. These populations include children and adolescent clients; active and veteran military personnel and their families; clients of color; adjudicated, involuntary, and incarcerated clients; aging clients; immigrant clients; gay, lesbian, bisexual, and transgendered clients; and clients served in rural settings.

LEARNING OBJECTIVES

After reading this chapter, you will be able to do the following:

- Identify and describe special considerations and circumstances that may influence treatment among various populations

- Identify cultural factors relevant to the treatment of specific client populations served in various clinical mental health settings (CACREP 5C-2-j)

- Describe various strategies, techniques, and interventions for prevention and treatment of a broad range of mental health issues within specific populations (CACREP 5C-3-b)

CHILDREN AND ADOLESCENT CLIENTS

Special Considerations and Circumstances

Working with children and adolescent clients can be a transformative experience for both client and counselor. However, for beginning-level counselors it is easy to feel overwhelmed by addressing the plethora of unique needs inherent to this specific population. Depending on the age of the client, counselors may find it challenging to establish a working alliance, alter language to match their client's developmental level, keep sessions progressing, identify the root cause of the problem, establish treatment goals and objectives meaningful to both the child or adolescent client and their parents, and balance parental rights and client confidentiality. Plus, the developmental process of children and adolescents in and of itself can pose many unique challenges for counselors throughout the counseling process. Counselors must consider the maturation and development of the child's or adolescent's brain, periods of rapid physical growth, and changes in cognitive functioning when working with this population. Table 15.1 provides an overview of the five psychosocial stages relevant to children and adolescents proposed by Erikson (1963).

TABLE 15.1 ■ Erikson's First Five Stages of Psychosocial Development	
Stage	**Description**
Trust vs. mistrust (birth to 18 months)	The infant lives in a world of uncertainty and continuously seeks out the primary caregiver for support and comfort. If the infant receives reliable and consistent care, he or she will develop a sense of trust that is carried forward in other relationships.
Autonomy vs. shame and doubt (age 18 months to 3 years)	The child is mobile, engaging in physical activities and discovering his or her independence while testing limits and boundaries. Children who experience encouragement and support by parents without facing shame feel secure and confident in their own abilities.
Initiative vs. guilt (age 4 to 5 years)	Children learn to be more assertive in action while interacting with other children. Central to this stage is play. Through play, children begin to explore and use their interpersonal skills, primarily through initiating activities with peers their own age.
Industry vs. inferiority (age 5 to 12 years)	Children learn to read, write, complete simple math functions, and how to do things independently. Peer groups are the main source of influence and most significant contributor to the child's self-esteem. Through seeking out approval, the child attempts to demonstrate competencies and develop a sense of pride that is reinforced by his or her social circle. If the child is discouraged or restricted, he or she begins to feel inferior instead of industrious.
Identity vs. role confusion (age 13 to 19 years)	The child transitions from child to adolescent, becoming more independent, thinking in terms of the future, how to fit within society, and so forth. The adolescent is developing a sense of independence from others and investigating his or her value and belief system. Mainly, the adolescent is learning the roles necessary to become an adult.

In addition to maturation and development, children and adolescents in today's society live in an information-driven world where access and exposure to almost anything imaginable is possible (Chapman & Rokutani, 2005). Although the information era can be beneficial to the development process (e.g., technology and education), it has the potential to cause harm during the formative years. For instance, the Internet provides access and exposure to pornography, gambling, cyberbullying, and so forth and can challenge both childhood development, especially during the transition period from adolescent to adulthood, and the counseling process. Other circumstances and special considerations that counselors should be aware of when working with this population include blended families, poverty or homelessness, divorce, domestic violence, physical or sexual abuse, death of a parent, bullying, relocating to a new city or school, and substance use. Being a child or adolescent is tough in today's society and is further complicated when life circumstances beyond their control are involved.

GUIDED PRACTICE EXERCISE 15.1

On your own, overview the five stages of Erikson's psychosocial development model pertinent to children and adolescents. If possible, consider your own development during this period. What additional developmental challenges do you foresee that may be important for counselors to be aware of when working with children and adolescent clients? Consider how U.S. culture may influence child or adolescent development.

Another area that may challenge the counseling process when working with children and adolescents is the ethical and legal responsibilities counselors have to minors and their parents. The most common include informed consent, confidentiality, and subpoenas and privileged communication. According to Remley and Herlihy (2015), **informed consent** is the process of providing clients with enough information so they are able to make an informed decision about entering into a counseling relationship. Do minors have the mental capacity to comprehend what counseling entails and what will be asked of them during the counseling process? For adolescents this may be less of a concern, but for younger children this may prove difficult. For example, Koralie, a 7-year-old, is brought to counseling for behavioral reasons occurring at school and home. It may be difficult for her to understand why counseling is necessary. Likewise, Aiden, a 16-year-old, is brought to counseling for thoughts of suicide. He most likely has the cognitive ability to understand what counseling is and is able to make an informed choice about entering into it. In the United States, minors are required to exercise legal rights through their parents (Kramer, 1994), to include consent, release of information, and access to medical records (Sori & Hecker, 2015). Therefore, parents are only able to consent to counseling services on behalf of their child, but counselors should seek assent from minors prior to engaging in a counseling relationship (American Counseling Association [ACA], 2014).

CASE ILLUSTRATION 15.1

Often, more experienced counselors report that a major challenge with working with children and adolescent clients involves what information to divulge to parents and the impact that has on the counselor-client relationship when information is shared against the child or adolescent client's wishes. Imagine working with a minor client. As the relationship begins showing signs of strengthening, the adolescent happens to mention that he is smoking marijuana. The child further adds that he does not do it often but does not plan to stop anytime soon and asks you not to share this information with his parents. This puts the counselor in a difficult situation. From an ethical and legal standpoint, the counselor has a responsibility to the adolescent's parents to ensure their child is safe from harm. In addition, the client's parents have a legal right to confidential information. Should the counselor choose not to disclose this information to the client's parents, he or she runs the risk of a malpractice lawsuit should the parents find out. Likewise, when the client finds out the counselor disclosed this information to his parents, the counselor-client relationship may be beyond repair.

Similar to the challenges associated with informed consent and minors is the ethical principle of confidentiality. **Confidentiality**, a foundational principle in counseling, is the counselor's obligation to keep any information related to counseling private (Sori & Hecker, 2015). However, a major challenge when working with children and adolescents is how much information to share with parents. Confidentiality, like informed consent, belongs to the parent or legal guardian in most states. Thus, when parents exert their right to confidential information, this can place counselors in a difficult position that may potentially challenge the counselor-client relationship. Similarly, breaching confidentially occurs when counselors believe minors may harm themselves or someone else or are being abused. In any of these instances, counselors have both an ethical and legal responsibility to protect a minor's welfare, informing both parents and appropriate authorities (when necessary) of the threat and faithfully continuing to work with the family to resolve the issue. The counseling relationship between minor and counselor and parent and counselor is never more challenged than in these types of situations. A final consideration related to confidentiality is subpoenas and privileged communication. A **subpoena** is a formal request made by the court soliciting information from the counselor or a request to appear in court. **Privileged communication** is a legal right of the client that prevents private information from being divulged in legal proceedings. Privileged communication is the legal side of confidentiality, and a subpoena is a legal form of breach in confidentiality. Privileged communication is a state status, that is, privilege varies from state to state. Similar to informed consent and issues surrounding confidentially, rights concerning privileged communication and subpoenas belong to the parents in most situations.

Many of the challenges when working with children and adolescents previously described can be mitigated during the initial session. Counselors who provide clear guidelines and policies regarding informed consent, confidentiality, and privileged communication and subpoenas in their professional disclosure statement and are aware of the legal statutes that guide counseling practice with minors can circumvent many of the ethical and legal challenges that may occur. As we move on to discuss various strategies found throughout the professional literature, keep in mind the circumstances and special considerations previously mentioned.

Strategies

Working with children and adolescents can be a rewarding experience for professional counselors. As children continue to grow and develop, certain cognitive, emotional, behavioral, and social milestones are anticipated; however, with life circumstances beyond the child's control, issues may arise requiring counseling as an intervention. Following are three strategies counselors should be aware of when working with children and adolescents: establishing a strong counselor-client relationship, play therapy, and art therapy.

Establishing a Strong Counselor-Client Relationship

Never underestimate the power of the counselor-client relationship. Rogers (1951) clearly understood the importance of the relationship when working with clients. Through his work, he established what are known as core conditions, which are evident in most counseling approaches. **Core conditions** are factors necessary for establishing a strong counselor-client relationship and creating personality change in counseling. According to Rogers (1951), clients need to experience counselors' communication of genuineness, unconditional positive regard, and empathy. These same core conditions are required when working with children and adolescents. In fact, Lambert (1992) and Miller, Duncan, and Hubble (1997) identified a four-factor model attempting to explain what contributes most to client outcomes. In their research, they hypothesized that the counseling relationship accounted for 30% of the outcome, which superseded the use of any model or technique used by the counselor (Miller et al., 1997).

Play Therapy

The Association for Play Therapy (APT; 2016) defines **play therapy** as "the systematic use of a theoretical model to establish an interpersonal process wherein trained play therapists use the therapeutic powers of play to help clients prevent or resolve psychosocial difficulties and achieve optimal growth and development" (para. 1). Similar to art-based therapy, play therapy takes into consideration the development level of the child and uses a medium—in this case, play—meant to encourage freedom of expression in a language universal to children. According to Bratton, Ray, Rhine, and Jones (2005), play therapy is an evidenced practice used to treat a range of emotional and behavioral disturbances among children. These include anger outburst, grief and loss, divorce, crisis and trauma, anxiety, depression, and attention deficit hyperactivity, just to name a few.

The process of play therapy is centered on the counselor-client relationship (Landreth & Bratton, 1999). Children, in a safe environment, act out their desires and feelings and explore their personal world through play. Externalization of internal experiences, traumas, frustrations, and so forth through play allows the transfer of anxieties and fears to objects instead of people (Landreth & Bratton, 1999). Throughout this process, the counselor is allowed to experience the inner workings of the child's world and given the opportunity to respond in a therapeutically beneficial way. Thus, the relationship between child and counselor facilitates this transformative and healing process, creating opportunities for the child to cope. To learn more about play therapy, see the Web Resources section at the end of this chapter.

Art Therapy

Art therapy is an intervention strategy used to provide individuals a safe outlet to creatively express thoughts and emotions that result from psychological distress (Eaton, Doherty, & Widrick, 2007). Art therapy is not "just arts and crafts," just like play therapy is not "just play." According to Malchiodi (2016), art therapy and play therapy are confused for one another. She further added that both art and play therapy, within the context of a counselor-client relationship, help children engage in self-exploration and meaning-making through art making. However, the difference is art therapy encourages the creation of tangible art products, whereas play therapy does not; art therapy is also focused on helping children visually express and record their thoughts, feelings, and emotions (Malchiodi, 2016).

Art therapy at the initial session includes the creation of art. The counselor provides the medium, tools, and encouragement throughout the creation process. As the session progresses, the child is asked to tell a story about the artwork created. The counselor's role at this point is to interpret the child's story, reflecting back to him or her those interpretations. The goal of this process is to distinguish what is real and what is fantasy, leading the child to self-discovery (St. Thomas & Johnson, 2002). As the child begins to accept reality, the counselor provides support and encouragement and promotes coping throughout. Finally, art therapy is built on a strong counselor-client relationship and these foundational principles (Malchiodi, 2016): (a) supports nonverbal communication and provides a sensory experience, (b) identifies growth and development, (c) promotes self-regulation and meaning-making, and (d) centers on attachment. To learn more about art therapy, see the Web Resources section at the end of this chapter.

ACTIVE AND VETERAN MILITARY PERSONNEL AND THEIR FAMILIES

Special Considerations and Circumstances

Another population clinical mental health counselors should carefully consider is active and veteran military personnel and their families. Recent global conflicts in Iraq and Afghanistan as well as recent health care initiatives (e.g., Joining Forces, Welcome Back Veterans) have brought attention to the myriad challenges military families experience. In 2008, the Veterans Administration (VA) estimated that of the 1.7 million Americans who served in Iraq and Afghanistan, 43% of service members had children (as cited in Acosta, 2013). Counselors working with this population need to be aware of the circumstances and give special consideration surrounding the challenges military personnel and their family may experience as a result of deployment, the aftereffects of war, reintegration into a noncombat living situation, and navigating the military health system and the U.S. Department of Veterans Affairs.

Deployment possesses challenges to the family. The parent deployed may experience anxiety, guilt, prolonged sadness, and isolation for leaving family for an extended period. Likewise, the parent not deployed takes on the brunt of the day-to-day home activities and caring for the children (Tanielian, Batka, & Meredith, 2017). Over time, this parent may feel overwhelmed, stressed, exhausted, and even resentment toward his or her spouse or partner for leaving and could easily develop his or her own mental health concerns (Acosta, 2013). Postdeployment families, particularly the parental unit, may experience a range of social, emotional, and behavioral related issues as a result of deployment: communication challenges, marital discourse, intimacy issues, domestic violence, divorce, and mental illness. Children postdeployment may experience anger outbursts, behavioral problems at home and school, mood dysregulation, poor academic performance, and mental illness. To meet the mental health needs of military families, many civilian and military veteran counselors, through TRICARE, work with military families.

Strategies

Considering the numerous challenges military personnel and their families face, clinical mental health counselors need to honor what is valued most by military families and establish a strong rapport before engaging in any specific intervention. Following are four strategies counselors should consider when working with this population: establishing trust, assisting with resource navigation, advocacy, and nature-based counseling.

Establishing Trust

Trust is a necessary quality in all counseling relationships. For military personnel and their families, building trust with persons outside of the military may prove challenging (Myers, 2013). A precursor to building trust is the counselor's own multicultural competence and awareness of personal values and biases related to working with the military population. For instance, some counselors may have strong personal values regarding war that if left unaddressed will negatively impact the counselor's ability to establish trust. For counselors to be successful in developing trust and a strong working relationship, consider military culture, demonstrate respect to military personnel and their families for the service they provided (e.g., honoring federally recognized military holidays), and remember that actions speak louder than words to military service members and their families. The infamous line of "I'm your counselor, you can trust me" has no bearing here, and likely nowhere else for that matter.

Assisting With Resource Navigation

Military personnel and their families may often be overwhelmed and uncertain as to how to acquire the wide array of services and resources available to them. It behooves counselors working with this population to be aware of the resources available at the federal, state, and local levels for military personnel and their families. Furthermore, counselors should be knowledgeable in what these resources offer clientele, educating them on how to access resources and assisting with applying for benefits when necessary. Although this may seem outside the scope of practice for some counselors, remember that with military personnel and their families actions tend to speak louder than words.

Advocacy

Another important strategy to keep in mind when working with military personnel and their families is advocacy. *Advocacy* in its most basic form means to "help or assist" another. Counselors can advocate for military personnel and their family by helping communicate their needs to other providers, linking them with community resources, and in some circumstances, joining them when meeting with other service providers to serve as a voice (Myers, 2014a). As a counselor in training, it is important to have the awareness, knowledge, and skills required to competently engage in advocacy. Thus, we recommend reviewing the Advocacy Competencies endorsed by the American Counseling Association (see Lewis, Arnold, House, & Toporek, 2003).

Nature-Based Counseling

A final strategy to consider is nature-based counseling (also known as ecotherapy). Nature-based counseling promotes emotional, physical, psychological, and spiritual health through nature and outdoor activities (Louv, 2008). Nature can provide military personnel the opportunity to reestablish a sense of peace in their life, one that was lost in combat, and serve as an alternative to medication treatment for disorders of PTSD, depression, and anxiety. What makes nature a wonderful medium for healing is the sense of calm it provides as well as the gentle stimuli available, such as the sound of birds chirping, the smell of flowers blooming, and the sight of endless greenery. Numerous interventions encompass nature-based counseling: nature meditation, horticultural therapy, equine-assisted therapy, exercising in nature, and mindfulness in nature. For military personnel, perhaps what makes nature-based approaches so appealing is the physical engagement available in these types of approaches. However, what matters most from this perspective is one's ability to reconnect with nature through establishing a physical presence.

A growing body of literature has demonstrated evidence for the effectiveness of nature-based approaches. In a recent study conducted by Stigsdotter et al. (2018), they demonstrated that nature-based counseling (i.e., 10-week group and individual therapy in nature, gardening, mindfulness, and relaxation) was just as effective as cognitive-behavioral counseling for treating stress-related illnesses. Among military personnel, nature outings have provided short-term relief in mental health symptoms and improved both social functioning and outlook on life (Duvall & Kaplan, 2014). Likewise, Poulsen (2017) completed a review on the evidence of nature-based therapy for veterans. Her findings indicate that nature-based therapy had a positive impact on PTSD symptoms, outlook on life, fostering hope, and returning to the workforce. Although preliminary evidence suggests that nature-based approaches are beneficial for veterans and military personnel, more research is needed to pinpoint which aspects of nature-based counseling are most advantageous.

CLIENTS OF COLOR

Special Considerations and Circumstances

According to the U.S. Census Bureau (2014), persons of color in the United States comprise approximately 37% of population. The term *persons of color* encompasses all non-White persons residing in the United States who share common experience, directly or indirect, with systemic racism (Franklin, Boyd-Franklin, & Kelly, 2006) and includes African Americans, Asian Americans, Latin Americans, and Native Americans (Sawyer-Kurian, Newsome, Dames, Horne, & Grant, 2017). Experiences of racism, discrimination, and oppression are prevalent among persons of color, enacted by both Whites and each other (Chou, Asnaani, & Hofmann, 2012; Sue & Sue, 2013). Within the current sociopolitical climate of the United States, African Americans experience the most discrimination, either directly in the form of blatant racism or indirectly in the form of microaggressions, followed by Hispanic Americans and Asian Americans (Chou et al., 2012). **Racism** occurs when someone from a race in power believes his or her race to be superior to the race of others not in power. A **microaggression** is a subtle form of discrimination communicated either verbally or nonverbally that insults disadvantaged groups. Recent events such as the Charleston church shooting, "Unite the Right" rally organized by White supremacists, fatal shooting of Michael Brown by a police officer, and Pulse Nightclub shooting in Florida demonstrate the unrest surrounding race in the United States.

Counselors working with clients of color need to be aware of this unrest, historical and present day, and the associated consequences that result from discrimination, such as oppression, marginalization, race-related stress, health care disparities, mental illness, and negative self-concept and low self-esteem, among many others (Carter & Reynolds, 2011; Chou et al., 2012; Sawyer-Kurian et al., 2017). Within the counseling process, racism, although unintentional, has a unique way of appearing. Counselors who take the position of "not seeing color," avoid discussing race or culture, accept stereotypes without challenge, and engage in microaggressions perpetuate racism (Williams, 2013). However, cultural competence is not a one-way street, reserved for only White counselors (Sawyer-Kurian et al., 2017). Counselors of color can have negative reactions to White clients, especially if they behave in a discriminatory or racist manner. In the counseling profession, persons of color represent 10.3% of all counselors (SAMHSA, 2013), and nearly half of clients served by counselors are White (Sawyer-Kurian et al., 2017). As such, it is important that all counselors develop the skills and competencies necessary to serve multiculturally diverse populations (Sue & Sue, 2013).

Strategies

Counselors working with clients of color need to consider the myriad factors that impact this population, both historically and today. Counselors working with this specific population want to avoid perpetuating messages of discrimination, acts of insensitivity, and making assumptions about one's culture and values based on stereotypes. Following are two strategies counselors should consider when working with clients of color: assessing one's biases and prejudices prior to serving in the role of counselor and serving as an agent of social change.

Assessing Biases and Prejudices

For many counselors in training and even some seasoned professionals, exploring and taking inventory of one's personal biases and prejudices can be uncomfortable—although necessary (Sue & Sue, 2013). To not do so would be a huge mistake. Sometimes biases and prejudices are well embedded into one's self, which can easily be overlooked and understood as truths that overtly or covertly govern the counseling process. In counselor preparation and training programs, counselors in training are encouraged to examine their own biases and prejudices in a supportive learning environment. However, examining one's biases and prejudices is not a one-time event but rather a commitment to the process of being culturally competent (Ratts, Singh, Nassar-McMillan, Butler, & McCullough, 2016). Counselors can examine their personal biases and prejudices through many avenues. For instance, taking inventory of your family history and culture or interviewing various family members can help in discovering your biases and prejudices. Likewise, recognizing one's privilege can be telling or listing personal assumptions about various minority groups may shed light on held biases and prejudices. Finally, counselors in training may want to consider engaging in their own counseling when challenged with recognizing personal biases and prejudices. The key to assessing and evaluating biases and prejudices is the willingness and act of doing so.

Agents of Social Change

It is no longer acceptable to remain passive in the social change process. As such, counselors are social change agents (Baker & Cramer, 1972), that is, they advocate for equality and serve disadvantaged groups in fighting the injustices experienced. This process begins with accepting the fact that social injustices and inequality exist in our society. It is easy to remain passive and maintain the status quo; however, clients of color have historically experienced exactly this from society. As counselors in training, it is important to recognize and acknowledge the barriers clients of color have endured and uncover how discrimination continues to impact their lives. Throughout the counseling process, counselors provide a platform for clients to express themselves and their concerns, communicate empathy and acceptance, and use their privilege to support equality among those who are disadvantaged. Remember, social change requires action and cultural competence, which extends beyond the counseling setting and into the community through social justice advocacy (Ratts et al., 2016).

ADJUDICATED, INVOLUNTARY, AND INCARCERATED CLIENTS

Special Considerations and Circumstances

If you remember the discussion at the beginning of the chapter regarding incarcerated clients, you may recognize some of the challenges surrounding their life circumstances and their risk for mental illness and substance use that may influence both treatment participation and outcomes. Let's continue this conversation regarding adjudicated and involuntary clientele. The term **adjudicated** is commonly associated with the legal system, meaning to settle or determine through judicial proceedings. In many states this is known as probation or deferred adjudication, although variations do exist, in which a person receives a court-ordered alternative to incarceration and is under the direct supervision of a probation officer (Petersilia, 1998). Another alternative to incarceration is parole. **Parole** refers to a period after incarceration when a person is under the direct supervision of a parole officer. Both parole and probation offer alternatives to incarceration; where the difference lies is when each occurs, before or after.

In 2016, an estimated 4,537,100 adults were under some type of probation or parole (Kaeble, 2018). Since 2007, the percentage of persons in U.S. correctional systems continues to decline (Kaeble & Cowhig, 2018). These statistics suggest that persons incarcerated are eventually reintegrating back into the community under the conditions of parole. Likewise, more persons are being placed under probation or deferred adjudication as a means to prevent incarceration. You may be asking yourself why this information is relevant. Well, it is not uncommon for clinical mental health counselors to find themselves working with clientele who are adjudicated or were previously incarcerated. In fact, many persons on probation and parole are placed under these mechanisms with conditions of participating in substance abuse treatment, anger management programs, parenting classes, self-help groups (e.g., Alcoholic Anonymous, Narcotics Anonymous), and counseling.

As such, counselors need to consider the life circumstances of persons in this population. Likewise, counselors need to address their personal values and beliefs and explore any potential biases that might impede their ability to work with this population. In addition to the life circumstances described previously for persons previously incarcerated are the challenges associated with reintegration. With only limited resources for securing basic needs of food, clothing, and housing, persons previously incarcerated face an uphill battle. Many fear how their criminal history will impede their ability to successfully obtain employment, as well as the financial challenges associated with probation and parole and daily living that may result in returning to a life of crime (Smith, 2016). In addition, counselors should be aware that many persons from this population may not value counseling or counseling-related services.

Although the term is not used or accepted by all counselors (e.g., Patterson, 1990), this clientele may be referred to as involuntary clients. An **involuntary client** is a person required or forced, usually through a court order, to attend and participate in treatment. Although the term *involuntary client* is commonly associated with the adjudicated and incarcerated populations, it includes any person not voluntarily seeking counseling services (e.g., older persons, parents, children, persons with addictions and mental illness). However, if a person seeking counseling services is involuntary, counselors need to consider client confidentiality and release of private information. Often, clientele under conditions of probation and parole are required to give permission to release personal and private information to their probation or parole officer. Counselors may be challenged in maintaining confidentiality and disclosure of private client information in these situations. It is imperative that counselors working with this population carefully consider the stipulations associated with providing court-ordered therapy and understand the privileged communication laws in their respective state.

Strategies

Similar to the military population, persons from this population have a natural tendency to mistrust those who provide help. It is not uncommon for beginning-level counselors to feel nervous, anxious, or even intimidated when working with this population. Here are three strategies counselors can employ: establish a strong counselor-client relationship, assist with employment, and experiment with motivational interviewing.

GUIDED PRACTICE EXERCISE 15.2

Working with adjudicated, involuntary, and incarcerated clients can be challenging and intimidating for many beginning-level counselors. With an in-class partner, explore your personal values, beliefs, and biases, if any, regarding this population. Remember, your values, beliefs, and biases are what make you human, and it is important to consider how they may impact your work with this population.

Establish a Strong Counselor-Client Relationship

According to Patterson (1964), there is no such thing as an involuntary or, for that matter, unmotivated client; rather, the client is highly motivated to avoid participating in counseling or treatment. Counselors working with this population may have an uphill battle, but when effort and energy are put into developing a counselor-client relationship, the result may be surprising. Respect, caring, and empathy exhibited by the counselor, regardless of the client's motivation to participate or change, over time, can lead to success. Work with this population is often slow-moving and the success rate can be less than desirable for some counselors. It is not uncommon for counselors, especially beginning-level counselors, to feel lost or even ineffective when working with this population. However, do not give up, do not lose hope, and do not underestimate the power of building a strong counselor-client relationship. If you find yourself feeling stuck, confused, annoyed, or even frustrated, remember to take a moment and walk a mile in their shoes.

Assist With Employment

A major hurdle for many clients in this population is gaining some type of employment. Usually a condition of probation or parole is finding employment, which can prove challenging for persons who wish not to disclose their criminal history. Likewise, job opportunities available to persons with a criminal history are sometimes dismal or do not meet their desired expectations. Counselors can assist clientele of this population by focusing on the skills necessary for gainful employment. It is easy to overlook the bigger picture and focus on the immediate. Working with clients to develop their interviewing skills, job search strategies, and resume can set them up for success. Offering encouragement and support and remaining transparent as clients begin to face the realities of their current life situation and career prospects will be paramount when working with this population.

Motivational Interviewing

Motivational interviewing (MI) is a person-centered, directive clinical approach used by counselors for enhancing peoples' intrinsic motivation to elicit change by resolving personal ambivalence (Miller & Rollnick, 2013). The implementation of change can be difficult and daunting for persons unsure if change is appropriate. In this case, persons are simultaneously in a position of "I want to change" and "I do not want to change." This ambivalence is a normal part of the change process (DiClemente, 2003) and is the crux of MI. This is not to say every person in need of change is even considering it, that is, their level of ambivalence may be minimal. In this case, their level of discrepancy between self and the status quo remains unchallenged in maladaptive ways. The term **discrepancy** in MI can be defined as the distance between one's personal goals and reality. According to Miller and Rollnick (2013), persons may experience discrepancies in three unique ways that result in unintended change: (1) the discrepancy may be insignificant or overwhelming, (2) the person may feel helpless in the situation and have low self-efficacy, or (3) the person simply avoids it altogether due to the unpleasant experience associated with the discrepancy. Let's direct our attention to the change process, discussed next, used in MI.

CASE ILLUSTRATION 15.2

Given the life circumstances of adjudicated, involuntary, and incarcerated clients, it may be difficult to implement change. The person-centered approach of motivational interviewing has been shown to be effective in helping persons of this population address their ambivalence about committing to change. Imagine a client who consumes alcohol in excess. The client does not see this as a problem in her life. However, she recently lost her job as a cashier at a local grocery store for being under the influence of alcohol while at work. The client further added that the job was important to her, yet she does not see the big deal regarding her being under the influence while at work. A counselor using motivational interviewing would quickly notice that the client's level of discrepancy between the self and status quo is nonexistent. Upon further exploration, the counselor learns the client is powerless against her drinking and doesn't foresee this changing any time soon. Remember, discrepancies exist in three forms: it may be insignificant or overwhelming, the person may feel helpless in the situation, or the person may avoid the situation because of the unpleasantness associated with it. Until a discrepancy between the client and her alcohol consumption exists that is manageable and realistic, the client's level of ambivalence will not emerge and change is not possible.

The change process in MI, although described here in abbreviated form, includes four phases: engaging, focusing, evoking, and planning. In the first phase of *engaging*, the counselor and client establish a relational connection and working relationship (Miller & Rollnick, 2013). The Rogerian principles (Rogers, 1951) of client-centered counseling hold true here. Being nonjudgmental, respecting the client's autonomy, accepting the person where he or she is, offering support and encouragement, and demonstrating accurate empathy are necessary counselor qualities to successfully develop a therapeutic relationship. The next phase, *focusing*, centers on the idea of creating direction as to why the client is seeking help, with the change being front and center. In other words, the focusing phase of MI is concerned with identifying the aspects the client hopes to change and maintaining a dialogue that is change focused. The third phase, *evoking*, is centered on the position of eliciting the client's motivation for change. In this phase, clients may describe their reasons for change and highlight the pros that may result from change and the cons associated with not changing. Counselors at this phase evoke the client's confidence and hope for change while offering support and encouragement. The last phase, *planning*, involves the client committing to the change process and developing a plan of action (Miller & Rollnick, 2013). Conversations between the counselor and client regarding the change process are action-oriented. The client may share his or her action process and throughout the counselor-client relationship collaboratively revisit the planning phase. As change proceeds, setbacks may occur or life circumstances arise that result in the counselor and client revisiting previous phases discussed. As such, each phase of MI builds on the other while maintaining the essence of previous phases. Although presented here in simple terms, MI is an advanced clinical approach that requires extensive training and supervised practice. For those interested in knowing more about MI, see the Web Resources located at the end of this chapter or Miller and Rollnick's (2013) third edition of *Motivational Interviewing: Helping People Change.*

AGING CLIENTS

Special Considerations and Circumstances

According to the U.S. Census Bureau's (2017) Nation Population Projections, the year 2030 will mark a significant shift in the U.S. population whereby persons age 65 or older will comprise one in every five residents. And by the year 2060, the number of Americans age 65 or older is expected to more than double from 46 million to 98 million (Mather, Jacobsen, & Pollard, 2015). The number of persons from this population continues to increase each year. Numerous factors have contributed to the healthy growth of this population: increased education level and average life expectancy, decreased gender gap, advances in technology and medicine, decline in poverty rates, and increased net worth (although significant disparities exist between races; Mather et al., 2015; National Institutes of Health, 2016; U.S. Census Bureau, 2017).

With longevity comes an abundance of risk factors counselors should be aware of when working with aging persons. According to the National Institutes of Health (2016), the concerns of tobacco and alcohol use, poor diet, and limited physical activity all contribute to the development of noncommunicable diseases (e.g., diabetes, obesity, cardiovascular disease; Mather et al., 2015; National Institutes of Health, 2016). Likewise, counselors should consider that persons from the aging population may be divorced and/or living alone, receive nursing home or home health care, suffer from cognitive decline, and feel challenged when navigating both social security and Medicare. Older persons are often subjected to negative age-related stereotypes and age discrimination and marginalized based on race, ethnicity, gender, and sexual orientation, which results in significant health disparities when compared to persons from the general population of similar age (Fredriksen-Goldsen, Kim, Bryan, Shiu, & Emlet, 2017; Meyers, 2014b).

A final concern related to this population is suicide. Although suicide rates are highest among younger and middle-aged populations (Conwell, Van Orden, & Caine, 2011), older adults attempting to end their own life are usually more methodical in planning their death and use deadlier means (Suicide Prevention Resource Center, 1994–2018). In fact, males aged 85 years or older have the highest rate of suicide of any group in the United States (Centers for Disease Control and Prevention, 2014). According to Conwell et al. (2011), mental illness, social connectedness, physical health, and functioning influence the risk of suicide among this population.

Strategies

Counselors working with aging clients need to consider the life circumstances previously mentioned as well as other life events (e.g., retirement, second career, death of friends and family of similar age) to meet the needs of this growing population. Following are three strategies counselors may find useful when working with aging clients: health care advocate, strength-based counseling, and fostering social connectedness.

Health Care Advocate

According to the 2015 United States of Aging Survey, the top three concerns for older Americans, from highest to lowest, are physical health, memory loss, and mental health (National Council on Aging, n.d.). Hence, counselors working with this population are in a prime position to assist in addressing these concerns in counseling. More specifically, counselors can serve in the role of advocate for health care needs and services. As you can imagine, health care for aging clients is a top priority, yet not every client has the capacity or capability to express their needs. Counselors in the role of health care advocate can collaborate with providers of care and clients to identify potential problems and solutions, improve communication between the client and provider, ensure continuity of information and treatment among health care providers, and provide resources and education to better understand their health care concerns and treatment options.

Strength-Based Counseling

Strength-based counseling can be understood as a framework of practice (Hirst, Lane, & Stares, 2013), although its origins are rooted in positive psychology (Rashid, 2015). Historically, mental health professionals have held a deficit- or problem-oriented philosophy to treating psychological, emotional, or behavioral issues; that is, a problem must be identified and defined at the onset of counseling. However, counselors who use strength-based approaches focus on clients' internal strengths and resources, rather than focusing on weaknesses and deficits that brought them to counseling in the first place. The majority of counseling, from a strength-based perspective, is helping clients uncover their personal strengths as they navigate the world in which they live (Hirst et al., 2013).

For aging clients, this perspective can help uncover personal strengths; shift attitude and mind-set surrounding a particular situation; and foster resiliency, vitality, and hope. Aging clients may face challenges with physical health, social isolation, finances, social support, basic resources, and so forth. However, persons from this population have a wealth of knowledge, experience, and strengths that can be used to solve current life circumstances. Counselors working with this population can help clients shift their negative thoughts to more positive ones, identify past successes to be used for current and future challenges, and increase client confidence and outlook on life. Interventions may include journaling, strengths assessment (e.g., Strengths and Difficulties Questionnaire [Goodman, 1997], Child and Adolescent Strengths Assessment Scale [Lyons, Howard, O'Mahoney, & Lish, 1997]), identifying strengths in others, and solution-focused brief therapy (Hirst et al., 2013).

Social Connectedness

Building and maintaining a social support network is essential for health and well-being (Reblin & Uchino, 2009). For aging clients, remaining socially connected with friends, family, and community is important and can lead to better health outcomes, being more adept at coping with mental illness (e.g., depression), and a more positive outlook on life. Counselors working with aging clients should recognize factors that may hinder social connectedness: mobility; health status; loss of spouse, family, or friends; changes in work status; and finances. Counselors can serve in the roles of educator, advocate, and case manager to support and improve aging clients' social connectedness. Counselors can help improve social connectedness for aging clients by encouraging clients to connect with community organizations and volunteerism through local charities, helping clients enroll in face-to-face or online classes, identifying support groups in the community, locating resources for learning how to use a computer and the Internet, and providing referrals to adjunctive therapies (e.g., group yoga for seniors) and other services.

IMMIGRANT CLIENTS

Special Considerations and Circumstances

According to the U.S. Census Bureau (2011), approximately 13% of the U.S population is foreign-born: 18.1 million are naturalized citizens, 11 million are authorized citizens, and 11 million are undocumented. It is anticipated that this specific population will continue to grow as individuals and families seek better opportunities for work, reunification with family, or aid and refuge from persecution by their home government. Since 1990, about 1 million new immigrants have entered the United States every year (American Psychological Association [APA], 2013). The process of immigration can take a toll on the person and result in major mental health challenges. When immigrating, persons face separation from family, country of origin, and familiar customs and traditions that may result in stress and challenges to mental well-being (APA, 2013).

Furthermore, once immigrated, persons face many challenges with acculturation. **Acculturation** is the process of blending one's social, psychological, behavioral, religious, and cultural aspects into the dominate culture (Casas & Pytluk, 1995). Immigrants often do not speak the language of the country in which they now reside, are unfamiliar with the availability of community resources, feel alone or isolated, reside in substandard living conditions, and experience employment challenges and discrimination and racism. Undocumented immigrants encounter myriad challenges different from those experienced by people who immigrated legally. Undocumented immigrants' journey to the United States can be characterized by "uncertainty, fear, injury, and death" (Chung, Bemak, Ortiz, & Sandoval-Perez, 2008, p. 311). Many are subjected to trauma, including encountering gangs, immigration raids, sexual assault and abuse, witnessing death, placement in detention camps, and deportation (APA, 2013). Adding further stress once in the United States is the constant fear of being discovered, detained, and subjected to legal proceedings and deportation. Considering the life circumstances immigrant clients experience and the myriad challenges they face once in the United States, counselors need to carefully attend to the previously discussed factors when working with this population.

Strategies

Counselors working with immigrant clients need to be prepared to address the many challenges that result from immigration and acculturation. In addition, counselors may feel challenged by their own preconceived notions and biases regarding immigrant clients, which may result in a strained counselor-client relationship if left unaddressed. Following are three strategies counselors may find useful when working with immigrant clients: working through fear, cultivating resiliency, and advocacy.

GUIDED PRACTICE EXERCISE 15.3

Many Americans have developed a negative perception of immigrants that has been perpetuated by media coverage on terrorism and spurred on by political groups. This has resulted in a culture of fear. Counselors should be aware of this fear and address their own fears regarding this population. As a class, each student will write down one to three fears on a sheet of paper. Be sure to make your list of fears anonymous. Next, the instructor will collect each student's list, fold it up, and place it in a basket. At random, the instructor chooses one list and reads it aloud. As a class, discuss the fears identified. Remember to keep an open mind and take a nonjudgmental position. Continue this process until a mixture of fears has been explored.

Working Through Fear

Once relocated into the United States, immigrant clients are exposed to and challenged with living in a culture that fears their presence (Chung, 2007). Many Americans have developed a negative perception of immigrants that has been perpetuated by media coverage on terrorism and spurred on by political groups. This is not to say every American feels this way, but overt and covert forms of racism regarding immigrants exist. Counselors working with this population need to be aware of the culture of fear and how it contributes to unconscious forms of prejudice and racism experienced by immigrants (Chung et al., 2008). Furthermore, counselors need to address their own fears associated with immigrant clients and challenge their personal biases, unconscious racism, and the culture of fear as a whole when preparing to work with immigrant clients.

Cultivating Resiliency

Another strategy counselors may find beneficial to the counseling process is cultivating immigrant clients' resiliency. According to Walsh (2006), *resiliency* is defined as the ability to recover from adverse challenges or circumstances while developing strengths and resources. Most, if not all, immigrant clients faced unimaginable circumstances that most people cannot even fathom. Within the context of a strong counselor-client relationship, counselors can help immigrant clients shape their experiences into personal strengths and resources that can be used to navigate the future. Over time, resilience can serve as a protective factor from mental illness and further traumatization associated with acculturation and the ever changing sociopolitical climate in the United States.

Advocacy

Rarely would a counselor find an immigrant client proactively walking through their door. Instead, immigrant clients often reach a tipping point in their lives. Faced with the daily stressor of acculturation and actively repressing painful memories of abuse and violence associated with their traumas, immigrant clients are often referred through social services or get entangled in the legal system and are mandated to seek counseling services. Counselors, through advocacy, can work with legal authorities, health agencies, and social services to ensure immigrant clients have fair access to counseling services and resources and are involved in the decision-making process. To learn more about immigration and how to access resources for immigrant clients, check out the Web Resources section located at the end of this chapter.

LESBIAN, GAY, BISEXUAL, AND TRANSGENDERED CLIENTS

Special Considerations and Circumstances

To provide competent care to lesbian, gay, bisexual, and transgender (LGBT) populations, counselors must understand LGBT culture within the context of the current sociopolitical climate and acknowledge the oppression, discrimination, and social injustices LGBT populations have endured (Association for Lesbian, Gay, Bisexual, and Transgender Issues in Counseling [ALGBTIC] Lesbian, Gay, Bisexual, Queer, Intersex, Questioning and Ally [LGBQIQA] Competencies Taskforce, 2012; Palma & Stanley, 2002). As such, counselors should familiarize themselves with current issues that affect the lives of many LGBT individuals. One significant advancement for the rights of LGBT persons occurred in 2015. The U.S. Supreme Court declared that all persons, regardless of gender, have the constitutional right to marry the person they love. However, there is no federal law protecting LGBT populations from employment discrimination based on sexual orientation or gender identity, although 22 states and the District of Columbia prohibit such discrimination (Out & Equal Workplace Advocates, n.d.).

Another area counselors should be aware of is violence. According to the Federal Bureau of Investigation's 2016 hate crime statistics report, 6,121 hate crimes were reported; of those crimes, 1,076 were based on sexual orientation and 124 were based on gender identity (Human Rights Campaign, 2018). These numbers represent a 5% increase from 2015. Likewise, some forms of sexual violence among LGBT persons are higher than those among heterosexuals. According to the Centers for Disease Control and Prevention's (2010) National Intimate Partner and Sexual Violence Survey, 1 in 8 lesbian women and nearly half of bisexual women and 4 in 10 gay men and nearly half of bisexual men have been raped in their lifetime. As a result of hate crimes, sexual violence, discrimination, and oppression, LGBT populations experience higher rates of suicidality, mental illness, and substance use (Milford, 2015). According to the National Alliance on Mental Illness (2018), LGBT individuals are 3 times more likely than their heterosexual counterparts to experience mental illness. A culmination of factors may contribute to this statistic, including coming out; oppression and discrimination; and fear of being rejected by society, community, family, and friends. As a result, LGBT individuals may hide their sexual orientation and mental illness from society.

Strategies

Counselors working with this population need to consider the life circumstances previously discussed, among many others not mentioned (e.g., reparative/conversion therapy and its impact on LGBT populations), when working with LGBT populations. In addition, counselors may feel challenged by their own preconceived notions and biases regarding LGBT populations, which may result in a strained counselor-client relationship if left unaddressed. Following are three strategies counselors may find useful when working with LGBT clients: communicating and demonstrating acceptance; developing partnerships with LGBT-welcoming providers; and remaining open, continuing to learn, and seeking supervision when necessary.

Communicating and Demonstrating Acceptance

First impressions can have a powerful, lasting effect with clients in general and LGBT populations specifically. The manner in which you communicate and demonstrate acceptance of LGBT persons is important. For instance, what does the reading material in your office say about you? How about the artwork on the wall? Although unintentional, heterosexual bias is present in many forms and can communicate a subtle, or not so subtle, message to LGBT persons. Consider including LGBT literature and artwork in your counseling space and indicate that your office space is a safe place for LGBT populations (e.g., displaying rainbow or safe zone symbols); display brochures about LGBT health concerns and clearly post a nondiscrimination statement for all to see (Shallcross, 2011). In doing so, the message sent to LGBT persons is one of inclusion and acceptance. Other areas to consider that may communicate heterosexual bias are assessment protocols and clerical paperwork. Do questions and statements include inclusive language? Because LGBT persons are asked to reveal personal information related to relationships and relationship status, it is judicious to include language in addition to *wife* and *husband*, such as *partner* or *significant other*. Finally, do not be afraid to ask how LGBT persons self-identify and which pronouns they prefer.

Developing Partnerships With LGBT-Welcoming Providers

Trust may be difficult for LGBT persons as a result of the discrimination and oppression experienced. Once counselors have established a strong counselor-client relationship based on trust, it is not uncommon for clients to ask for referrals to other health-related providers. Establishing relationships with other counselors, physicians, lawyers, social workers, and other professionals that are LGBT-welcoming can alleviate many of the fears and concerns LGBT clients may have about seeking help beyond counseling. Counselors should take a vested interest in the community they serve and establish strong partnerships with persons and agencies that are LGBT-welcoming.

Remaining Open, Continuing to Learn, and Seeking Supervision

Counselors working with LGBT populations for the first time may have personal values or beliefs that are distinctly different from those of LGBT clients. As such, counselors

GUIDED PRACTICE EXERCISE 15.4

Heterosexual bias is evident in the counseling practice (e.g., assessment protocols and counseling theories). In groups of four, consider how you would create a safe and inclusive counseling environment for LGBT clients.

must be prepared to address their biases, values, and beliefs that may impede their ability to effectively work with this population. The American Counseling Association (2013) Code of Ethics clearly outlines that counselors will not engage in or tolerate discrimination based on "gender, gender identity, sexual orientation, marital/partnership status" (C.5). Keeping an open mind is important, but if challenged, counselors need to take action. Actions taken on behalf of the counselor may include learning more about LGBT populations, seeking personal counseling, or engaging in continuing consultation and supervision with professionals who have experience working with the LGBT population. To learn more about the challenges this specific population experiences and how to competently work with LGBT populations, check out the Web Resources (e.g., ALGBTIC LGBQQIA Competencies) section at the end of this chapter.

CLIENTS IN RURAL SETTINGS

Special Considerations and Circumstances

According to the U.S. Census Bureau (2016), 97% of the nation's land area is rural, which is inhabited by only 19.3% of the U.S population. With the majority of the U.S. population living in urban or metropolitan areas, rural mental health is often overlooked in most conversations pertaining to counseling. So, what is meant by rural? According to the Health Resources and Services Administration (2017), **rural** is defined as any county consisting of fewer than 50,000 people and counties not economically linked to a metropolitan area. Often persons living in rural areas are stereotyped as being unsophisticated, violent, or morally deficient, when in fact the opposite is true. Rural life moves at a slower pace. Often persons living in rural areas have lower levels of anxiety, experience less crime and violence, and enjoy overall positive mental well-being as compared to persons living in major metropolitan areas.

Persons living in rural communities experience a wide range of challenges, including fewer health care providers, higher unemployment rates, limited education opportunities, a challenged economy, geographical isolation, higher incidents of alcohol and substance use, and poverty (Hasting & Cohn, 2013). Similarly, although unrelated, counselors working with this population may also face challenges living and practicing in these communities. Some challenges include the almost unescapable dual relationship, pressure by clients to work outside their competence, unavailability of community resources, and professional isolation (Schank, 1998). Despite the professional, ethical, and personal challenges faced by counselors living in rural areas, many find it a rewarding and an enjoyable experience.

Strategies

Counselors working with persons living in rural communities need to consider not only geographical but also cultural factors and how they intersect with mental health and well-being when working with this population. Following are three strategies counselors may find useful when working with clients living in rural communities: knowing the population served, taking a generalist approach to counseling, and maintaining counselor self-care.

Knowing the Population Served

Counselors working in rural areas are vital members of the community. This is not to say that counselors living in metropolitan areas are not also; rather, counselors working and living in rural communities can be easily recognized in their close-knit communities. As such, counselors should take an interest in knowing the community and the population served. Familiarizing themselves with the area's economy, sociopolitical climate, population demographics, social community events, and lifestyle provides counselors working in these settings a general understanding of daily life for this population. Furthermore, knowing this information may inform how you practice and how much to charge for counseling services.

CASE ILLUSTRATION 15.3

William, a licensed professional counselor-supervisor, decides to open a private practice in a rural community setting not knowing what his experience will be like. Being the only counselor within a 30-mile radius, his caseload fills up pretty quickly. Although his specialty is working with survivors of sexual assault, he finds himself working with community clients who are often in crisis or have marital issues. Rarely does William have the opportunity to work in his area of specialty. Instead, as he would put it, he finds himself putting out client fires and working with couples to prevent divorces, presenting issues he has come to enjoy. If William wanted to work only with clients within his specialty, his caseload would be small, and who knows how long he would stay in business. Even worse would be turning away clients he is qualified to help. In William's case, approaching counseling from a generalist lens seems fitting within his rural community setting. Counselors working in rural settings play an integral role in communities they serve and are often the only counseling services available within a reasonable distance.

Taking a Generalist Approach to Counseling

Although many counselors consider themselves specialists in certain areas such as addictions, trauma, or couples, the opposite seems to be true for counselors working in rural areas. Most rural counselors provide a wide array of services and address a multitude of problems. Thus, a specialist mind-set and method of practice is often met with clientele outside your defined problem areas. As such, counselors may feel compelled to refer that person to a counselor specializing in the present concern. However, a major challenge with rural counseling is the fact that counselors are in short supply, and there may not be another counselor to refer to. To complicate things further, often clients living in rural settings present for services only when a crisis strikes, and usually with a presenting concern the counselor is unfamiliar with. As such, counselors working in rural settings need to be effective in addressing a wide range of issues and take a generalist approach to counseling. This does not mean you are the expert in every issue that crosses your path; rather, it means you are continuously learning and staying current with the counseling literature and developing strong consultation and supervision relationships with other mental health providers.

Maintaining Counselor Self-Care

A final strategy for working with clients living in rural communities is the counselor tending to his or her self-care needs. Counselors living in rural areas can feel professionally isolated and alone. Counselors working in private settings as opposed to those working in large agency settings may not have strong work support systems or access to coworkers to consult on cases or share professional interests with. Over time, this lack of support may result in providing substandard counseling services and eventually burnout. Rural counselors need to develop creative strategies that keep them professionally engaged with other counselors (e.g., attending counseling conferences and seminars), as well as develop networks with other professionals within the local community. Taking care of yourself professionally (and personally) is always in your client's best interest.

Keystones

- Working with children and adolescent clients can pose many unique challenges. Counselors working with this population need to consider the maturation and development of the child or adolescent, how technology has influenced this development, and other life circumstances that may influence the counseling process. They should also consider the ethical and legal responsibilities counselors have to minors and their parent(s): informed consent, confidentiality, subpoena, and privileged communications. Play therapy, art therapy, and developing a strong therapeutic alliance have been effective with this population.

- When working with active and veteran military personnel and their families, counselors need to consider how deployment, aftereffects of war, postdeployment and reintegration, and navigating the military health system and the U.S. Department of Veterans Affairs impact this population and the counseling process. Establishing trust, assisting with resource navigation, advocating on behalf of the military personnel and their family members, and integrated

aspects of nature-based counseling will prove useful to the counseling process.

- When working with clients of color, counselors need to keep in mind the unrest associated with both historical and present-day discrimination and racism. Consequences of such unrest experienced by clients of color include oppression, marginalization, race-related stress, health care disparities, mental illness, and negative self-concept and low self-esteem. Assessing one's biases and prejudices prior to serving as a counselor and an agent of social change is crucial to the counseling process.

- When working with adjudicated, involuntary, or incarcerated clients, counselors need to keep in mind this group's life circumstances (e.g., poor outlook on life, at risk for mental illness and substance use) and the many challenges this population faces: unemployment, high recidivism, and the absence of autonomy. Establishing a strong counselor-client relationship, assisting with employment, and motivational interviewing are critical to the counseling process.

- When working with aging clients, counselors need to consider both risk factors and life circumstances specific to this population that impact health and well-being. Risk factors include tobacco and alcohol use, poor diet, limited physical activity, and disease. Life circumstances include divorce and/or living alone, nursing home or home health care, cognitive decline, mental illness, and navigating both social security and Medicare. Serving as a health care advocate, using strength-based counseling approaches, and increasing social connectedness are essential to the counseling process.

- When working with immigrant clients, counselors need to consider that each person's immigration process is unique. Many immigrants are subjected to trauma, including gang encounters, immigration raids, sexual assault and abuse, witnessing death, placement in detention camps, and deportation. Another challenge immigrants experience is the acculturation process and, if here illegally, the fear of being discovered and subject to deportation. Helping clients work through the culture of fear and cultivating resiliency and advocacy are important to a successful counseling process.

- When working with LGBT populations, counselors must gain an understanding of their culture within the context of the current sociopolitical climate and acknowledge the oppression, discrimination, and social injustices LGBT populations have endured. Challenges this population face include coming out; oppression and discrimination; and fear of being rejected by society, community, family, and friends. Demonstrating acceptance of LGBT persons, developing partnerships with LGBT-welcoming providers, remaining open, continuing to learn, and seeking supervision are necessary to build a successful therapeutic relationship and essential to the counseling process.

- When working with clients living in rural settings, counselors must consider how rural areas often have fewer health care providers, higher unemployment rates, limited education opportunities, a challenged economy, geographical isolation, higher incidence of alcohol and substance use, and poverty. Counselors working in rural areas also experience challenges, including dual relationships, pressure from clients to work outside their own competence, unavailability of community resources, and professional isolation. Becoming familiar with the population served, taking a generalist approach to counseling, and maintaining counselor self-care will help ensure a successful counseling process.

Key Terms

Web Resources

AFL-CIO: Immigration Resources (https://aflcio.org/about/programs/adelante-we-rise/immigration-resources)

ALGBTIC: Competencies for Counseling LGBQQIA Individuals (www.counseling.org/docs/ethics/algbtic-2012-07)

Association for Lesbian, Gay, Bisexual & Transgender Issues in Counseling (www.algbtic.org)

Association for Multicultural Counseling and Development (https://multiculturalcounseling development.org)

Association for Play Therapy (www.a4pt.org)

Association of Nature & Forest Therapy: Guides & Programs (www.natureandforesttherapy.org)

Case Western Reserve University: Motivational Interviewing (www.centerforebp.case.edu/practices/mi)

Counselors for Social Justice (https://counseling-csj.org)

Ecotherapy: What Is Ecotherapy? (www.ecotherapy heals.com/whatisecotherapy.html)

Futures Without Violence: Resources for Working With Immigrant Women (www.futureswithout violence.org/resources-for-working-with-immigrant-women)

Health Advocates for Older People (www.hafop.org)

Immigrant Legal Resource Center: Community Resources (www.ilrc.org/community-resources)

Motivational Interviewing Network of Trainers (http://motivationalinterviewing.org)

Multicultural and Social Justice Counseling Competencies (www.counseling.org/docs/default-source/competencies/multicultural-and-social-justice-counseling-competencies.pdf?sfvrsn=20)

NASW: Military and Veterans (www.socialworkers.org/practice/military-veterans)

National Council on Aging: The United States of Aging Survey (www.ncoa.org/news/resources-for-reporters/usoa-survey)

Out & Equal Workplace Advocates: Fact Sheet (http://outandequal.org/2017-workplace-equality-fact-sheet)

Psychology Today: Child Art Therapy: How It Works (www.psychologytoday.com/us/blog/arts-and-health/201601/child-art-therapy-how-it-works)

Psychotherapy.net: Motivational Interviewing Video With William Miller (www.psychotherapy.net/video/miller-motivational-interviewing?gclid=Cj0KCQjwu_jYBRD8ARIsAC3EGCLJeKshC5orveuwdxiq6SXZaIp g0hhpQB4kBiXo2QszKsZTfd_jMZoaAtYoEALw_wcB)

SAMHSA: Motivational Interviewing (www.integration.samhsa.gov/clinical-practice/motivational-interviewing)

SAMHSA: Other Specific Populations (www.samhsa.gov/specific-populations/other)

U.S. Department of Veterans Affairs: Mental Health (www.mentalhealth.va.gov/index.asp)

References

Acosta, G. (2013). *The impact of war: Mental health of veterans and their families.* Washington, DC: American Psychological Association.

American Counseling Association. (2014). *ACA code of ethics.* Alexandria, VA: Author.

American Psychological Association. (2013). Working with immigrant-origin clients: An update for mental health professionals. Retrieved from http://www.apa.org/topics/immigration/immigration-report-professionals.pdf

Association for Lesbian, Gay, Bisexual, and Transgender Issues in Counseling Lesbian, Gay, Bisexual, Queer, Intersex, Questioning and Ally Competencies Taskforce. (2012). Association for Lesbian, Gay, Bisexual, and Transgender Issues in Counseling competencies for counseling with lesbian, gay, bisexual, queer, questioning, intersex and ally individuals. Retrieved from https://www.counseling.org/docs/ethics/algbtic-2012-07

Association for Play Therapy. (2016). Why play therapy? Retrieved from https://www.a4pt.org/general/custom.asp?page=WhyPlayTherapy

Baillargeon, J., Binswanger, I. A., Penn, J. V., Williams, B. A., & Murray, O. J. (2009). Psychiatric disorders and repeat incarcerations: The revolving prison door. *American Journal of Psychiatry, 166,* 103–109. doi:10.1176/appi.ajp.2008.08030416

Baker, S. B., & Cramer, S. H. (1972). Counselor or change agent: Support from the profession. *Journal of Counseling & Development, 50,* 661–665. doi:10.1002/j.2164-4918.1972.tb03447.x

Bratton, S. C., Ray, D., Rhine, T., & Jones, L. (2005). The efficacy of play therapy with children: A meta-analytic review of treatment outcomes. *Professional Psychology: Research and Practice, 36,* 376–390. doi:10.1037/0735-7028.36.4.376

Carter, R. T., & Reynolds, A. L. (2011). Race-related stress, racial identity status attitudes, and emotional reactions of black Americans. *Cultural Diversity and Ethnic Minority Psychology, 17,* 156–162. doi:10.1037/a0023358

Casas, J. M., & Pytluk, S. D. (1995). Hispanic identity development: Implications for research and practice. In J. G. Ponterotto, J. M. Casas, L. A. Suzuki, & C. M. Alexander (Eds.), *Handbook of multicultural counseling* (pp. 155–180). Thousand Oaks, CA: Sage.

Centers for Disease Control and Prevention. (2014). Fatal injury reports, national and regional, 1999–2014. Retrieved from http://webappa.cdc.gov/sasweb/ncipc/mortrate10_us.html

Chapman, C., & Rokutani, L. (2005). *Adolescents and substance abuse: What works and why?* Retrieved from https://www.counseling.org/docs/default-source/vistas/vistas_2005_vistas05-art09.pdf?sfvrsn=85470601_12

Chou, T., Asnaani, A., & Hofmann, S. G. (2012). Perception of racial discrimination and psychopathology across three U.S. ethnic minority groups. *Cultural Diversity and Ethnic Minority Psychology, 18,* 74–81.

Chung, R. C.-Y. (2007, February). *Breaking the culture of fear: Implications for multiculturalism and social justice.* Paper presented at the 24th Annual Teacher's College Winter Roundtable on Culture and Psychology and Education, New York.

Chung, R. C.-Y., Bemak, F., Ortiz, D. P., & Sandoval-Perez, P. A. (2008). Promoting the mental health of immigrants: A multicultural/social justice perspective. *Journal of Counseling & Development, 86,* 310–317.

Conwell, Y., Van Orden, K., & Caine, E. D. (2011). Suicide in older adults. *Psychiatric Clinics of North America, 34,* 451–468. doi:10.1016/j.psc.2011.02.002

DiClemente, C. C. (2003). *Addiction and change: How addictions develop and addicted people recover.* New York, NY: Guilford Press.

Durose, M. R., Cooper, A. D., & Snyder, H. N. (2014). *Special report: Recidivism of prisoners released in 30 states in 2005: Patterns from 2005 to 2010.* Retrieved from https://www.bjs.gov/content/pub/pdf/rprts05p0510.pdf

Duvall, J., & Kaplan, R. (2014). Enhancing the well-being of veterans using extended group-based nature recreation experiences. *Journal of Rehabilitation Research and Development, 51,* 685–696.

Eaton, L. G., Doherty, K. L., & Widrick, R. M. (2007). A review of research and methods used to establish art therapy as an effective treatment method for traumatized children. *The Arts in Psychotherapy*, *34*, 256–262. doi:10.1016/j.aip.2007.03.001

Erikson, E. H. (1963). *Childhood and society* (2nd ed.). New York, NY: Norton.

Franklin, A. J., Boyd-Franklin, N., & Kelly, S. (2006). Racism and invisibility. *Journal of Emotional Abuse*, *6*(2–3), 9–30. doi:10.1300/J135v06n02_02

Fredriksen-Goldsen, K. I., Kim, H.-J. K., Bryan, A. E. B., Shiu, C. & Emlet, C. A. (2017). The cascading effects of marginalization and pathways of resilience in attaining good health among LGBT older adults. *The Gerontologist*, *57*, S72–S83. doi:10.1093/geront/gnw170

Gonzalez, J. M. R., & Connell, N. M. (2014). Mental health of prisoners: Identifying barriers to mental health treatment and medication continuity. *American Journal of Public Health*, *104*, 2328–2333.

Goodman, R. (1997). The strengths and difficulties questionnaire: A research note. *Journal of Child Psychiatry*, *38*, 581–586.

Hasting, S. L., & Cohn, T. J. (2013). Challenges and opportunities associated with rural mental health practice. *Journal of Rural Mental Health*, *37*, 37–49. doi:10.1037/rmh0000002

Health Resources & Services Administration. (2017). Defining rural population. Retrieved from https://www.hrsa.gov/rural-health/about-us/definition/index.html

Hirst, S. P., Lane, A., & Stares, R. (2013). Health promotion with older adults experiencing mental health challenges: A literature review of strength-based approaches. *Clinical Gerontologist*, *36*, 329–355. doi:10.1080/07317115.2013.788118

Human Rights Campaign. (2018). New FBI data shows increased reported incidents of anti-LGBTQ hate crimes in 2016. Retrieved from https://www.hrc.org/blog/new-fbi-data-shows-increased-reported-incidents-of-anti-lgbtq-hate-crimes-i

Kaeble, D. (2018). Probation and parole in the United States, 2016. Retrieved from https://www.bjs.gov/index.cfm?ty=pbdetail&iid=6188

Kaeble, D., & Cowhig, M. (2018). Correctional populations in the United States, 2016. Retrieved from https://www.bjs.gov/index.cfm?ty=pbdetail&iid=6226

Kramer, D. T. (1994). *Legal rights of children* (2nd ed.). New York, NY: McGraw-Hill.

Lambert, M. J. (1992). Psychotherapy outcome research: Implications for integrative and eclectic therapists. In J. C. Norcross & M. R. Goldfried (Eds.), *Handbook of psychotherapy integration* (pp. 94–129). New York, NY: Basic Books.

Landreth, G., & Bratton, S. (1999). Play therapy. Retrieved from https://www.counseling.org/resources/library/ERIC%20Digests/99-01.pdf

Lewis, J. A., Arnold, M. S., House, R., & Toporek, R. L. (2003). ACA advocacy competencies. Retrieved from https://www.counseling.org/docs/default-source/competencies/aca-advocacy-competencies.pdf?sfvrsn=d177522c_4

Louv, R. (2008). *Last child in the woods: Saving our children from nature-deficit disorder*. Chapel Hill, NC: Algonquin.

Lyons, J. S., Howard, K. I., O'Mahoney, M. T., & Lish, J. (1997). *The measurement and management of clinical outcomes in mental health*. New York, NY: Wiley.

Malchiodi, C. (2016). Child art therapy: How it works. Retrieved from https://www.psychologytoday.com/us/blog/arts-and-health/201601/child-art-therapy-how-it-works

Mather, M., Jacobsen, L. A., & Pollard, K. M. (2015). *Aging in the United States. Population Bulletin*, *70*, 1–19. Retrieved from https://www.prb.org/wp-content/uploads/2016/01/aging-us-population-bulletin-1.pdf

Meyers, L. (2014a). Advocacy in action. *Counseling Today*. Retrieved from https://ct.counseling.org/2014/04/advocacy-in-action/

Meyers, L. (2014b). Ages and stages. *Counseling Today*. Retrieved from https://ct.counseling.org/2014/03/ages-and-stages/

Milford, P. C. (2015). 3 things to know when working with LGBT clients. Retrieved from https://www.socialworkhelper.com/2015/07/02/3-things-know-working-lgbt-clients/

Miller, S. D., Duncan, B. L., & Hubble, M. A. (1997). *Escape from Babel: Toward a unifying language for psychotherapy practice*. New York, NY: Norton.

Miller, W. R., & Rollnick, S. (2013). *Motivational interviewing: Helping people change* (3rd ed.). New York, NY: Guilford Press.

Myers, K. (2013). Effective treatment of military clients. *Counseling Today*. Retrieved from https://ct.counseling.org/2013/08/effective-treatment-of-military-clients/

National Alliance on Mental Illness. (2018). LGBTQ. Retrieved from https://www.nami.org/Find-Support/LGBTQ

National Council on Aging. (n.d.). The United States of Aging Survey. Retrieved from https://www.ncoa.org/news/resources-for-reporters/usoa-survey/

National Institutes of Health. (2016). World's older population grows dramatically. Retrieved from https://www.nih.gov/news-events/news-releases/worlds-older-population-grows-dramatically

Out & Equal Workplace Advocates. (n.d.). 2017 workplace equality fact sheet. Retrieved from http://outandequal.org/2017-workplace-equality-fact-sheet/

Palma, T. V., & Stanley, J. L. (2011). Effective counseling with lesbian, gay, and bisexual clients. *Journal of College Counseling, 5*, 74–89. doi:10.1002/j.2161-1882.2002.tb00208.x

Patterson, C. H. (1964). A unitary theory of motivation and its counseling implications. *Journal of Individual Psychology, 20*, 17–31.

Patterson, C. H. (1990). Involuntary clients: A person-centered view. *Person-Centered Review, 5*, 316–320.

Petersilia, J. (1998). Probation in the United States. *Crime and Justice, 22*, 149–200.

Poulsen, D. V. (2017). Nature-based therapy as a treatment for veterans with PTSD: What do we know? *Journal of Public Mental Health, 16*, 15–20. doi:10.1108/JPMH-08-2016-0039

Rashid, T. (2015). Positive psychotherapy: A strength-based approach. *Journal of Positive Psychology, 10*, 25–40. doi:10.1080/17439760.2014.920411

Ratts, M. J., Singh, A. A., Nassar-McMillan, S., Butler, S. K., & McCullough, J. R. (2016). Multicultural and social justice counseling competencies: Guidelines for the counseling profession. *Journal of Multicultural Counseling and Development, 44*, 28–48. doi:10.1002/jmcd.12035

Reblin, M., & Uchino, B. N. (2009). Social and emotional support and its implication for health. *Current Opinion in Psychiatry, 21*, 201–205. doi:10.1097/YCO.0b013e3282f3ad89

Remley, T. P. Jr., & Herlihy, B. (2015). *Ethical, legal, and professional issues in counseling* (5th ed.). Boston, MA: Pearson Education.

Rogers, C. R. (1951). *Client-centered therapy*. Boston, MA: Houghton Mifflin.

Sawyer-Kurian, K. M., Newsome, G. K., Dames, L. S., Horne, R. A., & Grant, W. (2017). *Preparing counselors of color for diverse cultural contexts: A review of multicultural textbooks used in CACREP-accredited programs*. Retrieved from https://www.counseling.org/docs/default-source/vistas/preparing-counselors-of-color.pdf?sfvrsn=ebc24a2c_4

Schank, J. A. (1998). Ethical issues in rural counselling practice. *Canadian Journal of Counselling, 32*, 270–283.

Shallcross, L. (2011). "Come and be who you are." *Counseling Today, 53*, 24–32. Retrieved from https://www.counseling.org/resources/library/Counseling%20Today/May2011CTOnline.pdf

Smith, K. (2016). Seeing people, not prisoners. *Counseling Today*. Retrieved from https://ct.counseling.org/2016/09/seeing-people-not-prisoners/

Sori, C. F., & Hecker, L. L. (2015). Ethical and legal considerations when counselling children and families. *Australian and New Zealand Journal of Family Therapy, 36*, 450–464. doi:10.1002/anzf.1126

St. Thomas, B., & Johnson, P. (2002). In their own voices: Play activities and art with traumatized children. *Groupwork, 13*, 34–48.

Stigsdotter, U. K., Corazon, S. S., Sidenius, U., Nyed, P. K., Larsen, H. B., & Fjorback, L. (2018). Efficacy of nature-based therapy for individuals with stress-related illnesses: Randomised controlled trial. *British Journal of Psychiatry, 0*, 1–8. doi:10.1192/bjp.2018.2

Substance Abuse and Mental Health Services Administration. (n.d.). Other specific populations. Retrieved from https://www.samhsa.gov/specific-populations/other

Substance Abuse and Mental Health Services Administration. (2013). *Report to Congress on the nation's substance abuse and mental health workforce issues.* Rockville, MD: Author. Retrieved from http://store.samhsa.gov/shin/content/PEP13-RTC-BHWORK/PEP13-RTC-BHWORK.pdf

Sue, D. W., & Sue, D. (2013). *Counseling the culturally diverse: Theory and practice* (6th ed.). New York, NY: Wiley.

Suicide Prevention Resource Center. (1994–2018). Older adults. Retrieved from https://www.sprc.org/populations/older-adults

Tanielian, T., Batka, C., & Meredith, L. S. (2017). *The changing landscape for veterans' mental health care.* Santa Monica, CA: RAND Corporation. Retrieved from https://www.rand.org/pubs/research_briefs/RB9981z2.html.

U. S. Census Bureau. (2011). Current population survey – March 2011 detail tables. Retrieved from https://www.census.gov/data/tables/2011/demo/foreign-born/cps-2011.html

U.S. Census Bureau. (2014). Quick facts. Retrieved from http://www.census.gov/quickfacts/table/PST045215/00

U.S. Census Bureau. (2016). New census data shows differences between urban and rural populations. Retrieved from https://www.census.gov/newsroom/press-releases/2016/cb16-210.html

U.S. Census Bureau. (2017). 2017 National population projections tables. Retrieved from https://www.census.gov/data/tables/2017/demo/popproj/2017-summary-tables.html

Walsh, F. (2006). *Strengthening family resilience* (2nd ed.). New York, NY: Guilford Press.

Williams, M. T. (2013). How therapists drive away minority clients. *Psychology Today.* Retrieved from https://www.psychologytoday.com/us/blog/culturally-speaking/201306/how-therapists-drive-away-minority-clients

GLOSSARY

Acculturation: the process of blending one's social, psychological, behavioral, religious, and cultural aspects into the dominate culture.

Action potential: the stimulation of a neuron that fundamentally changes its electrical state and leads to the production of a nerve impulse.

Active listening: a process involving three stages—sensing, processing, and responding—that occurrs throughout the interviewing process.

Actualizing tendency: the force that guides us to grow and reach our full potential.

Adaptation: the degree to which a client's level of functioning is altered as a result of changes made in lifestyle and thought processing.

Adherence: the extent to which a client takes his or her prescribed medication at the correct time and in the correct dosage.

Adjudicated: commonly associated with the legal system, this term means to settle or determine through judicial proceedings.

Advocacy: those actions taken by counselors to remove the environmental barriers hampering client well-being.

Aggregate limit: the maximum amount an insurer is willing to pay for the lifetime of the policy, which is renewed annually.

Appeal: an action taken by a counseling provider regarding payment decisions made by an insurance company.

Art therapy: an intervention strategy used to provide individuals a safe outlet to creatively express thoughts and emotions that result from psychological distress.

Assent: a personal agreement to engage in therapeutic activities with a counselor.

Assessment: the collection of information to identify, analyze, evaluate, and address the problems, issues, and circumstances of clients in the counseling relationship.

Asynchronous technology: technology that allows supervisors and supervisees to communicate online at their own pace and on their own schedule.

Autonomy: one's basic right to control the direction of one's life and the counselor's responsibility to engage the client in ways that both respect and support the client's individuality.

Axon: a long slender tube that transports nerve impulses away from the cell body to other cells.

Behavioral medicine: a multidisciplinary science that integrates knowledge from various fields related to health and illness and applies that knowledge to the treatment and prevention of illness through use of behavioral interventions.

Beneficence: the counselor's responsibility to work for the good of the individual and society by promoting mental health and well-being.

Biomedical model: the way health professionals diagnose and treat disease, focusing primarily on biology while disregarding psychological and social factors that contribute to disease and illness.

Biopsychosocial model: a philosophy of client care and approach to clinical practice in treating disease and illness where the causes of disease and illness are thought to be the result of interactions among biological (e.g., genetic, sex), psychological (e.g., personality, self-esteem), and social factors (e.g., culture, peers).

Case conceptualization: a clinical tool used by counselors to organize client information—behaviors, thoughts, feelings, and physiology—in a manner that explains the client's perspective from the counselor's theoretical orientation.

Case notes: the session-to-session archives counselors keep about their work with clients.

Cell body: the center of a neuron containing several parts, the most important of which is the cell nucleus.

Certification: the process by which counselors are identified as meeting national standards set by the counseling profession.

Certified clinical mental health counselor: established in 1993 jointly by the National Academy of Clinical Mental Health Counselors (NACMH) and the National Board for Certified Counselors (NBCC), the CCMHC is a voluntary credential designed to recognize those individuals who meet a set of uniform competency standards for professional clinical mental health counselors.

Client-centered care: an approach to providing care that is respectful of and responsive to individual client preferences, needs, and values and ensures that client values guide all clinical decisions.

Clinical documentation: any written and/or electronic record pertaining to contact between the client and counselor and work that has occurred within the counseling relationship.

Clinical interview: an action-oriented intervention in which a counselor solicits information about a client and the client's past using a series of questions, assesses the client's verbal and nonverbal responses to those questions, and uses that information to formulate a diagnosis for the client.

Clinical mental health counseling: the provision of counseling services in institutions of higher education and community-based human service agencies.

Clinical supervision: a relational experience between an experienced senior counselor and a less experienced junior counselor designed to develop the skills, abilities, and personal attributes the junior counselor needs to be an effective clinician.

Closed-ended questions: questions designed to tailor a conversation to a specific point or event.

Cognitive processing therapy (CPT): an evidence-based treatment for PTSD and related symptomatology that consists of 12 weekly sessions delivered in group, individual, or combined group and individual formats.

Cognitive theory: a viewpoint asserting that a person's perceptions (thoughts) of an event are the primary determinant of one's behaviors, emotions, and physiology.

Collaborative care: an umbrella term used to describe a health care philosophy that systematically combines treatment of mental illness, substance use, and primary health diseases in primary or behavioral health care settings.

Compliance: the extent to which a client takes medication as prescribed.

Confidentiality: the counselor's obligation to keep counseling and any information related to counseling private.

Consent: an agreement from individuals over the age of 18 and with legal ability to do so to participate in counseling.

Construct bias: occurs when a construct of interest being measured (e.g., IQ, depression, despair, satisfaction) is conceptualized or understood differently across groups.

Continuum of care: a system that guides and tracks clients over time through a comprehensive array of health services spanning all levels and intensity of care.

Coping: cognitive or behavioral actions that individuals use to deal with stressors.

Core conditions: the factors necessary for establishing a strong counselor-client relationship and creating personality change in counseling.

Counseling: a professional relationship that empowers diverse individuals, families, and groups to accomplish mental health, wellness, education, and career goals.

Counseling strategies: techniques and interventions used with children, adolescents, and adults to meet treatment goals.

Credentialing: a formalized process of obtaining, verifying, and assessing the qualifications and competence of an individual by a third party with the relevant authority to issue such credentials.

Crisis: a perception or experiencing of an event that disrupts or undermines normal human functioning.

Cross-cutting assessments: tools that measure symptomatology common across diagnoses.

Deidentification: a process used to prevent a client's identity from relating to information found in a case file.

Dendrites: branch-like structures that act as receptors and help the neuron receive messages from other neurons.

Developmental crisis: a traumatic event expected as part of the normal developmental cycle.

Dialectic: the belief that two opposing perspectives can be true at the same time.

Differential diagnosis: a systematic process of ruling out competing diagnoses, using prior evidence, that share common symptomatology criteria.

Discrepancy: a motivational interviewing term referencing the distance between one's personal goals and reality.

Downcoding: when counselors give clients with more severe problems a less severe problem classification.

Drug: any substance that brings about a change in biological function through its chemical actions.

Effect size: the standardization of research findings across measures, variables, and populations.

Emotional symptoms: a collection of signs or indicators representing an individual's affectual response to a traumatic experience including but not limited to feelings of sadness and anger.

Empathy: the ability to perceive the internal frame of reference of another with accuracy, and with the emotional components and meanings, as if one were the other person.

Empirically supported treatment: a specific technique, intervention, or treatment shown to be efficacious in previous research.

Empowerment: the act or action of empowering someone or something.

Evidence: available facts and information supporting the truth and validity of a belief or proposition.

Evidence-based practice: the integration of the best available research with clinical expertise in the context of patient characteristics, culture, and preferences.

Eye movement desensitization and reprocessing (EMDR): exposure-based therapy that involves incorporating physiological aspects with the psychological components of trauma-based treatments.

Fee-for-service system: a payment model that itemizes each service component thereby maximizing the quantity of services provided.

Fidelity: counselors' responsibility to be true to their word, uphold their commitments and promises, and be trustworthy in their actions.

First messenger effect: the process through which information gained during the initial binding stage helps determine how polarized the neuron will become and how strong the action potential will be when released.

First responders: individuals with specialized training in crisis and emergency management who often provide onsite care and services following an accident, disaster, or other traumatic event.

Formal assessment strategies: an assessment approach that follows a specific, standardized set of procedures and yields quantifiable data that can be compared to a normative population.

Formative evaluation methods: evaluation strategies used to assess a client's experience in real time.

FREEDOM: a treatment approach for PTSD in which clients are led through a seven-step sequence of skills designed to assist them in understanding their trauma-related reactions and gain control of triggers associated with current daily life stresses.

Gatekeeping: the process by which individuals are policed by the larger community to ensure adherence to established community values, beliefs, and standards of practice.

Grounding: a technique by which a counselor distracts clients from their inner pain and has them focus on their external world though mental, physical, and self-soothing techniques.

Half-life: the amount of time it takes the body to eliminate 50% of a drug from the body.

Holding environment: a place for supervisees to share their experiences as a counselor including their knowledge, skills, fears, struggles, difficulties, and successes.

Holistic wellness counseling: a therapeutic approach in which counselors take the entire human experience into account when assessing and treatment planning.

Impact factor: the calculation of the number of citations received by a journal from other journals catalogued in the Web of Science database.

Informal assessment strategies: an assessment approach that does not follow a strict set of procedures and is not concerned with comparing results to a normative sample.

Informed consent: the process of providing clients with enough information so they are able to make an informed decision about entering into a counseling relationship.

Informed consent documents: paperwork that contains a variety of information describing what the counseling process will look like, what the client can expect from the counselor, what the client will be expected to do, how services will be arranged and how they will be paid for, and what recourse the client has should the services provided be deemed inappropriate or ineffective.

Intake interview: an assessment technique that provides counselors with information about clients' past functioning and how it relates to their current situation and the problems they are facing.

Integrated care treatment: the systematic coordination of general and behavioral health care.

Involuntary client: a person required or forced, usually through a court order, to attend and participate in treatment.

Isomorphism: a repetitive relational pattern occurring in supervisory relationships where the roles of supervisor and supervisee mirror those of counselor and client.

Item bias: occurs when items are poorly worded or seem ambiguous or unclear that results in differences in scores among groups. Generally speaking, the presence of test bias is usually the result of some type of cultural bias.

Justice: engaging clients equitably and fostering fairness and equality.

Latent construct: an abstract concept that is theoretical and therefore not directly measurable.

Lateralization: the belief that brain functioning is specialized to either hemisphere of the brain.

Laws: sets of rules decided on by legislative bodies for the purpose of governing a particular activity within society.

Licensed professional counselor: an individual who has met all state requirements and has the legal right to use of title and practice of profession.

Licensure: the process by which individual state legislatures regulate the use of title and practice of a profession in their jurisdiction to individuals with specific training and certification.

Licensure portability: the ability of a professional counselor licensed at the independent practice level to transfer a license to another state or U.S. jurisdiction when the counselor changes residence to that state or jurisdiction.

Loading dose: the amount of a drug initially given that is typically higher than what will be subsequently prescribed.

Localizationism: the belief that mental function is fixed to certain physical regions of the brain.

Longitudinal studies: studies where observational data are gathered repeatedly over time.

Maintenance dose: the regular dose of the medication that maintains the steady state plasma concentration in the therapeutic range.

Managed care: an umbrella term used to describe a practice or set of practices that provide oversight in the delivery of health care services.

Medical necessity: services, procedures, or supplies used to treat and diagnose health conditions that are justifiable and meet accepted standards of medicine.

Medicare: the federally funded health insurance program for persons 65 years of age or older, certain younger people with disabilities, and people with end-stage renal disease requiring dialysis and/or transplant.

Mental health: a state of well-being that encompasses all aspects of psychological and emotional wellness.

Mental status examination: a structured assessment of a client's behavioral and cognitive functioning.

Method bias: occurs when differences in scores are the result of factors surrounding the test administration (e.g., environment, length of test) rather than the construct of interest being measured.

Microaggression: a subtle form of discrimination communicated either verbally or nonverbally that insults disadvantaged groups.

Mindfulness: a way of being in which individuals focus their attention on what is happening in the present and how they are experiencing the moment.

Model of practice: a phenomenon or an aspect of a phenomenon in simplistic terms.

Motivational interviewing: a person-centered, directive clinical approach used by counselors for enhancing peoples' intrinsic motivation to elicit change by resolving personal ambivalence.

National certified counselor: the most established and perhaps the most widely recognized national counseling certification offered through the NBCC. To become an NCC, an individual needs to (a) hold a degree from either a CACREP-accredited counseling program or from a master's-level program in counseling with a minimum of 48 graduate-level semester hours or 72 quarter hours, (b) document a minimum of 100 hours of counseling supervision, (c) complete a minimum of 3,000 clock hours of post-master's counseling experience within a 24-month period, (d) demonstrate satisfactory performance on the National Counselor Examination (NCE), and (e) ensure that his or her behavior adheres to the standards identified in the current version of the NBCC Code of Ethics.

Nerve cells: the core components of the brain, spinal cord, and peripheral nervous system.

Neural stem cells: cells capable of self-renewal and differentiation into other cells to repair damaged brain areas as in the case of stroke, traumatic brain injury, or neurological degenerative diseases.

Neurocounseling: the integration of neuroscience into the practice of counseling, by teaching and illustrating the physiological underpinnings of many of our mental health concerns.

Neurogenesis: see *neuronal pruning*.

Neuron: see *nerve cells*.

Neuronal pruning: the processes by which the brain is remodeled in response to both internal metabolic conditions and external environmental factors.

Neuroplasticity: the processes by which the brain is remodeled in response to both internal metabolic conditions and external environmental factors.

Neurotransmitters: chemicals in the brain that help facilitate transmission of nerve impulses.

Nonmaleficence: the counselor's responsibility to avoid harming the client in any way.

Nonverbal body language: everything other than words that communicates messages to the client.

Occurrence limit: the maximum amount an insurer is willing to pay for any one claim.

Open-ended questions: questions that encourage clients to speak without reservation throughout the interview process.

Operational definition: clear and concise statement or set of statements, known as facets, of how something is measured.

Overjustification: occurs when the external source of motivation diminishes the internal source of self-regulation.

Parallel process: an intrapsychic phenomenon that unconsciously occurs on the part of the supervisee and originates in a relationship in one setting and is reflected in a relationship in a different setting.

Parity: the practice whereby insurers or health care service plan providers are prohibited by law from discriminating between coverage offered for mental illness, serious mental illness, substance abuse, and other physical disorders and diseases.

Parole: a period of time after incarceration when a person is under the direct supervision of a parole officer.

Pharmacodynamics: the study of the processes by which drugs affect the mind and body.

Pharmacokinetics: the in vivo (occurring inside the body) drug processes that include the administration, absorption, distribution, metabolism, and excretion of drugs.

Physical symptoms: a collection of signs or indicators representing the body's response to a traumatic experience including but not limited to headaches, loss of appetite, pain, and fatigue.

Play therapy: the systematic use of a theoretical model to establish an interpersonal process wherein trained play therapists use the therapeutic powers of play to help clients prevent or resolve psychosocial difficulties and achieve optimal growth and development.

Policy: a document that outlines what a governing body hopes to achieve for its constituents and the methods and principles it will use to achieve its goals.

Positive psychology: the scientific study of what makes life worth living.

Positive psychology interventions: interventions developed within the positive psychology framework that aim to create positive outcomes for clients

Posttraumatic growth (PTG): a process by which individuals who have endured some form of trauma experience positive change.

PRACTICE: acronym referencing the progressive intervention stages used in TF-CBT: psychoeducation and parenting strategies, relaxation, affect modulation, cognitive coping, trauma narrative, cognitive processing, and in vivo exposure.

Practice-based evidence: counselors' firsthand clinical experiences with their clients that are used to inform research.

Preauthorization: prior authorization to determine whether prescriptions, procedures, or services are medically necessary and appropriate.

Privileged communication: a legal right of the client that prevents private information from being divulged in legal proceedings.

Productivity: the ratio representing the number of billable hours a counselor generates in a day divided by the total number of hours spent onsite.

Provider status: the credentialing process that designates a health care provider as being approved by an insurance company or MCO to provide a specific service or set of services.

Psychosocial assessment: a comprehensive evaluation of a client's mental health, well-being, and social functioning.

Psychological symptoms: a collection of signs or indicators representing an individual's cognitive response to a traumatic experience including but not limited to depressive and anxious thoughts.

Psychological test: an instrument used to measure a latent construct of interest, such as depression, anxiety, wellness, or job satisfaction.

Racism: when a person from a race in power believes his or her race to be supervisor to that of others not in power.

Randomized control trials: studies where separate groups created by chance are used to compare treatments or interventions.

Recovery: a process of change through which individuals improve their health and wellness, live a self-directed life, and strive to reach their full potential.

Reflection of content: the process of stating back to the client the essence of what was said in a nonjudgmental or leading manner.

Reflection of feeling: similar to reflection of content; however, there is an explicit identification of feelings, and feeling words are included in the statement.

Registration: the process of recognizing individuals for successfully completing requirements mandated for the practice of mental health counseling.

Regulations: mandates prescribed by a governing body with the intent of carrying out legislation enacted by elected officials.

Relapse prevention plan: a step-by-step plan that identifies a client's possible triggers (e.g., stimuli, persons, situations, events, environmental settings) and outlines a systematic course of action by the client if faced with the potential to relapse.

Relevance: congruence between the available evidence and the stated purposes and uses of a specific practice.

Reliability: the ability of test scores to be interpreted in a consistent and dependable manner across multiple test administrations.

Resiliency: the ability to recover from adverse challenges or circumstances while developing strengths and resources.

Resting potential: a relaxed state where the amount of available electrical charge is greater outside the cell than it is within.

Reuptake: the process of retrieving any unused neurotransmitters and recycling them for future use.

Robustness: a method for evaluating incongruent evidence.

Rural: any county consisting of fewer than 50,000 people and counties not economically linked to a metropolitan area.

Second messenger effect: the process by which the exact state of the incoming message is confirmed, and the cell nucleus begins to actively increase or decrease receptor cell production depending on the state of the message received.

Secondary trauma: secondhand exposure to an event.

Selective norepinephrine reuptake inhibitors (SNRIs): third-generation antidepressants that retard the reuptake process and increase the amount of the targeted chemical in the brain, in this case norepinephrine.

Selective serotonin reuptake inhibitors (SSRIs): second-generation antidepressants that help to alleviate depressive symptoms by blocking the reabsorption of serotonin—a neurotransmitter associated with mood.

Self-injury: direct and deliberate bodily harm in the absence of suicidal intent.

Serious mental illness: a classification of mental health diagnoses of major depression, bipolar disorder, and schizophrenia.

Situational crisis: a traumatic event that is unanticipated and outside the expected course of events.

Social crisis: a traumatic event originating from an uncontrollable cultural event.

Social justice: the promotion of equity and fairness in the distribution of opportunities, resources, and privileges among all members of a society.

Soma: see *cell body.*

Spiritual symptoms: a collection of signs or indicators representing an individual's spiritual response to a traumatic experience including but not limited to a lack of purpose or sense of meaning in life.

Spirituality: an individualized practice extending beyond religious dogma and practice that serves to connect a person to a power greater than themselves and bring them peace.

Steady state: the amount of time required for a drug to reach a stable concentration level in the bloodstream.

Stress: a condition where a person's response to either a positive (e.g., birth of a child) or negative (e.g., loss of a loved one) situation leads to symptoms of physical or emotional tension and feeling anxious or threatened.

Subpoena: a formal request made by the court soliciting information from the counselor or a request to appear in court.

Summative evaluation methods: evaluation strategies used at set time points (e.g., every 2 weeks, once a month) throughout the counseling process.

Supervisee: a junior member of a profession who works with a senior member of the same profession to further his or her professional development and receive feedback on services provided to clients.

Supervisor: a senior member of a profession who works with a junior member in the same profession to enhance his or her professional functioning and monitor the quality of services provided.

Synapse: the gap between the ends of two neurons.

Synchronous technology: technology that allows supervisors and supervisees to communicate via distance in real time.

Telehealth: the use of electronic information and telecommunication technologies to support and promote long-distance clinical health care, patient and professional health-related education, public health, and health administration.

Terminal button: the storage center for neurotransmitters.

Test bias: when scores of one group are significantly different from scores of another group based solely on group membership.

Theory of practice: a set of principles or guidelines that describes and explains a phenomenon in its totality.

Therapeutic index: the difference between the therapeutic dose and toxic dose of a drug.

Titration: the art and science involved with balancing a drug dose against the client's symptoms.

Trauma: emotional responses to events such as an accident, rape, or natural disaster that challenge one's beliefs, security, thoughts, and feelings and undermine one's ability to cope.

Trauma-focused cognitive behavioral therapy (TC-CBT): evidence-based treatment developed to assist children and adolescents in recovering after a traumatic event.

Treatment plan: synopsis of a counselor's work with a client that includes a description of the client's presenting problem or issue, any potential diagnosis that may apply, goals established, and strategies or interventions planned to help reach those goals.

Triadic supervision: a supervision session including one supervisor and two supervisees.

Tricyclics: the second class of first-generation antidepressants that work by inhibiting the reuptake of serotonin, norepinephrine, and to a lesser extent dopamine.

Upcoding: when counselors give clients with less severe problems a more severe problem classification.

Utilization management: a set of techniques used by or on behalf of purchasers of health care benefits to manage health care costs by influencing patient care decision-making through case-by-case assessments of the appropriateness of care prior to its provision.

Validity: the degree to which evidence and theory support the interpretations of test scores entailed by proposed uses of test.

Veracity: the requirement that professional counselors remain truthful and honest in all professional interactions.

INDEX